German
ALL-IN-ONE

FOR DUMMIES®
A Wiley Brand

by Wendy Foster with Paulina Christensen, PhD, and Anne Fox

FOR DUMMIES®
A Wiley Brand

German All-in-One For Dummies®

Published by
John Wiley & Sons, Inc.
111 River St.
Hoboken, NJ 07030-5774
www.wiley.com

Copyright © 2013 by John Wiley & Sons, Inc., Hoboken, New Jersey

Published simultaneously in Canada

For general information on our other products and services, please contact our Customer Care Department within the U.S. at 877-762-2974, outside the U.S. at 317-572-3993, or fax 317-572-4002.

For technical support, please visit www.wiley.com/techsupport.

Wiley publishes in a variety of print and electronic formats and by print-on-demand. Some material included with standard print versions of this book may not be included in e-books or in print-on-demand. If this book refers to media such as a CD or DVD that is not included in the version you purchased, you may download this material at http://booksupport.wiley.com. For more information about Wiley products, visit www.wiley.com.

Library of Congress Control Number: 2013935672

ISBN 978-1-118-49140-9 (pbk); ISBN 978-1-118-61260-6 (ebk); ISBN 978-1-118-61270-5 (ebk); ISBN 978-1-118-61271-2 (ebk)

Manufactured in the United States of America

10 9 8

About the Authors

Wendy Foster was born in Connecticut and grew up in Scituate, Massachusetts. While studying in France, she traveled around Europe and became curious about the German language and culture. After graduating with a teaching certificate and a degree in French, she decided to return to Europe to study German. Her love of the Alps inspired her to live in Munich, where she spent 30 years. During that time, she completed her German studies at the Sprachen-und-Dolmetscher-Institut in Munich and later her MA in French at Middlebury College in Paris. Her professional experience includes teaching Business English, German, French, and intercultural communication skills. She also does editing for online German education programs. A few years ago, she returned to her New England roots. When she's not teaching ESL or German at the Boston Language Institute, she works from her home overlooking a spectacular salt marsh that constantly beckons her to go kayaking, exploring, and swimming.

Paulina Christensen has been working as a writer, editor, and translator for almost ten years. She holds a degree in English and German literature and has developed, written, and edited numerous German-language textbooks and teachers' handbooks for Berlitz International. Her work as a translator ranges from new media art to science fiction (*Starlog* magazine). She occasionally works as a court interpreter and does consulting and interpreting at educational conferences, as well as voice-overs for educational videos and CDs. Dr. Christensen received her MA and PhD from Düsseldorf University, Germany, and has taught at Berlitz Language Schools, New York University, and Fordham University.

Anne Fox has been working as a translator, editor, and writer for the past 12 years. She studied at Interpreters' School, Zurich, Switzerland, and holds a degree in translation. Her various assignments have taken her to outer space, hyperspace, and around the world. She has also taught at Berlitz Language Schools and worked as a legal and technical proofreader in the editorial departments of several law firms. Most recently she has been developing, writing, and editing student textbooks and teacher handbooks for Berlitz.

Dedication

This book is dedicated to all those who enjoy speaking German and appreciate the rich cultural heritage of German-speaking people. I also dedicate this work to Phil Kehoe, whose unflagging support of my endeavors serves as a constant inspiration to me. — Wendy Foster

Author's Acknowledgments

I would like to express my deep appreciation to the editorial staff at Wiley for their insight, patience, and expertise, especially my project editor Vicki Adang, copy editor Amanda Langferman, acquisitions editor Michael Lewis, and technical editors Candis Carey and Susan Reinhardt. The careful guidance provided by these professionals has greatly enhanced the quality of this book. My sincere thanks to all of you. — Wendy Foster

Publisher's Acknowledgments

We're proud of this book; please send us your comments at http://dummies.custhelp.com. For other comments, please contact our Customer Care Department within the U.S. at 877-762-2974, outside the U.S. at 317-572-3993, or fax 317-572-4002.

Some of the people who helped bring this book to market include the following:

Acquisitions, Editorial, and Vertical Websites

Senior Project Editor: Victoria M. Adang

Acquisitions Editor: Michael Lewis

Copy Editor: Amanda M. Langferman

Assistant Editor: David Lutton

Editorial Program Coordinator: Joe Niesen

Technical Editors: Candis Carey, Susan Reinhardt

Vertical Websites: Melanie Orr, Josh Frank, Doug Kuhn

Editorial Manager: Michelle Hacker

Editorial Assistants: Rachelle Amick, Alexa Koschier

Cover Photo: © iStockphoto.com / Nikada

Composition Services

Project Coordinator: Patrick Redmond

Layout and Graphics: Carrie A. Cesavice, Jennifer Creasey

Proofreaders: John Greenough, Tricia Liebig

Indexer: Potomac Indexing, LLC

Publishing and Editorial for Consumer Dummies

    Kathleen Nebenhaus, Vice President and Executive Publisher

    David Palmer, Associate Publisher

    Kristin Ferguson-Wagstaffe, Product Development Director

Publishing for Technology Dummies

    Andy Cummings, Vice President and Publisher

Composition Services

    Debbie Stailey, Director of Composition Services

Contents at a Glance

Table of Contents

Introduction

Starting out on the journey of speaking another language and discovering a foreign culture is like opening a window to the world. By learning to speak German, you're preparing yourself to communicate in the most widely spoken language of the European Union. Perhaps you're getting ready for a business or pleasure trip to Europe, perhaps you're studying German in school, or maybe you're simply curious about exploring Germany and its culture, including its language.

As you consider the plethora of language learning options out there, you'll find methods that promise you'll succeed in just a few easy steps, or better yet, while you're sleeping. Other programs take a significant chunk out of your budget and your spare time yet still don't deliver on their promises. This book lets you delve into the language at your own pace, and you can study the chapters in any order you want. Ample cross-referencing allows you to easily find any supporting information you need. Whatever your reasons for wanting to acquire some German, choosing *German All-in-One For Dummies* offers you a great opportunity to reach your goals.

About This Book

With *German All-in-One For Dummies*, you find a wealth of resources in one volume. You get straightforward information on the nuts and bolts of understanding and using the language as it's spoken today in German-speaking countries.

You can go through the chapters in this book in any order you choose, zeroing in on your priorities. You can skim or, better yet, skip over the lessons you don't need. Use the book to find answers to specific questions you may have on a topic that comes up while you're learning to use the language. Without even realizing it, your German vocabulary expands as you cruise through the book.

This book is chock-full of everyday phrases and words with pronunciation guidelines so you can practice the language right away. You find in-depth grammar explanations that answer your questions about how to build sentences in German. Throughout the book, you also get plenty of words, dialogues, and phrases related to specific situations you may come across in different settings. The appendixes offer more support in understanding grammar points, and the mini-dictionaries give you the translations of important words that appear in the book. The audio CD inside the back cover provides audio tracks of the German alphabet and listening practice for various dialogues in the book. (If you're reading a digital version of this book, go to http://booksupport.wiley.com for the audio tracks.) Most importantly, as you go through this book, **Viel Spaß!** (feel shpahs!) (*Have a lot of fun!*)

Conventions Used in This Book

To make your progress go as smoothly as possible, we use the following conventions in this book. They can help you spot essential elements in the text.

- ✔ We use **boldface** to highlight German words, example sentences, and the essential elements in verb tables, which may be information like verb endings or irregular conjugations.

- ✔ We *italicize* English translations that accompany German words and sentences. You'll find them set in parentheses following the pronunciation of German terms or sentences. Within the German pronunciations, we italicize the syllables that are stressed in words with two or more syllables. Finally, we italicize English terms that we define.

- ✔ In some cases, German speakers use the same pronunciation as English speakers for words, many of which are borrowed from English or other languages. When such words are pronounced the same way in German as in English, you see the English word in the pronunciation followed by the notation "as in English" rather than the usual phonetic pronunciation. Of course, if the pronunciation differs between the English and the German, we include the German pronunciation as usual.

- ✔ Verb *conjugations* (lists that show you the forms of a verb) are given in tables in this order:

  - The "I" form

  - The "you" (singular, informal [or sing. inf.]) form

  - The "he, she, it" form

  - The "we" form

  - The "you" (plural, informal [or pl. inf.]) form

  - The "they" form

  - The "you" (singular, formal [or sing. form.] and plural, formal [or pl. form.]) form

For example, here's what the present-tense conjugation of the verb **sein** (*to be*) looks like:

sein (*to be*)	
ich **bin**	wir **sind**
du **bist**	ihr **seid**
er/sie/es **ist**	sie **sind**
Sie **sind**	
Sind Sie Herr Schumpich? (*Are you Mr. Schumpich?*)	

To help you make fast progress in German, this book includes a few elements to help you along:

- ✔ **Talkin' the Talk dialogues:** The best way to learn a language is to see and hear how it's used in conversation, so we include dialogues throughout Books I and II. The dialogues come under the heading "Talkin' the Talk" and show you the German words, their pronunciations, and the English translations. For your listening and learning pleasure, we also include a number of these dialogues on the CD tucked into the back cover of your book. If you're reading a digital version of this book, you can find the audio tracks at `http://booksupport.wiley.com`.

- ✔ **Words to Know blackboards:** Acquiring key words and phrases is also important in language learning, so we collect these important words in sections that resemble chalkboards, with the heading "Words to Know." *Note:* In the pronunciations given in these sections, the stressed syllables are underlined rather than italicized.

- ✔ **Fun & Games activities:** If you want to flex your new language muscles, you can use the Fun & Games activities in Appendix D to reinforce what you learn. These activities are fun ways to check your progress.

Also note that, because each language has its own ways of expressing ideas, the English translations that we provide for the German terms may not be exactly literal. We want you to know the essence of what's being said, not just the meanings of single words. For example, the phrase **Es geht** (ês geyt) can be translated literally as *It goes,* but the phrase is actually the equivalent of *So, so,* or *Okay,* which is what you see as the translation.

Foolish Assumptions

In writing *German All-in-One For Dummies,* we made the following assumptions about you, dear reader:

✔ You're a German student looking for an in-depth, easy-to-use reference.

✔ You know very little or no German — or if you took German back in school, you remember very little of it.

✔ Your goal is to expand your knowledge of German. You don't want to be burdened by long-winded explanations of unnecessary grammatical terms, nor do you care to hold a scholarly discussion in German about Goethe's *Faust*. You just want to express yourself in clear and reasonably accurate German.

✔ You're enthusiastic about having some fun while honing your German skills.

If any or all of these statements describe you, then you're ready to get started using this book. **Willkommen!** (vil-*kom*-en!) (*Welcome!*)

How This Book Is Organized

This book is actually five books in one, each of which tackles a different aspect of German language acquisition. The following sections provide a brief description of what types of information you can find in each book.

Book I: Getting Started with German

In this book, you acquaint yourself with the world of popular German phrases and pronunciations. You get a broad base in the language of meeting and greeting people and talking about yourself and others. One chapter deals with everyday topics such as talking about the weather. Another contains practical vocabulary and expressions you need for speaking in business situations and using telecommunications. In Book I, you also gain insight into the world of German news media. You get practice in the language you need for buying clothes and food, as well as the ins and outs of having a pleasant dining experience.

Book II: Speaking German on the Go

Book II gets you up to speed on finding your way around in a German-speaking environment. You get practice in asking how to get somewhere and in understanding directions. You find useful input on the language you need for making reservations at a hotel, booking a trip, and going through airports. Book II also offers essential language for dealing with money matters like exchanging money and going to an ATM. And just in case, this book rounds out with a primer on going to the doctor and handling emergencies.

Book III: Assembling the Grammatical Foundations for Communication

In this book, you move onto the basics of grammar. You see the mysteries of gender and case unveiled, and you get an up-close look at the intricacies of combining nouns and pronouns with verbs. Here, you also find out how to construct sentences in the present tense, how to ask and answer questions, and how to agree and disagree. Book III delves into the finer points of expressing yourself using adjectives and adverbs. It shows you the six modal verbs that help you be polite, ask for help, and talk about what you can do, want to do, should do, or must do. Finally, you get the lowdown on how to make commands and how to use tricky two-part verbs.

Book IV: Building Detail and Precision in Your Communication

This book helps you become acquainted with past and future verb tenses. You get a handle on the difference between the conversational past and the simple (narrative) past, and you see how to choose the correct verb form to express yourself in the future. Here, you find out how to express yourself using reflexive verbs and how to connect shorter ideas with conjunctions to build more complex sentences. You find out the intricacies of using prepositions in German. Finally, you discover how to express certainty and uncertainty and how to make wishes and requests using subjunctive verbs.

Book V: The Appendixes

The five appendixes in this book provide an assortment of references to help you in expressing yourself confidently in German. The first appendix includes verb tables for conjugating verbs, as well as case-ending tables to help you use nouns, pronouns, and adjectives correctly. Appendixes B and C are two mini-dictionaries that allow you to find the meaning of a German word you don't understand or the German equivalent of an English word. Appendix D is the Fun & Games activities section. The last appendix, E, is devoted to the CD element of this book. It contains the listing of audio tracks that appear as dialogues throughout the book.

Icons Used in This Book

The following icons help you make the most of your journey through this book. You find them in the left-hand margin next to key points you don't want to miss. Here's what each icon means:

The Tip icon highlights helpful hints that'll make it a whole lot easier for you to feel comfortable using German, whether you're traveling abroad or just using it at home or in the workplace.

This icon alerts you to key information that's worth revisiting. You want to stash this info in your mind because you'll end up using it again and again.

If you're looking for information and advice about culture and travel, look for this icon. It draws your attention to interesting tidbits about the countries in which German is spoken.

The audio CD that comes with this book gives you the opportunity to listen to real German speakers so you can get a better understanding of what German sounds like. This icon marks the Talkin' the Talk dialogues in Books I and II that you can listen to on the CD. If you're using a digital version of this book, go to http://booksupport.wiley.com to download the audio tracks. You can also access the audio tracks at www.dummies.com/go/germanaio.

Where to Go from Here

For starters, try scanning the table of contents. Select a chapter that piques your interest and take it from there. Read the section in the chapter that presents a conversation in an everyday situation, a point of grammar, or some other information you want to know more about. Study the example dialogues and the details on forming useful language. You'll soon discover what you know or don't know, and when your curiosity is satisfied, flip back to the table of contents and find another chapter you're ready to tackle.

Whenever you feel like you're losing steam, **mach eine Pause** (mâH *ayn*-e *pou*-ze) (*take a break*), close your eyes, and dream about **die Romantische Straße** (dee ro-*mân*-tish-e *shtrah*-se) (*the Romantic Road* — an enchanting route through some of the most picturesque parts of southern Germany). Before you know it, you'll be dreaming of storybook castles and court jesters **auf Deutsch** (ouf doych) (*in German*)!

Book I
Getting Started with German

Contents at a Glance

Chapter 1

Warming Up to German Basics

In This Chapter
▶ Recognizing the German you already know
▶ Spotting words that aren't what they seem
▶ Understanding German pronunciation

*T*he best way to learn a new language is to jump right in — no tiptoeing around. In this chapter, you get a head start in German by seeing bits of the language you're already familiar with. You find out some popular German expressions, and you get the hang of why you need to be careful with words known as "false friends," that is, words that seem to be the same in both languages but actually have different meanings. In the section on pronunciation, you familiarize yourself with the German alphabet and find out how to pronounce words so you can start to sound just like a native.

Starting with What You Already Know

Because German and English are both Germanic languages, quite a few words are either identical or similar in the two languages. Words that share a common source are called *cognates*. Another group of words common to German and English stem from Latin-based words that English speakers are familiar with. Many of these words have direct equivalents in German (for example, nouns that end in -tion).

Friendly allies: Kindergarten and more (perfect cognates)

The following words are spelled the same way and have the same meaning in German and in English. The only difference is the pronunciation, as shown in parentheses; in a few instances, the German and English pronunciation for the word is the same, so you see the English word in the pronunciation (followed by the notation "as in English"). The other quirk you may notice is that in German, nouns are always capitalized. In addition, German nouns have one of three genders, as noted in this list by the words **der** (masculine), **die** (feminine), and **das** (neuter) in front of each noun. See Chapter 2 in Book III for details on what gender is all about.

- **der Arm** (dêr ârm)
- **der Bandit** (dêr bân-*deet*)
- **die Bank** (dee bânk)
- **die Basis** (dee *bah*-zis)
- **blind** (blint)
- **die Butter** (dee *boot*-er)
- **digital** (di-gi-*tâl*)
- **elegant** (êl-ê-*gânt*)
- **die Emotion** (dee ê-moh-tsee-*ohn*)
- **emotional** (ê-moh-tsee-oh-*nahl*)
- **der Export** (dêr ex-*port*)
- **der Finger** (dêr *fing*-er)
- **die Hand** (dee hânt)
- **das Hotel** (dâs hotel [as in English])
- **die Immigration** (dee im-i-grâ-tsee-*ohn*)
- **der Import** (dêr im-*port*)
- **die Inflation** (dee in-flâ-tsee-*ohn*)
- **die Information** (dee in-for-mâ-tsee-*ohn*)
- **die Inspiration** (dee in-spi-râ-tsee-*ohn*)
- **das Instrument** (dâs in-stroo-*mênt*)
- **international** (in-ter-nâ-tsee-oh-*nahl*)
- **irrational** (ir-râ-tsee-oh-*nahl*)
- **legal** (ley-*gahl*)

- **liberal** (lee-bêr-*ahl*)
- **der Mast** (dêr mast)
- **die Mine** (dee *meen*-e)
- **modern** (moh-*dêrn*)
- **der Moment** (dêr moh-*mênt*)
- **die Motivation** (dee moh-ti-vâ-tsee-*ohn*)
- **das Museum** (dâs mooh-*zey*-oohm)
- **der Name** (dêr *nah*-me)
- **die Nation** (dee nâ-t see-*ohn*)
- **normal** (nor-*mahl*)
- **die Olive** (dee oh-*lee*-ve)
- **parallel** (pâr-â-*leyl*)
- **der Pilot** (dêr pee-*loht*)
- **der Professor** (dêr pro-fessor [as in English])
- **das Radio** (dâs *rah*-dee-oh)
- **die Religion** (dee rey-li-gee-*ohn*)
- **das Restaurant** (dâs rês-tuh-*ron*)
- **die Rose** (dee *roh*-ze)
- **der Service** (dêr *ser*-vis)
- **das Signal** (dâs zig-*nahl*)
- **der Sport** (dêr shport)
- **die Statue** (dee *shtah*-tooh-e)
- **der Stress** (dêr shtrês)

- **das System** (dâs zers-*teym*)
- **das Taxi** (dâs *tâx*-ee)
- **der Tiger** (dêr *tee*-ger)
- **tolerant** (to-lêr-*ânt*)

- **die Tradition** (dee trâ-di-tsee-*ohn*)
- **der Tunnel** (dêr *toohn*-el)
- **wild** (vilt)
- **der Wind** (dêr vint)

Kissing cousins (near cognates)

Many words, like the ones shown in Table 1-1, are spelled almost the same in German as in English and have the same meaning. Table 1-1 also shows you a few common German spelling conventions:

- The English *c* is a **k** in most German words.
- The *ou* in English words like *house* or *mouse* is often equivalent to **au** in German words.
- Many English adjectives ending in *-ic* or *-ical* have an **-isch** ending in German.
- Some English adjectives ending in *-y* are spelled with **-ig** in German.
- Some English nouns ending in *-y* have an **-ie** ending in German.
- Some English nouns ending in *-ly* have a **-lich** ending in German.

Table 1-1	Words Similar in Meaning but Slightly Different in Spelling
German	*English*
die Adresse (dee ah-*drês*-e)	*address*
der Aspekt (dêr âs-*pêkt*)	*aspect*
der Bär (dêr bear [as in English])	*bear*
blond (blont)	*blond(e)*
die Bluse (dee *blooh*-ze)	*blouse*
braun (brown [as in English])	*brown*
die Demokratie (dee dê-moh-krâ-*tee*)	*democracy*
direkt (di-*rêkt*)	*direct*
der Doktor (dêr *dok*-tohr)	*doctor*
exakt (êx-*âkt*)	*exact*

(continued)

Table 1-1 *(continued)*

German	English
exzellent (êx-tsel-*ênt*)	*excellent*
fantastisch (fân-*tâs*-tish)	*fantastic*
der Fisch (dêr fish)	*fish*
das Glas (dâs glahs)	*glass*
das Haus (dâs hous)	*house*
hungrig (*hoong*-riH)	*hungry*
indirekt (in-di-*rêkt*)	*indirect*
die Industrie (dee in-dooh-*stree*)	*industry*
die Infektion (dee in-fêk-tsee-*ohn*)	*infection*
das Insekt (dâs in-*zêkt*)	*insect*
der Kaffee (dêr *kâf*-ey)	*coffee*
das Knie (dâs knee)	*knee*
die Komödie (dee koh-*mer*-dee-e)	*comedy*
die Kondition (dee kon-di-tsee-*ohn*)	*condition*
konservativ (*kon*-sêr-vâ-teef)	*conservative*
der Kontinent (dêr kon-ti-*nênt*)	*continent*
das Konzert (dâs kon-*tsêrt*)	*concert*
die Kultur (dee kool-*toohr*)	*culture*
logisch (*loh*-gish)	*logical*
das Mandat (dâs mân-*daht*)	*mandate*
der Mann (dêr mân)	*man*
die Maschine (dee mâ-*sheen*-e)	*machine*
die Maus (dee mouse [as in English])	*mouse*
die Methode (dee mê-*toh*-de)	*method*
die Mobilität (dee moh-bi-li-*tait*)	*mobility*
die Musik (dee mooh-*zeek*)	*music*
die Nationalität (dee nât-see-oh-nahl-i-*tait*)	*nationality*
die Natur (dee nâ-*toohr*)	*nature*
offiziell (oh-fits-ee-*êl*)	*official* (adjective)
der Ozean (dêr *oh*-tsê-ân)	*ocean*

German	English
das Papier (dâs pâ-*peer*)	paper
das Parlament (dâs pâr-lâ-*mênt*)	parliament
perfekt (pêr-*fêkt*)	perfect
politisch (poh-*li*-tish)	political
potenziell (po-tên-tsee-*êl*)	potential (adjective)
praktisch (*prâk*-tish)	practical
das Programm (dâs proh-*grâm*)	program
das Salz (dâs zâlts)	salt
der Scheck (dêr shêk)	check (bank or traveler's)
sonnig (*zon*-iH)	sunny
der Supermarkt (dêr *zooh*-pêr-mârkt)	supermarket
das Telefon (dâs *tê*-le-fohn)	telephone
die Theorie (dee tey-ohr-*ee*)	theory
die Tragödie (dee trâ-*ger*-dee-e)	tragedy
die Walnuss (dee *vahl*-noohs)	walnut

False friends

Like every language, German contains some false friends — words that look very similar to English but have a completely different meaning. As you read the following list, you can see why you have to treat any new German word with kid gloves, especially if it looks like an English word, until you find out for sure what it means in English:

- ✔ **After** (*ahf*-ter): If you want to avoid embarrassment, remember the meaning of this word. Its German meaning is *anus*, not *after*. The German word for *after* is **nach** (nahH) or **nachdem** (nahH-*deym*).

- ✔ **aktuell** (âk-tooh-*êl*): This word means *up-to-date* and *current*, not *actual*. The German translation for *actual* is **tatsächlich** (tât-*sêH*-liH).

- ✔ **also** (*âl*-zoh): This one means *so, therefore,* or *thus*, not *also*. The German word for *also* is **auch** (ouH).

- ✔ **bald** (bâlt): This word means *soon*. It isn't a description for someone with little or no hair. The German word for *bald* is **kahl** (kahl) or **glatzköpfig** (*glâts*-kerpf-iH).

- **bekommen** (be-*kom*-en): This verb is an important one to remember. It means *to get*, not *to become*. The German word for *to become* is **werden** (*vêr*-den).

- **Boot** (boht): This is a *boat* and not a *boot*, which is **Stiefel** (*shteef*-el) in German. A *sailboat* is called a **Segelboot** (*zey*-gêl-boht).

- **brav** (brahf): This word means *well-behaved*, not *brave*. The German word for *brave* is **tapfer** (*tâp*-fer).

- **Brief** (breef): This is a noun that means *letter*, not *brief*. The German translation for the English adjective *brief* is **kurz** (koorts), and for the English noun, **Auftrag** (*ouf*-trahk) or **Unterlagen** (*oon*-ter-lah-gen).

- **Chef** (shêf): This is the German word for a person you take orders from (in other words, your *boss* or *supervisor*), not someone who's in charge of the cooking. The German word for *chef* is **Küchenchef** (*kueH*-ên-shêf) or **Chefkoch** (*shêf*-koH). Otherwise, a plain *cook* is called a **Koch** (koH) in German.

- **eventuell** (ey-vên-tooh-*êl*): This one means *possible* or *possibly*, not *eventual* or *eventually*, both of which would be **schließlich** (*shlees*-liH) in German.

- **fast** (fâst): This is an adjective that means *almost* — not the speeds at which Formula One drivers race. The German word for *fast* is **schnell** (shnêl) or **rasch** (râsh).

- **genial** (gê-nee-*ahl*): This adjective describes an idea or person *of genius* and has nothing to do with *genial*. The German word for *genial* is **heiter** (*hay*-ter).

- **Gift** (gift [as in English]): The German meaning is *poison*, so when you're giving your German-speaking host a *present*, you should say you have a **Geschenk** (gê-*shênk*), that is, unless you really are giving something like weed killer or a green mamba.

- **Handy** (*hân*-dee): This is the German word for *cellphone*. The German equivalent of *handy* is **praktisch** (*prâk*-tish), **geschickt** (ge-*shikt*), or **handlich** (*hânt*-liH).

- **Hut** (hoot): This word means *hat*. The German word for *hut* is **Hütte** (*hueH*-tê).

- **Kind** (kint): This is the German word for *child*. It has nothing to do with the English *kind*, which is **nett** (nêt), **lieb** (leep), or **liebenswürdig** (*lee*-bens-vuerd-iH) in German.

- **Komfort** (kom-*fohr*): This word means *amenity*, for example, the amenities you expect in a five-star hotel, not *comfort*. The German verb meaning *to comfort* [someone] is **trösten** (*trers*-ten).

✔ **Kost** (kost): This is the German word for *food or fare*. For example, the term **Feinkost** (*fayn*-kost) refers to gourmet food or a delicatessen where you can buy fine food products. The German word meaning *to cost* is **kosten** (*kos*-ten).

✔ **kurios** (koohr-ee-*ohs*): This word means *strange*, not *curious*. The German word for *curious* is **neugierig** (*noy*-geer-iH).

✔ **Mist** (mist [as in English]): Be careful not to misuse this word that actually means *manure* in German! It doesn't describe heavy moisture resembling a fine rain, which is called **Nebel** (*ney*-bel) or **Dunst** (doonst).

✔ **Mobbing** (mobbing [as in English]): The meaning of this word is *bullying* or *harassing*. The German word for a *mob* is **Pöbel** (*per*-bel) or **Rotte** (*rot*-e), and the verb *to mob (someone)* is **anpöbeln** (*ân*-per-beln).

✔ **Most** (most): This is the German word for unfermented fruit juice, and in southern German-speaking regions, a young fruit wine. The German word for the English *most* is **das meiste** (dâs *mays*-te); for example, **die meisten Leute** (die *mays*-ten *loy*-te) (*most people*).

✔ **Oldtimer** (oldtimer [as in English]): Germans use this word to refer to a *vintage car*. An *old man*, like the kind you see in a rocking chair smoking a pipe is an **alter Hase** (*âlt*-er *hâz*-e), which actually means *old rabbit*.

✔ **ordinär** (or-di-*nair*): This word means *vulgar* rather than *ordinary*. The German word for *ordinary* is **normal** (nor-*mahl*) or **gewöhnlich** (ge-*vern*-liH).

✔ **pathetisch** (pâ-*tey*-tish): This one means *overly emotional*, not *pathetic*, which, in German, is **jämmerlich** (*yêm*-er-liH) or **armselig** (*ârm*-zey-liH).

✔ **plump** (ploomp): The German meaning is *clumsy* or *tactless*, not *roundish*, which in German is **rundlich** (*roont*-liH).

✔ **Präservativ** (prê-zêr-vah-*teef*): You can avoid another embarrassing moment when you remember that this word means *condom* in German. The German equivalent of *preservative* is **Konservierungsmittel** (kon-sêr-*yeer*-oongs-mit-el).

✔ **Provision** (proh-vi-zee-*ohn*): The meaning of this word is *commission*, not *provision*. The German word for *provision* is **Vorsorge** (*fohr*-zor-ge) or **Versorgung** (fêr-*zohrg*-oong).

✔ **Rat** (*rât*): This word means *advice* or *counsel*. In German, **Ratte** (*rah*-te) is the word for *rat*.

✔ **Rock** (rok): The meaning of this word is *skirt*. The German word for *rock* is **Fels** (fels). Germans do, however, use the word **Rockmusik** (rok moo-*zeek*) to refer to *rock music*.

✔ **See** (zey): This word means *lake* (**der See**) (deyr zey) or *sea* (**die See, das Meer**) (dee zey, dâs mêr). In German, the verb *to see* is **sehen** (*zey*-en).

✔ **sensibel** (zen-*zee*-bel): The meaning of this word is *sensitive* rather than *sensible,* which translates as **vernünftig** (fêr-*nuenf*-tiH).

✔ **Smoking** (smoking [as in English]): In German, this word means *tuxedo* or *dinner jacket.* The verb *to smoke* is **rauchen** (*rouH*-en).

✔ **spenden** (*shpen*-den): The German meaning is *to donate,* not *to spend,* which in German is **ausgeben [money]** (*ous*-gey-ben).

✔ **sympathisch** (zerm-*pah*-tish): This word means *likeable* or *congenial,* not *sympathetic.* The German word for *sympathetic* is **mitfühlend** (*mit*-fuel-ent) or **verständnisvoll** (fêr-*shtênd*-nis-fol).

✔ **Taste** (*tahs*-te): The meaning of this word is *key,* like the key of a musical instrument or a button on a computer or a machine. The German word for *taste* is **Geschmack** (ge-*shmâk*). The word for the item you use to lock or unlock a door is **Schlüssel** (*shlues*-el).

Lenders and borrowers

A few German words have been adopted by the English language and have retained their meaning, such as **Kindergarten** (*kin*-der-gâr-ten), **Angst** (ânkst), **kaputt** (kâ-*poot*), **Ersatz** (êr-*zats*), **Sauerkraut** (*zou*-er-krout), **Zeitgeist** (*tsayt*-gayst), and **Wanderlust** (*vân*-der-loost).

However, the number of these German words is minimal compared to the number of English words that have made their way into the German language. At times, the combination of English and German makes for somewhat curious linguistic oddities. For example, you may hear **das ist total in/out** (dâs ist toh-*tahl* in/out [as in English]) (*that's totally in/out*) or **Sie können den File downloaden** (zee *kern*-en deyn file [as in English] *doun*-lohd-en) (*You can download the file*).

The following is a list of German words that have been borrowed from the English language. Note that they all retain their English pronunciations, with one slight exception: The borrowed verbs are "Germanified," which simply means they combine the English verb, such as *kill* or *jog,* with **-en,** the German suffix that creates the infinitive form (*to kill* and *to jog*). Go to Chapter 1 of Book III for more on German verbs and infinitive forms.

- ✔ das Baby
- ✔ der Boss
- ✔ das Business
- ✔ das Catering
- ✔ die City (*downtown*)
- ✔ der Computer
- ✔ cool
- ✔ das Design
- ✔ das Event
- ✔ Fashion (used without article)
- ✔ das Fast Food
- ✔ das Feeling
- ✔ flirten (*to flirt*)
- ✔ der Headhunter
- ✔ Hi
- ✔ hip
- ✔ der Hit
- ✔ das Hotel
- ✔ das Internet
- ✔ das Interview
- ✔ der Jetlag
- ✔ der Job
- ✔ joggen (*to jog*)
- ✔ killen (*to kill*)

- ✔ klicken (*to click*)
- ✔ managen (*to manage*)
- ✔ der Manager
- ✔ das Marketing
- ✔ das Meeting
- ✔ Okay
- ✔ online
- ✔ outsourcen (*to outsource*)
- ✔ die Party
- ✔ pink
- ✔ das Shopping
- ✔ die Shorts
- ✔ die Show/Talkshow
- ✔ das Steak
- ✔ stoppen (*to stop*)
- ✔ surfen (*to surf waves or the Internet*)
- ✔ das Team
- ✔ der Thriller
- ✔ der Tourist
- ✔ der Trainer
- ✔ das T-Shirt
- ✔ der Workshop
- ✔ Wow

Book I

Getting Started with German

Talkin' the Talk

Read the following conversation with a grain of salt — and a smile. It gives you an idea of how many English words have slid into German. However, you're not likely to overhear this many examples of mixed language in a single conversation. In this scenario, two friends, Claudia and Jana, meet on the street. Notice how some terms have a slightly different meaning in German.

Claudia: **Hi Jana, wie geht's? Wie ist der neue Job?**
Hi [as in English] *yâ*-nâ, vee geyts? vee ist dêr *noy*-e job [as in English]?
Hi Jana, how are you? How's the new job?

Jana: **Super! Heute war meine erste Presentation vor meinem big Boss, und er war total cool.**
super [as in English]! *hoy*-te vahr *mayn*-e *êrs*-te pre-zen-tât-see-*ohn* fohr *mayn*-êm big boss [as in English], oont êr vahr toh-*tahl* cool [as in English].
Super! Today was my first presentation in front of my big boss, and he was totally cool.

Claudia: **Wow! In meinem Office gibt es nur Stress. Mein Boss kann nichts managen. Mein Kollege checkt nichts, und denkt, er ist ein Sonnyboy, und alle anderen spinnen.**
wow [as in English]! in *mayn*-êm office [as in English] gipt ês noohr shtrês. mayn boss kân niHts *mân*-â-jen. mayn kol-*ey*-ge checkt niHts, oont dênkt, êr ist ayn sonny boy [as in English], oont *âl*-e *ân*-der-en *spin*-en.
Wow! In my office there's nothing but stress. My boss can't manage anything. My colleague isn't "with it," and thinks he's a hot shot, and all the others are crazy.

Jana: **Ich gehe shoppen. Kommst du mit?**
iH *gey*-e *shop*-en. Komst dooh mit?
I'm going shopping. Do you want to come along?

Claudia: **Nein, danke. Gestern war ich in einem Outlet und habe ein T-Shirt in pink und eine Jeans im Boyfriend-Look gekauft. Ich gehe jetzt joggen. Bye-bye!**

nayn, *dân*-ke. *gês*-têrn vahr iH in *ayn*-em outlet [as in English] oont *hah*-be ayn T-shirt [as in English] in pink [as in English] oont *ayn*-e jeans [as in English] im boyfriend-look [as in English] ge-*kouft*. iH *gey*-e yêtst *jog*-en [jog as in English]. bye-bye [as in English]!
No, thanks. Yesterday I went to an outlet and bought a pink T-shirt and a pair of jeans in boyfriend look. I'm going jogging now. Bye!

Jana: **Schade. Bye-bye!**
shah-de. bye-bye!
Too bad. Bye!

Using Popular Expressions

Just like English, German has many *idioms,* or expressions typical of a language and culture. When you translate these idioms word for word, they may sound obscure, silly, or just plain meaningless, so to use them appropriately, you need to find out what they really mean.

Some expressions have an English equivalent that's recognizable, so using them correctly isn't too hard. For example, the German idiom **ein Fisch auf dem Trockenen** (ayn fish ouf deym *trok*-ên-en) literally translates into *a fish on the dry,* which somewhat resembles the English *a fish out of water.* Other German expressions are a little harder to figure out. For instance, if you were to take apart the German expression **Da liegt der Hund begraben** (da leekt dêr hoont be-*grah*-ben) word for word, you'd probably feel sorry for the poor dog, because in essence, it means something like *That's where the dog is buried.* However, the English equivalent is *That's the heart of the matter.*

A few other typical German idioms are

Die Daumen drücken. (dee *doum*-en *druek*-en.) (*Press the thumbs.*) The English meaning is *Keep your fingers crossed.*

Wo sich Fuchs und Hase gute Nacht sagen (voh ziH fooks oont *hah*-ze *gooh*-te nâHt *zah*-gen) (*where fox and hare say good night to one another*), which means *in the middle of nowhere* or *in the sticks.*

Ich bin fix und fertig. (iH bin fix oont *fêr*-tiH.) (*I'm quick and ready.*) This means *I'm wiped out* or *I'm exhausted.*

Du nimmst mich auf den Arm! (dooh nimst miH ouf deyn ârm!) (*You're taking me on your arm!*) In English, this means *You're pulling my leg!*

Das ist ein Katzensprung. (dâs ist ayn *kâts*-en-shproong.) (*That's a cat's jump.*) The English meaning is *It's a stone's throw away.*

Schlafen wie ein Murmeltier. (*shlâf*-en vee ayn *moor*-mel-teer.) (*Sleep like a woodchuck [marmot].*) In English, you say *Sleep like a log.*

Apart from such idioms, many handy and frequently used German expressions are easy to learn. Here are some of the most common ones:

Prima!/Klasse!/Toll! (*pree*-mah!/*klâs*-e!/tôl!) (*Great!*)

Fertig. (*fêrt*-iH.) (*Ready./Finished.*) This can be either a question or a statement.

Genau. (ge-*nou*.) (*Exactly./Precisely.*) This can be used to tell someone that you really agree.

Es tut mir leid. (*ês* toot mir layd.) (*I'm sorry.*) Use this when you apologize for something.

Aber . . . (*ah*-ber) (*But . . .*)

Quatsch! (qvâch!) (*Nonsense!/How silly of me!*)

Einverstanden. (*ayn*-fêr-shtând-en.) (*Agreed./Okay.*)

Vielleicht. (fee-*layHt*.) (*Maybe./Perhaps.*)

Eventuell. (ê-ven-too-*êl*.) (*Maybe./Possibly.*) You can use this alone or in a statement.

Mach's gut. (vîrt ge-*mâHt*.) (*Take it easy.*) This is a casual way of saying *goodbye*.

Wie, bitte? (vee, *bi*-te?) (*[I beg your] pardon?/What did you say?*)

Das macht nichts. (dâs mâHt niHts.) (*Never mind./That's okay.*)

Nicht der Rede wert. (niHt dêr *rey*-de vêrt.) (*Don't mention it.*)

Schade! (*shah*-de!) (*Too bad!/What a pity!*)

So ein Pech! (zoh ayn pêH!) (*Bad luck!*)

Viel Glück! (feel gluek!) (*Good luck!*)

Oder?/Nicht? (*oh*-der?) (*Isn't that true?/Don't you think so?*)

Bis dann! (bis dân!) (*See you then!*)

Bis bald! (bis bâlt!) (*See you soon!*)

Handling Basic Pronunciation

Speaking a foreign language correctly is all about mastering the basics of pronunciation. The key to mastering pronunciation is to start small by figuring out how the individual letters sound. Then you can expand to syllables, words, and finally, sentences. The rest is practice, practice, practice.

Understanding stress in German

This type of stress doesn't have anything to do with meeting deadlines or having a BMW tailgate you at 110 miles per hour on the Autobahn. Instead, it's about knowing which syllables to stress in German words. In the pronunciation key that you see in parentheses following each word, the syllables you should stress are in *italics*.

Constructing the alphabet blocks

The German alphabet has all the letters that English does — 26 of 'em — plus four special letters: **ä**, **ö**, **ü**, and **ß**. The good news is that German words are generally pronounced just as they're spelled, so things aren't as confusing as they are in English with the likes of *bow (tie)*, *(take a) bow,* and *(tree) bough.* The bad news is that many of the familiar letters are pronounced differently from their English counterparts.

Table 1-2 shows you the sound of each letter of the alphabet when it's pronounced alone. Knowing how to say each individual letter comes in handy, for example, when you need to spell your name to make a table reservation at a German restaurant, book a room with a hotel receptionist, or compete in a German spelling bee with a grand prize of 500,000 euros.

Track 1 gives you the sounds of the letters in the German alphabet as shown in Table 1-2. Note that the German pronunciation of a single letter may be different from the way you pronounce it within a German word.

Table 1-2		Pronouncing the German Alphabet
Letter	*German Pronunciation*	*German Word*
a	ah	**Ahnen** (*ahn*-en) (*ancestors*)
b	bey	**Bild** (bilt) (*image, picture*)
c	tsey	**Café** (kâ-*fey)* (*café*)
d	dey	**durstig** (*doohrs*-tiH) (*thirsty*)
e	ey	**Ehe** (*ey*-e) (*marriage*)
f	êf	**Feuer** (*foy*-er) (*fire*)
g	gey	**geben** (*gey*-ben) (*give*)
h	hah	**Haus** (house [as in English]) (*house*)
i	ee	**ihn** (een) (*him*)
j	yot	**Januar** (*yahn*-oo-âr) (*January*)
k	kah	**Kilometer** (ki-loh-*mey*-ter) (*kilometer*)
l	êl	**Liebe** (*lee*-be) (*love*)
m	êm	**Manager** (manager [as in English]) (*manager*)
n	ên	**Name** (*nah*-me) (*name*)
o	oh	**ohne** (*oh*-ne) (*without*)
p	pey	**Pause** (*pou*-ze) (*break, intermission*)
q	kooh	**Quatsch** (kvâch) (*nonsense*)
r	êr	**rot** (roht) (*red*)
s	ês	**S-Bahn** (*es*-bahn) (*suburban train*)
t	tey	**Taxi** (*tâx*-ee) (*taxi*)
u	ooh	**U-Boot** (*ooh*-boht) (*submarine*)
v	fou	**Vogel** (*foh*-gel) (*bird*)
w	veh	**Wald** (vâlt) (*forest*)
x	iks	**Fax** (fâx) (*fax*)
y	*uep*-si-lon	**System** (zers-*teym*) (*system*)
z	tset	**Zeit** (tsayt) (*time*)
ä	ah-*oom*-lout (Umlaut)	**Bäcker** (*bêk*-er) (*baker*)
ö	oh-*oom*-lout (Umlaut)	**schön** (shern) (*beautiful*)
ü	ooh-*oom*-lout (Umlaut)	**Tür** (tuer) (*system*)
ß	ês-*tsêt*	**Straße** (*strah*-se) (*street*)

Pronouncing vowels

In German, vowels (**a, e, i, o,** and **u**) can generally be pronounced in two ways — as short or long vowel sounds. The *short* vowel sounds are "clipped," meaning they're pronounced shorter than their English equivalents. *Long* vowel sounds are "steady-state" or "pure," meaning the sound quality doesn't change even though it's a long sound. Here are the basic rules:

- A vowel is long when it's followed by the letter *h,* as in **Stahl** (shtahl) (*steel*) or **ihn** (een) (him).

- A vowel is generally long when it's followed by a single consonant, as in **Tag** (tahk) (*day*).

- A vowel is long when it's doubled, as in **Teer** (teyr) (tar) or **Aal** (ahl) (*eel*).

- The vowels **a, e,** and **i** sound long before a single consonant, as in **beten** (*bey*-ten) (*to pray*).

- In general, a vowel is short when followed by two or more consonants, as in **Tanne** (*tân*-e) (*fir tree*).

Table 1-3 shows you how to pronounce German vowels by providing some examples and the letter combinations that serve as the English equivalent of the German letter's pronunciation (called the *phonetic script*). In this book's phonetic script, two short vowel sounds have a little "hat" over the letter, so they look like this: â and ê. (Note that the phonetic spelling of ê in Table 1-3 is the same as that of the German short umlaut sound ä in Table 1-4.) Listen to Track 2 to hear how to pronounce these German vowels.

Table 1-3		Pronouncing German Vowels	
German Letter	*Phonetic Symbol*	*As in English*	*German Example*
a (long)	ah	father	**Bahnhof** (*bahn*-hohf) (*station*)
a (short)	â	adore (clipped "a")	**Banner** (*bân*-er) (*banner*)
e (long)	ey	vein	**Leben** (*ley*-ben) (*life*)
e (short/ stressed)	ê	bet (clipped "e")	**Bett** (bêt) (*bed*)
e (short/ unstressed)	e	pocket	**Lachen** (*lâH*-en) (*laughter*)

(continued)

Table 1-3 *(continued)*

German Letter	Phonetic Symbol	As in English	German Example
i (long)	ee	see	**isoliert** (eez-o-*leert*) (*isolated*)
i (short)	i	winter	**Mitte** (*mit*-e) (*middle*)
o (long)	oh	mope	**Lob** (lohp) (*praise*)
o (short)	o	gonna	**Sonne** (*zon*-e) (*sun*)
u (long)	ooh	moon	**Grube** (*grooh*-be) (*pit*)
u (short)	oo	push (clipped "u")	**muss** (moos) (*have to/must*)

Pronouncing ä, ö, and ü

German has three extra vowels: **ä**, **ö**, and **ü**. The German word for those curious double dots over the vowels is **Umlaut** (*oom*-lout) (*umlaut*). Umlauts slightly alter the sound of the vowels **a**, **o**, and **u**, as outlined in Table 1-4. These sounds have no equivalent in English, so listen to them on Track 3 to find out how to pronounce them.

Table 1-4		Pronouncing Vowels with Umlauts	
German Letter	Phonetic Symbol	As in English	German Example
ä (long)	ai	say ("ay" in "say" with spread lips)	**nächste** (*naiH*-ste) (*next*)
ä (short)	ê	bet (clipped "e")	**fällen** (*fêl*-en) (*to fell* [*a tree*])
ö	er	her (without the "r" sound)	**schön** (shern) (*pretty*) (remember: no "r" sound)
ü	ue	lure ("ooh" with pursed lips)	**Tür** (tuer) (*door*)

To make your German vowels **ä**, **ö**, and **ü** sound a bit more authentic, try progressing through the **ä**, **ö**, and **ü** sounds, pronouncing the vowels as though you're getting ready to kiss someone — in other words, round your lips and pucker up, baby! The **ü** sound is pronounced with very pursed lips.

Pronouncing diphthongs

Diphthongs, which you can hear on Track 4, are combinations of two vowels in one syllable (as in the English "lie"). Table 1-5 lists the German diphthongs and shows you how to pronounce them.

Table 1-5		Pronouncing German Diphthongs	
German Diphthong	**Phonetic Symbol**	**As in English**	**German Example**
ai/ei/ay	ay	cry	**Mais** (mays) (*corn*)/**ein** (ayn) (*a*)/**Bayern** (*bay*-ern) (*Bavaria*)
au	ou	loud	**laut** (lout) (*noisy*)
äu/eu	oy	boy	**Häuser** (*hoy*-zer) (*houses*)/**Leute** (*loy*-te) (*people*)
ie	ee	see	**Miete** (*meet*-e) (*rent*)

Both the long German vowel **i** and the German vowel combination **ie** are pronounced like the English letter *e* in *see,* but the German **ei**, **ai**, and **ay** are pronounced like the English letter *y* in *cry.*

Pronouncing consonants

Ahh, relief! The sounds of German consonants are easier to master than the German vowel sounds. In fact, they're pronounced either almost the same as their English equivalents or like other English consonants. Of course, you'll find a couple of oddities and exceptions, but don't worry. The following sections explain what you need to know.

Pronouncing f, h, k, m, n, p, t, x, and ß

As part of a word, the letters **f**, **h**, **k**, **m**, **n**, **p**, **t**, and **x** are pronounced the same in German as they are in English. The letter **ß**, on the other hand, doesn't exist in English. It's kind of cool looking, though, don't you think? But even if you don't care about looks, you'll be glad to know that you pronounce it just like *ss* or *s.*

As far as the written language goes, whether a given German word is spelled with **ss** or **ß** depends on a couple of rules. Here's the scoop:

- ✔ After a long vowel or a diphthong, the *s* sound is spelled **ß** — for example, **Fuß** (foohs) (*foot*).

- ✔ After a short vowel, the *s* sound is spelled **ss** — for example, **Fass** (fâs) (*barrel*).

Note: In Switzerland, the **ß** isn't used at all. Instead, the Swiss always spell words with the double **ss.**

Table 1-6 tells you how to pronounce the rest of the German consonants by providing you with examples and a phonetic script. To hear them all, listen to Track 5.

Table 1-6	Pronouncing Selected German Consonants		
German Letter	*Phonetic Symbol*	*As in English*	*German Example*
b* (end of a word or syllable or before voiceless consonants)	p	*up*	**Abfahrt** (*âp*-fahrt) (*departure*)
b	b	*bright*	**Bild** (bilt) (*image, picture*)
c (beginning of a word)	k	*cat*	**Café** (kâ-*fey*) (*café*)
c (mostly words of foreign origin)	ts	*tsar*	**Celsius** (*tsêl*-zee-oos) (*Celsius*)
c (mostly words of foreign origin)	ch	*cello*	**Cello** (*chêl*-oh) (*cello*)
d* (end of a word or syllable or before voiceless consonants)	t	*moot*	**blind** (blint) (*blind*)
d	d	*do*	**Dunst** (doonst) (*mist, haze*)
g	g	*go*	**geben** (*gey*-ben) (*give*)
g* (end of a word or syllable or before voiceless consonants)	k	*lag*	**Tag** (tahk) (*day*)
j	y	*yes*	**ja** (yah) (*yes*)
qu	kv	*kv* (pronounced together)	**Quatsch** (kvâch) (*nonsense*)
s (beginning of a word)	z	*zoo*	**sieben** (*zee*-ben) (*seven*)
s (middle/end of a word)	s	*sit*	**Haus** (house [as in English]) (*house*)

German Letter	Phonetic Symbol	As in English	German Example
v	f	*fire*	**Vogel** (*foh*-gel) (*bird*)
v (words of foreign origin)	v	*velvet*	**Vase** (*vah*-ze) (*vase*)
w	v	*vice*	**Wald** (vâlt) (*forest*)
y (mostly words of foreign origin)	y	*yes*	**Yoga** (*yoh*-gâ) (*yoga*)
y (mostly middle a of word)	er	*her* (without the "r" sound)	**System** (zers-*teym*) (*system*)
z	ts	*ts* as in *tsunami*	**Zahl** (tsahl) (*number*)
ß	s	*guess*	**Straße** (shtrah-se) (*street*)

*Note: When the letters **b**, **d**, and **g** are at the end of a word or syllable or before voiceless consonants like **s** or **t**, they change sounds. The **b** changes to a p sound, **d** changes to t, and **g** changes to k.*

Pronouncing the German r and l

You pronounce the letters **r** and **l** differently in German than you do in English:

- ✔ To replicate the "gargled" pronunciation of the German **r**, try making a gargling sound before saying *aahh*, so you're saying *ra*. Also, don't roll the tip of your tongue or use it to pronounce the German **r**.

- ✔ To correctly pronounce the German letter **l**, you have to position your tongue differently than you do when you pronounce the English letter *l*. In English, you pronounce the *l* with your tongue in a spoon shape, hollowed out in the middle. To make the German **l**, you press the tip of your tongue against your gum ridge (just as you do in English), but you keep it flat instead of spoon-shaped. The German **l** sound is clipped, not drawled.

Listen to Track 6 to hear how to pronounce these letters. Here are some sample words:

- ✔ **l** as in **Bild** (bilt) (*picture*)
- ✔ **r** as in **richtig** (*riH*-tiH) (*correct*)

Pronouncing consonant combinations

The German language has a few consonant sounds that are either different or don't occur in English. Fortunately, most of them are easy to pronounce.

The German letter combination **ch** is the trickiest one for English speakers to pronounce. There's absolutely no equivalent for it in English (that's why it's represented by a capital *H* in this book's phonetic script), and you actually have to learn a new sound — a kind of gentle "dry" gargling sound — in order to say it. The sound is a bit like trying to pronounce *hch* and not a *k* sound. The sound is similar to the guttural *ch* in Scottish, like in *Loch Ness*.

The good news is that in a few words, the **ch + s** combo is simply pronounced as an *x* sound, for example in **Wachs** (vâks) (*wax*) or **Fuchs** (fooks) (*fox*). In a few other words (generally French foreign words), the **ch** is pronounced like the sound *sh* in English, for example in **Champignon** (shâm-peen-yon) (*mushroom*) or **Champagner** (shâm-*pân*-yer) (*champagne*).

Table 1-7 shows you how to pronounce the common consonant combinations of **ch**, **ck**, **sch**, **sp**, **st**, and **tsch**. Listen to Track 7 to hear how to pronounce these combinations.

Table 1-7	Pronouncing ch, ck, sch, sp, st, and tsch		
German Letter	*Phonetic Symbol*	*As in English*	*German Example*
ch	H	*Loch (Ness)*	**mich** (miH) (*me*)
ck	k	*check*	**Dreck** (drêk) (*dirt*)
sch	sh	*shut*	**Tisch** (tish) (*table*)
sp (beginning of a word or a syllable)	shp	*sh* as in *shut*, *p* as in *people*	**spät** (shpait) (*late*)
st (beginning of a word or a syllable)	sht	*sh* as in *shut*, *t* as in *table*	**Stadt** (shtât) (*city*)
st (middle/end of a word)	st	*stable*	**fast** (fâst) (*almost, nearly*)
tsch	ch	*switch*	**Deutsch** (doych) (*German*)

The English *th* sound doesn't exist in the German language. The **th** combination is pronounced one of two ways in German:

- ✔ The **h** is silent, as in the words **Theorie** (tey-oh-*ree*) (*theory*) and **Theologie** (tey-oh-loh-*gee*) (*theology*).

- ✔ The **t** and **h** are pronounced separately because they actually belong to different components of a compound noun, as in the words **Gasthaus** (*gâst*-hous) (*inn*), which is a combination of the German words for *guest* and *house,* or **Basthut** (*bâst*-hooht) (*straw hat*), a combo of the German words for *raffia* and *hat.*

Chapter 2

Handling Numbers, Times, Dates, and Measurements

. . . .

In This Chapter

▶ Naming numbers and counting

▶ Tackling time and the days of the week

▶ Managing months and calendars

▶ Getting familiar with metric measurements

. . . .

*I*n German-speaking countries, the servers in street cafés often walk around with a bulging black leather change purse either tucked in the back of the pants (the male version) or attached at the waist in front, neatly camouflaged under a starched white apron (the female version). When you say **die Rechnung, bitte** (dee *rêH*-noong *bi*-te), or its more informal version, **Zahlen, bitte** (*tsahl*-en *bi*-te) (*the check, please*), they have a crafty way of whipping the change purse out of hiding and opening it wide, ready for action. The next part is the best: watching the seasoned waiter take a quick look, add up the tab without pen and paper, and blurt out, **"Das macht siebenundzwanzig Euro."** (dâs mâHt *zee*-ben-oont-*tsvân*-tsiH *oy*-roh.) (*That'll be twenty-seven euros.*) That's the moment of reckoning: How good are you at understanding numbers in German?

In this chapter, you work with basic building blocks: numbers, dates, times, and measurements. If you feel confident that you can use these elements without any hesitation, you're ready to feed the waiter's portable cash wallet. You can also understand which **Bahnsteig** (*bahn*-shtayg) (*track*) the train is leaving from (and at what time) and jump on the correct train when there's been a last-minute track change.

Doing the Numbers

Chances are you'll encounter German numbers in all kinds of situations: when you're trying to decipher prices, for example, or street numbers, departure times, exchange rates, and so on. Knowing German numbers makes counting anything easy. (For money matters, such as changing currency and accessing funds, see Book II, Chapter 3.)

Counting off with cardinal numbers

Cardinal numbers have nothing to do with religious numbers colored red or a songbird that can sing numbers. These numbers are just plain, unadulterated numbers like 25, 654, or 300,000. In this section, you get a list of cardinal numbers and details on the differences between German and English numbers.

It's always good to start at the very beginning (as Julie Andrews pointed out in *The Sound of Music*), so here are the basic numbers and their German pronunciations. Listen to Track 8 to hear how to pronounce them:

- **0: null** (nool)
- **1: eins** (ayns)
- **2: zwei** (tsvay)
- **3: drei** (dray)
- **4: vier** (feer)
- **5: fünf** (fuenf)
- **6: sechs** (zêks)
- **7: sieben** (*zee*-ben)
- **8: acht** (âHt)
- **9: neun** (noyn)
- **10: zehn** (tseyn)
- **11: elf** (êlf)
- **12: zwölf** (tsverlf)
- **13: dreizehn** (*dray*-tseyn)
- **14: vierzehn** (*feer*-tseyn)
- **15: fünfzehn** (*fuenf*-tseyn)

- 16: **sechzehn** (*zêH*-tseyn)
- 17: **siebzehn** (*zeep*-tseyn)
- 18: **achtzehn** (*âHt*-tseyn)
- 19: **neunzehn** (*noyn*-tseyn)
- 20: **zwanzig** (*tsvân*-tsiH)
- 21: **einundzwanzig** (*ayn*-oont-tsvân-tsiH)
- 22: **zweiundzwanzig** (*tsvay*-oont-tsvân-tsiH)
- 23: **dreiundzwanzig** (*dray*-oont-tsvân-tsiH)
- 24: **vierundzwanzig** (*feer*-oont-tsvân-tsiH)
- 25: **fünfundzwanzig** (*fuenf*-oont-tsvân-tsiH)
- 30: **dreißig** (*dray*-siH)
- 40: **vierzig** (*feer*-tsiH)
- 50: **fünfzig** (*fuenf*-tsiH)
- 60: **sechzig** (*zêH*-tsiH)
- 70: **siebzig** (*zeep*-tsiH)
- 80: **achtzig** (*âHt*-tsiH)
- 90: **neunzig** (*noyn*-tsiH)
- 100: **hundert** (*hoon*-dert)
- 101: **hunderteins** (*hoon*-dert-ayns)
- 102: **hundertzwei** (*hoon*-dert-tsvay)
- 103: **hundertdrei** (*hoon*-dert-dray)
- 104: **hundertvier** (*hoon*-dert-feer)
- 111: **hundertelf** (*hoon*-dert-êlf)
- 112: **hundertzwölf** (*hoon*-dert-tsverlf)
- 113: **hundertdreizehn** (*hoon*-dert-*dray*-tseyn)
- 114: **hundertvierzehn** (*hoon*-dert-*feer*-tseyn)
- 200: **zweihundert** (*tsvay*-hoon-dert)
- 300: **dreihundert** (*dray*-hoon-dert)
- 400: **vierhundert** (*feer*-hoon-dert)
- 500: **fünfhundert** (*fuenf*-hoon-dert)

Notice that, as words, the numbers between 21 and 25 in the preceding list appear to be backward. Take the number *21,* **einundzwanzig,** for example. In German, you actually say, "One and twenty." Just remember to stick to this pattern for all the double-digit numbers, except for numbers in multiples of ten, like 30, 40, 50, and so on.

Pay close attention to the number 30. Unlike the other multiples of ten (40, 50, and so on), 30 is spelled slightly differently. **Dreißig** has no *z* in its ending, whereas the other double-digits do (**vierzig, fünfzig,** and so on).

When dealing with numbers made up of three digits, keep in mind that the last two digits in a three-digit sequence are spoken "backward." So for a number like 679, you say "six hundred nine and seventy." Check out the following examples of triple-digit numbers:

- ✔ **223 zweihundertdreiundzwanzig** (*tsvay*-hoon-dert-dray-oont-*tsvân*-tsiH) (*two hundred three and twenty*)

- ✔ **548 fünfhundertachtundvierzig** (*fuenf*-hoon-dert-āHt-oont-*feer*-tsiH) (*five hundred eight and forty*)

- ✔ **752 siebenhundertzweiundfünfzig** (*zee*-ben-hoon-dert-tsvay-oont-*fuenf*-tsiH) (*seven hundred two and fifty*)

Watching out for spelling and pronunciation changes

Not surprisingly, German numbers have a few of their own oddities that keep native English speakers on their toes. Here are some of the most common spelling and pronunciation changes related to numbers that you need to be familiar with:

- ✔ When you use the number **eins** to describe *one* thing in a sentence, it changes spelling because, in these situations, **eins** is working as an adjective, and it's the equivalent of using *a* or *an.* In German, adjectives go through all kinds of spelling changes in a sentence. (See Chapter 5 in Book III for more info on adjectives.) Consider this example:

  Er hat einen großen Hund. (ēr hât *ayn*-en *grohs*-en hoont.) (*He has a large dog.*)

- ✔ In spoken German, people commonly pronounce the digit 2 as **zwo** (tsvoh) instead of **zwei** (tsvay). Doing so helps avoid the confusion — acoustically speaking — with **drei** (dray) (*three*). To double-check that you heard **zwei** and not **drei** in credit card numbers, prices, telephone numbers, room numbers, and so on, simply ask, or repeat the number(s) using **zwo.** Say, for example, **Ich wiederhole vier-zwo-acht.** (iH vee-der-*hoh*-le feer-tsvoh-āHt.) (*I'll repeat four-two-eight.*)

✔ Especially in spoken German, you can use **einhundert** (ayn *hoon*-dert) (*one hundred*) in place of **hundert** (*hoon*-dert) (*hundred*). This change makes the number clearer to the listener.

✔ When referring to currency, you change the numerical value of the bill to a noun to talk about the bill itself. Imagine you're cashing €400 in traveler's checks and you want three €100 bills and five €20 bills. You say **Ich möchte drei Hunderter und fünf Zwanziger.** (iH *merH*-te dray *hoon*-dert-er oont fuenf *tsvân*-tsiH-er.) (*I'd like three hundreds [euro bills] and five twenties.*) The numbers **Hunderter** and **Zwanziger** are nouns, and you form them like this: Take the number, for example **hundert,** and add **-er** to the end of the number: **hundert** + **-er** = **Hunderter.**

✔ Germans often "spell" their phone numbers in pairs of numbers. If, for example, your number is 23 86 50, you say **dreiundzwanzig sechsundachtzig fünfzig** (*dray*-oont-tsvân-tsiH *zêks*-oont-âH-tsiH fuenf-tsiH). If you read the numbers one by one, you may say the number 2, or **zwei** (tsvay), pronounced as **zwo** (tsvoh), making 23 86 50 sound like **zwo drei acht sechs fünf null** (tsvoh dray âHt zeks fuenf nool). Numbers in groups of three, such as area codes, are usually read one by one. For example, the area code for München is 089, so you would say **null acht neun** (nool âHt noyn).

Thinking grand with large numbers and punctuating properly

For numbers higher than 999, look at the following list. Notice that the decimal point in German numbers represents the comma in English:

✔ **1.000: tausend** (*tou*-zent) or **ein tausend** (ayn *tou*-zent) (*1,000*)

✔ **1.000.000: Million** (mee-lee-*ohn*) or **eine Milllion** (*ayn*-e mee-lee-*ohn*) (*1,000,000*)

✔ **1.650.000: eine Million sechshundertfünzigtausend** (*ayn*-e mee-lee-*ohn* zêks *hoon*-dert *fuenf*-tsiH *tou*-zent) (*1,650,000*)

✔ **2.000.000: zwei Millionen** (tsvay mee-lee-*ohn*-en) (*2,000,000*)

✔ **1.000.000.000: eine Milliarde** (*ayn*-e mee-lee-*ahr*-de) (*1,000,000,000; one billion*)

✔ **2.000.000.000: zwei Milliarden** (tsvay mee-lee-*ahr*-den) (*2,000,000,000; two billion*)

✔ **1.000.000.000.000: eine Billion** (*ayn*-e bil-ee-*ohn*) (*1,000,000,000,000; one trillion*)

In English, you use a comma to indicate thousands and a period to show decimals. German (and many other languages) does the reverse: It uses a period (**Punkt**) (poonkt) to indicate thousands and the comma (**Komma**) (*ko*-mâ) to work as a decimal point. Consider these examples:

1 Zoll (ayn tsol) (*one inch*) = **2,54 Zentimeter** (tsvay *ko*-mâ foonf feer *tsen*-ti-mey-ter) (*two comma five four centimeters*)

1 Zentimeter (ayn *tsen*-ti-mey-ter) (*one centimeter*) = **0,39 Zoll** (noohl *ko*-mâ dray noyn tsol) (*zero comma three nine inches*)

Mount Everest ist 8.848 Meter hoch. (mount everest [as in English] ist âHt-*tou*-zent âHt *hoon*-dert âHt-oont-*feer*-tsiH *mey*-ter hohH.) (*Mount Everest is eight thousand eight hundred forty-eight meters high.*)

And this is how you say one of these numbers: 20,75 = **zwanzig Komma sieben fünf** (*tsvân*-tsiH *ko*-mâ *zee*-ben fuenf). The English equivalent has a decimal point in place of the comma in German, so you'd say the number as *twenty point seven five*.

Getting in line with ordinal numbers

Ordinal numbers are the kinds of numbers that show what order things come in. You need ordinal numbers when you're talking about **das Datum** (dâs *dah*-toom) (*the date*), **die Feiertage** (dee *fay*-er-*tah*-ge) (*the holidays*), **die Stockwerke in einem Hotel** (dee *shtok*-ver-ke in *ayn*-em hoh-*tel*) (*the floors in a hotel*), and stuff like that.

Ordinal numbers function as adjectives, so they have the adjective endings you normally use in a sentence. (Go to Chapter 5 in Book III for specifics on adjectives.) The general rule for forming ordinal numbers is to add **-te** to the numbers 1 through 19 and then **-ste** to the numbers 20 and higher. For example, **Nach der achten Tasse Kaffee, ist er am Schreibtisch eingeschlafen.** (naH dêr *âHt*-en *tah*-se *kâ*-fey ist êr âm *shrayp*-tish *ayn*-ge-*shlâf*-en.) (*After the eighth cup of coffee, he fell asleep on the desk.*)

This rule has four exceptions:

- **erste** (*êrs*-te) (*first*)
- **dritte** (*dri*-te) (*third*)
- **siebte** (*zeep*-te) (*seventh*)
- **achte** (*âHt*-e) (*eighth*)

For example, **Reinhold Messner war der erste Mensch, der Mount Everest ohne Sauerstoffmaske bestieg.** (*rayn*-hold *mês*-ner vahr dêr *êrs*-te mênsh, dêr mount everest [as in English] *oh*-ne zou-er-shtof-*mahs*-ke be-*shteeg*.) (*Reinhold Messner was the first person to climb Mt. Everest without an oxygen mask.*)

Here are two other adjectives you need to know when putting things in order: **letzte** (*lets*-te) (*last*) and **nächste** (*naiH*-ste) (*next*). You can use them to refer to any sequence of numbers, people, or things.

To write dates as numerals, write the digit followed by a period: **Der 1. Mai ist ein Feiertag in Deutschland.** (dêr *êrs*-te may ist ayn *fay*-er-tâg in *doych*-lânt.) (*May 1st is a holiday in Germany.*) In case you're wondering, the same sentence with a spelled-out date looks like this: **Der erste Mai ist ein Feiertag in Deutschland.**

Look at the examples of ordinal numbers in Table 2-1. The first column shows the ordinal numbers as numerals, or digits, the second column shows the same ordinal numbers as words, and the third column shows how to say *on the . . . fifth floor, sixth of December, and so on.*

Table 2-1	Ordinal Numbers	
Ordinals as Numerals	**Ordinals as Words**	**On the . . .**
1st	**der erste** (dêr *êrs*-te) (*the first*)	**am ersten** (âm *êrs*-ten) (*on the first*)
2nd	**der zweite** (dêr *tsvay*-te) (*the second*)	**am zweiten** (âm *tsvay*-ten) (*on the second*)
3rd	**der dritte** (dêr *dri*-te) (*the third*)	**am dritten** (âm *dri*-ten) (*on the third*)
4th	**der vierte** (dêr *feer*-te) (*the fourth*)	**am vierten** (âm *feer*-ten) (*on the fourth*)
5th	**der fünfte** (dêr *fuenf*-te) (*the fifth*)	**am fünften** (âm *fuenf*-ten) (*on the fifth*)
6th	**der sechste** (dêr *zêks*-te) (*the sixth*)	**am sechsten** (âm *zêks*-ten) (*on the sixth*)
7th	**der siebte** (dêr *zeep*-te) (*the seventh*)	**am siebten** (âm *zeep*-ten) (*on the seventh*)
18th	**der achtzehnte** (dêr *âHt-* tseyn -te) (*the eighteenth*)	**am achtzehnten** (âm *âHt-* tseyn-ten) (*on the eighteenth*)
22nd	**der zweiundzwanzigste** (dêr *tsvay*-oont-*tsvân*-tsiH-ste) (*the twenty-second*)	**am zweiundzwanzigsten** (âm *tsvay*-oont-*tsvân*-tsiH-sten) (*on the twenty-second*)

Note: In Table 2-1, you see how to formulate the expression *on the (first)*. It's **am** (âm) + *ordinal number* + **en** (en). **Am** is the contraction of **an** (ân) (*on*) + **dem** (deym) (*the*); you form it by taking the preposition **an,** which uses the dative case here, plus **dem,** the masculine dative of **der** (dêr) (*the*). You need to show dative case agreement with the adjective **erste** (*first*), so you add **-n: erste** + **n** = **ersten.** (See Chapter 2 in Book IV for more on prepositions.)

Telling Time

You're in **Interlaken, in der Schweiz** (*in*-têr-lâ-ken in dêr shvayts) (*Interlaken, in Switzerland*) and you want to know what time it is. You have four choices: Look at your own watch; look at the nearest clock tower (most are absolutely stunning) and find out just how accurate the Swiss are in keeping time (very!); buy a Rolex for 1,399 Swiss francs (no euros in Switzerland); or practice understanding German clock time by asking someone on the street, **Wie viel Uhr ist es?** (vee feel oohr ist ês?) (*What time is it?*) You're just about guaranteed whomever you ask will tell you the precise time.

German speakers have two systems for telling time: one using the numbers 1–12 on a standard clock and one using a 24-hour format. They use the 12-hour system in casual conversation and the 24-hour system when they want to avoid any chance of misunderstanding. Unlike in the United States, Germans don't use the a.m./p.m. system.

When you need to ask someone for the time, you can use either one of the following two phrases:

> **Wie viel Uhr ist es?** (vee feel oohr ist ês?) (*What time is it?*)

> **Wie spät ist es?** (vee shpait ist ês?) (*What time is it?*)

To make your request for the time a little more polite, simply add the phrase **Entschuldigen Sie, bitte** (ênt-*shool*-di-gen zee, *bi*-te) (*Excuse me, please*) to the beginning of your question.

Using the 12-hour clock

Many German speakers use the 12-hour clock format when talking casually. This system is one you're already familiar with: You use the numbers 1 through 12 on a standard clock. However, German doesn't have the expressions a.m. and p.m., so German speakers revert to the 24-hour format to avoid potential misunderstandings, for example, when discussing schedules and the like. (For more about the 24-hour system, head to the upcoming section.)

On the hour

At the top of the hour, telling time is very easy. You just say

> **Es ist . . . Uhr.** (ês ist . . . oohr.) (*It's . . . o'clock.*)

Of course, you include the number of the appropriate hour before the word **Uhr.**

Note: You say **Es ist ein Uhr** (ês ist ayn oohr) (*It's one o'clock*), not **eins Uhr** (ayns oohr). However, you can also say **Es ist eins** (ês ist ayns) (*It's one*) and leave out the word **Uhr** (oohr) (*o'clock*).

Before and after the hour

Indicating times like quarter past three, ten to eight, or half past eleven is a little more complicated, but you still need to know only three key expressions.

To use the German word for quarter, you include **Viertel** (*feer*-tel) (*quarter*) plus the word **nach** (nâH) (*past/after*) or **vor** (fohr) (*to/before*) followed by the appropriate hour, as shown in these examples:

> **Es ist Viertel nach. . . .** (ês ist *feer*-tel nâH. . . .) (*It's quarter past. . . .*)
>
> **Es ist Viertel vor. . . .** (ês ist *feer*-tel fohr. . . .) (*It's quarter to. . . .*)

Expressing the half hour isn't quite as straightforward. In German, the word **halb** (hâlp) (*half*) indicates half of the hour to come rather than the past hour. You use the phrase **Es ist halb. . . .** (ês ist hâlp. . . .) (*It's half an hour before. . . .*) followed by the appropriate hour. For example, when it's 4:30, you say this:

> **Es ist halb fünf.** (ês ist hâlp fuenf.) (*It's half an hour before 5:00.*)

A few minutes before or after

When you need to break down the time in terms of minutes before or after the hour, you use **nach** (nâH) (*past/after*) and **vor** (fohr) (*to/before*), like this:

> **Es ist fünf Minuten vor zwölf.** (ês ist fuenf mi-*nooh*-ten fohr tsverlf.) (*It's five minutes to twelve.*)
>
> **Es ist zwanzig Minuten nach sechs.** (ês ist *tsvân*-tsiH mi-*nooh*-ten nâH zêks.) (*It's twenty minutes past six.*)

If you're looking for a shortcut, you can leave out the word **Minuten.** For example, you can say either **Es ist fünf vor zwölf** or **Es ist fünf Minuten vor zwölf.** Both phrases mean the same thing: *It's five [minutes] to twelve.* The same goes for talking about the full hour. You don't need to use the word **Uhr.** You can say either **Es ist acht** or **Es ist acht Uhr.** Both phrases mean *It's eight [o'clock.].*

Book I

Getting Started with German

Using the 24-hour system

Like the a.m./p.m. system, the 24-hour system prevents misunderstanding, which is why all kinds of German businesses — banks, stores, airlines, theaters, museums, cinemas, and so forth — use it to tell time.

Here's how the 24-hour system works: After you reach 12, you keep adding hours (13, 14, 15, and so on) until you get to 24 or **Mitternacht** (*mit*-er-nâHt) (*midnight*), which is also called **null Uhr** (nool oohr) (literally: *zero hour*).

Time tables are published using the 24-hour system, so it's a good idea to become familiar with this format before heading off to Europe.

In this system of telling time, you don't use phrases like "half past" or "a quarter to" (the hour). Those expressions are only used for 12-hour time. With 24-hour time, everything is expressed in terms of minutes after the hour. Note in the following examples how the hour comes first, followed by the minutes:

> **Es ist fünfzehn Uhr dreißig.** (ês ist *fuenf*-tseyn oohr *dray*-siH.) (*It's fifteen hours and thirty.*) This corresponds to 3:30 p.m.
>
> **Es ist einundzwanzig Uhr fünfzehn.** (ês ist *ayn*-oont-*tsvân*-tsiH oohr *fuenf*-tseyn.) (*It's twenty-one hours and fifteen.*) That's 9:15 p.m.
>
> **Es ist zweiundzwanzig Uhr vierundvierzig.** (ês ist *tsvay*-oont-*tsv*ân-tsiH oohr *feer*-oont-feer-tsiH.) (*It's twenty-two hours and forty-four.*) You got it — 10:44 p.m.
>
> **Es ist null Uhr siebenundreißig.** (ês ist nool oohr *zee*-ben-oont-*dray*-siH.) (*It's zero hours and thirty-seven.*) That's the early, early morning — 12:37 a.m.!

When writing the time numerically, German traditionally uses a period where English uses a colon. Note that when you read the time, you say **Uhr** (*o'clock*) where the period appears. Alternatively, you can leave out the **Uhr,** just as you can leave out the *o'clock* in English. For example, **Um wie viel Uhr kommst du? Um sechs oder um sieben?** (oom vee feel oohr komst dooh? oom zêks *oh*-der oom *zee*-ben?) (*What time are you coming? At six or at seven?*) Note also that the word **Uhr** in the question means the word *time* in English. You can also say **Die Bank öffnet um 8.30 Uhr.** (dee bank *erf*-net oom âHt oohr *dray*-siH.) (*The bank opens at 8:30 a.m.*)

Describing times of the day

When you want to talk about a slice of the day, such as morning or afternoon, you have several options in German. However, take the following time periods with a grain of salt; they're meant as guidelines. After all, night owls and early morning joggers have different ideas about when one part of the day starts and another ends.

- **der Morgen** (dêr *mor*-gen) (*morning;* 4:00 a.m. to noon)

- **der Vormittag** (dêr *fohr*-mi-tahk) (*morning;* 9:00 a.m. to noon)

- **der Mittag** (dêr *mi*-tahk) (*noon;* 12 noon to 2:00 p.m.)

- **der Nachmitag** (dêr *nâH*-mi-tahk) (*afternoon;* 2:00 p.m. to 6:00 p.m.)

- **der Abend** (dêr *ah*-bent) (*evening;* 6:00 p.m. to 12:00 a.m.)

- **die Nacht** (dee nâHt) (*night;* 12:00 a.m. to 4:00 a.m.)

Expressing Dates

To express dates correctly, you first need to know how to use **die Tage der Woche** (dee *tah*-ge dêr *voH*-e) (*the days of the week*), **die Jahreszeiten** (dee *yahr*-es-tsay-ten) (*the seasons*), and **die Monate** (dee *moh*-nâ-te) (*the months*) in your writing and speech. That way, you can clearly and correctly ask and answer **Was ist das Datum?** (vâs ist dâs *dah*-toom?) (*What is the date?*)

Recounting the days

Looking at a German calendar, you find that *the week,* **die Woche** (dee *woH*-e), starts on a Monday. In addition, the days of the week are all the same gender — masculine (**dêr**) — but they're generally used without an article. For example, if you want to say that today is Monday, you say **Heute ist Montag.** (*hoy*-te ist *mohn*-tahk.)

Here are the days of the week followed by the abbreviations you often see on schedules:

- **Montag** (*mohn*-tahk) (Mo) (*Monday*)

- **Dienstag** (*deens*-tahk) (Di) (*Tuesday*)

- **Mittwoch** (*mit*-voH) (Mi) (*Wednesday*)

- **Donnerstag** (*don*-ers-tahk) (Do) (*Thursday*)

- **Freitag** (*fray*-tâk) (Fr) (*Friday*)

- **Samstag/Sonnabend** (*zâms*-tahk/*zon*-ah-bênt) (Sa) (*Saturday*)

- **Sonntag** (*zon*-tahk) (So) (*Sunday*)

In northern Germany, *Saturday* is called **Sonnabend**, while people living in southern Germany, Austria, and German-speaking Switzerland use the term **Samstag.**

To indicate that something always happens on a particular day of the week, you add an **s** to the word and lowercase it. For example, you may get to a museum or a restaurant on a Monday and find it closed, in which case you're likely to see a sign on the door that says **montags geschlossen** (*mohn*-tahks ge-*shlos*-en*) (closed on Mondays*).

Sometimes you want to be more casual in your references to days and use words like *tomorrow* or *yesterday* rather than the specific name of the day. Say it's Tuesday and you want to confirm that you've planned to meet someone the next day. You can ask whether you're meeting on Wednesday, or you can ask whether the meeting is tomorrow. The following list helps you refer to specific days without saying them by name:

- ✔ **heute** (*hoy*-te) (*today*)

- ✔ **gestern** (*gês*-tern) (*yesterday*)

- ✔ **vorgestern** (*fohr*-gês-tern) (*the day before yesterday*)

- ✔ **morgen** (*mor*-gen) (*tomorrow*)

- ✔ **übermorgen** (*ue*-ber-mor-gen) (*the day after tomorrow*)

To speak precisely about a particular time on a specific day, you can combine the preceding words with the times of day discussed in the earlier section "Describing times of the day." Try the following examples on for size:

heute Morgen (*hoy*-te *mor*-gen) (*this morning*)

heute Vormittag (*hoy*-te *fohr*-mi-tahk) (*this morning*)

gestern Abend (*gês*-tern *ah*-bent) (*yesterday evening/last night*)

The word **morgen** (*mor*-gen) shows up in two different versions. Written with a lowercase *m*, **morgen** means *tomorrow*. The noun **der Morgen,** written with an uppercase *m*, means *morning*. Theoretically, **morgen Morgen** should mean *tomorrow morning,* but German speakers don't say that. Instead, they say **morgen früh** (*mor*-gen frue) (*early tomorrow*).

Knowing the names of the months and seasons

When writing and speaking German, you need to have a firm grasp of the seasons and months because they're part of dates, too. (The last thing you want to do is invite someone to your July barbeque and tell him it's in the winter.) The good news is that some of the months of the calendar year in German are quite similar to their English counterparts. The only caveat is that the pronunciation of the German months is a bit different from English.

The following list shows you the names of the months. Although you don't use an article when speaking generally about a particular month, all the months' names are masculine, meaning that their article is **der:**

- **Januar** (*yâ-*noo-ahr) (*January*) or **Jänner** (*yên-*er) (*January*), which is often used in Austria
- **Februar** (*fey-*broo-ahr) (*February*)
- **März** (mêrts) (*March*)
- **April** (ah-*pril*) (*April*)
- **Mai** (may) (*May*)
- **Juni** (*yooh-*nee) (*June*)
- **Juli** (*yooh-*lee) (*July*)
- **August** (ou-*goost*) (*August*)
- **September** (zêp-*têm-*ber) (*September*)
- **Oktober** (ok-*toh-*ber) (*October*)
- **November** (no-*vêm-*ber) (*November*)
- **Dezember** (dey-*tsêm-*ber) (*December*)

Instead of saying Juni (*yooh-*nee) (*June*), some German speakers say **Juno** (*yooh-*noh) (*June*) to distinguish it, acoustically speaking, from **Juli** (*yooh-*lee) (*July*).

The following sentences explain the basic *calendar,* **der Kalender** (der kâ-*lên-*der), in German:

> **Ein Jahr hat 12 Monate.** (ayn yahr hât tsverlf *moh-*nâ-te.) (*A year has 12 months.*)

> **Ein Monat hat 30 oder 31 Tage.** (ayn *moh-*nât hât *dray-*siH *oh-*der *ayn-*oont-dray-siH *tah-*ge.) (*A month has 30 or 31 days.*)

> **Der Februar hat 28 oder 29 Tage.** (dêr *fey-*broo-ahr hât *âHt-*oont-tsvân-tsiH *oh-*der *noyn-*oont-tsvân-tsiH *tah-*ge.) (*February has 28 or 29 days.*)

> **Eine Woche hat 7 Tage.** (*ayn-*e voH-e hât *zee-*ben *tah-*ge.) (*A week has seven days.*)

Here's a look at *the seasons,* **die Jahreszeiten** (dee *yahr*-es-tsayt-en), in German:

- **der Frühling** (dêr *frue*-leeng) (*the spring*) or **das Frühjahr** (dâs *frue*-yahr) (*the spring*); these terms are interchangeable in German-speaking regions
- **der Sommer** (dêr *zom*-er) (*the summer*)
- **der Herbst** (dêr *hêrpst*) (*the autumn*)
- **der Winter** (dêr *vin*-ter) (*the winter*)

Writing dates the European way

In German (and other European languages), you write dates in the order of day-month-year, such as in this sentence: **Die Berliner Mauer ist am 09.11.1989 gefallen.** (dee bêr-*leen*-er *mou*-er ist âm *noyn*-ten *êlf*-ten *noyn*-tseyn-*hoon*-dert-*noyn*-oont-*âHt*-tsiH ge-*fâl*-en.) (*The Berlin Wall fell on 11/09/1989* or *The Berlin Wall fell on November 9, 1989.*) You need the periods in dates in German, just as you need to write the date in English with a slash between the month, day, and year.

To write out the date with the words for the ordinal numbers, you'd write **Die Berliner Mauer ist am neunten elften neunzehnhundertneunundachtzig gefallen.** (dee bêr-*leen*-er *mou*-er ist âm *noyn*-ten-*êlf*-ten-*noyn*-tseyn-*hoon*-dert-noyn-oont-*âHt*-tsiH ge-*fâl*-en.) (*The Berlin Wall fell on November 9, 1989.*) Alternatively, you could say **am neunten November** (âm *noyn*-ten no-*vêm*-ber) (*on the ninth of November*).

Those are the long versions. You often see or hear a shorter version. For example, you would write **14.10.2014**, and you would say **vierzehnter zehnter zweitausend vierzehn** (*feer*-tseyn-ter *tseyn*-ter tsvay-*tou*-zênt *feer*-tseyn) (*[the] 14th of October, 2014*). Note the periods after the numerals (both the day and month are ordinals).

If you want to find out what today's date is, simply ask

Welches Datum ist heute? (*vêlH*-es *dah*-toom ist *hoy*-te?) (*What's today's date?*)

The answer will be one of the following:

Heute ist der (achte April). (*hoy*-te ist dêr [*aH*-te ah-*pril*].) (*Today is the [eighth of April].*)

Heute haben wir den (achten April). (*hoy*-te *hah*-ben veer deyn [*aH*-ten ah-*pril*].) (*Today we have the [eighth of April].*)

Words to Know

das Jahr	dâs yahr	year
der Monat	dêr <u>moh</u>-nât	month
die Woche	dee <u>voH</u>-e	week
der Tag	dêr tahk	day
das Datum	dâs <u>dah</u>-toom	date
der Kalender	dêr kâ-<u>lên</u>-der	calendar

You may hear the name of a year integrated into a sentence in one of two ways. The first, longer way uses the preposition **im** to create the phrase **im Jahr . . .** (im yahr) (*in the year*). The second, more common, and shorter way omits this phrase. The following sentences show you examples of both ways of talking about the year:

> **Im Jahr 2010 arbeitete Herr Diebold in den USA.** (im yahr tsvay-*tou*-zênt-tseyn *âr*-bay-te-te hêr *dee*-bolt in deyn ooh-ês-*ah*.) (*In the year 2010, Mr. Diebold worked in the United States.*)

> **2008 war er in Kanada.** (tsvay-*tou*-zênt-*âHt* vâr êr in *kâ*-nâ-dâ.) (*In 2008, he was in Canada.*)

Referring to specific dates

When you refer to the days of the week, seasons, and months, keep in mind the following rules:

✔ They're all masculine, except for **das Frühjahr** (dâs *frue*-yahr) (*the spring*).

✔ When speaking or writing days of the week and months, you generally leave out the article **der.** However, some combinations with the dative prepositions **an** (*on*) and **in** (*in*) do include **der** in the dative form (see Book IV, Chapter 2 for more on prepositions).

✔ Seasons use the definite article.

Take a look at the following examples, two of which include **an** and **in** with the article **der:**

Gestern war Dienstag, heute ist Mittwoch, und morgen ist Donnerstag. (*gês*-tern vahr *deens*-tahk, *hoy*-te ist *mit*-voH, oont *mor*-gen ist *don*-ers-tahk.) (*Yesterday was Tuesday, today is Wednesday, and tomorrow is Thursday.*) The article **der** isn't used; you're referring to the name of the day of the week.

Am kommenden Freitag fahre ich nach Flensburg. (âm *kom*-en-den *fray*-tahk *fahr*-e iH naH *flêns*-boorg.) (*I'm driving to Flensburg this coming Friday.*) **An** + **dem** = **am; an** is a dative preposition, and **dem** is the dative masculine article derived from **der.** The phrase **am kommenden Freitag** describes the specific Friday; it literally means *on this coming Friday.*

Im Frühling gibt es viele Feiertage in Deutschland. (im *frue*-leeng gipt ês *fee*-le *fay*-er-tah-ge in *doych*-lânt.) (*In [the] spring there are a lot of holidays in Germany.*) **In** + **dem** = **im; in** is a dative preposition, and **dem** is the dative masculine article. You combine the name of the season or month with the preposition **im** (im) (*in*) when something takes place during a particular time.

Warum trägst du Sommerkleidung bei herbstlichen Temperaturen? (vah-*roohm* trêgst dooh *zom*-er-klai-doong bay *hêrpst*-leeH-en têmp-er-â-*toohr*-en?) (*Why are you wearing summer clothes during fall-like temperatures?*) **Bei** is a dative preposition, so to form the dative plural ending with the adjective **herbstlich** (*hêrpst*-leeH) (*fall-like*), you add **-en.** *Note:* **Sommerkleidung** (*zom*-er-klai-doong) (*summer clothes*) is a combination of two nouns. Because the last word of any noun combination determines the gender, you have **der Sommer** + **die Kleidung** = **die Sommerkleidung** (dêr *zom*-er + dee *klai*-doong = dee *zom*-er-klai-doong). In the prepositional phrase **bei herbstlichen Temperaturen** (*during fall-like temperatures*), the preposition **bei** (bay) (*during*) takes the dative case, so the adjective **herbstlichen** (*hêrpst*-leeH-en) (*fall-like*) is in the dative plural.

Naming specific times in the months

If you need to be more specific about a particular time of the month, the following phrases help narrow down the field:

Anfang Januar (*ân*-fâng *yân*-oo-ahr) (*in the beginning of January*)

Mitte Februar (*mit*-e *fey*-broo-ahr) (*in the middle of February*)

Ende März (*ên*-de mêrts) (*at the end of March*)

Of course, you can substitute the name of any month after **Anfang**, **Mitte**, and **Ende:**

> **Anfang April fliegen wir nach Berlin.** (*ân*-fâng â-*pril fleeg*-en veer nahH bêr-*leen*.) (*In the beginning of April, we're flying to Berlin.*)

> **Ich werde Ende Mai verreisen.** (iH *vêr*-de *ên*-de may fêr-*ray*-zen.) (*I'll go traveling at the end of May.*)

> **Herr Behr wird Mitte Februar in den Skiurlaub fahren.** (hêr beyr virt *mit*-e *fey*-broo-ahr in deyn *shee*-oor-loup *fahr*-en.) (*Mr. Behr is going on a skiing trip in the middle of February.*)

Celebrating holidays

People in German-speaking countries have a rich tradition of holidays that they celebrate throughout the year. In addition to the six weeks of paid vacation that most Germans enjoy, the country celebrates a number of **Festtage** (*fêst*-tah-ge) (*festive days*) and **Feiertage** (*fay*-er-tah-ge) (*legal holidays*) when people have the day off work. Some parts of Germany, Austria, and Switzerland have more legal holidays than others, but everyone has ample occasions to get together with family and friends to celebrate.

Here are a few of the holidays that various German-speaking regions of Europe celebrate:

- ✔ **Silvester** (sil-*vês*-ter) (*New Years Eve*) and **Neujahr** (*noy*-yahr) (*New Year's Day*) are celebrated mostly the same in German-speaking Europe as in other parts of the world. On **Silvester,** people join together for an elegant festive dinner or go to parties and spend the night dancing. To ring in the New Year, plenty of fireworks light up the sky.

- ✔ **Carnival** (*kâr*-ni-vâl) (*carnival*) or **Mardi Gras** (*mardi gras* [same as English]) (*Mardi gras*) season is one of the most popular celebrations that takes place in Germany, Austria, and German-speaking Switzerland. It has different names in different regions: **Karneval** (*kâr*-nê-vâl) in the German Rhineland, **Fasching** (*fâsh*-eeng) in Bavaria and Austria, and **Fastnacht** (*fâst*-nâHt) or **Fastnet** (*fâst*-nêt) in southwestern Germany and Switzerland. They all mean the same thing — a period of merrymaking, costume balls, parades, and generally crazy-fun days that precede the Lent period, which is when Catholics traditionally fast in preparation for Easter. Depending on the region, the festivities last anywhere from a few days up to several months. For the people of the Rhineland, **Fastnacht** begins each year on the 11th day of the 11th month at 11:11. The carnival season is jokingly referred to as **die fünfte Jahreszeit** (dee *fuenf*-te *yahr*-ês-tsayt) (*the fifth season*).

✔ **Tag der Arbeit** (tahk dêr *âr*-bayt) (*Labor Day*) takes place on the first of May in European countries. In ancient times, people held festivities to celebrate the beginning of spring on May 1. Nowadays, trade unions hold large public rallies to generate support for social reform.

✔ **Jahrmarkt** (*yahr*-mârkt) is one of several terms for a local annual fair held throughout German-speaking regions in late spring and summer. Depending on the region, other names for this type of fair are **Kirmes** (*kêr*-mês), **Kerb** (kêrb), and **Dult** (doolt). These annual fairs feature all kinds of regional food and drink specialties, rides, contests, booths, and live entertainment. Another general term for any kind of large celebration of this type is **Volksfest** (*folks*-fêst). In some areas, the annual celebration focuses on the founding of the local church and is called **Kirchweih** (*kirH*-vay), which means *blessing of the church*.

✔ **Oktoberfest** (ok-*toh*-ber-fêst) (*Octoberfest*) takes place in Munich, Germany, and is the largest **Volksfest** of its kind in the world. It's 16 days of beer drinking accompanied by oompah music in enormous specially erected **Bierzelte** (*beer*-zêlt-e) (*beer tents*), each of which features one locally brewed beer. On a sunny weekend day, **Oktoberfest**-goers consume more than 1 million **Maß Bier** (mahs beer) (*liter mugs of beer*) and thousands of servings of **Schweinshaxe** (*shvayns*-hâx-e) (*pork knuckle*) and grilled **Hähnchen** (*hain*-Hen) (*chicken*). Other attractions at the **Oktoberfest** include enormous roller coasters, a traditional merry-go-round, a hall of mirrors, and a real flea circus.

✔ **Weihnachtsmarkt** (*vay*-nâHts-mârkt) (*Christmas market*) is a four-week-long market that many cities hold in their center, where people set up booths to sell Christmas ornaments, gift items, and seasonal specialties like **Lebkuchen** (*leyb*-koohH-en) (*gingerbread*) and **Glühwein** (*glue*-vayn) (*hot mulled wine*).

✔ **Weihnachten** (*vay*-nâHt-en) (*Christmas*) is one celebration that happens quietly at home. Many families carry on the tradition of lighting the Christmas tree with real candles on **Allerheiligen** (âl-er-*hay*-lee-gen) (*Christmas Eve*). Christmas Day, December 25, is an official holiday. Families serve a traditional, festive meal that, depending on the region, may include **Gans** (gâns) (*goose*), **Karpfen** (*kârp*-fen) (*carp*), or **Würstchen mit Kartoffelsalat** (*wuerst*-Hen mit kâr-*tof*-el-zâ-laht) (*sausage with potato salad*). The day after Christmas is also an official holiday.

Germany, Austria, and Switzerland also have a few **Nationalfeiertage** (nâ-tsee-oh-*nahl*-fay-er-tah-ge) (*national days*) with unique historical backgrounds:

✔ **Der 3. Oktober** (dêr *drit*-te ok-*toh*-ber) (*October 3*): Germany's national day is officially called **Tag der Deutschen Einheit** (tahk dêr *doych*-en *ayn*-hayt) (*Day of German Unity*). It marks the day in 1990 when the German Democratic Republic ceased to exist and was officially united with the Federal Republic of Germany.

✔ **Der 26. Oktober** (dêr zeHs-oont-*tsvân*-tsig-ste ok-*toh*-ber) (*October 26*): Austria's national holiday commemorates the day in 1955 when Austria declared permanent neutrality after World War II and regained its status as an independent and sovereign nation.

✔ **Der 1. August** (dêr *êrs*-te ou-*goost*) (*August 1*): The national day of Switzerland dates back to 1291 when three cantons formed an historic alliance and the Swiss Confederation was founded.

Measurements, Quantities, and Weights

You use the metric system in German-speaking countries, as well as most other countries around the globe. The various metric units crop up in all sorts of everyday situations, so familiarizing yourself with the various equivalents for units of length, weight, and capacity is definitely worth your time. Here are a few examples to get you in the metric mood:

✔ You buy milk by the **Liter** (*lee*-ter) (*liter*) rather than the quart.

✔ Speed limits are in **Kilometer** (*kee*-lo-*mey*-ter) (*kilometers*) per hour (1 kilometer = 0.6 mile) rather than miles.

✔ A 2.2-pound sack of potatoes sells as a unit of 1 **Kilo(gramm)** (*kee*-loh-[gram]) (*kilo[gram]*). **Note:** German speakers refer to 1,000 grams as either **Kilo** or **Kilogramm**, and neither one has an *s* in the plural form.

If you want to buy some amount of something at a tantalizing open-air market, all you have to say is

Ich hätte gern. . . . (iH *hêt*-e gêrn. . . .) (*I would like to have.* . . .)

At the end of the phrase, simply say how much you want, which could include any of the following weights and measurements. Note that the plural forms for most of these measurements are the same as the singular form.

ein/zwei Kilo (ayn/tsvay *kee*-loh) (*1 kilogram/2 kilograms*) (1 kilogram = 2.2 pounds)

ein/zwei Pfund (ayn/tsvay pfoont) (*1 pound/2 pounds*) (1 metric pound = 500 grams) (In the U.S., a pound is 454 grams.)

ein/einhundert Gramm (ayn/ayn-*hoon*-dêrt grâm) (*1 gram/100 grams*)

ein/zwei Stück (ayn/tsvay shtuek) (*one piece/two pieces*)

eine Scheibe/zwei Scheiben (*ayn*-e *shay*-be/tsvay *shay*-ben) (*one slice/two slices*)

Words to Know

das Kilo	dâs kee-loh	kilogram
das Pfund	dâs pfoont	pound
das Gramm	dâs grâm	gram
wie viel	vee feel	how much
wie viele	vee _fee_-le	how many
Das wär's.	dâs vêrs.	That's it.
Was darf es sein?	vâs dârf ês zayn?	What would you like?
Sonst noch etwas?	zonst noH _êt_-vâs?	Anything else?

To specify exactly what you want, simply add the appropriate word to the end of the whole phrase. For example, if you want one **Kilo** of apples, you say

Ich hätte gern ein Kilo Äpfel. (iH _hêt_-e gêrn ayn _kee_-loh _êp_-fel.) (_I'd like to have one kilogram of apples._)

Talkin' the Talk

Frau Bauer buys all her produce at the open-air market. Today she needs apples and tomatoes. Looking at the various stands, she approaches one where she's bought produce before and speaks to the **Verkäuferin** (_saleswoman_). (Track 9)

Verkäuferin: **Guten Tag. Was darf es sein?**
gooh-ten tahk. vâs dârf ês zayn?
Hello. What would you like?

Frau Bauer: **Zwei Kilo Äpfel und ein Pfund Tomaten, bitte.**
tsvay _kee_-loh _êp_-fel oont ayn pfoont toh-_mah_-ten, _bi_-te.
Two kilograms of apples and one pound of tomatoes, please.

Verkäuferin: **Sonst noch etwas?**
zonst noH *êt*-vâs?
Anything else?

Frau Bauer: **Danke, das ist alles.**
dân-ke, dâs ist *âl*-ês.
Thank you, that's all.

Next, Frau Bauer goes to a stand that sells dairy products.

Frau Bauer: **Ich hätte gern etwas von dem Gouda.**
iH *hêt*-e gêrn *êt*-vâs fon deym *gou*-dâ.
I'd like to have some Gouda.

Verkäuferin: **Wie viel hätten Sie denn gern?**
vee-feel *hêt*-en zee dên gêrn?
How much would you like?

Frau Bauer: **Zweihundert Gramm, bitte.**
tsvay-hoon-dert grâm, *bi*-te.
Two hundred grams, please.

Verkäuferin: **Sonst noch etwas?**
zonst noH *êt*-vâs?
Anything else?

Frau Bauer: **Nein, danke. Das wär's.**
nayn, *dân*-ke. dâs vêrs.
No, thank you. That's it.

Chapter 3

Meeting and Greeting: Guten Tag!

In This Chapter

▶ Addressing people formally or informally

▶ Greeting others and saying goodbye

▶ Talking about yourself and saying where you're from

▶ Discussing the weather

Greetings and introductions are your crucial first steps in establishing contact with other people and making a positive first impression. To that end, this chapter helps you determine whether to use formal or informal language in various situations. It also introduces the basic expressions of polite conversation: how to say hello and goodbye, how to ask and answer the universal question "How are you?," and how to make introductions.

Engaging in small talk is one way to develop contacts and improve your German at the same time. Lucky for you, starting up a light and casual conversation isn't too difficult. Whether you're meeting somebody at a party or you want to talk to the person sitting next to you on the train, plane, or bus, you have several topics you can use as openers: yourself, your job, where you're from, and of course, the weather. Throughout this chapter, you become familiar with discussing these topics.

Getting Formal or Informal

German speakers generally place great value on showing respect toward each other and strangers. The language itself allows the speaker to make a clear distinction between formal and informal ways of saying *you.* (Once upon a time, English did this, too, but English speakers dropped the *thee* and *thou* forms long ago.) In German, you use either the formal **Sie** (zee) (*you*) or one of the two informal forms: **du** (dooh) (*you*), if you're talking to one person, or **ihr** (eer) (*you, you guys, you all*), if you're addressing two or more people.

Making the distinction between the informal and formal *you* forms is important. Why? Because people are likely to consider you impolite and disrespectful if you use the informal way of addressing them in a situation that calls for more formality.

In general, you use the formal **Sie** for everyday communication with people *outside* your circle of family and friends. Even among people who are in regular contact with one another (neighbors or coworkers, for example), **Sie** is often used as a means of showing respect. As you get to know somebody better, you may switch to **du.**

However, no hard and fast rules apply when it comes to using **du** or **Sie.** In fact, many exceptions exist. For example, suppose a German friend takes you to a party. Even though you and the other guests are complete strangers, the other guests may just address you with **du** — especially if they're easygoing — so you may address them with **du** as well. For more details on deciding when to use **Sie, du,** or **ihr,** go to Book III, Chapter 3.

If you're the least bit unsure of whether to use **du** or **Sie,** use **Sie** until the person you're addressing asks you to use **du** or addresses you with **du.**

Saying "Hello," "Goodbye," and "How Are You?"

Getting your hellos and goodbyes straight in German is a matter of keeping in mind how well you know someone. If you're on formal terms — in other words, if you're addressing one or more people with **Sie** (zee) (*you,* formal) — then you have one set of expressions. When you're on **du** (dooh) (*you,* informal) terms of address, you go with the more informal expressions.

Saying "Guten Tag" and "Auf Wiedersehen"

The first part of your greeting is a basic hello. How you say hello depends on what time of day it is. The following list includes both the standard, formal expressions for saying hello and the more casual, informal expressions:

Guten Morgen! (*gooh-*ten *mor-*gen!) (*Good morning!*) This is the standard, formal greeting you use in the morning (until about noon).

Guten Tag! (*gooh*-ten tahk!) (*Hello!*) This is the most common formal greeting you use, except early in the morning and late in the day.

Guten Abend! (*gooh*-ten *ah*-bent!) (*Good evening!*) Obviously, this is the formal greeting of choice in the evening.

Hallo! (*hâ*-loh!) (*Hello!*) You should be pretty comfortable with this informal greeting because it's very similar to English's *hello*.

When the time comes to part, you can say:

Auf Wiedersehen! (ouf *vee*-der-zey-en!) (*Goodbye!*) This is the standard, formal goodbye.

Gute Nacht! (*gooh*-te nâHt!) (*Good night!*) You use this standard, formal farewell when you say goodbye late at night.

War nett, Sie kennenzulernen. (vahr nêt, zee *kên*-en-tsoo-lêrn-en.) (*It was nice meeting you.*) You use this formal phrase to tell people that you enjoyed meeting them for the first time.

Tschüs! (chues!) (*Bye!*) This is the informal way of saying goodbye.

People in Southern Germany, Austria, and German-speaking Switzerland certainly understand you when you wish them **Guten Morgen/Guten Tag/Guten Abend** (depending on the time of day). However, people in these regions also use some other greetings:

✔ In Switzerland, you hear **Grüezi** (*grue*-e-tsee) (hello) most often, and people who know each other well use **salut** (sâ-*lue*) to say both *hi* and *bye*.

✔ In Southern Germany and Austria, you say *hello* with **Grüß Gott** (grues got) or its informal version, **Grüß dich** (grues diH). Good friends express both *hi* and *bye* with the casual **Servus** (*sêr*-voohs).

Especially among younger German speakers, you hear the informal *goodbye*, **Ciao** (chou) or the German-spelled version **Tschau** (chou), which has made its way north across the Alps from Italy.

Talkin' the Talk

In the next two conversations, people on a train are saying goodbye as the train comes into a station. In the first dialogue, Frau Stein is getting ready to exit the train. (Track 10)

Frau Stein: **Das ist meine Station. War nett, Sie kennen-zulernen, Frau Boch.**
dâs ist *mayn*-e shtâts-ee-*ohn*. vahr nêt, zee *kên*-en-tsoo-lêrn-en, frou boH.
This is my stop. It was nice to meet you, Ms. Boch.

Frau Boch:	**Ganz meinerseits. Auf Wiedersehen, Frau Stein.** gânts *mayn*-er-zayts. ouf *vee*-der-zey-en, frou shtayn. *And nice to meet you. Goodbye, Ms. Stein.*
Frau Stein:	**Auf Wiedersehen.** ouf *vee*-der-zey-en. *Goodbye.*

In this conversation, Hubert and Isgard are getting off the train as well, but before they do, they say goodbye to another passenger they met during their trip.

Hubert und Isgard:	**Tschüs Ludwig.** chues *lood*-vig *Bye, Ludwig.*
Ludwig:	**Tschüs Isgard, tschüs Hubert. Schöne Ferien!** chues *is*-gârd, chues *hooh*-bert. *shern*-e fê-ree-en! *Bye Isgard, bye Hubert. Have a nice vacation!*

Asking "Wie geht es Ihnen?"

The next step after greeting someone in German is asking the question *How are you?* Whether you use the formal or the informal version of the question depends on whom you're talking to. Sound complicated? Well, figuring out which form to use is easier than you may think.

The following three versions of *How are you?* use three dative-case pronouns that represent *you*. **Ihnen** (*een*-en) is the dative equivalent of **Sie, dir** (deer) represents **du,** and **euch** (oyH) stands in for **ihr.** (See Book III, Chapter 2 for more information on personal pronouns in the dative case.) Here's a breakdown of what to use when:

Wie geht es Ihnen? (vee geyt ês *een*-en?) (*How are you?*) This is the formal version.

Wie geht es dir? (vee geyt ês deer?) (*How are you?*) This is the informal, singular version.

Wie geht's? (vee geyts?) (*How's it going?*) When you know someone really well, you can use this casual question.

Wie geht es euch? (vee geyt ês oyH?) (*How are you?*) Use this when talking to several people informally.

Greetings and introductions are often accompanied by some form of bodily contact. In Germany, Austria, and Switzerland, hand-shaking is the most common form of bodily contact during greetings and introductions. Female friends may kiss each other on the cheek or give each other a hug. Men usually don't kiss or hug each other, although they may greet a woman friend with a hug (and a kiss). You may notice that people in Europe often stand closer to you than you're used to, for example, in stores, on the bus or subway, or during conversations with you.

Giving a response to "Wie geht es Ihnen?"

In English, the question *How are you?* is often just a way of saying hello, and no one raises an eyebrow if you don't answer. In German, however, a reply is customary. Germans expect a reply because for the German speaker, asking **"Wie geht es Ihnen?"** isn't the same as a casual *hello* but rather is a means of showing genuine interest in someone. The following are acceptable answers to the question **Wie geht es Ihnen?** (*How are you?*):

Danke, gut. (*dân*-ke, gooht.) (*Thanks, I'm fine.*) or **Gut, danke.** (gooht, *dân*-ke.) (*Fine, thanks.*)

Sehr gut. (zeyr gooht.) (*Very good.*)

Ganz gut. (gânts gooht.) (*Really good.*)

Es geht. (ês geyt.) (*So, so.*) This German expression actually means *it goes*.

Nicht so gut. (niHt zoh gooht.) (*Not so good.*)

As in English, you would usually accompany your reply with the question *And (how are) you?* Here's the formal version:

Und Ihnen? (oont *een*-en?) (*And you?*)

Here's how to pose the question informally:

Und dir? (oont deer?) (*And you?*) (singular, informal *you*)

Und euch? (oont oyH?) (*And you?*) (plural, informal *you*)

Talkin' the Talk

In the following dialogue, you find some phrases that German speakers commonly use for greetings in a more formal setting. (Track 11)

Herr Schulte: **Guten Tag, Frau Berger!**
gooh-ten tahk, frou *bêr*-ger!
Hello, Ms. Berger!

Frau Berger: **Herr Schulte, guten Tag! Wie geht es Ihnen?**
hêr *shool*-te, *gooh*-ten tahk! vee geyt ês *een*-en?
Mr. Schulte, hello! How are you?

Herr Schulte: **Danke, gut! Und Ihnen?**
dân-ke, gooht! oont *een*-en?
Thanks, I'm fine! And how are you?

Frau Berger: **Danke, gut.**
dân-ke, gooht.
Thanks, I'm fine.

Talkin' the Talk

Check out this dialogue between Mike and Christa, two old friends who run into each other on the street. (Track 12)

Mike: **Hallo Christa!**
hâ-loh christa [as in English]!
Hello Christa!

Christa: **Mike, hallo! Wie geht's?**
mike [as in English], *hâ*-loh! vee geyts?
Mike, hello! How's it going?

Mike: **Danke, mir geht's gut! Und selbst?**
dân-ke, meer geyts gooht! oont zêlpst?
Thanks, I'm fine! And yourself?

Christa: **Auch gut.**
ouH gooht.
I'm fine, too.

Introducing Yourself and Your Friends

Meeting and greeting often require introductions. Your friends may want you to meet someone they know, or you may have to introduce your significant other to your colleague at a formal occasion. This section gives you the low-down on how to do so.

Introducing your friends

Commonplace, everyday introductions are easy to make. You start with

> **Das ist . . .** (dâs ist . . .) (*This is . . .*)

Then you simply add the name of the person. Or if you're introducing a friend, begin with

> **Das ist eine Freundin von mir** (female)/**ein Freund von mir** (male) . . . (dâs ist *ayn*-e *froyn*-din fon mir/ayn froynt fon mir . . .) (*This is a friend of mine . . .*)

If you're introduced to someone, you may want to indicate that you're pleased to meet that person. In German, the casual way of responding to someone you've just met is to simply say **Hallo** (*hâ*-loh) (*hello*) or **Guten Tag** (*gooh*-ten tahk) (*hello*).

If the introductions have been more formal, you express *Nice to meet you* by saying

> **Freut mich.** (froyt miH.) (*Nice to meet you.*)

The person you have been introduced to may then reply by saying

> **Mich auch.** (miH ouH.) (*Pleased to meet you, too.*)

Making introductions for special occasions

If you were to find yourself in a situation that calls for a high level of formality, you'd need to know the following introductory phrases:

> ✔ **Darf ich Ihnen . . . vorstellen?** (dârf iH *een*-en . . . *fohr*-shtêl-len?) (*May I introduce you to. . . ?*)

> ✔ **Freut mich, Sie kennenzulernen.** (froyt miH, zee *kên*-en-tsoo-lêrn-en.)
> (*I'm pleased to meet you.*)
>
> ✔ **Meinerseits.** (*mayn*-er-zayts.)/**Ganz meinerseits.** (gânts *mayn*-er-zayts.)
> (*The pleasure is all mine.* Literally: *Mine* or *All mine.*)

Sometimes you need to use formal titles in your introduction. **Herr** (hêr) is the German word for *Mr.,* and **Frau** (frou) expresses *Mrs.* The same word, **die Frau** (dee frou), also means *woman,* as well as *wife,* as in **meine Frau** (*mayn*-e frou) (*my wife*). No German equivalent for the English *Ms.* exists, so you need to use **Frau.**

German also has the word **Fräulein** (*froy*-layn), which used to be the German version of *Miss* and was the proper way to address an unmarried woman. However, those days are long gone. So address a woman as **Frau,** regardless of her marital status. Or when in doubt, leave it out.

Talkin' the Talk

In this dialogue between the directors of two companies, listen to Herr Kramer and Herr Huber. They meet at an official function, and Herr Huber introduces his wife.

Herr Kramer: **Guten Abend, Herr Huber.**
gooh-ten *ah*-bent, hêr *hooh*-ber.
Good evening, Mr. Huber.

Herr Huber: **Guten Abend, Herr Kramer. Darf ich Ihnen meine Frau vorstellen?**
gooh-ten *ah*-bent, hêr *krah*-mer. dârf iH *een*-en *mayn*-e frou *fohr*-shtêl-len?
Good evening, Mr. Kramer. May I introduce my wife to you?

Herr Kramer: **Guten Abend, Frau Huber. Freut mich sehr, Sie kennenzulernen.**
gooh-ten *ah*-bent, frou *hooh*-ber. froyt miH zeyr, zee *kên*-en-tsoo-*lêrn*-en.
Good evening, Mrs. Huber. Very nice to meet you.

Frau Huber: **Ganz meinerseits, Herr Kramer.**
gânts *mayn*-er-zayts, hêr *krah*-mer.
And nice to meet you, Mr. Kramer.

Words to Know

auch	ouH	also
gut	gooht	good
sehr	zeyr	very
freuen	froy-en	to be glad/pleased
kennenlernen	kên-en-lêrn-en	to become acquainted with/to get to know
vorstellen	fohr-shtêl-len	to introduce
der Freund (m)	der froynt	friend
die Freundin (f)	dee froyn-din	friend

Introducing yourself

You can't always rely on someone else to introduce you. In such situations, you simply introduce yourself. Even in more formal settings, you can often introduce yourself simply by stating your name:

> **Mein Name ist. . . .** (mayn *nah*-me ist. . . .) (*My name is. . . .*)

Or use the verb that expresses the same idea, **heißen** (*hay*-sen) (*to be called*):

> **Ich heiße. . . .** (iH *hay*-se. . . .) (*My name is. . . .*)

Talkin' the Talk

In the following conversation, Herr Hauser arrives at a meeting with several people he hasn't been introduced to yet. He's looking for a seat at the conference table.

Herr Hauser: **Guten Tag. Ist dieser Platz noch frei?**
gooh-ten tahk. îst *dee*-zer plâts noH fray?
Hello. Is this seat still free?

Frau Berger: **Ja. Nehmen Sie doch bitte Platz.**
yah. *ney*-men zee doH *bi*-te plâts.
Yes, it is. Do sit down.

Herr Hauser: **Vielen Dank. Mein Name ist Max Hauser.**
fee-len dânk. mayn *nah*-me ist mâx *houz*-er.
Thank you very much. My name is Max Hauser.

Frau Berger: **Freut mich. Ich heiße Karin Berger.**
froyt miH. iH *hay*-se *kah*-rin *bêr*-ger.
Pleased to meet you. I'm Karin Berger.

The preceding conversation would sound very different among younger people meeting in an informal setting, like a party. They'd probably introduce each other like this:

Martin: **Hallo, wie heißt du?**
hâ-loh, vee hayst dooh?
Hello, what's your name?

Susanne: **Ich heiße Susanne. Und du?**
iH *hay*-se zooh-*zân*-e. oont dooh?
My name is Susanne. And you?

Martin: **Ich bin der Martin. Und wer ist das?**
iH bin dêr *mâr*-tin. oont vêr ist dâs?
I'm Martin. And who is that?

Susanne: **Das ist meine Freundin Anne.**
dâs ist *mayn*-e *froyn*-din *ân*-e.
This is my friend Anne.

Talking about Yourself

When you talk about yourself to a new acquaintance, you often answer many of the same key questions: What kind of job do you do? Where do you work? Are you self-employed? Are you a student? Where do you live? Later on in a conversation, your acquaintance may ask for your address and phone number. Because you'll encounter these topics often, you need to be prepared. The following sections provide you with the information you need.

Describing your work

Say you start chatting with a guy you meet at a friend's party. He may ask you what you do for a living. For example, he may ask any of the following:

Bei welcher Firma arbeiten Sie? (bay *vêlH*-er *fir*-mâ *âr*-bay-ten zee?) (*What company are you working for?*)

Was machen Sie beruflich? (vâs *mâH*-en zee be-*roohf*-liH?) (*What kind of work do you do?*)

Sind Sie berufstätig? (zint zee be-*roohfs*-tê-tiH?) (*Are you employed?*)

A few simple words and expressions help you describe your job and company. In most cases, you can describe what kind of work you do by connecting **Ich bin . . .** (iH bin . . .) (*I am . . .*) with the name of your occupation, without using any article. Most names for jobs exist in a female and male form. The male form frequently ends with **-er**; the female form usually ends with **-in**. Here are some examples:

Ich bin Handelsvertreter (m)/**Handelsvertreterin** (f). (iH bin *hân*-dels-fêr-trey-ter/*hân*-dels-fêr-trey-ter-in.) (*I am a sales representative.*)

Ich bin Student (m)/**Studentin** (f). (iH bin shtoo-*dênt*/shtoo-*dên*-tin.) (*I am a student.*)

If you're a student, you may want to say what you're studying. You do this with the phrase **Ich studiere . . .** (iH shtoo-*dee*-re . . .) (*I am studying . . .*). At the end of the sentence, you add the name of your field (without any article). Some fields you may use include the following:

✔ **Architektur** (âr-Hi-têk-*toohr*) (*architecture*)

✔ **Betriebswirtschaft** (be-*treeps*-virt-shâft) (*business administration*)

✔ **Softwaretechnik** (soft-wair-*têH*-nik) (*software engineering*)

✔ **Kunst** (koonst) (*art*)

✔ **Literaturwissenschaft** (li-te-rah-*toohr*-vis-en-shâft) (*literature*)

✔ **Biochemie** (bee-oh-Hey-*mee*) (*biochemistry*)

You also can describe what you do with the phrase **Ich bin . . .** (iH bin . . .) (*I am . . .*). You end the phrase with an appropriate adjective. For example, you may say any of the following:

Ich bin berufstätig/nicht berufstätig. (iH bin be-*roohfs*-tê-tiH/niHt be-*roohfs*-tê-tiH.) (*I am employed/not employed.*)

Ich bin pensioniert. (iH bin *pân*-zee-o-neert.) (*I am retired.*)

Ich bin oft geschäftlich unterwegs. (iH bin oft ge-*shêft*-liH oon-ter-*veyks.*) (*I often travel on business.*)

Ich bin selbständig. (iH bin *zelpst*-shtênd-iH.) (*I am self-employed.*)

Your company name, place of work, or line of work may be almost as important as the actual work you do. The phrase **Ich arbeite bei . . ./in . . .** (iH *âr*-bay-te bay . . ./in . . .) (*I work at . . ./in . . .*) tells someone, in a nutshell, where you earn your money. Consider these examples:

Ich arbeite bei der Firma. . . . (iH *âr*-bay-te bay dêr *fir*-mâ. . . .) (*I work at the company. . . .*) After the word **Firma**, you simply insert the name of the company you work for.

Ich arbeite in einem Krankenhaus. (iH *âr*-bay-te in ayn-em *krânk*-en-hous.) (*I work in a hospital.*)

Ich arbeite in der Gentechnik/in der Umweltforschung. (iH *âr*-bay-te in dêr *geyn*-teH-nik/in dêr *oom*-velt-fohrsh-oong.) (*I work in genetic engineering/in environmental research.*)

Ich arbeite in einem Architekturbüro/in einem Forschungslabor. (iH *âr*-bay-te in *ayn*-em âr-Hi-têk-*toohr*-bue-roh/in *ayn*-em *forsh*-oongs-lah-bor.) (*I work at an architecture office/in a research lab.*)

Providing names and numbers

Telling people where you live and how they can reach you is the key to growing your social and business relationships. The following sections give you everything you need to know to offer your personal information to others.

A business card is worth a thousand words, especially if your German is a little shaky. So if someone asks you about your personal info and you have your business card with you, why not save yourself the struggle of saying your vital statistics and present your card instead? Just hand it over and say **Hier ist meine Visitenkarte.** (heer ist *mayn*-e vi-*zeet*-en-kâr-te.) (*Here is my business card.*) For detailed information on personal pronouns like **mein** (mayn) (*my*) and **Ihr** (eer) (*your*), go to Book III, Chapter 2.

Telling someone where you live

When someone asks you **Wo wohnen Sie?** (voh *vohn*-en zee?) (*Where do you live?*), you can respond with any of the following:

Ich wohne in Berlin/in einem Vorort von Berlin. (iH *vohn*-e in bêr-*leen*/ in *ayn*-em *fohr*-ort von bêr-*leen*.) (*I live in Berlin/in a suburb of Berlin.*) Simply insert the name of your city in this expression.

Ich wohne in einer Kleinstadt/auf dem Land. (iH *vohn*-e in *ayn*-er klayn-shtât/ouf deym lânt.) (*I live in a small town/in the country.*)

Ich habe ein Haus/eine Wohnung. (iH *hah*-be ayn hous/*ayn*-e *vohn*-oong.) (*I have a house/an apartment.*)

Depending on the circumstances, someone may ask you **Wie ist Ihre Adresse?** (vee ist *eer*-e â-*drês*-e?) (*What is your address?*) When you want to get down to specifics on where you live, use the following words:

- ✔ **die Adresse** (dee â-*drês*-e) (*address*)
- ✔ **die Straße** (dee *shtrah*-se) (*street*)
- ✔ **die Hausnummer** (dee *hous*-noom-er) (*house/building number*)
- ✔ **die Postleitzahl** (dee *post*-layt-tsahl) (*zip code*)

When you tell someone your address, substitute the appropriate word into the following sentence: **Die Adresse/Straße/Hausnummer/Postleitzahl ist. . . .** (dee â-*drês*-e/*shtrah*-se/*hous*-noom-er/*post*-layt-tsahl ist. . . .) (*The address/ street/house number/zip code is. . . .*)

German addresses place the house number after the street, and the zip code before the city, such as this address: **Herr Peter Schmidt, Schulstraße 22, 07749 Jena, Deutschland.**

Handing out your phone number and e-mail address

If a new acquaintance asks you for your phone number and e-mail address, don't worry. You can easily provide your contact information. Here's what you say:

Die Telefonnummer/die Handynummer/die Vorwahl/die Nebenstelle ist. . . . (dee *tê*-le-fohn-noom-er/dee *hân*-dee-noom-er/dee *fohr*-vahl/dee *ney*-ben-shtêl-e ist. . . .) (*The telephone number/the cellphone number/the area code/the extension is. . . .*)

Meine E-mail Adresse ist . . . @ . . . dot com/net. (*mayn*-e e-mail [as in English] a-*drês*-e ist . . . at . . . dot com/net [as in English].) (*My e-mail address is . . . at . . . dot com/net.*)

Talkin' the Talk

Kurt Hanser is on the plane from München to Frankfurt. His seat is next to Frau Schneider, a businesswoman. After the two have introduced themselves, they talk about their jobs. (Track 13)

Herr Hanser:	**Was machen Sie beruflich, wenn ich fragen darf?** vâs *mâH*-en zee be-*roohf*-liH, vên iH *frah*-gen dârf? *What kind of work do you do, if I may ask?*
Frau Schneider:	**Ich arbeite als Biochemikerin bei der Firma Agrolab.** iH *âr*-bay-te âls bee-oh-*Hê*-mee-ker-in bay dêr *fir*-mâ â-groh-lâb. *I work as a biochemist at a company called Agrolab.*
Herr Hanser:	**Das ist ja interessant. Haben Sie eine Visitenkarte?** dâs ist yah in-te-re-*sânt*. *hah*-ben zee *ayn*-e vi-*zeet*-en-kâr-te? *That's interesting. Do you have a business card?*
Frau Schneider:	**Ja, hier bitte. Und was machen Sie beruflich?** yah, heer *bi*-te. oont vâs *mâH*-en zee be-*roohf*-liH? *Yes, here it is. And what kind of work do you do?*
Herr Hanser:	**Ich arbeite in einem Architekturbüro. Leider habe ich meine Visitenkarte nicht dabei.** iH *âr*-bay-te in *ayn*-em âr-Hi-têk-*toohr*-bue-roh. lay-der *hah*-be iH *mayn*-e vi-*zeet*-en-kâr-te niHt dâ-*bay*. *I work at an architecture office. Unfortunately, I don't have my business card with me.*
Frau Schneider:	**Ist Ihre Firma in Frankfurt?** ist *eer*-e *fir*-mâ in *frânk*-foort? *Is your company in Frankfurt?*
Herr Hanser:	**Ja, unser Büro ist in der Bockenheimer Straße 27.** yah, *oon*-zer *bue*-roh ist in deyr *bok*-en-haym-er *shtrah*-se zee-ben-oont-tsvân-tsiH. *Yes, our office is at Bockenheimer Street 27.*

Words to Know

fragen	<u>frah</u>-gen	to ask
geben	<u>gey</u>-ben	to give
dabei haben	dâ-<u>bay</u> <u>hah</u>-ben	to have on/with oneself
leider	<u>lay</u>-der	unfortunately

Discussing Cities, Countries, and Nationalities

When you're getting to know someone, at some point, the conversation will probably turn to familial origins. Using the handful of vocabulary words from this section, you can describe where you come from with confidence. You can also ask people where they come from and what languages they speak.

Saying where you come from

Saying where you're from in German is fairly easy. The magic words are

Ich komme aus . . . (iH *kom*-e ous . . .) (*I come from . . .*)

Ich bin aus . . . (iH bin ous . . .) (*I am from . . .*)

These few words go a long way. They work for countries, states, and cities. Take a look at these examples:

Ich komme aus Amerika. (iH *kom*-e ous â-*mey*-ree-kâ.) (*I come from America.*)

Ich bin aus Pennsylvania. (iH bin ous pennsylvania [as in English].) (*I am from Pennsylvania.*)

Ich komme aus Zürich. (iH *kom*-e ous *tsue*-riH.) (*I come from Zurich.*)

Ich bin aus Wien. (iH bin ous veen.) (*I am from Vienna.*)

The German language can be a bit challenging at times, so watch your step when discussing your origins. Here are a few specifics to be aware of:

- **Some countries' and regions' names are considered plural.** In this case, they use the plural definite article, **die** (dee) (*the*). The United States of America (USA) is one such country. In German, it's referred to as **die USA** (dee ooh-ês-*ah*) or **die Vereinigten Staaten** (dee fer-*ay*-nik-ten *shtah*-ten). Saying **Ich bin aus Amerika** (iH bin ous â-*mey*-ree-kâ) (*I'm from America*) is easy; however, technically, you could be referring to one of two American continents. So to be a little more specific, you may say **Ich bin aus den USA.** (iH bin ous deyn ooh-ês-*ah*.) (*I'm from the USA.*) Or you may want to challenge yourself with **Ich bin aus den Vereinigten Staaten.** (iH bin ous deyn fer-*ay*-nik-ten *shtah*-ten.) (*I'm from the United States.*)

- **Some countries' names are considered female.** Switzerland, for example, is **die Schweiz** (dee shvayts) in German. Ms. Egli, whom you meet later in this chapter in a Talkin' the Talk dialogue, is Swiss. So to say where Ms. Egli is from, you say **Frau Egli ist aus der Schweiz.** (frou *ey*-glee ist ous dêr shvayts.) (*Ms. Egli is from Switzerland.*) The article **die** changes to the dative case — **der** — when it's combined with the preposition **aus** (ous) (*from*). (See Book III, Chapter 2 for more info on the dative case.)

Asking people where they come from

To ask people where they're from, you first need to decide whether to use the formal term of address **Sie** or one of the two informal terms, **du** (for one person) or **ihr** (for several people). (For more information on when to use **Sie, du,** or **ihr,** turn to the section "Getting Formal or Informal.") Then you choose one of these three versions of the question:

Woher kommen Sie? (voh-*hêr* kom-en zee?) (*Where are you from?*)

Woher kommst du? (voh-*hêr* komst doo?) (*Where are you from?*)

Woher kommt ihr? (voh-*hêr* komt eer?) (*Where are you [all] from?*)

Talkin' the Talk

Frau Egli and Frau Myers are on a train. During their trip, they strike up a conversation. They have just introduced themselves and are curious to learn a little more about each other.

Frau Egli: **Und woher kommen Sie, Frau Myers?**
oont voh-*hêr kom*-en zee, frou myers [as in English]?
And where do you come from, Ms. Myers?

Frau Myers: **Ich komme aus den USA, aus Pennsylvania.**
IH *kom*-e ous deyn ooh-ês-ah, ous pennsylvania [as in English].
I come from the USA, from Pennsylvania.

Frau Egli: **Aus den USA, wie interessant. Kommen Sie aus einer Großstadt?**
ous deyn ooh-ês-*ah*, vee in-te-re-*sânt*. *kom*-en zee ous *ayn*-er *grohs*-shtât?
From the USA, how interesting. Do you come from a large city?

Frau Myers: **Nein, ich komme aus Doylestown, eine Kleinstadt, aber es ist sehr schön. Und Sie, Frau Egli, woher kommen Sie?**
nayn, iH *kom*-e ous Doylestown [as in English], *ayn*-e *klayn*-shtat, *ah*-ber ês ist zeyr shern. oont zee, frou *ey*-glee, voh-*hêr kom*-ên zee?
No, I come from Doylestown, a small town, but it's very pretty. And you, Ms. Egli, where do you come from?

Frau Egli: **Ich komme aus der Schweiz, aus Zürich.**
iH *kom*-e ous dêr shvayts, ous *tsue*-riH.
I'm from Switzerland, from Zurich.

In the next compartment, Claire and Michelle, two young back-packers, are getting to know Mark, another backpacker. Being easygoing teenagers, they use the informal address **du** and **ihr** right from the start.

Claire: **Kommst du aus Deutschland?**
komst dooh ous *doych*-lânt?
Are you from Germany?

Mark: **Nein, ich komme aus Österreich, aus Wien. Und ihr, woher kommt ihr?**
nayn, iH *kom*-e ous *er*-ste-rayH, ous veen. oont eer, voh-*hêr* komt eer?
No, I'm from Austria, from Vienna. And you, where do you come from?

Michelle: **Wir kommen aus Frankreich. Meine Freundin Claire kommt aus Lyon, und ich komme aus Avignon.**
veer *kom*-en ous *frânk*-rayH. *mayn*-e *froyn*-din claire [as in English] komt ous lee-*on*, oont iH *kom*-e ous ah-vee-*nyon*.
We're from France. My friend Claire comes from Lyon, and I come from Avignon.

Discovering nationalities

Unlike English, which describes nationality by using the adjective of a country's name (such as *She is French*), German indicates nationality with a noun. As you probably already know, genders are important in German, so it's no surprise that these nationality nouns have genders, too. Consider these examples:

ein Amerikaner (ayn â-mey-ree-*kah*-ner) (*American man or boy*)

eine Amerikanerin (*ayn*-e â-mey-ree-*kah*-ner-in) (*American woman or girl*)

You find more specifics on nouns and gender in Book III, Chapter 2.

Table 3-1 lists the names of a few countries along with the corresponding nationality (a noun) and adjective.

Table 3-1	Country Names, Nouns, and Adjectives		
Country in English	*Country in German*	*Nationality (Noun)*	*Adjective*
Belgium	**Belgien** (*bêl*-gee-ên)	**Belgier(-in)** (*bêl*-gee-êr[-in])	**belgisch** (*bêl*-gish)
Germany	**Deutschland** (*doych*-lânt)	**Deutsche(r)** (*doych*-e[r])	**deutsch** (doych)
England	**England** (*êng*-lânt)	**Engländer(in)** (*êng*-lain-der[-in])	**englisch** (*êng*-lish)
France	**Frankreich** (*frânk*-rayH)	**Franzose/ Französin** (frân-*tsoh*-ze/frân-*tser*-zin)	**französisch** (frân-*tser*-zish)
Italy	**Italien** (i-*tah*-lee-ên)	**Italiener(in)** (i-tah-*lee-eyn*-er[-in])	**italienisch** (i-tah-lee-*eyn*-ish)
Austria	**Österreich** (*er*-ste-rayH)	**Österreicher(in)** (*er*-ste-rayH-er[-in])	**österreichisch** (*er*-ste-rayH-ish)
Switzerland	**die Schweiz** (dee shvayts)	**Schweizer(in)** (*shvayts*-er[-in])	**schweizerisch** (*shvayts*-er-ish)
USA	**die USA** (dee ooh-ês-*ah*)	**Amerikaner(in)** (â-mey-ree-*kah*-ner[-in])	**amerikanisch** (â-mey-ree-*kah*-nish)

Here are a few examples of how you may use these words in sentences:

Herr Marsh ist Engländer. (hêr marsh [as in English] ist *êng*-lain-der.) (*Mr. Marsh is English.*)

Maria ist Italienerin. (mah-*ree*-ah ist i-tah-lee-*eyn*-er-in.) (*Maria is Italian.*)

Ich bin Schweizerin. (iH bin *shvayts*-er-in.) (*I am Swiss.*) In this example, a girl or a woman is speaking.

Ich bin Österreicher. (iH bin *er*-ste-rayH-er.) (*I am Austrian.*) In this sentence, a boy or a man is speaking.

Chatting about languages you speak

To tell people what language you speak, you use the verb **sprechen** (*shprêH*-en) (*to speak*) and combine it with the language's name. If you want to ask somebody whether he speaks English, for example, the question is (informally):

Sprichst du Englisch? (shpriHst dooh *êng*-lish?) (*Do you speak English?*)

Here's the formal version:

Sprechen Sie Englisch? (*shprêH*-en zee *êng*-lish?) (*Do you speak English?*)

Talkin' the Talk

Claire, Michelle, and Mark are talking about languages they speak.

Claire: **Sprichst du Französisch?**
shpriHst dooh frân-*tser*-zish?
Do you speak French?

Mark: **Nein, überhaupt nicht. Aber ich spreche Englisch. Und ihr?**
nayn, ue-ber-*houpt* niHt. *ah*-ber iH *shprêH*-e *êng*-lish. oont eer?
No, not at all. But I speak English. How about you?

Michelle: **Ich spreche ein bisschen Englisch, und ich spreche auch Spanisch.**
iH *shprêH*-e ayn *bis*-Hen *êng*-lish, oont iH *shprêH*-e ouH *shpah*-nish.
I speak a little English, and I speak Spanish, too.

Claire: **Spanisch spreche ich nicht, aber ich spreche Englisch sehr gut. Englisch finde ich leicht.**
shpah-nish shprêH-e iH niHt, ah-ber iH shprêH-e êng-lish zeyr gooht. êng-lish fin-de iH layHt.
I don't speak Spanish, but I speak English very well. I think English is easy.

Mark: **Deutsch ist auch leicht, oder?**
doych ist ouH layHt, oh-der?
German is easy, too, isn't it?

Claire: **Für mich nicht. Deutsch kann ich überhaupt nicht aussprechen!**
fuer miH niHt. doych kân iH ue-ber-houpt niHt ous-sprê-Hen!
Not for me. I can't pronounce German at all!

Words to Know

leicht	layHt	easy/simple
groß	grohs	large/big
interessant	in-te-re-sânt	interesting
klein	klayn	small
schön	shern	pretty
aber	ah-ber	but
ein bisschen	ayn bis-Hen	a little (bit)
überhaupt nicht	ue-ber-houpt niHt	not at all
sein	zayn	to be
sprechen	shprêH-en	to speak

Making Small Talk about the Weather

People everywhere love to talk about **das Wetter** (dâs *vêt*-er) (*the weather*).
After all, it affects major aspects of life — your commute to work, your plans
for outdoor activities, and sometimes even your mood. Plus, it's always a safe
topic of conversation that you can rant or rave about! You can ask about the
weather with the question **Wie ist das Wetter?** (vee ist dâs *vêt*-er?) (*What's
the weather like?*) In the following sections, you get comfortable making small
talk about the goings-on outside.

Noting what it's like out there

The phrase **Es ist . . .** (ês ist . . .) (*It is . . .*) helps you describe the weather no
matter what the forecast looks like. You simply supply the appropriate adjective at the end of the sentence. Check out these examples:

> **Es ist kalt.** (ês ist kâlt.) (*It is cold.*)
>
> **Es ist heiß.** (ês ist hays.) (*It is hot.*)
>
> **Es ist schön.** (ês ist shern.) (*It is beautiful.*)

The following vocabulary allows you to describe almost any kind of weather:

- **bewölkt** (be-*verlkt*) (*cloudy*)
- **eiskalt** (*ays*-kâlt) (*freezing*)
- **feucht** (foyHt) (*humid*)
- **kühl** (kuehl) (*cool*)
- **neblig** (*neyb*-liH) (*foggy*)
- **regnerisch** (*reyk*-ner-ish) (*rainy*)
- **schwül** (shvuel) (*muggy*)
- **sonnig** (*son*-iH) (*sunny*)
- **warm** (vârm) (*warm*)
- **windig** (*vin*-diH) (*windy*)

You can also use the following phrases to give your personal weather report:

Die Sonne scheint. (dee *son*-e shaynt.) (*The sun is shining.*)

Es regnet/schneit. (ês *reyk*-nêt/shnayt.) (*It is raining/snowing.*)

Es gibt ein Unwetter. Es blitzt und donnert. (ês gipt ayn *oon*-vêt-er. ês blitst oont *don*-ert.) (*There's a storm. There's lightning and thunder.*)

Es wird hell/dunkel. (ês virt hêl/*doon*-kel.) (*It is getting light/dark.*)

Discussing the temperature

In the old country, 30-degree weather means you can break out your swimming gear, not your skis! In Europe (and most everywhere else in the world), the temperature is measured in degrees Celsius (*tsêl*-zee-oos) (also called *Centigrade*), not degrees Fahrenheit (as it is in the United States). If you want to convert Celsius to Fahrenheit or the other way around, just use these formulas:

- ✔ **Celsius to Fahrenheit:** Multiply the Celsius temperature by 1.8 and then add 32.

- ✔ **Fahrenheit to Celsius:** Subtract 32 from the Fahrenheit temperature and multiply the result by 0.5.

You may want to take note of the following conversions:

- ✔ 0 degrees Celsius = 32 degrees Fahrenheit
- ✔ 10 degrees Celsius = 50 degrees Fahrenheit
- ✔ 20 degrees Celsius = 68 degrees Fahrenheit
- ✔ 30 degrees Celsius = 86 degrees Fahrenheit

When the temperature is the topic of conversation, the following phrases are sure to come up:

Es ist zehn Grad. (ês ist tseyn graht.) (*It's ten degrees.*) Of course, you substitute the appropriate number before the word **Grad.** (See Book I, Chapter 2 for more information on numbers.)

Es ist minus zehn Grad. (ês ist *mee*-noos tseyn graht.) (*It is minus ten degrees.*) Again, substitute the proper number before **Grad.**

Es ist zehn Grad unter Null. (ês ist tseyn graht *oon*-ter nool.) (*It is ten degrees below zero.*)

Die Temperatur fällt/steigt. (dee *têm*-pê-rah-*toohr* fêlt/shtaykt.) (*The temperature is falling/is rising.*)

Describing the day's weather

Any of the following phrases can get the ball rolling on a discussion of the weather:

Was für ein herrliches/prächtiges Wetter! (vâs fuer ayn *hêr*-liH-ês/ *praiH*-tig-es *vêt*-er!) (*What wonderful/glorious weather!*)

Was für ein schreckliches/schlechtes Wetter! (vâs fuer ayn *shrêk*-liH-ês/ *shlêHt*-ês *vêt*-er!) (*What horrible/bad weather!*)

Was für ein schöner/herrlicher Tag! (vâs fuer ayn *shern*-er/*hêr*-liH-er tahk!) (*What a beautiful/lovely day!*)

Talkin' the Talk

Anita and Rolf live across the hall from each other in the same apartment building. They have been planning to go to the park this Sunday afternoon. On Sunday morning, Rolf knocks on Anita's door to discuss their plans. (Go to www.dummies.com/go/ germanaio to listen to this bonus track.)

Rolf:	**Was machen wir jetzt? Bei so einem Wetter können wir nicht in den Park gehen. Es ist regnerisch und windig.** vâs *mâH*-en veer yêtst? bay zoh *ayn*-em *vêt*-er *kern*-nen veer niHt in deyn pârk *gey*-en. ês ist *reyk*-ner-ish oont *vin*-diH. *What do we do now? We can't go to the park in this weather. It's rainy and windy.*
Anita:	**Ja, ja, ich weiß. Aber gegen Mittag soll es aufhören zu regnen.** yah, yah, iH vays. *ah*-ber *gey*-gen *mi*-tahk zoll ês *ouf*- herr-en tsooh *reyk*-nen. *Yeah, yeah, I know. But around noon it's supposed to stop raining.*
Rolf:	**Wirklich? Ich sehe nur Wolken am Himmel . . .** *virk*-liH? iH *zey*-he noohr *vol*-ken âm *him*-el . . . *Really? I only see clouds in the sky . . .*
Anita:	**Keine Panik! Heute Mittag scheint bestimmt wieder die Sonne.** *kayn*-e *pah*-nik! *hoy*-te *mi*-tahk shaynt be-*stimmt* vee- der dee *zon*-e. *Don't panic! Surely the sun will shine again around noon today.*

Rolf: **Na gut. Vielleicht hast du recht. Ich kann bis Mittag warten.**
nâ gooht. vee-*layHt* hâst dooh rêHt. iH kân bis *mi*-tahk *vâr*-ten.
Okay. Perhaps you're right. I can wait until noon.

Anita: **Okay, bis später! Tschüs!**
okay [as in English], bis *shpai*-ter! chues!
Okay, see you later! Bye!

Words to Know

machen	<u>mâH</u>-en	to do
sehen	<u>zey</u>-hen	to see
wissen	<u>vis</u>-en	to know
recht haben	rêHt <u>hah</u>-ben	to be right
vielleicht	vee-<u>layHt</u>	perhaps
wirklich	<u>virk</u>-liH	really
bis später	bis <u>shpai</u>-ter	til later

Chapter 4

Talking about Home, Family, Friends, and Daily Life

In This Chapter

▶ Describing your home and everything in it

▶ Sharing info about your family and friends

▶ Talking about your daily routine and discussing your interest in sports

*T*alking about where you live and describing your family are great ways to open the lines of communication to a new acquaintance. In this chapter, you go on a tour of the rooms in the home and discover useful information on German domestic lifestyles. You identify names of family members, including pets, and find out how to talk about them. Finally, you build your vocabulary with words that describe your daily routine at home as well as sports.

Describing Where You Live

A far greater number of Germans live in apartments, either rented or owned, than do North Americans, and great value is placed on being able to own a single-family dwelling. Land and construction materials are very costly, so German living quarters tend to be smaller and more energy efficient than their North American counterparts.

Typical homes in German-speaking regions are solidly built using materials such as bricks or concrete with stucco-coated walls and slate or clay tile roofs. More traditional homes are half-timbered, and some have thatched roofs. Homes often include a full basement that many Germans use for storage or as a work room. Windows in homes and apartments often have shutters that unroll vertically over the windows, shutting out all daylight when closed. Windows can be opened fully inward or tipped open a bit for air, and screens are rare. Air-conditioning and clothes dryers are quite uncommon. Smaller kitchens mean smaller appliances, so you're unlikely to encounter massive, American-sized fridges.

The following sections help you talk about your own living quarters — from what type of building you live in to the type of furniture and accessories you have in your living room.

Looking at your living quarters: Mein Haus

Here's some basic vocabulary you need to know to describe rooms in a home, along with a few other residence-related details:

- **das Apartment** (dâs â-*pârt*-ment) (*studio, efficiency apartment*)
- **das Arbeitszimmer** (dâs *âr*-bayts-tsi-mer) (*workroom/study*)
- **das Bad/das Badezimmer** (dâs baht/dâs *bah*-de-tsi-mer) (*bathroom*)
- **der Balkon** (dêr bâl-*kon*) (*balcony*)
- **der Boden** (dêr *boh*-den) (*floor*)
- **der Dachboden** (dêr *dâH*-boh-den) (*attic*)
- **die Decke** (dee *dêk*-e) (*ceiling*)
- **die Eigentumswohnung** (dee *ay*-gên-tooms-vohn-oong) (*condominium*)
- **das Einfamilienhaus** (dâs *ayn*-fâ-mi-lee-en-hous) (*single-family home*)
- **das Esszimmer** (dâs *ês*-tsi-mer) (*dining room*)
- **das Fenster** (dâs *fêns*-ter) (*window*)
- **der Gang** (dêr gâng) (*hallway*)
- **die Garage** (dee gâ-*rah*-je) (*garage*)
- **der Garten** (dêr *gâr*-ten) (*yard/garden*)
- **der Keller** (dêr *kêl*-er) (*basement*)
- **die Küche** (dee *kueH*-e) (*kitchen*)
- **die Mietwohnung** (dee *meet*-vohn-oong) (*rented apartment*)
- **das Reihenhaus** (dâs *ray*-ên-hous) (*townhouse*)
- **das Schlafzimmer** (dâs *shlahf*-tsi-mer) (*bedroom*)
- **das Studentenwohnheim** (dâs shtoo-*dênt*-en-vohn-haym) (*student residence hall*)
- **das Studio** (dâs *shtooh*-dee-oh) (*studio/studio apartment*)
- **die Terrasse** (dee têr-*âs*-e) (*terrace*)

✔ **die Treppe** (dee *trêp*-e) (*stairs*)

✔ **die Tür** (dee tuer) (*door*)

✔ **die Wand** (dee vând) (*wall*)

✔ **die Wohnung** (dee *vohn*-oong) (*apartment*)

✔ **das Wohnzimmer** (dâs *vohn*-tsi-mer) (*living room*)

✔ **das Zimmer** (dâs *tsi*-mer) (*room*)

When you want to tell people what type of place you live in, use the verb **wohnen** (*vohn*-en) (*to live*). Consider the following examples:

> **Ich wohne in einer Eigentumswohnung.** (iH *vohn*-e in *ayn*-er *ayg*-en-tooms-vohn-oong.) (*I live in a condominium.*)
>
> **Wir wohnen in einem Einfamilienhaus.** (veer *vohn*-en in *ayn*-em *ayn*-fâ-mee-lee-en-hous.) (*We live in a single-family home.*)
>
> **Ich wohne mit meiner Frau in einem Reihenhaus.** (iH *vohn*-e mit *mayn*-er *frou* in *ayn*-em *ray*-en-hous.) (*I live with my wife in a townhouse.*)

Here are some ways you can describe your home:

> **Wir haben einen großen Garten.** (veer *hah*-ben ayn-en *grohs*-en *gâr*-ten.) (*We have a large garden.*)
>
> **Das Haus hat drei Schlafzimmer.** (dâs hous hât dray *shlahf*-tsi-mer.) (*The house has three bedrooms.*)
>
> **Das Wohnzimmer ist sehr bequem.** (dâs *vohn*-tsi-mer ist zeyr be-*kveym*.) (*The living room is very comfortable.*)
>
> **Unsere Wohnung hat einen schönen Balkon.** (*oon*-ser-e *vohn*-oong hât ayn-en *shern*-en *bâl*-kon.) (*Our apartment has a nice balcony.*)

Naming furnishings and appliances

When you furnish your home, your personal style influences what you choose to include in each room. Germans take great pride in having a home that's **gemütlich** (ge-*muet*-liH), a quintessential word that embodies the feeling of a place that's *cozy, comfortable,* and *homey.*

The following sections give you the basic vocabulary for home furnishings and other accessories you may find in the living room, bedroom, kitchen, and bathroom.

Das Wohnzimmer: The living room

The German-style **Wohnzimmer** (*vohn*-tsi-mer) (*living room*) is similar to what you're familiar with in North America, although German living spaces tend to be smaller. So you're unlikely to encounter mammoth sectional furniture and massive flat screen TVs. Instead, you often find a large *wall unit,* **die Schrankwand** (dee *shrânk*-vând), in the living room, which doubles as storage space and a place to display decorative or practical items.

Here's a list of other furnishings you typically find in a living room:

- ✔ **die Couch** (dee couch [as in English]) (*couch*)
- ✔ **der Couchtisch/der Kaffeetisch** (dêr *kouch*-tish/dêr *kâf*-e-tish) (*coffee table*)
- ✔ **der Fernseher** (dêr *fêrn*-zey-er) (*TV*)
- ✔ **die Gardinen/die Vorhänge** (dee gâr-*deen*-en/dee *for*-hêng-e) (*curtains*)
- ✔ **die Lampe** (dee *lâm*-pe) (*lamp*)
- ✔ **der Sessel** (dêr *zês*-el) (*armchair*)
- ✔ **das Sofa** (dâs sofa [as in English]) (*sofa*)
- ✔ **die Stehlampe** (dee *shtey*-lâm-pe) (*floor lamp*)
- ✔ **die Stereoanlage** (dee *shtêr*-ee-oh-ân-lâ-ge) (*stereo*)
- ✔ **der Teppich** (dêr *têp*-iH) (*carpet/rug*)
- ✔ **der Teppichboden** (dêr *têp*-iH-boh-den) (*wall-to-wall carpet*)

Using these words, you can talk about your living room, as in these examples:

In meinem Wohnzimmer gibt es zwei Sofas und einen Sessel. (in *mayn*-em *vohn*-tsi-mer gipt ês tsvay *soh*-fas oont *ayn*-en *zês*-el.) (*In my living room there are two sofas and an armchair.*)

Unsere Familie sieht dort fern, besonders am Abend. (*oon*-zer-e fâ-*mee*-lee-e zeet dort fêrn, be-*zon*-dêrs âm *ah*-bent.) (*Our family watches TV there, especially in the evening.*)

Die Couch ist sehr groß. (dee kouch ist zeyr grohs.) (*The couch is very large.*)

Das Schlafzimmer: The bedroom

When you need a bit of privacy or you want to sleep, **das Schlafzimmer** (dâs *shlahf*-tsi-mer) (*bedroom*) is where you go. Germans are great fans of fresh air, and even in winter, they like to sleep with the window open and the bedroom door closed. If you're wondering how they stay warm in a cold bedroom, well, the secret is a **Federbett** (*fey*-der-bêt) (*down-filled comforter*), which keeps them toasty warm, even when snow's blowing in the window.

Here are some of the other furnishings you find in a **Schlafzimmer:**

- ✔ **das Bett** (dâs bêt) (*bed*)

- ✔ **das Bettlaken** (dâs *bêt*-lâk-en) (*sheet*)

- ✔ **die Decke** (dee *dêk*-e) (*blanket*)

- ✔ **der Kleiderschrank** (dêr *klay*-dêr-shrânk) (*[clothes] closet*)

- ✔ **die Kommode** (dee ko-*moh*-de) (*dresser*)

- ✔ **das Kopfkissen** (dâs *kopf*-kis-en) (*pillow*)

- ✔ **der Nachttisch** (dêr *nâHt*-tish) (*nightstand*)

- ✔ **der Schrank** (dêr shrânk) (*closet*)

- ✔ **der Wecker** (dêr *vêk*-er) (*alarm clock*)

Die Küche: The kitchen

The heart of many homes is **die Küche** (dee kueH-e) (*kitchen*), where family and friends congregate while home-cooked meals are prepared.

Here's a list of what you may find in a typical **Küche:**

- ✔ **der Backofen** (dêr *bâk*-oh-fen) (*oven*)

- ✔ **die Geschirrspülmaschine** (dee ge-shir-shpuel-mâ-*sheen*-e) (*dishwasher*)

- ✔ **der Herd** (dêr hêrd) (*stove*)

- ✔ **der Kühlschrank** (dêr *kuel*-shrânk) (*refrigerator*)

- ✔ **der Mikrowellenherd** (dêr *meek*-roh-vêl-en-hêrd) (*microwave oven*)

- ✔ **der Mülleimer** (dêr *muel*-aym-er) (*garbage can*)

- ✔ **das Regal** (dâs rey-*gahl*) (*shelf*)

- ✔ **der Schrank** (dêr shrânk) (*cabinet/cupboard*)

- ✔ **das Spülbecken** (dâs *shpuel*-bêk-en) (*sink*)

- ✔ **der Stuhl** (dêr shtoohl) (*chair*)

- ✔ **die Theke** (dee *tey*-ke) (*counter*)

- ✔ **das Tiefkühlfach** (dâs *teef*-kuel-fâH) (*freezer*)

- ✔ **der Tisch** (dêr tish) (*table*)

- ✔ **der Wasserhahn** (dêr *vâs*-er-hahn) (*faucet*)

Book I

Getting Started with German

German homes may or may not have a dining room, depending on how they're designed. In cities where living space is at a premium, smaller apartments don't have a dining room, so people eat in the kitchen, or even in the living room, where you may find **der Esstisch** (dêr *ês*-tish) (*dining table*). Another alternative to eating at a regular dining table in the dining room is **die**

Eckbank (dee *êk*-bânk) (*corner bench*). This neat, space-saving seating arrangement found in the kitchens of farmhouses and city apartments alike consists of a corner bench and a table that can accommodate four or more people in a relatively small space. The bench seats may even flip up, offering plenty of storage below the seat for kitchen items.

Das Badezimmer: The bathroom

You may find yourself in an uncomfortable situation if you ask to use the **Badezimmer** (*bad*-e-tsi-mer) (*bathroom*), when what you're probably looking for, believe it or not, is **die Toilette** (dee toy-*lêt*-e) (*the toilet*). What constitutes a "bathroom" in German homes differs from the definition you may be accustomed to. In Germany, the bathroom is a room where you can take a bath or shower, but it may or may not have a toilet. The toilet may be located in a separate room, euphemistically described in real-estate lingo as a *half-bath*. So to avoid any confusion, whatever the plumbing situation may be, here's what you ask when you have to go:

Darf ich ihre Toilette benutzen? (dârf iH *eer*-e toy-*lêt*-e be-*noots*-en?) (*May I use the bathroom?* Literally: *May I use the toilet?*)

Here are some things you commonly find in a **Badezimmer:**

- **die Badewanne** (dee *bahd*-e-vân-e) (*bathtub*)
- **die Dusche** (dee *dooh*-she) (*shower*)
- **die Haarbürste** (dee *hahr*-buers-te) (*hairbrush*)
- **der Kamm** (dêr *kâm*) (*comb*)
- **der Rasierapparat** (dêr râ-*zeer*-âp-âr-aht) (*razor*)
- **die Seife** (dee *zay*-fe) (*soap*)
- **der Spiegel** (dêr *spee*-gel) (*faucet*)
- **das Tuch** (dâs toohH) (*towel*)
- **das Waschbecken** (dâs *vâsh*-bêk-en) (*bathroom sink*)
- **die Zahnbürste** (dee *tsahn*-buers-te) (*toothbrush*)
- **die Zahnpaste** (dee *tsahn*-pâs-te) (*toothpaste*)

If you're missing an item in the bathroom, either at somebody's house or in a hotel room, use the following question starters to find it:

Wo ist. . . ? (voh ist. . . ?) (*Where is. . . ?*) For example, **Wo ist das Badetuch?** (voh ist dâs *bahd*-e-toohH?) (*Where is the bathtowel?*)

Haben Sie. . . ? (hah-ben zee. . . ?) (*Do you have. . . ?*) For example, **Haben Sie Seife?** (hah-ben zee *zay*-fe?) (*Do you have soap?*)

Talking about Family

In the United States, discussing family, **die Familie** (dee fâ-*mee*-lee-e), is a great way to get to know someone. Some people may even show off their photos of family members. However, talking at great length about little Gretchen and Hansi, Jr. is a far less popular pastime in Germany, perhaps because Germans place a lot of value on privacy. Even so, you need to know how to talk about family, just in case the topic ever comes up.

Naming your relatives

The following list includes most, if not all, of the members of your family tree. Even if you don't have kids or in-laws, get familiar with these words so you can recognize them when discussing someone else's family (see Figure 4-1):

- **der Bruder** (dêr *brooh*-der) (*brother*)
- **der Cousin** (dêr *kooh*-zen) (*male cousin*)
- **die Cousine** (dee kooh-*zeen*-e) (*female cousin*)
- **die Eltern** (dee *êl*-tern) (*parents*)
- **die Frau** (dee frou) (*woman/wife*)
- **die Geschwister** (dee ge-*shvis*-ter) (*siblings*)
- **die Großeltern** (dee grohs-*êl*-tern) (*grandparents*)
- **die Großmutter** (dee *grohs*-moot-er) (*grandmother*)
- **der Großvater** (dêr *grohs*-fah-ter) (*grandfather*)
- **der Junge** (dêr *yoong*-e) (*boy*)
- **die Kinder** (dee *kin*-der) (*children, kids*)
- **das Mädchen** (dâs *maid*-Hên) (*girl*)
- **der Mann** (dêr mân) (*man/husband*)
- **die Mutter** (dee *moot*-er) (*mother*)
- **der Onkel** (dêr *on*-kel) (*uncle*)
- **die Schwester** (dee *shvês*-ter) (*sister*)
- **der Sohn** (dêr zohn) (*son*)
- **die Tante** (dee *tân*-te) (*aunt*)
- **die Tochter** (dee *toH*-ter) (*daughter*)
- **der Vater** (dêr *fah*-ter) (*father*)

Figure 4-1:
Who's who
in the family.

Illustration by Elizabeth Kurtzman

Use the following words for the in-laws:

- ✔ **der Schwager** (dêr *shvah*-ger) (*brother-in-law*)
- ✔ **die Schwägerin** (dee *shvai*-ger-in) (*sister-in-law*)
- ✔ **die Schwiegereltern** (dee *shvee*-ger-êl-tern) (*parents-in-law*)
- ✔ **die Schwiegermutter** (dee *shvee*-ger-moot-er) (*mother-in-law*)
- ✔ **der Schwiegersohn** (dêr *shvee*-ger-zohn) (*son-in-law*)
- ✔ **die Schwiegertochter** (dee *shvee*-ger-toH-ter) (*daughter-in-law*)
- ✔ **der Schwiegervater** (dêr *shvee*-ger-fah-ter) (*father-in-law*)

To express the term *step-*, you use the prefix **Stief-** with the name of the relative, like in this example: **Stiefbruder** (*steef*-brooh-der) (*step-brother*). The term for a *half* relative uses the prefix **Halb-**, so *half-sister* looks like this: **Halbschwester** (*hâlp*-shvês-ter).

German-speaking children use the following terms to talk about their parents and grandparents:

- ✔ **die Mama** (dee *mâ*-mâ) (*mom*)
- ✔ **die Mutti** (dee *moot*-ee) (*mommy*)

✔ **die Oma** (dee *oh*-mâ) (*grandma*)

✔ **der Opa** (der *oh*-pâ) (*grandpa*)

✔ **der Papa** (dêr *pâ*-pâ) (*dad*)

✔ **der Vati** (dêr *fâ*-tee) (*daddy*)

When directly addressing their elders, children leave out the articles **dee** (dee) (*the*) and **der** (dêr) (*the*). For example, **Mama! Komm her!** (*mâ*-mâ!! kom hêr!) (*Mom! Come here!*)

To say that you have a certain type of relative, simply use the following phrase:

> **Ich habe einen + masculine noun/eine + feminine noun/ein + neuter noun/(nothing before plurals). . . .** (îH *hah*-be *ayn*-en/*ayn*-e/ayn. . . .) (*I have a. . . .*)

The correct form of the indefinite article **einen** (masculine)/**eine** (feminine)/**ein** (neuter) (*ayn*-en/*ayn*-e/ayn) (*a*) depends on both gender and case. In the preceding phrase, you're using the accusative (direct object) case. The feminine and the neuter indefinite articles happen to be the same in the nominative (subject) case and the accusative (direct object) case, so their spelling doesn't change. The masculine indefinite article, however, takes a different form in the accusative. (Flip to Book III, Chapter 2 for more details on articles, gender, and case.)

So what do you do if you want to express that you don't have any siblings, a dog, a house, or whatever it may be? In English, you would say, "I don't have any siblings/a dog/a house." In German, you just use the negative, accusative form of the indefinite article **einen/eine/ein,** which you form by adding the letter **k** to the beginning of the word: **keinen/keine/kein** (*kayn*-en/*kayn*-e/kayn) (*no*). Look at the negative, accusative forms in the following sentences for some examples:

✔ **Masculine nouns:** Masculine nouns, such as **der Schwiegervater,** use **keinen: Ich habe keinen Schwiegervater.** (iH *hah*-be *kayn*-en *shvee*-ger-fah-ter.) (*I don't have a father-in-law.*)

✔ **Feminine nouns:** Feminine nouns, such as **die Familie,** use **keine: Ich habe keine große Familie.** (iH *hah*-be *kayn*-e groh-se fâ-*mi*-lee-e.) (*I don't have a large family.*)

✔ **Neuter nouns:** Neuter nouns, such as **das Haus,** use **kein: Ich habe kein Haus.** (iH *hah*-be kayn house.) (*I don't have a house.*)

✔ **Plural nouns:** Nouns in their plural form or those that are always plural, like **die Geschwister,** use **keine: Ich habe keine Geschwister.** (iH *hah*-be *kayn*-e ge-*shvis*-ter.) (*I don't have any siblings.*)

Family pets

Some families have other members besides the two-legged variety. In fact, **Haustiere** (*hous*-teer-e) (*house pets*) play an important role in many households.

The following list includes the typical animals that Germans have as pets:

- **der Fisch** (dêr fish) (*fish*)
- **der Goldfisch** (dêr goldfish [as in English]) (*goldfish*)
- **der Hund** (dêr hoont) (*dog*)
- **das Kaninchen** (dâs kân-*een*-Hen) (*rabbit*)
- **die Katze** (dee *kâts*-e) (*cat*)
- **das Meerschweinchen** (dâs *meyr*-shvayn-Hen) (*guinea pig*)
- **der Vogel** (dêr *foh*-gel) (*bird*)
- **der Wellensittich** (dêr *vêl*-en-zit-iH) (*parakeet*)

Here's a list of some activities you may do with your pet:

- **den Hund spazieren führen** (deyn hoont shpâts-*eer*-en *fuer*-en) (*to take the dog for a walk*)
- **den Hund anleinen** (deyn hoont *ân*-layn-en) (*to put a leash on the dog*)
- **mit dem Hund spielen** (mit deym hoont *spee*-len) (*to play with the dog*)
- **die Katze futtern** (dee *kât*-se *foot*-ern) (*to feed the cat*)

In Germany, **Hunde** (*hoon*-de) (*dogs*) are such beloved family members that, in some restaurants, they're allowed to sit under their master's table, provided they stay there.

Talkin' the Talk

Herr Hanser and Frau Schneider have just met at a symposium in Frankfurt. They're talking about their families during a coffee break. (Track 14)

Herr Hanser: **Wohnen Sie in Frankfurt?**
vohn-en zee in *frânk*-foort?
Do you live in Frankfurt?

Frau Schneider:	**Nicht direkt. Mein Mann und ich haben ein Reihenhaus in Mühlheim. Und Sie?**
	niHt *dee*-rêkt. mayn mahn oont iH *hah*-ben ayn *ray*-ên-hous in *muel*-haym. oont zee?
	Not exactly. My husband and I have a townhouse in Mühlheim. And you?

Herr Hanser:	**Wir haben eine Wohnung in der Innenstadt, aber unser Sohn wohnt in München. Haben Sie Kinder?**
	veer *hah*-ben ayn-e *vohn*-oong in dêr *in*-en-shtât, *ah*-ber oon-zer zohn vohnt in *muen*-Hen. *hah*-ben zee *kin*-der?
	We have an apartment in the center of the city, but our son lives in Munich. Do you have any kids?

Frau Schneider:	**Ja, zwei Kinder. Mein Sohn Andreas arbeitet bei Siemens, und meine Tochter Claudia wohnt mit ihrem Mann in Italien.**
	yah, tsvay *kin*-der. mayn zohn ân-*drey*-âs *âr*-bay-tet bay *zee*-mens, oont *mayn*-e *toH*-ter *klou*-dee-â vohnt mit *eer*-em mân in i-*tah*-lee-en.
	Yes, two children. My son Andreas works at Siemens, and my daughter Claudia lives with her husband in Italy.

Herr Hanser:	**Ach, meine Frau kommt aus Italien, aber ihre Eltern und ihre vier Geschwister wohnen alle in Deutschland.**
	âH, *mayn*-e frou komt ous i-*tah*-lee-en, *ah*-ber *eer*-e *êl*-tern oont *eer*-e feer ge-*shvis*-ter *vohn*-en *âl*-e în *doych*-lânt.
	Oh, my wife is from Italy, but her parents and her four siblings all live in Germany.

Discussing Friends, Acquaintances, and Neighbors

You may find yourself describing people you know as your friends, even if you aren't in close contact with them. In the German-speaking world, people have more distinct boundaries between those they consider as **Freunde** (*froyn*-de) (*friends*) and those they describe as **Bekannte** (bê-*kân*-te) (*acquaintances*).

For many Germans, **Freunde** are part of a smaller, tighter knit circle than those you may include in your group of *friends*. Aside from family and friends, other people you may know are **Nachbarn** (*nâH*-bârn) (*neighbors*) or **Arbeitskollegen** (*âr*-bayts-koh-ley-gen) (*coworkers*).

Here are some example sentences you may use to describe your friends, acquaintances, and neighbors:

> **Ich habe einen sehr guten Freund, der in New York lebt.** (iH *hah*-be *ayn*-en zeyr *gooh*-ten froynd, dêr in new york [as in English] lêpt.) (*I have a very good [male] friend who lives in New York.*)

> **Ich habe eine sehr gute Freundin, die in New York lebt.** (iH *hah*-be *ayn*-e zeyr *gooh*-te *froyn*-din, dee in new york [as in English] lêpt.) (*I have a very good [female] friend who lives in New York.*)

> **Er ist ein Bekannter von mir.** (êr ist ayn bê-*kân*-ter fon meer.) (*He's an acquaintance of mine.*)

> **Sie ist eine Bekannte von mir.** (zee ist *ayn*-e bê-*kân*-te fon meer.) (*She's an acquaintance of mine.*)

> **Ich kenne meine Nachbarn nicht sehr gut.** (iH *kên*-e *mayn*-e *nahH*-bârn niHt zeyr gooht.) (*I don't know my neighbors very well.*)

Note: In the previous example sentences, the German nouns for *friend* and *acquaintance* have different spellings, depending on whether you're talking about a male or a female. Some German nouns have this type of spelling change. For more on figuring out how to use such German nouns, see Book III, Chapter 2.

Spending Time at Your Home or Someone Else's

The time you spend at home is an important part of your life that defines who you are. It's where you prepare meals, relax, entertain friends, do work, and much more. This section provides you with useful vocabulary so you can describe the activities you do at home both during the week and on the weekends. It also explains what you need to know about being a guest at someone else's home.

Daily routine

Everyone has some sort of daily routine, starting with getting up in the morning and followed by a number of steps, like taking a shower, getting dressed, and having a bite to eat. The evening routine probably includes some of the same steps, only in reverse order. This section gets you up to speed on describing what you do on a daily basis.

Some German verbs that you use to describe your daily actions have an unusual construction. They're the equivalent of *reflexive verbs* in English. Verbs in this group use a reflexive pronoun like *myself* or *ourselves* to empha-size the information about who is carrying out the action of the verb. When you say, "*Cats wash themselves very thoroughly,*" you're using the reflexive pronoun *themselves* together with the verb *wash* to talk about what cats do. For more information on reflexive verbs, go to Book IV, Chapter 3.

Another set of verbs you use to describe your daily routine includes *separable-prefix verbs* and *inseparable-prefix verbs*. These verbs are similar to English verbs that have two parts, such as *look at* or *get up*. To find out more about using separable- and inseparable-prefix verbs, see Book III, Chapter 8.

Here's a list of typical daily routine activities. Some of the verbs in the list are regular, some are reflexive, and some are separable prefix. For the reflexive and separable-prefix verbs, you see a note after the English meaning of the word:

- **aufstehen** (*ouf*-shtey-en) (*to get up*) (separable prefix)
- **sich duschen** (zeeH *doohsh*-en) (*to take a shower*) (reflexive)
- **sich anziehen** (zeeH *ân*-tsee-en) (*to get dressed*) (reflexive/separable prefix)
- **frühstücken** (*frue*-shtuek-en) (*to eat breakfast*)
- **in die/zur Arbeit gehen** (in dee/tsoor *âr*-bayt *gey*-en) (*to go into/to work*)
- **zu Mittag essen** (tsooh *mit*-âk *ês*-en) (*to have lunch*)
- **nach Hause kommen** (nâH-*houz*-e kom-en) (*to come home*)
- **zu Abend essen** (tsooh ah-bent *ês*-en) (*to have dinner*)
- **fernsehen** (*fêrn*-zey-en) (*to watch TV*) (separable prefix)
- **den Wecker stellen** (deyn *vêk*-er *shtêl*-en) (*to set the alarm clock*)
- **sich ausziehen** (zeeH *ous*-tsee-en) (*to get undressed*) (reflexive/separable prefix)
- **ins Bett gehen** (ins bêt *gey*-en) (*to go to bed*)

Use the following sentences to describe your daily routine or someone else's:

Ich stehe um (7) Uhr auf. (iH shtey-e oom [*zee*-ben] oohr ouf.) (*I get up at [seven] o'clock.*)

Ich ziehe mich an. (iH *tsee*-e meeH ân.) (*I get dressed.*)

Wir kommen spät nach Hause. (veer *kom*-en shpait nâH *houz*-e.) (*We're coming home late.*)

Abends sehe ich oft fern. (*ah*-bents *zey*-e iH oft fêrn.) (*I often watch TV in the evening.*)

Sie geht um zehn Uhr ins Bett. (zee geyt oom tseyn oohr ins bêt.) (*She goes to bed at ten o'clock.*)

Das Wochenende: The weekend

Das Wochenende (dâs *voH*-en-*ên*-de) (*the weekend*) is the time to relax, or, expressed in German, **sich entspannen** (zeeH ênt-*shpân*-en) (*to relax*), especially for anyone who has a typical Monday through Friday work routine. On the weekend, you may have a number of chores to catch up on, but you may also get up a little later and have a relaxing breakfast first.

The following is a list of some typical weekend chores and activities. For verbs that are separable-prefix verbs, you see a note in parentheses after the English translation. For details on using separable-prefix verbs, see Book III, Chapter 8.

- **abwaschen** (*âp*-vâsh-en) (*to do the dishes*) (separable prefix)
- **das Auto waschen** (dâs *ou*-toh *vâsh*-en) (*to wash the car*)
- **einkaufen** (*ayn*-kouf-en) (*to shop*) (separable prefix)
- **faulenzen** (*foul*-ênts-en) (*to lounge around*)
- **Freunde einladen** (*froyn*-de *ayn*-lâd-en) (*to invite friends over*) (separable prefix)
- **die Hausarbeit machen** (dee *hous*-âr-bayt *mâH*-en) (*to do the housework*)
- **im Internet surfen** (im Internet [as in English] *soorf*-en) (*to surf the Internet*)
- **kochen** (*koH*-en) (*to cook*)
- **Musik hören** (moo-*zeek her*-en) (*to listen to music*)
- **saubermachen** (*zou*-ber-*mâH*-en) (*to clean up*) (separable prefix)
- **spät aufstehen** (shpait *ouf*-shtey-en) (*to get up late*) (separable prefix)
- **staubsaugen** (*shtoup*-zoug-en) (*to vacuum*) (separable prefix)
- **die Wäsche waschen** (dee *vaish*-e *vâsh*-en) (*to do the laundry*)

Here are some sentences you can use to talk about what you or other people do on weekends:

Ich lade Freunde ein. (iH *lâ*-de *froyn*-de ayn.) (*I'm inviting friends over.*)

Ich mache die Hausarbeit gern. (iH *mâH*-e dee *hous*-âr-bayt gêrn) (*I like to do the housework.*)

Er macht heute Nachmittag sauber. (êr mâHt *hoy*-te *nâH*-mi-tahk *zou*-ber.) (*He's cleaning up this afternoon.*)

Steht sie Sonntags spät auf? (shteyt zee *zon*-tahks spait ouf?) (*Does she get up late on Sundays?*)

Until a few years ago, strict laws in Germany, Austria, and Switzerland regulated when stores were allowed to be open, particularly on weekends. On Saturday mornings, people rushed to shop for food because supermarkets closed in the early afternoon, and no stores of any kind were open on Sundays. Although the regulations for opening and closing hours have been relaxed, people still like to get out early on Saturday to buy fresh **Brötchen** (*brert*-Hen) (*rolls*) from the local bakery. After doing some shopping and a number of household chores on Saturday morning, Germans enjoy taking a long **Spaziergang** (shpâts-*eer*-gâng) (*walk*), **Fahrradfahren** (*fahr*-râd-*fahr*-en) (*bicycling*), or doing any number of outdoor recreation activities.

Sunday is traditionally a day of rest and a time for families to enjoy a home-cooked meal together at midday, followed by a leisurely stroll. At around 4 p.m., many families share **Kaffee und Kuchen** (*kah*-fey oont *koohH*-en) (*coffee and cake*) or, for the indulgent, a big dollop of unsweetened **Schlagsahne** (shlâg-zahn-e) (*whipped cream*) on top of a slice of homemade **Apfelstrudel** (âp-fêl-shtrooh-del) (*apple strudel*). Mmm!

All day on Sundays and on weekdays usually between 1 p.m. and 3 p.m. and after 10 p.m., certain loud activities, such as mowing the lawn, playing loud music, and doing laundry, are prohibited in accordance with the "quiet time" law.

Doing and saying the right thing

Knowing what to do when you're a guest in someone's home is a simple matter of being aware of the differences in the conventions of others and then observing them. This section outlines some of the things you need to know before visiting someone's home in a German-speaking country.

Living behind closed doors

Privacy plays an important role in German-speaking countries, so in general, people close doors between rooms in homes and office buildings. As an added benefit to maintaining privacy, closed doors keep noise levels down and may conserve energy. When you're in doubt about whether it's okay to enter a room with a closed door, simply knock and say,

Darf ich? (dârf iH?) (*May I?*)

Helping yourself

When you're at home, you think nothing of going to the fridge to help yourself to something to drink. Your friends may do the same in your home. Germans tend to be more formal about opening up the fridge door in someone else's home without asking. If you're thirsty and you want something to drink, you can say,

> **Könnte ich etwas zu trinken haben?** (*kern*-te iH *êt*-vâs tsooh *trin*-ken *hah*-ben?) (*Could I have something to drink?*)

Behaving politely at the dinner table

Table etiquette in German-speaking countries involves a couple of polite phrases at the start of the meal, as well as appropriate eating customs. Before beginning a meal, Germans often say **Guten Appetit** (*gooh*-ten âp-e-*teet*) (*enjoy your meal*) or its more informal version, **Mahlzeit** (*mâl*-tsayt) (*enjoy your meal*). You may also hear **Mahlzeit** used as a means of greeting colleagues at the workplace around lunchtime. People gathered around a dinner table use the phrase **zum Wohl** (tsoom vohl) (*cheers*) as they raise their glasses before taking the first sip of something like wine. **Prost** (prohst) (*cheers*) is an alternative, informal expression more typically associated with drinking only.

Table manners in the German-speaking world deem it polite to have both hands on the table but not the elbows. In fact, your fellow diners would consider you strange if you kept your hands hidden in your lap during a meal. (No funny business under the table, please!) By the same token, eating with your fork while holding your knife in the other hand is acceptable.

During meal preparation, if you'd like to offer your help, by all means do so. You may use either the formal or informal version of *you*. Here's the formal *you* formulation:

> **Kann ich Ihnen helfen?** (kân iH *een*-en *hêlf*-en?) (*Can I help you?*)

The informal *you* version looks like this:

> **Kann ich dir helfen?** (kân iH deer *hêlf*-en?) (*Can I help you?*)

In another situation, you may be offered something (more) to eat or drink. Check out the question and some replies:

> **Darf/Kann ich Ihnen . . . anbieten?** (dârf/kân iH *een*-en . . . *ân*-beet-en?) (*May/Can I offer you. . . ?*)
>
> **Ja, bitte. Ich möchte. . . .** (yah, *bi*-te. iH *merH*-te. . . .) (*Yes, please. I'd like. . . .*)
>
> **Danke, nein.** (*dân*-ke, nayn.) (*No, thank you.*)

Playing Sports

Europeans, like Americans and people all over the world, enjoy participating in and watching a wide variety of indoor and outdoor sports. By far the most popular **Sport** (shport) (*sport*) is soccer, known to Germans as **Fußball** (*foohs*-bâl). It's not to be confused with **Football** (football [as in English]) (*American football*), which isn't played much in Europe. Other traditional German favorites include volleyball, bicycling, skiing, and hiking. Some relative newcomers are tennis, golf, and windsurfing. By using the words and phrases in this section, you can share your interest in sports with other people **auf Deutsch** (ouf doych) (*in German*)!

Playing around with the verb "spielen"

You can talk about playing many sports by using the verb **spielen** (*shpeel*-en) (to play) and the noun that describes the sport in the following phrase:

> **Ich spiele gern. . . .** (iH *shpeel*-e gêrn. . . .) (*I like to play. . . .*)

Just insert the names of the following sports at the end of the sentence and let the games begin!

- ✔ **Basketball** (basketball [as in English]) (*basketball*)
- ✔ **Fußball** (*foohs*-bâl) (*soccer*)
- ✔ **Golf** (golf [as in English]) (*golf*)
- ✔ **Tennis** (tennis [as in English]) (*tennis*)
- ✔ **Volleyball** (volleyball [as in English]) (*volleyball*)

Verbalizing sports you enjoy

Some sports you express as verbs, so you don't use the verb **spielen** to talk about them. Instead, you use the following expression:

> **Ich möchte gern. . . .** (iH *merH*-te gêrn. . . .) (*I would like to. . . .*)

To complete the sentence, you simply tack on the verb that expresses the sport — no conjugating necessary — at the end of the expression. For example:

> **Ich möchte gern segeln.** (iH *merH*-te gêrn *zey*-geln.) (*I would like to sail.*)

Here are a few other verbs that describe sports:

- ✔ **(Fahr)rad fahren** (*[fahr]*-rât *fahr*-en) (*to ride a bike*)

- ✔ **joggen** (*jog*-en) (*to jog*)

- ✔ **schwimmen** (*shvim*-en) (*to swim*)

- ✔ **Ski fahren** (shee *fahr*-en) (*to ski*) (***Note:*** Pronunciation is "*shee*," not "*skee*.")

- ✔ **windsurfen** (*vint*-soorf-en) (*to windsurf*)

The following construction provides another way to discuss your favorite activities:

Ich . . . gern. (iH . . . gêrn.) (*I like to. . . .*)

Here you need to remember to conjugate the verb (drop the **-n** for the **ich** forms, keep the **-n** for the **wir, sie/Sie** [we, they/you formal]) that you put in the blank. Check out these examples:

Ich schwimme gern. (iH *shvim*-e gêrn.) (*I like to swim.*)

Ich fahre gern Fahrrad. (iH *fahr*-e gêrn *fahr*-rât.) (*I like to bike.*)

Inviting someone to play

To ask someone to join you in an activity, use one of the following expressions and add either the verb (in infinitive form) that expresses the sport or the noun that expresses the sport plus the verb **spielen:**

Lass uns . . . gehen! (lâs oons . . . *gey*-en!) (*Let's go. . . !*)

Möchtest du. . . ? (*merH*-test dooh. . .) (*Would you like to. . . ?*)

Take a look at these two examples:

Lass uns windsurfen gehen! (lâs oons *vint*-soorf-en *gey*-en!) (*Let's go windsurfing!*)

Möchtest du Volleyball spielen? (*merH*-test dooh volleyball *speel*-en?) (*Would you like to play volleyball?*)

Words to Know

etwas vorhaben	êt-wâs <u>for</u>-hah-ben	to have some plans
mitkommen	<u>mit</u>-kom-en	to come along
ja, sicher	jâh, <u>zeeH</u>-er	yes, sure
wohin	voh-<u>hin</u>	where to
abgemacht	ahp-ge-mâHt	that's a deal
bis morgen	bis <u>mor</u>-gen	until tomorrow

Talkin' the Talk

It's Friday afternoon, and Michael spots his friend Ingo on the subway. (Track 15)

Michael: **Grüß dich Ingo. Was machst du morgen?**
grues dîH *een*-goh. Vâs mâHst dooh *mor*-gên?
Hi Ingo. What are you doing tomorrow?

Ingo: **Nichts Besonderes. Joggen oder schwimmen. Was hast du vor?**
niHts be-*zon*-der-es. *jog*-en *oh*-der *shvim*-en. vâs hâst du for?
Nothing special. Jogging or swimming. What are your plans?

Michael: **Ich möchte gern Fahrrad fahren. Kommst du mit?**
iH *merH*-te gêrn *fahr*-rât *fahr*-en. Komst du mit?
I'd really like to take a bike ride. Want to come along?

Ingo: **Ja, sicher. Wohin fahren wir?**
yâh, *zeeH*-er. voh-*hin fahr*-en veer?
Yes, sure. Where shall we go?

Michael: **Lass uns zum Starnberger See fahren. Wir können dort in den Biergarten gehen.**
lâs oons tsoom *shtahrn*-bêr-ger zey *fahr*-en. veer *kern*-en dort in deyn *beer*-gâr-ten *gey*-en.
Let's ride to Starnberger Lake. We can go to the beergarden there.

Ingo: **Abgemacht! Bis morgen!**
ahp-ge-mâHt. bis *mor*-gen!
That's a deal! Until tomorrow!

Chapter 5

Talking Telecommunications, Business, and Current Events

In This Chapter

▶ Placing phone calls

▶ Sending letters, faxes, and e-mails

▶ Becoming familiar with business terminology

▶ Understanding media and current events

Telecommunications increasingly drive daily interaction with others, from ordering pizza to conducting business between continents. The first step is deciding which interface you want to use to convey your message — phone, e-mail, fax, or a good old-fashioned letter. This chapter delves into each of these media. It also offers a brief primer in office terminology and some tips on conducting business. Finally, it includes a quick overview of the news media so you can keep up with current events.

Making a Phone Call

When German speakers pick up **das Telefon** (dâs *tē*-le-fohn) (*the telephone*), they usually answer the call by stating their last name — particularly when they're at the office. If you call somebody at home, you sometimes may hear a simple **Hallo?** (hâ-*loh?*) (*Hello?*).

If you want to express that you're going to call somebody or that you want somebody to call you, use the verb **anrufen** (*ân*-roohf-en) (*to call*). It's a separable verb, so the prefix **an** (ân) (*to*) gets separated from the stem **rufen** (*roohf*-en) (*call*) when you conjugate it, as you can see here:

anrufen (*to call*)	
ich ruf**e** an	wir ruf**en** an
du ruf**st** an	ihr ruft an
er/sie/es ruft an	sie ruf**en** an
Sie ruf**en** an	
Ich **rufe** später noch einmal **an.** (*I'll call again later.*)	

For more info on separable verbs, see Book III, Chapter 8.

Asking for your party

If the person you want to speak to doesn't pick up the phone, you need to ask for your party. As in English, you have several options to express that you want to speak with somebody:

Ich möchte gern Herrn/Frau . . . sprechen. (īH *merH*-te gêrn hêrn/frou . . . *shprêH*-en.) (*I would like to talk to Mr./Mrs. . . .*)

Ist Herr/Frau . . . zu sprechen? (ist hêr/frou . . . tsooh *shprêH*-en?) (*Is Mr./Mrs. . . . available?*)

Kann ich bitte mit Herrn/Frau . . . , sprechen? (kân īH *bi*-te mit hêrn/frou . . . , *shprêH*-en?) (*Can I speak to Mr./Mrs. . . . , please?*)

Herrn/Frau . . . , bitte. (hêrn/frou . . . , *bi*-te.) (*Mr./Mrs. . . . , please.*)

If you find that somebody on the other end of the line talks too fast for you to understand, try using these questions to slow down the conversation:

Können Sie bitte langsamer sprechen? (*kern*-en zee *bi*-te *lâng*-zahm-er *sprêH*-en?) (*Could you please talk more slowly?*)

Können Sie das bitte wiederholen? (*kern*-en zee dâs *bi*-te vee-der-*hoh*-len?) (*Could you repeat that, please?*)

And if the person on the other end starts speaking English in response to your question, don't consider it a failure on your part. The other person probably just wants to practice his or her English!

Using the phone while visiting Germany

If you'd like the convenience of using a cellphone while you're in Germany, or almost anywhere in Europe for that matter, shop around before you leave for your destination. You may want a prepaid SIM card for your cellphone, but you need to ask your provider beforehand whether it works in Europe. Your other options are to get a prepaid cellphone or to use a rental cellphone.

If you want to make a call from a public phone — **die Telefonzelle** (dee tê-le-*fohn*-tsêl-e) (*the*

phone booth) — in Germany, be prepared to do some sleuthing to find one. When you do, you'll need to figure out how it works, and you'll probably need to purchase a telephone card — **Telefonkarte** (tê-le-*fohn*-kâr-te) — elsewhere beforehand. You may find telephone cards for sale at tobacco shops. However, it may be easier to get your own cellphone — **das Handy** (dâs *hên*-dee) — at a telephone shop in Germany.

Making the connection

After you ask to speak to a specific person, you may hear any number of responses depending on whom you're calling and where that person is when you call:

> **Am Apparat.** (âm â-pâ-*raht*.) (*Speaking*. [Literally: *On the phone.*])

> **Einen Moment bitte, ich verbinde.** (*ayn*-en moh-*mênt* bi-te, îH fêr-*bin*-de.) (*One moment please, I'll put you through.*)

> **Er/sie telefoniert gerade.** (êr/zee tê-le-fohn-*eert* ge-*rah*-de.) (*He/she is on the telephone right now.*)

> **Bitte, bleiben Sie am Apparat.** (*bi*-te *blay*-ben zee âm â-pâ-*raht*.) (*Please hold.*)

> **Die Leitung ist besetzt.** (dee *lay*-toong ist be-*zêtst*.) (*The line is busy.*)

> **Können Sie später noch einmal anrufen?** (*kern*-en zee *shpai*-ter noH *ayn*-mahl *ân*-roohf-en?) (*Could you call again later?*)

> **Kann er/sie Sie zurückrufen?** (kân êr/zee zee tsoo-*ruek*-roohf-en?) (*Can he/she call you back?*)

> **Hat er/sie Ihre Telefonnummer?** (hât êr/zee *eer*-e tê-le-*fohn*-noom-er?) (*Does he/she have your phone number?*)

Here are some expressions that may be helpful if something goes wrong with your connection:

Es tut mir leid. Ich habe mich verwählt. (ês tooht meer layt. iH *hah*-be miH fer-*vailt.*) (*I'm sorry. I have dialed the wrong number.*)

Die Verbindung ist schlecht. (dee fêr-*bin*-doong ist shlêHt.) (*It's a bad connection.*)

Er/sie hebt nicht ab. (êr/zee hêpt niHt âp.) (*He/she doesn't answer the phone.*)

Ich werde später noch einmal versuchen. (iH *vêr*-de *shpait*-er *noH* ayn-mâl vêr-*zoohH*-en.) (*I'll try again later.*)

You may hear the following expressions when you're in the process of making your connection and you reach someone's answering machine:

Hier ist der Anrufbeantworter von. . . . (heer ist dêr *ân*-roohf-be-ânt-for-ter fon. . . .) (*This is the answering machine of. . . .*)

Sie können eine Nachricht hinterlassen. (zee *kern*-en *ayn*-e *nâH*-reeHt *hin*-ter-lâs-en.) (*You can leave a message.*)

Sprechen Sie bitte nach dem Piepton. (*sprêH*-en zee *bi*-te nâH deym peep-tohn.) (*Please speak after the beep.*)

Talkin' the Talk

The following is a conversation between Frau Bauer, the personal assistant of Herr Huber, and Herr Meißner, a client of the company. (Track 16)

Frau Bauer: **Firma TransEuropa, Bauer. Guten Morgen!**
fir-mâ *trâns*-oy-*roh*-pâ, *bou*-er. gooh-ten *mor*-gen!
TransEuropa company, (Mrs.) Bauer speaking. Good morning!

Herr Meißner: **Guten Morgen! Herrn Huber, bitte.**
gooh-ten *mor*-gen! hêrn *hooh*-ber, *bi*-te.
Good morning! Mr. Huber, please.

Frau Bauer: **Wie ist Ihr Name, bitte?**
vee ist eer *nah*-me, *bi*-te?
What is your name, please?

Herr Meißner: **Meißner. Ich bin von der Firma Schlecker.**
mays-ner. iH bin fon dêr *fir*-mâ *shlêk*-er.
(This is Mr.) Meißner. I'm from the Schlecker company.

Frau Bauer:	**Ich verbinde . . . Tut mir leid. Herr Huber ist in einer Besprechung. Kann er Sie zurückrufen?** iH fêr-*bin*-de . . . tooht meer layt. hêr *hooh*-ber ist in *ayn*-er be-*shprêH*-oong. kân êr zee tsoo-*ruek*-roohf-en? *I'll connect you . . . I'm sorry. Mr. Huber is in a meeting. Can he call you back?*
Herr Meißner:	**Selbstverständlich. Er hat meine Telefonnummer.** zêlpst-fêr-*shtant*-liH. êr hât *mayn*-e tê-le-*fohn*-noom-er. *Of course. He has my telephone number.*
Frau Bauer:	**Gut, Herr Meißner. Auf Wiederhören!** gooht, hêr *mays*-ner. ouf *vee*-der-herr-en! *Good, Mr. Meißner. Goodbye!*
Herr Meißner:	**Vielen Dank. Auf Wiederhören!** *fee*-len dânk. ouf *vee*-der-herr-en! *Thanks a lot. Goodbye!*

Words to Know

das Telefon	dâs <u>tê</u>-le-fohn	phone
das Handy	dâs <u>hên</u>-dee	cellphone
anrufen	<u>ân</u>-roohf-en	to call
zurückrufen	tsoo-<u>ruek</u>-roohf-en	to call back
auf Wiederhören!	ouf <u>vee</u>-der-herr-en	Goodbye! (on the phone)
das Telefonbuch	dâs tê-le-<u>fohn</u>-boohH	phone book
das Telefongespräch	dâs tê-le-<u>fohn</u>-ge-shpraiH	phone call
die Telefonnummer	dee tê-le-<u>fohn</u>- noom-er	phone number
der Anrufbeantworter	dêr <u>ân</u>-roohf-be-ânt-for-ter	answering machine

Saying goodbye on the phone

Does **auf Wiederhören!** (ouf *vee*-der-herr-en!) sound somewhat familiar? It's the phone equivalent to **auf Wiedersehen** (ouf *vee*-der-zey-en), the expression you use if you say goodbye to somebody you've just seen in person. **Auf**

Wiedersehen combines **wieder** (*vee*-der) (*again*) with the verb **sehen** (*zey*-en) (*to see*), whereas **auf Wiederhören** uses the verb **hören** (*herr*-en) (*to hear*), so it literally means "hear you again." Makes sense, doesn't it?

Making appointments

You may need to make an appointment to see someone. Here are some expressions that can help you get past the gatekeepers:

> **Ich möchte gern einen Termin machen.** (iH *merH*-te gêrn *ayn*-en têr-meen mâH-en.) (*I would like to make an appointment.*)

> **Kann ich meinen Termin verschieben?** (kân iH *mayn*-en têr-*meen* fêr-shee-ben?) (*Can I change my appointment?*)

Here are some of the responses you may hear:

> **Wann passt es Ihnen?** (vân pâst ês *een*-en?) (*What time suits you?*)

> **Wie wäre es mit. . . ?** (vee *vai*-re ês mit. . . ?) (*How about. . . ?*)

> **Heute ist leider kein Termin mehr frei.** (*hoy*-te ist *lay*-der kayn têr-*meen* meyr fray.) (*Unfortunately, there is no appointment available today.*)

Talkin' the Talk

Frau Bauer has to make an appointment at the doctor's office. She is talking to the doctor's assistant, Liza.

Liza: **Praxis Dr. Eggert.**
          prâx-is *dok*-tor *êg*-ert.
          Dr. Eggert's office.

Frau Bauer: **Guten Tag, Anita Bauer. Ich möchte einen Termin für nächste Woche machen.**
          gooh-ten tahk, â-*nee*-tâ *bou*-er. iH *merH*-te *ayn*-en têr-*meen* fuer *naiH*-ste *voH*-e *mâH*-en.
          Hello. (This is) Anita Bauer. I would like to make an appointment for next week.

Liza:	**Wann passt es Ihnen?** vân pâst ês *een*-en? *What time suits you?*
Frau Bauer:	**Mittwoch wäre gut.** *mit*-vôH *vai*-re gooht. *Wednesday would be good.*
Liza:	**Mittwoch ist leider kein Termin mehr frei. Wie wäre es mit Donnerstag?** *mit*-voH îst *lay*-der kayn têr-*meen* meyr fray. vee *vai*-re ês mit *don*-ers-tahk? *Unfortunately, there is no appointment available on Wednesday. How about Thursday?*
Frau Bauer:	**Donnerstag ist auch gut. Geht fünfzehn Uhr?** *don*-ers-tahk ist ouH gooht. geyt *fuenf*-tseyn oohr? *Thursday is good, too. Does 3:00 p.m. work?*
Liza:	**Kein Problem. Dann bis Donnerstag.** kayn proh-*bleym*. dân bis *don*-ers-tahk. *No problem. Until Thursday.*
Frau Bauer:	**Danke schön. Auf Wiederhören.** *dân*-ke shern. ouf *vee*-der-*herr*-en. *Thank you very much. Goodbye.*

Leaving messages

Unfortunately, you often don't get through to the person you're trying to reach, and you have to leave a message. In that case, some of the following expressions may come in handy:

Kann ich ihm/ihr eine Nachricht hinterlassen? (kân îH eem/eer *ayn*-e *nahH*-riHt hin-ter-*lâs*-en?) (*Can I leave him/her a message?*)

Kann ich ihm/ihr etwas ausrichten? (kân iH eem/eer *êt*-vâs *ous*-riH-ten?) (*Can I give him/her a message?*)

Möchten Sie eine Nachricht hinterlassen? (*merH*-ten zee *ayn*-e *naH*-riHt hin-ter-*lâs*-en?) (*Would you like to leave a message?*)

Ich bin unter der Nummer . . . zu erreichen. (iH bin *oon*-ter dêr *noom*-er . . . tsooh êr-*ayH*-en.) (*I can be reached at the number. . . .*)

Talkin' the Talk

Frau Bauer, an assistant at the company TransEuropa, answers a phone call from Hans Seibold, who is an old friend of her boss, Herr Huber.

Frau Bauer: **Firma TransEuropa, guten Tag!**
fir-mâ *trâns-oy-roh*-pâ, *gooh*-ten tahk!
TransEuropa company, hello!

Herr Seibold: **Guten Tag, Seibold hier. Kann ich bitte mit Herrn Huber, sprechen?**
gooh-ten tahk, *zay*-bolt heer. kân iH *bi*-te mit hêrn *hooh*-ber, *shprêH*-en?
Hello, (this is Mr.) Seibold. Can I speak to Mr. Huber, please?

Frau Bauer: **Guten Tag, Herr Seibold. Einen Moment bitte, ich verbinde.**
gooh-ten tahk hêr *zay*-bolt. *ayn*-en moh-*mênt bi*-te, iH fêr-*bin*-de.
Hello, Mr. Seibold. One moment, please. I'll connect you.

(After a short moment)

Frau Bauer: **Herr Seibold? Herr Huber spricht gerade auf der anderen Leitung. Möchten Sie ihm eine Nachricht hinterlassen?**
hêr *zay*-bolt? hêr *hooh*-ber shpriHt ge-*rah*-de ouf dêr *ân*-de-ren *lay*-toong. *merH*-ten zee eem *ayn*-e *nahH*-riHt hin-ter-*lâs*-en?
Mr. Seibold? Mr. Huber is on the other line. Would you like to leave him a message?

Herr Seibold: **Ja bitte. Ich bin unter der Nummer 089 57 36 488 zu erreichen.**
yah, *bi*-te. iH bin *oon*-têr dêr *noom*-er nool âHt noyn fuenf *zee*-ben dray zeks feer âHt âHt tsooh êr-*rayH*-en.
Yes, please. I can be reached at the number 089 57 36 488.

Frau Bauer: **Ich werde es ausrichten!**
iH *vêr*-de ês *ous*-riH-ten!
I'll forward the message!

Herr Seibold: **Vielen Dank! Auf Wiederhören!**
fee-len dânk! ouf *vee*-der-*herr*-en!
Thanks a lot! Goodbye!

Writing Your Message

Considering all the tasks you can accomplish with a (cell)phone, you may ask yourself why anyone would bother with the hassle of putting pen to paper, or fingers to keyboard, for that matter. Yet people still like, and need, to send written correspondence from time to time. Entire books have been written about the art of writing letters in German; this section gives you just enough information to write and send a letter or e-mail.

Beginning and ending a letter

You use certain conventions in German, just as you do in English, to write letters. The form of address varies, depending on whether you know the name of the person you're writing to. The greeting in the letter is followed by a comma. Contrary to English convention, the first letter of the first word in the opening sentence of a German letter isn't capitalized, unless it's a noun. The following sections provide more details on how to start and finish a letter in German.

Formal style

In formal German, when you know the name of the person you're writing to, the phrase you begin with is **Sehr geehrte Frau/Sehr geehrter Herr . . .** (zeyr ge-*eyr*-te frou/zeyr ge-*eyr*-ter hêr) (*Dear Mrs./Dear Mr. . . .*). You add the person's last name after the form of address of **Frau** or **Herr.** The term **Fräulein** (*froy*-layn) (*Miss*) is no longer used.

Here's an example of a formal style opening salutation:

> **Sehr geehrter Herr Schneider,** (zeyr ge-*eyr*-ter hêr *schnayd*-er,) (*Dear Mr. Schneider,*)

When you don't know the name of the person or people you're writing to, you write **Sehr geehrte Damen und Herren,** (zeyr ge-*eyr*-te *dâm*-en oont *hêr*-en,) (*Dear ladies and gentlemen,*).

When the person you're writing to has a title, be sure to include that in the salutation. The following list shows some commonly used titles, their abbreviated forms, and an example of how to use the title in the salutation of a letter:

- ✔ **Professor** (pro-*fês*-or) (*Professor*) (male)/**Professorin** (pro-*fês-or*-in) (*Professor*) (female): **Prof.** is the abbreviated form. You write the full title **Professor** or **Professorin** in the salutation of a letter like this:

> **Sehr geehrter Herr Professor Schlagbaum,** (zeyr ge-*eyr*-ter hêr proh-*fês*-or *shlahk*-boum,) (*Dear Professor Schlagbaum,*)

✔ **Doktor** (*dok*-tor) (*Doctor*) (male and female): **Dr.** is the abbreviation. In the German-speaking world, you use the title **Doktor** to address both people who are medical doctors as well as those with doctorate degrees. Write the abbreviated form in salutations like this:

> **Sehr geehrte Frau Dr. Prediger,** (zeyr ge-*eyr*-te frou *dok*-tor *prey*-dee-ger,) (*Dear Doctor Preydiger,*)

✔ **Diplom-Ingenieur** (di-*plohm*-in-gen-er) (*graduate engineer*): **Dipl.-Ing.** is the abbreviation. You use this title for people with advanced engineering degrees. Write the abbreviated form in salutations like this:

> **Sehr geehrter Herr Dipl.-Ing. Morgenstern,** (zeyr ge-*eyr*-ter hêr di-*plohm*-in-gen-er *mor*-gen-shtêrn,) (*Dear Mr. Morgenstern,*)

The phrase most often used to sign off a letter is **Mit freundlichen Grüßen** (mit *froynt*-liH-en *grues*-en) (*Sincerely*). Unlike the closing greeting in English, you don't follow this expression with a comma. Your signature goes below the closing, and you add your full name and contact information below the signature, as you do in English.

Informal style

When you know people well enough to be on a first-name basis, you use the informal **du** (dooh) (informal *you*) when you're speaking to them and the informal style of opening and closing a letter when writing to them. If you're not sure whether to address someone formally or informally, err on the side of caution and stick with formal usage. But when you're writing to people you know well, use the informal letter style for salutations and closings. Use **Liebe** (*leeb*-e) (*Dear*) to address a female and **Lieber** (*leeb*-er) (*Dear*) to address a male. Follow the greeting with the person's first name. For example:

> **Liebe Heidi,** (*leeb*-e *hay*-dee,) (*Dear Heidi,*)

The informal closing to a letter looks like this:

> **Herzliche Grüße** (*hertz*-leeH-e *grues*-e) (*kind regards*)

Sending mail the old-fashioned way

When you're ready to send someone **der Brief** (dêr breef) (*letter*), **die Postkarte** (dee *post*-kâr-te) (*postcard*), **die Ansichtskarte** (dee *ahn*-zîHts-kâr-te) (*picture postcard*), or **das Paket** (dâs pâ-*keyt*) (*package*), you need to be prepared with some simple phrases that get you in and out of **das Postamt** (dâs *post*-âmt) (*post office*) as quickly and hassle-free as possible.

Buying stamps

In Germany, you usually buy **Briefmarken** (*breef*-mâr-ken) (*stamps*) — or, if you need only one, **die Briefmarke** (dee *breef*-mâr-ke) (*stamp*) — at the post office. To get your stamps, say the following to the postal worker:

> **Ich möchte gern Briefmarken kaufen.** (iH *merH*-te gern *breef*-mâr-ken *kouf*-en.) (*I would like to buy stamps.*)

To specify how many stamps and what values you want, state your request like this:

> **5-mal 50 Cent und 10-mal 20 Cent.** (*fuenf*-mahl *fuenf*-tsiH sent oont *tseyn*-mahl *tsvân*-tsiH sent.) (*5 times 50 cents and 10 times 20 cents.*)

If you want to know the postage for an item you're sending to the U.S. — for example, a letter or a postcard — ask the following as you hand your correspondence over the counter:

> **Wie viel kostet es, diesen Brief/diese Ansichtskarte nach Amerika zu schicken?** (vee feel *kos*-tet ês, *deez*-en breef/*deez*-e *ahn*-ziHts-*kâr*-te nahH â-*mey*-ree-kah tsooh *shik*-en?) (*How much does it cost to send this letter/ picture postcard to the U.S.?*)

Putting your mail in the mailbox

As in the U.S., you can give your mail to a postal worker, drop it into one of the receptacles at the post office (those slits in the wall), or put it into a **Briefkasten** (*breef*-kâst-en) (*mailbox*) found on street corners or in front of post offices (in Germany, mailboxes are yellow, not blue). Sometimes separate mailboxes are available: one for the city you're in and the surrounding area, and another one for other places. So the mailboxes may have signs saying, for example, **Köln und Umgebung** (kerln oont oom-*gey*-boong) (*Cologne and surrounding area*) and **andere Orte** (*ân*-de-re *or*-te) (*other places*).

In Germany, you can't put items to mail in your mailbox to be picked up.

Asking for special services

If you want to send an express letter, airmail, certified mail, or a package, you need to be familiar with these words:

- ✔ **der Eilbrief** (dêr *ayl*-breef) (*express letter*)
- ✔ **das Einschreiben** (dâs *ayn*-shrayb-en) (*registered letter/certified mail*)
- ✔ **die Luftpost** (dee *looft*-post) (*airmail*)
- ✔ **das Paket** (dâs pâ-*keyt*) (*package*)

To get these special pieces of mail on their way, use one of these expressions:

> **Ich möchte diesen Brief per Eilzustellung/per Luftpost/per Einschreiben schicken.** (īH *merH*-te *deez*-en breef pêr *ayl*-tsooh-shtêl-oong/pêr *looft*-post/pêr *ayn*-shrayb-en *shik*-en.) (*I would like to send this letter express/by air mail/by registered mail.*)

> **Ich möchte dieses Paket absenden.** (iH *merH*-te *deez*-es pâ-*keyt* âp-zên-den.) (*I would like to send this package.*)

The following words come in handy when you're sending mail (and you find them on the form you have to fill out to send certified mail):

- **der Absender** (dêr *âp*-zên-der) (*sender*)
- **der Empfänger** (dêr êm-*pfêng*-er) (*addressee*)
- **das Porto** (dâs *por*-toh) (*postage*)

Talkin' the Talk

Frau Bauer's workday is almost over, and she has to mail a package at the post office. Listen in on her conversation with **der Postangestellte** (dêr *post*-ân-ge-shtêl-te) (*post office worker*).

Frau Bauer: **Guten Tag. Ich möchte ein Paket absenden.**
gooh-ten tahk. iH *merH*-te ayn pâ-*keyt* *ouf*-gey-ben.
Hello. I would like to send a package.

Der Postangestellte: **Jawohl. Füllen Sie bitte dieses Formular aus.**
yah-*vohl*. *fuel*-en zee *bi*-te *deez*-es fohr-moo-*lahr* ous.
Certainly. Please fill out this form.

Frau Bauer: **Was für ein Formular ist das?**
vâs fuer ayn fohr-moo-*lahr* ist dâs?
What kind of a form is that?

Der Postangestellte: **Es ist eine Zollerklärung.**
ês ist *ayn*-e *tsol*-êr-klair-oong.
It's a customs declaration.

Frau Bauer fills out the form and hands it back.

Frau Bauer: **Bitte.**
bi-te
Here you are.

Der Postangestellte: **Also, das macht 12,60 Euro.**
âl-*zoh*, dâs maHt tsverlf *oy*-roh sêH-tsiH.
So, that'll be 12 euros 60.

E-mailing and faxing

If you want to catch up on your e-mail while in Germany, your hotel will probably have Wi-Fi Internet access. Otherwise, head for a cybercafé or ask whether a (free) Wi-Fi hotspot is nearby.

The great thing about e-mail and the Internet is that they involve an international language — the language of computers, which is, for the most part, English. However, being aware of the German equivalents for a few words connected with e-mailing is still a good idea:

- ✔ **der Computer** (dêr computer [as in English]) (*computer*)
- ✔ **die E-mail** (dee e-mail [as in English]) (*e-mail*)
- ✔ **die E-Mail Adresse** (dee e-mail ah-*drês*-e) (*e-mail address*)
- ✔ **e-mailen** (e-mail-en) (*to e-mail*)
- ✔ **der Hotspot** (der *hot*-spot [as in English]) (*hot spot*)
- ✔ **das Internet** (dâs Internet [as in English]) (*Internet*)

If you can't conveniently use somebody's **Faxgerät** (*fâx*-ge-rêt) (*fax machine*), you should be able to send a **Fax** (fâx) (*fax*) from most cybercafés, hotels, and some copy shops. Just walk up to the counter and say the following:

Ich möchte etwas faxen. (iH *merH*-te êt-vâs *fâx*-en.) (*I would like to fax something.*)

After you find a place that can send your fax, the person operating the machine will ask you for **die Faxnummer** (dee *fâx*-noom-er) (*the fax number*).

Settling In at the Office

When it comes to the workplace, Germans have a reputation for being straightforward, productive, and efficient, but statistically speaking, they don't work as many hours as Americans do. Not that people don't work late, but Germans enjoy much more generous vacation time. Many companies also close early on Fridays.

When you're working in a German-speaking **Büro** (*bue*-roh) (*office*), you're assigned various tasks, or **Büroarbeit** (bue-*roh*-âr-bayt) (*office work*). What do you call all that paraphernalia on your desk or all the stuff in the supply closet? Read on. After you have these terms down, you need to know how to describe what to do with them. Time to get to work!

Organizing your desk and supplies

Typically, you may find — or hope to find — the following items on or around your **Schreibtisch** (*shrayp*-tish) (*desk*):

- **der Brief** (dêr breef) (*letter*)
- **der Bürostuhl** (dêr bue-*roh*-shtool) (*office chair*)
- **der Computer** (dêr computer [as in English]) (*computer*)
- **der Drucker** (dêr *drook*-er) (*printer*)
- **das Faxgerät** (dâs *fâx*-gê-reyt) (*fax machine*)
- **der Fotokopierer** (dêr foh-toh-ko-*peer*-er) (*copy machine*)
- **die Lampe** (dee *lâm*-pe) (*lamp*)
- **die Maus** (dee mouse [as in English]) (*mouse*)
- **die Tastatur** (dee tâs-tâ-*toohr*) (*keyboard*)
- **das Telefon** (dâs *tê*-le-fohn) (*telephone*)
- **die Unterlagen** (dee *oon*-ter-lah-gen) (*documents, files*)

Sooner or later, you're likely to need one of the following supplies:

- **der Bleistift** (dêr *blay*-shtift) (*pencil*)
- **der Kugelschreiber/der Kuli** (dêr *kooh*-gel-schrayb-er/dêr *kooh*-lee) (*pen*) (**Note:** People use the term **der Kuli** in spoken German.)
- **das Papier** (dâs pâ-*peer*) (*paper*)
- **der Umschlag** (dêr *oom*-shlahk) (*envelope*)

When you need some of these supplies and you can't find them on your own after rummaging around, ask a colleague to help you find them by saying one of the following:

Haben Sie einen Kuli/einen Umschlag für mich? (*hah*-ben zee *ayn*-en *kooh*-lee/*ayn*-en *oom*-shlahk fuer miH?) (*Could you give me a pen/ envelope? Literally: Do you have a pen/envelope for me?*)

Können Sie mir sagen, wo ich Umschläge/Bleistifte/Papier finde? (*kern*-en zee meer *zah*-gen, voh iH *oom*-shlê-ge/*blay*-shtift-e/pâ-*peer fin*-de?) (*Could you tell me where I would find envelopes/pencils/paper?*)

Interacting with coworkers

Comprehensive job training plays an important role in forming Germany's hardworking, qualified working population. To learn traditional trades such as **Bäcker** (*bêk*-er) (*baker*) or **Zimmerman** (*tsim*-er-mân) (*carpenter*) that don't require a university degree, as well as for positions in offices and the service sector, young people start out in their job field as a **Lehrling** (*lêhr*-leeng) (*apprentice*) and go through a three-year **Lehrzeit** (*lêhr*-tsayt) (*apprenticeship*). When they complete the training, they're well-qualified to enter the workforce in their job field.

The atmosphere between coworkers tends to be quite formal, so when you address people in the workplace, use the formal **Sie** (zee) (formal *you*).

Naming jobs and occupations

Many German job titles have two versions to show whether a man or a woman is doing that job. Often, the title for men ends in **–er,** and the counterpart title for women ends in an additional **-in,** as in the case of the term for a male manager, **der Manager** (dêr manager [as in English]), and the term for a female manager, **die Managerin** (dee manager-in). In the following list of common office jobs, those that follow a different pattern for male and female jobs are indicated with both terms:

✔ **der Angestellte/die Angestellte** (dêr *ân*-gê-shtêl-te/dee *ân*-gê-shtêl-te) (*clerk, employee*)

✔ **der Arbeitskollege/die Arbeitskollegin** (dêr âr-bayts-koh-*leyg*-e/dee âr-bayts-koh-*leyg*-in) (*coworker*)

✔ **der Assistent/die Assistentin** (dêr âs-is-*tênt*/dee âs-is-*tênt*-in) (*assistant*)

✔ **der Chef/die Chefin** (dêr shêf/die *shêf*-în) (*boss*)

✔ **der Direktor/die Direktorin** (dêr di-*rêk*-tohr/dee di-rêk-*tohr*-in) (*director*)

✔ **der Firmenchef/die Firmenchefin** (dêr *firm*-en-shêf/die *firm*-en-*shêf*-în) (*president [of a company]*)

✔ **der Geschäftsführer** (dêr gê-*shâfts*-fuer-er) (*business manager/CEO*)

✔ **der Geschäftsman/die Geschäftsfrau** (dêr gê-*shâfts*-mân/dee gê-*shâfts*-frou) (*businessman/businesswoman*)

✔ **der Leiter** (dêr *layt*-er) (*director*)

✔ **der Mitarbeiter** (dêr *mit*-âr-bay-ter) (*associate, colleague, staff member*)

✔ **der Sekretär/die Sekretärin** (dêr zê-krê-*têr*/dee zê-krê-*têr*-in) (*secretary*)

Talking about common duties

Here are a few expressions that come into play in everyday office situations; they also come in handy when you need help with a task:

Wo finde ich den Fotokopierer/das Faxgerät? (voh *fin*-de iH deyn foh-toh-ko-*peer*-er/dâs *fâx*-gê-reyt?) (*Where can I find the copy machine/fax machine?*)

Können Sie mir bitte zeigen, wie das funktioniert? (*kern*-en zee meer *bi*-te *tsay*-gen, vee dâs foonk-tsee-oh-*neert*?) (*Could you please show me how that works?*)

Würden Sie bitte diesen Brief für mich übersetzen? (*vuer*-den zee *bi*-te *deez*-en breef fuer miH ue-ber-*zêts*-en?) (*Would you translate this letter for me, please?*)

Doing business in German

Just like everywhere else, German-speaking countries have their own business world with their own culture and specialized language. To be successful at doing business in German, non-native speakers study for many years, taking special courses on holding meetings, negotiating, telephoning, and giving speeches. This chapter (or book, for that matter) doesn't have the space to provide all the details you need to communicate at the business level — and you probably don't have the time it would take to learn everything you'd need to know. But you may find yourself in a situation where a few business terms — and a little advice on how to proceed — can come in handy.

Here are a few common office terms:

- **anrufen** (*ân*-roohf-en) (*to phone*)
- **der Arbeitsplatz** (dêr *âr*-bayts-plâts) (*workplace*)
- **die Besprechung** (dee be-*shprêH*-oong) (*informal meeting*)
- **der Besprechungsraum** (dêr be-*shprêH*-oongs-room) (*meeting room*)
- **das Büro** (dâs buer-*oh*) (*office*)
- **das Großraumbüro** (dâs *grohs*-room-buer-oh) (*open-plan office*)
- **das Meeting** (dâs meeting [as in English]) (*formal meeting*)
- **die Telefonkonferenz** (dee *tê*-le-fohn-kon-fêr-ênts) (*conference call*)
- **der Termin** (dêr têr-*meen*) (*appointment*)
- **die Videokonferenz** (dee *vid*-ee-oh-kon-fêr-ênts) (*video conference*)
- **die Visitenkarte** (dee vi-*zeet*-en-kâr-te) (*business card*)

If you plan to perform business with German speakers, you may want to call ahead and ask whether the services of **der Dolmetscher** (dêr *dol*-mêch-er) (*interpreter*) or **der Übersetzer** (dêr ue-ber-*zêts*-êr) (*translator*) can be made available to you. Also find out whether the translator will take **die Notizen** (dee noh-*tits*-en) (*notes*) in English during the meeting so you have a written record of the goings-on. Don't feel the slightest bit shy about asking for an interpreter or a translator. Business people all over the world respect someone who knows when it's time to delegate.

Book I

Getting Started with German

Following are a few more steps to take before you start doing business **auf Deutsch** (ouf doych) (*in German*):

- ✔ Study up on the formal introductions in Book I, Chapter 3. Nailing the introductions shows your interest in the proceedings, even if you don't understand much more of what's being said.

- ✔ Read the section "Talking about Yourself" in Book I, Chapter 3. It arms you with a few words you need to make small talk about your job.

- ✔ Before you start doing business, make sure you have plenty of business cards to hand out.

Germans get far more vacation time than Americans: 30 workdays of vacation plus paid holidays (and some states of Germany have as many as 12 legal holidays). However, Germans typically have trouble finding the time to actually take vacations. Thus, vacation time is sometimes carried over into the next year.

Talkin' the Talk

Listen in on the following conversation between Frau Seifert and her assistant, Frau Remmert. Frau Seifert has come to the office early because she has an important meeting.

| Frau Seifert: | **Guten Morgen, Frau Remmert.**
gooh-ten *mor*-gen, frou *rêm*-ert.
Good morning, Ms. Remmert. |
| --- | --- |
| Frau Remmert: | **Guten Morgen, Frau Seifert.**
gooh-ten *mor*-gen, frou *zayf*-êrt.
Good morning, Ms. Seifert. |
| Frau Seifert: | **Wissen Sie, ob Herr Krause heute im Hause ist?**
vis-en zee, op hêr *krouz*-e *hoy*-te im *houz*-e ist?
Do you know if Mr. Krause is in the office today? |

Frau Remmert:	**Ich glaube ja.** iH *glou*-be yah. *I think so.*
Frau Seifert:	**Ich muss dringend mit ihm sprechen.** iH moos *dring*-end mit eem *shprêH*-en. *I have to speak to him urgently.*
Frau Remmert:	**In Ordnung. Ach ja, Frau Hoffmann von der Firma Solag hat angerufen.** in *ord*-noong. *ahH* yah, frou *hof*-mân fon dêr *fir*-mâ *soh*-lahk hât *ân*-gê-roohf-en. *Okay. Oh yes, Ms. Hoffman from (the company) Solag called.*
Frau Seifert:	**Gut, ich rufe sie gleich an. Und würden Sie bitte diesen Brief für mich übersetzen?** gooht, iH *roohf*-e zee glayH *ân*. oont *vuer*-den zee *bi*-te *deez*-en breef fuer miH ue-ber-*zêts*-en? *Good, I'll call her right away. And would you translate this letter for me, please?*
Frau Remmert:	**Wird gemacht, Frau Seifert.** virt gê-*mâHt* frou *zayf*-êrt *I'll do that, Ms. Seifert.*

Words to Know

gleich	glayH	right away
dringend	drîng-end	urgently
im Hause/ Büro sein	im houz-e/ buer-oh zayn	to be in the building/ office
in Ordnung	in ord-noong	okay
Wird gemacht	virt ge-mâHt	I'll do that. (Literally: It will be done.)

Tuning In to Current Events

Germans are known to be avid readers of newspapers and magazines that cover international current events. Both Germany and Austria have far higher per capita newspaper circulation rates than the United States, so you shouldn't be surprised to find out that many Europeans are just as informed about events in the U.S. as Americans themselves. German-speaking television channels devote a great deal of time to both international and local news, and the Internet provides online access to international newspapers, magazines, TV stations, and radio programs.

Newspapers and magazines

Several major German daily **Zeitungen** (*tsayt*-oong-en) (*newspapers*) offer in-depth coverage of international, national, and local news, and almost all German newspapers offer comprehensive online versions. In addition, some broadsheets offer special sections in English. The following sections and headings generally appear in large German daily papers:

- **Börse** (*ber*-ze) (*stock market*)
- **Kultur** (kool-*toohr*) (*culture*)
- **Politik** (pol-i-*teek*) (*politics*)
- **Sport** (shport) (*sports*)
- **Wetter** (vêt-er) (*weather*)
- **Wirtschaft** (*virt*-shâft) (*economy*)

The following sections, topics, and columns may appear daily or on certain days of the week, depending on the newspaper:

- **Bildung** (*bild*-oong) (*education*)
- **Briefe** (*breef*-e) (*letters*)
- **Gesellschaft** (gê-*zêl*-shâft) (*society*)
- **Gesundheit** (gê-*zoond*-hayt) (*health*)
- **Immobilienmarkt** (im-oh-*bee*-lee-en-mârkt) (*real estate market*)
- **Karriere** (kâr-ee-*êr*-e) (*careers*)
- **Kinoprogramm** (*kee*-noh-proh-*grâm*) (*movie program*)
- **Medien** (*mey*-dee-en) (*media*)

- **Meinung** (*mayn*-oong) (*opinion*)
- **Multimedia** (moohl-tee-*mey*-dee-â) (*multimedia*)
- **Spiele** (*shpee*-le) (*games*)
- **Stellenmarkt** (*shtêl*-en-mârkt) (*job market*)
- **Trends** (trends [as in English]) (*trends*)
- **TV-Programm** (tee-*fou*-proh-*grâm*) (*TV program*)
- **Umwelt** (*oohm*-vêlt) (*environment*)
- **Unterhaltung** (oon-ter-*hâlt*-oong) (*entertainment*)
- **Wissenschaft** (*vis*-en-shâft) (*science*)

Table 5-1 lists the largest newspapers in Germany and one in Switzerland.

Table 5-1	Largest Newspapers in Germany	
Newspaper	**Description**	**Website**
Bild (bilt)	Known for its focus on sensational news; high ratio of photos to text (**Bild** means *picture*)	www.bild.de
Frankfurter Allgemeine Zeitung (*frank*-foort-er âl-ge-*mayn*-e *tsayt*-oong) (abbreviation: **FAZ**) (êf-ah-*tset*)	One of the most widely read quality newspapers among German readers inside and outside of Europe	www.faz.net
Handelsblatt (*hân*-dêls-blât)	Strong focus on the world of business and finance	www.handels blatt.com
Die Neue Zürcher Zeitung (dee *noy*-e *tsuerH*-er *tsayt*-oong) (abbreviation: **NZZ**) (ên-tset-*tset*)	Swiss daily newspaper based in Zurich	www.nzz.ch
Die Süddeutsche Zeitung (dee *sued*-doych-e *tsayt*-oong) (abbreviation: **SZ**) (ês-*tset*)	Internationally recognized newspaper that has earned a reputation for solid journalism	www.sued deutsche.de
Die Welt (dee vêlt)	Focuses on world news, as well as local news in Germany; has a Sunday publication called **Die Welt am Sonntag** (dee vêlt am *zon*-tahk)	www.welt.de

The largest weekly magazines are **Bunte** (*boon*-te), **Focus** (*fohk*-oos), **Der Spiegel** (der *speeg*-el), and **Stern** (shtêrn). **Die Zeit** (dee tsayt) is a weekly newspaper that covers international and national news.

Television, radio, and the web

The government-funded German television stations **ARD** and **ZDF** are terrific ways to get excellent quality news in German. Simply go to their websites — www.ard.de and www.zdf.de — and choose the type of information you're interested in: politics, culture, sports, or of course, **Nachrichten** (*nâH*-reeH-ten) (*news*). At **ARD,** you can watch a classic weekly TV series, **Tatort** (*taht*-ort) (*Crime Scene*), a murder mystery/thriller.

You may also want to try **Deutsche Welle** (*doy*-che *vêl*-e) (*German radio*) (www.dw-world.de), which broadcasts both radio and TV programs in many languages, including German and English, or **radioWissen** (*rah*-dee-oh *vis*-en) (*radio knowledge*), which offers quality radio broadcasts in German (www.br-online.de/bayern2/radiowissen).

Looking for something else in German? Just type the topic into a major search engine, plus the international code: .de for Germany, .at for Austria, and .ch for Switzerland. For a directory of German news online, go to: http:// www.onlinenewspapers.com/germany.htm. Another great resource is http://www.goethe.de/enindex.htm.

Chapter 6

Shopping Simplified

· ·

In This Chapter

▶ Deciding where and when to shop

▶ Finding items, browsing, and asking for help

▶ Focusing on clothes as you shop

▶ Making purchases after you find what you need

· ·

Shopping in another country can be a fun way to dive into the culture and rub elbows with the locals. In many large European cities, you can either hunt for unique items in small shops and boutiques or, if you're in the mood for one-stop shopping, head for the major department stores.

When you're traveling, whether for business or pleasure, you probably want to bring back one or two **Andenken** (*ān*-dênk-en) (*souvenirs*) to remind you of the time you spent abroad. Whether you choose to buy an article of clothing, a knife set, or a beer mug, picking just the right item is part of the fun of going on a trip.

In this chapter, you become familiar with the terms and phrases you would use during a shopping trip — from browsing and asking for help to trying on and purchasing your finds.

Getting Familiar with the German Shopping Experience

City centers often have large pedestrian zones featuring all kinds of stores and restaurants, making them ideal settings for leisurely strolls and window shopping, which is called **Schaufensterbummel** (*shou*-fêns-ter-*boom*-el). When you're tired of shopping, you can sit down at a café in the pedestrian zone and watch the passers-by before doing some more shopping.

Identifying types of shops

Like the U.S., Germany offers plenty of shopping opportunities in places like the following:

- **die Apotheke** (dee ah-poh-*tey*-ke) (*pharmacy*)
- **das Blumengeschäft** (dâs *blooh*-men-ge-*shêft*) (*flower shop*)
- **die Boutique** (dee boutique [as in English]*)* (*boutique*)
- **die Buchhandlung** (dee *boohH*-hând-loong) (*bookstore*)
- **der Computerladen** (dêr computer [as in English] *lah*-den) (*computer store*)
- **die Drogerie** (dee drohg-êr-*ee*) (*drug store*) (**Note:** This is a store that sells toiletry items and over-the-counter medicines. For prescription drugs, go to **die Apotheke.**)
- **das Einkaufszentrum** (dâs *ayn*-koufs-*tsên*-troom) (*shopping center*)
- **das Fachgeschäft** (dâs *fâH*-ge-shêft) (*store specializing in a line of products*)
- **der Flohmarkt** (dêr *floh*-mârkt) (*flea market*)
- **die Fußgängerzone** (dee *foohs*-gêng-er-*tsoh*-ne) (*pedestrian zone*)
- **das Geschäft** (dâs ge-*shêft*) (*business, store*)
- **das Juweliergeschäft** (dâs yoo-ve-*leer*-ge-*shêft*) (*jewelry store*)
- **das Kaufhaus** (dâs *kouf*-hous) (*department store*)
- **der Kiosk** (dêr *kee*-osk) (*newsstand*)
- **der Laden** (dêr *lah*-den) (*store, shop*)
- **das Schreibwarengeschäft** (dâs *shrayb*-vâr-en-ge-*shêft*) (*stationery store*)
- **das Schuhgeschäft** (dâs *shooh*-ge-*shêft*) (*shoe store*)
- **der Souvenirladen, der Andenkenladen** (dêr zoo-ven-*eer-lah*-den, dêr *ân*-dênk-en-*lah*-den) (*souvenir shop*)
- **das Spielwarengeschäft** (dâs *speel*-vâr-en-ge-*shêft*) (*toy store*)
- **das Sportgeschäft** (dâs shport-ge-shêft) (*sporting goods store*)

Determining a store's hours

Shopping hours in Germany aren't what you're used to in the U.S. because German law regulates when stores can be open. For the most part, stores open at 6 a.m. and close by 8 p.m. Monday through Saturday, although Saturday hours may vary. In small towns, some stores close between noon and 2 p.m. for lunch. Most banks are open only until 4 p.m.; however, you may find some banks that stay open until 6 p.m. on Thursdays. Most businesses are closed Sundays.

Bakeries, which sell fresh rolls, or **Brötchen** (*brert*-Hen), are an exception to the rule that businesses are closed on Sundays, and some stores may be open in popular resort towns. If you're looking for a place to buy sandwich fixings on a Sunday afternoon, search for 24/7 gas stations that sell a wide variety of grocery items. Or check out the shops at train stations in larger cities.

To find out a store's open hours, ask the following questions:

- **Wann öffnen Sie?** (vân *erf*-nen zee?) (*When do you open?*)

- **Wann schließen Sie?** (vân *shlees*-en zee?) (*When do you close?*)

- **Haben Sie mittags geöffnet?** (*hah*-ben zee *mi*-tahks ge-*erf*-net?) (*Are you open during lunch?*)

Finding your way around a department store

If you need help finding a certain item or section in a department store, you can consult the information desk — **die Auskunft** (dee *ous*-koonft) or **die Information** (dee in-for-mâ-tsee-*ohn*). The people there should have all the answers you need. Plus, talking to the folks at the information desk provides you with a terrific opportunity to practice your questioning skills.

If you're searching for a certain item, you can ask for it by name with either of these phrases (at the end of the phrase, just fill in the plural form of the item you're looking for):

- **Wo bekomme ich. . . ?** (voh be-*kom*-e iH. . . ?) (*Where do I get. . . ?*)

- **Wo finde ich. . . ?** (voh *fin*-de iH. . . ?) (*Where do I find. . . ?*)

If you want to sound particularly nice as you ask for help, use the polite phrase **Entschuldigen Sie, bitte.** (ent-*shool*-di-gen zee, *bi*-te.) (*Excuse me, please.*) Consider, for example, the following polite question (turn to Chapter 3 in Book I for more details on polite expressions):

> **Entschuldigen Sie, bitte, wo ist die Rolltreppe?** (ent-*shool*-di-gen zee, *bi*-te, voh ist dee *rol*-trêp-e?) (*Excuse me, please, where is the escalator?*)

When you question the people at the information desk, they may say **. . . führen wir nicht** (. . . *fuer*-en veer niHt) (*We don't carry . . .*). Or they may direct you to the appropriate section of the store, using one of the following phrases:

- **Im Erdgeschoss/Parterre.** (im *êrt*-ge-shos/pâr-*têr*.) (*On the ground floor.*)
- **Im Untergeschoss.** (im *oon*-ter-ge-shos.) (*In the basement.*)
- **In der . . . Etage.** (in dêr . . . ê-*tah*-zhe.) (*On the . . . floor.*)
- **Im . . . Stock.** (im . . . shtok.) (*On the . . . floor.*)
- **Eine Etage höher.** (*ayn*-e ê-*tah*-zhe *her*-her.) (*One floor above.*)
- **Eine Etage tiefer.** (*ayn*-e ê-*tah*-zhe *teef*-er.) (*One floor below.*)

Germans (and other Europeans) look at buildings differently than Americans do. They don't count the ground floor, **das Erdgeschoss/das Parterre,** as the first floor. They start numbering with the floor above the ground floor. That system makes the American second floor the German first floor, and so on, all the way to the top.

If you'd like to browse through a section of the store or you're looking for a special feature of the store, you can use the phrase **Wo finde ich. . . ?** (voh *fin*-de iH. . . ?) (*Where do I find. . . ?*), ending the phrase with one of the following expressions:

- **den Aufzug/den Fahrstuhl** (deyn *ouf*-tsook/deyn *fâr*-shtoohl) (*elevator*)
- **die Damenabteilung** (dee *dah*-mên-âp-*tay*-loong) (*ladies' department*)
- **die Herrenabteilung** (dee *hêr*-en-âp-*tay*-loong) (*men's department*)
- **die Kasse** (dee *kâs*-e) (*checkout counter*)
- **die Kinderabteilung** (dee *kin*-der-âp-*tay*-loong) (*children's department*)
- **die Rolltreppe** (dee *rol*-trêp-e) (*escalator*)
- **die Schmuckabteilung** (dee *shmook*-âp-*tay*-loong) (*jewelry department*)
- **die Schuhabteilung** (dee *shooh*-âp-*tay*-loong) (*shoe department*)
- **die Toiletten** (dee toy-*lêt*-en) (*restrooms*)
- **die Umkleidekabinen** (dee *oom*-klayd-e-kâ-*been*-en) (*fitting rooms*)

Chapter 6: Shopping Simplified *123*

Book I

Getting
Started
with
German

Browsing and responding to "Kann ich Ihnen helfen?"

Sometimes you just want to check out the merchandise in the store on your own without anybody breathing down your neck. However, store assistants may offer their help by saying something like the following:

Kann ich Ihnen helfen? (kân iH *een*-en *hêlf*-en?) (*Can I help you?*)

Kann ich Ihnen behilflich sein? (kân iH *een*-en be-*hilf*-liH zayn?) (*Can I help you?*)

Suchen Sie etwas Bestimmtes? (*zoohH*-en zee *êt*-vâs be-*shtim*-tes?) (*Are you looking for something in particular?*)

When all you want to do is browse, use this phrase to politely turn down help:

Ich möchte mich nur umsehen. (iH *merH*-te miH noohr *oom*-zey-en.) (*I just want to look around.*)

The store assistant will probably tell you it's okay to keep browsing by saying either of the following:

Aber natürlich. Sagen Sie Bescheid, wenn Sie eine Frage haben. (*ah*-ber nâ-*tuer*-liH. *zah*-gen zee be-*shayt*, vên zee *ayn*-e *frah*-ge *hah*-ben.) (*Of course. Just let me know if you need help.*)

Rufen Sie mich, wenn Sie eine Frage haben. (*rooh*-fen zee miH, vên zee *ayn*-e *frah*-ge *hah*-ben.) (*Call me if you have a question.*)

Getting assistance

In some situations, you may want or need assistance while you're shopping. Here are some useful phrases you can use to get the help you need:

Würden Sie mir bitte helfen? Ich suche. . . . (*vuer*-den zee meer *bi*-te *hêl*-fen. iH *zoohH*-e. . . .) (*Would you help me, please? I'm looking for. . . .*)

Aber gern, hier entlang bitte. (*ah*-ber gêrn, heer *ênt*-lâng *bi*-te.) (*Certainly. This way please.*)

Welche Größe suchen Sie? (*vêl*-He *grer*-se *zoohH*-en zee?) (*What size are you looking for?*)

Haben Sie so etwas in Größe/in rot, blau. . . ? (*hah*-ben zee zoh *êt*-vâs in *grer*-se/in roht, blou. . . ?) (*Do you have something like this in size/in red, blue. . . ?*)

Wie gefällt Ihnen diese Farbe? (vee ge-*fêlt een*-en *deez*-e *fâr*-be?) (*How do you like this color?*)

Thanks to the education system, most sales people in Austrian, German, and Swiss stores are competent and knowledgeable. As is the case in most trades, salespeople generally complete a comprehensive three-year apprenticeship that combines on-the-job training with trade school instruction.

Shopping for Clothes

When you're shopping for clothes, you have to decide what you want in terms of item, color, size, fabric, style, and, so on. This section breaks down these criteria to help make your shopping experience go as smoothly as possible. Notice that some terms for clothing are the same in English and others that appear to be English words have different meanings in German.

Characterizing various clothing items

Some clothing items are unisex, while others are typical for either men or women. In this section, you get to know all the different types of clothes you may see in a German store, including casual and formal attire, outerwear, and accessories. You also find out how to describe fabrics, styles, and colors.

Some terms that apply to female clothes include the following:

- ✔ **der Badeanzug** (dêr *bah*-de-ân-tsook) (*bathing suit*)
- ✔ **die Bluse** (dee *blooh*-ze) (*blouse*)
- ✔ **der Hosenanzug** (dêr *hoh*-zen-ân-tsook) (*pantsuit*)
- ✔ **das Kleid** (dâs klayt) (*dress*)
- ✔ **das Kostüm** (dâs kos-*tuem*) (*suit, fancy dress*)
- ✔ **der Rock** (dêr rok) (*skirt*)
- ✔ **die Strumpfhose** (dee *shtroompf*-hoh-ze) (*panty hose*)

The following words usually apply to clothing for men:

Book I

Getting
Started
with
German

- ✔ **der Anzug** (dêr *ân*-tsook) (*suit*)
- ✔ **die Badehose** (dee *bah*-de-hoh-ze) (*swimming trunks*)
- ✔ **die Krawatte** (dee krâ-*vât*-e) (*tie*)

Generally speaking, both men and women wear the following items:

- ✔ **der Blazer** (dêr *bley*-zer) (*blazer*)
- ✔ **das Hemd** (dâs hêmt) (*shirt*)
- ✔ **die Hose** (dee *hoh*-ze) (*pants*)
- ✔ **das Jackett/die Jacke** (dâs jhâ-*kêt*/dee *yâ*-ke) (*jacket*)
- ✔ **die Jeans** (dee jeans [as in English]) (*jeans*)
- ✔ **der Mantel** (dêr *mân*-tel) (*coat*)
- ✔ **der Pullover/der Pulli** (dêr pool-*oh*-ver/dêr *poo*-lee) (*sweater*)
- ✔ **der Pullunder** (dêr poo-*loon*-der) (*tank top*)
- ✔ **der Pyjama** (dêr pêr-*jah*-mâ) (*pajamas*)
- ✔ **der Regenmantel** (dêr *rey*-gen-mân-tel) (*raincoat*)
- ✔ **die Sandalen** (dee zân-*dahl*-en) (*sandals*)
- ✔ **die Schuhe** (dee *shooh*-e) (*shoes*)
- ✔ **die Shorts/die kurze Hose** (dee shorts [as in English]/dee *koorts*-e-hoh-ze) (*shorts*)
- ✔ **die Socken/die Strümpfe** (dee *zok*-en/dee *shtruempf*-e) (*socks*)
- ✔ **die Stiefel** (dee *shteef*-el) (*boots*)
- ✔ **die Strickjacke** (dee *shtrik*-yâ-ke) (*cardigan*)
- ✔ **das Sweatshirt** (dâs sweatshirt [as in English]) (*sweatshirt*)
- ✔ **das T-Shirt** (dâs T-shirt [as in English]) (*T-shirt*)
- ✔ **die Unterwäsche** (dee *oon*-ter-vêsh-e) (*underwear*)
- ✔ **die Volkstracht** (dee *folks*-trâHt) (*folk costume*)
- ✔ **die Weste** (dee *vês*-te) (*vest*)

You may find the following items listed in a store directory as **das Zubehör** (dâs *tsooh*-bê-herr) (*accessories*):

- ✔ **der Gürtel** (dêr *guer*-tel) (*belt*)
- ✔ **die Handschuhe** (dee *hând*-shooh-e) (*gloves*)
- ✔ **die Handtasche** (dee *hând*-tâsh-e) (*purse, handbag*)
- ✔ **der Hut** (dêr hooht) (*hat*)
- ✔ **die Mütze** (dee *muets*-e) (*cap*)
- ✔ **der Schal** (dêr shâl) (*scarf*)
- ✔ **der Schmuck** (dêr shmook) (*jewelry*)
- ✔ **die Sonnenbrille** (dee *zon*-en-bril-e) (*sunglasses*)

Clothing and accessory items such as the ones in the preceding lists can come in any number of fabrics, including the following:

- ✔ **die Baumwolle** (dee *boum*-vol-e) (*cotton*)
- ✔ **der Flanell** (dêr flan-*êl*) (*flannel*)
- ✔ **das Fleece** (dâs fleece [as in English]) (*fleece*)
- ✔ **der Kord** (dêr kord) (*corduroy*)
- ✔ **die Kunstfaser** (dee *koonst*-fâz-er) (*synthetic material*)
- ✔ **das Leder** (dâs *ley*-der) (*leather*)
- ✔ **das Leinen** (dâs *layn*-en) (*linen*)
- ✔ **das Nylon** (dâs *ner*-lon) (*nylon*)
- ✔ **der Polyester** (dêr po-lee-*êst*-er) (*polyester*)
- ✔ **der Samt** (dêr zâmt) (*velvet*)
- ✔ **die Seide** (dee *zay*-de) (*silk*)
- ✔ **der Wildleder** (dêr *vilt*-ley-der) (*suede*)
- ✔ **die Wolle** (dee *vol*-e) (*wool*)

Clothing items can also come in any number of styles, including the following:

- ✔ **bunt** (boont) (*multicolored*)
- ✔ **einfarbig** (*ayn*-fâr-biH) (*solid color*)
- ✔ **elegant** (ê-le-*gânt*) (*elegant*)

✔ **gepunktet** (ge-*poonk*-tet) (*with dots*)

✔ **gestreift** (ge-*shtrayft*) (*striped*)

✔ **kariert** (kâr-*eert*) (*checkered*)

✔ **lässig** (*lês*-iH) (*casual*)

✔ **modisch** (*moh*-dish) (*fashionable*)

✔ **sportlich** (*shport*-liH) (*sporty*)

Figure 6-1 shows a variety of clothing items with their German names.

Whether you're looking for a new dress, a belt, or a pair of pants, you probably have a particular color in mind (or a color that you absolutely will not wear!). The basic **Farben** (*fâr*-ben) (*colors*) are

✔ **beige** (beige [as in English]) (*beige*)

✔ **blau** (blou) (*blue*)

✔ **braun** (brown [as in English]) (*brown*)

Figure 6-1:
Common
clothing
items.

Illustration by Elizabeth Kurtzman

- **gelb** (gêlp) (*yellow*)
- **gold** (golt) (*gold*)
- **grau** (grou) (*gray*)
- **grün** (gruen) (*green*)
- **lila** (*lee*-lâ) (*purple*)
- **orange** (o-*rânch*) (*orange*)
- **rosa** (*roh*-za) (*pink*)
- **rot** (roht) (*red*)
- **schwarz** (shvârts) (*black*)
- **silber** (*zil*-ber) (*silver*)
- **türkis** (tuer-*kees*) (*turquoise*)
- **violett** (vee-oh-*lêt*) (*violet*)
- **weiß** (vays) (*white*)

To describe dark and light shades of colors, use the following terms:

- **dunkel** (*doon*-kel) (*dark*)
- **hell** (hêl) (*light*)

Combine **dunkel** or **hell** with a color like this:

- **dunkelblau** (*doon*-kel blou) (*dark blue*)
- **hellgrün** (hêl gruen) (*light green*)

All these color words are adjectives. To find out how to fit them into phrases and sentences, check out Chapter 5 in Book III.

Knowing your size

Finding the right size clothing can be a pain in the neck in any shopping situation. When shopping in German-speaking countries, though, you get a double whammy: Clothes sizes aren't the same as they are in the U.S. The charts in this section provide useful guidelines to help you crack the code.

Here are the approximate equivalents for sizes of women's clothes. You simply add 30 to the American size to get the German size.

American	4	6	8	10	12	14	16	18	20
German	34	36	38	40	42	44	46	48	50

For men's jacket and suit sizes, use the following approximate conversions. You just add 10 to the American size to get the German size.

American	34	36	38	40	42	44	46	48	50
German	44	46	48	50	52	54	56	58	60

For men's shirts, keep in mind these approximate neck size conversions:

American	14	14.5	15	15.5	16	16.5	17	17.5	18
German	36	37	38	39	40	41	42	43	44

The following chart shows approximate equivalents for women's shoe sizes:

American	5	5½	6	6½	7	7½	8	8½	9½	9½
German	35–36	36	36–37	37	37–38	38	38–39	39	39–40	40
American	10	10½	11							
German	40–41	41	41–42							

For men's shoe sizes, refer to the following approximate equivalents:

American	6½	7	7½	8	8½	9	9½	10	10½
German	39	40	40–41	41	41–42	42	42–43	43	43–44
American	11	11½	12	13					
German	44	44–45	45	46					

Talkin' the Talk

Frau Schulte is in the ladies' section of a department store. She wants to buy a blouse and is getting assistance from a **Verkäuferin** (*saleswoman*). (Track 17)

Verkäuferin: **Kann ich Ihnen behilflich sein?**
kân iH *een*-en be-*hilf*-liH zayn?
Can I help you?

Frau Schulte: **Ja bitte. Ich suche eine Bluse.**
yah *bi*-te. iH *zooH*-e *ayn*-e *blooh*-ze.
Yes, please. I'm looking for a blouse.

Verkäuferin: **Hier entlang, bitte. Welche Farbe soll es denn sein?**
heer ênt-lang, *bi*-te. *vêlH*-e *fâr*-be zol ês dên zayn?
Please come this way. What color do you want?

Frau Schulte: **Weiß.**
Vays.
White.

Verkäuferin: **Suchen Sie etwas Lässiges?**
zoohH-en zee êt-vâs *lês*-ee-ges?
Are you looking for something casual?

Frau Schulte: **Nein, eher etwas Elegantes.**
nayn, ê-her êt-vâs ey-le-gân-tes.
No, rather something elegant.

Verkäuferin: **Gut. Welche Größe haben Sie?**
gooht. *vêlH*-e *grer*-se *hah*-ben zee?
Good. What is your size?

Frau Schulte: **Größe 38.**
grer-se *âHt*-toon-*dray*-siH.
Size 38.

Verkäuferin: **Wie gefällt Ihnen dieses Modell?**
vee ge-*fêlt* een-en *deez*-es mo-*dêl*?
How do you like this style?

Frau Schulte: **Sehr gut.**
zeyr gooht.
Very much.

Trying on clothes

When you find an article of clothing that looks promising, you may want to try it on. In that case, you can ask the sales assistant the following question, inserting the name of the article you want to try on:

Kann ich . . . anprobieren? (kân iH . . . *ân*-pro-bee-ren?) (*Can I try . . . on?*)

Or a sales assistant may anticipate your question and ask this question:

Möchten Sie . . . anprobieren? (*merH*-ten zee . . . *ân*-pro-bee-ren?) (*Would you like to try . . . on?*)

Words to Know

(zu) eng	(tsooh) êng	(too) tight
weit	vayt	loose
lang	lâng	long
kurz	koorts	short
groß	grohs	big
klein	klayn	small
die Abteilung	dee âb-<u>tay</u>-loong	department
die Größe	dee <u>grer</u>-se	size
die Farbe	dee <u>fâr</u>-be	color
das Modell, der Stil	dâs mo-<u>dêl</u>, der shtil	style
anprobieren	<u>ân</u>-pro-bee-ren	to try on
bringen	<u>bring</u>-en	to bring
passen	<u>pâs</u>-en	to fit
stehen	<u>stey</u>-en	to suit
gefallen	ge-<u>fâl</u>-en	to like
gefällt mir	ge-<u>fêlt</u> meer	I like
hier entlang	heer <u>ênt</u>-lâng	this way
die Umkleidekabine	dee <u>oom</u>-klay-de-kâ-<u>been</u>-e	fitting room
kaufen	<u>kouf</u>-en	to buy

In either case, the next step is going to the dressing rooms, which you can ask about by saying:

Wo sind die Umkleidekabinen? (voh zint dee *oom*-klay-de-kâ-*been*-en?) (*Where are the fitting rooms?*)

After you try on your item, the sales assistant may ask you one of the following questions to find out what you think of it:

Passt. . . ? (pâst. . . ?) (*Does . . . fit?*)

Wie passt Ihnen. . . ? (wie pâst *een*-en. . . ?) (*How does . . . fit you?*)

Gefällt Ihnen. . . ? (ge-*fēlt een*-en. . . ?) (*Do you like. . . ?*)

You can answer with any of the following, depending on how things went when you tried on your item:

Nein, . . . ist zu lang/kurz/eng/weit/groß/klein. (nayn, . . . ist tsooh lâng/koorts/ēng/vayt/grohs/klayn.) (*No, . . . is too long/short/tight/loose/big/small.*)

Können Sie mir eine andere Größe bringen? (*kern*-en zee meer *ayn*-e *ân*-de-re *grer*-se *bring*-en?) (*Can you get me another size?*)

. . . passt sehr gut. (. . . pâst zeyr gooht.) (. . . *fits very well.*)

. . . steht mir. (. . . shteyt meer.) (. . . *suits me.*)

. . . gefällt mir. (. . . ge-*fēlt* meer.) (*I like . . .*)

Ich nehme. . . . (IH *ney*-me. . . .) (*I'll take. . . .*)

Talkin' the Talk

Frau Schulte likes the blouse the saleswoman has shown her and wants to try it on. Here's a look at their conversation. (Track 18)

Frau Schulte: **Ich möchte diese Bluse anprobieren. Wo sind die Umkleidekabinen, bitte?**
iH *merH*-te *deez*-e *blooh*-ze *ân*-pro-bee-ren. voh zint dee *oom*-klay-de-kâ-*been*-en, *bi*-te?
I would like to try on this blouse. Where are the fitting rooms, please?

Verkäuferin: **Ja, natürlich. Da drüben sind die Umkleidekabinen.**
yah, nâ-*tuer*-liH. dâ *drue*-ben zint dee *oom*-klay-de-kâ-*been*-en.
Of course. The fitting rooms are over there.

(A few minutes later Frau Schulte returns.)

Verkäuferin: **Passt die Bluse?**
pâst dee *blooh*-ze?
Does the blouse fit?

Frau Schulte: **Ja. Ich nehme die Bluse.**
yah. iH *ney*-me dee *blooh*-ze.
Yes. I'll take the blouse.

Making Your Purchase

After selecting one or more items that you really like, you're ready to make your purchase. You're standing, sweater in hand, at the **Kasse** (*kâs*-e) (*checkout counter, cash register*), and the moment of reckoning comes when you have to pay.

Preparing to pay for your items

Stores in Europe generally accept most major credit cards, although some small shops and places like flea markets take only cash. Even at stores that take credit cards, however, you may prefer to withdraw money at an ATM before you shop and then use cash to pay for whatever you buy. At any rate, before you leave the U.S., find out about any fees your credit card company may charge you for using your card outside the U.S.

Here are some terms you may find useful to know when you're getting ready to make your purchases:

- **der Beleg** (dêr be-*leyk*) (*receipt, slip*)
- **der Bruttobetrag** (dêr *broot*-oh-be-trâk) (*total amount*)
- **die Kasse** (dee *kâs*-e) (*checkout counter, cash register*)
- **der Nettobetrag** (dêr *nêt*-oh-be-trâk) (*net amount*)
- **die Mehrwertsteuer** (dee *meyr*-vêrt-shtoy-er) (*sales tax*)
- **der Preis** (dêr prays) (*price*)
- **die Quittung** (dee *kvit*-oong) (*receipt*)
- **die Waren** (dee *vahr*-en) (*goods, merchandise*)

Occasionally, you may find yourself in a situation where you need to ask about the price (**der Preis**) of an item. Price tags, being the devious little critters that they are, have a way of falling off or being indecipherable, especially when handwritten. Consider this case in point: The German number **1** can look a lot like the American number *7* when scrawled by hand. But not to worry. The following simple phrases take care of the price question should you need to ask it:

Was kostet. . . ? (vâs *kos*-tet. . . ?) (*What does . . . cost?*)

Wie viel kostet. . . ? (vee *feel kos*-tet. . . ?) (*How much does . . . cost?*)

After you decide to purchase something, the following questions may help you as you proceed to the cash register:

Wo ist die Kasse? (voh ist dee *kâs*-e?) (*Where is the checkout counter?*)

Kann ich mit Kreditkarte bezahlen? (kân iH mit krê-*dit*-kâr-te be-*tsahl*-en?) (*Can I pay with a credit card?*)

You may hear the salesperson say one of the following in response:

Ja, sicher. (Ya, *zeeH*-er.) (*Yes, certainly.*)

Ja, selbstverständlich. (Ya, zêlps*t*-fêr-*shtênt*-liH.) (*Yes, of course.*)

Aber, natürlich. (*ah*-ber nâ-*tuer*-liH.) (*But, of course.*)

Es tut mir leid. Wir nehmen nur Bargeld. (ês toot mir layd. veer *ney*-men noor *bâr*-gêlt.) (*I'm sorry. We only accept cash.*)

Talkin' the Talk

Frau Schulte heads to the cash register to pay for her purchase. Consider how her conversation with the **Kassiererin** (*cashier*) goes.

Kassiererin: **Das macht 49 Euro.**
dâs mâHt *noyn*-oont-*feer*-tsiH *oy*-roh.
That's 49 euros, please.

Frau Schulte: **Nehmen Sie Kreditkarten?**
ney-men see krey-*dit*-kâr-ten?
Can I pay by credit card?

Kassiererin:	**Kein Problem.**
	kayn pro-*bleym.*
	No problem.

Frau Schulte:	**Hier bitte.**
	heer *bi*-te.
	Here you are.

Kassiererin:	**Danke. Würden Sie bitte unterschreiben? Und hier ist Ihre Quittung.**
	dân-ke. *wuer*-den zee *bi*-te un-ter-*schray*-ben? oont heer ist *eer*-e *kvit*-oong.
	Thanks. Would you please sign here? And here is your receipt.

Frau Schulte:	**Danke!**
	dân-ke!
	Thanks!

Getting a tax refund on your purchases

Most of the time, when you go shopping, every piece of merchandise has a tag that tells you exactly how much it costs. The price you see on a price tag is what you pay for the item at the cash register, including sales tax, called the VAT (or value added tax). The German word for VAT is **die Mehrwertsteuer (MwSt)** (dee *mêr*-vêrt-*shtoy*-er).

In Germany, most items, including clothing, are taxed at 19 percent, although some select goods are taxed at 7 percent. The good news is, you may be able to get a tax refund on items of value.

If you don't reside in a country of the European Union (EU), you usually can get a refund for the VAT tax when you leave the EU. The VAT refund is referred to as — take a deep breath — **die Mehrwertsteuerrückerstattung** (dee *mêr*-vêrt-shtoy-er-*ruek*-êr-shtât-oong). Although the German word for the VAT refund looks a bit daunting, the process for getting it back is usually simple. Just ask for a VAT refund form when you pay at the register. Collect all the receipts and forms for merchandise you're taking out of the EU, and then you can have a customs agent at the airport approve everything before you leave the EU to return home. (Because you must show the items, don't pack them with your checked luggage!)

Words to Know

kosten	<u>kos</u>-ten	to cost
der Preis	dêr prays	price
die Mehrwertsteuer (MwSt)	dee <u>mêr</u>-vêrt-<u>shtoy</u>-er	tax (VAT)
die Mehrwertsteuer rückerstattung	dee <u>mêr</u>-vêrt-shtoy-er-<u>ruek</u>-êr-shtât-oong	VAT refund

Chapter 7

Dining Out and Buying Food: Guten Appetit!

In This Chapter

▶ Talking about hunger, thirst, and meals

▶ Eating out at a restaurant or other eatery

▶ Buying food at a grocery store or outdoor market

*E*xploring the food and eating habits of people in another country is one of the most interesting — and tasty — ways to learn about their culture. One of the first differences you may notice when dining in Europe is the slower pace, which allows you time to linger after eating your food, even in simpler locales. You don't feel pressured by the service personnel to finish up, pay, and vacate the table for the next patrons. The epitome of life in the slow lane can still be experienced at traditional cafés, the most famous of which are in Vienna. You grab a newspaper conveniently attached to a stick with a handle, order a cup of coffee served with a glass of water on a small silver tray, and read to your heart's content.

When eating out in German-speaking Europe, one thing that isn't much different from what you're probably used to is the way the food is prepared. A traditional German meal consists of meat, potatoes, and vegetables or a salad. However, local cuisines vary from region to region, and we heartily suggest you try them whenever you can.

Whether you're interested in having a business lunch or enjoying a casual dinner, this chapter helps you find your way around food. You get the hang of deciphering a menu, ordering in a restaurant, and buying food items at an open air market. You get the lowdown on the standard practice of seating yourself in many restaurants. You discover how to get the server's attention, and you find out about tipping. In short, this chapter gets you ready to eat and drink your way through Germany, Austria, and Switzerland.

Talking about Eating and Drinking

The geographical features of German-speaking regions play a role in the types of food found on menus and in food markets. For instance, in the north of Germany, you find fresh fish from the North Sea. Traveling south, you come across some well-known foods, like **Schweinebraten** (*shvayn*-e-brât-en) (*roast pork*), as well as some surprises, like **weißer Spargel** (*vays*-er *shpâr*-gel) (*white asparagus*), a delicacy only available for a short period of time in the spring. Switzerland produces some world-famous alpine cheeses like **Emmentaler** (*êm*-en-tâl-er) (*emmentaler*) and **Appenzeller** (*âp*-en-tsêl-er) (*appenzeller*). A pleasant surprise in the form of a spreadable fresh cheese is **Quark** (kvârk) (*quark*), a common dairy product hardly known in North America. You find **Quark** in cheesecake, dips, and spreads. Potatoes and cabbage are grown in many regions, as well as a number of lesser known vegetables like **Kohlrabi** (*kohl*-râ-bee) (*kohlrabi*), **Lauch** (louH) (*leeks*), and **Sellerie** (*zêl*-êr-ee) (*celeriac*). You find these ingredients in hearty meat and vegetable stews.

Germans also have some great snacks you may like to try. Often, the best **Bratwurst** (*brât*-voorst) (*bratwurst*) are served at unassuming fast-food stands. Three of the most popular snacks you can enjoy in a Bavarian **Biergarten** (*beer*-gâr-ten) (*beer garden*) are mammoth-sized, freshly baked **Brezen** (*breyt*-tsen) (*pretzels*), often eaten together with **Obatzter** (*oh*-bats-ter) (*a spreadable blend of camembert cheese,* **Quark** [kvârk] [*quark*]*, and diced onions*), **Steckerlfisch** (*shtêk*-erl-fish) (*fish on a stick*), and a long piece of artfully sliced giant white radish called **Radi** (*râ*-dee) that looks like a curlicue streamer.

Germany, Austria, and Switzerland each have variations in their cooking styles and tastes, yet German-speaking regions and their cuisines extend beyond these three countries. In the region of **Elsaß** (*êl*-zâs) (*Alsace*) in eastern France, people still speak a dialect of German, and their cuisine reflects a remarkable blend of French and German cuisine. The northern part of Italy known as **Südtirol** (*zued*-tir-ol) (*south Tyrol*) is partly German speaking, so you may find menus that reflect a blend of Italian and German cuisine. Want to know more about German food? Read on.

Whatever meal you decide to enjoy, remember to say **Guten Appetit** (*gooh*-ten âp-e-*teet*) (*enjoy your meal*) as the Germans do with each other before they start to eat!

Saying you're hungry and thirsty: Hast du Hunger? Hast du Durst?

When it comes to food, expressing your hunger and thirst are important. Otherwise, you have no cure for your grumbling stomach and parched throat. Here's how you talk about being hungry or thirsty in German:

Ich habe Hunger/Durst. (iH *hah*-be *hoong*-er/doorst.) (*I am hungry/thirsty.* Literally: *I have hunger/thirst.*)

Ich bin hungrig/durstig. (iH bin *hoong*-riH/*door*-stiH.) (*I am hungry/thirsty.*)

To satisfy your hunger or thirst, you have to eat — **essen** (*ês*-en) — and you have to drink — **trinken** (*trin*-ken). Here are the conjugations for **essen**, which is an irregular verb, and **trinken** (see Book III, Chapter 3 for more information on conjugating verbs in the present tense):

essen (*to eat*)	
ich ess**e**	wir ess**en**
du **isst**	ihr esst
er/sie/es **isst**	sie ess**en**
Sie essen	
Wir **essen** gern Fisch. (*We like to eat fish.*)	

trinken (*to drink*)	
ich trink**e**	wir trink**en**
du trink**st**	ihr trink**t**
er/sie/es trink**t**	sie trink**en**
Sie trink**en**	
Trinkst du Bier? (*Do you drink beer?*)	

Talking about meals: Guten Appetit!

German meals and meal times don't differ too much from their American counterparts. The three **Mahlzeiten** (*mahl*-tsayt-en) (*meals*) of the day are

- **das Frühstück** (dâs *frue*-shtuek) (*breakfast*)
- **das Mittagessen** (dâs *mi*-tahk-ês-en) (*lunch*)
- **das Abendessen** (dâs *ah*-bent-ês-en) (*dinner*)

In most cafés and hotels, breakfast is served from 7 a.m. to 10 a.m., and it's often more substantial than the typical continental breakfast served in North America. In lodgings such as hostels and bed-and-breakfasts, breakfast may end at 9 a.m., so it's a good idea to check first before turning in for the night. In smaller eateries, a hot lunch is usually served only between 11:30 a.m. and 2:00 p.m. For some Germans, lunch is the main meal of the day; for others, the main meal comes at dinnertime. In restaurants, a full menu is generally available between 6:30 p.m. and 9:00 p.m. In larger cities, restaurants may offer a full menu until 11 p.m. In addition, fast-food places abound, including several well-known American hamburger restaurant chains, where, interestingly enough, you can order beer.

The traditional cold evening meal in German homes consists of bread with cold meats, cheeses, salad, and other cold dishes. This same fare is what families and friends in southern Germany have at the local **Biergarten** (dêr *beer*-gâr-ten) (*beer garden*), where they spread their food out on a picnic table and enjoy warm summer evenings with **eine Maß Bier** (*ayn*-e mahs beer [as in English]) (*a liter of beer*).

You may occasionally hear people say **Mahlzeit!** (*mahl*-tsayt) as a greeting at lunchtime. Roughly translated, the word means *mealtime* in English. This greeting is especially common among colleagues at the workplace. If someone says this to you, just say the same — **Mahlzeit!** — and smile.

Setting the table

The German table features all the same items that you find on your table at home, including the following:

- ✔ **der Becher** (dêr *bêH*-er) (*mug*)
- ✔ **das Besteck** (dâs be-*shtêk*) (*a set of a knife, fork, and spoon*)
- ✔ **die Gabel** (dee *gah*-bel) (*fork*)
- ✔ **das Glas** (dâs glahs) (*glass*)
- ✔ **der Kaffeelöffel/der Teelöffel** (*kâf*-ey-ler-fel/*tey-ler*-fel) (*teaspoon*)
- ✔ **der Löffel** (dêr *ler*-fel) (*spoon*)
- ✔ **das Messer** (dâs *mês*-er) (*knife*)
- ✔ **die Serviette** (dee *sêr*-vee-êt-e) (*napkin*)
- ✔ **der Suppenlöffel/der Esslöffel** (dêr *zoop*-enler-fel/dêr *ês-ler*-fel) (*soup spoon*)
- ✔ **der Suppenteller** (dêr *zoop*-en-têl-er) (*soup bowl*)
- ✔ **die Tasse** (dee *tâs*-e) (*cup*)
- ✔ **der Teller** (dêr *têl*-er) (*plate*)
- ✔ **die Tischdecke** (dee *tish*-dêk-e) (*tablecloth*)
- ✔ **der Unterteller** (dêr *oon*-ter-têl-er) (*saucer*)

If you're in a restaurant and need an item not found on the table (for example, a spoon, fork, or knife), call the waiter over by saying the following:

Entschuldigen Sie, bitte! (ênt-*shool*-di-gen zee, *bi*-te!) (*Excuse me, please!*)

After you get the waiter's attention, ask for what you need:

Kann ich bitte einen Löffel/eine Gabel/ein Messer haben? (kân iH *bi*-te *ayn*-en *ler*-fel/*ayn*-e gah-bel/ayn mês-er *hah*-ben?) (*Can I please have a spoon/a fork/a knife?*)

Going to a Restaurant: Das Restaurant

Eating out is quite popular in Germany, and you'll find a couple of differences between going to a restaurant in Germany and going to one in the U.S. For instance, in many German restaurants, you don't have to wait to be seated as you do in the U.S. However, in more upscale places, the server usually does take you to your table. Also, doggie bags aren't common practice in Germany. But, surprisingly, dogs are generally welcome in many restaurants if they sit under the table.

Europeans in general place great value on the dining experience. Overall, you can expect a more leisurely pace while enjoying your meal in Europe. In fact, don't expect your server to bring the check after you've finished your meal — until you ask for it.

In the following sections, you become acquainted with dining out in Germany so you can get the most from your experience.

Deciding where to eat

Most German eateries post a menu (see Figure 7-1) at their entrances, so you can easily tell what kind of dining experience you would have there. This display is helpful when you're looking for a place to eat. However, if you want to ask someone about a particular kind of eatery, you need to know what kinds are available. Here are the most common ones:

✔ **der Biergarten** (dêr *beer*-gâr-ten) (*beer garden*): This outdoor Bavarian institution is a casual family place that serves snacks and beer in 1-liter mugs. At a traditional **Biergarten**, you sit at picnic tables under the shade of chestnut trees, and you may bring your own food and a tablecloth.

- **die Bierhalle** (dee *beer*-hâl-e)/**die Bierstube** (dee *beer*-shtooh-be) (*beer hall*): Beer halls, of course, specialize in beer served from huge barrels. But besides beer, you can also order hot dishes (usually deciding among a few dishes of the day), salads, and pretzels. The best-known beer halls are in Munich, Bavaria, where the **Oktoberfest** (ok-*toh*-ber-fêst) takes place for two weeks beginning in late September. At this event, each Munich brewery sets up a massive **Bierzelt** (*beer*-tsêlt) (*beer tent*).

- **das Café** (dâs café [as in English]) (*café*): Cafés may range from places to have **Kaffee und Kuchen** (*kâf*-ey oont *koohH*-en) (*coffee and cake*) to upscale establishments with full menus. Vienna's café tradition is famous. In these cafés, you can sit down for a leisurely cup of fine coffee and read the newspaper.

- **das Gasthaus** (dâs *gâst*-hous)/**der Gasthof** (dêr *gâst*-hohf) (*inn*): You usually find these inns in the country. They often offer home cooking, and the atmosphere may be rather folksy. In rural areas, some offer lodging.

- **die Gaststätte** (dee *gâst*-shtêt-e) (*local type of restaurant*): This restaurant is a simpler type where you're likely to find local specialties.

- **der Heuriger** (dêr *hoy*-ree-ger) (*wine tavern*): Located in the wine-producing regions of eastern Austria, these tradition-bound taverns are open for only a few weeks each year, at which time they may serve their own most recently produced wine of that year, together with a selection of locally made cold foods.

- **die Kneipe** (dee *knayp*-e) (*bar-restaurant*): This type of bar-restaurant combination is similar to what you may find in the U.S. You usually find a casual atmosphere here where the locals hang out.

- **die Raststätte** (dee *râst*-shtêt-e) (*roadside restaurant*): These restaurants usually are found on the Autobahn. They provide service station facilities and sometimes even lodging. ***Note:*** In Austria, these restaurants are called **der Rasthof** (dêr *râst*-hohf).

- **der Ratskeller** (dêr *rahts*-kêl-er): This type of restaurant is named after an eatery in the **Keller** (*kêl*-er) (*cellar*) of the **Rathaus** (*raht*-hous) (*town hall*). You often find these in historic buildings.

- **das Restaurant** (dâs rês-tuh-*ron*) (*restaurant*): You find a similar variety of restaurants in Germany that you find in the U.S., ranging from simple to fancy establishments with corresponding menus and prices.

- **der (Schnell)imbiss** (dêr [*shnêl*-]im-bis) or **der (Steh)imbiss** (dêr [*shteyl*-]im-bis) (*snack bar, fast-food restaurant*): Here, you can get food like **Wurst** (woorst) (*sausage*) and **Pommes frites** (pom frit) (*french fries*).

- **die Weinstube** (dee *vayn*-shtooh-be) (*wine bar*): At this cozy restaurant, often found in wine-producing areas, you can sample wine with bar food and snacks.

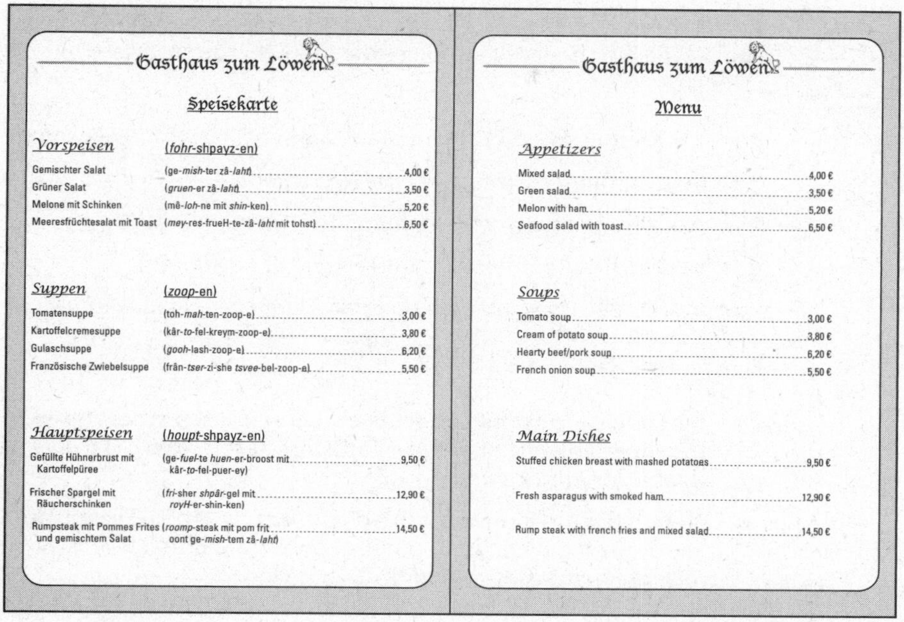

Figure 7-1:
German
restaurants
typically
post a menu
near the
door.

Illustration by Elizabeth Kurtzman

Making reservations

Making reservations isn't always necessary in Germany. In fact, during the week you may be able to get a table without a reservation — unless you're going to a particularly trendy place or one with limited seating. You usually don't make reservations at a **Kneipe** or **Gaststätte;** you get a table on a first-come, first-served basis. However, if you want to be on the safe side, call ahead to make a reservation.

When making a reservation, consider using the following expressions:

Ich möchte gern einen Tisch reservieren/bestellen. (iH *merH*-te gêrn *ayn*-en tish rê-zêr-*vee*-ren/be-*shtêl*-en.) (*I would like to reserve a table.*)

Haben Sie um . . . Uhr einen Tisch frei? (*hah*-ben zee oom . . . oohr *ayn*-en tish fray?) (*Do you have a table free at . . . o'clock?*)

Ich möchte gern einen Tisch für . . . Personen um . . . Uhr. (iH *merH*-te gêrn *ayn*-en tish fuer . . . pêr-*zohn*-en oom . . . oohr.) (*I would like a table for . . . people at . . . o'clock.*)

To get more specific about when you want the reservation, you can add the specific day of the week or one of the following appropriate phrases to your request:

- **am Freitag Abend** (âm *fray*-tahk *ah*-bent) (*on Friday evening*)
- **heute Abend** (*hoy*-te *ah*-bent) (*this evening*)
- **morgen Abend** (*mor*-gen *ah*-bent) (*tomorrow evening*)
- **heute Mittag** (*hoy*-te *mi*-tahk) (*today at lunchtime*)
- **morgen Mittag** (*mor*-gen *mi*-tahk) (*tomorrow at lunchtime*)

Here's what you may say:

Ich möchte gern für heute Abend einen Tisch reservieren. (iH *merH*-te gêrn fuer *hoy*-te *ah*-bent *ayn*-en tish rê-zêr-*vee*-ren.) (*I would like to reserve a table for this evening.*)

Haben Sie am Sonntag Abend um . . . Uhr einen Tisch frei? (*hah*-ben zee âm *zon*-tahk *ah*-bent oom . . . oohr *ayn*-en tish fray?) (*Do you have a table free on Sunday evening at . . . o'clock?*)

Talkin' the Talk

Mike and his friend Ute want to check out the trendy new Restaurant Galleria. Mike calls the restaurant to make a reservation.

Restaurant: **Restaurant Galleria.**
rês-tuh-*ron* gâ-le-*ree*-â.
Restaurant Galleria.

Mike: **Guten Tag. Ich möchte gern einen Tisch für heute Abend bestellen.**
gooh-ten tahk. iH *merH*-te gêrn *ayn*-en tish fuer *hoy*-te *ah*-bent be-*shtêl*-en.
Hello. I would like to reserve a table for this evening.

Restaurant: **Für wie viele Personen?**
fuer vee *fee*-le pêr-*zohn*-en?
For how many people?

Mike: **Zwei Personen, bitte. Haben Sie um acht Uhr einen Tisch frei?**
tsvay pêr-*zohn*-en, *bi*-te. *hah*-ben zee oom âHt oohr *ayn*-en tish fray?

Two people, please. Do you have a table free at eight o'clock?

Restaurant: **Tut mir leid. Um acht Uhr ist alles ausgebucht. Sie können aber um acht Uhr dreißig einen Tisch haben.**
tooht meer layt. oom âHt oohr ist *âl*-ês *ous*-ge-boohHt. zee *kern*-en *ah*-bêr oom âHt oohr *dray*-siH *ayn*-en tish *hah*-ben.
I'm sorry. At 8:00 everything's booked. But you could have a table at 8:30.

Mike: **Acht Uhr dreißig wäre auch gut.**
âHt oohr *dray*-siH *vai*-re ouH gooht.
8:30 would be good, too.

Restaurant: **Und Ihr Name, bitte?**
oont eer *nah*-me, *bi*-te?
And your name, please?

Mike: **Evans.**
evans [as in English].
Evans.

Restaurant: **Geht in Ordnung, ich habe den Tisch für Sie reserviert.**
geyt in *ort*-noong, iH *hah*-be deyn tish fuer zee rê-zêr-*veert*.
That's all set. I have reserved the table for you.

Mike: **Vielen Dank. Bis heute Abend.**
fee-lên dânk. bis *hoy*-te *ah*-bent.
Thank you very much. Until this evening.

Occasionally, you may call for a reservation and discover that no tables are available. In those instances, you may hear the following:

Es tut mir leid. Wir sind völlig ausgebucht. (ês tooht meer layt. veer zint *fer*-liH *ous*-ge-boohHt.) (*I'm sorry. We are totally booked.*)

If you show up at a busy restaurant without making a reservation, expect to hear one of the following:

In . . . Minuten wird ein Tisch frei. (in . . . mi-*nooh*-ten virt ayn tish fray.) (*In . . . minutes a table will be free.*)

Können Sie in . . . Minuten wiederkommen? (*kern*-en zee in . . . mi-*nooh*-ten *vee*-der-kom-en?) (*Could you come back in . . . minutes?*)

Arriving and being seated

When you arrive at a restaurant, you want to take your seat, **Platz nehmen** (plâts *neym*-en), and get your **Speisekarte** (*shpayz*-e-kâr-tê) (*menu*). In casual restaurants, you seat yourself. In upscale restaurants, a waiter, **der Kellner** (dêr *kêl*-ner), or a waitress, **die Kellnerin** (dee *kêl*-ner-in), directs you to your table.

With the exception of upscale restaurants, sharing a table with strangers isn't unusual. Sharing is especially common in places that tend to be crowded and in places with large tables. If seats are still available at the table where you're sitting, someone may ask you **Ist hier noch frei?** (ist heer noH fray?) (*Is this place still available?*) or **Können wir uns dazu setzen?** (*kern*-en veer oons dâ-tsooh *zêts*-en?) (*May we sit down with you?*) It's a very casual arrangement, and you don't have to start up a conversation with the party who's sharing the table with you. Some people may find the lack of privacy a little irritating, but it's also a good opportunity to meet the locals.

Talkin' the Talk

Mike and Ute have been looking forward to eating at Restaurant Galleria since Mike made the reservation. They arrive at the restaurant and are seated. (Go to www.dummies.com/go/germanaio to listen to this bonus track.)

Mike: **Guten Abend. Mein Name ist Evans. Wir haben einen Tisch für zwei Personen bestellt.**
gooh-ten *ah*-bent. mayn *nah*-me ist evans [as in English]. veer *hah*-ben *ayn*-en tish fuer tsvay pêr-*zohn*-en be-*shtêlt*.
Good evening. My name is Evans. We reserved a table for two people.

Kellner: **Guten Abend. Bitte, nehmen Sie hier vorne Platz.**
gooh-ten *ah*-bent. *bi*-te, *neym*-en zee heer *forn*-e plâts.
Good evening. Please take a seat over here.

Ute: **Könnten wir vielleicht den Tisch dort drüben am Fenster haben?**
kern-ten veer *fee*-layHt deyn tish dort *drue*-ben âm *fên*-ster *hah*-ben?
Could we perhaps have the table over there by the window?

Kellner: **Aber sicher, kein Problem. Setzen Sie sich. Ich bringe Ihnen sofort die Speisekarte.**
ah-ber *ziH*-er, kayn pro-*bleym*. *zêts*-en zee ziH. iH *bring*-e *een*-en zo-*fort* dee *shpayz*-e-kâr-te.
But of course, no problem. Have a seat. I'll bring you the menu right away.

Words to Know

bringen	<u>bring</u>-en	to bring
vielleicht	<u>fee</u>-layHt	perhaps
hier vorne	heer <u>forn</u>-e	over here
dort drüben	dort <u>drue</u>-ben	over there
Setzen Sie sich.	<u>zêts</u>-en zee ziH.	Have a seat.
Tut mir leid!	tooht meer layt!	I'm sorry!
Geht in Ordnung!	geyt in <u>ort</u>-noong!	That's all set.

Checking Out the Menu: Die Speisekarte

After you decide where to eat and then get a reservation and table, you're ready for the fun part — deciding what to eat! Of course, what's on **die Speisekarte** (dee *spayz*-e-kâr-te) (*the menu*) depends entirely on what kind of place you choose. Unlike in the U.S., the prices shown on a German menu normally include taxes and service.

If you go to a French, Spanish, or Chinese restaurant, the menu may be in the language of the respective country, with a German translation below the original name of the dish. In popular tourist areas, you may even find an English translation.

Looking at breakfast, lunch, and dinner items

The following sections tell you about foods you may find in European restaurants. Keep in mind, however, that these sections don't tell you about local cuisine, which differs substantially from region to region. For example, you commonly find certain regional dishes on the menu in Bavaria or southern Germany but never in Hamburg or the northern parts of the country. Austria and Switzerland also have their own regional specialties.

Breakfast

The following items may be offered **zum Frühstück** (tsoom *frue*-shtuek) (*for breakfast*) in a German-speaking country:

- ✔ **der Aufschnitt** (dêr *ouf*-shnit) (*cold meats and cheese*)
- ✔ **das Brot** (dâs broht) (*bread*)
- ✔ **das Brötchen** (dâs *brert*-Hên) (*roll*)
- ✔ **die Butter** (dee *boot*-er) (*butter*)
- ✔ **die Cornflakes** (dee *cornflakes [as in English]*) (*cornflakes*)
- ✔ **das Ei** (dâs ay) (*egg*)
- ✔ **die Haferflocken** (dee *hahf*-er-flok-en) (*oatmeal*)
- ✔ **die Margarine** (dee mâr-gâr-*een*-e) (*margarine*)
- ✔ **die Marmelade** (dee mâr-me-*lah*-de) (*marmelade, jam*)
- ✔ **die Milch** (dee milH) (*milk*)
- ✔ **das Müsli** (dâs *mues*-lee) (*muesli*)
- ✔ **die Rühreier** (dee *ruehr*-ay-er) (*scrambled eggs*)
- ✔ **der Saft** (dêr zâft) (*juice*)
- ✔ **der Schinken** (dêr *shin*-ken) (*ham*)
- ✔ **das Spiegelei** (dâs *shpee*-gêl-ay) (*fried egg, sunny side up*)
- ✔ **der Toast** (dêr tohst) (*toast*)
- ✔ **die Wurst** (dee voorst) (*sausage*)

In Germany, **Brötchen** are popular for breakfast; however, you also may get all kinds of bread or croissants. Eating cold cuts for breakfast is also common in Germany. If you order an egg without specifying that you want it scrambled or sunny side up, you'll get it soft-boiled, or **weichgekocht** (*vayH*-ge-koHt), served in an egg cup.

Appetizers

For **Vorspeisen** (*fohr*-shpayz-en) (*appetizers*), you may see the following German favorites:

- ✔ **Gemischter Salat** (ge-*mish*-ter zâ-*laht*) (*mixed salad*)
- ✔ **Grüner Salat** (*gruen*-er zâ-*laht*) (*green salad*)
- ✔ **Meeresfrüchtesalat mit Toast** (*meyr*-es-frueH-te-zâ-laht mit tohst) (*seafood salad with toast*)
- ✔ **Melone mit Schinken** (mê-*loh*-ne mit *shin*-ken) (*melon with ham*)

Soups

You may see the following **Suppen** (*zoop*-en) (*soups*) on a German menu:

- ✔ **Französische Zwiebelsuppe** (frân-*tser*-zi-she *tsvee*-bel-zoop-e) (*French onion soup*)

- ✓ **Gulaschsuppe** (*gooh*-lash-zoop-e) (*hearty beef and occasionally pork soup*)
- ✓ **Kartoffelcremesuppe** (kâr-*tof*-el-kreym-zoop-e) (*cream of potato soup*)
- ✓ **Tomatensuppe** (to-*mah*-ten-zoop-e) (*tomato soup*)

Book I

Getting
Started
with
German

Main dishes

Hauptspeisen (*houpt*-shpayz-en) (*main dishes*) are as diverse in Germany as they are in any culture; here are some you may find on a German menu:

- ✓ **Fisch des Tages** (fish dês *tah*-ges) (*fish of the day*)
- ✓ **Frischer Spargel mit Räucherschinken** (*frish*-er *shpâr*-gel mit *royH*-er-shin-ken) (*fresh white asparagus with smoked ham*)
- ✓ **gefüllte Hühnerbrust mit Kartoffelpüree** (ge-*fuel*-te *huen*-er-broost mit kâr-*tof*-el-puer-ey) (*stuffed chicken breast with mashed potatoes*)
- ✓ **Kalbsschnitzel nach Art des Hauses** (*kâlps*-shnits-el nahH ârt dês *houz*-es) (*chef's style veal cutlet*). This dish is often referred to as **Wienerschnitzel** (*veen*-er-shnits-el).
- ✓ **Lachs an Safransoße mit Spinat und Salzkartoffeln** (lâks ân *zâf*-rahn-zohs-e mit shpi-*naht* oont *zâlts*-kâr-tof-eln) (*salmon in saffron sauce with spinach and boiled potatoes*)
- ✓ **Lammfrikassee mit Reis** (lâm-frik-â-sey mit rays) (*lamb fricassee with rice*). With chicken, it's called **Hühnerfrikassee** (*huen*-er-frik-â-sey) (*chicken fricassee*).
- ✓ **Rumpsteak mit Pommes Frites und gemischtem Salat** (*roomp*-steak mit pom frit oont ge-*mish*-tem zâ-*laht*) (*rump steak with french fries and mixed salad*)

Side dishes

You can sometimes order **Beilagen** (*bay*-lah-gen) (*side dishes*) separately from your main course. Consider the following popular items:

- ✓ **Butterbohnen** (*boot*-er-bohn-en) (*buttered beans*)
- ✓ **Gurkensalat** (*goork*-en-zâ-laht) (*cucumber salad*)
- ✓ **Kartoffelkroketten** (kâr-*tof*-el-kroh-ket-en) (*potato croquettes*)

Dessert

German restaurants commonly offer many fine dishes **zum Nachtisch** (tsoom *naH*-tish) (*for dessert*), including the following:

- ✓ **Apfelstrudel** (*âp*-fel-shtrooh-del) (*apple strudel*)
- ✓ **Frischer Obstsalat** (*frish*-er *ohpst*-zâ-laht) (*fresh fruit salad*)

- **Gemischtes Eis mit Sahne** (ge-*mish*-tes ays mit *zahn*-e) (*mixed ice cream with whipped cream*)
- **Rote Grütze mit Vanillesoße** (*roh*-te *grue*-tse mit vâ-*ni*-le-zohs-e) (*red berry compote with vanilla sauce*)

Understanding cooking terms

When you're reading a menu in German, you can understand a great deal of the dishes when you're familiar with the various terms that describe methods of preparation such as frying or broiling. Here are some cooking terms you may see on a German menu, with examples of food prepared using such cooking methods:

- **eingelegt, mariniert** (*ayn*-ge-leygt, *mâr*-i-neert) (*pickled, marinated*): **eingelegter Hering** (*ayn*-ge-leygt-er *hêr*-ing) (*pickled herring*)

- **frittiert** (fri-*teert*) (*deep-fat fried*): **frittierte Zwiebelringe** (fri-*teer*-te *tsvee*-bel-ring-e) (*fried onion rings*)

- **gebacken** (ge-*bâk*-en) (*baked*): **gebackene Kartoffel** (ge-*bâk*-en-e kâr-*tof*-el) (*baked potatoes*)

- **gebraten** (ge-*brât*-en) (*roasted*): **gebratenes Hähnchen** (ge-*brât*-en-es *hain*-Hen) (*roasted chicken*)

- **gedampft** (ge-*dâmpft*) (*steamed*): **gedampftes Gemüse** (ge-*dâmpf*-tes ge-*muez*-e) (*steamed vegetables*)

- **gefüllt** (ge-*fuelt*) (*stuffed/filled*): **gefüllte Hühnerbrust** (ge-*fuel*-te *huen*-er-broost) (*stuffed chicken breast*)

- **gekocht** (ge-*koHt*) (*boiled/cooked*): **ein weichgekochtes Ei** (ayn *vayH*-ge-*koHt*-es ay) (*a soft-boiled egg*)

- **geräuchert** (ge-*royH*-êrt) (*smoked*): **geräucherte Forelle** (ge-*royH*-êrt-e for-*êl*-e) (*smoked trout*)

- **heiß** (hays) (*hot* [as in temperature]): **eine Tasse heisse Schokolade** (*ayn*-e *tâs*-e *hays*-e shok-oh-*lah*-de) (*a cup of hot chocolate*)

- **kalt** (kâlt) (*cold*): **eine kalte Suppe** (*ayn*-e *kal*-te *zoop*-e) (*a cold soup*)

- **roh** (roh) (*raw*): **rohe Austern** (*roh*-e *ous*-têrn) (*raw oysters*)

- **sauer** (*sou*-er) (*sour*): **Sauerkirschen** (*sou*-er-*keersch*-en) (*sour cherries*)

- **scharf** (shârf) (*hot* [as in spicy]): **eine scharfe Soße** (*ayn*-e *shârf*-e *zohs*-e) (*a spicy sauce*)

- **süß** (sues) (*sweet*): **Süßkirschen** (sues-*keersch*-en) (*sweet cherries*)

- **überbacken** (ue-ber-*bâk*-en) (*scalloped/au gratin*): **überbackene Aubergine** (ue-ber-*bâk*-en-e oh-bêr-*jeen*-e) (*eggplant Parmesan*)

Menus may also include some of the ingredients used in preparing a particular dish. Knowing some of the basics can help you better understand what you're ordering. The following is a list of condiments and ingredients commonly used in German-style cooking:

- ✔ **der Essig** (dêr *ês*-iH) (*vinegar*)
- ✔ **die Gewürze** (dee ge-*vuerts*-e) (*spices*)
- ✔ **der Honig** (dêr *hohn*-iH) (*honey*)
- ✔ **der Ketchup** (dêr ketchup [as in English]) (*ketchup*)
- ✔ **die Kräuter** (dee *kroyt*-er) (*herbs*)
- ✔ **der Meerrettich** (dêr *meyr*-rêt-iH) (*horseradish*)
- ✔ **das Öl** (dâs erl) (*oil*)
- ✔ **der Pfeffer** (dêr *pfêf*-er) (*pepper*)
- ✔ **die Sahne** (dee *zah*-ne) (*cream*)
- ✔ **die Salatsoße** (dee zâ-*laht*-zohs-e) (*dressing*)
- ✔ **das Salz** (dâs zâlts) (*salt*)
- ✔ **der Senf** (dêr zênf) (*mustard*)
- ✔ **die Soße** (dee *zohs*-e) (*sauce*)
- ✔ **der Zucker** (dêr *tsook*-er) (*sugar*)

Quenching your thirst

If you want to order **Wasser** (*vâs*-er) (*water*) at a German restaurant, you have the choice between the carbonated or noncarbonated kind — **ein Wasser mit Kohlensäure** (ayn *vâs*-er mit *koh*-len-zoy-re) (*carbonated water*) or **ein Wasser ohne Kohlensäure** (ayn *vâs*-er *oh*-ne *koh*-len-zoy-re) (*noncarbonated water*). If you ask the server for **ein Mineralwasser** (ayn min-êr-*ahl*-vâs-êr) (*mineral water*), you get carbonated water. Germans usually don't drink **Leitungswasser** (*lay*-toongs-*vâs*-er) (*tap water*). However, if you'd like a glass of tap water, you can say this:

> **Ein Glas Leitungswasser, bitte.** (ayn glahs *lay*-toongs-vâs-er, *bi*-te.)
> (*A glass of tap water, please.*)

You can order **Wein** (vayn) (*wine*) by the bottle — **die Flasche** (dee *flâsh*-e) — or by the glass — **das Glas** (dâs glahs). Occasionally, you also can get a carafe of wine, which is **die Karaffe** (dee kah-*râf*-e).

In the following list, you find some common beverages, **Getränke** (gê-*train*-ke), that you may see on a German menu:

- **Bier** (beer [as in English]) (*beer*)
- **das Bier vom Fass** (dâs beer fom fâs) (*draft beer*)
- **das Export** (dâs export [as in English]) (*smooth lager beer*)
- **helles/dunkles Bier** (*hel*-es/*dunk*-les beer) (*light/dark beer*) (**Helles** refers to the beer's light color, not its alcoholic content.)
- **der Kaffee** (dêr *kâf*-ê) (*coffee*)
- **das Pils/Pilsner** (dâs pils/pilsner [as in English]) (*pale lager beer*)
- **der Rotwein** (dêr *roht*-vayn) (*red wine*)
- **der Tafelwein** (dêr *tahf*-el-vayn) (*table wine, lowest quality*)
- **der Tee** (dêr tey) (*tea*)
- **Wein** (vayn) (*wine*)
- **der Weißwein** (dêr *vays*-vayn) (*white wine*)

Placing Your Order

As in English, you use a variety of common expressions, including the following, to order your food in German. Luckily, they aren't too complicated, and you can use them for ordering anything from food to drinks and for buying food at a store.

> **Ich hätte gern . . .** (iH *hêt*-e gêrn . . .) (*I would like to have . . .*)
>
> **Für mich bitte . . .** (fuer miH *bi*-te . . .) (*For me . . . please*)
>
> **Ich möchte (gern) . . .** (iH *merH*-te [gêrn] . . .) (*I would like to have . . .*)

When ordering, you may decide to be adventurous and ask the server to suggest something for you. Here's how:

> **Könnten Sie etwas empfehlen?** (*kern*-ten zee *êt*-vâs êm-*pfey*-len?) (*Could you recommend something?*)

Be prepared for your server to rattle off names of dishes you may be unfamiliar with. To avoid any confusion, try holding out your menu so the server can point at specific dishes when responding.

Ordering politely

Take a closer look at the verb forms **hätte**, **könnten**, and **möchte** in the preceding section. These verbs are in the subjunctive. The *subjunctive* has a number of uses in German, such as describing a wish or condition or expressing your opinion. For more information on the subjunctive, go to Book IV, Chapter 7. In the examples in this section, you use the subjunctive for making polite requests. Basically, the subjunctive acts like the English *would*.

Ich hätte . . . (iH *hêt*-e . . .) (*I would have . . .*) comes from **haben** (*hah*-ben) (*to have*). The big difference between the German and the English usage is that in German you can combine *would* and *have* into one word: **hätte**. Add **gern** (gêrn) (*gladly, willingly*) to **hätte** and presto! You have the form for ordering: **Ich hätte gern . . .** (iH *hêt*-e gêrn) (*I would like to have . . .*)

You also have **Ich möchte . . .** (iH *merH*-te . . .) (*I would like . . .*), which comes from **mögen** (*mer*-gen) (*to like*). **Möchte** basically corresponds to the English *would like*. You use it in a similar way when ordering. Consider the following example:

> **Ich möchte gern ein Glas Mineralwasser.** (iH *merH*-te gêrn ayn glahs min-êr-*ahl*-vâs-er.) (*I would like a glass of mineral water.*)

Note: Both **hätte** and **möchte** are commonly used without the infinitive of a verb.

The phrase **Ich könnte . . .** (iH *kern*-te . . .) (*I could . . .*) comes from the verb **können** (*kern*-en) (*to be able to* or *can*). **Könnte** combines with the infinitive of a verb to make the following request:

> **Könnten Sie uns helfen?** (*kern*-ten zee oons *helf*-en?) (*Could you help us?*)

Talkin' the Talk

Mike and Ute have had a chance to look at the menu. The waiter returns to take their orders. (Track 19)

Kellner:	**Darf ich Ihnen etwas zu trinken bringen?**
	dârf iH *een*-en êt-vâs tsooh *trin*-ken *bring*-en?
	May I bring you something to drink?

Mike:	**Ja, ich möchte gern ein Bier.**
	yah, iH *merH*-te gêrn ayn beer.
	Yes, I'd like a beer.

Kellner:	**Pils oder Export?**
	pils *oh*-der export?
	A pilsner or an export?
Mike:	**Export, bitte.**
	export, *bi*-te.
	Export, please.
Kellner:	**Ein Export. Und was darf es für Sie sein?**
	ayn export. oont vâs dârf ês fuer zee zayn?
	One export. And what would you like?
Ute:	**Mmm . . . Soll ich den Sylvaner oder den Riesling bestellen?**
	Mmm . . . zol iH deyn Sylvaner [as in English] *oh*-der deyn Riesling [as in English] be-*shtêl*-en?
	Mmm. Should I order the Sylvaner or the Riesling?
Kellner:	**Ich kann Ihnen beide Weißweine empfehlen.**
	iH kahn *een*-en *bay*-de *vays*-vayn-e êm-*pfey*-len.
	I can recommend both white wines.
Ute:	**Gut. Ich hätte gern ein Glas Sylvaner.**
	gooht. iH *hêt*-e gêrn ayn glahs Sylvaner.
	Good. I would like to have a glass of Sylvaner.

Asking for assistance

When you're asking someone for help, you want to be polite, so you formulate a question or make a statement using the verbs **darf, soll,** and **kann:**

✔ **Ich darf . . .** (iH dârf . . .) (*I may/I'm allowed to . . .*) comes from the verb **dürfen** (*duerf*-en) (*may/to be allowed to*).

✔ **Ich soll . . .** (iH zol . . .) (*I should . . .*) comes from the verb **sollen** (*zol*-en) (*should*).

✔ **Ich kann . . .** (iH kân . . .) (*I can . . .*) comes from the verb **können** (*kern*-en) (*can*).

These verbs help you further determine or modify the action expressed by another verb (that's why they're called *modal auxiliaries*), and they work in a similar way as their English equivalents *may, should,* and *can.* **Möchte,** which we discuss in the preceding section, does double duty as a modal auxiliary and as a subjunctive verb. For more information on modal auxiliaries, check out Book III, Chapter 6.

Here are some example sentences to familiarize you with **darf, soll,** and **kann:**

> **Darf ich die Speisekarte haben?** (dârf iH dee *shpayz*-e-kâr-te *hah*-ben?) (*May I have the menu, please?*)

> **Dürfen wir dort drüben sitzen?** (*duerf*-en veer dort *drueb*-en *zits*-en?) (*May we sit over there?*)

> **Sie sollten den Apfelstrudel bestellen.** (zee *zol*-ten den *âp*-fel-shtrooh-del be-*shtêl*-en.) (*You should order the apple strudel.*)

> **Soll ich Ihnen zwei Löffel bringen?** (zol iH *een*-en tsvay *ler*-fel *bring*-en?) (*Shall I bring you two spoons?*)

> **Kann ich bitte eine Serviette haben?** (*kân* iH *bi*-te *ayn*-e sêr-vee-*êt*-e *hah*-ben?) (*Can I have a napkin, please?*)

> **Können Sie uns bitte noch zwei Bier bringen?** (*kern*-en zee oons *bi*-te noH tsvay beer *bring*-en?) (*Can you bring us two more beers, please?*)

Ordering something special

People all over the world are now more conscientious than ever about what they're eating, whether due to health or ethical concerns. So you may need the following phrases to order something a little out of the ordinary:

> **Haben Sie vegetarische Gerichte?** (*hah*-ben zee vey-gê-*tahr*-ish-e ge-*riH*-te?) (*Do you have vegetarian dishes?*)

> **Ich kann nichts essen, was . . . enthält** (iH kân niHts *ês*-en, vâs . . . ênt-*hailt*) (*I can't eat anything that contains . . .*)

> **Haben Sie Gerichte für Diabetiker?** (*hah*-ben zee ge-*riH*-te fuer dee-â-bey-ti-ker?) (*Do you have dishes for diabetics?*)

> **Haben Sie Kinderportionen?** (*hah*-ben zee *kin*-der-por-tsee-ohn-en?) (*Do you have children's portions?*)

If you order meat — steak, for example — the server may ask you **Wie hätten Sie das Steak gern?** (vee *hêt*-en zee dâs steak gêrn?) (*How would you like your steak?*) You can respond with any of the following, depending on your tastes:

- ✔ **englisch** (*êng*-lish) (*rare*)

- ✔ **medium** (*mey*-dee-oom) (*medium*)

- ✔ **durchgebraten** (*doorH*-ge-braht-en) (*well-done*)

Finishing Your Meal and Getting the Check

When you're nearing the end of your meal, you may be thinking about having a cup of coffee or ordering some dessert, or you may just want the check. If the server doesn't stop by to ask you how you're doing, you have to take the initiative. To get your server's attention, try politely raising your hand. You can also say **Entschuldigen Sie, bitte!** (ênt-*shool*-di-gen zee, *bi*-te!) (*Excuse me, please!*)

Replying to "How did you like the food?" "Hat es Ihnen geschmeckt?"

After a meal, the server typically asks you whether you liked the food. The following is the question you hear:

> **Hat es Ihnen geschmeckt?** (hât ês *een*-en ge-*shmêkt?*) (*Did you enjoy the food?*)

Hopefully, you enjoyed your meal and can honestly answer the question with one of the following:

- **Danke, gut.** (*dân*-ke, gooht.) (*Thanks, good.*)
- **Sehr gut.** (zeyr gooht.) (*Very good.*)
- **Ausgezeichnet.** (ous-ge-*tsayH*-net.) (*Excellent.*)

After your server asks you how you liked the food, she may ask you the following as a way to bring your meal to a close and to find out whether you're ready for the check:

> **Sonst noch etwas?** (zonst noH *êt*-vâs?) (*Anything else?*)

Unless you'd like to order something else, it's time to pay **die Rechnung** (dee *rêH*-noong) (*bill*).

Asking for the check

In German-speaking regions, you have to ask for the check when you want to pay. Otherwise, your server will let you sit at your table indefinitely. After all, he would be considered pushy and impolite if he were to put the check on your table before you requested it. So when you're ready to pay, ask for the bill in one of the following ways:

> **Ich möchte bezahlen.** (iH *merH*-te be-*tsahl*-en.) (*I would like to pay.*)

> **Die Rechnung, bitte.** (dee *rêH*-noong, *bi*-te.) (*The check, please.*)

If you want to, you can pay together with the other people you're dining with. In that case, use this phrase: **Alles zusammen, bitte.** (*âl*-es tsoo-*zâm*-en, *bi*-te.) (*Everything together, please.*). Or you can ask to pay separately with **Wir möchten getrennt bezahlen.** (veer *merH*-ten ge-*trênt* be-*tsahl*-en.) (*We would like to pay separately.*)

Some German restaurants, especially upscale establishments, allow you to pay with a credit card — **die Kreditkarte** (dee krê-*dit*-kâr-te). These restaurants have signs in the window or at the door, indicating which cards they take (just as American restaurants do). If you must pay with a credit card, simply look for these signs.

If you need a **Quittung** (*kvit*-oong) (*receipt*), ask the server for one after you've asked for the check:

> **Und eine Quittung, bitte.** (oont *ayn*-e *kvit*-oong, *bi*-te.) (*And a receipt, please.*)

In more casual establishments, such as a **Kneipe,** you may simply tell the server that you want to pay and then make the payment directly at the table, usually with cash.

Don't feel like you have to tip as much as you do in North America. The servers receive a salary, and they don't live off their tips. If you're paying cash for the check at your table, just round up the bill by 5 percent. Consider using the phrase **Stimmt so.** (shtimt zoh.) (*Keep the change.*) It tells the server that the sum added on to the bill is the tip and that you don't need any change back. You need to hand the tip to the server, as leaving money on the table is not customary in Europe. Alternatively, if the check is 36€ and you only have a 50€ bill, you can say **Machen Sie es 38€** (*mâH*-en zee ês âHt-oont-*dray*-siH oy-roh.) (*Make that 38€.*) The server will hand you back 12€. In high-end restaurants with great service, you may want to leave a somewhat larger tip, and conversely, if you're in a simple establishment with minimal service, you may simply round off the amount to the next euro if the check is small.

Talkin' the Talk

Mike and Ute have enjoyed a great meal. They ask for the check, pay, and then tip the waiter. (Track 20)

Mike: **Die Rechnung, bitte.**
dee *rêH*-noong, *bi*-te.
The check, please.

Kellner: **Sofort. Das macht 45 Euro 80.**
zoh-*fort*. dâs mâHt fuenf-oont-*feer*-tsiH oy-roh *âHt*-tsiH.
Coming right up. That would be 45 euros 80 cents.

Mike puts 50 euros on the table.

Mike: **Stimmt so.**
shtimt zoh.
Keep the change.

Kellner: **Vielen Dank.**
fee-len dânk.
Thank you very much.

Mike: **Bitte.**
bi-te.
You're welcome.

Words to Know

bezahlen	be-<u>tsahl</u>-en	to pay
die Kreditkarte	dee krê-<u>dit</u>-kâr-te	credit card
die Quittung	dee <u>kvit</u>-oong	receipt
in bar bezahlen	in bâr be-<u>tsahl</u>-en	to pay cash
die Rechnung	dee rêH-noong	bill
Stimmt so.	shtimt zoh.	Keep the change.
Bitte.	<u>bi</u>-te.	You're welcome./Please.

Shopping for Food

Sometimes you may not feel like eating out. You may prefer to buy food for a picnic or to do the cooking yourself. If you want to shop for food, you need to know where to go and what to buy.

The following sections provide you with words for types of stores and food. To find out about how to order specific quantities of food, check out the section in Book I, Chapter 2 on weights and measurements.

Knowing where to shop

Although supermarkets are an obvious place to pick up the makings of a meal, you may not find one nearby. The local neighborhood grocery store, butcher shop, or bakery may be more convenient, and don't forget that in such stores you have the opportunity to interact in German.

Other shopping options include the open-air food stands and markets common in Germany, Austria, and Switzerland. Some are open on a regular basis, others are open only once a week, and a few may be seasonal, but all of them sell quality produce and food items that are fresh and tasty. Whether you want to buy something for a snack or a whole week's worth of groceries, you can stock up at the local market and practice your German at the same time. The food is often artfully displayed, tempting you to reach for that delicious-looking piece of fruit. However, restrain yourself and wait to be served. Outdoor-market etiquette is different from supermarket-style, self-serve shopping. You're better off resisting temptation to help yourself, lest you hear the words of warning: **Nicht anfassen!** (niHt *ân*-fâs-en!) (*Don't touch!*)

Here are just some of the stores and shops you can visit if you want to buy food:

- **die Bäckerei** (dee bêk-e-*ray*) (*bakery*)
- **der Bioladen, das Reformhaus** (dêr *bee*-oh-*lah*-den, dâs rê-*form*-hous) (*organic food store, health-food store*)
- **das Feinkostgeschäft** (dâs *fayn*-kost-ge-shêft) (*delicatessen*)
- **der Getränkemarkt** (dêr ge-*trênk*-e-markt) (*store selling alcoholic and nonalcoholic beverages*)
- **die Konditorei** (dee kon-dee-to-*ray*) (*cake and pastry shop*)
- **das Lebensmittelgeschäft** (dâs *ley*-benz-mit-el-ge-shêft) (*grocery store*)
- **der Markt** (dêr mârkt) (*market, usually outdoors*)
- **die Markthalle** (dee *mârkt*-hâl-e) (*covered market, often with stands selling fresh food items*)

- **der Marktplatz** (dêr *mârkt*-plâts) (*outdoor market place, often in the center of town near the town hall*)

- **die Metzgerei, die Fleischerei** (dee mêts-ge-*ray*, dee flaysh-er-*ay*) (*butcher shop*)

- **der Supermarkt** (dêr *zooh*-pêr-mârkt) (*supermarket*)

- **die Weinhandlung** (dee *vayn*-hând-loong) (*wine store*)

You may purchase beer, wine, and other alcoholic beverages in German supermarkets, grocery stores, discount stores, and even some gas stations. Large train stations may also have stores that sell food and alcoholic beverages, and some of the larger department stores have a full-fledged supermarket located in the basement.

Finding what you need

After you decide where you want to shop, you have to decide what you want to buy. Often making that decision requires talking to the shopkeeper or market seller. For instance, some shopkeepers pride themselves on their fine cheeses, olives, or other deli items and may be willing to let you try something before you decide to buy. All you have to do is ask. The following expressions may come in handy when you're interacting with a shopkeeper:

Ich hätte gern . . . (iH *hêt*-e gêrn . . .) (*I'd like . . .*)

Was ist das? (vâs ist dâs?) (*What is that?*)

Könnte ich das probieren? (*kern*-te iH dâs proh-*beer*-en?) (*Could I try that?*)

Das schmeckt sehr gut. (dâs shmêkt zeyr goot.) (*That tastes really good.*)

Ein Stück, bitte. (ayn shtueck, *bi*-te.) (*One piece, please.*)

300 Gramm, bitte. (dray *hoon*-dêrt grâm, *bi*-te.) (*Three hundred grams, please.*)

Das wär's/Das war's. (dâs vêrs/dâs vârs.) (*That's all.*)

You may hear the shopkeeper ask you the following:

Kann ich Ihnen behilflich sein/helfen? (kân iH *eehn*-en be-*hilf*-liH zany/ *hêlf*-en?) (*Can I help you?*)

Was darf es sein? (vâs dârf es zayn?) (*What would you like?*)

Am Stück oder geschnitten? (âm shtuek *oh*-der ge-*shnit*-en?) (*A piece or sliced?*)

Sonst noch etwas? (zonst noH *êt*-vâs?) (*Anything else?*)

Here are the main types of foods you may find in the shops and markets listed in the preceding section:

- ✔ **die Backwaren** (dee *bâk*-vâr-en) (*bakery goods*)

- ✔ **das Gebäck** (dâs ge-*bêk*) (*cookies, pastries*)

- ✔ **das Gemüse** (dâs ge-*mue*-ze) (*vegetables*)

- ✔ **der Fisch** (dêr fish) (*fish*)

- ✔ **das Fleisch** (dâs flaysh) (*meat*)

- ✔ **das Obst** (dâs ohpst) (*fruit*)

Some common grain and dairy items you may be interested in purchasing include

- ✔ **das Brot** (dâs broht) (*bread*)

- ✔ **das Brötchen** (dâs *brert*-Hen) (*roll*)

- ✔ **die Butter** (dee *boot*-er) (*butter*)

- ✔ **der Käse** (dêr *kai*-ze) (*cheese*)

- ✔ **der Kuchen** (dêr *koohH*-en) (*cake*)

- ✔ **die Milch** (dee milH) (*milk*)

- ✔ **der Reis** (dêr rays) (*rice*)

- ✔ **das Roggenbrot** (dâs *rog*-en-broht) (*rye bread*)

- ✔ **die Sahne** (dee *zahn*-e) (*cream*)

- ✔ **das Schwarzbrot** (dâs *shvârts*-broht) (*brown bread*)

- ✔ **die Torte** (dee *tor*-te) (cake, often multilayered)

You may be interested in buying the following types of **Fisch** (fish) (*fish*) and **Meeresfrüchte** (*meyr*-es-frueH-te) (*seafood*):

- ✔ **die Austern** (dee *ous*-têrn) (*oysters*)

- ✔ **die Flunder** (dee *floon*-der) (*flounder*)

- ✔ **die Forelle** (dee fohr-*e*-le) (*trout*)

- ✔ **der Heilbutt** (dêr *hayl*-boot) (*halibut*)

- ✔ **der Hering** (dêr *hêr*-ing) (*herring*)

- ✔ **der Kabeljau** (dêr *kah*-bel-you) (*cod*)

- ✔ **die Krabben** (dee *krâb*-en) (*shrimp*)

- ✔ **der Krebs** (dêr kreyps) (*crab*)

- **der Lachs** (dêr lâx) (*salmon*)

- **die Muscheln** (dee *moosh*-eln) (*mussels*)

- **der Schellfisch** (dêr *shêl*-fish) (*haddock*)

- **die Seezunge** (dee *zey*-tsoong-e) (*sole*)

- **der Thunfisch** (dêr *toohn*-fish) (*tuna*)

Here are some types of **Fleisch** (flaysh) (*meat*) you may want to buy:

- **die Bratwurst** (dee *braht*-voorst) (*fried sausage*)

- **die Ente** (dee *ên*-te) (*duck*)

- **der Fasan** (dêr fâ-*zân*) (*pheasant*)

- **die Gans** (dee gâns) (*goose*)

- **das Geflügel** (dâs ge-*flueg*-el) (poultry)

- **das Hackfleisch** (dâs *hâk*-flaysh) (*hamburger meat*)

- **das Hähnchen** (dâs *hain*-Hen) (*chicken*)

- **das Kalbfleisch** (dâs *kâlp*-flaysh) (*veal*)

- **das Kanninchen** (dâs kân-*een*-Hen) (*rabbit*)

- **das Lammfleisch** (dâs *lâm*-flaysh) (*lamb*)

- **das Rehfleisch** (dâs *rey*-flaysh) (*venison*)

- **das Rindfleisch** (dâs *rint*-flaysh) (*beef*)

- **der Schinken** (dêr *shin*-ken) (*ham*)

- **das Schweinefleisch** (dâs *shvayn*-e-flaysh) (*pork*)

- **der Speck** (dêr shpêk) (*bacon*)

- **der Truthahn, die Pute** (dêr *trooht*-hahn, dee *pooh*-te) (*turkey*)

- **das Wild** (dâs vilt) (*game*)

- **die Wurst** (dee voorst) (*sausage*)

Here are some types of **Obst** (opst) (*fruit*) and **Gemüse** (ge-*mue*-ze) (*vegetables*) you may want to purchase:

- **die Ananas** (dee *ân*-ân-âs) (*pineapple*)

- **der Apfel** (dêr *âp*-fel) (*apple*)

- **die Aubergine** (dee oh-bêr-*jeen*-e) (*eggplant*)

- **die Banane** (dee bâ-*nah*-ne) (*banana*)

- ✔ **die Birne** (dee *birn*-e) (*pear*)
- ✔ **die Blaubeere/Heidelbeere** (dee *blou*-beyr-e/*hay*-del-beyr-e) (*blueberry*)
- ✔ **der Blumenkohl** (dêr *bloom*-en-kohl) (*cauliflower*)
- ✔ **die Bohne** (dee *bohn*-e) (*bean*)
- ✔ **der Brokkoli** (dêr *broh*-ko-lee) (*broccoli*)
- ✔ **der Champignon** (dêr *shâm*-peen-yon) (*mushroom*)
- ✔ **die Erbse** (dee *êrp*-se) (*pea*)
- ✔ **die Erdbeere** (dee *eyrt*-beyr-e) (*strawberry*)
- ✔ **der Grünkohl** (dêr *gruen*-kohl) (*kale*)
- ✔ **die Gurke** (dee *goork*-e) (*cucumber*)
- ✔ **die Himbeere** (dee *him*-beyr-e) (*raspberry*)
- ✔ **die Karotte/Möhre** (dee kâ-*rot*-e/*mer*-e) (*carrot*)
- ✔ **die Kartoffel** (dee kâr-*tof*-el) (*potato*)
- ✔ **die Kirsche** (dee *kirsh*-e) (*cherry*)
- ✔ **die Kiwi** (dee *kee*-vee) (*kiwi*)
- ✔ **der Knoblauch** (dêr *knoh*-blouH) (*garlic*)
- ✔ **der Kohl** (dêr kohl) (*cabbage*)
- ✔ **der Kohlrabi** (dêr kohl-*râ*-bee) (*kohlrabi*)
- ✔ **der Kopfsalat** (dêr *kopf*-zâ-laht) (*lettuce*)
- ✔ **der Kürbis** (dêr *kuer*-bis) (*pumpkin*)
- ✔ **der Lauch** (dêr lauH) (*leek*)
- ✔ **die Olive** (dee oh-*leev*-e) (*olive*)
- ✔ **die Orange** (dee oh-*ron*-ge [g as in the word *genre*]) (*orange*)
- ✔ **der Paprika** (dêr *pâp*-ree-kah) (*bell pepper*)
- ✔ **der Pfirsich** (dêr *pfir*-siH) (*peach*)
- ✔ **die Pflaume** (dee *pflau*-me) (*plum*)
- ✔ **der Pilz** (dêr pilts) (*mushroom*) (often: *wild mushroom*)
- ✔ **die Preiselbeere** (dee *pray*-zêl-beyr-e) (*cranberry*)
- ✔ **der Rotkohl** (dêr *roht*-kohl) (*red cabbage*)
- ✔ **der Salat** (dêr zâ-*laht*) (*salad*)
- ✔ **das Sauerkraut** (dâs *zou*-er-krout) (*sauerkraut*)

- ✔ **die saure Gurke** (dee *zou*-re *goork*-e) (*sour pickle*)
- ✔ **der Sellerie** (dêr *zêl*-êr-ee) (*celeriac*)
- ✔ **der Spargel** (dêr *shpâr*-gêl) (*asparagus*)
- ✔ **der Spinat** (dêr shpi-*naht*) (*spinach*)
- ✔ **die Tomate** (dee to-*mah*-te) (*tomato*)
- ✔ **die Zitrone** (dee tsi-*trohn*-e) (*lemon*)
- ✔ **die Zucchini** (dee tsoo-*kee*-ni) (*zucchini*)
- ✔ **die Zwiebel** (dee *tsvee*-bel) (*onion*)

If you go shopping at a supermarket in Germany, you'll quickly notice that shoppers don't get free plastic or paper bags to put their groceries in. You either have to bring your own bag or pay a small amount for a plastic bag at the checkout. So why not go with the flow and purchase a few cloth bags that you can reuse? Oh, and keep in mind that bagging your own groceries is customary.

Book II
Speaking German on the Go

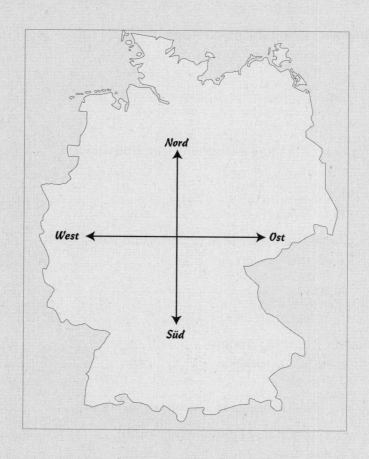

Contents at a Glance

Chapter 1

Locating Places

- -

In This Chapter

▶ Asking about the places you want to go

▶ Getting your directions straight

▶ Going by car or other vehicle

- -

T he key to getting around is knowing how to get where you're going. Before you hop on that bus or train, or set out on your journey by car or on foot, you naturally want to plan your trip. Being able to ask about the location of a train station, open-air market, or museum is a good start.

Of course, you also want to understand the directions someone gives you to your destination. For example, someone may say that the market is across from the subway station, behind the hotel, or next to the post office. Or they may tell you to take the second street on the left, turn right at the third traffic light, and so on. If you don't relish the thought of getting lost, read on.

Getting Yourself Oriented

You emerge from the subway station in the middle of a large city square and don't see any street signs near you, so you rotate your map, trying to make sense of the buildings around you. Finding your way at this point may be a bit confusing, so unless you have a reliable GPS with you, the next step is to ask someone for help locating your destination. This section points you in the right direction.

Finding out where something is

Where am I? Where do we go from here? Where would you be without the word *where?* Probably lost. Luckily, asking where something is in German is pretty easy. You start with the word **wo** (voh) (*where*) and frame your question like this:

> **Wo ist. . . ?** (voh ist. . . ?) (*Where is. . . ?*)

Whenever you ask a stranger a question, you sound more polite (and therefore are more likely to get more or better assistance) if you preface the question with the following:

> **Entschuldigen Sie, bitte** . . . (ênt-*shool*-di-gen zee, *bi*-te . . .)
> (*Excuse me, please . . .*)

After you flag down a stranger and start your question with **Entschuldigen Sie, bitte, wo ist . . .,** finish the question by supplying the name of the location you're looking for, which may include one of the following:

- **der Bahnhof** (dêr *bahn*-hohf) (*train station*)
- **die U-Bahnstation** (dee *ooh*-bahn-shtât-see-ohn) (*subway station*)
- **die Bank** (dee bânk) (*bank*)
- **die Bushaltestelle/die Straßenbahnhaltestelle** (dee *boos*-hâl-te-shtêl-e/ dee *shtrah*-sen-bahn-hâl-te-shtêl-e*) (*bus stop/streetcar or tram stop*)
- **das Café** (dâs kâf-*ey*) (*café*)
- **der Dom** (dêr dohm) (*cathedral*)
- **der Flughafen** (dêr *floohk*-hah-fen) (*airport*)
- **der Hafen** (dêr *hah*-fen) (*harbor*)
- **das Hotel** (dâs hotel [as in English]) (*hotel*)
- **das Kino** (dâs *kee*-noh) (*movie theater*)
- **die Kirche** (dee *kirH*-e) (*church*)
- **der Markt** (dêr mârkt) (*market*)
- **das Museum** (dâs moo-*zey*-oom) (*museum*)
- **der Park** (dêr pârk) (*park*)
- **der Platz** (dêr plâtz) (*[town] square*)
- **die Post** (dee post) (*post office*)
- **das Restaurant** (dâs rês-tuh-*ron*) (*restaurant*)
- **der Taxistand** (dêr *tâx*-ee-shtânt) (*taxi stand*)
- **das Theater** (dâs tey-*ah*-ter) (*theater*)

Of course, if you're in a town of any size at all, a general question like "Where is the bus stop?" or "Where is the bank?" may be met with a quizzical look. After all, multiple bus stops and banks may be in close proximity. To make your questions as specific as possible, include the proper name of the bus stop, theater, church, or other location in your question. Here are some examples:

> **Wo ist die Bushaltestelle Karlsplatz?** (voh ist dee *boos*-hâl-te-shtêl-e *kârlz*-plâts?) (*Where is the bus stop Karlsplatz?*)

> **Wo ist das Staatstheater?** (voh ist dâs *shtâts*-tey-ah-ter?) (*Where is the Staatstheater?*)

> **Wo ist der Marktplatz?** (voh ist dêr *mârkt*-plâts?) (*Where is the open-air market?*)

Book II

Speaking German on the Go

If you don't know the proper name of your destination, you can ask for directions to the nearest of whatever you're looking for. You simply insert the word **nächste** (*naiH*-ste) (*nearest*) after the article of the location in question. Check out the following questions that use **nächste**:

> **Wo ist der nächste Park?** (voh ist dêr *naiH*-ste pârk?) (*Where is the nearest park?*)

> **Wo ist die nächste Bank?** (voh ist dee *naiH*-ste bânk?) (*Where is the nearest bank?*)

> **Wo ist das nächste Hotel?** (voh ist dâs *naiH*-ste hotel?) (*Where is the nearest hotel?*)

When it comes to getting around and asking for directions, the following expressions help you to say that you don't know your way around:

> **Ich bin Tourist.** (iH bin toor-*ist.*) (*I'm a tourist.*)

> **Ich bin nicht von hier.** (iH bin niHt fon heer.) (*I'm not from here.*)

With the following helpful verb, you can indicate that you don't know your way around a place: **auskennen** (*ous*-kên-en) (*to know one's way around*). Here's an expression using this verb that you may want to memorize:

> **Ich kenne mich hier nicht aus.** (iH *kên*-e miH heer niHt *ous.*) (*I don't know my way around here.*)

The verb **auskennen** belongs to a group of verbs called *separable verbs.* They all have a prefix that separates from the main part of the verb and gets shoved to the end of the sentence. The prefix of the verb **auskennen** is **aus-**. Notice how this prefix appears at the very end of the sentence in the preceding example. For more information on separable verbs, turn to Book III, Chapter 8.

Asking how far something is:
Ist es weit von hier?

Before you decide whether you want to walk to your destination or take public transportation, you need to find out how far away your destination is. You have a few ways to discover how distant a location is, and the key word to know is **weit** (vayt) (*far*):

> **Ist . . . weit entfernt/weit von hier?** (ist . . . vayt ênt-*fêrnt*/vayt fon heer?) (*Is . . . far away/far from here?*)

Just fill in the name of the location you're asking about. So, for example, if you're headed to the art museum, you may ask someone one of the following:

> **Ist das Kunstmuseum weit entfernt?** (ist dâs *koonst*-moo-*zey*-oom vayt ênt-*fêrnt?*) (*Is the art museum far [away]?*)

> **Ist das Kunstmuseum weit von hier?** (ist dâs *koonst*-moo-*zey*-oom vayt fon heer?) (*Is the art museum far from here?*)

Hopefully, you get the answer

> **Nein, das Kunstmuseum ist nicht weit von hier.** (nayn, dâs *koonst*-moo-*zey*-oom ist niHt vayt fon heer.) (*No, the art museum isn't far from here.*)

If you want to know specifically how far away a location is, you can use this question:

> **Wie weit ist . . . von hier?** (vee vayt ist . . . fon heer?) (*How far is . . . from here?*)

You may also approach the issue the other way around and find out how close something is by using the word **nah** (nah) (*near*). You usually find the word **nah** in the following combination: **in der Nähe** (in dêr *nai*-he) (*nearby*). You can ask the question

> **Ist . . . in der Nähe?** (ist . . . in dêr *nai*-he?) (*Is . . . nearby?*)

Getting more specific directions

The words **hier** (heer) (*here*) and **dort** (dort) (*there*) may be small words, but they play an important part in communicating directions. How? Well, like their English equivalents, they make directions just a little more concrete.

Look at the following sample sentences to see how **hier** and **dort** work in explaining directions:

Das Museum ist nicht weit von hier. (dâs moo-*zey*-oom ist niHt vayt fon heer.) (*The museum isn't far from here.*)

Das Hotel ist dort, neben dem Café. (dâs hotel [as in English] ist dort, *ney*-ben deym café [as in English].) (*The hotel is there, next to the café.*)

Some key words that answer the question "where?" more specifically are easier to remember when you recognize them in commonly used word combinations. Try these combos on for size:

- ✔ **hier vorne** (heer *forn*-e) (*here in front*)
- ✔ **dort drüben** (dort *drue*-ben) (*over there*)
- ✔ **ziemlich weit/sehr weit** (*tseem*-leeH vayt/zeyr vayt) (*quite far/very far*)
- ✔ **gleich um die Ecke** (glayH oom dee *êk*-e) (*just around the corner*)
- ✔ **direkt gegenüber** (di-*rêkt* gey-gen-*ue*-ber) (*directly opposite*)

Check out the following sentences that use some of the preceding expressions:

Der Hauptbahnhof ist gleich um die Ecke. (dêr *houpt*-bahn-hohf ist glayH oom dee *êk*-e.) (*The main train station is just around the corner.*)

Die U-Bahnstation ist dort drüben. (dee *ooh*-bahn-shtât-see-ohn ist dort *drue*-ben.) (*The subway station is over there.*)

Asking How to Get from One Place to Another

When you want to ask "How do I get there?" you use the verb **kommen** (*kom*-en), which means both "to come" and, when used with a preposition, "to get to." Refer to Book I, Chapter 3 for the conjugation of **kommen**.

The basic form of the question "How do I get there?" is

Wie komme ich. . . ? (vee *kom*-e iH. . . ?) (*How do I get. . . ?*)

To finish the rest of the sentence, you need to use a preposition to help you say "to the train station" or "to the city center." At this point, you need to shift into high gear — that is, high grammar gear.

In German, you don't just deal with one preposition as you do in English, in which you would simply use *to* (*How do I get to. . . ?*). In fact, you may need to use any of a number of prepositions, all of which can mean "to." The most commonly used "to" prepositions in German are the following:

- ✔ **in** (in)
- ✔ **nach** (nahH)
- ✔ **zu** (tsooh)

The following sections discuss each of these prepositions and explain how to use them.

Asking how to get to a location

You use the preposition **in** (in) when you want to get to or into a certain location, such as the city center, the zoo, or the mountains. For example:

> **Wie komme ich in die Innenstadt?** (vee *kom*-e iH in dee *in*-ên-shtât?) (*How do I get to the center of the city?*)

When you use the preposition **in** this way, the article that comes after it goes into the accusative case, meaning that some of the articles change form slightly. Book IV, Chapter 2 has a complete explanation of the accusative case, but here's a quick reminder of how the articles change (or don't change):

- ✔ **der** (dêr) becomes **den** (deyn) (masculine)
- ✔ **die** (dee) stays **die** (feminine)
- ✔ **das** (dâs) stays **das** (neuter)
- ✔ **die** (dee) stays **die** (plural)

For example, the article of a feminine noun like **die City** (dee *si*-tee) (*city center*) stays the same:

> **Wie komme ich in die City?** (vee *kom*-e iH in dee *si*-tee?) (*How do I get to the city center?*)

The article of a masculine noun like **der Zoo** (dêr tsoh) (*zoo*) changes like this:

> **Wie kommen wir zum Zoo?** (vee *kom*-en veer tsoohm tsoh?) (*How do we get to the zoo?*)

The article of a plural noun like **die Berge** (dee *bêr*-ge) (*mountains*) stays the same:

> **Wie komme ich in die Berge?** (vee *kom*-e iH in dee *bêr*-ge?) (*How do I get to the mountains?*)

The article of a neuter noun like **das Zentrum** (dâs *tsên*-troom) (*center*) stays the same, but when the preposition **in** is used with neuter nouns in the accusative case, the preposition and article contract to form the word **ins** (ins):

> **in** + **das** = **ins**

This contraction is almost always used, giving you phrases like

> **Wie komme ich ins Zentrum/ins Museum/ins Cafe?** (vee *kom*-e iH ins *tsên*-troom/ins mooh-*zey*-oom/ins kâf-*ey*?) (*How do I get to the city center/ museum/café?*)

Book II

Speaking German on the Go

Asking how to get to a city or country

Luckily, the preposition **nach** (nahH) comes into play only in one specific context — when you want to get to a city or country:

> **Wie komme ich nach Köln?** (vee *kom*-e iH nahH kerln?) (*How do I get to Cologne?*)

You have no troublesome articles to bother with when using **nach** because city names and most country names don't need articles.

Asking how to get to a specific building

If you're asking how to get to a place such as a train station or a museum, the preposition **zu** (tsooh) is a pretty safe bet. However, it may go through a slight spelling change when used in a sentence. For example:

> **Wie kommen wir zum Flughafen/zum Theater/zum Restaurant/zum Café?** (vee *kom*-en veer tsoom *floohk-hâ*-fen/tsoom tey-*ah*-ter/tsoom rês-tuh-*ron*/tsoom kâf-*ey*?) (*How do we get to the airport/theater/ restaurant/café?*)

> **Wie komme ich zur Deutschen Bank/zur Apotheke?** (vee *kom*-e iH tsoor *doych*-en bânk/tsoor âp-oh-*teyk*-e?) (*How do I get to the German bank/ pharmacy?*)

The preposition **zu** requires the dative case. (See Book IV, Chapter 2 for a complete explanation of the dative case.) As a result, the articles used right after **zu** change in the following ways:

- ✔ **der** (dêr) becomes **dem** (deym) (masculine)
- ✔ **die** (dee) becomes **der** (dêr) (feminine)
- ✔ **das** (dâs) becomes **dem** (deym) (neuter)
- ✔ **die** (dee) becomes **den** (deyn) (plural)

When **zu** is used with masculine nouns, like **der Bahnhof,** and neuter nouns, like **das Hotel,** the preposition and article contract to form the word **zum.** In other words, **zu + dem = zum.** The following two examples both use **zum:**

> **Wie komme ich zum Bahnhof?** (vee *kom*-e iH tsoom *bahn*-hohf?) (*How do I get to the train station?*)

> **Wie komme ich zum Hotel Kempinski?** (vee *kom*-e iH tsoom hotel kêm-*pin*-skee?) (*How do I get to Hotel Kempinski?*)

Similarly, take a look at how **zu** combines with a feminine noun like **die Post** (dee post) (*post office*) in its dative form, **der Post: zu + der = zur.** Here's an example:

> **Wie komme ich zur Post/zur Bäckerei/zur Kirche?** (vee *kom*-e iH tsoor post/tsoor bêk-er-*ay*/tsoor *kirH*-e?) (*How do I get to the post office/bakery/church?*)

To use plural nouns like **die Souvenirläden** (dee zoo-ven-*eer*-lê-den) (*souvenir shops*) together with **zu,** you simply change the article to **den,** like this:

> **Wie kommen wir zu den Souvenirläden/zu den Restaurants/zu den Cafés?** (vee *kom*-en veer tsooh deyn zoo-ven-*eer*-lê-den/tsooh deyn rês-toh-*rons*/kâf-*eyz*?) (*How do we get to the souvenir shops/restaurants/cafés?*)

Describing Where Something Is Located

After you ask for directions, you have to be ready to understand the answers you may receive. After all, if you don't understand how a language describes how to get from one place to another, you'll have a hard time following directions. In this section, you can put an end to your helplessness by mastering the few simple words you need to understand (and ask about) the various directions in German. You also get up to speed on common prepositions used to describe locations, and you get a handle on how to follow instructions on turning left or right and how to understand compass points.

Locating one place in relation to another

People commonly express the location of a place in relation to a well-known landmark or location. You can use quite a few prepositions to describe locations in this way. Luckily, all the prepositions used in this context use the dative case, so any articles after the preposition behave just as they do when used with **zu,** as described in the preceding section. In addition, the preposition **bei** (bay) (*near/next to*) and the article **dem** almost always contract like this: **bei + dem = beim** (baym).

Table 1-1 shows you some common prepositions that are used to express the location of one thing in relation to another.

Book II

Speaking German on the Go

Table 1-1	Prepositions That Express Locations		
Preposition	*Pronunciation*	*Meaning*	*Example*
an	ân	*at*	**an der Ecke** (ân dêr *êk*-e) (*at the corner*)
auf	ouf	*on*	**auf der Museumsinsel** (ouf dêr moo-*zey*-ooms-in-sel) (*on the Museum Island*)
bei	bay	*near/next to*	**beim Bahnhof** (baym *bahn*-hohf) (*near the train station*)
hinter	*hin*-ter	*behind*	**hinter der Kirche** (*hin*-ter dêr *kirH*-e) (*behind the church*)
neben	*ney*-ben	*next to*	**neben der Bank** (*ney*-ben dêr bânk) (*next to the bank*)
vor	fohr	*in front of*	**vor der Post** (fohr dêr post) (*in front of the post office*)
zwischen	*tsvi*-shen	*between*	**zwischen dem Theater und der Bank** (*tsvish*-en deym *tey-ah*-ter oont dêr bânk) (*between the theater and the bank*)

Talkin' the Talk

Mike is on a business trip to **München** (*muen*-Hen) (*Munich*), a city he hasn't visited before. He wants to take a cab to get to a friend's house, but he needs some help finding the nearest taxi stand. So he approaches a woman on the street. (Track 21)

Mike: **Entschuldigen Sie, bitte, wo ist der nächste Taxistand?**
ênt-*shool*-di-gen zee, *bi*-te, voh ist dêr *naiH*-ste *tâx*-ee-shtant?
Excuse me, where is the nearest taxi stand?

Frau: **In der Sonnenstraße.**
in dêr *zon*-en-shtrah-se.
On Sonnen Street.

Mike: **Ich kenne mich in München leider nicht aus. Wie komme ich zur Sonnenstraße?**
iH *kên*-e miH in *muen*-Hen *lay*-der niHt ous. vee *kom*-e iH tsoor *zon*-en-shtrah-se?
Unfortunately, I don't know my way around Munich. How do I get to Sonnen Street?

Frau: **Sehen Sie die Kirche dort drüben? Hinter der Kirche ist der Sendlinger-Tor-Platz und direkt gegenüber ist der Taxistand.**
zey-en zee dee *kirH*-e dort *drue*-ben? *hin*-ter dêr *kirH*-e ist dêr zênd-leeng-er-*tohr*-plâts oont *di*-rêkt gey-gen-*ue*-ber ist dêr *tâx*-ee-shtânt.
Do you see the church over there? Behind the church is Sendlinger-Tor Square and directly opposite is the taxi stand.

Mike: **Vielen Dank!**
fee-len dânk!
Thank you very much!

Words to Know

Wo ist...?	voh ist...?	Where is...?
nächste	<u>naiH</u>-ste	nearest
sich auskennen	ziH <u>ous</u>-kên-en	to know one's way around
weit	vayt	far
in der Nähe	in dêr <u>nai</u>-he	nearby
hinter	<u>hin</u>-ter	behind
vor	fohr	in front of
neben	<u>ney</u>-ben	next to
an	ân	at

Going left, right, straight ahead: Links, rechts, geradeaus

Unless you tackle the words for the various directions such as left, right, or straight ahead, you may find yourself trying to find the town hall by tugging at some stranger's sleeve and chanting **Rathaus** (*rât*-hous) over and over, hoping he'll lead you to the right building.

To avoid that embarrassing situation, commit the following directional words to memory:

- **links** (links) (*left*)
- **rechts** (rêHts) (*right*)
- **geradeaus** (ge-rah-de-*ous*) (*straight ahead*)

If you want to express that something is located to the left or right of something else, you add the preposition **von** (fon) (*of*), making the following:

- **links von** (links fon) (*to the left of*)
- **rechts von** (rêHts fon) (*to the right of*)

Check out these examples that use **von** and a defining position:

> **Der Markt ist links von der Kirche.** (dêr mârkt ist links fon dêr *kirH*-e.) (*The market is to the left of the church.*)

> **Die U-Bahnstation ist rechts vom Theater.** (dee *ooh*-bahn-shtât-see-ohn ist rêHts fom tey-*ah*-ter.) (*The subway station is to the right of the theater.*)

When the preposition **von** combines with **dem** (deym), it usually contracts like this: **von** + **dem** = **vom** (fom). (**Dem** is the dative form of the masculine definite article **der** and the neuter definite article **das.** Book IV, Chapter 2 gives you more info on the dative case.)

You also may hear the word for side, **die Seite** (dee *zay*-te), in connection with directions. **Seite** can help directions be more specific. For example:

> **Das Museum ist auf der linken Seite.** (dâs moo-*zey*-oom ist ouf dêr *lin*-ken *zay*-te.) (*The museum is on the left side.*)

> **Die Bank ist auf der rechten Seite.** (dee bânk ist ouf dêr *rêHt*-en *zay*-te.) (*The bank is on the right side.*)

Using compass points

Instead of using left, right, or straight ahead, some folks give directions by using the points of the compass (also called *cardinal points*). These points are

- **der Norden** (dêr *nor*-den) (*the north*)
- **der Süden** (dêr *zue*-den) (*the south*)
- **der Osten** (dêr *os*-ten) (*the east*)
- **der Westen** (dêr *wês*-ten) (*the west*)

If someone uses cardinal points to tell you the specific location of a place, you may hear something like

> **Der Hafen liegt im Norden/Süden/Osten/Westen.** (dêr *hah*-fen leekt im *nor*-den/*zue*-den/*os*-ten/*vês*-ten.) (*The harbor lies [is] in the north/south/east/west.*)

To describe a location, for example, in the north, you use the preposition **in** with a definite article in the dative case. When the definite article is masculine (**der**) or neuter (**das**), it changes to **dem** (deym), and the preposition **in** usually contracts to **im** like this: **in** + **dem** = **im** (im).

Understanding Where to Go

You ask where something is located, and a kind stranger rattles off some details that include landmarks and street names you're unfamiliar with. One way to make sure you understand is to repeat what you've heard, especially the information about when to turn left or right and when to go straight ahead. If that doesn't work, you can always approach another person and ask where to go.

Book II

Speaking German on the Go

Pointing out the first, second, or third street

When you ask for directions, you may get the answer that you should take a specific street — the second street on the left or the first street on the right, for example. *One, two, three, four,* and similar numbers are referred to as *cardinal numbers,* while numbers like *first, second, third,* and *fourth* are called *ordinal numbers.* Ordinal numbers indicate the specific order of something. For example, to answer the question "Which house?" you use an ordinal number to say, "The fifth house on the left."

In German, you form ordinal numbers by adding the suffix **-te** to the cardinal numbers for numbers between 1 and 19 — with the following exceptions:

- **eins** (ayns) (*one*)/**erste** (êrs-te) (*first*)
- **drei** (dray) (*three*)/**dritte** (drit-e) (*third*)
- **sieben** (*zee*-ben) (*seven*)/**siebte** (*zeep*-te) (*seventh*)
- **acht** (âHt) (*eight*)/**achte** (âHt-e) (*eighth*)

Ordinals 20 and above all add the suffix **-ste** to the cardinal number. Table 1-2 shows how to form the ordinal numbers 1 through 10, including one example of an ordinal number formed with a "-teen" number and another example for an ordinal above 20.

Table 1-2	Sample Cardinal and Ordinal Numbers
Cardinal Number	*Ordinal Number*
eins (ayns) (*one*)	**der/die/das erste** (êrs-te) (*first*)
zwei (tsvay) (*two*)	**zweite** (*tsvay*-te) (*second*)
drei (dray) (*three*)	**dritte** (*drit*-e) (*third*)
vier (feer) (*four*)	**vierte** (*feer*-te) (*fourth*)
fünf (fuenf) (*five*)	**fünfte** (*fuenf*-te) (*fifth*)
sechs (zêks) (*six*)	**sechste** (*zêks*-te) (*sixth*)
sieben (*zeeb*-en) (*seven*)	**siebte** (*zeep*-te) (*seventh*)
acht (âHt) (*eight*)	**achte** (*âHt*-e) (*eighth*)
neun (noyn) (*nine*)	**neunte** (*noyn*-te) (*ninth*)
zehn (tseyn) (*ten*)	**zehnte** (*tseyn*-te) (*tenth*)
siebzehn (*zeep*-tseyn) (*seventeen*)	**siebzehnte** (*zeep*-tseyn-te) (*seventeenth*)
vierzig (*fir*-tsiH) (*forty*)	**vierzigste** (*fir*-tsiH-ste) (*fortieth*)

See Book I, Chapter 2 for more information about cardinal and ordinal numbers.

Because they're used like adjectives, the ordinal numbers take the gender and case of the noun they refer to. Table 1-3 shows you how the adjective **erste** and the article that comes before it changes in each case.

Table 1-3	Breaking Down an Ordinal Number by Case and Gender: Erste (êrs-te) (*first*)			
Noun's Gender	*Nominative*	*Genitive*	*Dative*	*Accusative*
Masculine (**der**)	der erste	des ersten	dem ersten	den ersten
Feminine (**die**)	die erste	der ersten	der ersten	die erste
Neuter (**das**)	das erste	des ersten	dem ersten	das erste
Plural (**die**)	die ersten	der ersten	den ersten	die ersten

Following directions: Take this street

When you give or receive directions, you need to be familiar with the verbs **gehen** (*gey*-en) (*to go*) and **nehmen** (*ney*-men) (*to take*) in the imperative. (For the moment, just focus on the word order. You find out more about imperative sentences — those that give commands — in Book III, Chapter 7.) With the imperative, the verb goes at the beginning of the sentence. For example:

> **Nehmen Sie die zweite Straße links.** (*ney*-men zee dee *tsvay*-te *shtrah*-se links.) (*Take the second street on the left.*)

> **Gehen Sie die erste Straße rechts.** (*gey*-en zee dee *êrs*-te *shtrah*-se rêHts.) (*Go down the first street on the right.*)

If you simply have to go straight ahead, you may hear these instructions:

> **Gehen Sie immer geradeaus.** (*gey*-en zee *im*-er ge-rah-de-*ous*.) (*Go straight ahead.*)

If you're looking for a specific building, you may hear something like this:

> **Es ist das dritte Haus auf der linken Seite.** (ês ist dâs *drit*-e house [as in English] ouf dêr *lin*-ken *zay*-te.) (*It is the third house on the left side.*)

Book II

Speaking German on the Go

Talkin' the Talk

 Erika is in town on business and wants to meet an old friend who also happens to be in town on business. She has the address of the hotel where her friend is staying, but she isn't sure where the street is located, so she asks for help. (Track 22)

Erika: **Entschuldigung?**
ênt-*shool*-di-goong?
Excuse me?

Mann: **Ja, bitte?**
yah, *bi*-te?
Yes, please?

Erika : **Wie komme ich zur Beethovenstraße?**
vee *kom*-e iH tsoor *bey*-toh-fên-shtrah-se?
How do I get to Beethoven Street?

Mann: **Nehmen Sie die U-Bahn am Opernplatz.**
ney-men zee dee *ooh*-bahn âm *oh*-pêrn-plâts.
You have to take the subway at Opera Square.

Erika: **Und wo ist der Opernplatz?**
oont voh ist dêr *oh*-pêrn-plâts?
And where is Opera Square?

Mann:	**Gehen Sie die Wodanstraße geradeaus. Dann gehen Sie links in die Reuterstraße. Rechts liegt die Post und direkt gegenüber ist der Opernplatz.**
	gey-en zee dee *voh*-dahn-shtrah-se ge-rah-de-*ous*. dân *gey*-en zee links in dee *roy*-ter-shtrah-se. rêHts leekt dee post oont dee-*rêkt gey*-gen-*ue*-ber ist dêr *oh*-pêrn-plâts.
	Go straight down Wodan Street. Then go left onto Reuter Street. On the right you see the post office and directly opposite is Opera Square.
Erika:	**Und welche U-Bahn nehme ich?**
	oont vêlH-e *ooh*-bahn *ney*-me iH?
	And which subway do I take?
Mann:	**Die U5 bis zur Station Beethovenstraße.**
	dee ooh fuenf bis tsoor *shtat*-tsee-ohn *bey*-toh-fên-shtrah-se.
	Take the subway 5 to the stop Beethoven Street.
Erika:	**Vielen Dank!**
	fee-len dânk!
	Thank you very much!

Words to Know

links	links	left
rechts	rêHts	right
Wo ist. . .?	voh ist. . .?	Where is. . .?
Nehmen Sie . . .	*ney*-men zee . . .	Take . . .
Gehen Sie . . .	*gey*-en zee . . .	Go . . .
die U-Bahn	dee *ooh*-bahn	subway

Traveling by Car — das Auto — or Other Vehicle

In English, whether you're going by car or on foot doesn't make much difference; distance aside, you're still going somewhere. However, the German verb **gehen** (*gey*-en) (*to go*) isn't that flexible. You may "go" on foot, which would require **zu Fuß gehen** (tsooh foohs *gey*-en). But if you take the car, the bus, a bicycle, or another form of transportation, you're "driving," which takes **fahren** (*fahr*-en) — not **gehen** — even if you aren't behind the wheel.

When using **fahren** in a sentence, you need three things: the word for the type of vehicle in which you're traveling, the preposition **mit** (mit) (*with*), and the dative version of the vehicle's article. Here's an example of how you use the verb **fahren** in a sentence to say that you're taking a specific type of transportation:

> **Ich fahre mit dem Auto/mit dem Bus/mit dem Rad.** (iH *fahr*-e mit deym *ou*-toh/mit deym boos/mit deym râd.) (*I'm going by car/by bus/by bicycle.* Literally: *I'm driving with the car/with the bus/with the bicycle.*)

You use the verb **fahren** whether you're describing turns you or someone else makes on a bike, in a pair of inline skates, or on a snowboard. You simply say

> **Fahren Sie links/rechts.** (*fahr*-en zee links/rêHts.) (*Go left/right.* Literally: *Drive left/right.*)

If you get lost driving around, always remember to pull this expression from your memory:

> **Ich habe mich verfahren. Ich suche . . .** (iH *hah*-be miH fêr-*fahr*-en. iH *zoohH*-e . . .) (*I've lost my way. I'm looking for . . .*)

See Book II, Chapter 5 for more information on words you need for getting around in a car or other vehicle.

Talkin' the Talk

Paula has rented a car to go to Frankfurt for a day trip. She's on her way to Bockenheim, a district of Frankfurt, and she stops at a gas station to ask the pump attendant (**Tankwart**) for directions.

Paula:	**Entschuldigen Sie, wie komme ich nach Bockenheim?** ênt-*shool*-di-gên zee, vee *kom*-e iH nahH *bok*-en-haym? *Excuse me, how do I get to Bockenheim?*
Tankwart:	**Nehmen Sie die Ausfahrt Frankfurt-Messe. Das sind ungefähr vier Kilometer von hier.** *ney*-men zee dee *ous*-fahrt *frânk*-foort *mês*-e. Dâs zint *oon*-ge-fair feer ki-lo-*mey*-ter fon heer. *Take the exit Frankfurt-Messe. That is approximately 4 kilometers from here.*
Paula:	**Alles klar! Danke.** *âl*-es klahr! *dân*-ke. *Okay! Thank you.*

Paula makes it to Bockenheim but then seems to have lost her way. She stops her car and asks a policeman (**Polizei**) for directions.

Paula:	**Entschuldigen Sie, ich habe mich verfahren. Ich suche den Hessenplatz.** ênt-*shool*-di-gên zee, iH *hah*-be miH fêr-*fahr*-en. iH *zoohH*-e deyn *hês*-ên-plâts. *Excuse me, I've lost my way. I'm looking for Hessen Square.*
Polizei:	**An der nächsten Kreuzung fahren Sie rechts. Dann fahren Sie geradeaus, ungefähr einen Kilometer. Der Hessenplatz liegt auf der linken Seite.** ân dêr *naiH*-sten *kroy*-tsoong *fahr*-en zee rêHts. dân *fahr*-en zee ge-rah-de-*ous*, *oon*-ge-fair *ayn*-en ki-lo-*mey*-ter. dêr *hês*-en-plâts leekt ouf dêr *lin*-ken *zay*-te. *Go left at the next intersection. Then go straight on, approximately one kilometer. Hessen Square is on the left side.*
Paula:	**Vielen Dank!** *fee*-len dânk! *Thank you very much!*

Chapter 2

Going Out on the Town

. . . .

In This Chapter

▶ Doing some sightseeing

▶ Going to the movies, the museum, a concert, or a party

▶ Talking about an event you attend

. . . .

You find a surprisingly large number of cultural venues in Germany and most of the rest of Europe. Not only do the arts receive state and federal funds to support their efforts, but Europeans also have a long-standing appreciation of their cultural assets. So if you're interested in visiting a museum and you happen to be in Berlin, you have more than 170 to choose from! **Das Pergamonmuseum** (dâs *pêr*-gâ-mon-moo-*sey*-oom) (*Pergamon Museum*) is a great place to start, with its priceless world treasures that include ancient Greek, Roman, and Etruscan artifacts.

To get a taste of German culture, check the media to find out what's going on. Along with local websites, the local newspapers and other media offer weekly guides of local events by publishing a **Veranstaltungskalender** (fêr-*ân*-shtâl-toongs-kâ-*len*-der) (*calendar of events*).

However you decide to spend your time, you're sure to enjoy it more when you make some careful plans beforehand. This chapter helps you decide what you want to see and do when you're visiting a new place and how to do it.

Taking in the Sights

When you're deciding what you want to do and see, you may want to take in the sights and activities that are unique to that place. Europe is steeped in a rich culture and lifestyle that ranges from cafés to classical music, from museums to mountain climbing, and most everything in between. When you're planning your day, you may find it best to begin with the most ambitious activities, such as hiking around the ramparts of a **Burg** (boork) (*castle*) perched atop the city of Salzburg, and allow for some down time in the afternoon before attending a **Konzert** (kon-*tsērt*) (*concert*) in the evening.

In case you're not the planning type, you can take a **Stadtrundfahrt** (*shtāt*-roond-fahrt) (*city tour*) and let the experts show you the highlights of the city. Many of the same organizations that offer city tours can help you book an interesting **Tagesausflug** (dēr *tahg*-es-ous-floohk) (*day trip*) to any number of outlying areas around the city you're visiting.

This section gives you useful terms and expressions for talking about various sightseeing options. You may want to join a guided tour through a castle or go on a city bicycle tour with a small group or set out on your own to explore the sights.

Deciding what to see

When you travel, you first have to figure out what sorts of places to see and then decide how to get to them in the amount of time you have. If you're doing a lot of traveling, you may consider mixing a morning **Stadtrundfahrt** (*shtāt*-roond-fahrt) (*city tour*) with some other type of afternoon activity, such as **Menschen beobachten** (*mēn*-shēn be-*oh*-bāHt-en) (*people watching*) from the vantage point of a **Café** (kāf-*ey*) (*café*), or taking a **Spaziergang** (shpāts-*eer*-gāng) (*walk/stroll*) through a city park to see how the natives spend their free time.

Some of the sights you find in and around cities include the following:

- **der botanische Garten** (dēr boh-*tān*-ish-e *gār*-ten) (*botanical garden*)
- **die Burg** (dee boork) (*castle*) (usually on a hill)
- **das Denkmal** (dās *dēnk*-māl) (*monument*)
- **die Galerie** (dee gāl-ēr-*ee*) (*gallery*)
- **die Kirche** (dee *kirH*-e) (*church*)
- **der Markt** (dēr mārkt) (*market*)
- **das Monument** (dās mon-oo-*mēnt*) (*monument*)
- **das Museum** (dās moo-*sey*-oom) (*museum*)
- **der Palast** (dēr pā-*lāst*) (*palace*)
- **der Park** (dēr park [as in English]) (*park*)

- **der Platz** (dêr plâts) (*square*)

- **das Rathaus** (dâs *rât*-hous) (*town hall*)

- **das Schloss** (dâs shlos) (*castle*)

- **das Stadion** (dâs *shtah*-dee-on) (*stadium*)

- **die Statue** (dee *shtât*-oo-e) (*statue*)

- **das Theater** (dâs tey-*ah*-ter) (*theater*)

- **der Tierpark** (dêr *teer*-park [as in English]) (*zoo*)

When you're deciding what to see and do, you may notice that place names may or may not have the identifying word for that particular sight. It's easy to decipher what sort of place the **Olympiastadion** (oh-*lerm*-pee-â-*shtah*-dee-on) (*Olympic stadium*) is when you break down the two words. Other places may not be so obvious because they don't contain a word that describes what that place is. Take, for example, **der Friedensengel** (dêr *freed*-enz-êng-el) (*angel of peace*), which is found in both Berlin and Munich. The term is a combination of the two words, **Frieden** (*freed*-en) (*peace/freedom*) and **Engel** (*êng*-el) (*angel*), and it describes a monument with a golden angel mounted on a pedestal. When you're on the street asking someone where to find such a location, the natives are much more likely to understand you when you use the German term for that place, even if your pronunciation isn't perfect.

Try asking about places like this:

> **Entschuldigen Sie, bitte. Wo ist der Friedensengel?** (ent-*shool*-di-gen zee, *bi*-te. voh ist dêr *freed*-enz-êng-el?) (*Excuse me, please. Where is the angel of peace?*)

> **Entschuldigen Sie, bitte. Ist das der Reichstag?** (ent-*shool*-di-gen zee, *bi*-te. ist dâs dêr *reyHs*-tahk?) (*Excuse me, please. Is that the German parliament building?*)

Taking a sightseeing tour

German-speaking cities offer guided tours of all kinds, and you can often choose a tour in English if you don't feel confident listening to German for several hours. You may also be interested in getting outside of the bustling city atmosphere by booking a day excursion to an outlying tourist destination like the castle **Neuschwanstein** (noy-*shvân*-shtayn), which inspired Disneyland's fantasy castle. Your choices are practically boundless, so you only have to decide what suits you. If you don't like being in a group, ask about hiring a private guide.

Book II

Speaking German on the Go

Here are some terms for sightseeing tours you may encounter:

- **die City-Sightseeing** (dee city sightseeing [as in English]) (*city sightseeing*)

- **die Fahrradtour** (dee *fahr*-râd-toor) (*bicycle tour*)

- **die Gruppenführung** (dee *groop*-en-fuer-oong) (*group tour*)

- **die Hafenrundfahrt** (dee *hah*-fên-roond-fahrt) (*harbor boat tour*)

- **die Schiffsrundfahrt** (dee *shifs*-roond-fahrt) (*boat tour*)

- **die Stadtführung** (dee *shtât*-fuer-oong) (*city tour*)

- **die Stadtrundfahrt** (dee *shtât*-roond-fahrt) (*city tour*)

- **die Stadttour** (dee *shtât*-tour) (*city tour*)

- **der Tagesausflug** (dêr *tahg*-es-ous-floohk) (*day trip*)

- **Hamburg by Night** (Hamburg by Night [as in English]) (*Hamburg by night;* a tour of some of the popular night spots in the lively St. Pauli quarter of Hamburg; other cities offer the same)

When you're trying to decide what sort of sightseeing tour to take, you may want to know some specific information about the tour. Here are some questions you may find useful:

Wie lange dauert die Führung? (vee *lâng*-e *dou*-êrt dee *fuer*-oong?) (*How long does the tour last?*)

Wo ist der Treffpunkt? (voh ist dêr *trêf*-poonkt?) (*Where is the meeting point?*)

Ist das Mittagessen im Preis enthalten? (ist dâs *mi*-tahk-ês-en im prays ênt-*hâlt*-en?) (*Is lunch included in the price?*)

Gibt es eine Tour auf Englisch? (gipt ês *ayn*-e tour [as in English] ouf *êng*-lish?) (*Is there a tour in English?*)

Making plans

Sometimes you may want to go out by yourself, and other times you may want company. If you're in the mood for companionship and want to toss around ideas with someone about what to do, you can ask

Was wollen wir unternehmen? (vâs *vol*-en veer oon-ter-*ney*-men?) (*What do we want to do?*)

Use the following phrases if you want to find out about somebody's plans or if you want to know whether somebody is available:

Haben Sie (heute Abend) etwas vor? (*hah*-ben zee [*hoy*-te *ah*-bênt] *êt*-vâs fohr?) (*Do you have anything planned [for this evening]?*)

Haben Sie (heute Abend) Zeit? (*hah*-ben zee [*hoy*-te *ah*-bênt] tsayt) (*Do you have time this evening?*)

Hast du (morgen Vormittag) etwas vor? (hâst dooh [*mor*-gen *fohr*-mi-tahk] *êt*-vâs fohr?) (*Do you have anything planned [for tomorrow morning]?*)

Use the formal **Sie** (zee) (*you*) when you don't know the person you're speaking with very well; use the informal **du** (dooh) (*you*) only when you're on mutually familiar terms. Notice that the form of the verb changes along with the **Sie** and **du** forms: **Haben Sie. . . ?** and **Hast du. . . ?**

Book II

Speaking German on the Go

Heading to the Movies

Watching films in a language you want to learn is a terrific way of getting your ear accustomed to how the language sounds. At the same time, you can get used to understanding many different speakers. All around the world, in fact, people learn English by watching American movies.

When you want to tell someone that you're interested in going to the movies, you can use the following phrases:

Ich möchte ins Kino gehen. (iH *merH*-te ins *kee*-noh *gey*-en.) (*I would like to go to the movies.*)

Ich möchte einen Film sehen. (iH *merH*-te *ayn*-en film *zey*-en.) (*I would like to see a film.*)

Going to the show

If you're searching for a movie to go to, your best bet is to check out local websites, weekly guides of local events, or newspaper listings. The listings usually tell you everything you need to know about **der Film** (dêr film) (*movie*) or **die Vorstellung** (dee *fohr*-stêl-oong) (*the show*): when and where the movie is playing, who the actors are, and whether the movie is in its original language. Here are some terms that may come in handy:

- ✔ **im Original** (im o-ri-gi-*nahl*) (*original*)
- ✔ **OmU**, which stands for **Original mit Untertiteln** (o-ri-gi-*nahl* mit *oon*-têr-ti-teln) (*original with subtitles*)
- ✔ **synchronisiert** (zyn-kro-nee-*zeert*) (*dubbed*)

If you don't have access to the Internet or other sources of information, the following phrases can help you ask for information about a movie:

In welchem Kino läuft. . . ? (in *vêlH*-êm *kee*-noh loyft. . . ?) (*In which movie theater is . . . showing?*)

Wo läuft. . . ? (voh loyft. . . ?) (*Where is . . . playing?*)

Um wie viel Uhr beginnt der Film? (oom *vee* feel oohr be-*gint* dêr film?) (*At what time does the movie start?*)

Läuft der Film im Original oder ist er synchronisiert? (loyft dêr film im o-ri-gi-*nahl oh*-der ist êr zyn-kro-nee-*zeert?*) (*Is the film shown in the original [language] or is it dubbed?*)

Most foreign films shown in Germany are dubbed into German, although some movie theaters, especially the small independents, specialize in showing foreign films in the original language with German subtitles — **Originalfassung mit deutschen Untertiteln** (o-ri-gi-*nahl*-fâs-oong mit *doy*-chen oon-têr-ti-teln) (*original version with German subtitles*). So if you're not into the mind-altering experience of listening to Hollywood actors assume strange voices and speak in tongues, keep an eye open for the undubbed version of the film or go see movies filmed in German exclusively. If you do go to the **Originalfassung mit Untertiteln** (o-ri-gi-*nahl*-*fâs*-oong mit *oon*-têr-ti-teln) (*original version with subtitles*) of an American movie, you have the advantage of reading the German as you listen to the English, and you may pick up some useful expressions. From the standpoint of language input, you may enjoy the ads and the trailers just as much as the actual movie, so be sure to get to the movie theater in time to catch these parts of the **Vorstellung** (*fohr*-shtêl-oong) (*show*).

Buying tickets

You can use the following phrase whenever you want to buy tickets, whether they're for the opera, the movies, or the museum:

Ich möchte (zwei) Karten/Eintrittskarten für . . . (iH *merH*-te [tsvay] *kâr*-ten/*ayn*-trits-*kâr*-ten fuer . . .) (*I would like [two] tickets/entrance tickets for . . .*)

After buying your tickets for a movie, you may get some information from the ticket seller, including the following:

Der Film hat schon begonnen. (dêr film hât shon be-*gon*-en.) (*The movie has already started.*)

Der . . . Uhr Film ist leider ausverkauft. (dêr . . . film ist *lay*-der ous-fêr-kouft.) (*The . . . o'clock movie is unfortunately sold out.*)

Wir haben noch Karten für den Film um . . . Uhr. (veer *hah*-ben noH *kâr*-ten fuer deyn film . . . oohr.) (*There are tickets left for the movie at . . . o'clock.*)

Note: German has two words that mean *ticket (for a show)* — **Karte** and **Eintrittskarte.** The difference is simply the fact that **Eintrittskarte** is a compound word that translates roughly as *entrance ticket.* You come across many such compound words in German, and they're frequently a combination of two words, in this case, **Eintritt(s)** and **Karte.**

Book II

Speaking German on the Go

Talkin' the Talk

Antje is talking to her friend Robert on the phone. Antje wants to go to the movies. After greeting her friend, Antje gets right to the point. (Go to www.dummies.com/go/germanaio to listen to this bonus track.)

Antje:	**Der neue Zeichentrickfilm von Pixar Studios soll super witzig sein.** dêr *noy*-e *tsayH*-en-trik-film fon *pix*-ahr *shtooh*-dee-ohs sol *sooh*-per *vits*-eeH zayn. *The new animated film from Pixar Studios is supposed to be incredibly funny.*
Robert:	**Wann willst du gehen?** vân vilst dooh *gey*-en? *When do you want to go?*
Antje:	**Morgen Abend habe ich Zeit.** *mor*-gen *ah*-bênt *hah*-be iH tsayt. *I have time tomorrow evening.*
Robert:	**Morgen passt mir auch. In welchem Kino läuft der Film?** *mor*-gen pâst meer ouH. in *vêlH*-êm *kee*-noh loyft dêr film? *Tomorrow works for me as well. In which movie theater is the film showing?*

Antje: **Im Hansatheater. Der Film beginnt um 20 Uhr.**
im *hân*-sâ-*tey-ah*-ter. dêr film be-*gint* oom *tsvân*-tsiH oohr.
In the Hansa Theater. The movie starts at 8 p.m.

Robert: **Gut, treffen wir uns um Viertel vor acht vor dem Kino.**
gooht, *trêf*-en veer oons oom *fir*-tel fohr âHt fohr deym *kee*-noh.
Okay. Let's meet at a quarter to eight in front of the movie theater.

Antje: **Prima. Bis morgen dann.**
pree-mâ. bis *mor*-gen dân.
Great. Until tomorrow then.

Words to Know

das Kino	dâs <u>kee</u>-no	movie theater
der Spielfilm	dêr <u>shpeel</u>-film	feature film
der Film	dêr film	film
die Vorstellung	dee <u>fohr</u>-shtêl-oong	show
die Karte	dee <u>kâr</u>-te	ticket
die Eintrittskarte	dee <u>ayn</u>-trits-<u>kâr</u>-te	entrance ticket
witzig	<u>vits</u>-eeH	funny
sehen	<u>zey</u>-en	to see
laufen	<u>louf</u>-en	to show

Going to the Museum

Germany has a long and rich museum tradition with many world-renowned museums sprinkled across the country. Most German museums receive state or federal funds and, as a result, often charge surprisingly low entrance fees.

Discovering different types of museums

If you're into art, keep an eye open for the **Kunstmuseum** (koonst-moo-*sey*-oom) (*art museum*). If you want to find out more about the traditional lifestyle of a certain area, go to the **Freilichtmuseum** (*fray*-leeHt-moo-*sey*–oom) (*open-air museum*). In Germany, you can find museums for virtually everything a human being might fancy, including a **Biermuseum** (beer-moo-*sey*-um) (*beer museum*) in Munich and several other locations!

Museum mavens beware: German museums, like many European museums and other cultural centers, are closed on Mondays — **montags geschlossen** (mohn-tahks ge-*shlos*-en). Others are closed on **dienstags** (deens-tahks) (*Tuesdays*). Make sure to check **die Öffnungszeiten** (dee *erf*-noongs-*tsayt*-en) (*the opening hours*) before heading out. Many museums, performances, and other places offer discount tickets to students, so you may want to take advantage of these discounts by getting an international student ID before you leave home.

Book II

Speaking German on the Go

Talking about museums

When you want to catch an exhibition — **Ausstellung** (*ous*-shtêl-oong) — the following phrases come in handy:

> **Ich möchte ins Museum gehen.** (iH *merH*-te ins moo-*sey*-oom *gey*-en.) (*I would like to go to the museum.*)

> **Ich möchte die . . . Ausstellung sehen.** (iH *merH*-te dee . . . *ous*-shtêl-oong *zey*-en.) (*I would like to see the . . . exhibition.*)

> **In welchem Museum läuft die . . . Ausstellung?** (in *vêlH*-em moo-*sey*-oom loyft dee . . . *ous*-shtêl-oong?) (*At which museum is the . . . exhibit running?*)

> **Ist das Museum montags geöffnet?** (ist dâs moo-*sey*-oom *mohn*-tahks ge-*erf*-net?) (*Is the museum open on Mondays?*)

> **Um wie viel Uhr öffnet das Museum?** (oom *vee* feel oohr *erf*-net dâs moo-*sey*-oom?) (*At what time does the museum open?*)

> **Gibt es eine Sonderausstellung?** (gipt ês *ayn*-e *zon*-der-*ous*-shtêl-oong?) (*Is there a special exhibit?*)

Talkin' the Talk

Jan and Mona are planning a trip to a museum. They invite their friend Ingo to join them.

Jan:	**Hallo, Ingo. Wir wollen morgen ins Städtische Museum.** *hâ-lo, in-go. veer vol-en mor-gen ins shtê-ti-she moo-sey-oom.* *Hi, Ingo. We want to go to the city museum tomorrow.*
Mona:	**Wir wollen uns die Ausstellung über die Bronzezeit ansehen. Kommst du mit?** *veer vol-en oons dee ous-shtêl-oong ue-ber dee bron-tse-tsayt ân-zey-en. komst dooh mit?* *We want to see the exhibit about the Bronze Age. Do you want to come along?*
Ingo:	**Hmm, ich weiß nicht. Die Ausstellung habe ich schon letzte Woche gesehen.** *hmm, iH vays niHt. dee ous-shtêl-oong hah-be iH shohn lets-te voH-e ge-zey-en.* *Hmm, I don't know. I already saw the exhibit last week.*
Mona:	**Hat sie dir gefallen?** *hât zee deer ge-fâl-en?* *Did you like it?*
Ingo:	**Ja. Vielleicht komme ich noch einmal mit.** *yah. fee-layHt kom-e iH noH ayn-mahl mit.* *Yes. Maybe I'll come along for a second time.*
Jan:	**Wir wollen morgen um 10.00 Uhr in die Ausstellung.** *veer vol-en mor-gen oom tseyn oohr in dee ous-shtêl-oong.* *We want to go to the exhibit tomorrow at ten o'clock.*
Ingo:	**Gut. Ich treffe euch dort.** *gooht. iH trêf-e oyH dohrt.* *Good. I'll meet you there.*

Attending Cultural Performances

Wherever you may be staying in Europe, you're probably just a short trip away from cultural centers that present such events as **Oper** (*oh*-per) (*opera*), **Konzert** (kon-*tsêrt*) (*concert*), **Sinfonie** (sin-foh-*nee*) (*symphony*), and **Theater** (tey-*ah*-ter) (*theater*). After all, performing arts centers abound in Europe.

Summertime is when you find the greatest number of musical performances ranging from techno to opera and just about everything in between. When you're thinking about taking in some musical entertainment, pick up a local newspaper, go to a ticket agency, or go online to the city website to find out what's happening where.

Book II

Speaking German on the Go

Deciding where to go

With all the entertainment options available in Germany (and elsewhere in Europe), you may want to consider doing something that you normally can't do when you're at home. For instance, if you aren't familiar with opera, now would be a great opportunity to try it.

If you're up for going out on the town, say

> **Ich möchte heute Abend ausgehen.** (iH *merH*-te *hoy*-te *ah*-bênt *ous-gey*-en.) (*I would like to go out this evening.*)

The following words and phrases may be helpful during a night out:

> **Ich möchte ins Theater/Konzert gehen.** (iH *merH*-te ins tey-*ah*-ter/kon-*tsert gey*-en.) (*I would like to go to the theater/a concert.*)

> **Ich möchte in die Oper gehen.** (iH *merH*-te in dee *oh*-per *gey*-en.) (*I would like to go to the opera.*)

> **Gehen wir ins Theater/Konzert.** (*gey*-en veer ins tey-*ah*-ter/kon-*tsert*.) (*Let's go to the theater/a concert.*)

> **Gehen wir ins Ballet.** (*gey*-en veer ins bâ-*lêt*.) (*Let's go to the ballet.*)

> **Wann ist die Premiere von. . . ?** (vân ist dee prêm-*yee*-re fon. . . ?) (*When is the opening night of. . . ?*)

> **In welchem Theater spielt. . . ?** (in *vêlH*-em tey-*ah*-ter shpeelt. . . ?) (*In which theater is . . . showing?*)

Worried about the dress code? It's relatively liberal, although Europeans do enjoy getting decked out for opera and symphony performances, especially for **Premiere** (prêm-*yee*-re) (*opening night*) or a **Galavorstellung** (*gâ*-lâ-fohr-shtêl-oong) (*gala performance*). Other than that, as long as you stay away from the T-shirt, jeans, and sneakers look, you won't stick out like a sore thumb.

Words to Know

das Theater	dâs tey-<u>ah</u>-ter	theater
die Oper	dee <u>oh</u>-per	opera/opera house
die Sinfonie	dee sin-foh-<u>nee</u>	symphony
das Ballett	dâs bâ-<u>lêt</u>	ballet
die Pause	dee <u>pou</u>-ze	intermission
der Sänger/die Sängerin	dêr <u>zên</u>-ger/dee <u>zên</u>-ge-rin	singer
der Schauspieler/ die Schauspielerin	dêr <u>shou</u>-shpee-ler/ dee <u>shou</u>-shpee-le-rin	actor/actress
der Tänzer/die Tänzerin	dêr <u>tên</u>-tser/dee <u>tên</u>-tse-rin	dancer
singen	<u>zing</u>-en	to sing
tanzen	<u>tân</u>-tsen	to dance
klatschen	<u>klâch</u>-en	to clap
der Beifall	dêr <u>bay</u>-fâl	applause
die Zugabe	dee <u>tsooh</u>-gah-be	encore
die Kinokasse/ Theaterkasse	dee <u>kee</u>-noh-kâs-e/ tey-<u>ah</u>-ter-kâs-e	movie/theater box office
der Platz	dêr plâts	seat

Going to a concert

Getting a taste of the music scene while you're in a foreign country is a terrific way to relax and get to know the culture of the people. After all, many of the greatest composers of classical music were Austrian or German. Think Mozart, Haydn, Beethoven, Bach. . . . Germany, Austria, and Switzerland enjoy an overwhelmingly rich classical music **Kulturerbe** (kool-*toohr*-êr-be) (*cultural heritage*), which is one reason why old music traditions are so alive there today.

Some of the most famous summer music festivals in Europe take place in Germany, Austria, and Switzerland. They include

- **Richard Wagner Festspiele** (*riH*-ârd *vahg*-ner *fêst*-spee-le) (*Richard Wagner Music Festival*): An annual Wagnerian opera festival that takes place in Bayreuth

- **Salzburger Festspiele** (*zâlts*-boorg-er *fêst*-spee-le) (*Salzburg Music Festival*): A six-week-long music festival in Salzburg, Austria

- **Bregenzer Festspiele** (brêg-*ênts*-er *fêst*-spee-le) (*Bregenz Music Festival*): A music festival that takes place in Bregenz, Austria

At such performances, a great number of prominent people, including political dignitaries and movie actors from Europe and beyond, can be spotted posing for photographers in front of lavish concert halls.

You may have a hard time getting tickets to the top-notch performances, and prices can be astronomical. But don't worry; Germany, Austria, and Switzerland offer plenty of other lesser-known events for **Otto Normalverbraucher** (*ot*-oh nor-*mâl*-fêr-brouH-er) (*average Joe*).

The following are some general terms and types of musical events that may interest you:

- **die BallettFestwoche** (die bâl-*êt-fêst*-woH-e) (*ballet festival week*)
- **die Jazzmusik** (dee jazz-[as in English]-moo-*zeek*) (*jazz music*)
- **die Kammermusik** (dee *kâm*-er-moo-*zeek*) (*chamber music*)
- **die Kirchenmusik** (dee *kirH*-en moo-*zeek*) (*church music*)
- **die klassische Musik** (dee *klâs*-ish-e moo-*zeek*) (*classical music*)
- **der Konzertsaal** (dêr kon-*tsêrt*-zâl) (*concert hall*)
- **das Musikfest** (dâs moo-*zeek*-fêst) (*music festival*)
- **das Musikfestival** (dâs moo-*zeek*-fês-ti-vâl) (*music festival*)

Book II

Speaking German on the Go

- **die Opernfestspiele** (dee *oh*-pern-fêst-*spee*-le) (*opera festival*)

- **die Philharmonie** (dee fil-hâr-mon-*ee*) (*philharmonic orchestra*)

- **das Quartett** (dâs kvâr-*têt*) (*quartet*)

- **der Rap** (dêr rap [as in English]) (*rap*)

- **die Rockmusik** (dee *rok*-moo-*zeek*) (*rock music*)

- **die Sinfonie** (dee sin-fon-*ee*) (*symphony*)

- **der Techno** (dêr *têH*-noh) (*techno*)

When the audience wants the performers to play more music, they shout **Zugabe!** (*tsoo*-gâ-be) (*encore*). So if you like the music you hear on your next night out, feel free to join in the shouting. Oh, and of course, you can show your appreciation with **klatschen** (*klatsh*-en) (*clapping*).

How Was It? Talking about Entertainment

One of the best parts about watching a movie, going to a concert, or attending some other kind of performance is that you're part of a captive audience. Afterward, you may want to compare your impressions with others who shared the evening. When you want to talk about your experience, you need to know how to express yourself using the past tense.

You get a complete look at the past tense in Chapters 4 and 5 of Book IV; here you get a quick sample of things to say when you want to talk about what you did or saw on your night out. You find out how to ask others how they liked the entertainment and how to give your opinions on the evening's experience.

Asking about the entertainment

When it comes to entertainment, everybody seems to have an opinion. So why miss out on the fun? Somebody may ask you one of the following questions — or you may pose one of them to someone else — to start a conversation about an exhibition, film, or performance:

Hat Ihnen die Ausstellung/der Film/die Oper gefallen? (hât *een*-en dee *ous*-shtêl-oong/dêr film/dee *oh*-per ge-*fâl*-en?) (*Did you* [formal] *like the exhibition/the movie/the opera?*)

Hat dir die Ausstellung/der Film/die Oper gefallen? (hât deer dee *ous*-shtêl-oong/dêr film/dee *oh*-per ge-*fâl*-en?) (*Did you* [informal] *like the exhibition/the movie/the opera?*)

Hast du eine Theaterkarte bekommen? (hâst dooh *ayn*-e tey-*ah*-ter-*kâr*-te be-*kom*-en?) (*Did you get a theater ticket?*)

Habt ihr Karten für die Matinee gekauft? (hâpt eer *kâr*-ten fuer dee mâ-tee-*ney* ge-*kouft?*) (*Did you buy tickets for the matinee?*)

Telling people what you think

Now comes the fun part — telling people what you thought about a film or performance you've just seen. For starters, you can say whether you liked the entertainment. Try one of the following on for size:

Die Ausstellung/der Film/die Oper hat mir (sehr) gut gefallen. (dee *ous*-shtêl-oong/dêr film/dee *oh*-per hât meer [zeyr] gooht ge-*fâl*-en.) (*I liked the exhibition/the movie/the opera [a lot].*)

Die Ausstellung/der Film/die Oper hat mir (gar) nicht gefallen. (dee *ous*-shtêl-oong/dêr film/dee *oh*-per hât meer [gâr] niHt ge-*fâl*-en.) (*I didn't like the exhibition/the movie/the opera [at all].*)

Wir haben das Kino nach 20 Minuten verlassen. (veer *hah*-ben dâs *kee*-noh nâH *tsvân*-tsiH mi-*nooh*-ten vêr-*lâs*-en.) (*We left the movie theater after 20 minutes.*)

Ich habe viel gelacht. (iH *hah*-be feel ge-*lâHt*.) (*I laughed a lot.*)

You may want to follow up your statement with a reason. Start out by saying

Die Ausstellung/der Film/die Oper war wirklich . . . (dee *ous*-shtêl-oong/dêr film/dee *oh*-per vahr *virk*-liH . . .) (*The exhibition/the movie/the opera was really . . .*)

Finish the thought with any of the following adjectives that apply. You can always string a few of them together with the conjunction **und** (oont) (*and*) to add even more zest to your statement:

- **aufregend** (*ouf*-rey-gent) (*exciting*)
- **ausgezeichnet** (ous-ge-*tsayH*-net) (*excellent*)
- **enttäuschend** (ênt-*toy*-shênt) (*disappointing*)
- **fantastisch** (fân-*tâs*-tish*) (*fantastic*)
- **langweilig** (*lâng*-vay-liH) (*boring*)
- **sehenswert** (*zey*-êns-veyrt) (*worth seeing*)
- **spannend** (*shpân*-ênt) (*thrilling, suspenseful*)
- **unterhaltsam** (oon-ter-*hâlt*-tsahm) (*entertaining*)
- **wunderschön** (*voon*-der-shern) (*beautiful*)

Book II

Speaking German on the Go

Talkin' the Talk

 Frau Peters went to the theater last night. Today at the office, she's telling her colleague Herr Krüger about the show. (Track 23)

Herr Krüger: **Sind Sie nicht gestern im Theater gewesen?**
zint zee niHt *gês*-tern im teh-*ah*-ter ge-*vey*-zen?
Weren't you at the theater last night?

Frau Peters: **Doch. Ich habe das neue Ballet gesehen.**
doH. iH *hah*-be dâs *noy*-e bâ-*lêt* ge-*zey*-en.
Indeed. I saw the new ballet.

Herr Krüger: **Wie hat es Ihnen gefallen?**
vee hât ês *een*-en ge-*fâl*-en?
How did you like it?

Frau Peters: **Die Tänzer waren fantastisch. Die Vorstellung hat mir ausgezeichnet gefallen.**
dee *tên*-tser *vahr*-ren fân-*tâs*-tish. dee *fohr*-shtêl-oong hât meer ous-ge-*tsayH*-net ge-*fâl*-en.
The dancers were fantastic. I liked the performance very much.

Herr Krüger: **War es einfach, Karten zu bekommen?**
vahr ês *ayn*-fâH, *kâr*-ten tsooh be-*kom*-en?
Was it easy to get tickets?

Frau Peters: **Ja. Ich habe die Karte gestern Morgen an der Theaterkasse gekauft.**
yah. iH *hah*-be dee *kâr*-te *gês*-tern *mor*-gen ân dêr tey-*ah*-ter-*kâs*-e ge-*kouft*.
Yes. I bought the ticket at the box office yesterday morning.

Going to a Party

Just as Americans do, German speakers have different ideas about what makes a good party. They enjoy organizing all kinds of gatherings, ranging from formal sit-down dinners to Sunday afternoon barbecues. If you're invited to a formal gathering at somebody's home, take a small gift, such as a bottle of wine or a bouquet of flowers, with you.

If you're invited to an informal get-together, your host or hostess may ask you to bring along something to eat or drink. You can also take the initiative and ask whether you should bring anything by saying

> **Soll ich etwas mitbringen?** (zol iH _êt_-vâs _mit_-bring-en?) (_Do you want me to bring anything?_)

If you're invited to **Kaffee und Kuchen** (_kâ_-fey oont _koohH_-en) (_coffee and cake_) in the afternoon, a German institution, make sure you arrive on time. In fact, some Germans like to arrive ten minutes early just to be on the safe side, and they wait out on the street until the exact hour to ring the doorbell. Don't expect to stay for dinner. You may be asked, but don't count on it.

Getting an invitation

You may hear any of the following common phrases when receiving an invitation — **die Einladung** (dee _ayn_-lah-doong) — to a party:

> **Ich würde Sie gern zu einer Party einladen.** (iH _vuer_-de zee gêrn tsooh _ayn_-er _pâr_-tee _ayn_-lah-den.) (_I would like to invite you to a party._)

> **Wir wollen ein Fest feiern. Hast du Lust zu kommen?** (veer _vol_-en ayn fêst _fay_-ern. hâst dooh loost tsooh _kom_-en?) (_We want to have a party. Do you feel like coming?_)

If you can't make it (or don't want to go for some reason), you can politely turn down the invitation by saying one of the following:

> **Nein, tut mir leid, ich kann leider nicht kommen.** (nayn, toot meer layt, iH kân _lay_-der niHt _kom_-en.) (_No, sorry, unfortunately I won't be able to make it._)

> **Nein, da kann ich leider nicht. Ich habe schon etwas anderes vor.** (nayn, dâ kân iH _lay_-der niHt. iH _hah_-be shohn _êt_-vâs _ân_-de-res fohr.) (_No, unfortunately I won't be able to make it. I have other plans._)

If you'd like to go, you can accept the invitation with one of the following phrases:

> **Vielen Dank. Ich nehme die Einladung gern an.** (_fee_-len dânk. iH _neh_-me dee _ayn_-lah-doong gêrn ân.) (_Thank you very much. I'll gladly accept the invitation._)

> **Gut, ich komme gern.** (gooht, iH _kom_-e gêrn.) (_Good, I'd like to come._)

Talking about the party

When someone asks you something like **Wie war die Party am Samstag?** (vee vahr dee *pâr*-tee âm *zâms*-tahk?) (*How was the party on Saturday?*), you can reply with any of these responses:

> **Toll, wir haben bis . . . Uhr gefeiert.** (tol, veer *hah*-ben bis . . . oohr ge-*fay*-êrt.) (*Great. We partied until . . . o'clock.*)
>
> **Wir haben uns ausgezeichnet unterhalten.** (veer *hah*-ben oons ous-ge-*tsayH*-net oon-ter-*hâl*-ten.) (*We had a great time.*)
>
> **Das Essen war. . . .** (dâs *ês*-en vahr. . . .) (*The food was. . . .*)
>
> **Wir haben sogar getanzt.** (veer *hah*-ben zoh-*gahr* ge-*tântst*.) (*We even danced.*)
>
> **Die Musik war. . . .** (dee mooh-*zeek* vahr. . . .) (*The music was. . . .*)
>
> **Das Fest war. . . .** (dâs fêst vahr. . . .) (*The party was. . . .*)

Check out the list of adjectives in the earlier section "Telling people what you think" for some appropriate descriptions to use with the preceding phrases.

Chapter 3

Planning a Pleasure Trip: Gute Reise!

Would you like to go hiking in the Alps or head to the sea? How about a one-day **Ausflug** (*ous*-floohk) (*excursion*), perhaps from Munich to the pristine Bavarian lake of **Königsee** (*ker*-nig-zee)? Or what about a weeklong vacation **Pauschalreise** (pou-*shahl*-ray-ze) (*package tour*) to the **Nordseeinseln** (*nord*-zee-in-zêln) (*North Sea islands*)?

No matter what destination you decide on, every trip requires some preparation. You need to check your calendar and set the dates, make sure your passport is valid for six months past the length of your trip (especially if you're traveling across borders), make reservations, and so on. This chapter gives you some helpful language input to make your trip go as smoothly as possible.

Getting Ready for Your Trip

Exploring new places while traveling can be very exciting, but before you can start exploring, you need to make enough plans that you know what to expect without burdening yourself with a strict itinerary that leaves no room for spontaneity. Whether you prefer gathering information online or working directly with a travel agent when planning a trip, you'll find the information in this section useful.

Finding travel information online

You may want to go online to find more information about the destinations you're interested in. With so many sites out there, you may have a hard time finding what you're looking for. Don't give up! A great deal of tourist information is available in multiple languages, including English. Simply go to the site you're interested in and choose the English option if you don't want to try to translate the German. If you don't have a specific site in mind, do some **googeln** (*goo*-geln) (*googling*); start with google.de for Germany, google.at for Austria, and google.ch for Switzerland. Or simply type the name of a location into your browser and add the country address, like *Innsbruck.at* for Innsbruck, Austria.

If you're feeling adventurous, try looking at websites in German. Although it may seem more complicated at first, it's actually a great way to expand your knowledge of the language and do some armchair traveling to **Deutschland** (*doych*-lânt), **Österreich** (*er*-stê-rayH), and **die Schweiz** (dee shvayz) (*Germany, Austria, and Switzerland*) at the same time.

The following general terms are helpful when you want to check out information on German language websites:

- ✔ **Angebote finden** (*find offers*)
- ✔ **anmelden** (*sign in*)
- ✔ **Hilfe** (*help*)
- ✔ **Login** (*log in*)
- ✔ **mehr** (*more*)
- ✔ **Startseite** (*home*)
- ✔ **Suche** (*search*)
- ✔ **Tipps** (*tips*)
- ✔ **zum Seitenanfang** (*return to top*)

Europeans have more vacation time at their disposal than North Americans, so many of them enjoy taking several **Kurzurlaubsreisen** (*koorts*-oohr-loups-ray-zen) (*short vacation trips*) interspersed throughout the year as well as a longer **Urlaub** (*oohr*-loup) (*vacation*) of two or three weeks. While you're in Europe, you may want to book a short three-day trip to a city like **Berlin** (bêr-*leen*) (*Berlin*) or **Salzburg** (*zâlts*-boorg) (*Salzburg*) or a week-long **Pauschalreise** (pou-*shâl*-ray-ze) (*all-inclusive trip*) to a popular warm-weather destination like **Gran Canaria** (grân câ-*nahr*-ee-â) (*Gran Canaria*), a Spanish island off the coast of northern Africa, or **Antalya** (ân-*tahl*-yâ) (*Antalya*), a city on the Mediterranean coast of Turkey.

You may come across the following terms as you're looking at travel websites or travel brochures:

- **Ferienunterkünfte** (*fêr*-ee-en-oon-têr-kuenf-te) (*vacation rentals*)
- **Flug & Hotel** (floohk) (*flight & hotel*)
- **Flüge** (*flueg*-e) (*flights*)
- **Hotels** (hotels [as in English]) (*hotels*)
- **Last Minute Reisen** (last minute [as in English] *rayz*-en) (*last-minute trips*)
- **Reiseziele** (*ray*-ze-tsee-le) (*travel destinations*)
- **Restaurants** (rêst-uh-*rons*) (*restaurants*)
- **Spezialangebote** (spêts-ee-*ahl*-ân-gê-boh-te) (*special deals*)
- **Städtereisen** (*shtêt*-e-ray-zen) (*city trips*)
- **Urlaubsreisen** (*oor*-loups-ray-zen) (*vacation trips*)
- **Wellness Urlaub** (wellness [as in English] *oor*-loup) (*spa-type vacation*)

Book II

Speaking German on the Go

Hotels may quote room prices like this:

Einzelzimmer 95€ (*ayn*-tsêl-tsi-mer 95 *oy*-roh) (*single room 95 euros*)

Doppelzimmer ab 170€ (*dop*-el-tsi-mer âp 170 *oy*-roh) (*double room starting at 170 euros*)

Trip organizers may quote prices on a **p. P.** (proh pêr-*zohn*) (*per person*) basis, as shown in these examples:

Preise bereits ab 495€ p. P. (*prayz*-e be-*rayts* âp 495 *oy*-roh proh pêr-*zohn*) (*prices starting at 495 euros per person*)

Flug & Hotel ab 650€ p. P. (floohk & hotel [as in English] âp 650 *oy*-roh proh pêr-*zohn*) (*flight & hotel starting at 650 euros per person*)

The large number of **Kurorte** (*koohr*-ort-e) (*spa towns*) in Europe stems from a centuries-old culture that involved the "taking of the waters," in which the elite spent time at a luxurious hotel going in and out of **Thermen** (*têr*-men) (*thermal springs*) and saunas. Nowadays, many spa venues are reasonably priced, especially when you go for just the day. One of the most well-known **Kurorte** in Germany is **Baden-Baden** (*bah*-den-*bah*-den) (*Baden-Baden*), located near the French border. Locations where you can find spas are frequently named **Bad** (baht) (*bath*) followed by the name of the town; for example, two spa towns are **Bad Reichenhall** (baht *rayH*-en-hâl) in Germany and **Bad Gastein** (baht gash-*tayn*) in Austria.

Getting help from a travel agent

Booking your trip online is fast and convenient, yet you may find that a travel agent can better serve your needs when you're already in Europe and want to plan a short trip from there. After all, you don't want to get stuck spending five nights at a hotel that blasts ear-splitting music 24/7 from its poolside disco!

When you first contact a travel agency, **das Reisebüro** (dâs *ray-*ze-bue-*roh*), say to the travel agent

> **Ich möchte gern . . .** (iH *merH-*te gêrn . . .) (*I would like to . . .*)

At the end of this phrase, say any of the following to specify what you want the agent to do for you:

> **. . . einen Flug nach . . . buchen.** (. . . *ayn-*en floohk nahH . . . *boohH-*en.) (. . . *book a flight to. . . .*)

> **. . . am . . . abfliegen.** (. . . âm . . . *âp-*fleeg-en.) (. . . *depart [fly] on the. . . .*)

> **. . . am . . . zurückfliegen.** (. . . âm . . . tsoo-*ruek-*fleeg-en.) (. . . *return [fly back] on the. . . .*)

> **. . . eine (Pauschal)reise nach . . . buchen.** (. . . *ayn-*e [pou-*shahl*]-ray-ze nahH . . . *boohH-*en.) (. . . *book a vacation [package] to. . . .*)

> **. . . einen Ausflug nach . . . buchen.** (. . . *ayn-*en *ous-*floohk nahH . . . *boohH-*en.) (. . . *book an excursion to. . . .*)

> **. . . ein Hotelzimmer reservieren.** (. . . ayn hoh-*tēl-*tsi-mer rê-zêr-*vee-*ren.) (. . . *reserve a hotel room.*)

Talkin' the Talk

Frau Burger wants to book a vacation package to the Spanish island of **Mallorca** (may-*yor-*kâ), a very popular destination for Germans. She calls a travel agency to book her trip. (Go to www. dummies.com/go/germanaio to listen to this bonus track.)

Angestellter: **Reisebüro Kunze, guten Tag!**
ray-ze-bue-*roh* koon-tse, *gooh*-ten *tahk!*
Travel agency Kunze, hello!

Frau Burger: **Guten Tag. Ich möchte eine Pauschalreise für eine Woche nach Mallorca buchen.**
*gooh-*ten *tahk.* iH *merH-*te *ayn-*e pou-*shâl-*ray-ze fuer *ayn-*e *woH-*e naH may-*yor-*kâ *boohH-*en.
Hello, I'd like to book a one-week vacation package to Mallorca.

Angestellter: **Gut. Wann möchten Sie hinfliegen?**
gooht. vân *merH*-ten zee *hin*-fleeg-en?
Good. When do you want to fly there?

Frau Burger: **Im Oktober. Aber wie sind die Preise?**
im ok-*toh*-ber. *ah*-ber vee zint dee *pray*-ze?
In October. But what are the prices like?

Angestellter: **Keine Sorge. Oktober ist Nebensaison. Möchten Sie am 5. Oktober abfliegen?**
kayn-e *zohr*-ge. ok-*toh*-ber ist *ney*-ben-zey-zon.
merH-ten zee âm *fuenf*-ten ok-*toh*-ber *âp*-fleeg-en?
Not to worry. October is the low season. Would you like to leave on the fifth of October?

Book II

Speaking German on the Go

Frau Burger: **Perfekt. Das passt ausgezeichnet.**
pêr-*fêkt*. dâs pâst *ous*-ge-*tsayH*-nêt.
Perfect. That suits me perfectly.

Angestellter: **Sehr gut. Ich buche den Flug und die Übernachtung für Sie. Ich empfehle Ihnen das fûnf Stern Hotel Eden.**
zeyr gooht. iH *boohH*-e deyn floohk oont dee ue-ber-*nâHt*-oong fuer zee. iH em-*pfey*-le *een*-en dâs fuenf shtêrn hotel [as in English] *ey*-den.
Very good. I'll book the flight and accommodation for you. I recommend the five-star Hotel Eden.

Frau Burger: **Danke.**
dân-ke.
Thank you.

Words to Know

die Reise	dee <u>ray</u>-ze	trip
reisen	<u>ray</u>-zen	to travel
buchen	<u>boohH</u>-en	to book
das Reisebüro	dâs <u>ray</u>-ze-bue-roh	travel agency
die Übernachtung	dee ue-ber-<u>nâHt</u>-oong	accommodation

Packing your bags

Preparing for a trip always includes packing your bags, though seasoned travelers manage to get around with a minimum of **das Gepäck** (dâs gê-*pêk*) (*luggage*). Particularly when you have to fly to your destination, the ideal **Gepäck** consists of one manageable checked bag and a small carry-on.

The following are some types of luggage people use when traveling:

- **das Handgepäck** (dâs *hânt*-ge-pêk) (*hand luggage*)
- **die Handtasche** (dee *hânt*-tâsh-e) (*handbag*)
- **der Koffer** (dêr *kof*-er) (*suitcase*)
- **der Rollkoffer** (dêr *rol*-kof-er) (*wheeled suitcase*)
- **der Rucksack** (dêr *rook*-zâk) (*backpack*)
- **die Tasche** (dee *tâsh*-e) (*bag*)

What separates the novice packer from the expert is a matter of planning what to take and, possibly even more important, what not to take. Wrinkle-free clothing items with multiple uses are a good starting point. For example, women should take a couple of silk or pashmina scarves that double as a means of dressing up any basic black outfit and as a cover-up on chilly evenings. In the shoe department, a pair of sensible shoes are a must for walking around European cities with expansive pedestrian zones.

Are you planning to take any electronic devices? If so, remember to pack the right power converters and adapter plugs for Europe.

Among the obvious items you have to remember to take are your up-to-date passport, some small euro bills, any medications you normally take, and reading materials. Here's a list of some miscellaneous items besides clothes that you may want to take on your trip:

- **der Fotoapparat/die Kamera** (dêr *foh*-to-âp-â-rât/dee *kâm*-êr-ah) (*camera*)
- **das Handy** (dâs *hên*-dee) (*cellphone*)
- **der iPad/iPod** (dêr iPad/iPod [as in English]) (*iPad/iPod*)
- **der Laptop** (dêr laptop [as in English]) (*laptop*)
- **der Rasierapparat** (dêr râ-*zeer*-âp-â-rât) (*razor*)
- **die Reiseapotheke** (dee *ray*-ze-âp-oo-tey-ke) (*travel first-aid kit*)
- **der Reisewecker** (dêr *ray*-ze-vêk-er) (*travel alarm clock*)
- **die Sonnenbrille** (dee *zon*-en-bril-e) (*sunglasses*)

✔ die **Sonnenschutzcreme** (dee *zon*-en-shoots-kreym) (*sunscreen*)

✔ der **Tablet-Computer** (dêr tablet [as in English] computer [as in English]) (*tablet*)

✔ die **Taschentücher** (dee *tâsh*-en-tueH-er) (*tissues*)

✔ die **Toilettenartikel** (dee toy-*lêt*-en-âr-ti-kel) (*toilet articles*)

✔ die **Zahnbürste** (dee *tsahn*-buers-te) (*toothbrush*)

✔ die **Zahnpaste** (dee *tsahn*-pâs-te) (*toothpaste*)

In case you forget to bring toiletries and sundry items, not to worry. After you're in German-speaking Europe, you just need to head to **eine Drogerie** (*ayn*-e *drohg*-êr-ee), which is like an American drugstore except that it doesn't sell prescription drugs.

When you're packing summer clothes, remember to include some items of clothing that cover your shoulders and legs so you blend in with the natives. Why? You don't want to contradict local customs if you go into places of worship where tank tops and short skirts are frowned upon.

Exploring the Outdoors

Within German-speaking Europe, you can enjoy a vast range of sports and recreation opportunities. All you have to do is decide which ones you want to try! You can sail on one of many lakes, ski in the mountains, go mountain biking, relax at the shore, or simply enjoy nature in a park. Or maybe you just want to get away from the busyness of life and experience the great outdoors alone or with your family and friends. In that case, lace up your hiking boots and grab your binoculars and guidebook. Just don't forget to pack a lunch because you may not find a snack bar at the end of the trail!

Getting out and going

If you're interested in walking and hiking, the following phrases can help get you on your way:

Wollen wir spazieren/wandern gehen? (*vol*-en veer shpâ-*tsee*-ren/ *vân*-dern *gey*-en?) (*Should we take a walk/go hiking?*)

Ich möchte spazieren/wandern gehen. (iH *merH*-te shpâ-*tsee*-ren/ *vân*-dern *gey*-en.) (*I would like to take a walk/go hiking.*)

Things to see along the way

When you return from your tour of the great outdoors, you can tell people about what you saw by saying

Ich habe . . . gesehen. (iH *hah*-be . . . gê-*zey*-en.) (*I saw. . . .*)

Ich habe . . . beobachtet. (iH *hah*-be . . . bê-*oh*-bâH-tet.) (*I was watching. . . .*)

Just fill in the blanks. You may encounter any of the following along the way:

- ✔ **der Baum** (dêr boum) (*tree*)
- ✔ **der Fluss** (dêr floos) (*river*)
- ✔ **die Kuh** (dee kooh) (*cow*)
- ✔ **das Meer** (dâs meyr) (*sea, ocean*)
- ✔ **das Pferd** (dâs pfêrt) (*horse*)
- ✔ **das Reh** (dâs rey) (*deer*)
- ✔ **das Schaf** (dâs shahf) (*sheep*)
- ✔ **der See** (dêr zey) (*lake*)
- ✔ **der Vogel** (dêr *foh*-gel) (*bird*)

Remember that you use the accusative case when completing these sentences. (See Book III, Chapter 2 for details on the accusative case.) For masculine nouns, phrase your sentences in this way:

Ich habe einen Adler gesehen. (iH *hah*-be *ayn*-en *âd*-ler ge-*zey*-en.)
(*I saw an eagle.*)

For feminine nouns, use this phrasing:

Ich habe eine lilafarbene Kuh gesehen! (iH *hah*-be *ayn*-e lee-lâ-fâr-bên-e kooh ge-*zey*-en!) (*I saw a purple-colored cow!*) Well, maybe not in the Alps, but you can see the purple cow on the wrapper of a well-known brand of chocolate.

Express neuter nouns this way:

Ich habe ein Reh gesehen. (iH *hah*-be ayn rey ge-*zey*-en.) (*I saw a deer.*)

Or you may want to use the plural form, which is generally easier:

Ich habe viele Vögel gesehen. (iH *hah*-be *fee*-le *fer*-gel ge-*zey*-en.) (*I saw a lot of birds.*)

Talkin' the Talk

Mr. and Mrs. Paulsen are in a small town in the mountains. Today they want to go hiking. They are speaking with Frau Kreutzer at the local tourist information office to find out about hiking trails in the area. (Track 24)

Book II

Speaking German on the Go

Frau Paulsen: **Guten Morgen. Wir möchten eine Wanderung machen.**
gooh-ten *mor*-gen. veer *merH*-ten *ayn*-e *vân*-der-oong *mâH*-en.
Good morning. We would like to go hiking.

Frau Kreutzer: **Ich kann Ihnen eine Wanderkarte für diese Gegend geben.**
iH kân *een*-en *ayn*-e *vân*-dêr-*kâr*-te fuer *deez*-e *gey*-gend *gey*-ben.
I can give you a hiking map of this area.

Herr Paulsen: **Das ist genau das, was wir brauchen.**
dâs ist ge-*nou* dâs, vâs veer *brouH*-en.
That's exactly what we need.

Frau Kreutzer: **Wie wäre es mit dem Hornberg? Wenn Sie Glück haben, können Sie sogar einige Murmeltiere sehen.**
vee vair-e ês mit deym *hohrn*-bêrg? vên zee gluek *hah*-ben, *kern*-en zee zoh-*gâr ayn*-ee-ge *moor*-mel-teer-e *zey*-en.
How about Horn mountain? If you're lucky, you can even see some marmots.

Herr Paulsen: **Das klingt gut. Können Sie uns den Weg auf der Karte markieren?**
dâs klinkt gooht. *keer*-en zee oons deyn vêg ouf dêr *kâr*-te *mâr*-*keer*-en?
Sounds good. Can you mark the trail for us on the map?

Frau Kreutzer: **Ja, natürlich.**
yah, nâ-*tuer*-liH.
Yes, of course.

Frau Paulsen: **Vielen Dank für ihre Hilfe.**
fee-len dânk fuer *eer*-e *hil*-fe.
Thank you very much for your help.

Going to the mountains

Whether you plan to explore the ever-popular Alps or one of the other mountain ranges, you're sure to meet the locals. In fact, you're likely to see whole families out hiking if you venture out on a Sunday afternoon. Before you join them, fortify yourself with some sustaining vocabulary:

- **der Berg** (dêr bêrg) (*mountain*)
- **das Gebirge** (dâs ge-*bir*-ge) (*mountain range*)
- **der Gipfel** (dêr *gip*-fel) (*peak*)
- **der Hügel** (dêr *hue*-gel) (*hill*)
- **das Naturschutzgebiet** (dâs nâ-*toohr*-shoots-ge-beet) (*nature preserve*)
- **das Tal** (dâs tahl) (*valley*)

Here are a few examples of sentences:

Wir fahren in die Berge. (veer *fahr*-en in dee *bêr*-ge.) (*We're going to the mountains.*)

Wir wollen im Naturschutzgebiet wandern gehen. (veer *vol*-en im nâ-*toohr*-shoots-ge-beet *vân*-dern *gey*-en.) (*We want to go hiking in the nature preserve.*)

Ich will bis zum Gipfel bergsteigen. (iH vil bis tsoom *gip*-fel *bêrg*-shtayg-en.) (*I want to climb to the peak.*)

The Alps offer a variety of hiking opportunities for the casual hiker as well as for the expert climber. When you meet German-speaking people in the mountains and strike up a conversation, you're bound to notice that complete strangers may address each other with **du.** Using the familiar form is a means of showing camaraderie with others interested in the experience of hiking.

Words to Know

wandern	<u>vân</u>-dern	to go hiking
spazieren gehen	shpâ-<u>tsee</u>-ren <u>gey</u>-en	to take a walk
die Wanderung	dee <u>vân</u>-der-oong	hike
die Karte	dee <u>kâr</u>-te	map
der Weg	dêr veyk	trail, path, way
die Gegend	dee <u>gey</u>-gent	area

Talkin' the Talk

Herr Mahler meets Frau Pohl on his way home from work. They start talking about their travel plans.

Frau Pohl: **Tag Herr Mahler. Na, haben Sie schon Urlaubspläne gemacht?**
tahk hêr *mah*-ler. nah, *hah*-ben zee shon *oor*-loups-plên-e ge-*mâHt*?
Hello, Mr. Mahler. So, have you made plans for your vacation yet?

Herr Mahler: **Aber ja, meine Frau und ich werden wieder in die Berge fahren.**
ah-ber yah, *mayn*-e frou oont iH *vêr*-den *vee*-der in dee *bêr*-ge *fahr*-en.
Oh yes, my wife and I will go to the mountains again.

Frau Pohl: **Wieder in die Alpen?**
vee-der in dee *âlp*-en?
Back to the Alps?

Herr Mahler: **Nein, diesmal gehen wir in den Pyrenäen wandern. Und Sie?**
nayn, *dees*-mâl *gey*-en veer in deyn per-re-*nê*-en *vân*-dern. oont zee?
No, this time we're going hiking in the Pyrenees. And you?

Frau Pohl:	**Wir wollen im Herbst in die Dolomiten zum Bergsteigen.**
	veer *vol*-en im hêrpst in dee do-lo-*meet*-en tsoom *bêrg*-shtayg-en.
	We want to go mountain climbing in the Dolomite Alps in the fall.
Herr Mahler:	**Haben Sie schon ein Hotel gebucht?**
	hah-ben zee shohn ayn hotel [as in English] ge-*booHt*?
	Did you book a hotel yet?
Frau Pohl:	**Nein, wir werden in Berghütten übernachten.**
	nayn, veer *vêr*-den în *bêrg*-huet-en ue-ber-*nâH*-ten.
	No, we're going to stay in mountain huts.

Going to the country

Mountains aren't your idea of fun? How about some fresh country air then? Despite a population of about 82 million people in Germany, you can still find quiet rural areas and out-of-the-way places, sometimes surprisingly close to bustling urban centers. And it goes without saying that you can find peace and quiet in the Austrian and Swiss countryside. All you need to get started on your relaxing country vacation is the right vocabulary:

- **der Bauernhof** (dêr *bou*-ern-hohf) (*farm*)
- **das Dorf** (dâs dorf) (*village*)
- **das Feld** (dâs fêlt) (*field*)
- **das Land** (dâs lânt) (*countryside*)
- **der Wald** (dêr vâlt) (*forest*)
- **die Wiese** (dee *veez*-e) (*meadow*)

Here are a few sample sentences:

Wir fahren aufs Land. (veer *fahr*-en oufs lânt.) (*We're going to the countryside.*)

Wir machen Urlaub auf dem Bauernhof. (veer *mâH*-en *oor*-loup ouf deym *bou*-ern-hohf.) (*We're vacationing on a farm.*)

Ich gehe im Wald spazieren. (iH *gey*-e im vâlt shpâ-*tsee*-ren.) (*I'm going for a walk in the woods.*)

Talkin' the Talk

Daniel runs into his friend Ellen. After they greet each other, Daniel tells Ellen about his upcoming vacation.

Daniel: **Ich fahre in der letzten Woche in Juli aufs Land.**
iH *fahr*-e in dêr *lêts*-ten *voH*-e in *yooh*-lee oufs lânt.
I'm going to the countryside the last week in July.

Ellen: **Fährst du allein?**
fairst dooh *âl*-ayn?
Are you going alone?

Daniel: **Nein, ich verreise zusammen mit meiner Schwester und ihren Kindern.**
nayn, iH fêr-*ray*-ze tsoo-*zâm*-en mit *mayn*-er *shvês*-ter oont *eer*-en *kin*-dern.
No, I'm traveling together with my sister and her children.

Ellen: **Habt ihr eine Ferienwohnung gemietet?**
hahpt eer *ayn*-e *feyr*-ee-ên-*vohn*-oong ge-*meet*-et?
Did you rent a vacation apartment?

Daniel: **Nein. Wir übernachten auf einem Bauernhof in einem kleinen Dorf.**
nayn. veer ue-bêr-*nâHt*-en ouf *ayn*-em *bou*-ern-hohf in *ayn*-em *klayn*-en dorf.
No. We're staying on a farm in a small village.

Ellen: **Die Kindern freuen sich sicher.**
dee *kin*-dern *froy*-en ziH *ziH*-er.
The kids are surely looking forward to that.

Daniel: **Und wie!**
oont vee!
Oh, yes!

Going to the sea

If hiking through the mountains or countryside sounds somewhat dry and tame to you, maybe what you need is a stiff breeze and the cry of gulls overhead. Whether you decide to go to one of the windswept islands in the North

Sea or settle for the more serene Baltic Sea, you'll be able to enjoy nature and meet the locals at the same time, using the following words:

- **die Ebbe** (dee *êb*-e) (*low tide*)
- **die Flut** (dee flooht) (*high tide*)
- **die Gezeiten** (dee gê-*tsayt*-en) (*tides*)
- **die Küste** (dee *kues*-te) (*coast*)
- **das Meer** (dâs meyr) (*sea*)
- **die Nordsee** (dee *nort*-zey) (*North Sea*)
- **die Ostsee** (dee *ost*-zey) (*Baltic Sea*)
- **der Sturm** (dêr shtoorm) (*storm*)
- **die Wellen** (dee *vêl*-en) (*waves*)
- **der Wind** (dêr vint) (*wind*)

Talkin' the Talk

Udo and Karin are talking about their holiday trips. They both like the seaside but have different ideas about what's fun.

Udo: **Wir wollen dieses Jahr an die Ostsee.**
veer *vol*-en *deez*-es yahr ân dee *ost*-zey.
We want to go to the Baltic Sea this year.

Karin: **Toll! Und was macht ihr dort?**
Tol! oont vâs mâHt eer dort?
Cool! And what are you going to do there?

Udo: **Wir wollen windsurfen. Und ihr?**
veer *vol*-en *vint*-soorf-en. oont eer?
We want to go windsurfing. And you?

Karin: **Wir werden auf eine Nordseeinsel fahren. Wir wollen im Watt wandern gehen.**
veer *vêr*-den ouf *ayn*-e *nort*-zey-in-zel *fahr*-en. veer *vol*-en im vât *vân*-dern *gey*-en.
We'll go to a North Sea island. We want to go walking in the tidal flats.

Udo: **Ist das nicht gefährlich?**
ist dâs niHt ge-*fair*-liH?
Isn't that dangerous?

Karin:	**Nein, man geht bei Ebbe los, und dann hat man einige Stunden Zeit, bevor die Flut kommt.**
	nayn, mân geyt bay *êb*-e lohs, oont dân hât mân *ayn-ee*-ge *shtoon*-den tsayt, bê-*fohr* dee flooht komt.
	No, you set out at low tide, and then you have several hours before high tide sets in.

Dealing with Passports and Visas

Book II

Speaking German on the Go

Although the world seems to be shrinking faster and faster thanks to the Internet, you still need paperwork to travel out of the country. Specifically, you need a passport. (You know, that handy little booklet with the embarrassing picture that you always seem to misplace or let expire just before you're about to leave on a trip?) And then there's the issue of visas. The following sections cover both.

Keeping tabs on your passport

Before you leave on a trip, make sure your passport is valid for the entire length of your stay and then some (many countries allow you to stay for between three and six months total). After all, you don't want to spend your time away from home trying to find an American consulate to renew your passport. If you forget to take care of this very important task, you'll hear the following when you show your passport at the airline ticket counter, or worse yet, at the border:

Ihr Pass ist abgelaufen! (eer pâs ist *âp*-ge-louf-en!) (*Your passport has expired!*)

At that point, you'll be directed to the nearest American consulate — **das amerikanische Konsulat** (dâs â-mê-ree-*kah*-ni-she kon-zoo-*laht*) — where you can take care of the necessary paperwork.

In the event that you notice your passport is missing, head straight to the American consulate to report it. If necessary, you can stop a policeman or file a report at a police station. Just say the following to get help:

Ich habe meinen Pass verloren. (iH *hah*-be *mayn*-en pâs fêr-*lohr*-en.) (*I lost my passport.*)

Inquiring about visas

Most countries in Europe don't require you to have a visa if you're traveling on vacation and are planning to stay a few weeks or a couple of months. But just in case you like your destination so much that you want to stay longer or you decide to continue on to a place where you're required to have a visa, the following phrases can come in handy when you apply for one:

Braucht man ein Visum für Reisen nach. . . ? (brouHt mân ayn *vee*-zoom fuer *ray*-zen nahH. . . ?) (*Does one need a visa for trips to. . . ?*)

Ich möchte ein Visum beantragen. (iH *merH*-te ayn *vee*-zoom bê-*ân*-trah-gen.) (*I would like to apply for a visa.*)

Wie lange ist das Visum gültig? (vee *lâng*-e ist dâs *vee*-zoom *guel*-tiH?) (*For how long is the visa valid?*)

Talkin' the Talk

George Beck, an American living in Germany, wants to go on a trip to Phuket (fooh-*ket*), Thailand. As he's making the necessary arrangements at the travel agency, he talks to the agent about entering the country.

George: **Brauche ich ein Visum für Thailand?**
brouH-e iH ayn *vee*-zoom *fuer tay*-lânt?
Do I need a visa for Thailand?

Angestellte: **Nein, für Thailand nicht, aber Sie brauchen natürlich Ihren Reisepass. Ist er noch gültig?**
nayn, fuer *tay*-lânt niHt, aber zee *brouH*-en na-*tuer*-liH *eer*-en *ray*-ze-pâs. ist êr noH *guel*-tiH?
No, not for Thailand, but you need your passport, of course. Is it still valid?

George: **Ja, doch.**
yah, doH.
Yes, it is.

Angestellte: **Prima! Noch irgendwelche Fragen, Herr Beck?**
pree-mâ! noH *eer*-gênt-velH-ê *frah*-gen hêr bêk?
Great! Any other questions, Mr. Beck?

George: **Nein, das war's. Vielen Dank.**
nayn, dâs vahrs. *fee*-len dânk.
No, that was it. Thank you very much.

Angestellte: **Gern geschehen. Und, Gute Reise!**
gêrn ge-*shey*-en. oont, *gooh*-te *ray*-ze!
You're welcome. And have a nice trip!

Words to Know

der Reisepass	dêr <u>ray</u>-ze-pâs	passport
das Visum	dâs <u>vee</u>-zoom	visa
beantragen	bê-<u>ân</u>-trah-gen	to apply for
gültig/ungültig	<u>guel</u>-tiH/ <u>oon</u>-guel-tiH	valid/invalid
verlängern	fêr-<u>lêng</u>-ern	to renew, to extend
ablaufen	<u>âp</u>-louf-en	to expire
das Konsulat	dâs kon-zooh-<u>laht</u>	consulate
die Botschaft	dee <u>boht</u>-shâft	embassy

Handling Money

Money does indeed make the world go 'round. And Euroland is no different; it revolves around its multinational currency, the *euro*. When shopping and eating out, Germans use either paper (that is, hard currency) or plastic; however, many Germans prefer to use cash almost exclusively. Plastic, at least for Germans, refers to the electronic cash (EC) card, a debit card. Alternatively, Germans sometimes use credit cards, though many stores and restaurants don't readily accept them.

So what about the good old greenback? In this section, you get up to speed on exchanging your bucks for multicolored, multisized euros. Oh, and you get the lowdown on money in those countries such as Switzerland that still have their own respective currencies. Whether you're dealing with a personable teller or an impersonal ATM, a pocketful of the right expressions can get you, well, a pocketful of euros.

As a non-European, your credit card will work in much the same way as it does at home, but before traveling, check with the institution that issued your card to find out whether any transaction fees apply. When you want to use your credit card to withdraw cash at an ATM, you need to use your four-digit PIN.

Changing currency: Geldwechsel

Obtaining local currency in Europe is generally a hassle-free experience. Practically every bank is willing to accept your dollars and provide you with the local cash. You can also easily withdraw cash in the local currency from an ATM (see the later section for details), provided you're using a major credit card (preferably Visa or Mastercard) and you know your PIN.

You usually find a notice posted in or outside the bank with the current *exchange rates* (**Wechselkurse**) (*vêk*-sel-koorz-e). Look for the column marked **Ankauf** (*ân*-kouf) (*purchase/buy*). Then saunter up to the *teller window*, **der Schalter** (dêr *shâl*-ter). The **Bankangestellter** (*bânk*-an-ge-stêl-ter) (*bank teller*) at the counter will either complete your transaction on the spot or send you on to the **Kasse** (*kâs*-e) (*cashier*).

In airports and major train stations, you often find businesses that specialize in exchanging currencies, called **Wechselstube** (*vêk*-sel-stooh-be) in German. No matter where you decide to change your money, the whole process is simple. All you need are the following phrases:

> **Ich möchte . . . Dollar in Euro wechseln/tauschen.** (iH *merH*-te . . . *dol*-âr in *oy*-roh *vêk*-seln/*toush*-en.) (*I would like to change . . . dollars into euros.*) *Note:* Both **wechseln** and **tauschen** can mean *change* or *exchange* — in this case, money.

> **Wie ist der Wechselkurs?** (vee ist dêr *vêk*-sel-koors?) (*What's the exchange rate?*)

> **Wie hoch sind die Gebühren?** (vee hohH zint dee ge-*buer*-en?) (*How much are the transaction fees?*)

> **Nehmen Sie Reiseschecks?** (*ney*-men zee *ray*-ze-shêks?) (*Do you take traveler's checks?*)

When you exchange money, you'll probably have to show the teller your *passport* (**Reisepass**) (*ray*-ze-pâs). The teller will ask you

> **Haben Sie ihren Reisepass?** (*hah*-ben zee *eer*-en *ray*-ze-pâs?) (*Do you have your passport?*)

After you show your official mug shot — and assuming it appears to be you — the teller may ask you how you want the money:

Welche Scheine hätten Sie gern? (*vêlH-e shayn-e hêt-en zee gêrn?*)
(*What size denominations would you like?*)

You can respond with

In Zehnern/in Zwanzigern/in Fünfzigern/in Hundertern, bitte.
(in *tseyn-ern/in tsvân-zig-ern/in fuenf-tsig-ern/in hoon-dert-ern, bi-te.*)
(*In bills of 10/20/50/100, please.*)

Book II

Speaking German on the Go

Talkin' the Talk

Anne, an American tourist, heads to a bank to exchange money. (Track 25)

Bankangestellter:	**Guten Morgen.**
	gooh-ten mor-gen.
	Good morning.
Anne:	**Guten Morgen. Ich möchte 300 US-Dollar wechseln. Wie ist der Wechselkurs, bitte?**
	gooh-ten mor-gen. iH merH-te dray-hoon-dert ooh-ês dol-âr vêk-seln. vee ist dêr vêk-sel-koors, bi-te?
	Good morning. I'd like to change 300 U.S. dollars. What's the exchange rate, please?
Bankangestellter:	**Einen Moment, bitte. Für einen Dollar bekommen Sie 0,78 Euro.**
	ayn-en moh-ment, bi-te. fuer ayn-en dol-âr be-kom-en zee nool kom-â zee-ben âHt oy-roh.
	One moment, please. One dollar is currently 0.78 euros.
Anne:	**Können Sie mir bitte Reiseschecks über 300 Dollar in Euro wechseln?**
	kern-en zee meer bi-te ray-ze-shêks ue-ber dray-hoon-dêrt dol-âr in oy-roh vêk-seln?
	Could you exchange 300 dollars in traveler's checks into euros, please?
Bankangestellter:	**Kein Problem. Haben Sie ihren Reisepass?**
	kayn pro-bleym. hah-ben zee eer-en ray-ze-pâs?
	No problem. Do you have your passport?

Anne:	**Ja, hier ist er.**	
	yah, heer ist êr.	
	Yes, here it is.	

Bankangestellter:	**Für 300 Dollar bekommen Sie 234 Euro. Abzüglich 3,30 Euro Wechselgebühr macht das 230,70 Euro.**
	fuer *dray*-hoon-dert *dol*-âr bê-*kom*-en zee *tsvay*-hoon-dert-feer-oont-*dray*-siH *oy*-roh. *âb*-tsueg-liH dray *oy*-roh *dray*-siH *vêk*-sel-ge-buer mâHt dâs *tsvay*-hoon-dert-*dray*-siH *oy*-roh *zeep*-tsiH.
	For 300 dollars, you get 234 euros. Minus a 3.30 euro transaction fee, that's 230.70 euros.

Anne:	**Vielen Dank.**
	fee-len dânk
	Thank you very much.

Words to Know

Geld tauschen	gêlt <u>toush</u>-en	to change/exchange money
Geld wechseln	gêlt <u>vêk</u>-seln	to change/exchange money
das Bargeld	dâs <u>bâr</u>-gêlt	cash
in bar	in bâr	in cash
einen Reisescheck einlösen	<u>ayn</u>-en ray-ze-shêk <u>ayn</u>-ler-zen	to cash a traveler's check
eine Gebühr bezahlen	<u>ayn</u>-e ge-<u>buer</u> be-tsah-len	to pay a fee
der Wechselkurs	dêr <u>vêk</u>-sel-koors	exchange rate
der Ankauf	dêr <u>ân</u>-kouf	purchase, acquisition
der Verkauf	dêr <u>fêr</u>-kouf	sale

Understanding the euro and other currencies

With the introduction of the European Monetary Union in 2002, the euro became the currency for 12 countries, including Germany and Austria. *Euroland,* the term coined (no pun intended) for countries that have adopted the euro, currently comprises 17 nations, and the numbers are still growing. Switzerland, the U.K., Denmark, and Poland are among those countries that still use their respective currencies.

When referring to the plural of **der Euro** (dêr *oy*-roh) (*euro*), you have two choices, **die Euro** or **die Euros,** but whichever you choose, you pronounce them the same way (dee *oy*-roh) (*euros*). Each **Euro** has 100 **Cent** (sênt) (*cents*). The official abbreviation for the euro is EUR. When using the symbol for the euro, €, it appears after the number like this: 47€.

The currencies of other countries are as follows:

- ✔ **Czechoslovakia: die tschechische Krone** (dee *chêH*-ish-e *kroh*-ne) (*Czech crown*)

- ✔ **Denmark: die dänische Krone** (dee *deyn*-ish-e *kroh*-ne) (*Danish crown*)

- ✔ **Poland: der polnische Zloty** (dêr *poln*-ish-e *slo*-tee) (*Polish zloty*)

- ✔ **Switzerland: der schweizer Franken** (dêr *shvayts*-er *frân*-ken) (*Swiss franc*)

- ✔ **U.K.: das Pfund** (dâs pfoont) (*pound*)

- ✔ **United States: der Dollar** (dêr *dol*-âr) (*dollar*)

Heading to the ATM

Instead of changing money at the teller window of a bank, you can use a **Bankautomat** (*bânk*-ou-toh-maht) or **Geldautomat** (*gêlt*-ou-toh-maht) (*ATM machine*). Just look for your card symbol on the machine to make sure the machine takes your kind of card.

Many ATMs give you a choice of languages to communicate in, but just in case German is your only option, you need to be prepared. ATMs use phrases that are direct and to the point. A typical run-through of prompts may look like this:

Karte einführen (*kâr*-te *ayn*-fuer-en) (*Insert card*)

Sprache wählen (shprahH-e *vai*-len) (*Choose a language*)

Geheimzahl eingeben (ge-*haym*-tsahl *ayn*-gey-ben) (*Enter PIN*)

Betrag eingeben (be-*trahk ayn*-gey-ben) (*Enter amount*)

Betrag bestätigen (be-*trahk* be-*shtê*-ti-gen) (*Confirm amount*)

Karte entnehmen (*kâr*-te ênt-*ney*-men) (*Remove card*)

Geld entnehmen (gêlt ênt-*ney*-men) (*Take cash*)

Transaction completed. Your wallet should now be bulging with local currency — that is, unless something went wrong. The ATM may be out of order, in which case, you see the following message:

Geldautomat außer Betrieb. (*gêlt*-ou-toh-maht *ous*-er be-*treep*.) (*ATM out of service.*)

Or the ATM may spit out your card without parting with any of its largesse. In that case, you may receive this message:

Die Karte ist ungültig./Die Karte wird nicht akzeptiert. (dee *kâr*-te ist *oon*-guel-tiH./dee *kâr*-te virt niHt âk-tsep-*teert.*) (*The card is not valid./ The card can't be accepted.*)

The worst case scenario? The ATM may swallow your card whole, leaving you with only this message for consolation:

Die Karte wurde eingezogen. Bitte gehen Sie zum Bankschalter. (dee *kâr*-te *voor*-de ayn-ge-tsoh-gen. *bi*-te *gey*-en zee tsoom *bânk*-shâl-ter.) (*The card was confiscated. Please go to the counter in the bank.*)

ATMs and other machines often use terse-sounding phrases like **Geheimzahl eingeben** (*Enter PIN*). Although these phrases may not sound very polite, they're used as a way to save space. For example, a more polite way to say **Geheimzahl eingeben** would be

Bitte geben Sie Ihre Geheimzahl ein. (*bi*-te *gey*-ben zee *eer*-e ge-*haym*-tsahl ayn.) (*Please enter your PIN.*)

Grammatically speaking, such terse phrases are infinitives posing as *imperatives* (commands). You encounter these forms wherever language efficiency is of utmost importance to the writer or speaker or instructions are being given. (For more details about imperatives and commands, head to Book III, Chapter 7.)

Talkin' the Talk

Mike is about to meet his girlfriend for a cup of coffee when he realizes that he has only a 200-euro bill in his wallet. He goes to a bank to change his bill into smaller denominations.

Mike: **Können Sie bitte diesen 200-Euro-Schein in kleinere Scheine wechseln?**
kern-en zee *bi*-te *deez*-en *tsavy* hoon-dert-*oy*-roh-shayn in *klayn*-er-e *shayn*-e *vêk*-seln?
Could you exchange this 200-euro bill for smaller bills, please?

Bankangestellte: **Welche Scheine darf ich Ihnen geben?**
vêlH-e *shayn*-e dârf iH *een*-en *gey*-ben?
What denominations would you like?

Mike: **Ich hätte gern einen 50-Euro-Schein, 5 Zwanziger und 5 Zehner.**
iH *hêt*-e gêrn *ayn*-en *fuenf*-tsiH-oy-roh-shayn, fuenf *tsvân*-tsee-ger oont fuenf *tseyn*-er.
I'd like one 50-euro bill, five 20-euro bills, and five 10-euro bills.

Bankangestellte: **Bitte. Haben Sie sonst noch einen Wunsch?**
bi-te. *hah*-ben zee sonst noH *ayn*-en voonsh?
Here you are. Do you need anything else?

Mike: **Danke. Das ist alles.**
dân-ke. dâs ist *âl*-es.
Thanks. That's all.

Book II

Speaking German on the Go

Chapter 4

Finding a Place to Stay: Gute Nacht!

In This Chapter

▶ Choosing where to stay and making reservations

▶ Getting the most out of your stay — no matter how long it is

▶ Checking in and out and paying the bill

Regardless of whether you're traveling on business or taking a vacation, having a clean and comfortable place to spend the night is an important part of your trip. In this chapter, we help you with the vocabulary and phrases you need to know to find accommodations, inquire about facilities, make reservations, and check in and out.

Finding Accommodations

If you're one of those people who likes the adventure of doing things on the spur of the moment or if you simply need help finding a hotel after you get to your town, you can get reliable information about all types of accommodations through the local tourist information center, which is called **das Fremdenverkehrsbüro** or **Fremdenverkehrsamt** (dâs *frêm*-den-fêr-keyrs-bue-roh or *frêm*-den-fêr-keyrs-âmt). These tourist centers are often located conveniently in the center of town or next to the train station. Some information centers, called **Touristen-Information** (toor-*ist*-en-in-for-mâts-ee-*ohn*), are easily recognizable by a sign with a lowercase *I* on a red background. They may also help you get tickets to various events and attractions.

Of course, you can also ask other people you know or meet whether they can recommend a hotel. In this case, ask

> **Können Sie mir ein Hotel in . . . empfehlen?** (*kern*-en zee meer ayn hotel [as in English] in . . . êm-*pfey*-len?) (*Can you recommend a hotel in. . . ?*)

You can find a wide range of hotels and hotel-like accommodations in German-speaking countries. Outside urban areas, you're especially likely to see different types of lodging, including the following:

- **die Ferienwohnung** (dee *feyr*-ree-ên-vohn-oong): A furnished vacation apartment located in a popular tourist destination.

- **das Fremdenzimmer** (dâs *frêm*-dên-tsi-mer): A bed-and-breakfast, often with shared bathroom facilities.

- **das Gasthaus/der Gasthof** (dâs *gâst*-hous/dêr *gâst*-hohf): An inn that provides food, drinks, and often lodging.

- **das Hotel garni** (dâs hotel gâr-*nee*): A hotel that serves only breakfast.

- **die Jugendherberge** (die *yooh*-gênt-hêr-bêr-ge): A youth hostel, but not only for the under-25 crowd. This is an inexpensive option, but you generally need a Youth Hostel ID, which you can get before you travel.

- **die Pension** (dee pên-zee-*ohn*): A bed-and-breakfast type of place. In addition to breakfast, it may also serve lunch and dinner.

- **der Rasthof/das Motel** (dêr *râst*-hohf/dâs motel [as in English]): A roadside lodge or motel located just off a highway.

Making a Reservation

To avoid last-minute hassles, booking a hotel room in advance is best, especially during the peak season or when a special event in town may mean that hotels are booked solid for months in advance. If you're having difficulty finding a room, try looking outside of towns and city centers. Ask for some assistance at the **Fremdenverkehrsamt** (*frêm*-den-fêr-keyrs-âmt). (See the preceding section for more information on that helpful office with the long name.)

Of course, you can make reservations for hotel rooms online, but if you're using the phone, you may want to read Book I, Chapter 5 beforehand. When you call, the following sentence can help you explain the purpose of your call:

> **Ich möchte gern ein Zimmer reservieren.** (iH *merH*-te gêrn ayn *tsi*-mer rê-zêr-*vee*-ren.) (*I would like to reserve a room.*)

If you want to book more than one room, simply substitute the appropriate number — **zwei** (tsvay) (*two*), **drei** (dray) (*three*), and so on — in place of **ein.** Keep reading to find out what else you need to know when making reservations by phone.

Saying when and how long you want to stay

The person taking your reservation is likely to ask you a handful of questions before setting up your reservation. One of the first of these questions may be something like this:

> **Von wann bis wann möchten Sie das Zimmer reservieren?** (fon vân bis vân *merH*-ten zee dâs *tsi*-mer rê-zêr-*vee*-ren?) (*For what dates would you like to reserve the room?*)

To specify how many nights you want to stay or for what dates you want to reserve a room, you can say either of the following, depending on what suits your needs. (Book I, Chapter 2 gives more details on how to specify the date.)

> **Ich möchte gern ein Zimmer für . . . Nächte reservieren.** (iH *merH*-te gêrn ayn *tsi*-mer fuer . . . *naiHt*-e rê-zêr-*vee*-ren.) (*I would like to reserve a room for . . . nights.*)

> **Ich möchte gern ein Zimmer vom 11. 3. bis zum 15. 3. reservieren.** (iH *merH*-te gêrn ayn *tsi*-mer fom *êlf*-ten *drit*-en bis tsoom *fuenf*-tseyn-ten *drit*-en rê-zêr-*vee*-ren.) (*I would like to reserve a room from the 11th to the 15th of March.*)

Book II

Speaking German on the Go

Specifying the kind of room you want

The person taking your reservation is certain to ask you something like the following to find out what kind of room you want:

> **Was für ein Zimmer möchten Sie gern?** (vâs fuer ayn *tsi*-mer *merH*-ten zee gêrn?) (*What kind of room would you like?*)

Customer service people often ask **Was für. . . ?** (vâs fuer. . . ?) (*What kind of. . . ?*) when they want to know specifics about what you need. For example, someone at the **Fremdenverkehrsbüro** may want to find out exactly what you're looking for by asking questions like the following:

> **Was für eine Ferienwohnung möchten Sie gern?** (vâs fuer *ayn*-e *feyr*-ree-ê*n*-vohn-oong *merH*-ten zee gêrn?) (*What kind of vacation apartment would you like?*)

> **Was für eine Unterkunft suchen Sie?** (vâs fuer *ayn*-e *oon*-ter-koonft *zoohH*-en zee?) (*What kind of accommodation are you looking for?*)

The question **Was für. . . ?** is always used with the indefinite article in the accusative case. (See Book III, Chapter 2 for the lowdown on indefinite articles and the accusative case.)

Or you can take the initiative and state what kind of room you want with the phrase

Ich hätte gern. . . . (iH *hêt*-e gêrn. . . .) (*I would like. . . .*)

At the end of the phrase, add any of the following (or a combination of them) to specify exactly what kind of room you want to rest your weary bones in:

- **ein Doppelzimmer** (ayn *dôp*-el-tsi-mer) (*a double room*)

- **ein Einzelzimmer** (ayn *ayn*-tsêl-tsi-mer) (*a single room*)

- **ein Zimmer mit . . .** (ayn *tsi*-mer mit . . .) (*a room with . . .*) and then choose from the following features:

  - **Bad** (baht) (*bathroom*)

  - **Dusche** (*dooh*-she) (*shower*)

  - **einem Doppelbett** (*ayn*-êm *dôp*-el-bêt) (*one double bed*)

  - **zwei Einzelbetten** (tsvay *ayn*-tsêl-bêt-en) (*two twin beds*)

Asking about the price

Even if your last name is Moneybags, you probably want to find out what the room costs. Look at the following variations of this question, depending on whether you want to know the basic price or the price with other features included:

Was kostet das Zimmer pro Nacht? (vâs *kos*-tet dâs *tsi*-mer proh nâHt?) (*What does the room cost per night?*)

Was kostet eine Übernachtung mit Frühstück? (vâs *kos*-tet *ayn*-e ue-ber-*nâHt*-oong mit *frue*-shtuek?) (*What does accommodation including breakfast cost?*)

Was kostet ein Zimmer mit Halbpension/Vollpension? (vâs *kos*-tet ayn *tsi*-mer mit *hâlp*-pân-zee-ohn/*fol*-pân-zee-ohn?) (*What does a room with half board/full board cost?*) (*Half board* means two meals [breakfast and usually dinner], and *full board* means all three meals.)

Finalizing the reservation

If the room is available and the price doesn't cause you to faint, you can seal the deal by saying

Können Sie das Zimmer bitte reservieren? (*kern*-en zee dâs *tsi*-mer *bi*-te rê-zêr-*vee*-ren?) (*Could you reserve that room, please?*)

Talkin' the Talk

Klaus and Ulrike Huber want to take a vacation in **Österreich** (*erst*-êr-ayH) (*Austria*), and they've found a hotel on Lake Mondsee where they'd like to stay. Klaus calls the Hotel Alpenhof and talks to the receptionist. (Go to www.dummies.com/go/germanaio to listen to this bonus track.)

Rezeption: **Hotel Alpenhof, guten Tag.**
hotel [as in English] *âlp*-en-hohf, *gooh*-ten tahk.
Hello, Hotel Alpenhof.

Klaus: **Guten Tag. Ich möchte ein Zimmer vom 15. bis zum 23. Juni reservieren.**
gooh-ten tahk. iH *merH*-te ayn *tsi*-mer fom *fuenf*-tseyn-ten bis tsoom *dray*-oont-tsvân-tsiH-sten *yooh*-nee rê-zêr-*vee*-ren.
Hello. I'd like to book a room from the 15th to the 23rd of June.

Rezeption: **Ja, das geht. Was für ein Zimmer möchten Sie?**
yah, dâs geyt. vâs fuer ayn *tsi*-mer *merH*-ten zee?
Yes, that's fine. What kind of room would you like?

Klaus: **Ein Doppelzimmer mit Bad, bitte. Was kostet das Zimmer pro Nacht?**
ayn *dôp*-el-tsi-mer mit baht, *bi*-te. vâs *kôs*-tet dâs *tsi*-mer proh nâHt?
A double room with bathroom, please. What does the room cost per night?

Book II

Speaking German on the Go

Rezeption: **129 Euro für die Übernachtung mit Frühstück.**
ayn-hoon-dert-noyn-oont-*tsvân*-tsiH *oy*-roh fuer dee
ue-ber-*nâHt*-oong mit *frue*-shtuek.
129 euros for accommodation including breakfast.

Klaus: **Sehr gut. Können Sie es bitte reservieren? Mein
Name ist Huber.**
zeyr gooht. *kern*-en zee ês *bi*-te rê-zêr-vee-ren?
mayn *nah*-me ist *hooh*-ber.
That's very good. Could you please reserve it?
My name is Huber.

Rezeption: **Geht in Ordnung, Herr Huber.**
geyt in *ort*-noong, hêr *hooh*-ber.
Okay, Mr. Huber.

Klaus: **Vielen Dank!**
fee-len dânk!
Thank you very much!

Words to Know

das Fremdenverkehrsbüro	dâs frêm-den-fêrkeyrs-bue-roh	tourist information center
das Einzelzimmer	dâs ayn-tsêl-tsi-mer	single room
das Doppelzimmer	dâs dôp-el-tsi-mer	double room
das Bad	dâs baht	bathtub
die Dusche	dee dooh-she	shower
(Geht) in Ordnung!	(geyt) in ort-noong!	Okay!

Checking In

After you arrive at your hotel, you have to check in at the **Rezeption** (rê-tsêp-tsee-*ohn*)/**Empfang** (êm-*pfâng*) (*reception desk*). To let the receptionist know that you have made reservations, say

> **Ich habe ein Zimmer reserviert.** (iH *hah*-be ayn *tsi*-mer rê-zêr-*veert.*) (*I have reserved a room.*)

Of course, you also have to let the receptionist know what your name is:

> **Mein Name ist. . . .** (mayn *nah*-me ist. . . .) (*My name is. . . .*)

Book II

Speaking German on the Go

Stating how long you're staying

If you haven't made a reservation or the receptionist wants to double-check the length of your stay, you may hear the question

> **Wie lange bleiben Sie?** (vee *lâng*-e *blay*-ben zee?) (*How long are you going to stay?*)

You can reply with the phrase

> **Ich bleibe/Wir bleiben. . . .** (iH *blay*-be/veer *blay*-ben. . . .) (*I'm going to stay/ We're going to stay. . . .*)

Then end the phrase with any of the appropriate lengths of time:

> **nur eine Nacht** (noohr *ayn*-e nâHt) (*only one night*)
>
> **bis zum elften** (bis tsoom *êlf*-ten) (*until the 11th*)
>
> **eine Woche** (*ayn*-e *vôH*-e) (*one week*)

Filling out the registration form

At most hotels, you have to fill out **der Meldeschein** (dêr *mêl*-de-shayn) (*reservation form*), commonly referred to as **das Formular** (dâs for-mooh-*lahr*) (*the form*), as part of the check-in process. The receptionist will hand you the form, saying something like the following:

> **Bitte füllen Sie dieses Formular aus.** (*bi*-te *fuel*-en zee *deez*-ês for-mooh-*lahr* ous.) (*Please fill out this form.*)

The registration form asks you for all or most of the following information:

- **Tag der Ankunft** (tahk dēr *ān*-koonft) (*date of arrival*)
- **Name/Vorname** (*nah*-me/*fohr*-nah-me) (*surname/first name*)
- **Straße/Nummer (Nr.)** (*shtrah*-se/*noom*-er) (*street/number*)
- **Postleitzahl (PLZ)/Wohnort** (*post*-layt-tsahl/*vohn*-ort) (*zip code/town*)
- **Geburtsdatum/Geburtsort** (gē-*boorts*-dah-toohm/gē-*boorts*-ort) (*birth date/place of birth*)
- **Staatsangehörigkeit/Nationalität** (*stahts*-ân-ge-herr-iH-kayt/*nā*-tsee-oh-nahl-i-*tait*) (*nationality*)
- **Beruf** (bē-*roohf*) (*occupation*)
- **Passnummer** (*pās*-noom-er) (*passport number*)
- **Ort/Datum** (ort/*dah*-toohm) (*place/date*)
- **Unterschrift** (*oon*-ter-shrift) (*signature*)

Getting keyed in

After you check in, the receptionist hands you your room key and says something like

> **Sie haben Zimmer Nummer 203.** (zee *hah*-ben *tsi*-mer *noom*-er *tsvay*-hoon-dert-dray.) (*You have room number 203.*)

In some hotels, usually the more traditional ones, your room key is on a massive, metal key holder. You may be asked to leave your heavy metal key at the reception desk when you go out. When you arrive back at the hotel and need the key to your room, you can use the following phrase:

> **Können Sie mir bitte den Schlüssel für Zimmer Nummer . . . geben?** (*kern*-nen zee meer *bi*-te deyn *shlues*-êl fuer *tsi*-mer *noom*-er . . . *gey*-ben?) (*Could you give me the key for room number. . . ?*)

In all likelihood, you'll travel with some kind of **das Gepäck** (dâs ge-*pêk*) (*luggage*). Your luggage could be **der Koffer** (dēr *kof*-er) (*a suitcase*) or maybe even **die Koffer** (dee *kof*-er) (*suitcases*). No, that's not a mistake — the only difference between the singular and plural forms of *suitcase* is the article. (Book III, Chapter 2 gives you more details on plural endings for nouns.)

Although service charges are usually included in the price of your hotel room, you may want to give a **das Trinkgeld** (dâs *trink*-gêlt) (*tip*) to the porter who brings up your luggage. In this case, 1 or 2 euros per bag is a reasonable amount. On rare occasions, you also may see a little envelope in your room where you can leave money for the cleaning staff. Depending on the hotel and service, you can give a tip of 10 to 15 euros per week.

Asking about amenities and essentials

You may want to find out what kind of services and facilities the hotel offers. Does your room have Wi-Fi or a minibar? Does the hotel have a laundry service? This section helps you find out.

Book II

Speaking German on the Go

Your room

When you want to ask about specific features of your room, start with the phrase

Hat das Zimmer. . . ? (hât dâs *tsi*-mer. . . ?) (*Does the room have. . . ?*)

Then end the phrase with any of the following items:

einen Balkon (*ayn*-en bâl-*kohn*) (*a balcony*)

eine Minibar (*ayn*-e minibar [as in English]) (*a minibar*)

Satellitenfernsehen/Kabelfernsehen (zâ-tê-*lee*-ten-fêrn-zey-en/*kah*-bel-fêrn-zey-en) (*satellite TV/cable TV*)

ein Telefon (ayn *tê*-le-fohn) (*a phone*)

Wi-Fi (wee-fee) (*Wi-Fi*)

The hotel

The hotel may offer a number of services that are outlined in a brochure you find in your room. However, if you need to ask about the hotel's amenities before you arrive or because you misplaced your reading glasses, just ask

Hat das Hotel. . . ? (hât dâs hotel. . . ?) (*Does the hotel have. . . ?*)

You can then ask about any of the following services by ending the preceding phrase with

einen Fitnessraum (*ayn*-en *fit*-nes-room) (*a fitness room*)

eine Hotelgarage (*ayn*-e hoh-*têl*-gâ-*rah*-ge [second *g* pronounced as *g* in *genre*]) (*a hotel garage*)

eine Klimaanlage (*ayn*-e *klee*-mah-ân-lah-ge) (*air conditioning*)

einen Parkplatz (*ayn*-en *pârk*-plâts) (*a parking lot*)

eine Sauna (*ayn*-e *zou*-nâ) (*a sauna*)

ein Schwimmbad (ayn *shvim*-baht) (*a swimming pool*)

einen Wäschedienst (*ayn*-en *vêsh*-e-deenst) (*laundry service*)

Here are the questions that allow you to inquire about breakfast and room service:

Wann wird das Frühstück serviert? (vân virt dâs *frue*-shtuek zêr-*veert?*) (*At what time is breakfast served?*)

Gibt es Zimmerservice? (gipt ês *tsi*-mer-ser-vis?) (*Is there room service?*)

Talkin' the Talk

Klaus and Ulrike Huber arrive at the Hotel Alpenhof. They park their car at the entrance and go to the reception desk to check in. (Track 26)

Klaus: **Guten Abend! Mein Name ist Huber. Wir haben ein Zimmer reserviert.**
gooht-en *ah*-bent! mayn *nah*-me ist *hooh*-ber. veer *hah*-ben ayn *tsi*-mer rê-zêr-*veert.*
Good evening! My name is Huber. We've reserved a room.

Rezeption: **Ja richtig, ein Doppelzimmer mit Bad. Bitte füllen Sie dieses Formular aus.**
yah *riH*-tiH, ayn *dôp*-el-tsi-mer mit baht. *bi*-te *fuel*-en zee *deez*-es for-mooh-*lahr* ous.
Yes right, a double room with bath. Please fill out this form.

Klaus: **Haben Sie eine Garage oder einen Parkplatz?**
hah-ben zee *ayn*-e gâ-*rah*-ge *oh*-der *ayn*-en *pârk*-plâts?
Do you have a garage or a parking lot?

Rezeption: **Jawohl. Der Parkplatz ist hinter dem Hotel. Und hier ist Ihr Zimmerschlüssel, Nummer 203.**
yah-*vohl*. dêr *pârk*-plâts ist *hin*-ter deym hotel [as in English]. oont heer ist eer *tsi*-mer-*shlues*-êl, *noom*-er *tsavy*-hoon-dert-dray.
Yes, indeed. The parking lot is behind the hotel. And here is your key, number 203.

Ulrike: **Wann servieren Sie Frühstück?**
vân zêr-*vee*-ren zee *frue*-shtuek?
When do you serve breakfast?

Rezeption: **Von sieben bis zehn Uhr.**
fon *zee*-ben bis tseyn oohr.
From 7 to 10 o'clock.

Ulrike: **Vielen Dank.**
fee-len dânk
Thank you very much.

Words to Know

bleiben	<u>blay</u>-ben	to stay
das Formular	dâs for-mooh-<u>lahr</u>	form
ausfüllen	<u>ous</u>-fuel-en	to fill out
der Schlüssel	dêr <u>shlues</u>-êl	key
der Zimmerservice	dêr <u>tsi</u>-mer-ser-vis	room service
der Parkplatz	dêr <u>pârk</u>-plâts	parking lot

Making the Most of Your Stay

Whether you stay for just a few nights or several weeks, you'll likely have some interactions with the hotel staff. You may need to ask for certain items or request help in resolving a problem. The following sections provide the phrases you need to enjoy your stay.

Making special requests

After you're settled in your hotel room, you may discover that you need an extra pillow or that you'd like someone to recommend a good restaurant nearby. The following questions and requests may come in handy:

Können Sie mich bitte um 6 Uhr wecken? (*kern*-en zee miH *bi*-te oom zêks oohr *vêk*-en?) (*Could you wake me up at 6 o'clock, please?*)

Können Sie mir bitte noch ein Kopfkissen bringen? (*kern*-en zee mir *bi*-te noH ayn *kopf*-kis-en *bring*-en?) (*Could you bring me another pillow, please?*)

Könnte ich bitte noch ein (weiteres) Badetuch haben? (*kern*-te iH *bi*-te noH ayn [*vayt*-êr-ês] *bah*-de-tooH *hah*-ben?) (*Could I have [another] bath towel, please?*)

Können Sie mir ein gutes Restaurant in der Nähe empfehlen? (*kern*-en zee mir ayn *gooht*-es rês-tuh-*ron* in dêr *nai*-he êm-*pfey*-len?) (*Could you recommend a good restaurant nearby?*)

Gibt es hier in der Nähe eine U-Bahnstation? (gipt ês heer in dêr *nai*-he *ayn*-e *ooh*-bahn-shtât-see-ohn?) (*Is there a subway station near here?*)

Wo ist die nächste Bank? (voh ist die *naiH*-ste bânk?) (*Where is the nearest bank?*)

Wie funktioniert die Klimaanlage? (vee foonk-tsee-on-*eert* dee *klee*-mâ-ân-lâ-ge?) (*How does the air conditioning work?*)

Darf ich einen Fön ausleihen? (dârf iH *ayn*-en fern *ous*-lay-en?) (*May I borrow a hair dryer?*)

Many of the larger hotels will arrange sightseeing tours and excursions for you, as well as buy tickets to the theater or other events. You make your request known at the **Rezeption** (rê-zep-tsee-*ohn*) (*reception*) or, in some of the fancier hotels, at a separate desk where you can get help specifically with planning your stay in town. Here are a few phrases that may be helpful:

Ich möchte gern in die Berge fahren. (iH *merH*-te gêrn in dee *bêrg*-e *fahr*-hen.) (*I'd like to go to the mountains.*)

Könnten Sie mir bitte einen Tagesausflug buchen? (*kern*-ten zee mir *bi*-te ayn-en *tah*-ges-ous-floohk *booH*-en?) (*Could you book a day trip for me?*)

Ich möchte gern ins Theater gehen. (iH *merH*-te gêrn ins tey-*ah*-ter *gey*-en.) (*I'd like to go to the theater.*)

Könnten Sie mir bitte für heute Abend zwei Karten fürs Theater reservieren? (*kern*-ten zee mir *bi*-te fuer *hoy*-te *ah*-bênt tvsay *kâr*-ten fuers tey-*ah*-ter rêz-êr-*veer*-en?) (*Could you reserve two tickets for this evening?*)

Pointing out problems

Book II

Speaking German on the Go

German, Austrian, and Swiss hotels enjoy a solid reputation for top-notch service and superb cleanliness, along with a continental breakfast or breakfast buffet included in the room price. Yet even at first-rate hotels, you may experience a glitch in the otherwise perfect accommodations. To point out something that needs attention, you want to be polite, but you also want results.

Hopefully none of the following situations happen to you, but just in case one does, here's a helpful list of how to address the problem. For each situation, you get a statement of what's wrong, followed by a polite request for a solution:

Das Zimmer ist zu kalt. (dâs *tsi*-mer ist tsooh kâlt.) (*The room is too cold.*)

Können Sie mir bitte sagen, wie ich die Heizung aufdrehe? (*kern*-en zee mir *bi*-te *zah*-gen, vee iH dee *hayts*-oong *ouf*-drey-e?) (*Could you tell me how to turn up the heat, please?*)

Der Straßenlärm ist mir sehr unangenehm. (dêr *shtrah*-sen-lêrm ist mir zeyr *oon*-ân-ge-neym.) (*The street noise is very unpleasant.*)

Haben Sie vielleicht ein ruhigeres Zimmer zum Hinterhof? (*hah*-ben zee fee-*layHt* ayn *rooh*-ee-gêr-es *tsi*-mer tsoom *hin*-ter-hohf?) (*Do you have a quieter room facing the courtyard?*)

In meinem Zimmer gibt es keine Fernbedienung. (in *mayn*-em *tsi*-mer gipt ês *kayn*-e *fêrn*-be-deen-oong.) (*There is no remote control in my room.*)

Könnten Sie mir bitte eine bringen? (*kernt*-en zee mir *bi*-te *ayn*-e *bring*-en?) (*Could you bring me one, please?*)

Die Gäste im Zimmer nebenan machen zu viel Lärm. (dee *gês*-te im *tsi*-mer ney-ben-*ân* *mâH*-en tsooh feel lêrm.) (*The guests in the room next door are making too much noise.*)

Könnten Sie sie (darum) bitten, ruhiger zu sein? (*kern*-ten zee zee [*dâ*-room] *bi*-ten, *rooh*-ee-ger tsoo zayn?) (*Could you ask them to be quieter?*)

Ich kann das Fenster nicht öffnen. (iH kân dâs *fêns*-ter niHt *erf*-nen.) (*I can't open the window.*)

Können sie mir bitte zeigen, wie ich das Fenster öffne? (*kern*-en zee mir *bi*-te *tsay*-gen, vee iH dâs *fêns*-ter *erf*-ne?) (*Could you show me how I open the window, please?*)

Es gibt nur kaltes Wasser in der Dusche. (ês gipt noor *kâl*-tes *vâs*-er in dêr *dooh*-she.) (*There's only cold water in the shower.*)

Hätten Sie ein anderes Zimmer? (*hêt*-ten zee *ayn* ân-dêr-es *tsi*-mer?) (*Would you have another room?*)

Ich bin allergisch gegen den Federn in der Bettdecke. (iH bin â-*lêr*-gish *gey*-gen dên *fey*-dêrn in dêr *bêt*-dêk-e.) (*I'm allergic to the feathers in the quilt.*)

Können Sie mir bitte eine andere Bettdecke bringen? (*kern*-en zee mir *bi*-te *ayn*-e *ân*-dêr-e *bêt*-dêk-e *bring*-en?) (*Could you bring me another quilt, please?*)

Checking Out and Paying the Bill

The German language has no exact equivalent for the convenient English phrase "to check out." So you use **das Zimmer räumen** (dâs *tsi*-mêr *roy*-men), which literally translates into *to clear out the room*. If you want to ask what time you have to vacate your room, just say

Bis wann müssen wir/muss ich das Zimmer räumen? (bis vân *mues*-en veer/moos iH dâs *tsi*-mêr *roy*-men?) (*At what time do we/I have to check out of the room?*)

Asking for the bill

When you're ready to check out of the hotel, you can use the word **abreisen** (*âp*-ray-zen) (*to leave; literally: to travel on*). So when you want to leave, tell the receptionist

Ich reise ab. (iH *ray*-ze âp.) (*I'm leaving.*)

Wir reisen ab. (veer *ray*-zen âp.) (*We're leaving.*)

The preceding phrases will probably be enough to get the receptionist busy preparing your bill. However, if you need to drive home the point that you'd like to have your bill, you can say

> **Kann ich bitte die Rechnung haben?** (kân iH *bi*-te dee *rêH*-noong *hah*-ben?) (*Could I have the bill, please?*)

Book I, Chapters 6 and 7 tell you all about dealing with bills, paying with a credit card, and asking for a receipt.

Asking small favors

Book II

Speaking German on the Go

If you have to check out of the hotel before you're actually ready to continue on your trip, you may want to leave your luggage for a couple of hours. Fortunately, most hotels allow you to do this. Simply ask

> **Können wir unser/Kann ich mein Gepäck bis . . . Uhr hier lassen?** (*kern*-en veer *oon*-zer/kân iH mayn ge-*pêk* bis . . . oohr heer *lâs*-en?) (*Could we leave our/Could I leave my luggage here until . . . o'clock?*)

When you return to pick up your luggage, you can say

> **Können wir/Kann ich bitte unser/mein Gepäck haben?** (*kern*-en veer/ kân iH *bi*-te *oon*-zer/mayn ge-*pêk hah*-ben?) (*Could we/Could I get our/ my luggage, please?*)

Ready to go to the airport or train station? If you want the receptionist to call you a cab, ask

> **Können Sie mir bitte ein Taxi bestellen?** (*kern*-en zee meer *bi*-te ayn *tâx*-ee be-*shtêl*-en?) (*Could you call a cab for me?*)

The receptionist will need to know where you intend to go before calling for your taxi. The receptionist may ask you

> **Wo möchten Sie hin?** (voh *merH*-ten zee hin?) (*Where would you like to go?*)

Just make sure you know the name of the place you want to go before you approach the receptionist!

Talkin' the Talk

Klaus and Ulrike Huber are ready to move on and explore other parts of the country. They go to the reception desk to check out.

Klaus:	**Guten Morgen! Wir reisen heute ab. Kann ich bitte die Rechnung haben?**
	gooh-ten *môr*-gen! veer *ray*-zen *hoy*-te âp. kân iH *bi*-te dee *rêH*-noong *hah*-ben?
	Good morning! We're leaving today. May I have the bill, please?
Rezeption:	**Sicher, einen Moment bitte. Haben Sie gestern Abend noch etwas aus der Minibar genommen?**
	ziH-er, *ayn*-en moh-*mênt bi*-te. *hah*-ben zee *gês*-tern *ah*-bent nôH *êt*-vâs ous dêr minibar gê-*nôm*-en?
	Sure, one moment please. Did you take anything from the minibar last night?
Klaus:	**Ja, zwei Bier.**
	yah, tsvay beer.
	Yes, two beers.
Rezeption:	**Danke. Also, hier ist ihre Rechnung.**
	dân-ke. *al*-zoh, heer ist *eer*-e *rêH*-noong.
	Thank you. So, here is your bill.
Klaus:	**Kann ich mit Kreditkarte bezahlen?**
	kân iH mit krê-*dit*-kâr-te be-*tsahl*-en?
	Can I pay with a credit card?
Rezeption:	**Selbstverständlich. Unterschreiben Sie hier, bitte.**
	zêlpst-fêr-*shtênt*-liH. oon-ter-*shray*-ben zee heer, *bi*-te.
	Of course. Please sign here.
Klaus:	**Vielen Dank und auf Wiedersehen.**
	fee-len dânk oont ouf *vee*-der-zey-en.
	Thank you very much and goodbye.
Rezeption:	**Gute Reise!**
	gooh-te *ray*-ze!
	Have a good trip!

Chapter 5

Getting Around

● ●

In This Chapter

▶ Getting familiar with airport lingo

▶ Seeing Germany (or wherever you are) by car

▶ Traveling by train

▶ Taking a bus, streetcar, subway, or taxi

● ●

Planes, trains, taxis, streetcars, buses, subways, and automobiles — you have lots of options for how to get around German-speaking countries. In this chapter, you find out what you need to know to deal with ticket agents, customs officials, car-rental staff, and public transportation personnel. You also discover how to ask the occasional bystander for help, all while keeping a cool head, smiling, and being polite.

Going through the Airport

Most airline personnel speak several languages, so they can usually help you in English. But in case you need a little backup, this section provides you with enough vocabulary to navigate the airport with confidence and a smile.

Getting your ticket and checking in

Before you head to the airport, you may want to memorize the following three terms related to airplane tickets — just in case:

  ✔ **die Bordkarte** (dee *bord*-kâr-te) (*boarding pass*)

  ✔ **das Flugticket/der Flugschein** (dâs *floohk*-ti-ket/dêr *floohk*-shayn) (*airplane ticket*)

  ✔ **das Rückflugticket** (dâs *ruek*-floohk-ti-ket) (*round-trip ticket*)

If you can't print out your ticket and boarding pass before you get to the air-port, you'll have to find the appropriate airline counter. Hopefully the signs at the airport are clear enough, but if you're feeling like Alice in Wonderland and don't know which way to go, stop an employee and ask for directions to your airline's ticket counter:

> **Wo ist der . . . Schalter?** (voh ist dêr . . . *shâl*-ter?) (*Where is the . . . counter?*)

When you arrive at the ticket counter, just say the following to inquire about your ticket:

> **Ich möchte mein Ticket abholen.** (iH *merH*-te mayn ticket [as in English] *âp*-hoh-len.) (*I would like to pick up my ticket.*)

The attendant will ask you a few questions to prepare you for boarding the plane:

> **Haben Sie Gepäck?** (*hah*-ben zee ge-*pêk*?) (*Do you have luggage?*)

> **Wo möchten Sie sitzen, am Fenster oder am Gang?** (voh *merH*-ten zee *zits*-en, âm *fêns*-ter *oh*-der âm gâng?) (*Where would you like to sit, by the window or on the aisle?*)

In response to the question about where you want to sit, you can respond simply **am Fenster/am Gang** (âm *fêns*-ter/âm gâng) (*by a window/on the aisle*), according to your preference.

You may also want to ask the following questions to get some details about the flight:

> **Wie lange dauert der Flug?** (vee *lâng*-e *dou*-êrt dêr floohk?) (*How long is the flight?*)

> **Wann fliegt die Maschine/das Flugzeug ab?** (vân fleekt dee mâ-*sheen*-e/ dâs *floohk*-tsoyk âp?) (*When does the plane leave?*)

If you're at the airport to meet somebody who's arriving on another plane, you can ask

> **Wann kommt die Maschine aus . . . an?** (vân komt dee mâ-*sheen*-e ous . . . ân?) (*When does the plane from . . . arrive?*)

Words to Know

der Anschlussflug	dêr <u>ân</u>-shloos-floohk	connecting flight
das Flugticket/der Flugschein	dâs <u>floohk</u>-ti-ket/ dêr <u>floohk</u>-shayn	airplane ticket
das Rückflugticket	dâs <u>ruek</u>-floohk-ti-ket	round-trip ticket
die Bordkarte	dee <u>bord</u>-kâr-te	boarding pass
das Gepäck/ Handgepäck	dâs ge-<u>pêk</u>/ <u>hând</u>-ge-pêk	luggage/hand luggage
das Flugzeug/die Maschine	das <u>floohk</u>-tsoyk/ dee mâ-<u>shee</u>-ne	airplane
der Flug	dêr floohk	flight
abholen	<u>âp</u>-hoh-len	to pick up
dauern	<u>dou</u>-ern	to last, to take (time)

Book II

Speaking German on the Go

Talkin' the Talk

Frau Schöller is flying to Prague. At the airport she's getting her boarding pass at the Lufthansa counter. (Track 27)

Frau Schöller: **Guten Morgen. Ich brauche eine Bordkarte. Hier ist mein Ticket.**
gooh-ten *mor*-gen. iH *brauH*-e *ayn*-e *bord*-kâr-te. Heer ist mayn ticket.
Good morning. I need a boarding pass. Here is my ticket.

Angestellter: **Ihren Pass, bitte.**
eer-en pâs, *bi*-te.
Your passport, please.

Frau Schöller hands the counter agent her passport.

Frau Schöller: **Bitte schön.**
bi-te shern.
Here you are.

Angestellter: **Danke. Wo möchten Sie sitzen, am Fenster oder am Gang?**
dân-ke. voh *merH*-ten zee *zits*-en, âm *fêns*-ter *oh*-der âm gâng?
Thank you. Where would you like to sit, by the window or by the aisle?

Frau Schöller: **Am Fenster, bitte.**
âm *fêns*-ter, *bi*-te.
By the window, please.

Angestellter: **Sie haben Platz 15A, einen Fensterplatz. Hier ist Ihre Bordkarte. Haben Sie Gepäck?**
zee *hah*-ben plâts *fuenf*-tseyn ah, *ayn*-en *fêns*-ter-plâts. heer ist *eer*-e *bord-kâr*-te. *hah*-ben zee ge-*pêk*?
You have seat 15A, a window seat. Here is your boarding pass. Do you have any luggage?

Frau Schöller: **Ich habe nur Handgepäck, diese Tasche.**
iH *hah*-be noohr *hând*-ge-pêk, *deez*-e *tâsh*-e.
I only have a carry-on, this bag.

Angestellter: **Dann können Sie direkt zum Flugsteig gehen.**
dân *kern*-en zee di-*rêkt* tsoom *floohk*-shtayk *gey*-en.
Then you can go straight to the gate.

Frau Schöller: **Danke.**
dân-ke.
Thank you.

Words to Know

der Abflug	dêr âp-floohk	departure
die Ankunft	dee ân-koonft	arrival
der Flugsteig	dêr floohk-shtayk	gate
mitnehmen	mit-neym-en	to take along
einchecken	ayn-chêk-en	to check in
fliegen	fleeg-en	to fly
abfliegen	âp-fleeg-en	to leave (on a plane)
ankommen	ân-kom-en	to arrive
der Ausweis	dêr ous-vays	ID card
verspätet	fêr-shpey-tet	delayed

Book II

Speaking German on the Go

Going through passport control

Jet-lagged after a long flight across the Atlantic (or wherever you've come from), all you want to do is leave the airport. But first you have two hurdles to overcome — passport control and customs. To help you in your foggy state of mind, here are the words you may need to be familiar with when you go through **Passkontrolle** (dee *pâs*-kon-*trol*-e) (*passport control*) (see the next section for details on customs):

der Reisepass/der Pass (dêr *ray*-ze-pâs/dêr pâs) (*passport*)

EU-Bürger (ey-*ooh-buer*-ger) (*citizen of a country of the European Union*)

Nicht-EU-Bürger (*niHt*-ey-ooh-buer-ger) (*citizen of a country outside the EU*)

Here are some sentences you may need to use on your way:

Ich bin im Urlaub hier. (iH bin im *oor*-loup heer.) (*I'm here on vacation.*)

Ich bin geschäftlich hier. (iH bin ge-*shêft*-liH heer.) (*I'm here on business.*)

Ich bin auf der Durchreise nach. . . . (iH bin ouf dêr *doorH*-ray-ze nâhH. . . .) (*I am on my way to. . . .*)

Most of the time when you reach passport control, you get to choose between two lines: One is for **EU-Bürger** and the other is for **Nicht-EU-Bürger.** After passing through whichever line applies to you, you claim your baggage and go through **der Zoll** (dêr tsol) (*customs*), where you may have to open your luggage for inspection (see the next section).

Matters are more laid back when you're traveling from one member country of **die europäische Union** (dee oy-roh-*pey*-i-she oon-ee-*yohn*) (*the European Union*) to another by car or train. With the number of member states currently at 27 — and still counting — you may find yourself crossing many internal borders of the EU without being checked. So when you drive from Germany to France, for example, you may not even notice where the border is until you suddenly discover that the signs are all in French. You can also import virtually unlimited quantities of goods bought from one EU country to another country.

Going through customs

You passed the first hurdle and are on your way to customs. Are you one of those people who feels guilty even when you have nothing to hide? Customs officers can make you feel that way. It pays to know how to answer their questions succinctly so you can get past them as quickly as possible.

At **der Zoll** (dêr tsol) (*customs*), you usually get to choose between two options: the red exit for people who have to declare goods or the green exit for those people who are carrying only things they don't need to declare. Customs officers may use the following phrase to ask you personally whether you have anything to declare, in which case you may need to pay duty:

> **Haben Sie etwas zu verzollen?** (*hah*-ben zee *êt*-vâs tsooh fêr-*tsol*-en?)
> (*Do you have anything to declare?*)

To this question, you can respond with either of the following:

> **Ich möchte . . . verzollen.** (iH *merH*-te . . . fêr-*tsol*-en) (*I would like to declare. . . .*)

> **Ich habe nichts zu verzollen.** (iH *hah*-be niHts tsooh fêr-*tsol*-en.) (*I have nothing to declare.*)

Despite your most engaging smile, the customs officer may ask to have a look at your not-so-suspicious-looking stuff by saying

> **Bitte öffnen Sie diesen Koffer/diese Tasche.** (*bi*-te *erf*-nen zee *deez*-en *kof*-er/*deez*-e *tâsh*-e.) (*Please open this suitcase/bag.*)

When the customs officer asks what you're planning to do with a particular item in your bag, you may answer

> **Es ist für meinen persönlichen Gebrauch.** (ês ist fuer *mayn*-en pêr-*sern*-liH-en ge-*brouH.*) (*It's for my personal use.*)
>
> **Es ist ein Geschenk.** (ês ist ayn ge-*shênk.*) (*It's a gift.*)

Traveling by Car

Book II

Speaking German on the Go

Before setting out on a European road trip in a rental car, consider acquiring an **internationaler Führerschein** (*in*-têr-nâ-tee-oh-nâ-ler *fuer*-er-shayn) (*international driving permit*). You can apply for one at the local AAA (American Automobile Association) website. (Find your local club at www.aaa.com.) Even with an **internationaler Führerschein**, however, you still need a valid driver's license from your own country. The **internationaler Füherschein** is simply a document with translations of the license information into several major European languages. If you have both, you're all set to discover new territory.

To get from city to city in German-speaking countries, you're most likely to travel the following types of roads:

- ✔ **die Autobahn** (dee *ou*-toh-bahn) (*four- to six-lane freeway*)
- ✔ **die Bundesstraße** (dee *boon*-des-shtrah-se) or, in Switzerland, **Nationalstrasse** (nâ-tee-oh-*nahl*-shtrah-se) (*two- to four-lane highway*)
- ✔ **die Landstraße** (dee *länt*-shtrah-se) (*two-lane highway*)

Renting a car

You're likely to find that making car reservations is cheaper and more hassle-free if you do it before leaving for your European trip. However, if you decide to rent a car when you're already in Europe, you need to make your way to the **Autovermietung** (*ou*-toh-fêr-meet-oong) (*car rental agency*). When you arrive, start out by saying

> **Ich möchte ein Auto mieten.** (iH *merH*-te ayn *ou*-toh *meet*-en.) (*I would like to rent a car.*)

The attendant will ask you what kind of car you want by saying something like

> **Was für ein Auto möchten Sie?** (vâs fuer ayn *ou*-toh *merH*-ten zee?) (*What kind of car would you like?*)

You can respond with any of the following:

- ✔ **ein zweitüriges/viertüriges Auto** (ayn *tsvay*-tuer-ee-ges/*feer*-tuer-ee-ges *ou*-toh) (*a two-door/four-door car*)
- ✔ **einen Kleinwagen** (*ayn*-en *klayn*-wah-gen) (*compact car*)
- ✔ **mit Klimanlage** (mit *klee*-mâ-ân-lâ-ge) (*with A/C*)
- ✔ **mit Automatik** (mit ou-toh-*mah*-tik) (*car with automatic transmission*)
- ✔ **mit Gangschaltung** (mit *gâng*-shâlt-oong) (*car with standard transmission*)

The attendant may also ask you one or more of the following questions about your rental plans:

> **Ab wann möchten Sie den Wagen mieten?** (âp vân *merH*-ten zee deyn *vah*-gen *meet*-en?) (*When would you like to start renting the car?*)

> **Wann/Wo möchten Sie den Wagen zurückgeben?** (vân/voh *merH*-ten zee deyn *vah*-gen tsoo-*ruek*-gey-ben?) (*Where/When would you like to return the car?*)

Here are some possible answers:

> **Ich möchte den Wagen ab dem . . . mieten.** (iH *merH*-te deyn *vah*-gen âp deym . . . *meet*-en.) (*I would like to rent the car starting. . . .*)

> **Ich möchte den Wagen am . . . zurückgeben.** (iH *merH*-te deyn *vah*-gen âm . . . tsoo-*ruek*-gey-ben.) (*I would like to return the car on the. . . .*)

> **Ich möchte den Wagen in (Frankfurt) zurückgeben.** (iH *merH*-te deyn *vah*-gen in [*frânk*-foort] tsoo-*ruek*-gey-ben.) (*I would like to return the car in [Frankfurt].*)

During the rental process, you'll hear the following words as well:

- ✔ **der Führerschein** (dêr *fuer*-er-shayn) (*driver's license*)
- ✔ **die Vollkaskoversicherung** (dee *fol*-kâs-koh-fêr-*zeeH*-er-oong) (*comprehensive collision insurance*)
- ✔ **inbegriffen** (*in*-be-grif-en) (*included*)
- ✔ **ohne Kilometerbegrenzung** (*oh*-ne ki-lo-*mey*-ter-be-*grênts*-oong) (*unlimited mileage*)

Talkin' the Talk

Anke has just arrived in Frankfurt. After going through customs, she heads for a car rental agency where she talks to an employee.

Anke: **Guten Morgen. Ich möchte ein Auto mieten.**
gooh-ten *mor*-gen. iH *merH*-te ayn *ou*-toh *meet*-en.
Good morning. I would like to rent a car.

Angestellter: **Was für ein Auto möchten Sie?**
vâs fuer ayn *ou*-toh *merH*-ten zee?
What kind of car would you like?

Anke: **Einen Kleinwagen mit Automatik.**
ayn-en *klayn*-vah-gen mit ou-toh-*mah*-tik.
A compact car with automatic transmission.

Angestellter: **Wie lange brauchen Sie den Wagen?**
vee *lâng*-e *brouH*-en zee deyn *vah*-gen?
How long do you need the car?

Anke: **Eine Woche.**
ayn-e *voH*-e.
For one week.

Angestellter: **Ein VW Polo kostet für eine Woche ohne Kilometerbregrenzung 299 Euro inklusive Versicherung.**
ayn vou-*vey poh*-loh *kos*-tet fuer *ayn*-e *voH*-e oh-ne ki-lo-*mey*-ter-be-*grênts*-oong *tsvay*-hoon-dêrt-*noyn*-oont–*noyn*-tsiH oy-roh in-kloo-*zee*-ve fêr-*ziH*-er-oong.
A VW Polo costs 299 euros for one week, including unlimited mileage and insurance.

Making sense of road maps

A good map tells you plenty more than how to get from Point A to Point B, and it allows you to mark your route as you travel. Another advantage of maps is that they're primarily visual, so you don't have to know too much of the language to read one. However, you may find that knowing the words for different kinds of maps is helpful, in case you need to ask for one:

- ✔ **die Landkarte** (dee *lânt*-kâr-te) (*map*)
- ✔ **der Stadtplan** (dêr *shtât*-plahn) (*map of a city*)
- ✔ **die Straßenkarte** (dee *shtrah*-sen-kâr-te) (*road map*)

On a German map (and also on road signs), you may see the following words:

- **die Altstadt** (dee *âlt*-shtât) (*historic center*)
- **die Ausfahrt** (dee *ous*-fahrt) (*exit ramp*)
- **das Autobahndreieck** (dâs *ou*-toh-bahn-*dray*-êk) (*where one freeway splits off from another freeway*)
- **das Autobahnkreuz** (dâs *ou*-toh-bahn-kroyts) (*junction of two freeways*)
- **die Einfahrt** (dee *ayn*-fahrt) (*entrance ramp*)
- **die Fußgängerzone** (dee *foohs*-gên-ger-*tsohn*-e) (*pedestrian zone*)
- **die Kirche** (dee *kirH*-e) (*church*)
- **das Parkhaus** (dâs *pârk*-hous) (*parking garage*)
- **der Parkplatz** (dêr *pârk*-plâts) (*parking lot*)
- **das Theater** (dâs tey-*ah*-ter) (*theater*)

Understanding and observing road signs

No matter where you're driving, you surely don't want to get stopped for driving too fast in the wrong direction down a one-way street that's been closed for construction. To prevent a scenario like this, here are some of the most common road signs that you encounter in German-speaking countries:

- **Anlieger frei** (*ân*-lee-ger fray) (*access only; no exit*)
- **Baustelle** (*bou*-shtêl-e) (*construction site*)
- **Einbahnstraße** (*ayn*-bahn-*shtrah*-se) (*one-way street*)
- **Einordnen** (*ayn*-ord-nen) (*merge*)
- **50 bei Nebel** (*fuenf*-tsiH bay *ney*-bel) (*50 kilometers per hour when foggy*)
- **Gebührenpflichtig** (ge-*buer*-en-pfliHt-iH) (*subject to charges* — you have to pay toll; you see this sign at the beginning of bridges, tunnels, or turnpikes)
- **Gesperrt** (ge-*shpêrt*) (*closed*)
- **Licht an/aus** (liHt ân/ous) (*lights on/off* — you see these signs at tunnels)
- **Maut** (mout) (*toll*)
- **Stau** (shtou) (*traffic jam* — you see this message on electronic signage)
- **Umleitung** (*oom*-lay-toong) (*detour*)
- **Vorsicht Glätte** (fohr-ziHt *glêt*-e) (*slippery when wet*)

Identifying parts of a car

When you rent a car in Europe, you have the convenience of getting around to some of the most beautiful scenery imaginable, especially in the Alps. Driving up and down mountain passes is an exciting experience. In the unlikely event that something happens to your car and you need to go to an **Automechaniker** (*ou*-toh-mêH-*ân*-i-kêr) (*car mechanic*), you may want to be familiar with the parts of the car and some of the issues you could have with it:

- **abschleppen** (*âp*-shlêp-en) (*to tow*)
- **der Abschleppwagen** (*âp*-shlêp-vâ-gen) (*tow truck*)
- **das Auto** (dâs *ou*-toh) (*car*)
- **die Batterie** (dee bât-êr-*ee*) (*battery*)
- **das Benzin** (dâs bên-*tseen*) (*gasoline*)
- **der Blinker** (dêr *blink*-er) (*turn signal*)
- **bremsen** (*brêm*-zen) (*to brake*)
- **das Bremspedal** (dâs *brêmz*-pêd-âl) (*brake pedal*)
- **einstellen** (*ayn*-shtêl-en) (*to adjust*)
- **fehlen** (*fey*-len) (*to be missing*)
- **der Gang** (dêr gâng) (*gear*)
- **das Gaspedal** (dâs *gâs*-pêd-âl) (*gas pedal*)
- **halten** (*hâlt*-en) (*to stop*)
- **klopfen** (*klopf*-en) (*to knock*)
- **der Kotflügel** (dêr *koht*-flueg-el) (*fender*)
- **kuppeln** (*koop*-eln) (*to engage the clutch*)
- **die Kupplung** (dee *koop*-loong) (*clutch*)
- **der Lärm** (dêr lêrm) (*noise*)
- **lecken** (*lêk*-en) (*to leak*)
- **leer** (lêr) (*empty*)
- **lenken** (*lênk*-en) (*to steer*)
- **das Lenkrad** (dâs *lênk*-râd) (*steering wheel*)
- **liegen bleiben** (*lee*-gen *blay*-ben) (*to stall*)
- **der Motor** (dêr *moh*-tor) (*motor*)
- **die Notbremse** (dee *noht*-brêm-ze) (*emergency brake*)

Book II

Speaking German on the Go

- die **Panne** (dee *pân*-e) (*breakdown*)
- einen **Platten haben** (*ayn*-en *plât*-en *hah*-ben) (*to have a flat tire*)
- der **Reifen** (dêr *rayf*-en) (*tire*)
- der **Reifendruck** (dêr *rayf*-en-drook) (*tire pressure*)
- die **Reparatur** (dee rêp-âr-â-*toor*) (*repair*)
- **reparieren** (rêp-âr-*eer*-en) (*to repair*)
- **schalten** (*shâl*-ten) (*to shift gears*)
- der **Scheibenwischer** (dêr *shay*-ben-wish-er) (*windshield wiper*)
- die **Stoßstange** (dee *shtohs*-shtâng-e) (*bumper*)
- die **Tankstelle** (dee *tânk*-shtêl-e) (*gas station*)
- der **Unfall** (dêr *oon*-fâl) (*accident*)
- der **Wagen** (dêr *wah*-gen) (*car*)
- die **Zundkerze** (dee *tsoond*-kêrts-e) (*spark plug*)
- die **Zündung** (dee *tsuend*-oong) (*ignition*)

The following expressions may help you if you need to explain what's wrong with your car or what you want the mechanic to do to it:

Ich habe einen Platten. (iH *hah*-be *ayn*-en *plât*-en.) (*I have a flat tire.*)

Können Sie bitte den Reifen wechseln? (*kern*-en zee *bi*-te den *ray*-fen *vêk*-seln?) (*Can you change the tire, please?*)

Können Sie bitte den Reifendruck kontrollieren? (*kern*-en zee *bi*-te den *rayf*-en-drook kon-tro-*leer*-en?) (*Can you check the tire pressure, please?*)

Der Motor klopft. (dêr *moh*-tor klopft.) (*The motor knocks.*)

Der Wagen springt nicht an. (dêr *vah*-gen shprinkt niHt ân.) (*The car doesn't start.*)

Der Wagen bleibt liegen. (dêr *vah*-gen blaypt *lee*-gen.) (*The car has stalled.*)

Der Motor macht einen komischen Lärm. (dêr *moh*-tor mâHt *ayn*-en *koh*-mish-en lêrm.) (*The motor is making a strange noise.*)

Können Sie bitte das Auto sofort reparieren? (*kern*-en zee *bi*-te dâs *ou*-toh zoh-*fort* rêp-âr-*eer*-en?) (*Can you repair the car right away, please?*)

Wie lange dauert die Reparatur? (vee *lâng*-e *dou*-êrt dee rêp-âr-â-*toor*?) (*How long will the repair take?*)

Können Sie bitte einen Abschleppwagen schicken? (*kern*-en zee *bi*-te ayn-en *âp*-shlêp-vâg-en *shik*-en?) (*Can you send a tow truck, please?*)

Nehmen Sie Kreditkarten? (*ney*-men zee krê-*dit*-kâr-ten?) (*Do you accept credit cards?*)

Taking the Train

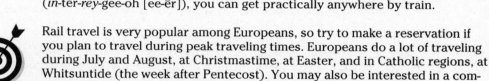

Traveling by rail is a very comfortable way of getting around Europe. Whether you want to whiz from Stuttgart to Paris on the **Intercity Express (ICE)** (*in*-têr-si-tee êks-*prês* [ee-tsey-*ey*]) or you want to head to the quaint towns along the Mosel River aboard the much slower **Interregio (IR)** (*in*-têr-*rey*-gee-oh [ee-êr]), you can get practically anywhere by train.

Rail travel is very popular among Europeans, so try to make a reservation if you plan to travel during peak traveling times. Europeans do a lot of traveling during July and August, at Christmastime, at Easter, and in Catholic regions, at Whitsuntide (the week after Pentecost). You may also be interested in a combination ticket that allows you to rent a bicycle or a car from a train station. Or if you're covering a lot of ground in a short time, go online and check out the various types of rail passes before you leave home.

Interpreting train schedules

Every train station displays schedules for all the trains that run through that particular station. However, with the flood of information displayed on these schedules, you may have a hard time figuring out what you need to know about the specific train you want to take. The following expressions provide some guidance for demystifying train schedules:

- ✔ **die Abfahrt** (dee *âp*-fahrt) (*departure*)
- ✔ **die Ankunft** (dee *ân*-koonft) (*arrival*)
- ✔ **der Fahrplan** (dêr *fahr*-plahn) (*train schedule*)
- ✔ **sonn- und feiertags** (*zon* oont *fay*-er-tâhks) (*Sundays and holidays*)
- ✔ **über** (*ue*-ber) (*via*)
- ✔ **werktags** (*vêrk*-tâhks) (*workdays*)

Getting more information

When you have questions about a train you want to take, head to **die Auskunft** (dee *ous*-koonft) (*the information counter*). There, you may ask any of the following questions:

> **Von welchem Gleis fährt der Zug nach . . . ab?** (fon *vêlH*-Hem glays fairt dêr tsoohk nahH . . . âp?) (*Which track does the train to . . . leave from?*)

> **Auf welchem Gleis kommt der Zug aus . . . an?** (ouf *vêlH*-em glays komt dêr tsoohk ous . . . ân?) (*Which track does the train from . . . arrive on?*)

> **Hat der Zug Verspätung?** (hât dêr tsoohk fêr-*shpêt*-oong?) (*Is the train delayed?*)

> **Muss ich umsteigen?** (moos iH *oom*-shtay-gen?) (*Do I have to change trains?*)

Many German verbs, including many of the verbs used in this chapter, have prefixes that are detachable from the body (stem) of the verb. When using *separable-prefix verbs,* as these verbs are called, the main verb stem with the appropriate ending goes in its usual place, and the prefix becomes the last word in the sentence. This rule works for the present and simple past tenses. (Turn to Book III, Chapter 8 for more on separable- and inseparable-prefix verbs.)

Take a look at this phenomenon in action, using the verb **ankommen** (*ân*-kom-en) (*to arrive*). Notice how the prefix always moves to the end of the sentence, no matter how many words come between it and the verb:

> **Der Zug kommt um 18.15 Uhr an.** (dêr tsoohk komt oom *âHt*-tseyn oohr *fuenf*-tseyn ân.) (*The train arrives at 6:15 p.m.*)

> **Auf welchem Gleis kommt der Zug aus Dessau an?** (ouf *vêlH*-em glays komt dêr tsoohk ous *dês*-ou ân?) (*Which track does the train from Dessau arrive on?*)

> **Wann fährt der Zug ab?** (vân fairt dêr tsoohk âp?) (*When does the train depart?*)

Here are a few other travel-related verbs that follow this pattern. Notice how the first syllable is stressed:

- **abfahren** (*âp*-fahr-en) (*to depart [on a train]*)
- **abfliegen** (*âp*-fleeg-en) (*to depart [on a plane]*)
- **anfangen** (*ân*-fâng-en) (*to start*)
- **ankommen** (*ân*-kom-en) (*to arrive*)
- **aussteigen** (*ous*-shtayg-en) (*to get off*)
- **einsteigen** (*ayn*-shtayg-en) (*to get on*)

Words to Know

der Bahnsteig	dêr <u>bahn</u>-shtayk	platform
das Gleis	dâs glays	track
die Verspätung	dee fêr-<u>shpêt</u>-oong	delay
einsteigen	<u>ayn</u>-shtayg-en	to get on
aussteigen	<u>ous</u>-shtayg-en	to get off
umsteigen	<u>oom</u>-shtayg-en	to change (trains, buses, and so on)
abfahren	<u>âp</u>-fahr-en	to leave
fahren	<u>fahr</u>-en	to go by, to travel

Book II

Speaking German on the Go

Buying train tickets

For train tickets, you need to go to **der Fahrkartenautomat** (dêr *fahr*-kâr-ten-ou-toh-mât) (*ticket machine*) or **der Fahrkartenschalter** (dêr *fahr*-kâr-ten-shâl-ter) (*ticket window/counter*). With the help of the words in this section, you can buy a ticket to virtually anywhere you want to go.

The basics

When it's your turn to talk to the ticket agent, just say the following to buy a ticket:

> **Eine Fahrkarte nach . . . , bitte.** (*ayn*-e *fahr*-kâr-te nahH . . . , *bi*-te.)
> (*A train ticket to . . . , please.*)

To find out whether you want a one-way or round-trip ticket, the ticket agent will ask

> **Einfach oder hin und zurück?** (*ayn*-fâH *oh*-der hin oont tsoo-*ruek?*)
> (*One-way or round-trip?*)

Then to find out whether you want a first-class or second-class ticket, the ticket agent will ask

> **Erster oder zweiter Klasse?** (*eyrs*-ter *oh*-der *tsvay*-ter *klâs*-e?) (*In first or second class?*)

Extras

On all trains, you pay a set base price per kilometer for first and second class. In addition, you have to pay **der Zuschlag** (dêr *tsooh*-shlahk) (*surcharge*) for the very fast trains marked **ICE** (*Intercity Express*), **IC** (*Intercity*), or **EC** (*Eurocity*). For these trains, the word **Zuschlag** usually appears on the train schedule or the board displaying departures.

On especially busy trains, you're better off reserving a seat in advance. To do so, simply ask

> **Ich möchte gern eine Platzkarte für den . . . von . . . nach. . . .** (iH *merH*-te gêrn *ayn*-e *plâts*-kâr-te fuer deyn . . . fon . . . nahH. . . .) (*I would like to reserve a seat on the . . . from . . . to. . . .*)

Words to Know

die Fahrkarte	dee <u>fahr</u>-kâr-te	train ticket
die erste Klasse	dee <u>êrs</u>-te <u>klâs</u>-e	first class
die zweite Klasse	dee <u>tsvay</u>-te <u>klâs</u>-e	second class
der Zuschlag	dêr <u>tsooh</u>-shlahk	surcharge
die Rückfahrkarte	dee <u>ruek</u>-fahr-kâr-te	round-trip ticket
die Platzkarte	dee <u>plâts</u>-kâr-te	reserved seat
hin und zurück	hin oont tsoo-<u>ruek</u>	round-trip
einfach	<u>ayn</u>-fâH	one-way

Navigating Buses, Subways, Streetcars, and Taxis

German cities and towns usually have excellent public transportation systems. A combination of **Bus** (boos) (*bus*), **U-Bahn** (*ooh*-bahn) (*subway*), **Straßenbahn** (*shtrah*-sen-bahn) (*streetcar*), and **S-Bahn** (*ēs*-bahn) (*light rail train to the suburbs*) can get you rapidly and safely where you want to go. Generally, your ticket allows you to ride on the various forms of transportation available. Of course, you can also take a taxi, if you prefer.

Book II

Speaking German on the Go

Purchasing a ticket

When you enter a subway station in a German-speaking country, you won't see any turnstiles. So how do people pay for the ride? They buy tickets first and then validate them by inserting the ticket into a validating machine in the bus or streetcar, and in the case of a subway, before proceeding to the platform. To buy a ticket, go to **der Fahrkartenautomat** (dēr *fahr*-kâr-ten-ou-toh-mât) (*ticket machine*) at bus and streetcar stops and in subway stations.

Here are three words you may see for *ticket* on the ticket machine or on the ticket itself:

- **der Fahrschein** (der *fahr*-shayn) (*ticket for transportation*)
- **die Fahrkarte** (dee *fahr*-kar-te) (*ticket for transportation*)
- **das Ticket** (dâs *ti*-ket) (*general word for ticket*)

The following are various types of tickets you can buy:

- **die Einzelfahrkarte** (dee *ayn*-zel-fahr-kâr-te) (*ticket*): A single-ride ticket; generally valid for up to two hours of travel in a single direction
- **die Streifenkarte** (dee *shtrayf*-en-kâr-te) (*strip ticket*): A strip ticket for multiple trips; you fold over the number of strips that the trip costs, depending on the number of zones you're traveling through
- **die Tageskarte** (dee *tâg*-es-kâr-te) (*one-day ticket*): A ticket valid for unlimited travel for one 24-hour period
- **die Partnertageskarte** (dee partner [as in English]-*tâg*-es-kâr-te) (*partner day ticket*): A ticket for two or more people — depending on the city — for unlimited travel within a 24-hour period

- ✔ **die Gruppentageskarte** (dee *groop*-en-*tãg*-es-kâr-te) (*group day ticket*): A ticket for a small group of people, for example, up to six — depending on the city — for unlimited travel within a 24-hour period

- ✔ **die Wochenkarte** (dee *woH*-en-kâr-te) (*weekly ticket*): A ticket for unlimited travel for one week

- ✔ **die Monatskarte** (dee *moH*-nâts-kâr-te) (*monthly ticket*): A ticket for unlimited travel for a month

After you purchase a ticket, don't forget to validate it before boarding the train, subway, streetcar, or bus. Plainclothes ticket inspectors make frequent checks, and anyone caught without a valid ticket can count on a hefty on-the-spot fine.

You validate your ticket by inserting the end of the ticket marked by an arrow or the word **entwerten** (ênt-*wêrt*-en) (*validate*) into the **Entwerter** (ênt-*wêrt*-er) (*validating machine*). You find **Entwerter** on buses and streetcars and in subway stations before you enter the subway. After you've validated your ticket, you can use it interchangeably on the various forms of transportation available.

Boarding the bus, subway, or streetcar

Getting on the right subway is easy when you know which direction to take. Take a look at the subway map to figure out where to go. If you're still unsure, ask one or, better yet, two different people the following question:

> **Ist das die richtige U-bahn zum (Stadion)?** (ist dâs dee *riH*-tee-ge *ooh*-bahn tsoom [*shtah*-dee-on]?) (*Is this the right subway to the [stadium]?*)

If you need help finding the right bus or streetcar to take, you can ask the agent at the **Fahrkartenschalter** (fahr-kâr-ten-shâl-ter) (*ticket window/counter*) or any bus driver (**der Busfahrer**) (dêr *boos*-fahr-er) or **Straßenbahnfahrer** (*shtrah*-sen-bahn-fahr-er) (*streetcar driver*) one of the following questions:

> **Welcher Bus fährt ins Stadtzentrum?** (*vêlH*-er boos fairt ins *shtât*-tsên-troom?) (Which bus goes to the city center?)

> **Muss ich umsteigen?** (moos iH *oom*-shtayg-en?) (*Do I have to switch [buses]?*)

> **Hält dieser Bus am Hauptbahnhof?** (hêlt *deez*-er boos âm *houpt*-bahn-hohf?) (*Does this bus stop at the main train station?*)

Words to Know

der Bus	dêr boos	bus
die U-bahn	dee <u>ooh</u>-bahn	subway
die S-Bahn	dee <u>ês</u>-bahn	local train
die Straßenbahn	dee <u>shtrah</u>-sen-bahn	streetcar
die Buslinie/ U-Bahnlinie	dee <u>boos</u>-leen-ye/ <u>ooh</u>-bahn-leen-ye	bus line/subway line
die Haltestelle	dee <u>hâl</u>-te-shtê-le	station, stop
halten	<u>hâl</u>-ten	to stop
die U-Bahnstation	dee <u>ooh</u>-bahn-shtâts-ee-ohn	subway station
das Taxi	dâs <u>tâx</u>-ee	taxi
der Taxistand	dêr <u>tâx</u>-ee-shtânt	taxi stand
der Fahrscheinautomat	dêr fahr-shayn-ou-toh-maht	ticket vending machine

Book II

Speaking German on the Go

Talkin' the Talk

Ben wants to take the bus to city hall, but he's not quite sure which bus he should take. So he approaches a teenager who is standing next to him at the bus stop. (Track 28)

Ben: **Entschuldigen Sie, bitte, hält hier der Bus Nummer 9?**
ênt-*shool*-dee-gen zee, *bi*-te, hêlt heer dêr boos-*noom*-er noyn?
Excuse me please, does the bus number 9 stop here?

Teenager: **Nein, hier hält nur die Linie 8. Wohin wollen Sie denn?**
nayn, heer hêlt noohr dee *leen*-ye âHt. vo-*hin vol*-en zee dên?
No, only number 8 stops here. Where do you want to go?

Ben:	**Zum Rathaus.**
	tsoom *raht*-hous.
	To the town hall.
Teenager:	**Fahren Sie mit der Linie 8 bis zum Goetheplatz, und dort steigen Sie in die Linie 9 um.**
	fahr-en zee mit dêr *leen*-ye âHt bis tsoom *ger*-te-plâts, oont dort *shtayg*-en zee in dee *leen*-ye noyn oom.
	Take this bus to Goetheplatz and switch there to number 9.
Ben:	**Wie viele Haltestellen sind es bis zum Goetheplatz?**
	vee *feel*-e *hâl*-te-shtêl-en zint ês bis tsoom *ger*-te-plâts?
	How many stops are there to Goetheplatz?
Teenager:	**Von hier sind es vier Haltestellen.**
	fon heer zint ês feer *hâl*-te-shtêl-en.
	It's four stops from here.
Ben:	**Vielen Dank für die Auskunft.**
	feel-en dânk fuer dee *ous*-koonft.
	Thank you very much for the information.

Getting a taxi

The secret to getting a taxi cab in Germany is making a phone call or walking to the nearest taxi stand. You may be used to the idea of hailing a cab on the street, but doing so isn't common practice in Germany — even in the larger cities. Why? Well, with the astronomical cost of gas in Europe, consider how much cab drivers would spend if they drove around until being hailed. So if you want to take a taxi, you can ask someone on the street where the nearest taxi stand is located and walk to it, or you can find out the phone number of the taxi stand closest to you and call it. If you're at a restaurant or some other business, you can ask an employee to call a cab for you. Of course, you also find taxi stands in front of airports, train stations, and major hotels.

Getting a taxi at a **Taxistand** (*tâx*-ee-shtânt) (*taxi stand*) isn't hard. Just go straight up to the first car in the line. When you get in, the **Taxifahrer** (*tâx*-ee-fahr-er) (*taxi driver*) will turn on the meter and ask you

> **Wohin möchten Sie?** (vo-*hin merH*-ten zee?) (*Where would you like to go?*)

At the end of the trip, you pay the price indicated on the meter, along with a modest tip of around 5 percent.

Many Germans taking a taxi alone sit in the passenger seat. You may enjoy doing the same. You have a far greater chance of seeing where you're going, and you can take the opportunity to ask questions and practice your German.

Chapter 6

Handling Emergencies: Hilfe!

In This Chapter

▶ Asking for assistance

▶ Getting help for a medical problem

▶ Communicating with the police

Hopefully, you'll never need to use the vocabulary and information in this chapter, but you never know, so read on. Aside from dealing with accidents and talking to the police, you may need to handle other kinds of emergencies — like what to do if you wake up in the morning with a bout of nausea and stomach cramps. This chapter assists you in dealing with various emergency situations, from seeking medical attention to reporting a theft.

Requesting Help

The hardest part of handling emergencies is keeping your cool so you can communicate the situation clearly and calmly to someone, be it a police officer, an emergency medical technician, or a doctor. So don't panic if you have to express the following unpleasant facts in German. In case you get tongue-tied, make sure you know how to ask for someone who speaks English.

Shouting for help

The following expressions come in handy if you need to grab someone's attention to get help in an emergency situation:

Hilfe! (*hilf*-e!) (*Help!*)

Rufen Sie die Polizei! (*roohf*-en zee dee po-li-*tsay!*) (*Call the police!*)

Rufen Sie einen Krankenwagen! (*roohf*-en zee *ayn*-en *krânk*-en-vahg-en!) (*Call an ambulance!*)

Rufen Sie die Feuerwehr! (*roohf*-en zee dee *foy*-er-veyr!) (*Call the fire department!*)

Holen Sie einen Arzt! (*hohl*-en zee *ayn*-en ârtst!) (*Get a doctor!*)

Feuer! (*foy*-êr!) (*Fire!*)

Reporting a problem

If you need to report an accident or let people know that you or other people are hurt, this basic vocabulary can help:

Ich möchte einen Unfall melden. (iH *merH*-te *ayn*-en *oon*-fâl *mêl*-den.) (*I want to report an accident.*)

Ich möchte einen Autounfall melden. (iH *merH*-te *ayn*-en *ou*-toh-oon-fâl *mêl*-den.) (*I want to report a car accident.*)

Ich bin verletzt. (iH bin fêr-*lêtst*.) (*I am hurt.*)

Es gibt Verletzte. (ês gipt fêr-*lêts*-te.) (*There are injured people.*)

In case of an emergency, you definitely want to have the right phone numbers handy. If you find yourself in an emergency situation while you're in European Union (EU) countries, including Germany and Austria, the crucial number you need to memorize or keep in your wallet is 112. Switzerland and most other non-EU countries in western Europe have also adopted the 112 number for emergencies. When you dial 112, which should work even from a cellphone, your call is routed to the nearest emergency call center. The center is prepared to dispatch the **Polizei** (po-li-*tsay*) (*police*), call the **Feuerwehr** (*foy*-êr-veyr) (*fire department*), or contact a **Rettungsdienst** (*rêt*-oongs-deenst) (*emergency service*).

If you're driving on the **Autobahn** (*ou*-toh-bahn) (*highway*) and you have to report an accident, the highway systems in Germany, Austria, Switzerland, and many other western European countries have motorist aid call boxes at regular intervals. On the **Autobahn** in German-speaking countries, such call boxes are labeled **Notruf** or **S.O.S.** (*noht*-roohf or s.o.s. [as in English]) (*emergency call* or *S.O.S.*). You'll also see arrows on guard rails or posts that point in the direction of the nearest emergency phone.

Accidents aside, you need to be prepared for other emergencies, such as a robbery or theft, as well:

Ich möchte einen Diebstahl/Raubüberfall melden. (iH *merH*-te *ayn*-en *deep*-shtahl/*roup*-ue-ber-fâl *mêl*-den.) (*I want to report a theft/robbery.*)

Halten Sie den Dieb! (*hâl*-ten zee deyn deep!) (*Catch the thief!*)

Asking for English-speaking help

If you aren't able to get the help you need by speaking German, ask this question:

Spricht hier jemand Englisch? (shpriHt heer *yey*-mânt *êng*-lish?)
(*Does anybody here speak English?*)

Words to Know

Hilfe!	<u>hilf</u>-e!	Help!
Rufen Sie die Polizei!	<u>roohf</u>-en zee dee po-li-<u>tsay</u>!	Call the police!
Feuer!	foy-êr!	Fire!

Handling Health Issues

Open your mouth and say, "Ahhhhhh." Good. Now breathe deeply. Relax. Breathe deeply again. Great! Now you, dear reader, should be relaxed enough to figure out how to explain what ails you. Hopefully, you won't need to seek medical assistance in a foreign country, but if you do, this section is exactly what the doctor ordered.

What kind of medical professional do you need? Where do you want to go? Here are a few words you need to know in case you're feeling out of sorts and need medical attention:

- ✔ **die Apotheke** (dee ah-poh-*tey*-ke) (*pharmacy*)
- ✔ **der Arzt/die Ärztin** (dêr ârtst/dee *êrts*-tin) (*male/female medical doctor*)
- ✔ **die Arztpraxis** (dee *ârtst*-prâx-is) (*doctor's office*)
- ✔ **der Doktor** (dêr *dok*-tohr) (*doctor* — profession and form of address)
- ✔ **das Krankenhaus** (dâs *krânk*-en-hous) (*hospital*)
- ✔ **die Notaufnahme** (dee *noht*-ouf-nah-me) (*emergency room*)
- ✔ **der Zahnarzt/die Zahnärztin** (dêr *tsahn*-ârtst/dee *tsahn*-êrts-tin) (*male/female dentist*)
- ✔ **die Zahnarztpraxis** (dee *tsahn*-ârtst-prax-is) (*dentist's office*)

If you need medical help, you can ask for a doctor or find out where the nearest doctor's office, hospital, or pharmacy is located by saying one of the following:

Ich brauche einen Arzt. (iH *brouH*-e *ayn*-en ârtst.) (*I need a doctor.*)

Wo ist die Notaufnahme? (voh ist dee *noht*-ouf-nah-me?) (*Where is the emergency room?*)

Wo ist die nächste Arztpraxis/das nächste Krankenhaus/die nächste Apotheke? (voh ist dee *naiH*-ste *ârtst*-prâx-is/dâs *naiH*-ste *krânk*-en-hous/ dee *naiH*-ste ah-poh-*tey*-ke?) (*Where is the nearest doctor's office/the nearest hospital/the nearest pharmacy?*)

Describing what ails you

Got a fever? Shooting pains down your leg? Nausea or worse? Then you've come to the right place. If you want to express that you aren't feeling well and explain where it hurts, use the following sentences:

Ich fühle mich nicht wohl. (iH *fuel*-e miH niHt vohl.) (*I'm not feeling well.*)

Ich bin krank. (iH bin krânk.) (*I am sick.*)

Mir geht es nicht gut. (meer geyt ês niHt gooht.) (*I don't feel well.*)

Mir ist schwindlig. (meer ist *shvind*-liH.) (*I feel dizzy.*)

Mir ist übel. (meer ist *ue*-bel.) (*I feel nauseous.*)

Ich glaube, ich bin erkältet. (iH *glou*-be, iH bin êr-*kêlt*-et.) (*I think I have a cold.*)

Ich habe einen starken Husten. (iH *hah*-be *ayn*-en *shtârk*-en *hooh*-sten.) (*I have a bad cough.*)

Ich habe geschwollene Drüsen. (iH *hah*-be gê-*shvol*-en-e *druez*-en.) (*I have swollen glands.*)

Ich leide an Verstopfung. (iH *lay*-de ân fêr-*shtopf*-oong.) (*I'm suffering from constipation.*)

Ich muss mich häufig übergeben. (iH moos miH *hoy*-fiH ue-ber-*gey*-ben.) (*I have to vomit frequently.*)

Ich habe Fieber/Durchfall. (iH *hah*-be *feeb*-er/*doorH*-fâl.) (*I have a fever/ diarrhea.*)

Mir tut der Fuß/Bauch/Rücken/Hals weh. (meer tooht dêr foohs/bouH/ *ruek*-en/hâls vey.) (*My foot/stomach/back/throat hurts.*)

Ich habe Schmerzen im Arm/Bauch/Brust(korb). (iH *hah*-be *shmêrts*-en im ârm/bouH/*broost*[korp].) (*I feel pain in my arm/stomach/chest.*)

Ich habe (starke) Bauchschmerzen/Kopfschmerzen. (iH *hah*-be [*shtârk*-e] *bouH*-shmêrts-en/*kopf*-shmêrts-en.) (*I have [a severe] stomachache/headache.*)

Ich habe Ohrenschmerzen/Zahnschmerzen. (iH *hah*-be *ohr*-en-shmêrts-en/*tsahn*-shmêrts-en.) (*I have a headache/toothache.*)

Ich habe Halsschmerzen/Rückenschmerzen. (iH *hah*-be *hâls*-shmêrts-en/*ruek*-en-shmêrts-en.) (*I have a sore throat/back pain.*)

Talking about any special conditions

An important part of getting treatment is letting the doctor know whether you're allergic to something or have any other medical conditions. To do so, start out by saying

Ich bin . . . (ih bin . . .) (*I am . . .*)

Then finish the sentence with any of the following:

allergisch gegen . . . (â-*lêr*-gish *gey*-gen . . .) (*allergic to . . .*)

behindert (bê-*hin*-dêrt) (*handicapped*)

schwanger (*shvâng*-er) (*pregnant*)

Diabetiker (dee-ah-*bey*-ti-ker) (*a diabetic*)

Epileptiker (ey-pi-*lêp*-ti-ker) (*an epileptic*)

A few specific conditions may require that you begin with the following:

Ich habe . . . (iH *hah*-be . . .) (*I have . . .*)

Then state the condition. Here are some examples:

eine Intoleranz gegen (Penizillin) (*ayn*-e *in*-tol-er-ants *gey*-gen [pê-ni-tsi-*leen*]) (*an intolerance to [penicillin]*)

ein Herzleiden (ayn *hêrts*-layd-en) (*a heart condition*)

zu hohen/niedrigen Blutdruck (tsooh *hoh*-en/*need*-reeg-gen *blooht*-drook) (*high/low blood pressure*)

Getting an examination

After you get into the examination room, you need to make sure you understand the doctor's questions and the instructions you have to follow to get the proper diagnosis. The doctor may ask you questions like

Was haben Sie für Beschwerden? (vâs *hah*-ben zee fuer be-*shveyr*-den?) (*What symptoms do you have?*)

Was fehlt Ihnen? (vâs feylt *een*-en?) (*What is wrong with you?*)

Haben Sie Schmerzen? (*hah*-ben zee *shmêrts*-en?) (*Are you in pain?*)

Wo tut es weh? (voh tooht ês vey?) (*Where does it hurt?*)

Tut es hier weh? (tooht ês heer vey?) (*Does it hurt here?*)

Wie lange fühlen Sie sich schon so? (vee *lâng*-e *fuel*-en zee ziH shon zoh?) (*How long have you been feeling this way?*)

Sind Sie gegen irgendetwas allergisch? (zint zee *gey*-gen *ir*-gênt-êt-vâs â-*lêr*-gish?) (*Are you allergic to anything?*)

Here are some (not-so-fun) instructions you may hear from the doctor:

Bitte streifen Sie den Ärmel hoch. (*bi*-te *shtrayf*-en zee deyn *êr*-mel hoH.) (*Please pull up your sleeve.*)

Bitte machen Sie den Oberkörper frei. (*bi*-te *māH*-en zee deyn *oh*-bêr-kerr-per fray.) (*Please take off your shirt.*)

Bitte legen Sie sich hin. (*bi*-te *ley*-gen zee ziH hin.) (*Please lie down.*)

Machen Sie bitte den Mund auf. (*māH*-en zee *bi*-te deyn moont ouf.) (*Please open your mouth.*)

Atmen Sie bitte tief durch./Einatmen./Ausatmen. (*aht*-men zee *bi*-te teef doorH/*ayn*-aht-men/*ous*-aht-men.) (*Please take a deep breath./Breathe in./Breathe out.*)

Husten Sie bitte. (*hoohs*-ten zee *bi*-te.) (*Please cough.*)

Ich werde Ihren Puls messen. (iH *wêr*-de *eer*-en pools *mês*-en.) (*I'm going to check your pulse.*)

Ich möchte Ihren Blutdruck messen. (iH *merH*-te *eer*-en *blooht*-drook *mês*-en.) (*I would like to check your blood pressure.*)

Wir müssen eine Blutuntersuchung/Stuhlprobe machen. (veer *mues*-en *ayn*-e *blooht*-oon-ter-zooH-oong/*shtoohl*-proh-be *maH*-en.) (*We need to take a blood sample/stool sample.*)

Ich gebe Ihnen eine Spritze. (iH *gey*-be *een*-en *ayn*-e *shprit*-se.) (*I'm giving you a shot.*)

Wir müssen eine Röntgenaufnahme machen. (veer *mues*-en *ayn*-e *rernt*-gên-ouf-nah-me *māH*-en.) (*We have to take an X-ray.*)

Sie müssen geröntgt werden. (zee *mues*-en ge-*rerngt* *vêr*-den.) (*You have to get an X-ray.*)

Specifying parts of the body

To the question **Wo tut es weh?** (voh tooht ês vey?) (*Where does it hurt?*), you can answer any of the following:

- **der Arm** (dêr ârm) (*arm*)
- **das Auge/die Augen** (dâs *oug*-e/dee *oug*-en) (*eye/eyes*)
- **der Bauch** (dêr bouH) (*stomach*)
- **das Bein** (dâs bayn) (*leg*)
- **die Brust** (dee broost) (*chest*)
- **der Daumen** (dêr *doum*-en) (*thumb*)
- **der Finger** (dêr *fing*-er) (*finger*)
- **der Fuß** (dêr foohs) (*foot*)
- **der Fußgelenk/Fußknöchel** (dêr *foohs*-ge-lênk/*foohs*-knerH-el) (*ankle*)
- **die Gelenke** (dee ge-*lênk*-e) (*joints*)
- **der Hals** (dêr hâls) (*throat, neck*)
- **die Hand** (dee hânt) (*hand*)
- **das Handgelenk** (dâs *hant*-gê-lênk) (*wrist*)
- **das Herz** (dâs hêrts) (*heart*)
- **die Hüfte** (dee *huef*-te) (*hip*)
- **der Kiefer** (dêr *keef*-er) (*jaw*)
- **das Knie** (dâs knee) (*knee*)
- **die Leber** (dee *ley*-ber) (*liver*)
- **die Lungen** (dee *loong*-en) (*lungs*)
- **der Magen** (dêr *mah*-gen) (*stomach*)
- **der Mund** (dêr moont) (*mouth*)
- **der Muskel** (dêr *moos*-kel) (*muscle*)
- **der Nacken** (dêr *nâk*-en) (*neck*)
- **die Nase** (dee *nah*-ze) (*nose*)
- **die Nieren** (dee *neer*-en) (*kidneys*)
- **der Oberschenkel** (dêr *oh*-bêr-shênk-el) (*thigh*)
- **das Ohr/die Ohren** (dâs ohr/dee *ohr*-en) (*ear/ears*)

Book II

Speaking German on the Go

✔ **der Rücken** (dêr *ruek*-en) (*back*)

✔ **die Schulter** (dee *shool*-ter) (*shoulder*)

✔ **der Zahn** (dêr tsahn) (*tooth*)

✔ **der Zeh** (dêr tsey) (*toe*)

✔ **die Zunge** (dee *tsoong*-e) (*tongue*)

Here are a few other parts of the body you may need to identify:

✔ **das Gesicht** (dâs ge-*ziHt*) (*face*)

✔ **das Haar** (dâs hahr) (*hair*)

✔ **der Kopf** (dêr kopf) (*head*)

✔ **die Lippe** (dee *lip*-e) (*lip*)

Understanding the diagnosis

After the doctor has gathered the information she needs, she'll tell you what she thinks is wrong. Here are some very useful words and phrases that keep you from being left in the dark:

die Diagnose (dee dee-âg-*noh*-ze) (*diagnosis*)

Sie haben . . . (zee *hah*-ben . . .) (*You have . . .*)

eine Erkältung (*ayn*-e êr-*kêlt*-oong) (*a cold*)

eine Grippe (*ayn*-e *grip*-e) (*the flu*)

eine Entzündung (*ayn*-e ênt-*tsuend*-oong) (*an inflammation*)

Blinddarmentzündung (*blint*-dârm-ênt-tsuend-oong) (*appendicitis*)

Lungenentzündung (*lung*-en-ênt-tsuend-oong) (*pneumonia*)

Mandelentzündung (*mân*-del-ênt-tsuend-oong) (*tonsillitis*)

Here are a few sample sentences you may hear:

Sie haben 39 Grad Fieber. (zee *hah*-ben noyn-oont-*dray*-siH grâd *feeb*-er.) (*You have a fever of 39 degrees.*)

Ihre Temperatur ist etwas erhöht. (*eer*-e têmp-êr-ah-*toohr* ist *êt*-vâs êr-*hert*.) (*You have a slight temperature.*)

Ihr Fußknöchel ist gebrochen/verstaucht/verrenkt. (eer *foohs*-knerH-êl ist ge-*broH*-en/fêr-*shtouHt*/fêr-*rênkt*.) (*Your ankle is broken/sprained/dislocated.*)

Sie müssen einen Spezialisten aufsuchen. (zee *mues*-en *ayn*-en shpêts-ee-â-*list*-en *ouf*-zooH-en.) (*You need to see a specialist.*)

If the doctor tells you that you need to see a specialist, you can ask about finding a specialist by saying

> **Können Sie mir bitte einen Spezialisten empfehlen?** (*kern*-en zee meer *bi*-te *ayn*-en shpêts-ee-â-*list*-en êm-*pfey*-len?) (*Could you recommend a specialist to me, please?*)

Talkin' the Talk

 Ulrich Lempert hasn't been feeling well for a couple of days and has made an appointment with his doctor, Dr. Grawen. (Track 29)

Book II

Speaking German on the Go

Dr. Grawen: **Guten Morgen, Herr Lempert. Was haben Sie für Beschwerden?**
gooht-en *mor*-gen, hêr *lêm*-pêrt. vâs *hah*-ben zee fuer be-*shveyr*-den?
Good morning, Mr. Lempert. What symptoms do you have?

Ulrich: **Ich fühle mich seit ein paar Tagen nicht wohl.**
iH *fuel*-e miH zayt ayn pahr *tah*-gen niHt vohl.
I haven't been feeling well for a couple of days.

Dr. Grawen: **Haben Sie Schmerzen?**
hah-ben zee *shmêrts*-en?
Are you in pain?

Ulrich: **Ja, ich habe starke Kopf- und Magenschmerzen.**
yah, iH *hah*-be *stâr*-ke kopf- oont *mah*-gen-*shmêrts*-en.
Yes, I have a severe headache and stomachache.

Dr. Grawen: **Bitte setzen Sie sich hier hin und machen Sie den Oberkörper frei.**
bi-te *zêts*-en zee ziH heer hin oont *mâH*-en zee deyn oh-*bêr*-kerr-pêr fray.
Please sit down here and take off your shirt.

Dr. Grawen starts examining Ulrich.

Dr. Grawen: **Machen Sie bitte den Mund auf — danke. Atmen Sie bitte tief durch. Husten Sie bitte.**
mâH-en zee *bi*-te deyn moont ouf — *dân*-ke. *aht*-mên zee *bi*-te teef doorH. *hoohs*-ten zee *bi*-te.
Please open your mouth — thank you. Take a deep breath, please. Please cough.

Ulrich: **Und, was stimmt nicht mit mir?**
oont, vâs shtimt niHt mit meer?
And what's wrong with me?

Dr. Grawen: **Sie haben eine Grippe. Ich gebe Ihnen ein Rezept.**
Und bleiben Sie die nächsten Tage im Bett.
zee *hah*-ben *ayn*-e *grip*-e. iH *gey*-be *een*-en ayn rê-
tsêpt. oont *blay*-ben zee dee *naiH*-sten *tah*-ge im bêt.
You have the flu. I'm giving you a prescription. And
stay in bed for the next few days.

Words to Know

Ich brauche einen Arzt.	iH <u>brouH</u>-e <u>ayn</u>-en ârtst.	I need a doctor.
Ich bin krank.	iH bin krânk.	I am sick.
Wo tut es weh?	voh tooht ês vey?	Where does it hurt?
Haben Sie Schmerzen?	<u>hah</u>-ben zee <u>shmêrts</u>-en?	Are you in pain?

Getting treatment

After the doctor tells you what the problem is, he will tell you what to do about it. The doctor may ask you one final question before deciding what treatment would be best for you:

Nehmen Sie noch andere Medikamente? (*ney*-men zee noH *ân*-de-re mey-dee-kâ-*mên*-te?) (*Are you taking any other medicine?*)

The doctor may then begin with

Ich gebe Ihnen . . ./Ich verschreibe Ihnen . . . (iH *gey*-be *een*-en . . ./ iH fêr-*shray*-be *een*-en . . .) (*I'll give you . . ./I'll prescribe for you . . .*)

He may end that statement with any of the following:

- ✔ **Antibiotika** (ân-tee-bee-*oh*-ti-kâ) (*antibiotics*)
- ✔ **das Medikament/die Medikamente** (dâs mey-dee-kâ-*mênt*/dee mey-dee-kâ-*mên*-te) (*medicine* [singular and plural])
- ✔ **ein Schmerzmittel** (ayn *shmêrts*-mit-el) (*a painkiller*)
- ✔ **Tabletten** (tâ-*blêt*-en) (*pills*)

Finally, the doctor may indicate that he wants to see you again by saying

> **Kommen Sie in . . . Tagen/einer Woche wieder.** (*kom*-en zee in . . . *tah*-gen/*ayn*-er *voH*-e *vee*-der.) (*Come back in . . . days/one week.*)

The doctor will give you a prescription, **das Rezept** (dâs rê-*tsêpt*), that you take to a pharmacy, called **die Apotheke** (dee âpo-*tey*-ke), to be filled.

The following phrases can help you understand the instructions for taking your medicine:

> **Bitte, nehmen Sie . . . Tabletten/Teelöffel . . .** (*bi*-te, *ney*-men zee . . . tah-*blêt*-en/*tey*-lerf-el . . .) (*Please take . . . pills/teaspoons . . .*)

> **dreimal am Tag/täglich** (*dray*-mahl âm tahk/*taig*-liH) (*three times a day/daily*)

> **alle . . . Stunden** (*âl*-e . . . *shtoon*-den) (*every . . . hours*)

> **vor/nach dem Essen** (fohr/naH deym *ês*-en) (*before/after meals*)

Going to a pharmacy

You may be used to getting your prescription medicine at a drugstore, but that isn't the case in Germany. The German equivalent of the *drugstore* is the **Drogerie** (droh-ge-*ree*), where you get everything from toothpaste to sunblock, as well as nonprescription drugs, such as aspirin and cough syrup. For prescription drugs, however, you have to go to the **Apotheke** (âpoh-*tey*-ke) (*pharmacy*). When it comes to prescriptions, German laws are very strict, meaning that a lot of the medicine (such as allergy medication) you can buy over the counter in the U.S. requires a prescription in Germany (and thus, a trip to the doctor).

While traveling, heading to the nearest pharmacy may be your best option if you don't have time to make a doctor's appointment or if you think what's ailing you can be remedied with over-the-counter medicine. As in North America, the pharmacists in German-speaking Europe are well-trained and

Book II

Speaking German on the Go

qualified to listen to their customers' ailments and recommend nonprescription medicine to alleviate the symptoms of the common cold, sore throat, coughing, diarrhea, constipation, skin rash, sunburn, and so on.

When you want to get help from the pharmacist, just ask one of these questions:

> **Können Sie mir bitte etwas gegen . . . geben?** (*kern*-en zee mir *bi*-te *êt*-vâs *gey*-gen . . . *gey*-ben?) (*Could you give me something for . . . , please?*)

> **Haben Sie etwas gegen. . . ?** (*hah*-ben zee *êt*-vâs *gey*-gen. . . ?) (*Do you have something for. . . ?*)

You can complete these questions with any of the following:

- ✔ **Durchfall** (*doorH*-fâl) (*diarrhea*)
- ✔ **eine Erkältung** (*ayn*-e êr-*kêlt*-oong) (*a cold*)
- ✔ **die Grippe** (dee *grip*-e) (*the flu*)
- ✔ **Husten** (*hoos*-tên) (*cough*)
- ✔ **Kopfweh** (*kopf*-wey) (*headache*)
- ✔ **Sonnenbrand** (*zon*-en-brânt) (*sunburn*)
- ✔ **Verstopfung** (fêr-*shtopf*-oong) (*constipation*)

The following questions may help you get more information about taking whatever medicine the pharmacist hands you:

> **Haben diese Tabletten eine starke Wirkung?** (*hah*-ben *dee*-ze tâ-*blêt*-en *ayn*-e *shtârk*-e *virk*-oong?) (*Do these tablets have a strong effect?*)

> **Wieviele Tabletten soll ich nehmen?** (vee *fee*-le tâ-*blêt*-en zol iH *ney*-men?) (*How many tablets should I take?*)

> **Wann soll ich dieses Medikament nehmen?** (vân zol iH *dee*-zes *mêd*-i-kâ-*mênt ney*-men?) (*When should I take this medicine?*)

Here are a few other items you may be looking for in the pharmacy:

- ✔ **Aspirin** (âs-pi-*reen*) (*aspirin*)
- ✔ **der (Heft-/Wund-)pflaster** (dêr [*hêft*-/voont-]pflâs-ter) (*band-aid*)
- ✔ **Hustenbonbons** (*hoohs*-ten-bon-bonz) (*cough drops*)
- ✔ **Hustensaft** (*hoohs*-ten-zâft) (*cough syrup*)
- ✔ **der Verband** (dêr fêr-*bânt*) (*bandage*)

Talkin' the Talk

After Ulrich gets his diagnosis, he takes the prescription to his neighborhood pharmacy and talks to the pharmacist.

Ulrich: **Guten Morgen. Mein Ärzt hat mir dieses Rezept gegeben.**
gooht-en *mor*-gen. *Mayn* ârtst hât meer *deez*-es rê-*tsêpt* ge-*gey*-ben.
Good morning. My doctor has given me this prescription.

Apothekerin: **Einen Moment.**
ayn-en moh-*ment.*
Just a moment.

The pharmacist fills Ulrich's prescription and returns.

So, Herr Lempert. Bitte nehmen Sie dreimal am Tag zwei von diesen Tabletten.
zoh, hêr *lêm*-pêrt. *bi*-te *ney*-men zee *dray*-mahl âm tahk tsavy fon *deez*-en tâ-*blêt*-en.
Okay, Mr. Lempert. Please take two of these pills three times a day.

Ulrich: **Vor oder nach dem Essen?**
fohr *oh*-der nahH deym *ês*-en?
Before or after meals?

Apothekerin: **Nach dem Essen.**
nahH deym *ês*-en.
After meals.

Ulrich: **Wird gemacht.**
virt ge-*mâHt.*
I'll do that.

Apothekerin: **Gute Besserung, Herr Lempert!**
gooh-te *bês*-er-oong, hêr *lêm*-pêrt!
Hope you feel better, Mr. Lempert!

Book II

Speaking German on the Go

Handling Police Matters

You've just discovered that your hotel room has been robbed. The thieves made off with a lot, but fortunately, they left *German All-in-One For Dummies* behind. Their loss, your gain!

Here are some helpful expressions for handling the situation:

Wo ist das nächste Polizeirevier? (voh ist dâs *naiH*-ste po-li-*tsay*-re-veer?) (*Where is the closest police station?*)

Ich möchte einen Diebstahl melden. (iH *merH*-te *ayn*-en *deep*-shtahl *mêl*-den.) (*I would like to report a theft.*)

Describing what was stolen

To describe a theft, you start out by saying

Man hat mir . . . gestohlen. (mân hât meer . . . ge-*shtohl*-en.) (*Someone has stolen. . . .*)

You can then finish the sentence by inserting any of the following:

- **mein Auto** (mayn *ou*-toh) (*my car*)
- **meine Brieftasche/mein Portemonnaie** (*mayn*-e *breef*-tâsh-e/mayn port-mon-*ey*) (*my wallet*)
- **mein Geld** (mayn gêlt) (*my money*)
- **meinen Pass** (*mayn*-en pâs) (*my passport*)
- **meine Tasche/Handtasche** (*mayn*-e *tâsh*-e/*hânt*-tâsh-e) (*my bag/handbag*)

If you want to express that someone has broken into your room or office, you use the verb **einbrechen** (*ayn*-brêH-en) (*to break into*):

Man hat bei mir eingebrochen. (mân hât bay meer *ayn*-ge-broH-en.) (*Someone has broken into [my room].*)

If you're talking about your car, however, you use a similar but slightly different verb, **aufbrechen** (*ouf*-brêH-en), which literally means *to break open*:

Man hat mein Auto aufgebrochen. (mân hât mayn *ou*-toh *ouf*-ge-broH-en.) (*Someone has broken into my car.*)

The indefinite pronoun **man** (mân), which means *one, someone,* or *you* (in the sense of people in general), comes in handy. It's easy to use because it always has the same form and spelling — **man.** Consider these examples:

> **Man hat seine Tasche gestohlen.** (mân hât *zayn*-e *tâsh*-e ge-*shtohl*-en.) (*Someone has stolen his bag.*)

> **Was macht man jetzt?** (vâs mâHt mân yêtst?) (*What does one do now?*)

Giving a description of the thief

So you got a good look at the thug. Was he or she tall or short, thin or fat, hairy or bald? The police will want to know everything. (As a bonus, after you know how to describe people, you'll also be ready to peruse personal ads.)

The police will ask

> **Können Sie die Person beschreiben?** (*kern*-en zee dee pêr-*zohn* be-*shrayb*-en?) (*Can you describe that person?*)

Your answer to this question can begin

> **Die Person/Er/Sie hatte . . .** (dee per-*zohn*/êr/zee *hât*-e . . .) (*The person/he/she had . . .*)

Then finish the sentence with any of the following. You can combine traits by saying **und** between them:

- ✔ **blonde/schwarze/rote/graue/lange/kurze Haare** (*blon*-de/*shvârts*-e/*roh*-te/*grou*-e/*lâng*-e/*koorts*-e *hahr*-e) (*blond/black/red/gray/long/short hair*)
- ✔ **einen Bart/einen Schnurrbart/keinen Bart** (*ayn*-en bahrt/*ayn*-en *shnoohr*-bahrt/*kayn*-en bahrt) (*a beard/a mustache/no beard*)
- ✔ **eine Glatze** (*ayn*-e *glâts*-e) (*a bald head*)
- ✔ **eine Brille** (*ayn*-e *bril*-e) (*glasses*)

Alternatively, your answer may begin with

> **Die Person/Er/Sie war . . .** (dee pêr-*zohn*/êr/zee vahr . . .) (*The person/he/she was . . .*)

You can then end with any of the following:

- ✔ **groß/klein** (grohs/klayn) (*tall/short*)
- ✔ **schlank/dick** (shlânk/dik) (*thin/fat*)

✔ **ungefähr . . . Meter groß** (*oon*-ge-fair . . . *mey*-ter grohs) (*approximately . . . meters tall*)

✔ **ungefähr . . . Jahre alt** (*oon*-ge-fair . . . *yahr*-e âlt) (*approximately . . . years old*)

The police may also ask you the following questions:

Was ist passiert? (vâs ist pâs-*eert?*) (*What happened?*)

Wann ist das passiert? (vân ist dâs pâs-*eert?*) (*When did it happen?*)

Wo waren Sie in dem Moment? (voh *vahr*-en zee in deym moh-*mênt?*) (*Where were you at that moment?*)

Getting legal help

Had enough for the day? If you're really not up to conversing with the law on your own, here are two very important phrases that you should know:

Ich brauche einen Anwalt. (iH *brouH*-e *ayn*-en ân-vâlt.) (*I need a lawyer.*)

Ich möchte das Konsulat anrufen. (iH *merH*-te dâs kon-zoo-*laht ân*-roohf-en.) (*I would like to call the consulate.*)

Talkin' the Talk

Erika Berger has to drop off some documents at her client's office. When she returns to her car half an hour later, she sees that somebody has broken into it and stolen her bag. Luckily, the nearest police station is right around the corner.

Erika: **Guten Tag. Ich möchte einen Diebstahl melden. Man hat mein Auto aufgebrochen und meine Tasche gestohlen.**
gooht-en tahk. iH *merH*-te *ayn*-en *deep*-shtahl *mêl*-den. mân hât mayn *ou*-toh *ouf*-ge-broH-en oont *mayn*-e *tâsh*-e ge-*shtohl*-en.
Hello. I would like to report a theft. Someone has broken into my car and stolen my bag.

Polizist: **Moment mal. Wie ist ihr Name?**
moh-*mênt* mâl. vee ist eer *nah*-me?
One moment. What is your name?

Erika: **Erika Berger.**
           êr-i-kâ *bêr*-ger.
           Erika Berger.

Polizist: **Wann ist das passiert?**
           vân ist dâs pâs-*eert?*
           When did it happen?

Erika: **Zwischen elf und halb zwölf.**
           tsvish-en êlf oont hâlp tsverlf.
           Between 11:00 and 11:30.

Polizist: **Und wo?**
           oont voh?
           And where?

Erika: **Gleich um die Ecke, in der Rothmundstraße.**
           glayH um dee *êk*-e, în dêr *roht*-moont-*shtrah*-se.
           Right around the corner, on Rothmundstraße.

Polizist: **Was war in Ihrer Tasche?**
           vâs vahr in *eer*-er *tâsh*-e?
           What was in your bag?

Erika: **Meine Brieftasche mit ungefähr fünfzig Euro, meine Kreditkarten und mein Führerschein!**
           mayn-e *breef*-tâsh-e mit *oon*-ge-fair *fuenf*-tsiH *oy*-roh, *mayn*-e krê-*deet*-kârt-en oont mayn *fuer*-er-shayn!
           My wallet with approximately 50 euros in it, my credit cards, and my driver's license!

Polizist: **Nun, ich habe noch einige Fragen. Wir erstatten dann Anzeige.**
           noon, iH *hah*-be noH *ayn*-ee-ge *frah*-gen. veer êr-*shtât*-en dân *ân*-tsayg-e.
           Now I have some more questions. Then we'll file a report.

Book III

Assembling the Grammatical Foundations for Communication

German Words That Mean *The*				
Case	*Masculine*	*Feminine*	*Neuter*	*Plural*
Nominative (subjects, predicate nouns)	der	die	das	die
Accusative (direct objects)	den	die	das	die
Dative (indirect objects)	dem	der	dem	den
Genitive (owned objects)	des	der	des	der

You're bound to have questions or need to ask someone for help during your time in Germany. To ensure you phrase your inquiries politely, check out the free article about asking questions in different situations at www.dummies.com/extras/germanaio.

Contents at a Glance

Chapter 1

Laying Out the Basics to Build Sentences

In This Chapter

▶ Identifying the parts of speech

▶ Combining words to create sentences

▶ Talking in terms of the past, present, and future

▶ Understanding how to use context and a bilingual dictionary to find meaning

*W*hen you think about grammar, imagine a big dresser with lots of drawers. Instead of being filled with all kinds of clothing, these drawers contain different types of words, called *parts of speech* — nouns, verbs, adjectives, adverbs, and so on. Each part of speech is in a separate drawer.

Now imagine it's early morning and you're about to utter your first German sentence of the day. To begin, you reach into the noun drawer and pull out the word **Socken** (*socks*). Next, to describe your socks, you reach into the adjective drawer and pull out two words, **neu** (*new*) and **schwarz** (*black*). To indicate what you do with your new black socks, you fish through the verb drawer and pull out the verb **anziehen** (*to put on*). And because you're running late, you dive straight into the adverb drawer and grab the word **schnell** (*quickly*). Now, to construct a whole sentence, you need another item, this one from the pronoun drawer: **ich** (*I*). Before you know it, you've pulled a complete sentence out of the dresser: **Ich ziehe schnell meine neuen schwarzen Socken an.** (*I am quickly putting on my new black socks.*)

To construct a correct sentence, you need to know how to string all these words together, and that's what grammar is all about. This chapter makes using grammar as easy as getting dressed in the morning. With a few basic rules in your back pocket, you'll be using grammar with confidence in no time. So arrange your thoughts, grab the words you need, and before you know it, you'll be out the door and speaking **auf Deutsch** (*in German*).

Identifying the Parts of Speech

To build a sentence, you need to figure out what you want to say, identify the parts of speech you need to express your ideas, and then decide which words to use and how to put them together. Table 1-1 lists the most essential parts of speech used in German sentences: nouns, pronouns, articles, verbs, adjectives, adverbs, conjunctions, and prepositions. The sections that follow the table give you the lowdown on each one.

Table 1-1		Parts of Speech	
Name	*Definition*	*Examples*	*Notes*
Noun	A person, place, animal, thing, quality, concept, and so on	**Dracula** **Hotel California** **Känguruh** (*kangaroo*) **Liebe** (*love*)	In German, they're always capitalized. (See Book III, Chapter 2.)
Pronoun	A word that replaces or stands for a noun	**er** (*he*) **sie** (*she*) **uns** (*us*)	German has far more pronoun variations than English; the four cases influence pronouns. (See Book III, Chapter 2.)
Article	A word that indicates the gender of a noun	**der/die/das** (*the*) **ein/eine/ein** (*a/an*)	German has three genders, so it uses three different articles for *the.* (See Book III, Chapter 2.)
Verb	A word that shows action or a state of being	**denken** (*to think*) **haben** (*to have*) **reisen** (*to travel*)	Verbs are conjugated according to person (I, you, he, and so on), tense (present, past, and future), and mood (for example, the difference between *it is* and *it would be*). (See Book III, Chapter 3 for details on present tense.)

Name	Definition	Examples	Notes
Adjective	A word that modifies or describes a noun or a pronoun	schön (*beautiful*) praktisch (*practical*) interessant (*interesting*)	Adjectives may or may not have case endings. (See Book III, Chapter 5.)
Adverb	A word that modifies or describes a verb, an adjective, or another adverb	schnell (*fast, quickly*) sehr (*very*) schrecklich (*terribly*)	In German, adjectives and adverbs can be the same word. (See Book III, Chapter 5.)
Conjunction	A word that connects other words or sentence parts together	und (*and*) aber (*but*) weil (*because*)	In German, some conjunctions affect the word order of the sentence. (See Book IV, Chapter 1.)
Preposition	A word that shows a relationship between its object (a noun or pronoun) and another word in a sentence	mit (mir) (*with [me]*) ohne (mich) (*without [me]*) während (des Tages) (*during [the day]*)	In German, a preposition uses case (dative, accusative, or genitive) to show the relationship to its object. (See Book IV, Chapter 2.)

Book III

Assembling the Grammatical Foundations for Communication

Nouns

A rose is a rose is a rose, right? Well, a rose is also a noun, and nouns aren't exactly the same in German and English. Although nouns in both languages name things (people, places, objects, concepts, and so on), the difference is that all German nouns are capitalized and have one of three genders: masculine, feminine, or neuter. The following sections go into more detail on gender and explain how to make singular German nouns plural.

Understanding a noun's gender

All German nouns have gender. That is, they are one of the following: masculine, feminine, or neuter. Unfortunately, the meaning of a noun isn't usually much help in predicting its grammatical gender. After all, in German, grammatical gender is an element of German grammar and isn't related to the meaning of the noun. Instead, it's a kind of marker that identifies how the noun fits into a sentence. So you simply have to memorize the gender that belongs with each noun. Fortunately, a few guidelines can get you started:

- Nouns for male persons, car makes, nationalities, occupations, seasons, days, and months are usually masculine.
- Nouns for most female persons, many flowers, and trees are feminine.
- Nouns beginning with **Ge-** are usually neuter.
- All verbs used as nouns, such as **das Schwimmen** (*swimming*) are neuter.
- Nouns ending in **-ist, -ich, -ismus,** and **-ner** are usually masculine.
- Nouns ending in **-heit, -keit, -ik, -schaft, -ei, -ie, -tät,** and **-ung** are feminine.
- Nouns ending in **-chen, -lein, -ium, -um,** and **-tum** are usually neuter.

Knowing a noun's gender becomes even more important when the noun is plopped into a sentence. How's that? Well, depending on the role the noun plays in the sentence, the three definite articles **der, die,** and **das,** all of which translate to the English *the,* can go through all kinds of spelling gyrations, and sometimes even the noun's spelling is altered. The same goes for the indefinite articles **ein, eine,** and **ein,** which correspond to the English *a* and *an.* The key to all this morphing is what's known as *case.* Later in this chapter, we shed more light on how to put German nouns and articles into sentences. (For detailed information on gender, go to Book III, Chapter 2.)

Making singular nouns plural

German has several ways to change a singular noun to its plural form. Fortunately, two groups of words are easy to deal with:

- **Nouns that are the same in both the singular and plural forms, like the English noun *sheep:*** Many of the nouns in this group are masculine- and neuter-gender words ending in **-er,** like **das Fenster/die Fenster** (*window/windows*) and **der Amerikaner/die Amerikaner** (*American/Americans*).
- **Nouns that are mostly of foreign origin:** The plural form of these nouns has an **-s** ending, for example **das Radio/die Radios** (*radio/radios*) and **das Café/die Cafés** (*café/cafés*).

Other plural form patterns include nouns that add **-e, -er,** or **–en;** nouns that add an umlaut (represented by two dots over a vowel, as in ä, ö, and ü); or nouns that do a combination of both. Following are three examples:

der Vater/die Väter (*father/fathers*), die Lampe/die Lampen (*lamp/lamps*), and das Buch/die Bücher (*book/books*). Sound complicated? You're right, so try to make a point of remembering the plural form of a noun (and its gender!) when you first incorporate it into your active vocabulary.

Pronouns

Pronouns are the handy group of words that can stand in for nouns so you don't have to sound redundant. They're extremely versatile because they turn up in so many places, so you need to be able to recognize them and know how to use them.

Figuring out which German pronoun to use takes some practice. To begin with, realize that both English and German pronouns have cases, which help show how a word functions in a sentence. (For more information on pronouns and their cases, go to Book III, Chapter 2.)

The following list gives you a quick overview of the types of pronouns in both English and German:

- *Personal pronouns* include **ich, mich, mir** (*I, me, me*), and others. These pronouns replace the word for a person, animal, object, idea, and so on. **Ich liebe dich** (*I love you*) has two personal pronouns: **ich** and **dich**. (Go to Book III, Chapter 2 for details on using personal pronouns.)

- *Demonstrative pronouns,* such as **der, das,** and **den** (*he/it, it, him/it;* also *this* and *that*), point to and identify the noun or pronoun that they replace. For example, when you're in an ice cream store, you point to the flavor you want as you say: **Das möchte ich.** (*That's the one I want.*) (Find out more about demonstrative pronouns in Book III, Chapter 2.)

- *Interrogative pronouns,* also called *question words* in this book, include **wer** (*who*), **was** (*what*), and other words that you use for asking questions. For example, **Was machen Sie?** (*What are you doing?*) (For more information on forming questions, turn to Book III, Chapter 4.)

- *Relative pronouns* help you include more information about a noun or pronoun that has been expressed beforehand in a sentence. Examples of relative pronouns are *who, that,* and *which.* In the following sentence, the relative pronoun is **den** (*whom*): **Das ist der Mann, den ich heiraten möchte.** (*That is the man [whom] I would like to marry.*) In English, you don't need to use the relative pronoun *whom* to connect the two parts of the sentence, but in German you do. (See Book IV, Chapter 1 for details on how to use the German relative pronouns.)

- *Possessive pronouns,* such as **mein, sein,** and **ihr** *(my, his,* and *her),* describe who owns or is in possession of a particular person or object. These words are actually considered adjectives, and they change form just as adjectives do — according to the gender and case they have. For example, in the question **Wo ist mein Handy?** *(Where is my cellphone?),* **mein** is the possessive for the word **Handy.** (For information on how to use possessives and adjectives, check out Book III, Chapter 5.)

- *Reflexive pronouns* refer to the subject of a clause or sentence and include *yourself* and *myself.* The following sentence has the reflexive pronoun **mir** *(myself):* **Ich kaufe mir ein neues Auto.** *(I'm buying [myself] a new car.)* Some German verbs require a reflexive pronoun. (You find information on reflexive pronouns in Book IV, Chapter 3.)

Articles

Nouns often appear in the company of a sidekick: a definite article (**der, die,** and **das,** which correspond to the English *the*) or an indefinite article (**ein, eine,** and **ein,** which correspond to *a* or *an*).

The definite articles ("der," "die," and "das")

While the definite article *the* has only one form in English, in German, it has three forms: **der** (masculine), **die** (feminine), and **das** (neuter). Which form you use depends on the gender of the German noun. **Der** is the definite article used with masculine nouns, **die** is used with feminine nouns, and **das** is used with neuter nouns.

When you meet a new noun, find out whether its definite article is **der, die,** or **das** — in other words, determine the gender of the noun. For example, memorize **der Garten** *(the garden)* rather than just **Garten** *(garden),* **die Tür** *(the door)* rather than **Tür** *(door),* and **das Haus** *(the house)* rather than **Haus** *(house).*

For plural nouns, things are comparatively easy. The definite article for all plural nouns, regardless of gender, is **die.** As in English, the indefinite article *a* just vanishes in the plural: *a garden* becomes *gardens.* (The next section explains indefinite articles in more detail.)

The indefinite articles ("ein," "eine," and "ein")

In English, you use the indefinite article *a* or *an* when you want to specify one of a particular thing. Because German has three different genders, you have to use three different indefinite articles. Luckily, the indefinite article for masculine and neuter nouns is the same:

✔ **For masculine nouns:** Use **ein** — for example, **ein Name** (*a name*), **ein Mann** (*a man*), and **ein Berg** (*a mountain*).

✔ **For neuter nouns:** Use **ein** — for example, **ein Problem** (*a problem*), **ein Museum** (*a museum*), and **ein Bier** (*a beer*).

✔ **For feminine nouns:** Add an **e** to **ein,** making **eine** — for example, **eine Nacht** (*a night*), **eine Adresse** (*an address*), and **eine Cousine** (*a female cousin*).

Not too difficult, right? Unfortunately, things can get a little more complicated. You know that the gender of a noun determines the articles you use with it. But the endings of the articles also change depending on whether the noun they're attached to is in the nominative, genitive, dative, or accusative case. The endings specified in the preceding list are those of the nominative case. (For more information about case and the effect it has on both definite and indefinite articles, head to Book III, Chapter 2.)

Adjectives

Adjectives describe nouns. In German, adjectives have different endings depending on the gender, case, and number (singular or plural) of the noun they accompany. Adjective endings also depend on whether the adjective is accompanied by a definite article, an indefinite article, or no article at all.

The following list shows the endings for adjectives accompanied by a definite article in the nominative case. (For more on case, see Book III, Chapter 2.) This list includes the adjectives **schön** (*beautiful*), **weiß** (*white*), **groß** (*large*), and **klein** (*small*). The adjective endings appear in italics.

✔ **der schön*e* Garten** (*the beautiful garden*)

✔ **die weiß*e* Tür** (*the white door*)

✔ **das klein*e* Haus** (*the small house*)

✔ **die groß*en* Häuser** (*the large houses*)

Following are the nominative case endings for adjectives used alone (that is, without an accompanying article) or adjectives accompanied by an indefinite article:

✔ **(ein) schön*er* Garten** (*[a] beautiful garden*)

✔ **(eine) weiß*e* Tür** (*[a] white door*)

✔ **(ein) klein*es* Haus** (*[a] small house*)

✔ **groß*e* Häuser** (*large houses*)

All the adjectives (and their corresponding endings) in the preceding examples are in the subject case (that is, the nominative case). (For more information on adjectives, go to Book III, Chapter 5.)

Verbs

Verbs express actions or states of being. The person doing the action is the verb's subject, and in both English and German, the verb always adjusts its ending for the subject. For example, you say *I open the door* and *the cat opens the door*. In the present tense in English, most verbs have two different forms, or spellings — for example, *open* and *opens*. Most German verbs, on the other hand, have four different forms. For example, the following table shows the endings (or forms) of the verb **sagen** (*to say*) in the present tense. You simply tack the appropriate ending onto the stem **sag-**, depending on how you're expressing the verb. (For more on conjugating verbs and dealing with tenses, check out Chapters 3, 7, and 8 in Book III and Chapters 4 through 7 in Book IV. Also refer to the later section "Conjugating verbs and understanding tenses.")

sagen (*to say*)	
ich sag**e**	wir sag**en**
du sag**st**	ihr sag**t**
er/sie/es sag**t**	sie sag**en**
Sie sag**en**	
Er **sagt**, dass er aus Deutschland kommt. (*He says that he's from Germany.*)	

Seems easy enough, right? But — as usual — some exceptions to the rule exist. When the stem of the verb ends in **-m, -n, -d,** or **-t,** you need to insert an **e** before the ending in the **du, er/sie/es,** and **ihr** constructions, as shown in the following examples:

> **du atm-e-st** (*you* [singular, informal] *breathe*)
>
> **er arbeit-e-t** (*he works*)
>
> **ihr bad-e-t** (*you* [plural, informal] *bathe*)

Why the added **e?** Try to pronounce "atmst" and you'll know.

Adverbs

Adverbs accompany verbs or adjectives in order to describe them. In English, most adverbs end with *-ly* (as in: I *quickly* put on my new black socks). In German, adverbs are generally spelled the same as their adjective counterparts in their barebones form, without special endings.

Take, for example, **vorsichtig** (*careful/carefully*), which has the same spelling for both its adjective and its adverb meaning. When you use **vorsichtig** in a sentence as an adverb, it keeps the same spelling — for example, **Fahren Sie vorsichtig!** (*Drive carefully!*) However, when you use **vorsichtig** in a sentence as an adjective, it changes its form (spelling) the way all German adjectives do; see the previous section about adjectives. The following sentence shows how **vorsichtig,** when used as an adjective, changes its spelling according to the noun it describes:

> **Sie ist eine vorsichtige Fahrerin.** (*She's a careful driver.*)

To find out more about using adverbs, go to Book III, Chapter 5.

Conjunctions

Conjunctions serve the purpose of linking words and parts of sentences together. You can divide conjunctions into two groups: coordinating conjunctions and subordinating conjunctions.

Three commonly used coordinating conjunctions are **und** (*and*), **aber** (*but*), and **oder** (*or*). Of the two types of conjunctions, the coordinating type are easier to use. The following example uses **oder** to link words:

> **Möchten Sie Kaffee oder Tee?** (*Would you like coffee or tea?*)

Subordinating conjunctions include words like **falls** (*in case*), **weil** (*because*), **dass** (*that*), and **wenn** (*if/when*). With German subordinating conjunctions, you have to use a comma to separate the two parts of the sentence being connected by the conjunction, and you need to know what word order to use. (For details on word order with conjunctions, go to Book IV, Chapter 1.) Look at the following examples:

> **Wir möchten, dass Sie am Samstag zu unserem Fest kommen.** (*We'd like you to come to our party on Saturday.* Literally: *We would like that you come to our party on Saturday.*)

> **Ich kann leider nicht, weil ich schon Pläne habe.** (*Unfortunately, I can't because I already have plans.*)

For more information on using conjunctions, turn to Book IV, Chapter 1.

Book III

Assembling the Grammatical Foundations for Communication

Prepositions

Prepositions show the relationship of a noun or a pronoun to some other word or words in the sentence. Some examples of prepositions are **mit** (*with*), **durch** (*through/by*), and **über** (*above/over*). In most instances, you place the preposition right before the word or words that it modifies. The preposition determines the case — accusative, dative, or genitive — that the modified word or words following it will have. Some prepositions can use either the accusative case or the dative case depending on the meaning. Here are a couple of examples with the prepositions **mit** and **durch:**

> **Ich fahre oft mit dem Zug.** (*I often take the train.*) The more literal translation is *I often travel with the train.* **Mit** is a dative preposition, so **dem Zug** is in the dative case.

> **Der Zug fährt durch den Tunnel.** (*The train is going through the tunnel.*) **Durch** is an accusative preposition, so **den Tunnel** is in the accusative case.

Head to Book IV, Chapter 2 for more information on how to use German prepositions and Book III, Chapter 2 for more details on case.

Understanding Grammar Terms

Before you can start building sentences in German, you need to be able to keep track of the many grammatical terms you encounter. This section clears up any fuzzy ideas you may have about the names for tools of German grammar, such as *conjugation, gender, case,* and *tense.*

Conjugating verbs and understanding tenses

The verb form in its basic, static state is called the *infinitive.* It's the form you see in dictionary entries, as in **wohnen** (*to live*). In English, the *to* indicates that the word is in infinitive form; the German equivalent is the **-en** ending on the verb, although a small number of verbs, including **tun** (*to do*), have the infinitive ending **-n.**

When you *conjugate* a verb, you change the verb form so it fits in your sentence to convey information such as which subject is doing the action and when something is happening. Conjugation involves breaking the verb into its usable parts. Look at the conjugation of the verb *to work: I work, you work, he/she/it works, we work, you work, they work.* English has only two different spellings of *work* (with and without *s*). The same conjugation in German — **ich arbeite, du arbeitest, er/sie/es arbeitet, wir arbeiten, ihr arbeitet, sie arbeiten, Sie arbeiten** — reveals four different verb endings: **-e, -est, -et,** and **-en.**

Verbs are conjugated in different *tenses,* which describe time. The three main descriptions of time are past, present, and future. Here's a brief look at the most frequently used tenses, with the relevant verbs underlined:

- ✔ **Present tense:** This tense describes actions that are happening now, habitual actions, or general facts. Look at the following sentence, which uses the verb **wohnen** (*to live*) in the present tense: **Ich wohne in den U.S.A.** You can translate it as *I live in the U.S.A.* or *I'm living in the U.S.A.* (See Book III, Chapter 3 for details on the present tense.)

- ✔ **Present perfect (conversational past):** In German, the present perfect describes something that happened in the past, whether finished or unfinished. It's used in conversational German. **Ich habe in den U.S.A. gewohnt** can mean *I have lived in the U.S.A.* or *I lived in the U.S.A.* (For more on the present perfect, go to Book IV, Chapter 4.)

- ✔ **Simple past:** The simple past is used in formal language to describe past actions. **Ich wohnte in den U.S.A.** means *I lived in the U.S.A.* (Find out more about the simple past in Book IV, Chapter 5.)

- ✔ **Future:** The future describes events that haven't yet occurred. **Ich werde in den U.S.A. wohnen** means *I will live in the U.S.A.* or *I'm going to live in the U.S.A.* German makes much less use of the future tense than English, often opting for the simple present instead. (Check out Book IV, Chapter 6 for more info on the future.)

English uses continuous (progressive) tenses — verbs with a form of *to be* and *-ing,* as in *am living* or *have been living* — to describe a temporary or ongoing action. But because German has no continuous forms, you can simply use the basic German tenses you see in the preceding list for the continuous form in English. German also uses other tenses slightly differently from English. (For more on these differences, go to Book IV, Chapters 4 and 6.)

The *subjunctive* is not a tense but rather a *mood,* something that indicates *how* you describe an action — for example, as a fact, a possibility, or an uncertainty. But as with tenses, the subjunctive gets its own conjugation. (Go to Book IV, Chapter 7 for more on the subjunctive.)

Book III

Assembling the Grammatical Foundations for Communication

Familiarizing yourself with gender, number, and case

The trio of gender, number, and case are closely linked to each other to help you make sense of single words and to connect them into sentences. You need to know how to use gender, number, and case to express your ideas in understandable language. Check out the following explanations (turn to Book III, Chapter 2 for more on any of these topics):

- ✔ **Gender:** People are one of two genders, masculine or feminine, right? Dogs and cats are, too. But do stones and water have a gender? In German, yes indeed! Every noun has a gender; **der** (*masculine*), **die** (*feminine*), and **das** (*neuter*) are the options. All three are the gender-specific versions of the English word *the*. (If this were a soccer game, the German team would've already won by a margin of two.)

   When looking at German words, don't confuse grammatical gender with the word's meaning. Gender has to do with the word itself, not the meaning of the word.

- ✔ **Number:** Number refers to singular and plural, like *one potato, two potatoes, three potatoes*. German plurals are more intricate than English plurals. In fact, German offers five major different types of plural endings. Some plurals compare with the irregular English plurals, like *man* and *men* (**der Mann** and **die Männer**).

- ✔ **Case:** German has four cases: nominative, accusative, dative, and genitive. But what does that actually mean? Cases help tell you what role the word plays in the sentence. They have to do with the difference between *I* and *me* or *she* and *her,* and they deal with the significance of the *to* in *give it to me* or the apostrophe *s* in *dog's Frisbee.*

   German case endings are numerous, and they show the relationship between the words having those cases. English uses case far less often.

Grammar terms that describe words, parts of words, and word groupings

Grammatically speaking, you need to know several terms that describe words that you put together to convey meaning — *sentence, clause, phrase,* and so on. The following list shows the most important key words you see in this book:

- ✔ **Phrase:** A group of words without a subject or a verb; most often used to describe a prepositional phrase, such as **ohne Zweifel** (*without a doubt*).

✔ **Clause:** A group of related words that has a subject and a verb, such as **wir arbeiten . . .** (*we're working . . .*).

✔ **Sentence:** A group of words that represents a complete thought and has a complete sentence structure — subject, verb, and punctuation — such as **Gehen wir!** (*Let's go!*)

✔ **Prefix:** A "word beginning" attached to the front of a word that alters the word's meaning, such as **un** (*un-*) + **freundlich** (*friendly*) = **un**freundlich (*unfriendly*) or **aus** (*out*) + **gehen** (*to go*) = **aus**gehen (*to go out*).

✔ **Suffix:** A "word ending" attached to the back of a word that alters the word's meaning, such as **(der) Kapital** + **ismus** = Kapital**ismus** (*capital + ism = capitalism*). Another example is the diminutive suffix **-chen,** which conveys the meaning of a smaller version of the original word, such as **(das) Haus** (*house*) + **-chen** = **Häuschen** (*small house, cottage, booth*). To form the diminutive **-chen,** you also need to add an *umlaut* over the letter **a,** as in **ä.**

✔ **Cognates:** Words that have the same meaning and the same (or nearly the same) spelling in two languages, such as **der Hammer** (*the hammer*) or **die Melodie** (*the melody*).

Note: Technically, *cognates* are simply two words that come from a common ancestor.

Book III

Assembling the Grammatical Foundations for Communication

Understanding Word Order

Nouns, verbs, adjectives, and other parts of speech aren't just thrown together helter-skelter to make a sentence. Instead, to create a logical sentence, you arrange words in a specific order. In some respects, German word order is more flexible than English word order because case plays a key role in clarifying the meaning of a sentence, something that's not nearly as powerful of a tool in English. When positioning words in a German sentence, however, you need to keep in mind a few major points. The following sections give you the skinny on word order.

Arranging words in the right order

Standard word order in German is much like English word order. The subject comes first, then the verb, followed by the rest of the sentence. Look at the following example sentence:

Subject	Verb	Object
Meine Freundin	**hat**	**einen Hund.**
My girlfriend	*has*	*a dog.*

Putting the verb in second place

One of the most important things to remember is the place of the verb in a German sentence. In freestanding, main clauses (known as *independent clauses*), like the one in the preceding section, a one-word verb is always in second place, no matter what. The term *second place,* however, doesn't necessarily mean the second *word* in the sentence. Rather, it refers to the second *placeholder,* which may be comprised of more than one word. For example, **meine Freundin,** the subject of the earlier sentence, consists of two words, but it's the first placeholder. In the following examples, the verb is **fahren** (*to drive*), and it follows the second place rule:

> **Meine Freundin fährt nach Dänemark.** (*My girlfriend is driving to Denmark.*)

How about adding some more information?

> **Meine Freundin fährt morgen nach Dänemark.** (*My girlfriend is driving to Denmark tomorrow.*)

Standard practice in German sentences is to place the reference to time, **morgen** (*tomorrow*), before the reference to place, **nach Dänemark** (*to Denmark*), as you can see in the previous sentence. What happens if you start the sentence with **morgen?**

> **Morgen fährt meine Freundin nach Dänemark.** (*Tomorrow my girlfriend is driving to Denmark.*)

Morgen is in first place, and because the verb has to be in second place, the subject follows the verb. Technically, this arrangement is called *inversion of the verb.* All it means is that the verb and the subject switch places. Inversion of the verb occurs whenever anything other than the subject occupies first place in a sentence.

Having said that, what about the statement **Meine Freundin hat einen Hund?** Can you give that one a twirl and change the word order? Absolutely, as long as the verb stays in second place, like this: **Einen Hund hat meine Freundin.** But why would you want to rearrange word order? Generally, you do so to shift emphasis in the meaning. For example, you may hear something along the lines of the following conversation:

> **Hat deine Schwester einen Hund?** (*Does your sister have a dog?*)

> **Nein, sie hat eine Katze. Einen Hund hat meine Freundin Heike.** (*No, she has a cat. It's my girlfriend Heike who has a dog.*)

Don't German speakers get all confused playing around with word order like that? That's where the (in)famous German case system comes into play. Adjectives and articles that appear alongside nouns and, in some instances, the nouns themselves, assume different endings depending on their function in a sentence. So no matter where a noun appears in a German sentence, you can figure out its role by checking the ending of the article, the noun itself, and/or the adjective. (See Book III, Chapter 2 for more on case.)

Pushing the verb to the end

The examples used so far in this section have all been independent, stand-alone sentences, but sometimes several thoughts combine to form a more complex structure:

> **Wir gehen nicht einkaufen, weil wir kein Geld haben.** (*We're not going shopping because we have no money.*)

The verb **gehen** (*go*) is in second place as you would expect, but the verb in the second part of the sentence, the part that begins with **weil** (*because*), gets kicked to the end. This arrangement of the verb happens in *dependent clauses.*

Dependent clauses typically start with *subordinating conjunctions* (words that link sentences) like **dass** (*that*), **weil** (*because*), **damit** (*so that*), **obwohl** (*although*), **bevor** (*before*), and **wenn** (*when*), and they always end with the verb. (Turn to Book IV, Chapter 1 for the lowdown on conjunctions.)

Forming questions

The German word order for asking yes or no questions is straightforward. You begin with a verb, and the subject follows, as in these examples:

> **Tanzen Sie gern?** (*Do you like to dance?*)

> **Spricht er Spanisch?** (*Does he speak Spanish?*)

Note that you don't have the verb *do* in German when forming questions.

Another way to elicit information is to form a question by using a question word like **wer** (*who*), **was** (*what*), **wo** (*where*), **wann** (*when*), **wie** (*how*), or **warum** (*why*). You can also form a question with words and phrases like **was für ein/e/en. . . ?** (*what kind of. . . ?*) or **welche/r/s. . . ?** (*which. . . ?*).

Book III

Assembling the Grammatical Foundations for Communication

When forming questions with these words, the verb goes in its usual place — second:

Was für ein Fahrrad kauft Helmut? (*What kind of bicycle is Helmut buying?*)

Wer kauft ein Rennrad? (*Who's buying a racing bicycle?*)

Wo kauft er das Rad? (*Where's he buying the bike?*)

Warum kauft er ein Rennrad? (*Why's he buying a racing bicycle?*)

(For more details on using question words and forming questions, go to Book III, Chapter 4.)

Checking Out the Tenses: Present, Past, and Future

In grammar, the word *tense* is what the layperson calls "time." You pick the appropriate tense to describe when the action you're talking about takes place. The ways to look at the concept of time differ slightly from one culture and language to the next, so the way tenses are used sometimes differs, too.

Looking at the present

The present tense is an incredibly useful tense in German. You can go a long way using just this one tense. The German present tense corresponds to three forms in English. For example, **ich denke** can mean the equivalent of *I think, I do think,* or *I am thinking* in English. And it gets even better: Depending on the context, the German present tense can correspond to the past or future tense in English.

The present tense can describe what's happening now:

Was machst du gerade? (*What are you doing right now?*)

Ich lese die Zeitung. (*I'm reading the newspaper.*)

Additionally, the present tense can describe what sometimes, usually, always, or never happens:

Freitags gehe ich oft ins Kino. (*I often go to the movies on Fridays.*)

The German present tense can also describe what's going to happen:

> **Wir fliegen im Dezember nach Portugal.** (*We're flying to Portugal in December.*)

> **Nächste Woche fahre ich nach Bremen.** (*Next week I'm going to drive to Bremen.*)

Using the present tense is a very common way of talking about future events in German, particularly if the sentence includes a time expression that anchors the action clearly in the future — for example, **im Dezember** (*in December*) or **nächste Woche** (*next week*).

Finally, Germans use the present tense to describe what's been happening up until now:

> **Ich lebe seit zehn Jahren in derselben Wohnung.** (*I've been living in the same apartment for ten years.*)

> **Wie lange lernst du schon Deutsch?** (*How long have you been learning German?*)

Note that English uses the present perfect tense to express the same thing.

Talking about the past

The perfect tense — as in **wir haben gegessen** (*we have eaten*) or **Jan hat gearbeitet** (*Jan has worked*) — is the main tense used to describe past events in spoken German. It's very versatile: You can use it to talk about most actions and situations in the past. Contrast this with the use of the English perfect tense (*I have gone, I have eaten,* and so on), which you can use only in specific contexts. For example, **Ich habe Anna letzte Woche gesehen** (*I have seen Anna last week*) is grammatically correct in German, even though it doesn't quite work in English.

In the preceding sentence, the verb has two parts, **habe** and **gesehen.** These two parts are described in grammatical terms as the *conjugated verb* (**habe** in this example) and the *past participle* (here, **gesehen**).

German word order for using verbs that have two or more parts follows specific rules. When forming a sentence with multiple verb parts, the *conjugated verb* takes second position in the sentence, and the other part(s) of the verb — in this instance, the *past participle* — goes all the way at the end of the sentence. This rule holds true for all verbs that have two or more parts.

Most verbs form the perfect tense by combining the conjugated form of the verb **haben** (*have*) and the past participle form of the verb. The following examples follow the German word order rule, meaning that the conjugated form of the verb **haben** is in second position in the sentence, and the past participle of the verb that's being expressed is kicked to the end of the sentence:

> **Luka hat mir geholfen.** (*Luka [has] helped me.*)
>
> **Gestern haben wir ein neues Auto gekauft.** (*Yesterday we bought a new car.*)
>
> **Hast du die Zeitung schon gelesen?** (*Have you read the newspaper yet?*)
>
> **Ich habe den Film vor einer Woche gesehen.** (*I saw the film a week ago.*)

Certain verbs require **sein** (*to be*) in combination with the past participle instead of **haben** (*to have*) to form the perfect tense. These verbs often describe a change of location, state, or condition. Here are a few examples:

> **Gestern bin ich ins Kino gegangen.** (*I went to the movies yesterday.*)
>
> **Ich bin in Hamburg gewesen.** (*I've been to Hamburg./I was in Hamburg.*)
>
> **Bist du mit dem Auto gekommen?** (*Did you come by car?*)
>
> **Sie ist nicht mit dem Zug gefahren.** (*She didn't take the train.*)

German verbs fall into two categories: weak and strong verbs. Regular verbs, known as weak verbs, make up the largest group of German verbs. The next two sections discuss how to form past participles of weak and strong verbs in German.

Forming the past participle of a weak verb

The past participle form of a weak verb begins with the past participle marker **ge-** like this:

> **ge** + verb stem (the infinitive minus **-en**) + **(e)t** = past participle

For example, for the verb **fragen** (*to ask*), the formula looks like this:

> **ge** + **frag** + **t** = **gefragt**

Some exceptions to this formula do exist. When the stem of the verb ends in **-m, -n, -d,** or **-t,** you need to insert an **-e** after the stem and before adding the **-t,** for example with the verbs **arbeiten** (to work) and **atmen** (to breathe) like this:

> **ge** + **arbeit** + **e** + **t** = **gearbeitet**
>
> **ge** + **atm** + **e** + **t** = **geatmet**

Forming the past participle of a strong verb

Here's the formula for constructing the past participle of a strong (irregular) verb:

ge + verb stem (the infinitive minus **-en**) + **en** = past participle

For the verb **kommen** (*to come*), the past participle is

ge + **komm** + **en** = **gekommen**

See Book IV, Chapter 4 for more information on the perfect tense.

Writing about the past

The simple past verb tense is very frequently used in English. Imagine you're sitting at the dinner table, telling about your day; you're bound to use the simple past tense. For example, in the following story, the simple past tense verbs are underlined: *There <u>was</u> a huge traffic jam, so I <u>got</u> to work late. My coworkers <u>looked at</u> me skeptically when I <u>rolled out</u> my usual excuse. Then I <u>spilled</u> coffee on my keyboard. The day <u>seemed</u> to get progressively worse after that.*

The simple past tense is used all the time in printed German, such as newspapers or books, but it's much less common in spoken German, like the dinner table story in the previous paragraph. One exception is the simple past tense of **sein** (*to be*), which is often preferable to the perfect tense in both speech and writing. The following table shows you the various forms of the simple past tense of the verb **sein**. (For more information on the simple past tense, check out Book IV, Chapter 5.)

sein (to be)	
ich **war**	wir **waren**
du **warst**	ihr **wart**
er/sie/es **war**	sie **waren**
Sie **waren**	
Ich **war** heute Nachmittag nicht zu Hause. (*I wasn't home this afternoon.*)	

Book III

Assembling the Grammatical Foundations for Communication

Talking about the future

The future tense isn't used as frequently in German as it is in English. In many situations, you can use the present tense instead. The way to form the future tense in German is pretty similar to English: You conjugate the verb **werden** (*will/to become*) and add an infinitive. The following table shows you the forms of the verb **werden** in the present tense.

werden (*will/to become*)	
ich werd**e**	wir werd**en**
du **wirst**	ihr werd**et**
er/sie/es **wird**	sie werd**en**
Sie werd**en**	
Wir **werden** im Herbst einen langen Urlaub machen. (*This fall we're going to take a long vacation.*)	

To incorporate the future tense of verbs into sentences, you follow the standard German word order for using verbs that have two parts: The *conjugated verb*, in this case, **werden,** takes second position in the sentence. The other verb part, which, for the future tense, is the *infinitive* of the verb, goes all the way at the end of the sentence, as the following examples show:

Ich werde viel Geld verdienen. (*I'm going to/I'll earn a lot of money.*)

Wir werden morgen skifahren. (*We'll go/We're going skiing tomorrow.*)

Es wird regnen. (*It's going to rain.*)

(Go to Book IV, Chapter 6 for more info on the future tense.)

Finding Meaning through Context

One essential tool for making sense of a foreign language is to consciously look for meaning through the context of the words. You probably do the same thing in your own language. Imagine you're reading a text that's not in your field of expertise. You instinctively look at any headings, scan the text rapidly, and get clues from any illustrations, charts, or tables. When you're looking at a text in German, you can figure out what it means by employing the same techniques you already use in your native language.

To understand what a whole sentence means, see how the words fit together. Identify the verb or verbs and a noun or pronoun, and you have the meat of your sentence. Then check out how the other words are related to the subject and verb — for example, look for a prepositional phrase or a conjunction. (See the earlier section for details on the parts of speech.) In short, use all the tools at your disposal to understand German sentences.

Before you start memorizing new words, you want to make sure you know how to use them. So after you figure out the meaning of a new word or expression by looking at it in its context, you may want to write it down. Putting words together in a phrase or a sentence — that is, in the context where you first discovered the word(s) — is a great way to improve your brain's ability to remember new words and their meanings.

 Unfortunately, you don't retain vocabulary, grammar, or what-have-you the first time you're exposed to it — or the second or third time. So use a system of recording important information that works well for you: Try making flashcards (color code the nouns according to gender — blue cards for masculine, pink for feminine, green for neuter), creating an alphabetical word list, writing new expressions in meaningful sentences, and incorporating new grammar points into a short dialogue.

Using a Bilingual Dictionary

Horses are only as good for riding as their training is. And dictionaries are only as useful for finding words as their owners' knowledge of how to use them. Except for the terms *breaking in a horse* and *breaking in a book,* that's about it for parallels (unless, of course, you want to speak German to your horse).

A bilingual dictionary can be a challenge to use at first. Take on the challenge by reading the information at the front of the dictionary on how to use it. The symbols and abbreviations are your key to successfully scouting for the right word. This section helps you sort out this handy tool.

Making the right choice

When choosing a bilingual dictionary, your first task is selecting the right dictionary. First and foremost is the size and quality. Don't scrimp here. Check out a few dictionaries by comparing their features. Does the dictionary use only a core vocabulary of, say, 2,000 words to explain the entries? Does it contain word partnership info? Does it show usage of the word in complete

Book III

Assembling the Grammatical Foundations for Communication

example sentences? Get the feel of the dictionary's distinguishing features and layout. Then compare three different entries. Start with a frequently used verb like **machen.** The following shortened dictionary entry for the verb **machen** shows you how a good dictionary organizes the information on the first two lines:

> **machen 1** *vt* (**a**) to do; (*herstellen, zubereiten*) to make. **was ~ Sie (beruflich)?** what do you do for a living?; **gut, wird gemacht** right, I'll get that done *or* will be done (*coll*).

You may notice two abbreviations and a symbol in this entry:

- The abbreviation *vt* stands for *transitive verb;* that's a verb that can take a direct object. Other verbs have the abbreviation *vi,* which stands for *intransitive verb;* that's a verb without a direct object.

- The second abbreviation *coll* stands for *colloquial;* expressions or words marked by this abbreviation are used in informal conversation.

- The ~ symbol represents the *headword* (the first word) **machen.** The complete expression is **Was machen Sie (beruflich)?**

Start your dictionary comparison task by following these steps:

1. **Look at how comprehensive the entries are.**

   Check for commonly used phrases, such as **was machst du denn da?** (*what in the world are you doing here?*), **mach schneller!** (*hurry up!*), or **mach's gut** (*take care*), and compare their translations for detail and content. You should be able to find complete sentences and phrases using **machen.** Comprehensive dictionaries should offer alternative words in German (at least for frequently used verbs such as **machen**), along with possible translations. For example, after **machen,** you may find **herstellen** (*to produce, manufacture*) or **zubereiten** (*to prepare*), as in the example entry.

2. **Ask yourself which dictionary is more user-friendly.**

   In other words, does the dictionary provide plenty of helpful abbreviations to help you understand the entries? Do you see clearly marked sections under the headword **machen?** They should be marked by numbers and letters in bold; in the example entry, you find **1** and (**a**). Some quality dictionaries indent the numbered sections to make them even easier to locate. You can compare whether there's a phonetic pronunciation for tricky words. Also, check that the dictionary makes ample use of symbols like *coll* to indicate usage of the word.

   Apart from the abbreviations that show part of speech, gender, number, case, and so on, you find many more details in any large, quality dictionary. A (very) short list of such abbreviated terms should include *fig* (figurative), *lit* (literal), *esp* (especially), *sl* (slang), *Tech* (technology), *Psych* (psychology), *Prov* (proverb), *Jur* (law), *spec* (specialist term), *Aus* (Austrian usage), and *Sw* (Swiss usage).

Make your choice wisely, and start enjoying your new **Wörterbuch** (*dictionary*).

If you prefer an online dictionary and you're not sure about how to make a good selection, follow the same criteria. Select a couple of reputable dictionary publishers, go to their online dictionaries, and find out how extensive and (hopefully accurate) they are. If you're not familiar with dictionary publishers, check out the dictionaries listed under "deutsch-englisches wörterbuch." Do a thorough online search to find what's available and compare the sources you find.

Online dictionaries are a good backup for finding out about words if you're on a limited budget. They often have the add-on feature of an audio recording of each word. This can be a great help in figuring out the pronunciation of the word.

Performing a word search

Whether you're using a hard copy or an online dictionary, you still have to know how to find the right word.

Familiarize yourself with the symbols and abbreviations used by looking up a few nouns, verbs, adjectives, and so on. See whether you understand them in the context of the dictionary entry. Instead of trying to memorize the meaning of all the abbreviations, make a photocopy of the list that you find at the front of the dictionary and keep it as a bookmark in your dictionary. Better yet, laminate it. That way you can use it as a mouse pad, a table mat, or whatever. You can then cross-check definitions to get more information on words you're looking up.

When you look up a word that has several definitions, read beyond the first or second entry line and try to decide which one suits your needs. Think about context and decide which word fits best into the rest of the sentence. Besides meaning, here are some other factors that may affect your word choice:

✔ **Nouns:** Think of gender and number as the vital statistics of a noun.

  • Gender is indicated by *m, f,* and *nt* (for masculine, feminine, and neuter) in some dictionaries.

Book III

Assembling the Grammatical Foundations for Communication

- Number is indicated with the plural ending form for that noun. There are five main groups of noun endings. A common ending is **-en;** other nouns add **-s.** With some nouns, you see the genitive case ending indicated for that noun in addition to the plural ending.

✔ **Verbs:** Verbs also have vital statistics you need to know.

- A verb is transitive or intransitive (symbols like *vt* and *vi*). A *transitive verb* takes a direct object; an *intransitive* verb doesn't.

- A transitive verb may have a separable prefix (*vt sep*) or an inseparable prefix (*vt insep*). If the prefix is separable, it usually gets booted to the end of the sentence when the verb is conjugated.

- Some verbs are reflexive (*vr*), meaning they require a reflexive pronoun (*myself, himself,* and so on).

- The simple past form and the past participle are also indicated (in some dictionaries with *pret* and *ptp,* respectively).

✔ **Prepositions:** Prepositions in German dictionary entries show which case they have: accusative (*prep + acc*), dative (*prep + dat*), or genitive (*prep + gen*). Some prepositions have more than one case, and most prepositions have more than one meaning.

✔ **Pronouns:** Pronouns include personal pronouns (*pers pron*), such as **ich** (*I*); demonstrative pronouns (*dem pron*), such as **denen** (*them*); relative pronouns (*rel pron*), such as **das** (*that*); and reflexive pronouns (*reflexive pron*), such as **mich** (*myself*). See Book III, Chapter 2 for details on pronoun types.

Chapter 2

Sorting Out Word Gender and Case

- -

- -

Most words in a German sentence take their cues from nouns (or their esteemed representatives — pronouns). When studying German, you really don't know a new noun unless you know its characteristics, including gender. So for each new noun you come across, accept its gender as a part of the word and commit it to memory.

To use nouns and pronouns (as well as adjectives and prepositions) in a German sentence, you have to know how they fit together; this is the role of case. In German, case endings on words show you how those words are being used in the sentence. Take, for example, nouns and their sidekicks, the articles. The case endings on these words indicate how the noun is working in the sentence — as the subject or object, for instance.

In this chapter, you get the lowdown on how gender and case work hand in hand to form various endings on the members of two large families of words: the article family and the pronoun family. You also see how case and gender affect certain verbs (called *dative verbs*) and adjectives.

Classifying Nouns and Pronouns with Gender

Not everything with gender lives and breathes. Listen to people talk about inanimate objects and you may hear them refer to the faithful bicycle they cherish, the noncompliant computer they want to throttle, or the old jalopy they're trying to coax up a hill as *he* or *she*. Like these other things you may have a love-hate relationship with, German *words* have gender.

In German grammar, *gender* is the classification of a noun or a pronoun into one of three categories: masculine, feminine, or neuter. These genders often have nothing to do with the meaning of the word; they're simply an identity bracelet. Note that *gender* refers to the word, not whatever the word represents. You need to know a word's gender because it can dictate the spelling of other words in the sentence. The following sections explain how to identify a word's gender.

Identifying German genders and figuring out which one to use

In English, you mark a noun as one of three genders: male (masculine), female (feminine), or inanimate/neither (neuter). The descriptions *male, female,* and *inanimate* refer to living beings and things. The words in parentheses — *masculine, feminine,* and *neuter* — refer to grammatical gender distinction, which is how German describes *noun gender.*

Gender distinction in English is *natural,* which means you need to know only whether the noun refers to a female being, a male being, or an inanimate object (neither male nor female). You can refer to the nouns as *he, she,* or *it.* The articles you use — such as *the, a,* and *an* — don't tell you anything about gender at all. Look at these examples:

- *Can you see the girl over there? She's really tall.* (You know the word *girl* refers to a female, so you use *she* when you refer back to her in the second sentence.)

- *The new German teacher is Herr Mangold. I think he comes from Bremen.* (The teacher is male, so you refer to him as *he.*)

- *Have you seen the cool guitar in the shop window? It has 12 strings.* (You refer to an inanimate object as *it.*)

In German, you have three genders just as you do in English; however, much of the gender designation in German is *unnatural,* meaning you won't find a silver bullet to help you remember the gender of a word. Instead of referring to a word's meaning, gender in German refers to the word itself. Thus, you use different gender markers to point out the gender of nouns. The three gender markers that mean *the* (singular) in German are **der** (masculine), **die** (feminine), and **das** (neuter). (These gender markers are also called *definite articles;* check out the later section "Mastering the Art of Articles" for details.)

For example, look at the words for eating utensils, where you have all three bases covered: **der Löffel** (*the spoon*), **die Gabel** (*the fork*), and **das Messer** (*the knife*). Why should a spoon be masculine, a fork feminine, and a knife neuter? See any logical pattern here? Neither do we.

So how do you know how to form/use genders correctly in German? First, remember that gender is an integral part of each noun; it's like a piece of the noun's identity. When you see a new noun, check a dictionary to find the gender; German dictionary entries identify nouns as **der, die,** or **das.** You can also use one of the noun gender categories listed in Tables 2-1 and 2-2 to help you make a good guess.

Some categories of nouns are consistently masculine, feminine, or neuter. For instance, noun gender usually follows the gender of people: **der Onkel** (*the uncle*) and **die Schwester** (*the sister*). In many other cases, the noun categories have to do with the ending of the noun. Tables 2-1 and 2-2 provide some fairly reliable categories of nouns and their genders; however, there are exceptions (big surprise, huh?). Among the exceptions are **der Kunde** (*customer*) and **das Messer** (*knife*).

Table 2-1   Common Genders by Noun Ending (Or Beginning)

Usually Masculine (der)	Usually Feminine (die)	Usually Neuter (das)
-er (especially when referring to male people/jobs)	**-ade, -age, -anz, -enz, -ette, -ine, -ion, -tur** (if foreign/borrowed from another language)	**-chen**
-ich	**-e**	**-ium**
-ismus	**-ei**	**-lein**
-ist	**-heit**	**-ment** (if foreign/borrowed from another language)
-ner	**-ie**	**-o**
	-ik	**-tum** or **-um**
	-in (when referring to female people/occupations)	**Ge-**
	-keit	
	-schaft	
	-tät	
	-ung	

Table 2-2	Common Genders by Noun Subject	
Usually Masculine (der)	*Usually Feminine (die)*	*Usually Neuter (das)*
Days, months, and seasons: **der Freitag** (*Friday*)	Many flowers: **die Rose** (*the rose*)	Colors (adjectives) used as nouns: **grün** (*green*) → **das Grün** (*the green*)
Map locations: **der Süd(en)** (*the south*)	Many trees: **die Buche** (*the beech*)	Geographic place names: **das Europa** (*Europe*)
Names of cars and trains: **der Audi** (*the Audi*), **der ICE** (*the Intercity Express*)	Names of aircraft and ships: **die Boeing 767** (*the Boeing 767*), **die Titanic** (*the Titanic*)	Infinitives used as nouns (gerunds): **schwimmen** (*to swim*) → **das Schwimmen** (*swimming*)
Nationalities and words showing citizenship: **der Amerikaner** (*the American*)	Cardinal numbers: **eine Drei** (*a three*)	Young people and animals: **das Baby** (*the baby*)
Occupations: **der Arzt** (*the doctor*)		Almost all the chemical elements and most metals: **das Aluminium** (*aluminum*), **das Blei** (*lead*)
Names of most mountains and lakes: **der Großglockner** (the highest mountain in Austria)		
Most rivers outside of Europe: **der Amazonas** (*the Amazon*)		

Eyeing nouns with more than one gender and meaning

Knowing the gender of a given German word is especially tricky (yet important) with groups of nouns that have more than one gender. Some of these nouns may have two different genders as a result of usage in different German-speaking regions. Other nouns have more than one gender and more than one meaning. Because there's no logic to explain why a word has more than one gender, the only way to keep track of such words is through memory. Table 2-3 shows some of the more frequently used nouns that have more than one gender and meaning.

Table 2-3 German Nouns with More Than One Gender and Meaning

German Nouns	English Translations	German Nouns	English Translations
der Band	volume (book)	das Schild	sign, name/number plate
die Band	band (music group)	der Schild	shield, shell (of a turtle)
das Band	tape, ribbon, band, wavelength (radio)		
das Golf	golf (game)	der See	lake
der Golf	gulf	die See	sea, ocean
der Kunde	customer	das Stift	foundation, seminary
die Kunde	tidings; the study of . . .	der Stift	pencil, pin, marker, pen (ballpoint)
der Leiter	director, leader, manager	das Tor	gate, gateway, goal
die Leiter	ladder	der Tor	fool (person)
das Messer	knife		
der Messer	surveyor, gauge		

Compound nouns (nouns with two or more nouns in one word) always have the gender of the last noun: **die Polizei** (*the police*) + **der Hund** (*the dog*) = **der Polizeihund** (*the police dog*).

Pinning Down Plurals

When you want to make a noun plural in English, all you usually have to do is add *-s* or *-es* to the end of the noun. In German, on the other hand, you have five ways to choose from when forming plural nouns. Before you throw your hands up in dismay, think about how English varies from the one standard form of making plurals with *-s* or *-es*. Think of *mouse/mice, tooth/teeth, child/children, shelf/shelves, phenomenon/phenomena, man/men,* and *country/countries.* Better yet, think about words like *hoof/hoofs/hooves* that have two plural forms. With both languages, you have a variety of plural endings and/or changes in the noun to remember.

Here's the good news: You don't have to worry much about gender when you're dealing with plural definite articles in German because **die** (*the* in plural form) is all you need (see the preceding section for more about

Book III

Assembling the Grammatical Foundations for Communication

gender). The article **die** corresponds to all three singular definite article forms: **der** (*the,* masculine), **die** (*the,* feminine), and **das** (*the,* neuter).

Although **die** has the double duty of being both a singular, feminine definite article and a plural definite article for all three genders, you can still distinguish between singular and plural. Just follow these tips:

- ✔ Find out the difference in noun endings for each feminine noun in its singular form and its plural form.

- ✔ Use the context in the sentence to figure out whether you're dealing with a singular or plural form of the noun. You always have the chance to check subject/verb agreement. To see how this works, look at the difference in meaning between the following two phrases: **die Schwester ist hier** (*the sister is here*) and **die Schwestern sind hier** (*the sisters are here*).

- ✔ Refer to the case of the noun for clues; check out the section "Calling All Cases: The Roles Nouns and Pronouns Play" for details.

Knowing the five plural forms

You can make nouns plural in five main ways in German. Table 2-4 shows you how. There's no hard and fast method of knowing which plural ending you need, but you can recognize some patterns as you expand your vocabulary. At any rate, you need to place high priority on memorizing plural forms and genders when you first learn a word. To get started, consider the following patterns for forming plural nouns (and keep in mind that there may be exceptions):

- ✔ Feminine nouns with the (feminine) suffixes **-heit, -keit,** and **-ung** usually have an **-en** plural ending: **die Möglichkeit** (*the possibility*) → **die Möglichkeiten** (*possibilities*).

- ✔ Singular nouns ending in **-er** may not have any ending in the plural form: **das Fenster** (*the window*) → **die Fenster** (*the windows*).

- ✔ Many nouns, including many one-syllable words, have an umlaut and an extra **-e** in the plural form: **der Kuss** (*the kiss*) → **die Küsse** (*the kisses*); **der Traum** (*the dream*) → **die Träume** (*the dreams*).

- ✔ Some German nouns are used only in the plural or in the singular: **die Ferien** (*the [often: school] vacation*) is always plural; **die Milch** (*the milk*) is always singular.

Table 2-4	The Five German Plural Groups		
Change Needed	*English Singular and Plural*	*German Singular*	*German Plural*
Add **-s**	*the car(s)*	**das Auto**	**die Autos**
	the office(s)	**das Büro**	**die Büros**
	the café(s)	**das Café**	**die Cafés**
	the boss(es)	**der Chef**	**die Chefs**
	the club(s)	**der Club**	**die Clubs**
	the pen(s)	**der Kuli**	**die Kulis**
No change, or add umlaut (¨)	*the computer(s)*	**der Computer**	**die Computer**
	the window(s)	**das Fenster**	**die Fenster**
	the garden(s)	**der Garten**	**die Gärten**
	the girl(s)	**das Mädchen**	**die Mädchen**
	the mother(s)	**die Mutter**	**die Mütter**
	the daughter(s)	**die Tochter**	**die Töchter**
	the father(s)	**der Vater**	**die Väter**
Add **-e** or umlaut (¨) + **-e**	*the train station(s)*	**der Bahnhof**	**die Banhöfe**
	the friend(s) (singular is male)	**der Freund**	**die Freunde**
	the problem(s)	**das Problem**	**die Probleme**
	the son(s)	**der Sohn**	**die Söhne**
	the city/cities	**die Stadt**	**die Städte**
	the chair(s)	**der Stuhl**	**die Stühle**
	the day(s)	**der Tag**	**die Tage**
Add **-er** or umlaut (¨) + **-er**	*the book(s)*	**das Buch**	**die Bücher**
	the bicycle(s)	**das Fahrrad**	**die Fahrräder**
	the house(s)	**das Haus**	**die Häuser**
	the child/children	**das Kind**	**die Kinder**
	the man (men)	**der Mann**	**die Männer**
	the castle(s)	**das Schloss**	**die Schlösser**

(continued)

Book III

Assembling the Grammatical Foundations for Communication

Table 2-4 (continued)

Change Needed	English Singular and Plural	German Singular	German Plural
Add **-n**, **-en**, or **-nen**	the idea(s)	**die Idee**	**die Ideen**
	the boy(s)	**der Junge**	**die Jungen**
	the lamp(s)	**die Lampe**	**die Lampen**
	the sister(s)	**die Schwester**	**die Schwestern**
	the student(s) (female)	**die Studentin**	**die Studentinnen**
	the university(-ies)	**die Universität**	**die Universitäten**
	the newspaper(s)	**die Zeitung**	**die Zeitungen**

Taking note of nouns that are only singular or plural

In both German and English, some nouns have only a plural form, and others have only a singular form. To keep things interesting, some nouns are plural in German and singular in English and vice versa. When you want to use a German noun that has no plural or one that has no singular form, you need to use the correct verb form in a sentence. For example, words like *pants* and *(eye)glasses* are singular in German and plural in English. Look at these two sentences:

Deine Hose passt dir nicht. (Literally: *Your pants doesn't fit you.*)

Wo ist meine Brille? (Literally: *Where is my glasses?*)

On the other hand, words such as *vacation* and *the United States* are plural in German and singular in English. The following sentences show how the German verb is plural to reflect the German use of the noun as a plural:

Wann beginnen die Ferien? (Literally: *When are the vacation beginning?*)

Die Vereinigten Staaten sind ein wunderbares Land. (Literally: *The United States are a wonderful country.*)

Table 2-5 shows commonly used nouns that are singular in German and plural in English.

Table 2-5   Nouns That Are Singular in German but Plural in English

German Noun	English Translation	German Noun	English Translation
die Brille	the (eye)glasses	das Mittelalter	the Middle Ages
die Dynamik	the dynamics	die Polizei	the police
das Feuerwerk	the fireworks	die Schere	the scissors
das Gemüse	the vegetables	die Statistik	the statistics
ein Gemüse (a single type of vegetable)	a vegetable		
die Hose	the pants	die Umgebung	the surroundings
der Inhalt	the contents	das Volk	the people (of a nation)

Table 2-6 shows frequently used nouns that are plural in German and singular in English.

Table 2-6   Nouns That Are Plural in German but Singular in English

German Noun	English Translation	German Noun	English Translation
die Depressionen	the depression (illness)	die Kosten	the cost(s)
die Ferien	the vacation	die Möbel	the furniture
die Haare (a head of hair), usually plural	hair	die Vereinigten Staaten	the United States (of America)
die Informationen	the information		

Book III

Assembling the Grammatical Foundations for Communication

Mastering the Art of Articles

Getting comfortable with using articles in German is a matter of determining whether you need the definite article **der/die/das** (*the*) or the indefinite article **ein/eine** (*a/an*) or the third option — no article at all.

Identifying singular nouns with indefinite articles

Just as English has two indefinite articles — *a* and *an* — that you use with singular nouns, German also has two indefinite articles (in the nominative case): **ein** for masculine- and neuter-gender words and **eine** for feminine-gender words. (See the later section "Calling All Cases: The Roles Nouns and Pronouns Play" for more on the nominative and other cases.)

An indefinite article has many of the same uses in both languages. For example, you use it before a singular noun that's countable the first time it's mentioned: **Ein Mann geht um die Ecke.** (*A man is walking around the corner.*) You also use it when a singular countable noun represents a class of things: **Ein Elefant vergisst nie.** (*An elephant never forgets.*) In addition, you can use **ein/eine** together with a *predicate noun* (a noun that complements the subject): **Willy Brandt war ein geschickter Politiker.** (*Willy Brandt was a skillful politician.*) (In case you're wondering, in the preceding example, **Politiker** is the predicate noun.)

Another similarity with English is that the German indefinite article **ein/eine** doesn't have a plural form. Depending on how you're describing something plural, you may or may not need to use the plural definite article. Consider the following generalized statement, which requires no article: **In Zermatt sind Autos verboten.** (*Cars are forbidden in Zermatt* [Switzerland].)

The following list shows you the definite articles and the corresponding indefinite articles (nominative case):

Gender/Number	Definite (the)	Indefinite (a/an)
Masculine	**der**	**ein**
Feminine	**die**	**eine**
Neuter	**das**	**ein**
Plural	**die**	(no plural form)

For tables with definite articles and indefinite articles, go to Appendix A.

Knowing when not to use articles

The following three guidelines explain when not to use an article in the sentence:

✔ Don't use the indefinite article when you mention someone's profession, nationality, or religion, all of which are nouns in German. Look at these three examples:

> **Mein Onkel war General bei der Bundeswehr.** (*My uncle was [a] general in the army.*)

> **Sind Sie Australier oder Neuseeländer?** (*Are you [an] Australian or [a] New Zealander?*)

> **Ich glaube, sie ist Lutheranerin.** (*I think she's [a] Lutheran.*)

✔ Just as in English, don't use the definite article in generalized statements using plural nouns in German. But do use the plural definite article when you're not making a generalization. Here are two examples:

> **Lügen haben kurze Beine.** (*You don't get far by lying.* Literally: *Lies have short legs.*) Both nouns, **Lügen** and **Beine,** are generalizations and need no article.

> **Die Bäume haben keine Blätter.** (*The trees have no leaves.*) The second plural noun **Blätter** is generalized; it needs no article.

✔ Although names of countries have genders in German — most often **das,** or *neuter* — you generally don't include the definite article. Of course, a few exceptions exist (see Chapter 3 of Book I for more on countries). Here are a few examples:

> **Viele berühmte Komponisten sind aus Deutschland oder Österreich.** (*Many famous composers are from Germany or Austria.*)

> **Die Schweiz gehört nicht zur Europäischen Union.** (*Switzerland doesn't belong to the European Union.*) Note **die,** the feminine definite article.

> **Die Vereinigten Staaten sind die größte Volkswirtschaft der Welt.** (*The United States has the largest economy in the world.*) Note **die,** the plural definite article.

Calling All Cases: The Roles Nouns and Pronouns Play

Cases indicate the role or function of nouns and pronouns in the sentence. English and German both have cases, as do most languages. This section identifies the four German cases and explains how they're used, as well as how English and German cases compare.

Identifying the four cases

When studying German, you have to get familiar with the four German cases because they're the reason nouns, pronouns, articles, and adjectives go through so many spelling changes from sentence to sentence. Here are the four cases:

- ✔ **Nominative case (nom.):** This case is for the subject of the sentence. The *subject* is a person or thing acting like the quarterback and calling the shots. In a sentence, it's who or what carries out the action. In the sentence **Brady wirft den Ball** (*Brady throws the ball*), **Brady** is the subject.

  Note: You also use the nominative case for *predicate nouns,* which are nouns (or noun phrases) that express more about the subject, such as a description or identification. For example, in the sentence **Er ist ein hervorragender Tennisspieler** (*He's an outstanding tennis player*), both the subject **Er** and the predicate noun phrase **ein hervorragender Tennisspieler** are in the nominative case.

- ✔ **Accusative case (acc.):** This case is for the direct object of the sentence. The *direct object* is a bit similar to the quarterback's ball — the subject is acting on it. In **Ein Zuschauer fängt den Ball** (*A spectator catches the ball*), **Ball** is the direct object.

- ✔ **Dative case (dat.):** This case is for the indirect object of the sentence. The *indirect object* receives the direct object — it's like the person the spectator gives the ball to. In **Der Zuschauer gibt seinem Sohn den Ball** (*The spectator gives his son the ball*), **seinem Sohn** (*his son*) is the indirect object, so it's in the dative case. In both German and English, you generally use the verb **geben** (*to give*) the same way; you *give* (the verb) something (**den Ball,** accusative case) to someone (**seinem Sohn,** dative case).

- ✔ **Genitive case (gen.):** This case shows possession. A person or thing can be the possessor, or owner. In **Die Mutter des Sohnes jubelt** (*The mother of the son cheers*), the son belongs to his cheering mother; **des Sohnes** is in the genitive case.

Note: Prepositions also use the accusative, dative, and genitive cases for the words they link with. (See Chapter 2 of Book IV for more on prepositions.)

The word endings of nouns, pronouns, articles, and adjectives alter slightly according to the case. These changes are necessary to identify what you want to express in a German sentence. (The case ending tables in Appendix A come in extremely handy when you want to find the correct word and its word ending.)

Eyeing the similarities and differences

When dealing with case, English and German have their share of similarities and differences. Before you can tackle the differences, you need to understand that German and English share the following case-related characteristics:

- **They share the same system of marking cases of personal pronouns.** In other words, pronouns have different forms (spellings) according to the case they're taking in a sentence. For example, in **Er lebt dort** (*he lives there*), the pronoun **er** (*he*) is the subject, so it's in the nominative case. However, in **Ich kenne ihn gut** (*I know him well*), **ihn** (*him*) is the direct object, so it's in the accusative case. Spelling changes indicate the role the pronoun is playing; for example, **ich** (*I*) changes to **mich** (*me*) and **wir** (*we*) changes to **uns** (*us*).

  The same is true for relative pronouns: **Der** (*who*) changes to **dessen** (*whose*). Skip to the later section "Putting Pronouns in Place" for more on this type of pronoun.

- **They use the nominative case — the same case you use for subjects — when you have a predicate noun as the object of a sentence.** A predicate noun states more about the subject. For English and German, the verb **sein** (*to be*) is the prime example of a verb that's followed by the predicate noun. German also uses the predicate noun with the verbs **bleiben** (*to stay, to remain*), **heißen** (*to be named, to be called*), and **werden** (*to become*). (In English, people often call these verbs *linking verbs.*) Consider this example: **Mein Zahnarzt ist auch der Zahnarzt meiner Eltern.** (*My dentist is also my parent's dentist.*) **Mein Zahnarzt** and **der Zahnarzt** are both in the nominative case.

As for differences, English doesn't have case endings for nouns (only for pronouns), so it relies on word order to indicate which grammatical hat the noun wears. The most common word order in an English sentence is subject-verb-object (or other information, such as a prepositional phrase). Hence, you can usually recognize the subject because you see it at the beginning of the sentence.

Because German has different case spellings/endings for both articles and nouns, word order in German sentences can be more flexible. Look at the word order of these two sentences, for example:

Der Junge liebt den Hund. (*The boy loves the dog.*)

Den Hund liebt der Junge. (*The boy loves the dog.*)

In both sentences, **der Junge** (*the boy*) is the subject and **den Hund** (*the dog*) is the object; as far as meaning goes, the two sentences are the same.

Book III

Assembling the Grammatical Foundations for Communication

However, you have a different case ending for the definite article (**der** in the first sentence and **den** in the second). In the nominative singular case, it's **der (Hund),** but in the accusative case, it's **den (Hund).** So why put **den Hund** (the direct object) at the beginning of the sentence? Because in German, you can use that word order to emphasize that **den Hund** (and not some other house pet) is the one the boy loves. To get that type of emphasis in English, you need to say something like *It's the dog that the boy loves.* English speakers tend to create this kind of emphasis vocally, whereas in German, you can accomplish such a nuance in both writing and speech.

Table 2-7 shows how the definite article *the* changes in both gender and case. You see the four cases and the three genders, plus the plural form of the definite article *the.* Appendix A shows the same type of table for indefinite articles.

Table 2-7	German Words That Mean *The*			
Case	*Masculine*	*Feminine*	*Neuter*	*Plural*
Nominative (subjects, predicate nouns)	der	die	das	die
Accusative (direct objects)	den	die	das	die
Dative (indirect objects)	dem	der	dem	den
Genitive (owned objects)	des	der	des	der

You have a grand total of six different definite articles in German and one lonely word, *the,* in English. Practice makes perfect, so set your standards high for mastering the definite article in German.

The following example sentences show you how definite articles appear in different cases. After each definite article and its noun, the information in parentheses tells you the gender and case of the definite article/noun duo and whether it's in the plural form. The following abbreviations are in parentheses: m. = masculine; f. = feminine; n. = neuter; pl. = plural; nom. = nominative; acc. = accusative; dat. = dative; and gen. = genitive. These abbreviations refer to the noun that directly precedes them.

- **Die Mannschaft** (f., nom.) **spielt sehr gut Fußball.** (*The team plays soccer very well.*)
- **Brauchst du den Kuli** (m., acc.)**?** (*Do you need the pen?*)
- **Das Radio** (n., nom.) **läuft nicht sehr gut.** (*The radio doesn't work very well.*)

- ✔ **Ich schreibe der Zeitung** (f., dat.) **einen Brief.** (*I'm writing the newspaper a letter.*)

- ✔ **Die Mädchen** (pl., nom.) **sind sehr freundlich.** (*The girls are very friendly.*)

- ✔ **Mir gefällt die Farbe der Krawatte** (f., gen.)**.** (*I like the color of the tie.*)

- ✔ **Kennen Sie die Leute** (pl., acc.) **da drüben?** (*Do you know the people over there?*)

Understanding nouns with case endings

Fortunately, most German nouns are spelled the same in all four cases. Of course, they have plural endings when necessary, but those endings don't change from one case to another. Unfortunately, some small groups of commonly used nouns do change spelling, depending on their case in a sentence. This group of nouns includes **der Fremde** (*the stranger*) and **der Junge** (*the boy*). What distinguishes them from most German nouns is that they both have an **-n** ending in accusative, dative, and genitive cases.

Here are the groups of nouns that have case endings:

- ✔ **Masculine nouns ending in -e:** In German, most nouns ending in **-e** are feminine, such as **die Blume** (*the flower*). The group of masculine nouns that end in **-e** generally has the case ending **-n** for all cases except the nominative case; in other words, these nouns add **-n** in the accusative, dative, and genitive cases. Some nouns of this type are **der Franzose** (*the Frenchman*), **der Kunde** (*the customer*), and **der Verwandte** (*the relative*). Consider this example sentence: **Wir empfehlen dem Fremden ein Restaurant.** (*We recommend a restaurant to the stranger.*) **Dem Fremden** (*to the stranger*) is the dative case for the noun **der Fremde.** You simply add the dative case ending **-n** to **der Fremde.**

- ✔ **Masculine nouns ending in -e with the genitive case ending -(e)ns:** This small subset of masculine nouns ending in **-e** has the case ending **-(e)ns** in the genitive case as well as the ending **-n** for the accusative and dative cases. Two examples of this type of noun are **der Name** (*the name*) and **der Glaube** (*the belief*). When used in the genitive case, these nouns are **des Namens** (*of the name*) and **des Glaubens** (*of the belief*).

- ✔ **Certain groups of masculine nouns:** The groups of nouns that refer to animals, people, professions, and titles of people add the ending **-en** in all cases except the nominative case. Some examples of these nouns are **der Präsident** (*the president*), **der Mensch** (*human being, person*), and **der Bär** (*the bear*). Here's a sample sentence: **Wir kennen den Präsidenten sehr gut.** (*We know the president very well.*) **Den Präsidenten** is the accusative case with the ending **-en** for the noun **der Präsident.**

Book III

Assembling the Grammatical Foundations for Communication

When Germans use these masculine nouns in everyday, casual situations, they often replace the genitive endings **-n** and **-en** with **-s** or **-es.** And in some instances, they drop the accusative and dative endings altogether.

For a list of nouns with case endings, go to Appendix A.

Putting Pronouns in Place

What's the big deal about pronouns like *you, me, it, them, this,* and *that?* First off, these plentiful, useful, and essential critters are lurking in various corners of many sentences. After all, they're great for replacing or referring to nouns elsewhere in a sentence. The bad news is that, like articles, they also change spelling/endings according to the role they play in a sentence (case) and the nouns they replace.

This section discusses three types of pronouns: personal, demonstrative, and relative. (See Book IV, Chapter 3 for details on a fourth type of pronoun — reflexive.) In German, pronouns are more affected by gender and case patterns than they are in English, so this section puts them into tables to help you see those patterns more easily. The case tables are arranged in order of frequency of use: nominative, accusative, dative, and genitive. You can also go to Appendix A for reference.

Note: One more group of pronouns, called the *possessive pronouns* — such as **mein** (*my*), **dein** (*your*), **unser** (*our*), and so on — are technically classified as adjectives; they have endings that resemble those of descriptive adjectives like *interesting, tiny,* and *pink.* (See Book III, Chapter 5 for more details on possessive adjectives/pronouns.)

Getting personal with personal pronouns

The personal pronoun family, shown in Table 2-8, comes in handy in all kinds of situations when you want to talk (or write) about people, including yourself, without repeating names all the time. You use the nominative case frequently because every sentence needs a subject. (See the earlier section "Identifying the four cases" for details on cases.)

With German personal pronouns, the biggest difference is that you have to distinguish among three ways to say *you:* **du, ihr,** and **Sie.** Other personal pronouns, like **ich** and **mich** (*I* and *me*) or **wir** and **uns** (*we* and *us*), bear a closer resemblance to English. *Note:* The genitive case isn't represented among the personal pronouns because it indicates possession; the personal pronouns represent only people, not something those people possess.

Check out Table 2-8 for a list of the personal pronouns. Notice that *you* and *it* don't change in English and the accusative (for direct objects) and dative (for indirect objects) pronouns are identical. The table lists the distinguishing factors for the three forms of you — **du, ihr,** and **Sie** — in abbreviated form. Here's what the abbreviations mean: s. = singular, pl. = plural, inf. = informal, form. = formal. (For detailed information on the difference between the formal and informal forms of *you,* go to Book III, Chapter 3.)

Table 2-8	German Personal Pronouns	
Nominative (nom.)	*Accusative (acc.)*	*Dative (dat.)*
ich (*I*)	**mich** (*me*)	**mir** (*me*)
du (*you*) (s., inf.)	**dich** (*you*) (s., inf.)	**dir** (*you*) (s., inf.)
er (*he*)	**ihn** (*him*)	**ihm** (*him*)
sie (*she*)	**sie** (*her*)	**ihr** (*her*)
es (*it*)	**es** (*it*)	**ihm** (*it*)
wir (*we*)	**uns** (*us*)	**uns** (*us*)
ihr (*you*) (pl., inf.)	**euch** (*you*) (pl., inf.)	**euch** (*you*) (pl., inf.)
sie (*they*)	**sie** (*them*)	**ihnen** (*them*)
Sie (*you*) (s. or pl., form.)	**Sie** (*you*) (s. or pl., form.)	**Ihnen** (*you*) (s. or pl., form.)

The following example sentences show you how the personal pronouns look when you place them in a sentence. After each pronoun, the notes in parentheses show the English equivalent of the German pronoun, followed by the abbreviations that identify the case of the pronoun in the sentence. If the pronoun is one of the three forms of *you* — **du, ihr,** or **Sie** — you see the same distinguishing factors for *you* that you see in Table 2-8:

> **Ich glaube, sie** (*she*, nom.) **arbeitet zu viel.** (*I think she works too hard.*)

> **Kennst du** (*you*, nom., s., inf.) **meine Schwester?** (*Do you know my sister?*)

> **Was kann ich** (*I*, nom.) **für Sie** (*you*, acc., s. or pl., form.) **tun?** (*What can I do for you?*)

> **Die Familie fährt ohne sie** (*her*, acc.) **nach Schweinfurt.** (*The family is traveling without her to Schweinfurt.*)

> **Thomas und Janina gehen mit Ihnen** (*you*, dat., s. or pl., form.) **ins Kino.** (*Thomas and Janina are going with you to the movies.*)

Book III

Assembling the Grammatical Foundations for Communication

Wohnen Sie (*you*, nom., s. or pl., form.) **in der Nähe?** (*Do you live nearby?*)

Wie gefällt euch (*you*, dat., pl., inf.) **der neue Bürgermeister?** (*How do you like the new mayor?*)

Relating to relative pronouns

You use relative pronouns (*who, whom, whose, that,* and *which*) to include extra information about a noun or pronoun. A relative pronoun typically appears at the front of a relative clause, where it refers back to the noun in the main clause.

In case you're wondering, a *main clause* is a part of a sentence that can stand on its own and still make sense. A *relative clause* is a type of *subordinate clause,* which, as you can probably guess, is a part of a sentence that can't stand alone (in other words, it's a sentence fragment). (If you're confused by all this talk of clauses, refer to Book III, Chapter 1 for clarification.)

The following guidelines help you put relative pronouns to use in your sentences:

- ✔ **In German, you must use a relative pronoun to connect a main clause and a relative clause.** In English, you don't always have to. For example, **Ist das der Mann, den du liebst?** (*Is that the man [whom, that] you love?*) In this sentence, the main clause is followed by the relative clause, **den du liebst.** The second **den** is the relative pronoun connecting the two parts of the sentence.

- ✔ **You place a comma between the main clause and the relative clause.** Remember that the relative clause begins with the relative pronoun. In English, people usually include this comma only before the relative pronoun *which.* For example: **Bestellen wir die Pizza, die wir meistens essen.** (*Let's order the pizza that we usually eat.*) No comma needed in English, but you do have a comma in German to separate the main clause **Bestellen wir die Pizza** from the relative clause **die wir meistens essen.**

- ✔ **Word order comes into play in relative clauses.** You push the conjugated verb to the end of the clause. For example, **Gestern habe ich eine gute Freundin getroffen, die ich seit Jahren nicht gesehen habe.** (*Yesterday I met a good [female] friend whom I haven't seen for years.*) In the relative clause **die ich seit Jahren nicht gesehen habe,** the verb has two parts, **gesehen,** the past participle, and **habe,** which is the conjugated part of the verb. **Habe** is the last word in the sentence. (For an in-depth look at the present perfect verb tense, go to Book IV, Chapter 4.)

Table 2-9 breaks down the relative pronouns (*who, whom, whose,* and *that*) by gender and case.

Table 2-9	Relative Pronouns			
Gender/Number of the Noun Being Replaced	**Nominative Case**	**Accusative Case**	**Dative Case**	**Genitive Case**
Masculine (m.)	der	den	dem	dessen
Feminine (f.)	die	die	der	deren
Neuter (n.)	das	das	dem	dessen
Plural (pl.)	die	die	denen	deren

The following sentences show relative pronouns that connect clauses. After each sentence, you see an explanation for the gender and case of the relative pronoun.

- ✔ **Ich kenne den Supermarkt, den du meinst.** (*I know the supermarket [that] you mean/are talking about.*) The pronoun **den** works as the masculine relative pronoun in the accusative case because it replaces the masculine noun **der Supermarkt** and is the direct object of the verb **meinen** (here: **meinst**).

- ✔ **Ist das die Frau, die bei der Polizei arbeitet?** (*Is that the woman who works for the police?*) The relative pronoun **die** is feminine and in the nominative case, reflecting the gender and case of **die Frau**, the noun it replaces in the relative clause.

- ✔ **Wie gefällt dir das Hemd, das ich anhabe?** (*How do you like the shirt [that] I'm wearing?*) **Das** replaces a neuter noun, **das Hemd,** and refers to the direct object (the accusative case) of **anhaben** in the relative clause.

- ✔ **Das ist der Mann, dessen Hund ein Kind gebissen hat.** (*That's the man whose dog bit a child.*) **Dessen** is the relative pronoun for the masculine gender, genitive case. **Dessen Hund** (*whose dog*) refers to the masculine gender noun **der Mann** (*the man*) in the main clause.

Book III

Assembling the Grammatical Foundations for Communication

Demonstrating demonstrative pronouns

Demonstrative pronouns (listed in Table 2-10) allow you to emphasize or point out the pronoun that's replacing a noun. Besides the pronouns *he, it, they,* and so on, which are the translations you see in Table 2-10, you can also translate these pronouns with the demonstratives *this, that, these,* or *those.* Like in English, the demonstrative pronoun generally comes at the beginning of a phrase. You use demonstrative pronouns in the nominative case to emphasize the subject or in the accusative case to emphasize the object.

Table 2-10	Demonstrative Pronouns	
Gender/Number of the Noun Being Replaced	*Nominative Case (Subjects and Predicate Nouns)*	*Accusative Case (Direct Objects)*
Masculine (m.)	**der** (*he/it*)	**den** (*him/it*)
Feminine (f.)	**die** (*she/it*)	**die** (*her/it*)
Neuter (n.)	**das** (*it*)	**das** (*it*)
Plural (pl.)	**die** (*they*)	**die** (*them*)

The only demonstrative pronoun that's different in the nominative case and the accusative case is the masculine pronoun. **Der** is the nominative, and **den** is the accusative case.

The following pairs of questions and answers show how demonstrative pronouns work in German. Each answer replaces a noun from the corresponding question with a relative pronoun.

Question: Ist der Flug ausgebucht? (*Is the flight completely booked?*)

Answer: Ja, der ist voll. (*Yes, it's full.*) **Der** is the subject of the sentence, so it's in the nominative case, and it replaces **der Flug,** which is masculine singular. **Der** is the masculine singular demonstrative pronoun in the nominative case.

Question: Ist die Straße relativ ruhig? (*Is the street relatively quiet?*)

Answer: Ja, die ist absolut ruhig. (*Yes, it's absolutely quiet.*) **Die** is the subject (nominative case) that replaces **die Straße,** a feminine singular noun, which is why you use the feminine singular nominative demonstrative pronoun.

Question: Wie findest du die Farbe? (*What do you think of this color?*)

Answer: Die finde ich zu dunkel. (*I think it's too dark.*) In this answer, **die** is the object in the accusative case. It replaces the feminine singular noun **die Farbe,** so you need the feminine singular accusative demonstrative pronoun.

Question: Sind die Pferde aggressiv? (*Are the horses aggressive?*)

Answer: Nein, die sind freundlich. (*No, they're friendly.*) **Die** is the subject, so it's in the nominative case. It stands in for **die Pferde,** which is plural, so you use the plural nominative demonstrative pronoun.

Discovering Dative Verbs

In German, a number of verbs are considered *dative verbs*. They distinguish themselves in two ways from the majority of German verbs:

- Generally speaking, dative verbs have only one object in a sentence.
- That object is in the dative case.

This group of verbs doesn't include such common verbs as **geben** (*to give*) and **zeigen** (*to indicate, to show*), which can have a dative object as well as an accusative object in the sentence. Table 2-11 shows a list of common German dative verbs with English equivalents and example sentences.

Table 2-11		Dative Verbs	
German Verb	*English Translation*	*Example Sentence*	*English Translation*
antworten	to answer	Antworten Sie mir, bitte.	Please answer me.
danken	to thank	Ich danke Ihnen.	I thank you.
folgen	to follow	Folgen Sie mir, bitte.	Please follow me.
gefallen	to like	Diese Schuhe gefallen mir.	I like these shoes.
gehören	to belong to	Die Jacke gehört ihr.	The jacket belongs to her.
geschehen	to happen (to)	Ist ihr etwas geschehen?	Did something happen to her?
glauben	to believe	Wir glauben seiner Geschichte.	We believe his story.
helfen	to help	Helfen Sie uns, bitte.	Please help us.
passieren	to happen (to)	Das ist mir nie passiert.	That's never happened to me.
raten	to advise	Ich rate dem Mann.	I advise the man.
wehtun	to hurt	Wo tut es Ihnen weh?	Where does it hurt you?
verzeihen	to forgive, to pardon	Verzeihen Sie mir.	Forgive me.
zuhören	to listen to	Hören Sie dem Piloten zu.	Listen to the pilot.

Book III

Assembling the Grammatical Foundations for Communication

Considering How Case Affects Adjectives

When you think of adjectives, you may think of words like *beautiful*, *interesting*, or *fast*. But these are just the tip of the iceberg of adjectives. The plethora of words that makes up the adjective family (in both German and English) is incredibly diverse. For instance, the sentence *My family is large* has two different types of adjectives. The first is *my,* which is a possessive adjective that gives more information about the noun *family.* The second adjective is *large*.

One important difference between German and English adjectives is that German adjectives change their spelling according to the case in which you use them. In English, you pay little or no attention to case because spelling changes in adjectives crop up only in the possessive adjectives.

How possessives change

Possessive adjectives establish ownership. They mark the difference between what belongs to you (*your* book), what belongs to me (*my* book), and so on. Here are the possessive adjective forms for the different persons:

- **mein** (*my*)
- **dein** (*your*) (informal, singular)
- **Ihr** (*your*) (formal, singular)
- **sein, ihr, sein** (*his, her, its*)
- **unser** (*our*)
- **euer** (*your*) (informal, plural)
- **Ihr** (*your*) (formal, plural)
- **ihr** (*their*)

Of course, each of these forms has different endings for the different cases. Table 2-12 presents all the forms of the possessive adjective **mein** (*my*). Fortunately, the other possessives take the same endings. These endings may look familiar because they're the same as those for the indefinite article **ein** (*a, an*), as well as for the adjective that negates a noun, **kein** (*no, not, not any*).

Table 2-12	Possessive Endings for Mein by Case			
Gender	**Nominative**	**Accusative**	**Dative**	**Genitive**
Masculine	mein	meinen	meinem	meines
Feminine	meine	meine	meiner	meiner
Neuter	mein	mein	meinem	meines
Plural	meine	meine	meinen	meiner

How adjective endings change

As you discover earlier in this chapter, adjectives and articles that accompany nouns change their endings according to the role the nouns play in the sentence. To illustrate the endings both adjectives and articles take based on the nouns they describe, check out Tables 2-13 and 2-14. Table 2-13 shows the endings with an indefinite article, and Table 2-14 shows them with the definite article.

The so-called **ein-** words follow the same pattern as indefinite articles, so Table 2-13 includes them, too. In case you need a quick refresher, **ein-** words include **kein** (*no, not, not any*) and the possessive adjectives (see the preceding section for a list). This table includes the word **kein** for the plural forms because the indefinite article has no plural. For more information on using **kein**, see Book III, Chapter 4.

Book III

Assembling the Grammatical Foundations for Communication

Table 2-13	Examples of Adjective Endings Preceded by Indefinite Articles or Ein- Words				
Gender/ Number	**Nominative**	**Accusative**	**Dative**	**Genitive**	**English Translation**
Masculine	ein schöner Garten	einen schönen Garten	einem schönen Garten	eines schönen Gartens	*a beautiful garden*
Feminine	eine weiße Tür	eine weiße Tür	einer weißen Tür	einer weißen Tür	*a white door*
Neuter	ein kleines Haus	ein kleines Haus	einem kleinen Haus	eines kleinen Hauses	*a small house*
Plural	keine großen Häuser	keine großen Häuser	keinen großen Häusern	keiner großen Häuser	*no large houses*

Table 2-14	Examples of Adjective Endings Preceded by Definite Articles				
Gender/ Number	Nominative	Accusative	Dative	Genitive	English Translation
Masculine	der schöne Garten	den schönen Garten	dem schönen Garten	des schönen Gartens	the beautiful garden
Feminine	die weiße Tür	die weiße Tür	der weißen Tür	der weißen Tür	the white door
Neuter	das kleine Haus	das kleine Haus	dem kleinen Haus	des kleinen Hauses	the small house
Plural	die großen Häuser	die großen Häuser	den großen Häusern	der großen Häuser	the large houses

Chapter 3

Dealing with the Here and Now: The Present Tense

*Y*ou*'re driving* down the road when you *see* a small herd of cows. Some *are grazing*, others *are chewing* their cud. Okay, so they *might be drooling*, too, but even so, it *gets* you on to thoughts about milk, and the idea *hits* you: You*'re going to get* some ice cream. You *say* to yourself, "I *think* I'*ll go* to Jan and Berry's because I really *do owe* myself a treat. After all, I'*ve been working* hard, and —" you *wake up* and realize you'*ve been dreaming* for the past five minutes. Darn!

Believe it or not, this isn't a plug for ice cream. It is, however, a superb example of how streamlined German can be, because you can put all the verbs in the preceding paragraph (marked in italics) in the present tense in German. This multitalented player stands in for the plain old simple present tense (*gets, wake up*), the present continuous (*are driving, are chewing*), an emphatic form (*do owe*), some futures (*are going to get, will go*), and even references to actions that started in the past (*have been working, have been dreaming*). **Das klingt gut, oder?** (*That sounds good, doesn't it?*) (For more information on the terminology of verb tenses, see Book III, Chapter 1.)

You probably thought we were going to start out with something along the lines of "First things first: The *present tense* is the verb form you use to talk about the present. Period." Well, that's true for sure, but there's more to it. In this chapter, you see how to use subject pronouns with the present tense and how to conjugate regular and irregular verbs. You also see how versatile the present tense is and how you can use both active and passive voice with it.

Grasping the Specifics of Subject Pronouns

Before you can understand the present tense (and all other verb tenses), you need a firm grasp of the subject pronouns and the way they work together with verbs to make logical sentences. You can't just pick out a pronoun and a verb, stick them together, and hope they make sense. If you don't observe certain conventions of how these two pieces go together, the sentence you create may sound more like mumbo-jumbo than a cohesive thought.

The subject pronouns stand in for long-winded nouns and pop up everywhere in any language, and they play a key role in helping you get your verbs in shape. You always see them in tables that conjugate verbs, so get familiar with them before you start work on the verbs that accompany them.

Assigning person and number to subject pronouns

You use *subject pronouns* — **ich** (*I*), **du** (*you*), **er** (*he*), **sie** (*she*), **es** (*it*), and so on — to express who or what is carrying out the action or idea of the verb. They refer to the noun without naming it, which means they can serve as placeholders so you don't have to sound redundant by repeating the noun. (For more on pronouns, check out Book III, Chapters 1 and 2.) To use subject pronouns, you need to know which *person* (first, second, or third) and *number* (singular or plural) the pronoun represents; for example, **ich** (*I*) = first person, singular. To connect the correct subject pronoun to a present-tense verb, you need to know which conjugated verb form to use. I lay out this information in the later section "Getting Your Verbs in Shape."

Table 3-1 shows you the breakdown of subject pronouns in German and English. Notice the format with singular on the left, plural on the right, and the pronoun **Sie** (*you*) at the bottom. You see the same setup throughout the verb tables in this book.

Table 3-1	Subject Pronouns	
Person	**Singular**	**Plural**
First	**ich** (*I*)	**wir** (*we*)
Second (familiar)	**du** (*you*)	**ihr** (*you*)
Third	**er** (*he, it*)	**sie** (*they*)
	sie (*she, it*)	
	es (*it*)	
Second (formal)	**Sie** (*you,* both singular and plural)	

Think of the subject pronouns as *persona* because they im*person*ate the subject that they represent. You characterize them by their grammatical *person* (based on who's speaking and listening), number (singular or plural), and sometimes formality (which we discuss in the next section). Here's a closer look at the three persons:

- **First person:** The one(s) speaking: **ich** (*I*) or **wir** (*we*).

- **Second person:** The one(s) spoken *to:* **du, ihr, Sie.** All three mean *you* in English; **du** is the singular, familiar form, which you'd use with a friend; **ihr** is the plural, familiar form, which you'd use with a group of friends; and **Sie** is the formal form, whether singular or plural, which you'd use with the chancellor of Germany and the cabinet ministers (and everyone else you're not on a first-name basis with).

- **Third person:** Who or what is spoken *about:* **er** (*he, it*), **sie** (*she, it*), or **es** (*it*) and **sie** (*they*). If you're talking about an inanimate object (*it*), the choice among **er, sie,** and **es** depends on the gender of the noun — see Book III, Chapter 2 for details.

Distinguishing among the three forms of "you"

If you're hobnobbing with some business moguls, the mayor, and a throng of socialites at the charity benefit of the year, we hope you're on your best behavior. On the other hand, most people do and say whatever they feel like while hanging out with their buddies at a backyard barbecue on a Saturday afternoon. That formality/informality factor is what you need to keep in mind when you address people in German because there are three ways to say *you:* **du, ihr,** and **Sie.**

Using Sie

Use **Sie**, which is always capitalized, to speak to one or more people with whom you have a more distant, formal relationship. It's appropriate

- ✔ When adults meet each other for the first time
- ✔ When you aren't sure about whether **du/ihr** or **Sie** is correct
- ✔ When you're not yet on a first-name basis with someone (for example, using Herr Kuhnagel or Frau Zitzelsberger, not Sigmund or Hildegard)
- ✔ When you're talking to adults you don't know well
- ✔ In business or at your place of work
- ✔ In public situations to service staff or a person in uniform (police officer, airport official, and other such individuals)

Using du and ihr

Use **du** when you talk to one person (or animal) in an informal way; use **ihr,** the plural version of **du,** to address more than one person (or animal) informally. An informal pronoun is appropriate

- ✔ When a German speaker invites you to use **du**
- ✔ For talking to a close friend or relative
- ✔ For addressing children and teens younger than 16 or so
- ✔ Among people who share a common bond — for example, members of a club, a sports team, or comrades in the military
- ✔ When you talk to pets

You may hear **du** among close work colleagues, students, members of a sports team, or people hiking in the mountains, but unless someone asks you, **"Wollen wir uns dutzen?"** (*Shall we say **du** to each other?*), try to stick with **Sie.**

Using first names and addressing people with **du** (or **ihr**) when doing so isn't appropriate can turn German speakers off — fast. Language and culture are bonded together with superglue, so avoid pasting your culture on the German-speaking world. Also, be careful with recent crossover scenarios at the workplace: people addressing each other with **Sie,** although they use first names: **Heinz, haben Sie meine E-mail gelesen?** (*Heinz, have you read my e-mail?*) If you use last names (**Frau Dinkelhuber** and **Herr Sternhagel**), using **Sie** is best.

The following three example questions asking for help show how this trio of **du, ihr,** and **Sie** play out. Notice that all three have the same English equivalent because English doesn't have differences between the singular and plural of *you* or for showing formality and informality:

> **Können Sie mir helfen?** (*Could you help me?*) This situation may involve a person at work seeking help from a colleague.

> **Kannst du mir helfen?** (*Could you help me?*) The situation may be someone asking a friend to help out.

> **Könnt ihr mir helfen?** (*Could you help me?*) In this situation, a teenager may be asking a couple of friends for some help.

Distinguishing among "she," "they," and the formal "you"

Look at Table 3-1, and you find the Three Musketeers, **sie** (*she*), **sie** (*they*), and **Sie** (*you*), lurking in their separate boxes. Seeing them in what look like random places may seem daunting, but a few clues can help you sort them out. First, you know the meanings by their context. The conjugated verb and capitalization also help reveal the meaning. Here's what to watch for:

- **Conjugation:** When **sie** means *she,* its verb form is distinct; in the present tense, the conjugated verb usually ends in **-t.** When **sie/Sie** means *they* or *you,* the present-tense verb ends in **-en.** (For more on conjugation, see the next section.)

- **Capitalization:** The *they* and *you* forms of **sie/Sie** have identical conjugations, but only the *you* version, which is formal, is capitalized.

The following examples show you how to figure out which one to use when:

> **Wo wohnt sie?** (*Where does she live?*) The verb is in third-person singular form.

> **Wo wohnen sie?** (*Where do they live?*) The verb is in third-person plural form, and **sie** isn't capitalized.

> **Wo wohnen Sie?** (*Where do you* [formal] *live?*) The verb is in second-person plural form (which is identical to the third-person plural form), and **Sie** is capitalized.

Book III

Assembling the Grammatical Foundations for Communication

When you're speaking, listen carefully for cues in the context that help you distinguish between sentences like **Wo wohnen sie?** and **Wo wohnen Sie?** If you're still not sure, just ask, **"Meinen Sie mich?"** (*Do you mean me?*). If you're on a first-name basis with the speaker, then you're all set; no confusion here because if someone asks you where you live, you hear the informal version: **Wo wohnst du?**

Getting Your Verbs in Shape

Most of us love to talk — about ourselves, our family, our friends, our job, and what's going on in our lives. Talking (and writing) about all these things and more in German is, for the most part, just a matter of knowing how to construct a verb in the present tense with the help of a noun (subject) and a few other elements. Most German verbs are *regular*, meaning they follow a standard pattern of conjugation. Think of conjugating as activating a verb from the sleepy infinitive form found in dusty dictionaries (**leben, lachen, lieben**) and its English equivalent with that pesky *to* (*to live, to laugh, to love*) into a form that's compatible with the subject.

This section shows you how to put verbs through their paces by conjugating them and combining them with nouns, pronouns, and other grammar goodies so you can start talking and writing with confidence in German.

Agreeing with the regulars

Regular verbs don't have any change in their basic form, or *stem.* You conjugate a verb by taking the stem — which is almost always the result of dropping **-en** from the infinitive form of the verb (the not-yet conjugated form) — and adding the right ending. In the present tense, English has only the ending *-s* or no ending at all (*I live, you live, he lives*), whereas German has four endings (**-e, -st, -t,** and **-en**).

To conjugate a regular verb in the present tense, just drop the **-en** from the infinitive and add the appropriate ending to the stem. The endings are **-e, -st, -t, -en, -t, -en,** and **-en.** The following verb table shows how to conjugate the verb **kommen** (*to come*). The present-tense endings are marked in bold. Notice that three of the conjugated forms — first-person plural **wir** (*we*), third-person plural **sie** (*they*), and formal second-person plural **Sie** (*you*) — are identical to the infinitive itself.

(Make sure you know the meanings of the subject pronouns by checking Table 3-1 earlier in this chapter.)

kommen (*to come*)	
ich komm**e**	wir komm**en**
du komm**st**	ihr komm**t**
er/sie/es komm**t**	sie komm**en**
Sie komm**en**	
Er **kommt** aus Irland. (*He comes from Ireland.*)	

If the verb stem ends in **-d** or **-t**, place an **e** in front of the verb endings **-st** and **-t.** The following table shows you how to conjugate the regular verb **arbeiten** (*to work*) in the present tense. The stem **arbeit-** ends in **-t**, so you add an **e** before the verb endings for the second- and third-person singular (**du arbeitest, er/sie/es arbeitet**) and the second-person plural familiar form (**ihr arbeitet**).

arbeiten (*to work*)	
ich arbeit**e**	wir arbeit**en**
du arbeit**est**	ihr arbeit**et**
er/sie/es arbeit**et**	sie arbeit**en**
Sie arbeit**en**	
Du **arbeitest** sehr schnell. (*You work very fast.*)	

Note: Both English and German sometimes insert extra vowels to make a verb understandable. Just try saying *she teachs* as one syllable — it's not easy. English adds an *e* before the *-s* so *teaches* expands to two syllables; the listener can then recognize that the speaker is using the third-person singular. German adds **-est** and **-et** to **du arbeit-** and **er/sie/es arbeit-** for the same reason: pronunciation. Adding the **e** lets speakers pronounce **arbeitet** with three syllables.

With a few verbs that don't have an **-en** infinitive ending, notably **wandern** (*to hike*) and **tun** (*to do*), drop **-n** from the infinitive and add only **-n** to

- ✔ The first-person plural form: **wir wandern** (*we hike*) and **wir tun** (*we do*)

- ✔ The third-person plural form: **sie wandern** (*they hike*) and **sie tun** (*they do*)

- ✔ The formal second-person singular and plural form: **Sie wandern** (*you hike*) and **Sie tun** (*you do*)

Here are some other common regular German verbs; you use the regular conjugation on all of them:

- **bringen** (*to bring*)
- **finden** (*to find, to have an opinion*)
- **gehen** (*to go, to walk*)
- **heißen** (*to be called, to be named*)
- **kaufen** (*to buy*)
- **kennen** (*to know [a person]*)
- **kosten** (*to cost*)

- **lernen** (*to learn*)
- **reisen** (*to travel*)
- **sagen** (*to say*)
- **schreiben** (*to write*)
- **spielen** (*to play [a game, cards]*)
- **wohnen** (*to live*)

The following examples show what a conjugated regular verb looks like in a sentence:

Was spielt ihr? (*What are you playing?*)

Sabina und Moritz reisen nach Australien. (*Sabina and Moritz are traveling to Australia.*)

Der Computer kostet 599€. (*The computer costs 599€.*)

Meine Großmutter und ich heißen beide Monika. (*My grandmother and I are both called Monika.*)

Schreibst du oft Briefe? (*Do you often write letters?*)

Ich wandere sehr gern in den Bergen. (*I like to hike in the mountains.*)

Manfred kommt heute Abend spät nach Hause. (*Manfred is coming home late this evening.*)

Kennt ihr den Mann da drüben? (*Do you know the man over there?*)

Ja, mein Mann arbeitet mit ihm in derselben Firma. (*Yes, my husband works with him in the same company.*)

Wohin gehen Sie? (*Where are you going?*)

Heute kaufen Florian und Maria ein Auto. (*Florian and Maria are buying a car today.*)

Conjugating verbs with spelling changes

The verbs in this section are more or less regular, but their stems undergo a few small changes in spelling. Luckily — or unluckily, depending on how you see it — many of the spelling-change verbs are frequently used, so perhaps you can acquire them by osmosis! You may notice that some of the verbs here are *cognates*, words that come from a common ancestor and are often similar in meaning and spelling. For instance, **fallen** and *to fall* are the same, taking into account the German infinitive ending **–en.** The same goes for **helfen** and *to help*.

These verbs with spelling changes are technically classified as verbs with stem-vowel changes because — you guessed it — the vowel(s) in the stem changes when you conjugate the verb. The *stem* is the part of the infinitive left after you slice off the **-en** ending: **Sprechen** (*to speak*) is the infinitive, and **sprech-** is the stem.

The stem-vowel changes take place in the **du** and **er/sie/es** forms (and in one verb type, the **ich** form). When dealing with these types of verbs, you encounter the following changes:

- **a→ä** and **au→äu** (**laufen** [*to run*])

- **e→i** (**geben** [*to give*])

- **e→ie** (**sehen** [*to see*])

- **e→i** (**nehmen** [*to take*]); also, consonant changes from **hm** to **mm** (see the **nehmen** verb table)

- **i→ei** (**wissen** [*to know as a fact*]); also, **ich** and **er/sie/es** forms have no endings (see the **wissen** verb table)

The next five tables show each of these stem-vowel changes, along with the additional changes in **nehmen** (*to take*) and **wissen** (*to know as a fact*). In these tables, only the stem-vowel changing verb forms are in bold.

Book III

Assembling the Grammatical Foundations for Communication

fahren (*to drive*): a→ä	
ich fahre	wir fahren
du **fährst**	ihr fahrt
er/sie/es **fährt**	sie fahren
Sie fahren	
Du **fährst** sehr vorsichtig. (*You drive very carefully.*)	

Other **a→ä** verbs include the following:

- **backen** (*to bake*)
- **fallen** (*to fall*)
- **gefallen** (*to like, to enjoy*)
- **halten** (*to stop, to think about*)

- **laufen** (*to run*)
- **schlafen** (*to sleep*)
- **tragen** (*to carry, to wear*)
- **waschen** (*to wash*)

sprechen (*to speak*): e→i	
ich spreche	wir sprechen
du **sprichst**	ihr sprecht
er/sie/es **spricht**	sie sprechen
Sie sprechen	
Adrienne **spricht** fließend Englisch, Deutsch, und Französisch. (*Adrienne speaks fluent English, German, and French.*)	

Here are some other **e→i** verbs:

- **essen** (*to eat*)
- **geben** (*to give*)
- **helfen** (*to help*)
- **vergessen** (*to forget*)

lesen (*to read*): e→ie	
ich lese	wir lesen
du **liest**	ihr lest
er/sie/es **liest**	sie lesen
Sie lesen	
Das Kind **liest** schon Romane. (*The child already reads novels.*)	

Sehen (*to see*) is also an **e→ie** verb.

nehmen (*to take*): e→i, hm→mm	
ich nehme	wir nehmen
du **nimmst**	ihr nehmt
er/sie/es **nimmt**	sie nehmen
Sie nehmen	
Du **nimmst** zu viele Kekse! (*You're taking too many cookies!*)	

wissen (*to know as a fact*): i→ei	
ich **weiß**	wir wissen
du **weißt**	ihr wisst
er/sie/es **weiß**	sie wissen
Sie wissen	
Weißt du, wer das ist? (*Do you know who that is?*)	

Note: When you use **wissen** to refer to information in the sentence, you use a comma to separate the two clauses.

The following examples illustrate how stem-vowel-change verbs appear in a sentence. Notice in these examples that the stem-vowel changes take place in the **du** and **er/sie/es** (second-person singular familiar and third-person singular).

Helena läuft am schnellsten. (*Helena runs the fastest.*)

Sie sieht sehr schlecht ohne Brille. (*She sees very poorly without glasses.*)

Mein Vater gibt mir viel Geld. (*My father gives/is giving me a lot of money.*)

Was esst ihr zum Frühstück? (*What do you eat/are you eating for breakfast?*)

Meistens schläft das Baby nur bis 5.00 Uhr. (*The baby usually sleeps only until 5 a.m.*)

Wohin fährst du am Wochenende? (*Where are you driving to/going on the weekend?*)

Ludwig spricht Deutsch mit einem schwäbischen Akzent. (*Ludwig speaks German with a Swabian accent.*) (Swabia is a region in the southwest of Germany.)

Book III

Assembling the Grammatical Foundations for Communication

Conjugating the irregulars haben and sein: To have and to be

To have and to be: It sounds like a cross between a book title by an adventurous journalist turned author and a famous quote in English literature or a remake of a movie from the 1940s. Whatever comes to mind when you think of these two verbs, **haben** (*to have*) and **sein** (*to be*) are stars in their own right.

These two common verbs are irregular. Just as in English, you come across them as full-fledged, free-standing, autonomous verbs and as auxiliary (helping) verbs. The auxiliary verb function of **haben** and **sein** is to work with other verbs in a frequently used verb tense: the *present perfect*. (For more on auxiliary verbs, see Book III, Chapter 6, and for more on the present perfect, go to Book IV, Chapter 4.) In this section, you see how **haben** and **sein** look in the present tense, and you discover how the English and German uses of these verbs compare.

Haben: Let me have it

Look at the conjugation of **haben** in the present tense. Notice that the verb actually has only two irregular verb forms: **du hast** and **er/sie/es hat**. The rest of the forms follow the regular verb conjugation pattern of taking the stem (in this case **hab-**) and adding the usual ending.

haben (*to have*)	
ich **habe**	wir **haben**
du **hast**	ihr **habt**
er/sie/es **hat**	sie **haben**
Sie **haben**	
Sie **hat** eine grosse Familie. (*She has a large family.*)	

German, like English, has many expressions that involve the verb *to have*. Many of them are the same in German and in English: **Zeit haben** (*to have time*). Others aren't. For example, English has two ways to express that something is absolutely necessary, *must* and *have to*. German has only one, **müssen** (*must*): **Ich muß anfangen.** (*I have to start.*) In other cases, like those that follow, German uses the verb **haben** when English has a different construction:

- **When expressing likes with haben and the adverb gern:** Gern means *gladly, with pleasure* when you use it alone, but it means *to like* when you pair it with **haben.** When expressing likes, you usually place **gern** at the end of the sentence: **Hast du klassische Musik gern?** (*Do you like classical music?*)

✔ **When talking about your birthday:** For example, **Ich habe am achten Oktober Geburtstag.** (*My birthday is on the eighth of October.*)

✔ **When using expressions that describe a physical condition, an emotional condition, or a state of being:** Some common expressions are

- **Angst haben** (*to be afraid*)

- **Dienst haben** (*to be on duty*)

- **Durst haben** (*to be thirsty*)

- **Glück haben** (*to be lucky, to be fortunate*)

- **Hunger haben** (*to be hungry*)

- **Lust haben** (*to feel like [doing something]*)

- **Recht haben** (*to be right*)

Look at the following example sentences that use the verb **haben:**

Hast du einen Hund? (*Do you have a dog?*)

Nein, ich habe eine Katze. (*No, I have a cat.*)

Wann habt ihr Zeit? (*When do you have time?*)

Wir haben kein Wasser. (*We don't have any water.*)

Ein Polizist hat immer Recht. (*A policeman is always right.*)

Sie haben wenig Geld. (*They have little money.*)

Sein: To be or not to be

Look at the conjugation of **sein** (*to be*) in the present tense. Notice that all the verb forms are irregular, although **wir sind, sie sind,** and **Sie sind** are identical. Remember that regular verb conjugations in the present tense also have the same endings for **wir, sie,** and **Sie** pronouns; consider the regular verb **gehen** (*to go, to walk*): **wir gehen, sie gehen,** and **Sie gehen.**

Book III

Assembling the Grammatical Foundations for Communication

sein (*to be*)	
ich **bin**	wir **sind**
du **bist**	ihr **seid**
er/sie/es **ist**	sie **sind**
Sie **sind**	
Sind Sie Herr Schumpich? (*Are you Mr. Schumpich?*)	

The verb **sein** is a true workhorse in German. Not only does it tell you what is and what isn't, but it can also help you form the present perfect — although **haben** is the main auxiliary verb for that task. (For more information on the present perfect tense, see Book IV, Chapter 4.)

German and English use the verb **sein** (*to be*) in similar ways. For example, *What's your boss like? Is it time yet? Who's that? Is it quiet? Are you ready? No, we're not. Am I too old? How much is that? What's up? Where are we? Isn't she funny? Where are you? I'm lost.* Here's how you can use **sein:**

- ✔ **With an adjective:**

  Du bist sehr lustig. (*You're very funny.*)

  Mein Sohn ist nicht musikalisch. (*My son is not musical.*)

  Some expressions in German use the verb **sein** with an adjective plus a noun or pronoun in the dative case. (For the lowdown on cases, refer to Book III, Chapter 2.) A couple of common expressions are

  Mir ist kalt/warm. (*I'm cold/warm.*) **Mir** is the dative case of the pronoun **ich.**

  Ihm ist schlecht/übel. (*He's feeling sick/sick to his stomach.*) **Ihm** is the dative case of the pronoun **er.**

- ✔ **With an adverb:**

  Wir sind morgen nicht hier. (*We're not here tomorrow.*)

  Sie ist dort. (*She's there.*)

- ✔ **With nouns:**

  Sind Sie Kanadier? (*Are you a Canadian?*)

  Ich bin Bauingenieur. (*I'm a civil engineer.*)

  Note that German leaves out the article **ein** (*a*) for professions and nationalities. (See Book III, Chapter 2 for more information.)

A few German expressions using **sein** are expressed slightly differently from their English equivalents:

- ✔ **Wie ist ihre Telefonnummer/Adresse?** (*What's your phone number/ address? Literally, **wie** means *how.*) (Book III, Chapter 4 deals with questions.)

- ✔ **Hier ist Frau Becker.** (*I'm Mrs. Becker.* You'd use this expression to identify yourself on the telephone.)

- ✔ **Ihr seid hier richtig.** (*You're in the right place.*)

Expressing yourself using haben and sein

You find all kinds of idioms that use the verbs **haben** and **sein** in German and English. German speakers use them in everyday situations when talking with people they know. So when you use such expressions, your German sounds more like a native's.

The idioms in the following lists are used in informal situations, so use them only with people you know fairly well. You can gauge the appropriateness of the expressions by looking at the English equivalent. The example sentences in these lists use a variety of personal pronouns so you can see the conjugations of the verbs **haben** and **sein**.

Here are some common (and colorful) idioms with **haben**:

- ✔ **Ich habe es satt.** (*I'm fed up with it.*)
- ✔ **Er hat die Nase voll.** (*He's fed up.*)
- ✔ **Ich hab's.** (*I get it!/I've got it!*)
- ✔ **Sie haben es eilig.** (*They're in a hurry.*)
- ✔ **Du hast einen Vogel.** (*You're crazy.*)
- ✔ **Sie hat nichts dagegen.** (*She has nothing against it.*)
- ✔ **Ich habe eine weiße Weste.** (*I have a clear conscience.*)
- ✔ **Er hat ein dickes Fell.** (*He's got a thick skin.*) (In other words, he doesn't get upset easily.)
- ✔ **Sie hat viel auf dem Gewissen.** (*She has a lot to answer for.*)
- ✔ **Ich habe zwei linke Hände.** (*I'm really clumsy.* Literally: *I have two left hands.*)
- ✔ **Wir haben alle Hände voll zu tun.** (*We've got our hands full.*)
- ✔ **Du hast eine lange Leitung.** (*You're slow on the uptake.*)
- ✔ **Er hat eine spitze Zunge.** (*He has a sharp tongue.*)
- ✔ **Sie hat Köpfchen/Verstand.** (*She's got brains/sense.*)

Here are a few common idioms with **sein**:

- ✔ **Sie sind in guten Händen.** (*You're in good hands.*)
- ✔ **Wir sind gut in Form.** (*We're going strong.*)
- ✔ **Er ist auf Draht.** (*He knows his stuff.*)
- ✔ **Das ist für die Katze.** (*It's for the birds.*)

Book III

Assembling the Grammatical Foundations for Communication

- ✔ **Ich bin mit meinem Latein am Ende.** (*I'm stumped.*)

- ✔ **Er ist pleite.** (*He's broke.*)

- ✔ **Du bist gut!** (*You're a fine one!*) This is a sarcastic type of comment.

- ✔ **Ich bin gespannt.** (*I'm curious.*)

- ✔ **Er ist ein Angsthase.** (*He's a wimp.*)

- ✔ **Er ist ein Spielverderber.** (*He's a spoilsport.*)

- ✔ **Du bist in guter Laune.** (*You're in a good mood.*)

The following expressions begin with **es ist** (*it is*):

- ✔ **Es ist nur eine Frage der Zeit.** (*It's only a matter of time.*)

- ✔ **Es ist gang und gäbe.** (*It's common practice.*)

- ✔ **Es ist höchste Zeit.** (*It's high time.*)

- ✔ **Es ist mir egal.** (*It's all the same to me./I don't care.*)

- ✔ **Es ist der Mühe wert.** (*It's worth the trouble.*)

Using the Very Versatile Present Tense

When you want to gain confidence speaking and writing in any language, you work on polishing your verb skills so you feel competent using the present, past, and future tenses. In German, grasping the present tense opens the door to several ways of expressing yourself.

When you want to talk about something in German, first figure out whether you can use the present tense. In virtually all the situations where you use the present in English, you also use the present in German. In addition, you have a lot of opportunities to use the present tense in German when you have to use other verb tenses in English.

The primary difference in usage is that English has a continuous verb form and German doesn't. English uses the present continuous (our guests *are staying* until Sunday) to indicate that an action is happening now, and it uses the present tense for habitual actions or facts without expressing whether the action is going on at the time (my brother *lives* on a lake). Because German doesn't verbally express such time distinctions, the listener can interpret sentences such as **Was denkst du?** in two ways: *What are you thinking?/What's on your mind?* or *What do you think?/What's your opinion?*

Look at Table 3-2 for three ways to translate one German sentence into English.

Table 3-2 English Present Tense Translations for German Present

German Present Tense	Possible English Translations	Intended Idea
Jörg spielt sehr gut Basketball.	*Jörg plays basketball very well.*	Stating a general fact, common knowledge (simple present)
Jörg spielt sehr gut Basketball.	*Jörg is playing basketball very well.*	Happening now, today, this week, and so on (present continuous)
Jörg spielt sehr gut Basketball.	*Jörg does play basketball very well.*	Showing emphasis or contradicting someone's opinion (simple present with auxiliary *do*)

We aren't kidding when we say the simple present tense in German is versatile! You even use it to talk about future plans, predictions, spontaneous decisions made at the time of speaking, and activities that started in the past and are still going on. Table 3-3 shows how German uses the present tense for talking about the future and the past.

Table 3-3 Future and Present Perfect Tense Translations for German Present

German Present Tense	English Translations with Other Tenses	Intended Idea
Wir treffen uns um acht Uhr, oder?	*We're meeting/going to meet at eight o'clock, aren't we?*	Stating a plan or intention
Vielleicht regnet es morgen.	*Maybe it'll rain tomorrow.*	Predicting or speculating
Warte mal, ich helfe dir. (colloquial)	*Wait a sec, I'll help you.*	Making a spontaneous decision at the time of speaking, such as offering help or promising
Sie arbeitet seit 20 Jahren bei der Firma.	*She's been working at the company for 20 years.*	Expressing an action that started in the past and is still going

Stating Information with the Passive

When you hear the term *passive* in relation to German grammar, it's not talking about a lion that lies on its back and lets you rub its tummy. What it is talking about is the *passive voice*. To really get a handle on passive voice, you first need to realize that it isn't a *tense*. Then you need to distinguish between *active voice* and *passive voice*.

When an action is in the active voice, the emphasis is on the subject of the sentence as the "agent" that carries out the action of the verb. In contrast, with the passive voice, the person or thing carrying out the action is de-emphasized; the receiver of the action is the focus of attention. In sentences that are in the passive voice, the subject may or may not be mentioned. English makes more use of the passive than German.

The following example sentences show how you can express the same basic information in the active voice and in the passive voice:

- **Jedes Jahr erntet der Bauer das Getreide.** (*The farmer harvests the grain every year.*) This is the active voice; the emphasis is on the agent, **der Bauer** (*the farmer*), who carries out the action of harvesting the grain.

- **Jedes Jahr wird das Getreide vom Bauer geerntet.** (*The grain is harvested every year by the farmer.*) This is the passive voice; the action of harvesting the grain is more important. The agent, **der Bauer** (*the farmer*), is less important.

- **Jedes Jahr wird das Getreide geerntet.** (*The grain is harvested every year.*) This is the passive voice; the important information is the action of harvesting the grain. The agent, **der Bauer** (*the farmer*), isn't even mentioned. In cases like this, it's often obvious or unnecessary to include the subject info.

Forming the passive

To understand how to form the passive, you need to keep in mind that passive (and active) voice forms aren't tenses. You can put the passive (and active) into the present, past, future, or any other tense. In this section, you see how to form the passive in the present tense.

To form the passive, German uses the verb **werden** as a helping (or auxiliary) verb together with the past participle form of the verb being expressed in the passive. English uses the verb *to be* as the helping verb to form the passive. In a passive sentence, you translate **werden** by using the corresponding conjugated form of the verb *to be*. Word order in passive sentences follows the basic rule for German sentences: The conjugated or auxiliary verb is in second position in the phrase or sentence, and the main verb (in this case, the past participle of the verb) goes at the end of the phrase or sentence. (For more information on word order, turn to Book III, Chapter 1.)

Werden is a multitalented verb that has several uses and several meanings. As a main verb, it can mean *to become* or *to get,* but it also acts as an auxiliary verb to form the future tense. In the future tense, it means *will.* (For the low-down on the future tense, flip to Book IV, Chapter 6.)

The following table shows the present tense conjugation of **werden,** which is what you use to form passive sentences in the present tense.

werden (*to be* in passive voice)	
ich **werde**	wir **werden**
du **wirst**	ihr **werdet**
er/sie/es **wird**	sie **werden**
Sie **werden**	
Die Benzinpreise **werden** ständig erhöht. (*Gasoline prices are raised/are being raised constantly.*)	

The following example illustrates how to form the German passive in the present tense:

> **Der President wird vom Volk gewählt.** (*The president is elected by the people.*)

In this sentence, you use the present tense form of **werden,** which is **wird,** and the past participle of **wählen,** which is **gewählt.**

To form other passive voice sentences in the past or the future, you use the corresponding verb tense of **werden** in combination with the past participle of the main verb. For example:

> **Die unendliche Geschichte wurde von Michael Ende geschrieben.** (The *Never Ending Story was written by Michael Ende.*)

Wurde is the simple past conjugated form of **werden. Wurde . . . geschrieben** (*was written*) is the past passive form of the verb **schreiben** (*to write*).

Book III

Assembling the Grammatical Foundations for Communication

In a passive sentence, you use **von** (*by*) to introduce the subject or agent when the agent is a person, as shown in the preceding example sentence. When the subject is a thing, you usually use **durch** (*by, through, by means of*). Look at the following example:

> **In fast jedem Krieg werden viele Zivlisten durch Bomben getötet.** (*In nearly every war, many civilians are killed by bombs.*)

An active sentence with the same information looks like this:

> **Bomben töten viele Zivilisten in fast jedem Krieg.** (*Bombs kill many civilians in nearly every war.*)

Using the passive

In German, you come across the passive far less often than in English. Where you do find it is in the written language, for example, in newspapers, instructions, and technical manuals. To illustrate how to use passive voice, Table 3-4 shows the same information in both active and passive voice.

Table 3-4	Contrasting Active and Passive Voice
Active Voice	*Passive Voice*
Die Werkstatt repariert heute mein Auto. (*The garage is repairing my car today.*)	**Mein Auto wird heute repariert.** (*My car is being repaired today.*)
Menschen verbreiten viele Gerüchte über das Internet. (*People spread a lot of rumors on the Internet.*)	**Viele Gerüchte werden über das Internet verbreitet.** (*A lot of rumors are spread on the Internet.*)
Lehrer unterrichten selten Deutsch an amerikanischen Gymnasien. (*Teachers seldom teach German in American high schools.*)	**Deutsch wird selten an amerikanischen Gymnasien unterrichtet.** (*German is seldom taught in American high schools.*)
Wir teilen uns die Hausarbeit. (*We share the housework.*)	**Die Hausarbeit wird von uns geteilt.** (*The housework is shared by us.*)
Man findet keine Pinguine in der Arktis. (*You don't find penguins in the Arctic.*)	**Pinguine werden in der Arktis nicht gefunden.** (*Penguins aren't found in the Arctic.*)

Recognizing the impersonal passive

The *impersonal passive* expresses action in the passive without a direct object of the sentence. Constructions like this don't exist in English, so the equivalent sentence in English may sound a bit unusual. The following list offers some important points about constructing impersonal passive sentences and provides examples:

✔ German impersonal sentences frequently use the placeholder **es.** For example, **Es wird gefeiert.** (*Partying is going on./There is partying going on.*) In this sentence, **es** (*it*) is a placeholder, not the subject of the sentence. The sentence doesn't have a direct object.

✔ Sometimes the placeholder **es** is absent, as in **Hier wird aufgeräumt.** (*Cleaning is going on here.*) Another way to convey this thought in English is *It's here that cleaning is going on.* Again, this sentence doesn't have a direct object.

✔ With passive sentences that have conjunctions such as **weil** (*because*) or **dass** (*that*), the placeholder **es** (*it*) is left out of the sentence. **Ich höre, dass heute nicht gearbeitet wird.** (*I hear that there's no work going on today./I hear no work is being done today.*)

Chapter 4

Asking and Answering Questions

Asking questions puts you in the conversational driver's seat. You use questions to initiate dialogues, find out what you need to know, and clarify information you're not sure about. When you're studying a new language, you may find that your counterpart is speaking so fast that you can barely understand the first word, let alone the barrage that follows. You feel like asking where the stop button (or at least the rewind button) is, but instead, you ask, **Können Sie das bitte wiederholen?** (*Could you repeat that, please?*) But you're still in the back seat, and your goal is to get behind the wheel. How you achieve that is simple: You implement effective question techniques.

Answering questions is just as important as asking them. Knowing how to formulate your replies to questions either positively or negatively involves a bit of diplomacy. After all, you want to sound polite. This chapter gets you up to speed on formulating all kinds of questions and answers, including the means to soften a blunt "no" reply.

Knowing How to Formulate Questions

Anytime you want to start a conversation with a stranger, you're bound to ask questions. For example, when you go into a store and need some help from the salesperson, you need to know how to ask a few basic questions about the merchandise. The following section guides you through some very useful language to get you up and running as you go out and ask questions.

Inverting word order for yes/no questions

German word order is easy to follow when you form a question that merits a yes or no answer. You simply flip the subject and the conjugated (main) verb: The verb is in first place, and the subject is in second place (where the verb usually goes in statements). English is more complicated because you usually use the auxiliary (helping) verb *to do* or *to be* together with the main verb; in English, only the auxiliary verb goes in first place. Take a look at the following German questions and their translations:

Leben Sie in einer Großstadt? (*Do you live in a large city?*)

Bleibt sie hier? (*Is she staying here?*)

Ist es kalt bei Ihnen im Winter? (*Is it cold where you live in the winter?*)

The German present tense encompasses two English verb tenses (and more). The present continuous doesn't exist in German, so in the second question here, you use the present. (See Book III, Chapter 3 for more on the present tense.) The inverted word order in German is the same for both the present tense and present continuous tense in English.

The following examples are a few yes/no questions you may hear or want to ask at a **Reiseauskunft** (*travel information*) counter when you're thinking of traveling to Berlin by train:

Kann ich hier Tickets kaufen? (*Can I buy tickets here?*) ***Note:*** You may also use the word **Fahrkarten** for *tickets*.

Reisen Sie nach Berlin hin und zurück? (*Are you going round-trip to Berlin?*)

Wollen Sie ein Ticket 1. Klasse oder 2. Klasse nehmen? (*Do you want a first- or second-class ticket?*)

Ist das Ticket 1. Klasse sehr teuer? (*Is the first-class ticket very expensive?*)

Fährt ein Zug am Nachmittag? (*Is there a train leaving in the afternoon?*)

Gibt es ein gutes Hotel am Bahnhof in Berlin? (*Is there a good hotel at the train station in Berlin?*)

Haben Sie viel Gepäck dabei? (*Do you have much luggage with you?*)

Gathering information with question words: Who, what, why, and more

When kids reach the age of asking why, it's marvelous at first, but after weeks of nonstop questioning, you may wonder whether they're practicing for a career in some government spy agency. Asking *why* is a kid's way of engaging an adult in conversation just as much as it's a way of gathering information. As you progress in German, you need question words (interrogative pronouns) such as *who, what, where,* and *when* to gather specific information, but you can also use the kid's tactic of asking **wer** (*who*), **was** (*what*), **warum** (*why*), and so on to engage people in conversation. This particular tactic is useful because it gives you more control over the direction of the discussion.

The inverted word order for yes/no questions (see the preceding section) is the same for information-gathering questions, only the question word (or phrase) comes first. Thus, the word order for info-gathering questions is question word + verb + subject, as in **Warum ist der Himmel blau?** (*Why is the sky blue?*) and **Wann fahren wir nach Hause?** (*When are we driving home?*)

Table 4-1 lists frequently used German question words and phrases, their English equivalents, and an example question for each.

Table 4-1	Question Words and Example Questions	
Question Word	*Example Question*	*English Translation*
wie (*how*)	**Wie heißen Sie?**	*What is your name?*
wie viele (*how many*)	**Wie viele Personen arbeiten in Ihrer Firma?**	*How many people work in your company?*
wie viel (*how much*)	**Wie viel kostet die Karte?**	*How much is the ticket?*
wie lange (*how long*)	**Wie lange dauert die Fahrt nach St. Anton?**	*How long does the trip take to St. Anton?*
wie oft (*how often*)	**Wie oft esst ihr Pizza?**	*How often do you eat pizza?*
wie weit (*how far*)	**Wie weit ist es bis Leipzig?**	*How far is it to Leipzig?*
was (*what*)	**Was machen wir nach der Pause?**	*What are we doing after the break?*
was für (*what kind of*)	**Was für ein Auto fahren Sie?**	*What kind of car do you drive?*
wann (*when*)	**Wann beginnt das Konzert?**	*When does the concert begin?*
wo (*where*)	**Wo wohnen Sie?**	*Where do you live?*
woher (*where . . . from*)	**Woher kommen Sie?**	*Where are you from?*
wohin (*where . . . [to]*)	**Wohin fährt der Bus?**	*Where does the bus go (to)?*

(continued)

Book III

Assembling the Grammatical Foundations for Communication

Table 4-1 *(continued)*

Question Word	Example Question	English Translation
welcher/welche/welches (*which*)	Welche Straßenbahn soll ich nehmen? (die Straßenbahn)	Which tram should I take?
wer (nominative) (*who*)	Wer ist Ihr Chef?	Who is your boss?
wen (accusative) (*whom, who*)		
wem (dative) (*who*)		
wessen (genitive) (*whose*)		
warum (*why*)	Warum hält der Zug jetzt (an)?	Why is the train stopping now?
weshalb (*why*)	Weshalb gibt es hier kein Wifi?	Why is there no WiFi here?
wieso (*why*)	Wieso lachst du?	Why are you laughing?
bis wann (*until when*)	Bis wann arbeitest du heute Abend?	Until what time are you working this evening?
für wen (*who . . . for*)	Für wen ist das Paket?	Who is the package for?
seit wann (*since when*)	Seit wann hast du ein Pferd?	Since when have you had a horse?

Here are a couple of points to keep in mind regarding Table 4-1:

- **Welcher/welche/welches** (*which*) is an interrogative pronoun with three versions to correspond with the three noun genders **der/die/das: welcher Computer** (*which computer*), **welche Frau** (*which woman*), **welches Auto** (*which car*). Remember that it has adjective endings — in other words, the case endings of the noun it's describing. For example, consider **Mit welchem Bus soll ich fahren?** (*Which bus should I take?* Literally: *With which bus should I drive/travel?*). The preposition **mit** uses the dative case, and **der Bus** is masculine, so **mit welchem Bus** uses the masculine dative singular form of **welch-** in the prepositional phrase.

  Note: **Welcher/welche/welches** words follow the same pattern of case and gender endings that you see in **der** words. (For more information on **der** words, go to Book III, Chapter 2.)

- **Wer** (*who*) is an interrogative pronoun that has three other forms. **Wer** is the nominative case, **wen** (*whom, who*) is accusative, **wem** (*who*) is dative, and **wessen** (*whose*) is genitive.

The following example questions are the type you may want to ask when you're inquiring about a language course at a **Sprachenschule** (*language school*):

> **Wie viel kostet so ein Sprachkurs?** (*How much does such a language course cost?*)
>
> **Wie viele Stunden ist es?** (*How many hours is it?*)
>
> **Warum ist es so teuer?** (*Why is it so expensive?*)
>
> **Wer macht den Unterricht?** (*Who is teaching the class?*)
>
> **Wie heißt die Lehrerin?** (*What is the teacher's name?*)
>
> **Woher kommt sie?** (*Where is she from?*)
>
> **Wann können wir anfangen?** (*When can we begin?*)

Forming indirect questions

Sometimes you want to find out something from someone, but you don't want to ask a direct question. If you want to be sneaky about getting answers, you can use an indirect question. For instance, when you're speculating about something and you want to pose a type of question that doesn't sound as much like a question, you can start with one of the following expressions:

> **Wissen Sie,** . . . . (*Do you know. . . ?*)
>
> **Können Sie mir sagen,** . . . . (*Can you tell me. . . ?*)
>
> **Ich frage mich,** . . . . (*I wonder. . . .*)
>
> **Wir möchten gern wissen,** . . . . (*We'd really like to know. . . .*)
>
> **Er hätte gern gewusst,** . . . . (*He was wondering. . . .*)
>
> **Jeder stellt sich die Frage,** . . . . (*Everyone is wondering. . . .*)
>
> **Mich würde interessieren,** . . . . (*I was wondering. . . .*)

To form the rest of the indirect question, you can use a couple of different types of words to connect the indirect expression (from the preceding list) with the thought that you're formulating. These include question words such as **wann** (*when*) or **wo** (*where*). When you don't want to use a question word, you use the conjunction **ob** (*whether/if*).

Here are two other practices to keep in mind when forming indirect questions:

- You need a comma after the expression. In English, you don't need a comma.

- In the phrase following the indirect question expression, the verb goes at the end of the sentence.

The following examples combine indirect question expressions with other information to make complete sentences:

Wissen Sie, wo die nächste U-Bahn Station ist? (*Do you know where the nearest subway station is?*)

Können Sie mir sagen, ob morgen ein Feiertag ist? (*Can you tell me if tomorrow is a holiday?*)

Ich frage mich, welche Familie hier lebt. (*I wonder which family lives here.*)

Wir möchten gern wissen, wann sie endlich heiraten. (*We'd really like to know when they're finally getting married.*)

Er hätte gern gewusst, warum sein Chef nicht im Büro ist. (*He was wondering why his boss isn't in the office.*)

Jeder stellt sich die Frage, ob dieser Winter wieder so kalt wird. (*Everyone is wondering whether this is going to be a cold winter again.*)

Mich würde interessieren, wie dieses Gerät funktioniert. (*I was wondering how this device works.*)

Checking information: Tag! You're it, aren't you?

When you're talking to someone and you want to check some information, you may say something like this, expecting the listener to agree with you: *The mall opens at 10, doesn't it?* The same tactic is handy when you're not sure whether the other person is actually listening to you or is more engrossed in the game on TV.

As you delve into the depths of the German language, you may wonder at how much more complicated German grammar seems than English grammar. Then you stumble upon the realm of tag questions, and you giggle at how simple it is to play tag in German. A *tag question* is simply what you tack onto the end of a statement to make it into a question. In English, the tag depends on the subject and verb in the statement. The possibilities are practically endless in English: *isn't she?, do you?, can't you?, wasn't it?, were you?, wouldn't it?, are you?,* and so on. The German equivalent is far simpler.

To form a tag question in German, just add **nicht?** (Literally: *not?*) or **nicht wahr?** (Literally: *not true?*) to the end of the sentence. Some more expressions that have the same function in German are **Stimmt das?** (*Is that true?*), **Oder?** (Literally: *Or?*), and **Richtig?** (*Correct?*). These expressions serve the same function as the long list of tag question equivalents in English: to elicit a sign of agreement or disagreement or even just a grunt of acknowledgment from the listener. You can use the tag questions interchangeably regardless of whether you're talking about something in the past, present, or future or something that's negative or positive, because they aren't grammatically linked to the first part of the sentence, as they are in English. Here are a couple of examples:

> **Sie fahren morgen nach Düsseldorf, richtig?** (*You're going/driving to Düsseldorf tomorrow, aren't you?*)

> **Der Film war nicht besonders gut, nicht?** (*The movie wasn't especially good, was it?*)

> **Sie wohnen in Graz, nicht wahr?** (*You live in Graz, don't you?*)

> **Wir haben noch eine Stunde Zeit, oder?** (*We have another hour, don't we?*)

> **Sie hat uns alle wichtigen Informationen gegeben, nicht?** (*She gave us all the important information, didn't she?*)

Making choices: Asking what kind of. . . ?

You're looking at a ticket machine for the public transportation system in a major German city. You know the system is really extensive because on the wall next to the machine is a huge subway/light rail map, the **U-Bahn/S-Bahn Netzplan.** (**U-Bahn** is short for **Untergrundbahn** [*subway*], and **S-Bahn** stands for **Schnellbahn** [*commuter rail/light rail*].) The shiny blue and silver ticket machine is a real gem from a technical standpoint, but it doesn't look very user-friendly to **Ausländer** (*foreigners*) like you. The machine must provide lots of ticket choices because it has all kinds of buttons to push and various slots for inserting money and taking out tickets; still, no one seems to be having any trouble. You have two choices: Pretend you're at a slot machine in Las Vegas, press a few buttons, and hope you get a ticket out of the deal, or use the phrase **was für (ein)** and ask a kind-looking passerby, **"Was für ein Ticket brauche ich?"** (*"What kind of ticket do I need?"*) — or, point to the ticket in her hand and ask, **"Was für ein Ticket ist das?"** (*"What kind of a ticket is that?"*)

Obviously, we suggest you try the second option: To form this type of question, you use the phrase **was für (ein)** with a noun as the subject (nominative case) or the direct object (accusative case) of a question. To see how this works, consider these two questions:

> **Was für ein Ticket ist das?** (*What kind of a ticket is that?*) In this question, you start with **was für.** Next, you add the subject of the sentence, **ein Ticket** (*a ticket*), and then the verb **ist** (*is*) and **das** (*that,* indicating the ticket the passenger is holding).

Book III

Assembling the Grammatical Foundations for Communication

Was für ein Ticket brauche ich? (*What kind of ticket do I need?*) This question starts the same way with **was für,** followed by **ein Ticket,** which is the object of the sentence. The verb **brauche** (*need*) comes next, followed by the subject of the question, **ich** (*I*).

If you're having trouble figuring out what a subject (nominative case) is and what a direct object (accusative case) is, turn the question into a normal, declarative sentence. To **Was für ein Ticket ist das?** you may hear the answer **Das ist eine Streifenkarte.** (*That's a strip ticket.*) **Eine Streifenkarte** is nominative case; you use it with the verb **sein** (*to be*). In response to **Was für ein Ticket brauche ich?** you may hear **Sie brauchen eine Streifenkarte.** (*You need a strip ticket.*) The subject is **Sie,** in nominative case, and the object is **eine Streifenkarte,** in accusative case.

Table 4-2 shows the breakdown of the grammatical structure for asking **was für ein. . . ?** (*what kind of. . . ?*) Notice the case and gender endings of the subject and object in each question. Remember that the preposition **für** in **was für** doesn't determine the case; rather, the other information in the question does so.

Table 4-2	Was Für: Showing Case and Gender Endings			
Gender/ Number	*Nominative (Was Für. . . ?)*	*Translation*	*Accusative (Was Für. . . ?)*	*Translation*
Masculine	**Was für ein Fahrschein ist das?**	*What kind of ticket is that?*	**Was für einen Fahrschein brauche ich?**	*What kind of ticket do I need?*
Feminine	**Was für eine Fahrkarte ist das?**	*What kind of ticket is that?*	**Was für eine Fahrkarte brauche ich?**	*What kind of ticket do I need?*
Neuter	**Was für ein Bier ist das?**	*What kind of beer is that?*	**Was für ein Bier trinken Sie?**	*What kind of beer are you drinking?*
Plural	**Was für Geschäfte sind hier im Ort?** (no article needed)	*What kinds of shops are (there) in this town?*	**Was für Geschäfte verkaufen Bierkrüge?**	*What kinds of shops sell beer steins?*

Answering with Yes

You're listening to your aunt as she talks on the phone in the room next to you; you know the conversation isn't very interesting because all you hear is *yes, yes, yeah, yes, yeah, yes.* Your aunt is probably employing most of those yeses for more than answering a question; she's likely signaling that she's still listening or is simply being polite. If she were in the same room as the person she's talking to, she probably wouldn't even need to talk — she could simply bob her head around, nodding in agreement or shaking it to express disagreement.

Knowing how to say **ja** (*yes*) in German is essential whether you're answering questions, responding to information, or agreeing with others, but in many situations, you need more than a one-word "yes" answer to clearly express yourself. Lucky for you, this section is here to help. In it, you discover various ways to clearly express yes.

Variations on yes

When you want to show someone that you understand, that you're listening, and so on, you use **ja** (*yes*) and its extended family: **Ja, das ist richtig.** (*Yes, that's right.*) In these instances, all you have to do is add **ja** to what you want to say. You use **ja** the way you do in English — to answer a question in the affirmative or to say that you agree to something. It can stand alone, or if **ja** is in a sentence, it generally comes at the beginning of an affirmative sentence, just as it does in English.

When you get bored with saying **ja** all the time, try a few variations that render the same meaning with slightly different emphasis. Table 4-3 lists nine alternatives for good old **ja.** The English explanations describe the implications behind these common substitutes, and the example sentences put them into context.

Book III

Assembling the Grammatical Foundations for Communication

Table 4-3	Alternatives for Ja		
Ja Equivalent	**Translation — Explanation**	**Example Sentence**	**Translation**
genau	*exactly, precisely* — sounds stilted in English, but not so to the German ear	**Genau, mein Familienname ist Schranner.**	*Exactly, my family name is Schranner.*

(continued)

Table 4-3 *(continued)*

Ja Equivalent	*Translation — Explanation*	*Example Sentence*	*Translation*
gewiss	*of course, sure enough — somewhat formal-sounding in German*	**Gewiss. Sie werden um 7.00 Uhr geweckt.**	*Of course. You'll be woken up at 7 a.m.*
ja, ja	*yes, yes — can express enthusiasm or skepticism*	**Ja, ja, das weiß ich schon.**	*Yes, yes, I already know that.*
jawohl	*exactly — has a somewhat formal ring*	**Jawohl, meine Frau kommt aus Sydney.**	*Exactly, my wife is from Sydney.*
klar	*of course (Literally: clear or clearly) — somewhat casual, colloquial tone*	**Klar kann ich segeln.**	*Of course I know how to sail.*
natürlich	*naturally — neutral, neither formal nor colloquial*	**Natürlich helfen wir Ihnen.**	*Naturally, we'll help you.*
richtig	*right — neutral, neither formal nor colloquial*	**Richtig. Er mietet ein Auto.**	*Right. He's renting a car.*
selbstverständlich	*certainly — good choice for business, formal situations*	**Selbstverständlich lade ich Sie zum Mittagessen ein.**	*Certainly, I'm inviting you to lunch.*
sicher	*certainly, sure*	**Sicher mache ich das Licht aus.**	*Sure, I'll turn off the light.*

Notice in the example sentences in Table 4-3, when the **ja** substitute is followed by a comma or a period, you start the next phrase in the usual German word order of subject followed by the verb in second position. (In the example sentences, the comma and period are interchangeable.) When the **ja** replacement word functions as the first element in the sentence (no comma or period), the verb follows in second position.

Emphasizing yes

When you want to add more emphasis to show that you really understand or agree with someone, you can add **ja** or **aber** (*but*) to the expressions in Table 4-3. Take a look at these examples:

> **Ja, klar!** (*Yes, of course!*)
>
> **Aber natürlich!** (*Certainly!*)
>
> **Aber selbstverständlich!** (*Why, certainly!*)
>
> **Ja, sicher!** (*Yes, sure!*)

These examples place the **ja** words at the beginning of the sentence. However, when you want to express understanding or agreement within a sentence, you can construct sentences that use these words in more or less fixed expressions like **genau richtig** (*exactly right*) or **es ist (mir) klar** (*it's clear to me*). In addition, **genau, gewiss, klar, natürlich, richtig, selbstverständlich,** and **sicher** can work as adjectives or in some cases as adverbs, and they have similar meanings. (See Book III, Chapter 5 for more on adjectives and adverbs.) The following list of example sentences shows you the context for how to use these *yes* expressions:

> **Das wird selbstverständlich gemacht.** (*That will certainly be done.*)
>
> **Es ist mir klar, daß ich abnehmen soll.** (*I realize that I should lose weight.* Literally: *It's clear to me that I should lose weight.*)
>
> **Die Straßen waren nach dem Sturm gewiss sehr gefährlich.** (*The streets were certainly very dangerous after the storm.*)
>
> **Natürlich können wir mit dem Zug nach Köln fahren.** (*Naturally, we can take the train to Cologne.*)
>
> **Richtig. Ich bin Herr Gravenstein.** (*Right. I'm Herr Gravenstein.*)
>
> **Klar geht die ganze Familie in Urlaub.** (*Of course the whole family is going on vacation.*)
>
> **Sicher, wir fliegen am Dienstag nach Genf.** (*Sure, we're flying to Geneva on Tuesday.*)
>
> **Sie haben es genau richtig geraten.** (*You guessed it exactly right.*)

Book III

Assembling the Grammatical Foundations for Communication

Responding with No: The Difference between Kein and Nicht

Saying *no* in German is plain and simple: **nein.** However, when you want to negate an action, an object, or a person, you have two ways to express *not* (or *not any*): **kein** and **nicht.** Which one you use depends on what they negate in a sentence. The word order of these negations is important to know, as is how to form the endings of **kein** (**nicht** doesn't change). In this section, we walk you through the steps of when and how to use **nicht** and **kein.** You also get the hang of how to avoid sounding too blunt when you're saying *no* in German by using various words and expressions that soften your message.

Negating with nicht

The nuts and bolts of **nicht** are straightforward as far as its form and use are concerned. In terms of form, **nicht** is all you need to know (unlike **kein,** which has case and gender endings — see the next section). As for use, **nicht** generally negates a verb — **nicht einladen** (*not to invite*), **nicht fahren** (*not to drive, not to travel*), **nicht feiern** (*not to celebrate*) — though it can also negate an adjective, as in **nicht interessant** (*not interesting*), or an adverb, as in **nicht pünktlich** (*not on time*).

What you have to figure out is how to position **nicht** in a sentence. Because **nicht** is an adverb, it negates the action of the verb or modifies an adjective or an adverb, and it's generally next to these parts of speech. For example:

Sie fliegen nicht nach London. (*They're not flying to London.*) **Nicht** directly follows the verb in this sentence, negating the idea that they're flying.

Martin spricht nicht gut Deutsch. (*Martin doesn't speak good German.*) In this sentence, **nicht** tells you that Martin's ability to speak German is not good, so **nicht** immediately follows the verb.

Gestern kamen wir nicht pünktlich zum Termin. (*Yesterday we didn't get to our appointment on time.*) **Nicht** links with the adverb **pünktlich** (*on time*) to mean *not on time,* so you place it before **pünktlich.**

Das Buch ist nicht interessant. (*The book isn't interesting.*) The negation connects the verb **ist** (*is*) and the adjective **interessant** (*interesting*); **nicht** modifies **interessant,** so you place it in front of the adjective.

Placement is the most complex part of **nicht,** but most of the time, even if you're not perfect with word order, your listeners will be able to understand you. Table 4-4 explains some guidelines to follow when using **nicht.**

Table 4-4	Guidelines for Positioning Nicht	
Position of Nicht	*Example Sentence*	*Translation*
Follows		
A conjugated verb	Maria fährt **nicht** nach Kiel.	*Maria isn't driving to Kiel.*
A conjugated verb and precedes a separable prefix	Felix und Gretl sehen **nicht** fern. (**Fernsehen** is a separable prefix verb.)	*Felix and Gretl aren't watching TV.*
Most specific adverbs of time	Ich war gestern **nicht** zu Hause. (**Gestern** is the specific adverb of time.)	*I wasn't at home yesterday.*
Comes at the end of		
Yes/no questions	Essen Sie den Apfel **nicht?**	*Aren't you going to eat the apple?*
A sentence or question with a direct object	Ich kenne diesen Mann **nicht.** (**Diesen Mann** is the direct object.)	*I don't know that man.*
Precedes		
Most adjectives	Das Hotel ist **nicht** gemütlich. (**Gemütlich** is the adjective.)	*The hotel isn't cozy.*
Most adverbs, except for specific adverbs of time	Ihr lauft **nicht** schnell. (**Schnell** is the adverb.)	*You don't run fast.*
Infinitives connected to a verb	Ich gehe **nicht** einkaufen. (**Einkaufen** is the infinitive.)	*I'm not going shopping.*
Most prepositional phrases	Dieser Käse kommt **nicht** aus Frankreich. (**Aus Frankreich** is the prepositional phrase.)	*This cheese isn't from France.*
The combinations of parts in a sentence (usually)	Matthias geht **nicht** sehr oft in die Bibliothek. (Two parts are here — **sehr oft** and **in die Bibliothek.**)	*Matthias doesn't go to the library very often.*

Book III

Assembling the Grammatical Foundations for Communication

The following pairs of questions and answers illustrate how to use **nicht**. After the answers, you see the reasons for the word order.

Ist das dein Haus? (*Is that your house?*)

Nein, das ist nicht mein Haus. (*No, it isn't my house.*) **Nicht** follows the verb.

Kommen Sie am Mittwoch zu uns? (*Are you coming to see us on Wednesday?*)

Nein, am Mittwoch kommen wir nicht zu Ihnen. (*No, we're not coming on Wednesday to see you.*) **Nicht** precedes the prepositional phrase **zu Ihnen.**

Gehen Sie jetzt Golf spielen? (*Are you going to play golf now?*)

Nein, ich gehe nicht Golf spielen. (*No, I'm not going to play golf.*) **Nicht** precedes the infinitive expression **Golf spielen.**

Trinken Sie den Orangensaft nicht? (*Aren't you going to drink the orange juice?*)

Nein, ich trinke ihn nicht. (*No, I'm not going to drink it.*) **Nicht** follows the direct object **ihn.**

Liegt Duisburg in einer schönen Gegend? (*Is Duisburg in a pretty area?*)

Nein, Duisburg liegt nicht in einer schönen Gegend. (*No, Duisburg isn't in a pretty area.*) **Nicht** precedes the prepositional phrase **in einer schönen Gegend.**

Here are a few ready-made expressions with **nicht** that may help you add your two cents when you want to start with something fancier than just **nein:**

Das ist nicht schlecht. (*That's not bad.*) Just as in English, depending on how you say this, it can mean that something is actually pretty good.

Das genügt nicht. (*That's not enough./That won't do.*)

Das mache ich nicht mit. (*I won't have a part in that.*)

Ich auch nicht. (*Neither am/do/can* [and so on] *I.*) In English, you use a helping verb to say what you can't do either; in German, you don't need a verb to express the same thing.

Negating with kein

Using **kein** (*no, not, not any*) is almost as easy as using **nicht** (see the preceding section). **Kein** functions as an adjective; it describes nouns by expressing negation such as **keiner Polizist** (*no policeman*), **keine Jeans** (*no jeans*), **kein Brot** (*no bread*), and so on. However, before you can jump in and start adding

kein to your sentences, you need to know the gender and case of the noun you're negating. Look at the following sentence:

Keiner Polizist hat einen leichten Job. (*No policeman has an easy job.*)

Keiner Polizist is the subject of the sentence, so it's in nominative case. **Polizist** is masculine (**der**), so you add **-er** to **kein = keiner Polizist. Keiner** is the singular masculine form of **kein** in nominative case. (See Book III, Chapter 2 for more on gender and case.)

When you look at **kein,** you see the indefinite article **ein** (*a, an*). More good news on the grammar front: The indefinite article **ein** and other very commonly used words are often referred to as **ein-** words because they follow the same pattern in case and gender endings. In the nominative case, **ein** and **kein** are the masculine and neuter forms, and **eine** and **keine** are the feminine and plural forms. That means you need to remember only one set of endings for the following words:

- ✔ **ein** (*a, an*), the indefinite article
- ✔ **kein** (*no, not, not any*), the adjective that negates a noun
- ✔ **mein** (*my*), **dein** (*your*), **sein** (*his*), **ihr** (*her*), **unser** (*our*), **eurer** (*your*), **ihr** (*their*), **Ihr** (*your*), the possessive adjectives

Table 4-5 shows how to remember the endings for **kein,** with the case and gender endings in bold. Masculine and neuter are grouped together, and feminine and plural are grouped together. This table is also valid for **ein-** words except for **ein** itself, which has no plural form.

Table 4-5	Endings of Kein	
Case	*Masculine/Neuter*	*Feminine/Plural*
Nominative	kein	kein**e**
Accusative	kein**en** (masc.), kein (n.)	kein**e**
Dative	kein**em**	kein**er** (fem.), kein**en** (pl.)
Genitive	kein**es**	kein**er**

Notice that the masculine and neuter endings are almost all the same for **kein** and **ein-** words; the accusative is the only one that differs. You can also remember feminine and plural together, keeping in mind that the dative is the only one that isn't the same. Look at these example sentences with **kein** in the four cases, followed by the English equivalent and the grammar note explaining the gender:

Book III

Assembling the Grammatical Foundations for Communication

- Nominative case: **Keine Menschen leben auf der Insel.** (*No people live on the island.*) **Menschen** (plural) is the subject of the sentence, so **keine Menschen** is nominative plural.

- Accusative case: **Nach dem grossen Abendessen hatte ich keinen Hunger.** (*I wasn't hungry after the big dinner.*) Literally, **ich hatte keinen Hunger** means *I had no hunger*. **Der Hunger** (masculine) changes to the accusative singular **keinen Hunger** because it's the object of the sentence.

- Dative case: **In keinem alten Auto gibt es Navi.** (*There's no GPS in any old car[s].* Literally: *In no old car is there GPS.*) The prepositional phrase **in keinem alten Auto** is in dative case; therefore, **das Auto** becomes **keinem (alten) Auto.**

- Genitive case: **Während keiner Nacht in der letzten Woche habe ich gut geschlafen.** (*I didn't sleep well [during] any night last week.* Literally: *During no night in the past week did I sleep well.*) **Während** (*during*) is a genitive preposition and **die Nacht** is feminine singular, so you need the genitive case ending **-er** for **kein.** (Book IV, Chapter 2 offers plenty more details on prepositions.)

When you're reading German, use the examples you see to understand the grammar involved. Train yourself to take a step back and think carefully about which word endings you're dealing with in a sentence. The pieces of the grammar puzzle begin to fit into place when you recognize which gender and case you're looking at.

Avoiding blunt negative replies

You don't want to sound overly negative when answering yes/no questions with a straight **nein.** Instead, you can cushion the impact and make a positive impression on German speakers when giving positive and even negative replies by using *idiomatic expressions* — fixed phrases. Consider this exchange:

> **Haben Sie Kleingeld für 2€?** (*Do you have change for 2€?*)
>
> **Nein, es tut mir leid.** (*No, I'm sorry. I don't.*)

In the response, you soften the blow of **nein** by adding the apology **es tut mir leid** (*I'm sorry*). You can also give an excuse (hopefully a plausible one) such as **Nein, da mein Portmonnaie zu Hause ist.** (*No, because my wallet is at home.*)

Table 4-6 provides a sampling of expressions that help you avoid sounding too negative.

Table 4-6	Avoiding Bluntness with Negative Answers	
Phrase	**English Equivalent**	**Comments**
Es tut mir leid	*I'm sorry*	The apology **Es tut mir leid** prefaces the rest of the information.
fast keine (Zeit)	*hardly any (time)*	**Fast keine Zeit** (*hardly any time*) is the same as **kaum Zeit.**
Im Grunde genommen	*basically*	The signal of a refusal — **Im Grunde genommen** — comes at the beginning of the sentence, softening the negative.
nicht hundertprozentig/ nicht ganz	*not 100%, not completely*	You don't need to admit that you understand only 70%. Chances are, the speaker will repeat him/herself. Stating **nein** flatly may not get you anywhere.
nicht nur (. . . sondern auch)	*not only (. . . but also)*	**nicht nur** (*not only*) can be linked like this: **Nicht nur** mein Vater, **sondern auch** mein Großvater kam aus Irland. (*Not only my father but also my grandfather came from Ireland.*)
Ich habe nicht die leiseste Ahnung	*I haven't the faintest idea*	This is a fixed expression that can also be stated like this: **Ich habe keine Ahnung.** (*I have no idea.*)
auch nicht	*[n]either*	To add that something else is not easy/useful/helpful, and so on, you can say **Das ist auch nicht leicht.** (*That's not easy, either.*)
doch nicht	*definitely not*	For emphasis, use **doch nicht** like this: **Ich fahre doch nicht mit.** (*I'm definitely not coming along.*) It implies you've changed your mind.
eigentlich nicht	*actually not*	You can clarify with **eigentlich nicht.** Example: **Das ist eigentlich nicht so einfach.** (*That's actually not so easy.*)
ja und nein	*yes and no*	When you're on the fence about answering with yes or no, say **ja und nein.**
jein	*yes-no*	Yes and no are combined together into one word with **jein** — the informal expression for those who can't make up their minds or who want to say that they partially agree with something.
nicht genau	*not exactly*	When you're not clear about something, you can say, **Ich weiß nicht genau.** (*I don't know exactly.*)
noch nicht	*not yet*	When you need to express that you're not yet ready, for example, you can say, **Ich bin noch nicht fertig.** (*I'm not ready yet.*)

Book III

Assembling the Grammatical Foundations for Communication

The following examples put the expressions from Table 4-6 to use in dialogue. For each example, a question is followed by an answer with a softener that avoids the bluntness of **kein** and **nicht.** The modifying words are set in bold:

- Können wir noch einen Kaffee trinken? (*Can we have another cup of coffee?*)

  Es tut mir leid, aber wir haben **fast keine** Zeit. (*I'm sorry, but we have hardly any time.*)

- Interessieren Sie sich für diese Musik? (*Are you interested in this music?*)

  Ich habe **praktisch kein** Interesse für solche Musik. (*I have practically no interest in such music.*)

- Können Sie in diesem Fall eine Ausnahme machen? (*Can you make an exception in this case?*)

  Im Grunde genommen, dürfen wir keine Ausnahmen machen. (*Basically, we can't make any exceptions.*) ***Note:*** You can also use **nicht** with a verb: **Im Grunde genommen,** geht das **nicht.** (*Basically, that won't work.*)

- Verstehen Sie, was ich meine? (*Do you understand what I mean?*)

  Nicht hundertprozentig/Nicht ganz. (*Not one hundred percent./Not completely.*)

- Sie Sind Engländer, nicht wahr? (*You're English, aren't you?*)

  Nicht nur Engländer, da mein Vater aus Irland kam. (*Not only English, because my father came from Ireland.*)

- Ändert sich das Klima heutzutage? (*Is the climate changing nowadays?*)

  Ich habe nicht die leiseste Ahnung. (*I haven't the faintest idea.*)

Asking and Answering Questions with Wo- and Da- Compound Words

If you don't want to ask a question by beginning with a basic question word like **wann** (*when*) or **wer** (*who*), you can mix things up a bit by combining the word **wo** (*where*) with various prepositions, like **mit** (*with*), to make a whole new question word — in this case, **womit** (*what . . . with*). In a question, this combo looks like this: **Womit schneidet er das Holz?** (*What's he cutting the wood with?*)

Another type of word combination you may come across in connection with German questions consists of **da-** together with a preposition like **zu** (*to, at*) to form the word **dazu** (*with it, in addition*). These **da-** compound words come in handy in answers to questions when you want to refer back to some information that's already been mentioned in a prepositional phrase without having to repeat the same words again. Imagine you're discussing your favorite dish, and someone asks you, **Trinken Sie Weißwein oder Rotwein mit dem Eintopf?** (*Do you drink white wine or red wine with the stew?*) Your answer: **Dazu trinkt man am besten Rotwein.** (*It's best to drink red wine with it.*) You simply replace the prepositional phrase **mit dem Eintopf** with **dazu**.

The following two sections take you through the ins and outs of using these two types of combination words.

Combining question words: Compounds with wo-

You're listening to the German businessman sitting next to you on the plane tell you something like **Ich bin gegen höhere Benzinpreise.** (*I'm against higher gas prices.*) You hear the first part of the statement, **ich bin gegen,** but you don't catch the rest — what's he against? That one song about **Benzin** (*gasoline*) by Rammstein? You ask, **Sie sind gegen was?** (*You're against what?*) The businessman can understand your question, but it sounds as though you're challenging his opinion. It's a bit like saying *Just what is it that you claim you're against?!* and insinuating that you don't agree at all. How do you communicate that you don't want to challenge his judgment, but you do need a repeat of the statement? You ask, **Wogegen sind Sie?** (*What are you against?*)

The question **Wogegen sind Sie** literally means *What against are you?* **Wogegen** asks for the object of the preposition **gegen** (*against*). In German, you stick **wo-** in front of the preposition to signal to the listener that a question about the object of the preposition is coming. The listener gets the most important information first in the question.

The German word order in questions beginning with **wo-** compounds like **worüber** (*what about, what over*) may seem odd at first: **Worüber spricht sie?** (*What's she talking about?* Literally: *What over [about] is she talking?*) However, compare it to a similar structure in formal English — *To whom am I speaking?* instead of the far more natural sounding *Who am I speaking to?* **Remember:** Such word order may seem odd in English, yet it's standard fare in German.

A second important function of the compound question words using **wo-** is to prompt the listener that the question you're asking allows an open-ended answer: **Wofür sind Sie?** (*What are you for?*) The listener may answer like this: **Ich bin für den Frieden** (*I'm for peace*) or **Ich bin für einen Spaziergang im Park** (*I'm [up] for a walk in the park*).

The meaning of the preposition in the compound with **wo-** may be different from the original meaning. Keep in mind that many German verbs require particular prepositions in particular contexts (check out Book IV, Chapter 2, for more on prepositions), which sometimes can determine which preposition you choose to combine with **wo-**, such as **Worauf warten Sie?** (*What*

Book III

Assembling the Grammatical Foundations for Communication

are you waiting for?) and **Ich warte auf den Bus.** (*I'm waiting for the bus.*) The person posing the question uses the phrase **warten auf . . .** in question form. The reply contains the complete phrase (**ich warte auf**) with the object of the preposition (**den Bus**).

When you know the most common verb-preposition combinations, you're on the road to success at forming **wo-** compounds. (Book IV, Chapters 2 and 3 help you with such combinations.) However, you also need to know which grammatical case to use with prepositions. Most important is being aware that prepositions can change meaning depending on the context of the sentence, so get to know how to use the **wo-** compounds in sentences.

Table 4-7 shows the most common compounds formed by adding **wo-** to the prepositions. The English equivalents can help you get a feel for the preposition, but they change meaning according to the context of the sentence. Notice that when the preposition begins with a vowel, you insert the letter **r** between the two elements of the question word (for instance, **wo + r + in = worin**).

Table 4-7	Questioning Using Wo- Compounds	
German Preposition	*Translation*	*Wo- Compound*
an	*on, at, to*	**woran**
auf	*on top of, to*	**worauf**
aus	*out of, from*	**woraus**
durch	*through, by*	**wodurch**
für	*for*	**wofür**
gegen	*against*	**wogegen**
hinter	*behind, after*	**wohinter**
in	*in, inside of*	**worin**
mit	*with, by*	**womit**
nach	*after, to*	**wonach**
über	*over, above*	**worüber**
um	*around*	**worum**
unter	*under*	**worunter**
von	*from, by*	**wovon**
vor	*in front of, before*	**wovor**
zu	*to, at*	**wozu**

The following examples show questions beginning with **wo-** compound words, followed by possible answers:

> **Woran leidet er? Er leidet an Bronchitis.** (*What is he suffering from? He's suffering from bronchitis.*)

> **Worüber spricht sie? Sie spricht über die Umwelt.** (*What is she talking about? She's talking about the environment.*)

> **Wozu brauchen Sie einen Hammer? Um ein Bücherregal zu bauen.** (*What do you need a hammer for? To build a bookshelf.*)

> **Wodurch wurden Sie krank? Durch schlechten Fisch wurde ich krank.** (*What did you get sick from? I got sick from bad fish.*)

> **Worauf wartest du? Ich warte auf meine Freundin.** (*What are you waiting for? I'm waiting for my [girl]friend.*)

Explaining yes and no answers by using da- compounds

You're probably aware of German's propensity for combining words or word fragments into one humongous word that's as long as its definition. Fortunately, **da-** compounds are far simpler because they combine only two parts: **da-** and a preposition. These compounds are handy for replacing the object of the preposition; **da-** translates as *it* or *that* and, in the case of plural nouns, *them*. You don't need to repeat the prepositional phrase, making you sound intelligent as well as fluent in German.

This section describes the ins and outs of **da-** compounds: how to form them and when and how to use them. (The preceding section "Combining question words: Compounds with **wo-**" deals with the kissing cousins of **da-** compounds, the **wo-** compounds, which you use in questions.)

Book III

Assembling the Grammatical Foundations for Communication

Forming da- compounds

To form compounds with **da-**, check out Table 4-8. The table shows the most common compounds formed by adding **da-** to the prepositions. The English equivalents help you get a feel for the preposition, but keep in mind that they can alter their meaning according to the context of the sentence. When the preposition begins with a vowel, you insert the letter **r** between the two elements of the word (as in **da + r + über = darüber**).

Table 4-8	Forming Da- Compounds	
German Preposition	*Translation*	*Da- Compound (Preposition + it, that, them)*
an	*on, at, to*	**daran**
auf	*on top of, to*	**darauf**
aus	*out of, from*	**daraus**
bei	*at, with*	**dabei**
durch	*through, by*	**dadurch**
für	*for*	**dafür**
gegen	*against*	**dagegen**
hinter	*behind, after*	**dahinter**
in	*in, inside of*	**darin**
mit	*with, by*	**damit**
nach	*after, to*	**danach**
neben	*next to*	**daneben**
über	*over, above*	**darüber**
um	*around*	**darum**
unter	*under*	**darunter**
von	*from, by*	**davon**
vor	*in front of, before*	**davor**
zu	*to, at*	**dazu**
zwischen	*between*	**dazwischen**

Putting da- compounds to work

Use combinations of **da-** + preposition when you want to refer to a prepositional phrase that someone has already mentioned without repeating it — for
example, in a reply to a question — just as you say something like *I like to
work with it* (**Ich arbeite gern damit**) in English. For instance, you can replace
the phrase **mit meinem neuen Computer** (*with my new computer*) with
damit, a combination of **da-** + **mit** (literally *it* + *with*).

Look at this example question with two different replies. Clearly, the second
reply is much less redundant than the first one, and you sound much more
like you know what you're talking about — even though you say that you **verstehe nichts davon** (*understand nothing about it*)!

> **Verstehen Sie etwas von dieser Grammatik?** (*Do you know/understand
> anything about this grammar?*)

Nein, ich verstehe nichts von dieser Grammatik. (*No, I don't know/ understand anything about this grammar.*)

Nein, ich verstehe nichts davon. (*No, I know/understand nothing about it.*)

Notice how **davon** translates in the second reply: *about it.* You can also translate **davon** as *about that,* even though in Table 4-8, **von** has only two translations, *from* and *by.* Why? Because the meaning of the preposition can change when you add it to a prepositional phrase or (especially) a verbal phrase (a *verbal phrase* is a more or less fixed expression that has a verb in it). The verbal phrase in the preceding example is **von etwas verstehen,** which is what you'd see in a dictionary entry under the headword **verstehen,** translated as *to know sth about* (*sth* is a standard abbreviation for *something*).

The following pairs of questions and answers show how **da-** compound words play out in sentences:

Denkst du oft an die Reise? (*Do you often think about the trip?*)

Ja, ich denke oft daran. (*Yes, I often think about it.*)

Warten Sie noch auf Ihre Bestellung? (*Are you waiting for your order?*)

Ja, ich warte noch darauf. (*Yes, I'm still waiting for it.*)

Schreibst du mit dem Laptop? (*Are you writing with the laptop?*)

Nein, ich schreibe nicht damit. (*No, I'm not writing with it.*)

Arbeitet er für 8€ in der Stunde? (*Does he work for 8€ an hour?*)

Nein, dafür arbeitet er nicht. (*No, he doesn't/won't work for that.*)

Steht der Stuhl vor dem Fenster oder hinter dem Tisch? (*Is the chair in front of the window or behind the table?*)

Der Stuhl steht nicht davor und nicht dahinter; er steht in einem anderen Zimmer. (*The chair isn't in front of or behind it; it's in another room.*)

Yet another frequently used **da-** compound is **darum** (*that is why, so, therefore, for this/that reason, on that account*), with its impressive number of meanings. When it's used as part of a fixed expression, the chameleon **darum** changes meanings again and again. Here are some common expressions that use **darum:**

Es geht darum, (dass) . . . (*The point is . . .*)

Es handelt sich darum, (dass) . . . (*The question is . . .*)

Sei's drum! (*So be it!*)

mit allem drum und dran (*with the whole works, the whole shebang*)

In the last two examples, the words **darum** and **daran** are shortened to form **drum** and **dran,** respectively.

Book III

Assembling the Grammatical Foundations for Communication

Sounding Diplomatic: Using Maybe, Suggesting, and Refusing Politely

Ever felt like blurting out a resounding *No!* in the middle of a meeting when you totally disagreed with the proposal being discussed? Ever wanted to shake someone who's always negative into saying an unequivocal *Yes* to something you suggested? If so, you likely used a bit more tact when you actually did speak up. Knowing how to couch your agreement or disagreement in diplomatic words is even more important when you speak another language. Although German may — acoustically speaking — sound direct and even harsh at times, you can sound more diplomatic and polite simply by adding a few measures of *maybes* and *wells* to replies that may otherwise sound too blunt.

Add words such as **vielleicht** (*maybe*) or **nun** (*well*) where you would in English, namely at the beginning of the idea that you intend to disagree with or answer with a negative reply. Longer diplomatic expressions generally go at the beginning of the sentence you're expressing doubts about; you just have to memorize them as fixed expressions. Here are a couple of examples:

> **Es kann sein, dass der Bericht einige Fehler hat.** (*It could be that the report has some mistakes.*) The expression **es kann sein** is a fixed expression connected to the rest of the sentence by the conjunction **dass.** (For details on conjunctions, see Book IV, Chapter 1.)

> **Um ehrlich zu sein, das wäre schwierig.** (*To be honest, that would be difficult.*) The expression **um ehrlich zu sein** is a fixed expression. Following it is the information that you're being honest about.

North Americans — and possibly even more so, the British — enjoy a great reputation for using a broad range of polite language when expressing indecision, agreement, and disagreement with others. The German language isn't quite as famous for sounding reserved. Why? The language itself has a stronger ring to the ears than English because of the **Tonfall** (*inflection* or *tone*) and the fact that it bunches more consonants together. Speakers of German don't deliberately try to be blunt; rather, the effect comes from the sound of the language. However, Germans do generally state their opinions more directly than North Americans do.

Table 4-9 walks you through a number of ways you can respond diplomatically when you want to signal your reservations about something. Each German expression is followed by an example phrase and its English equivalent. Some of the expressions are one-word introductory signals that you use to preface your opinion; others are longer phrases that you use in German to sound diplomatic, to qualify your standpoint, or to negotiate acceptance of your suggestion.

Another bonus for using such expressions is that you gain time while you decide whether you really want to agree or disagree with the person you're conversing with. That's a thankful bonus when you're speaking a language that isn't your own and you want to sound intelligent — and intelligible — in what you say.

Table 4-9	Diplomatic Answering Gambits	
German Expression	*Example Phrase*	*English Equivalent*
Expressing maybe/perhaps		
Vielleicht . . .	**Vielleicht kommt er** . . .	*Maybe he'll come* . . .
Eventuell . . .	**Eventuell kann man** . . .	*You could possibly* . . .
		***Note: Eventuell** means possibly or perhaps, not eventually.*
Möglicherweise . . .	**Möglicherweise regnet es nicht** . . .	*Perhaps it won't rain* . . .
Introducing doubt		
Nun . . .	**Nun, wenn es so ist** . . .	*Well, if it's like that* . . .
Eigentlich . . .	**Eigentlich dachte ich** . . .	*Actually, I thought* . . .
. . . **aber** . . .	**Ich verstehe, aber** . . .	*I understand, but* . . .
Mit allem Respekt . . .	**Mit allem Respekt muss ich dazu sagen** . . .	*With all due respect, I must say* . . .
Suggesting		
Machen wir so, . . .	**Machen wir so, wir schieben** . . .	*Let's do it like this: We'll delay* . . .
Wir könnten . . .	**Wir könnten morgen mit einander treffen** . . .	*We could meet tomorrow* . . .
Wie wäre es . . .	**Wie wäre es wenn wir versuchen würden** . . .	*How would it be if we tried* . . .
		*(The introduction to the sentence **wie wäre es** implies that it will continue in the subjunctive because you're imagining something.)*
Was halten Sie davon, wenn . . .	**Was halten Sie davon, wenn wir abwarten** . . .	*What do you think about waiting* . . .

(continued)

Table 4-9 *(continued)*

German Expression	Example Phrase	English Equivalent
Modifying negation		
. . . kaum . . .	Das ist kaum möglich . . .	*That's hardly possible . . .*
. . . fast nicht . . .	Das ist fast nicht machbar . . .	*That's just about impossible to do . . .*
Ich habe einige Bedenken . . .	Ich habe einige Bedenken dazu . . .	*I have a few doubts about that . . .*
. . . etwas zu . . .	Der Preis ist etwas zu hoch . . .	*The price is somewhat too high . . .*
. . . ein bißchen . . .	Wir brauchen ein bißchen mehr Zeit . . .	*We need a bit more time . . .*
Refusing diplomatically		
Leider . . .	Leider kann ich nicht mitkommen . . .	*Unfortunately, I can't come along . . .*
Es tut mir leid . . .	Es tut mir leid, aber das geht nicht . . .	*I'm sorry, but that won't work . . .*
Entschuldigung, aber . . .	Entschuldigung, aber ich habe wenig Zeit . . .	*Sorry, but I have little time . . .*
Ist das nicht . . .	Ist das nicht etwas früh?	*Isn't that a bit early?*

Chapter 5

Describing and Comparing with Adjectives and Adverbs

Adjectives and adverbs add spice, distinctive flavor, and creativity to a sentence. They dress it up for a vigorous winter workout in Arlberg. Why not leave out these extra words and stick with the basics? Cross out the adjective *vigorous* from *vigorous winter workout* in the previous sentence, and your listener still gets the picture. But she doesn't perk up and become involved. Adjectives add depth and character to the power of a noun, and adverbs add oomph to verbs and other parts of a sentence. Besides, they're **interessant** (*interesting*), **lustig** (*funny*), **unglaublich** (*incredible*), **ruhig** (*quiet*), and **praktisch** (*practical*).

Incorporating adjectives and adverbs into your sentences involves a bit of good news and a bit of not-so-good news. First the good news: Adverbs are no-nonsense words in that they don't go through any contortions of German grammar. In addition, there are quite a few cognates among German adjectives and adverbs. In the first paragraph, you probably recognize **interessant,** and you may get the meaning of **praktisch** if you know that the ending **-isch** often stands in for English adjective endings like *-ic* and *-ical*. The not-so-good news has to do with adjectives. When handling adjectives, you have to address grammar — gender, number, and case. Depending on where you place the adjective in the sentence, you may or may not need to make the adjective agree with the noun it modifies.

Keine Sorge. (*Not to worry.*) This chapter gives you the lowdown on adjectives and adverbs so you can start using them confidently in your descriptive German. Plus, you get up to speed on using them when making comparisons.

Organizing Adjectives: Opposites, Cognates, and Collocations

Adjectives are so numerous that you absolutely must find a system for categorizing them as a means of easy reference. When you encounter a new adjective, try to find a hook to hang it on or a group to put it in. You may be able to group them three different ways:

- **Opposites:** Some adjective types lend themselves to pairing up with an adjective of the opposite meaning.

- **Cognates:** *Cognates,* which are similar words in English and German, are instantly recognizable; after you check that the meaning is the same in both languages, you only need to know how to form their endings in sentences.

- **Collocations:** *Collocations* are semi-fixed, frequently used word combinations, so look for adjective + noun phrases.

  Get into the habit of recognizing collocations that include adjectives. Getting familiar with them takes a bit more work than figuring out what a solo adjective means, but in the end, it saves time. Add them to your range of expression, and you're on the path to successful, idiomatic German.

The following sections help you place adjectives in these three different groups. By doing so, you can more easily remember these descriptors, and then you can use them when you want to discuss appearance, personal traits, weather, and more.

Letting opposites attract

You can master many groups of descriptive adjectives as opposite pairs. Two common groups are the adjectives that describe people's appearance and personal traits and the adjectives that describe the weather.

Describing appearance and personal traits

When you want to say what people are like, you use descriptive adjectives to describe them; for example, **sie ist groß** (*she's tall*) or **er ist freundlich** (*he's friendly*). In Table 5-1, you see such adjectives grouped as opposites; looking at them this way saves you time when remembering them.

Table 5-1	Adjectives of Personal Appearance and Traits		
German Adjective	*English Translation*	**German Opposite**	*English Opposite*
attraktiv	*attractive*	**unattraktiv**	*unattractive*
freundlich	*friendly*	**unfreundlich**	*unfriendly*
glücklich	*happy*	**traurig/unglücklich**	*sad/unhappy*
heiter	*cheerful*	**ernst**	*serious*
interessant	*interesting*	**uninteressant/ langweilig**	*uninteresting/ boring*
jung	*young*	**alt**	*old*
klein	*short*	**groß**	*tall*
neu	*new*	**alt**	*old*
ruhig	*quiet*	**laut**	*loud*
schlank	*thin, slim*	**mollig**	*plump, chubby*
sportlich	*athletic*	**unsportlich**	*unathletic*
stark	*strong*	**schwach**	*weak*
sympathisch	*likable, friendly*	**unsympathisch**	*unpleasant, disagreeable*
tolerant	*tolerant*	**intolerant**	*intolerant*
zuverlässig	*reliable*	**unzuverlässig**	*unreliable*

The following example sentences contain adjectives that describe the appearance and personal traits of Paula and Philip, twins who couldn't be more opposite from each other:

> **Philip ist zuverlässig, aber Paula ist unzuverlässig.** (*Philip is reliable, but Paula is unreliable.*)

> **Paula ist klein, aber Philip ist groß.** (*Paula is short, but Philip is tall.*)

> **Paula ist attraktiv, aber Philip ist unattraktiv.** (*Paula is attractive, but Philip is unattractive.*)

> **Philip ist sympathisch, aber Paula ist unsympathisch.** (*Philip is likable, but Paula is disagreeable.*)

> **Philip ist stark, aber Paula ist schwach.** (*Philip is strong, but Paula is weak.*)

> **Paula ist unsportlich, aber Philip ist sportlich.** (*Paula is unathletic, but Philip is athletic.*)

Book III

Assembling the Grammatical Foundations for Communication

Describing the weather

No matter where you are, talking about **das Wetter** (*the weather*) is the perfect icebreaker. It also provides you with ammunition to make your friends jealous when you're writing them **Ansichtskarten** (*postcards*) while you're **im Urlaub** (*on vacation*). Look at the weather vocabulary in Table 5-2. Great news: Most of the adjectives have near opposites, so you can easily remember them in pairs.

Table 5-2		Adjectives of Weather	
German Adjective	*English Translation*	*German Opposite*	*English Opposite*
gut, schön	*good, nice*	**schlecht**	*bad*
sonnig	*sunny*	**wolkig/bewölkt**	*cloudy*
wunderschön	*delightful, lovely*	**furchtbar**	*awful*
warm	*warm*	**kühl**	*cool*
heiß	*hot*	**kalt**	*cold*
trocken	*dry*	**nass**	*wet*

More weather-related adjectives that don't have clear opposites include **frostig** (*chilly*), **schön warm** (*nice and warm*), **neb(e)lig** (*foggy*), **regnerisch** (*rainy*), **schwül** (*humid*), and **stürmisch** (*gusty, blustery*).

A family resemblance: Describing with cognates

Although German does have some incredibly foreign-sounding words, the number of cognates is surprisingly large. You can put them in several categories for easy access. Some example categories are based on the adjective's ending, as you can see in Table 5-3.

Table 5-3	Common Endings on German Adjectives	
German Ending	*Usual English Ending*	*German Examples*
-al	same	**diagonal, digital, emotional, formal, ideal, integral, interkontinental, international, irrational, kollegial, liberal, national, normal, optimal, original, sentimental, sozial, total, universal**

German Ending	Usual English Ending	German Examples
-ant or -ent	same	elegant, exzellent, intelligent, interessant, intolerant, kompetent, tolerant, uninteressant
-ell	-al	generell, individuell, informell, konventionell, kriminell, offiziell, partiell, rationell, sensationell, visuell
-isch	-ic or -ical	allergisch, alphabetisch, analytisch, charakteristisch, chemisch, dynamisch, egoistisch, elastisch, elektrisch, elektronisch, ethisch, exotisch, exzentrisch, fanatisch, fantastisch, klassisch, harmonisch, hygienisch, identisch, idiomatisch, idyllisch, ironisch, logisch, lyrisch, melodisch, militärisch, musikalisch, mythisch, patriotisch, philosophisch, politisch, praktisch, romantisch, sarkastisch, sporadisch, symmetrisch, systematisch, tropisch
-iv	-ive	aktiv, alternativ, exklusiv, explosiv, intensiv, interaktiv, kreativ, massiv, passiv
-lich or -ig	-y, -ly, or -ally	freundlich, frostig, hungrig, persönlich, sportlich, sonnig, unfreundlich, unpersönlich, unsportlich, windig

Some cognates — such as **bitter, blind, blond, fair, golden, human, illegal, legal, liberal, mild, modern, neutral, parallel, solid, uniform, warm,** and **wild** — have the same meaning and the same spelling, but you pronounce them according to German pronunciation. Others have a few spelling changes from English to German, such as

- ✔ *c* → **k: direkt, exakt, intakt, komplex, konstant, korrekt, nuklear**

- ✔ *c* → **k;** *ve* → **v: aktiv, effektiv, exklusiv, kreativ**

- ✔ *le* → **el: flexibel, kompatibel, miserabel, variabel**

- ✔ *d* → **t: hart, laut** (*loud*)

- ✔ *y* → **ig: frostig, hungrig, sonnig, windig**

Get in the habit of remembering cognates in groups. Repeat them out loud, alphabetically, and rhythmically. They'll stick with you and serve you well when you need them.

Book III

Assembling the Grammatical Foundations for Communication

Putting collocations and word partnerships into action

Acquiring word chunks is far more economical than studying isolated words. *Collocations* are word combos that are very predictable, some so predictable that they nearly always stick together. By some definitions, collocations include idioms and other fixed expressions. Collocations are made up of all kinds of word combinations: adjective + noun, noun + noun, adverb + adjective, and so on. In this section, we deal with adjective combos.

Some collocations translate well: **Starke Nerven** is the same as *strong nerves*. Other expressions aren't as close: **Das ist ein starkes Stück** in literal English means *that's a strong piece*. Yet in German, it's like saying *that's a bit too much*, as in *that's over the top*. Take a look at some other example collocations:

> **Unsere Produkte werden nur in umweltfreundlichen Verpackungen verkauft.** (*Our products are sold only in environmentally friendly packaging.*) The collocation is the combination of **umweltfreundlich(en)** + **Verpackung(en)** (*environmentally friendly* + *packaging*). Notice that the fixed combination *environmentally friendly* is an adverb + adjective in English; in German, it's a noun + adjective: **die Umwelt** (*the environment*) + **freundlich** (*friendly*).

> **Ich ärgere mich grün und blau.** (*I'm hopping mad.* Literally: *I'm annoyed green and blue.*) You can also describe this expression as an *idiom* (a group of words with a figurative meaning). Whatever the terminology, if you were to ask a German speaker to finish the sentence **ich ärgere mich . . . und . . .,** he wouldn't hesitate to add the right colors.

Use only German collocations or idioms you're sure about. Although you know a collocation in English, it may very well translate into German as nonsense. Take the German adjective **stark,** for example. Put the English collocation *stark raving mad* into German word for word, and you get gibberish. Why? The equivalent for this particular three-word chunk is the German collocation **total verrückt** (*totally crazy*). When you know that **stark** means *strong* in German, not *harsh* as in English, you're halfway on the road to using it correctly.

Read and listen actively to German. Make it your goal to recognize chunks of language, not just single words. Knowing a stack of collocations with adjectives offers you great opportunities for expressing yourself clearly and succinctly.

Look at the following German expressions using colors. Memorizing them as word combos rather than individual words can help you understand (and be understood) when you're conversing with a native German speaker.

Sie treffen ins Schwarze. (*They hit the bull's eye.*)

Sie sind blau. (*They're drunk.*)

Sie fahren schwarz. (*They're riding [the train] without a ticket.*)

Sie sind im Grünen. (*They're outdoors.*)

Sie werden rot. (*They're blushing.*)

Sie arbeiten schwarz. (*They're working illegally, not paying taxes.*)

Sie werden braun. (*They're getting tan.*)

Sie sind gelb vor Neid. (*They're green with envy.* Literally: *They're yellow with envy.*)

Sie machen blau. (*They're skipping work/school.*)

Helping Adjectives Meet a Satisfying End

Expanding your adjective arsenal is the first step to spicing up your German (see the preceding section); knowing how to form and use adjectives correctly in a sentence is the second step. This section helps you figure out whether the adjectives need endings and, if so, how to form those endings.

English uses adjectives as they come, straight up, no changes needed to plunk them into a combination with a noun. German is quite different. Before a German adjective can sidle up to a noun, it often needs an ending that reflects the gender and case of the noun it modifies. As in English, a German adjective usually comes right before the noun it describes: **meine schwarze Handschuhe** (*my black gloves*).

However, not all adjectives need special attention as far as ending changes are concerned. Adjectives that precede nouns are changed, but *post-position adjectives* — ones that follow later in a clause — are not. An adjective has no ending when it follows the verbs **sein** (*to be*), **werden** (*to become*), or **bleiben** (*to remain*) and modifies the subject. Consider these two examples:

Das Wetter bleibt warm. (*The weather remains warm.*)

Die Berge in Bayern sind wunderschön. (*The mountains in Bavaria are gorgeous.*)

Book III

Assembling the Grammatical Foundations for Communication

Work at recognizing the case and gender of nouns in the sentence and then adding the correct endings to their corresponding adjectives. In this section, you find out the difference between endings when an adjective stands alone in front of the noun — for example, **frisches Obst** (*fresh fruit*) — and when an adjective has a word such as **der, ein,** or **dieser** at the beginning of the phrase — for example, **das frische Obst** (*the fresh fruit*).

Forming endings on adjectives not preceded by der- or ein- words

When you describe something in general such as food prices, you simply say something like *fresh pineapples are expensive.* You don't need to add *the, those,* or *our.* It's the same in German, except you have to deal with the added factor of case endings for adjectives. In other words, when you say **frische Ananas sind teuer** (*fresh pineapples are expensive*), you need to know that the ending for **frisch** is **-e.** *Note:* In phrases that do have an article or modifier like *the, those,* or *our* (as in *those fresh pineapples*), the adjective endings are different. Check out the next section, "Adding endings for preceded adjectives," for details.

This section deals with endings for an adjective that modifies and precedes a noun but isn't preceded by an article (such as **der/die/das** or **ein/eine**) or other modifiers (**der-** words, such as **dieser** and **solcher,** and **ein-** words, such as **mein** and **kein**).

Here are the characteristics that define adjectives without **der-** or **ein-** words preceding them:

✔ Because no article or other modifier precedes the noun, the adjective must indicate gender and case of the noun; it has a double duty of adjective and article.

✔ These adjectives have mostly the same endings as **der-** words, with the exception of the masculine and neuter genitive, where the ending is **-en.**

To form these adjective endings, you need to know the gender, case, and number of the noun that the adjective modifies. For example, take the adjective **gut** (*good*). To say **guter Käse ist teuer** (*good cheese is expensive*), you need to know that **Käse** is masculine singular (**der Käse**) and that, in this sentence, it's in the nominative case (subject). Then you just add the nominative masculine ending **-er** onto **gut,** so you have **gut + -er = guter Käse.**

The four adjectives in Table 5-4 deal with food: **gut** (*good*), **schmackhaft** (*tasty*), **lecker** (*delicious, mouth-watering, scrumptious*), and **köstlich** (*delicious,* *luscious, exquisite*). The endings that agree in case, number, and gender with the noun they modify are in bold. For easy reference, the table also lists the adjective ending separately in bold with each example. Add these endings to adjectives that are not preceded by **der-** or **ein-** words.

Table 5-4   Adjective Endings Not Preceded by Der- or Ein- Words

Case	Masculine	Feminine	Neuter	Plural
Nominative (subject)	**-er** guter Käse (*good cheese*)	**-e** schmackhafte Wurst (*tasty sausage*)	**-es** leckeres Brot (*delicious bread*)	**-e** köstliche Kuchen (*delicious cakes*)
Accusative (direct object)	**-en** guten Käse	**-e** schmackhafte Wurst	**-es** leckeres Brot	**-e** köstliche Kuchen
Dative (indirect object)	**-em** gutem Käse	**-er** schmackhafter Wurst	**-em** leckerem Brot	**-en** köstlichen Kuchen
Genitive (possessive)	**-en** guten Käses	**-er** schmackhafter Wurst	**-en** leckeren Brotes	**-er** köstlicher Kuchen

Book III

Assembling the Grammatical Foundations for Communication

Check out some examples:

Leckeres Brot findet man überall in deutschen Bäckereien. (*You can find delicious bread everywhere in German bakeries.*) The adjective **lecker** + **-es** (*delicious*) describes the noun **(das) Brot** (*bread*); leckeres Brot is in the accusative case because it's the direct object. The singular, neuter accusative ending for unpreceded adjectives is **-es.**

Es gibt köstliche Kuchen in österreichischen Cafés. (*There are luscious cakes in Austrian cafés.*) The adjective **köstlich** + **-e** describes the noun **(der) Kuchen,** in plural form. **Köstliche Kuchen** is in the accusative case because it's the direct object. The plural accusative ending for unpreceded adjectives is **-e.**

Im Winter trinken wir gern heißen Tee. (*We like to drink hot tea in the winter.*) **Tee** is masculine. **Heißen Tee** is in accusative case; it's the direct object of the sentence. The masculine singular accusative ending for unpreceded adjectives is **-en.**

Adding endings for preceded adjectives

When you want to be specific about something, you use articles and modifiers like *the, those,* or *a* to say something like *the modern painting, those violent movies,* or *a fantastic restaurant.* In English, you simply add the adjective of your choice, and you're all set. Not so in German. Both the article/modifier and the adjective need to reflect the gender, number, and case of the noun they modify.

This section deals with endings for an adjective that modifies and precedes a noun that's preceded by an article (such as **der/die/das** or **ein/eine**) or other modifiers (**der-** words, such as **dieser** and **solcher,** and **ein-** words, such as **mein** and **kein**). (See Book III, Chapters 1 and 2 for information on articles and **der-** and **ein-** words.) *Preceded adjectives,* as they're called, appear in phrases with an article or other modifier, an adjective, and a noun.

Take the example **ein lockeres Hemd ist bequem** (*a loose shirt is comfortable*). **Hemd** is singular, neuter, and in the nominative case because it's the subject of the sentence, so the article **ein** and the adjective **lockeres** reflect the neuter gender, number, and case of **Hemd.** Check out Table 5-5 for a few more examples that show how the adjective ending reflects the gender of the noun when both the article and the adjective appear together preceding the noun.

Table 5-5	Preceded Adjective Endings			
Case	*Masculine*	*Feminine*	*Neuter*	*Plural*
Nominative (subject)	**der** lustig**e** Manne (*the funny man*) ein lustig**er** Mann (*a funny man*)	**die** glückliche Frau (*the happy woman*) eine glückliche Frau (*a happy woman*)	**das** brave Kind (*the well-behaved child*) ein braves Kind (*a well-behaved child*)	**die** braven Kinder (*the well-behaved children*) keine braven Kinder (*no well-behaved children*)
Accusative (direct object)	**den** lustig**en** Mann (*the funny man*) ein**en** lustig**en** Mann (*a funny man*)	**die** glückliche Frau (*the happy woman*) eine glückliche Frau (*a happy woman*)	**das** brave Kind (*the well-behaved child*) ein braves Kind (*a well-behaved child*)	**die** braven Kinder (*the well-behaved children*) keine braven Kinder (*no well-behaved children*)

Case	Masculine	Feminine	Neuter	Plural
Dative (indirect object)	**dem** lustig**en** Mann (*[to] the funny man*) **einem** lusti-g**en** Mann (*[to] a funny man*)	**der** glück-lich**en** Frau (*[to] the happy woman*) **einer** glücklich**en** Frau (*[to] a happy woman*)	**dem** brav**en** Kind (*[to] the well-behaved child*) **einem** brav**en** Kind (*[to] a well-behaved child*)	**den** brav**en** Kind**ern** (*[to] the well-behaved children*) **keinen** brav**en** Kind**ern** (*[to] no well-behaved children*)
Genitive (possessive)	**des** lustig**en** Mann**es** (*[of] the funny man*) **eines** lusti-g**en** Mann**es** (*[of] a funny man*)	**der** glück-lich**en** Frau (*[of] the happy woman*) **einer** glücklich**en** Frau (*[of] a happy woman*)	**des** brav**en** Kind**es** (*[of] the well-behaved child*) **eines** brav**en** Kind**es** (*[of] a well-behaved child*)	**der** brav**en** Kinder (*[of] the well-behaved children*) **keiner** brav**en** Kinder (*[of] no well-behaved children*)

Look at the following example sentences:

> **Letzte Woche habe ich ein neues Auto gekauft.** (*Last week I bought a new car.*) **Ein neues Auto** is the object of the sentence; it's in the accusative case. **Auto** is singular neuter, so the article **ein** and the adjective **neu** follow the gender, number, and case of the noun **Auto. Ein** needs no ending; the singular, neuter accusative ending for **neu** is **-es.**

> **Die hohen Berge sind schon schneebedeckt.** (*The high mountains are already snow-covered.*) **Die hohen Berge** is the subject of the sentence; it's in the nominative case and plural. **Die** and **hohen** reflect the nominative plural case. The nominative plural of **Berg** is **Berge.**

> **Salzburg hat eine herrliche Innenstadt.** (*Salzburg has a wonderful city center.*) **Eine herrliche Innenstadt** is the object of the sentence. **Innenstadt** is feminine singular; **eine** and **herrliche** both indicate the agreement with **Innenstadt** by tacking on the ending **-e.**

Using the right endings with possessive adjectives

Possessive adjectives are the words describing ownership, possession, or relationship, such as *my, your, his, her,* and so on. They're also referred to as *possessive pronouns*. (That's because technically speaking, a possessive adjective is a pronoun that's used as an adjective to show who "owns" the noun following it.) Identifying possessive adjectives is easy because they're grouped together with the **ein-** words (they have the same endings, even if they don't rhyme with **ein**). The **ein-** words include **ein, kein,** and all the possessive adjectives.

The singular possessive adjectives are **mein** (*my*), **dein** (*your*), **sein** (*his*), **ihr** (*her*), and **sein** (*its*). The plural possessive adjectives are **unser** (*our*), **euer** (*your*), **ihr** (*their*), and **Ihr** (*your* — formal, singular and plural).

Table 5-6 shows possessive adjective endings in all cases and genders; it follows the same pattern as **ein-** and **kein-** in Table 5-5. Note that the table shows **mein** and **unser** together; all other possessive adjectives use these same endings. The endings are shown separately in bold.

Table 5-6   Possessive Adjective Endings and First-Person Examples

Case	Masculine	Feminine	Neuter	Plural
Nominative (subject)	**-** mein, unser	**-e** mein**e**, unser**e**	**-** mein, unser	**-e** mein**e**, unser**e**
Accusative (direct object)	**-en** mein**en**, unser**en**	**-e** mein**e**, unser**e**	**-** mein, unser	**-e** mein**e**, unser**e**
Dative (indirect object)	**-em** mein**em**, unser**em**	**-er** mein**er**, unser**er**	**-em** mein**em**, unser**em**	**-en** mein**en**, unser**en**
Genitive (possessive)	**-es** mein**es**, unser**es**	**-er** mein**er**, unser**er**	**-es** mein**es**, unser**es**	**-er** mein**er**, unser**er**

The following example sentences show possessive adjectives with their endings:

> **Ich kann meine Schlüssel nicht finden.** (*I can't find my keys.*) **Meine** is plural accusative.

> **Deine Schlüssel liegen auf dem Tisch.** (*Your keys are on the table.*) **Deine Schlüssel** is plural nominative.

> **Und ist unser Gepäck schon fertig?** (*And is our luggage ready?*) **Unser Gepäck** is singular, neuter nominative.

Uli hat seinen Koffer noch nicht gepackt. (*No. Uli hasn't packed his suitcase yet.*) **Seinen Koffer** is singular, masculine accusative.

Na ja, unser Urlaub fängt schon mit vielen Problemen an. (*Oh well. Our vacation is already starting with a lot of problems.*) **Unser Urlaub** is singular, masculine nominative.

Understanding Types of Adverbs

Adverbs can modify verbs, adjectives, or other adverbs. (The verb **sein** [*to be*] is an exception: Adverbs can't modify the verb **sein**.) Some adverbs are exactly the same word as their adjective cousins, while others may resemble their cousins, except that they, like all adverbs, don't change form in a sentence. The fact that adverbs don't require different endings based on the words they modify makes life easier for you when you want to insert an adverb into a sentence. In this section, you get the lowdown on four main groups of adverbs: adverbs of time, adverbs of place, adverbs of manner and degree, and adverbs that indicate cause.

Describing time with adverbs

The adverbs that describe time (or express when an event or action takes place) include words like **gestern** (*yesterday*) and **jetzt** (*now*). Here are a few other frequently used adverbs of time:

- **bald** (*soon*)
- **bisher** (*up until now*)
- **damals** (*at that time*)
- **früher** (*before, formerly*)
- **gerade** (*just, currently*)
- **heute** (*today*)
- **heutzutage** (*nowadays*)
- **immer** (*always*)
- **jemals** (*ever*)
- **morgen** (*tomorrow*)
- **nachher** (*afterward*)
- **neuerdings** (*recently*)
- **nie/niemals** (*never*)
- **seitdem** (*since then*)
- **später** (*later*)
- **stets** (*always*)
- **übermorgen** (*the day after tomorrow*)
- **vorgestern** (*the day before yesterday*)
- **vorher** (*before/beforehand*)

Here are a few example sentences using these adverbs:

Heutzutage leben wenige Menschen auf dem Land. (*Nowadays, few people live in the countryside.*)

Das Flugzeug landet gerade. (*The plane is just landing.*)

Ich habe bisher keine neuen Informationen bekommen. (*I haven't received any new information up until now.*)

You can also express days of the week as well as a few other nouns that are related to time as adverbs. You simply add the letter **s** to the end of the noun. Here are some examples of such adverbs, which work as a reference to a habitual, recurring point in time:

- **sonntags, montags, dienstags, and so on.** (*Sundays, Mondays, Tuesdays, and so on*)
- **morgens** (*in the mornings*)
- **mittags** (*at noontime*)
- **nachmittags** (*in the afternoons*)
- **abends** (*in the evenings*)

The following sentences show how these adverbs express time:

Freitags kommt er meistens spät nach Hause. (*He usually gets home late on Fridays.*)

Ich arbeite ungern abends. (*I work reluctantly in the evenings.*)

Nachmittags spielen sie oft Golf. (*They often play golf in the afternoon[s].*)

Using adverbs to indicate place

An adverb of place indicates where the action expressed takes place. It's the type of adverb used to answer questions like **wo** (*where*), **wohin** (*where to*), and **woher** (*from where*). Some adverbs of this type, such as **hierhin** (*over here*) or **dort drüben** (*over there*), combine with other adverbs to form a one- or a two-word expression.

The following is a list of commonly used adverbs of place. Some appear together with adverbs of the opposite meaning to help you more easily remember them. These are separated by a forward slash (/). Synonyms (words that mean nearly the same) are separated by commas.

- **da/hier** (*there/here*)
- **dahin, dorthin/hierhin** (*over there/over here*)
- **draußen/drinnen** (*outside, outdoors/inside, indoors*)

- ✔ **drüben, da drüben, dort drüben** (*over there*)
- ✔ **geradeaus** (*straight ahead*)
- ✔ **links/rechts** (*left/right*)
- ✔ **nach links/nach rechts** (*to the left/to the right*)
- ✔ **nirgendwo/irgendwo** (*nowhere/somewhere*)
- ✔ **oben/unten** (*up/down*)
- ✔ **unterwegs** (*on the way/away [traveling]*)
- ✔ **vorn(e)/hinten** (*in front/behind*)
- ✔ **woanders** (*somewhere else*)

The following examples show how adverbs of place play out when they're in a sentence:

> **Der Geschäftsführer ist oft dienstlich unterwegs.** (*The director is often away on business.*)
>
> **Hier in diesem Raum befindet sich ein wunderschönes Gemälde.** (*There's a beautiful painting here in this room.*)
>
> **Zum Museum müssen Sie nach links gehen.** (*To get to the museum, you have to go left.*)

Looking at adverbs of manner and degree

Adverbs that show how or why a situation or an action occurs belong to one group described as adverbs of manner and degree. They answer such questions as **wie** (*how*) and **warum** (*why*). The following list contains common adverbs of manner and degree. Notice how some of these adverbs intensify the meaning of the sentence, while others describe how much or to what degree an action takes place.

- ✔ **allein** (*alone*)
- ✔ **bestimmt** (*certainly*)
- ✔ **etwa** (*approximately*)
- ✔ **eventuell** (*possibly, maybe*)
- ✔ **fast** (*almost*)
- ✔ **hoffentlich** (*hopefully*)
- ✔ **kaum** (*hardly*)
- ✔ **leider** (*unfortunately*)
- ✔ **natürlich** (*of course*)

- ✔ **nicht** (*not*)
- ✔ **sehr** (*very*)
- ✔ **unbedingt** (*absolutely*)
- ✔ **umsonst** (*for nothing*)
- ✔ **vielleicht** (*perhaps, maybe*)
- ✔ **wahrscheinlich** (*probably*)
- ✔ **wirklich** (*really, absolutely*)
- ✔ **zusammen** (*together*)

Book III

Assembling the Grammatical Foundations for Communication

The following sentences show how these adverbs work in a sentence:

Warten Sie, bitte. Ich bin fast fertig. (*Please wait. I'm almost ready.*)

Er konnte die Musik kaum hören. (*He could hardly hear the music.*)

Wir sind mit dem neun Bürgermeister sehr zufrieden. (*We're very pleased with the new mayor.*)

Der Film war wirklich lustig. (*The film was really funny.*)

Hoffentlich schneit es heute Abend. (*Hopefully it'll snow this evening.*)

Ich muss meine Schwester unbedingt anrufen. (*I absolutely have to call my sister.*)

In both English and German, you can use adverbs in this group alone in informal speech to add emphasis, as in this example dialogue:

Können Sie mir bitte helfen? (*Could you help me, please?*)

Aber, natürlich! (*But, of course!*)

Another type of adverb that belongs to this group is a cross between an adjective and an adverb. To put such adverbs into perspective, look at the following two example sentences with information on how the adjective/adverb in them differs:

Sie ist eine schnelle Läuferin. (*She's a fast runner.*) **Schnell** (*fast*) is an adjective here; it describes **Läuferin** (*runner*), which is a noun. The adjective precedes the noun, and it has to change spelling to fit with the noun in case and gender.

Sie läuft schnell. (*She runs fast.*) Technically speaking, when words like **schnell** follow a verb and describe the verb, they're adjectives that function as adverbs. They're classified as adverbs in the sense that they don't go through any of the changes to indicate agreement with case and gender that adjectives do. (For more information on the changes adjectives undergo, see the earlier section "Helping Adjectives Meet a Satisfying End.")

Eyeing adverbs that describe cause

Adverbs of cause indicate the purpose, reason, or consequence of a statement. They serve as a link between parts of a sentence. Here's a list of commonly used adverbs of cause:

- ✔ **also** (*so*)
- ✔ **darum** (*therefore, for that reason*)
- ✔ **deshalb** (*therefore*)
- ✔ **jedenfalls** (*anyway, in any case*)
- ✔ **nämlich** (*namely*)
- ✔ **somit** (*consequently, therefore*)
- ✔ **sonst** (*otherwise*)
- ✔ **trotzdem** (*nevertheless*)

Look at the following sentences to see how to use adverbs that describe cause:

> **Das Konzert war sehr schlecht, deshalb sind wir nach der Pause nach Hause gegangen.** (*The concert was very bad; therefore, we went home after the break.*)

> **Ich spreche ziemlich gut Deutsch, trotzdem möchte ich noch viel mehr lernen.** (*I speak fairly good German; nevertheless, I'd like to learn a lot more.*)

> **Ziehen Sie eine Winterjacke an, sonst wird es Ihnen kalt.** (*Put on a winter jacket; otherwise, you'll be cold.*)

Putting Adverbs and Adverbial Expressions in Their Proper Place

To put an adverb in a sentence, you have to keep in mind the following basic guidelines on word order, which are related to what type of adverb you're using, what the adverb is modifying, and how the adverb is being used in the sentence:

- ✔ Adverbs that provide more information about the verb in a main clause generally come after the conjugated verb: **Sie lachen oft über seine Witze.** (*They often laugh at his jokes.*) The adverb **oft** follows the verb **lachen.**

- ✔ When an adverb modifies another adverb, the two appear together, generally after the conjugated verb in a main clause, like this: **Sie schreibt sehr gut.** (*She writes very well.*) The adverb **sehr** (*very*) modifies the adverb **gut** (*well*). Note that **gut** can also be an adjective when it modifies a noun. However, when adjectives like **gut** follow a verb, they function as adverbs (For more on adjectives, check out the first half of this chapter.)

✔ When an adverb modifies an adjective, the adverb precedes the adjective, and they're generally placed after the conjugated verb in a main clause: **Es ist fast dunkel.** (*It's almost dark.*) The adverb **fast** precedes the adjective **dunkel.**

✔ Adverbs that refer to a noun follow the noun: **Der Hund dort drüben heißt Waldi.** (*The name of that dog over there is Waldi.*) **Dort drüben** is the adverb, and it follows the noun **der Hund.**

✔ Adverbs introduce subordinate clauses: **Fahren wir jetzt, sonst wird es zu spät.** (*Let's go now, otherwise it'll be too late.*) The adverb **sonst** begins the subordinate clause.

✔ The adverb can come before the verb when you want to stress the information it portrays: **Leider haben wir wenig Zeit.** (*Unfortunately, we have little time.*) The adverb **leider** (*unfortunately*) precedes the verb **haben** (*have*).

Word order in German sentences varies from English when the sentences include information about time, cause, manner, and place. In German, you put adverbial expressions in the following order:

1. **Expressions of time:** Answer the question **wann?** (*when?*)

2. **Expressions of cause:** Answer the question **warum?** (*why?*)

3. **Expressions of manner:** Answer the question **wie?** (*how?*)

4. **Expressions of place:** Answer the question **wo?** (*where?*)

Notice the word order in the following sentences, which contain two or more of these types of adverbial expressions:

Wir fahren heute Abend wegen des Wetters mit dem Auto zum Theater. (*We're going by car to the theater this evening because of the rain.*) The adverb of time, **heute Abend** (*this evening*), comes first, followed by the expressions of cause, manner, and place — **wegen des Wetters** (*because of the weather*), **mit dem Auto** (*by car*), and **zum Theater** (*to the theater*). As is the case with standard German word order, the subject is followed by the verb, which is in second position in the sentence.

Tanya und ich fahren heute mit dem Fahrrad an den See. (*Tanya and I are bicycling to the lake today.*) The adverb of time, **heute** (*today*), comes first, followed by the expressions of manner and place — **mit dem Fahrrad** (*by bicycle*) and **an den See** (*to the lake*). As is the case with standard German word order, the subject is followed by the verb, which is in second position in the sentence.

To add a little variety, you can rearrange the information in the preceding example as long as you adhere to the German word order of time, cause, manner, and place:

> **Heute fahren Tanya und ich mit dem Fahrrad an den See.** (*Tanya and I are bicycling to the lake today.*) The adverb of time, **heute,** is at the front of the sentence, the verb is in the second position, followed by the subject. The other adverbial elements are in the same order: **mit dem Fahrrad** comes before **an den See.**

The following sentences offer two more examples of how you can arrange information two different ways while still following the rules of word order:

> **Sie fliegen morgen mit der ersten Maschine nach Berlin.** (*They are flying to Berlin with the first plane this morning.*) The time expression **morgen** (*tomorrow*) comes before the expression of manner, **mit der Maschine** (*with the plane*), which answers the question *how.* **Nach Berlin** (*to Berlin*), the expression of place, is in last place in the sentence. As usual, the verb is in second position in the sentence.

> **Morgen fliegen Sie mit der ersten Maschine nach Berlin.** (*They are flying to Berlin with the first plane this morning.*) The first word, **morgen,** is the adverb of time. Next comes the verb, followed by the subject. The two elements of manner and place — **mit der ersten Maschine** and **nach Berlin** — are at the end of the sentence.

Comparing with Regular Adjectives and Adverbs: Fast, Faster, Fastest

You may be wondering why we mix adjectives and adverbs in the same section. Actually, we have some very good reasons. For one thing, both have the power to make comparisons. What's even better is that German adjectives and adverbs are one and the same word in many cases. Take, for instance, the adjective *good* and its adverbial counterpart *well.* The German equivalents are exactly the same for both adjective and adverb: **gut.** Best of all, using comparative and superlative forms of adjectives and adverbs offers great opportunities for making your language more precise, more useful, and more interesting.

In this section, you make comparisons by using the comparative and superlative forms of adjectives and adverbs — for example, **freundlich, freundlicher, am freundlichsten** (*friendly, friendlier, friendliest*). *Comparative* means that you compare two objects, people, activities, ideas, and so on (for example, *longer* is the comparative form of *long*); *superlative* means that you compare three or more objects, people, activities, ideas, and so on (*longest* is the superlative form).

Fortunately, many adjectives and adverbs follow a regular pattern for making words of comparison, and that pattern isn't too difficult to remember when you see the similarities to English. The endings that vary from the most frequent pattern mostly have to do with facilitating pronunciation. The guidelines that follow show how to add **-er** and **-(e)st** endings as well as the endings for adjectives that come before nouns. (See the earlier section "Helping Adjectives Meet a Satisfying End" for details on adjective agreement.)

Comparing two things

For both adjectives and adverbs, when you want to compare two things, people, and so on, take the base form (the adjective or adverb as you see it in the dictionary) and form the comparative by adding **-er** to the base form; for instance, **witzig** → **witziger** (*witty* → *wittier*). To express *than* in a comparison, use the German equivalent **als.** Consider these examples:

Mein Onkel Richard ist nett, aber meine Tante Christel ist netter als Onkel Richard. (*My Uncle Richard is nice, but my Aunt Christel is nicer than Uncle Richard.*) The adjective **nett** is the base form; **netter als** (*nicer than*) is the comparative form.

Onkel Richard fährt schnell, aber Tante Christel fährt schneller er. (*Uncle Richard drives fast, but Aunt Christel drives faster than he [does].*) The adverb **schnell** is the base form; **schneller als** (*faster than*) is the comparative form. *Note:* **Schnell** is both an adjective and an adverb, just as *fast* is in English.

Adjectives ending in **-el** and **-er** leave the last **-e** off the base form and then add **-er** to make the comparative: **dunkel** → **dunkler** (*dark* → *darker*) and **teuer** → **teurer** (*expensive* → *more expensive*).

When using a comparative adjective that precedes the noun, you follow the same guidelines as with other adjectives that precede the noun (see the earlier section "Helping Adjectives Meet a Satisfying End" for details). Look at the following examples, which show three different scenarios for preceded adjective endings:

Du hast ein neueres Auto als ich. (*You have a newer car than I do.*) The direct object, **ein neueres Auto,** is in accusative case, and it's singular. The indefinite article **ein** (*a*) has no ending in accusative singular case: It's neuter to reflect the neuter noun **(das) Auto.** The base form of the adjective **neu** (*new*) has the comparative ending **-er** + the neuter, singular ending **-es** to form **neueres (neu + -er + -es).**

Ich habe den kleineren Wagen. (*I have the smaller car.*) The direct object, **den kleineren Wagen,** is in accusative case, and it's singular. The definite article **den** (*the*) has the accusative masculine ending: It's masculine to reflect the masculine noun **(der) Wagen.** The base form of the adjective **klein** (*small*) has the comparative ending **-er** + the singular, masculine accusative ending **-en** to form **kleineren (klein + -er + -en).**

Köstlicheres Brot ist kaum zu finden. (*It's hard to find more delicious bread.*) The subject of the sentence, **köstlicheres Brot,** is in nominative case, and it's singular. The base form of the adjective **köstlich** (*delicious*) has the comparative ending **-er** + the neuter singular ending **-es** to reflect the neuter noun **(das) Brot.** The comparative **köstlicheres** is formed like this: **köstlich + -er + -es = köstlicheres.**

German doesn't use **mehr** (*more*) together with the **-er** ending. In English, the comparative adjective form can look like this: *more intelligent* or *more interesting.* German uses only the **-er** ending: **intelligenter** or **interessanter.**

Absolutely the most! Discussing superlatives

The superlative form for adverbs as well as for adjectives that follow a noun in a sentence is **am** + adjective/adverb + **-sten:**

Dieser Supermarkt ist am billigsten. (*This supermarket is the cheapest/ most inexpensive.*) **Billig** is the base form of the adjective, and **am billigsten** is the superlative.

Gisela läuft am schnellsten. (*Gisela runs the fastest.*) **Schnell** is the base form of the adverb; **am schnellsten** is the superlative form.

A superlative adjective often precedes the noun it modifies, which means it needs to reflect the noun's gender, number, and case. You get the superlative form of such adjectives by adding **-st** to the base form and then adding the appropriate adjective ending (see the previous section in this chapter on adjective endings): **höflich → höflichst-** + adjective ending (*polite → most polite*).

Manuela ist die höflichste Kollegin im Büro. (*Manuela is the most polite colleague in the office.*) **Höflich** is the base form of the adjective; **die höflichst-** + **-e (Kollegin)** is feminine, singular, nominative case.

Onkel Kalle hat das schönste Haus. (*Uncle Kalle has the nicest house.*) **Schön** is the base form of the adjective; **das schönst-** + **-e (Haus)** is the superlative form that reflects the neuter, singular accusative noun **das Haus.** *Note:* Here's the alternative form, which uses an adjective that follows the noun: **Sein Haus ist am schönsten.** (*His house is the nicest.*)

Book III

Assembling the Grammatical Foundations for Communication

You make the superlative form for adjectives ending in **-t** or **-z** (and a few others) by adding **-e** + **-st** = **-est** for ease of pronunciation, as in **elegantest-** (*most elegant*). For example, **Du findest die elegantesten Schuhe bei Salamander.** (*You find the most elegant shoes at Salamander [a well-known shoe store].*) **Elegant** is the base form of the adjective; **die elegant-** + **est-** + **-en** is the superlative form that reflects the accusative plural noun **Schuhe.**

Considering common comparisons

Table 5-7 lists some adjectives and adverbs that are frequently used to compare people and things. The fourth column shows any differences in spelling, as in **nett** → **netter** → **am nettesten,** where you add the **-e** in front of **-st.** The superlative form for all words is shown at first as **am + (e)sten.** You use this form when the adjective follows the noun and for adverbs. The form shown in parentheses is the form that you use when a superlative adjective precedes the noun. You add the adjective endings to that form.

Table 5-7		Regular Comparison Forms		
English	*Base*	*Comparative*	*Superlative*	*Spelling Changes*
modest	**bescheiden**	**bescheidener**	**am bescheidensten** (**bescheidenst-**)	
cheap, inexpensive	**billig**	**billiger**	**am billigsten** (**billigst-**)	
dark	**dunkel**	**dunkler**	**am dunkelsten** (**dunkelst-**)	drop the last **-e** in the comparative
elegant	**elegant**	**eleganter**	**am elegantesten** (**elegantest-**)	add **-e** + **st** in the superlative
fit, in shape	**fit**	**fitter**	**am fittesten** (**fittest-**)	double the **t**; add **-e** + **st** in the superlative
hard working, industrious	**fleißig**	**fleißiger**	**am fleißigsten** (**fleißigst-**)	
flexible	**flexibel**	**flexibler**	**am flexibelsten** (**flexibelst-**)	drop the last **-e** in the comparative

English	Base	Comparative	Superlative	Spelling Changes
friendly	freundlich	freundlicher	am freundlichsten (freundlichst-)	
generous	großzügig	großzügiger	am großzügigsten (großzügigst-)	
ugly	hässlich	hässlicher	am hässlichsten (hässlichst-)	
polite	höflich	höflicher	am höflichsten (höflichst-)	
pretty	hübsch	hübscher	am hübschesten (hübschest-)	add -e + st in the superlative
intelligent	intelligent	intelligenter	am intelligentesten (intellegentest-)	add -e + st in the superlative
musical	musikalisch	musikalischer	am musikalischsten (musikalischst-)	
brave	mutig	mutiger	am mutigsten (mutigst-)	
nice	nett	netter	am nettesten (nettest-)	add -e + st in the superlative
neat	ordentlich	ordentlicher	am ordentlichsten (ordentlichst-)	
chic, stylish	schick	schicker	am schicksten (schickst-)	
pretty, beautiful	schön	schöner	am schönsten (schönst-)	
athletic	sportlich	sportlicher	am sportlichsten (sportlichst-)	
expensive	teuer	teurer	am teuersten (teuerst-)	drop the last -e in the comparative
sensible	vernünftig	vernünftiger	am vernünftigsten (vernünftigst-)	
witty	witzig	witziger	am witzigsten (witzigst-)	

Book III

Assembling the Grammatical Foundations for Communication

When making a sentence, remember to add the appropriate endings to adjectives of comparison when needed. Adjectives following a noun don't need to reflect the gender, number, and case of the noun, but adjectives that precede the noun do need agreement.

The following example sentences use the comparative or superlative form of the adjective:

> **Mein Bruder ist witziger als ich.** (*My brother is wittier than I.*)
>
> **Wir waren vorher mutiger als jetzt.** (*We were braver then than now.*)
>
> **Siegbert machte den nettesten Eindruck.** (*Siegbert made the nicest impression.*)
>
> **Ich bin fitter als du.** (*I'm in better shape than you.*)
>
> **Am glücklichsten bin ich mit meiner Familie.** (*I'm happiest [when I'm] with my family.*)
>
> **Wiebke hat jetzt dunkleres Haar als früher.** (*Wiebke now has darker hair than before.*)

Adding the umlaut in regular comparisons

German wouldn't be the same without its three interesting-looking letters that have umlauts (not to mention that cool **ess-tset,** the letter **ß**). When forming the comparative and superlative forms of some adjectives and adverbs, be careful to add the umlaut when you need it.

The general guideline for adding umlauts in comparisons is simple to remember: Many adjectives and adverbs with one syllable and with an **-a, -o,** or **-u** in the base form add an umlaut in the comparative and superlative forms: **alt →
älter → ältest-** (*old → older → oldest*).

Of course, there are some exceptions: Some common one-syllable words with an **-a, -o,** or **-u** in the base form don't have an umlaut: **blond** (*blond[e]*), **bunt** (*colorful*), **falsch** (*wrong*), **froh** (*glad*), **klar** (*clear*), **toll** (*amazing, great*), **wahr** (*true*), and **laut** (*loud, noisy*). *Note:* **Laut** has **-au** in the base form, unlike the others in this list. We include it here because it doesn't add an umlaut in the comparative and superlative forms.

Here are a couple of examples:

Herr Diefenbacher ist alt, aber Frau Kolbe ist noch älter. (*Herr Diefenbacher is old, but Frau Kolbe is even older.*) The adjective **alt** (base form) changes to **älter,** with an umlaut in the comparative form.

Die ärmsten Länder brauchen sehr viel Unterstützung. (*The poorest countries need a lot of aid.*) The adjective **ärmsten** is the superlative form; **die ärmsten Länder** is the subject (nominative case), and it's plural. **Ärmsten** precedes the noun, so it needs the adjective ending to reflect **Länder.** You form it like this: **arm-** (base form) changes to **ärm-** (add the umlaut) + **-est** (superlative ending) + **en** (nominative plural ending).

Table 5-8 shows some common adjectives and adverbs together with the German base and the comparative and superlative forms that use an umlaut.

Table 5-8	Comparison Forms with Umlauts		
English Equivalent	*Base*	*Comparative*	*Superlative*
old	**alt**	**älter**	**am ältesten**
poor	**arm**	**ärmer**	**am ärmsten**
stupid	**dumm**	**dümmer**	**am dümmsten**
crude, coarse	**grob**	**gröber**	**am gröbsten**
large, big, tall	**groß**	**größer**	**am größten**
hard, tough	**hart**	**härter**	**am härtesten**
young	**jung**	**jünger**	**am jüngsten**
cold	**kalt**	**kälter**	**am kältesten**

Using Irregular Comparison Forms

German has some wayward characters among its adjectives and adverbs, but luckily, a few of these irregular types have parallels to English odd ducks. The classic example is **gut → besser → am besten,** which is easily recognizable in English as *good → better → best*. These irregular words are very common, and there are only a few of them, so getting them into your active vocabulary should be a snap. All you need to do is memorize the list of frequently used irregular comparison forms shown in Table 5-9.

Table 5-9	Irregular Comparison Forms		
English Equivalent	*Base*	*Comparative*	*Superlative*
soon, sooner, soonest	**bald**	**eher**	**am ehesten**
like/enjoy (doing something), prefer, like most of all	**gern**	**lieber**	**am liebsten**
good, better, best	**gut**	**besser**	**am besten**
high, higher, highest	**hoch**	**höher**	**am höchsten**
near, nearer, nearest	**nah**	**näher**	**am nächsten**
much, more, most	**viel**	**mehr**	**am meisten**

The use of **gern** (the base form of the word meaning *to like, to enjoy [doing something]*) is easiest to remember in the context of some common expressions:

✔ **Ich spiele gern Klavier./Ich tanze gern./Ich esse gern Fisch.** (*I like to play the piano./I like to dance./I like to eat fish.*) You use this construction to express that you like an activity, sport, game, food, and so on. Also: **Ich spiele lieber Tennis./Ich trinke am liebsten Wasser.** (*I prefer playing tennis./I like drinking water most of all.*) The base forms of these sentences are **Ich spiele gern Tennis** and **Ich trinke gern Wasser** (*I like to play tennis* and *I like to drink water*).

✔ **Ich möchte gern wissen, ob . . .** (*I wonder if . . .*)

✔ **Was möchtest du lieber . . . ?** (*Which would you rather . . . ?*)

✔ **Am liebsten möchte ich . . .** (*Most of all, I'd like to . . .*) Use this expression to talk about an activity/food/place that you like or would like to do/eat/go to/and so on.

Comparing Equals and Nonequals

When you were a kid, you probably boasted about yourself, saying you were better than the rest. Now that you've grown up, you have to consider a few more factors in your comparisons with others, and you may want to sound more diplomatic. Using the expressions in this section, you can sound smooth enough (and diplomatic enough) to impress almost anyone.

Table 5-10 lists some commonly used expressions that describe equality or inequality between things, people, or ideas. The example sentences show how these expressions fit into sentences. Notice the word order of the information in each example sentence; with the exception of **je . . . desto** (*the . . .*

-er, the . . . -er), you use the same word order in German and English to make comparisons using these expressions. The adjective or adverb that you're using as a comparison is in the middle of the two parts of the expression. For example, if you use the adverb **schnell** (*fast*) to say *just as fast as* . . . , you say **genauso schnell wie . . .** in German.

Table 5-10	Comparison Forms of Equals/Nonequals		
Comparison of Equals/Nonequals	*English Equivalent*	*Example Sentence*	*English Translation*
genauso . . . wie . . .	*just as . . . as . . .*	Mein Auto fährt **genauso** schnell **wie** sein Motorrad.	*My car goes just as fast as his motorcycle.*
halb so . . . wie . . .	*half as . . . as . . .*	Das Ergebnis war nur **halb so** schlimm **wie** wir erwarteten.	*The result was only half as bad as we expected.*
nicht so . . . wie . . .	*not as . . . as . . .*	Ich bin **nicht so** stark **wie** ich dachte.	*I'm not as strong as I thought.*
so . . . wie . . .	*as . . . as . . .*	Unsere Produkte sind **so** zuverlässig **wie** importierte Produkte.	*Our products are as reliable as imported products.*
je . . . , desto . . . (comparative words follow **je . . . , desto . . .**)	*the . . . -er, the . . . -er* (adjectives or adverbs in comparative form)	**Je mehr** Sie lesen, **desto besser** informiert werden Sie. (***Note:*** The word order is different in English.)	*The more you read, the better informed you'll be.*

Look at these example sentences, along with a few notes on word order:

> **Ein neuer BMW kostet so viel wie ein neuer Mercedes.** (*A new BMW costs as much as a new Mercedes.*) Note that you can also say this in reverse order: **Ein neuer Mercedes kostet so viel wie ein neuer BMW.** (*A new Mercedes costs as much as a new BMW.*)

> **Ein Baseballspieler läuft halb so viel wie ein Fußballspieler.** (*A baseball player runs half as much as a soccer player.*)

> **Je mehr er Poker spielt, desto reicher wird er.** (*The more he plays poker, the richer he becomes.*) This one has a tricky word order.

Die neuen Autos benutzen nicht so viel Benzin wie die alten Modelle. (*The new cars don't use as much gas as the old models.*) You can also say this one in reverse order.

Schwarz-Weiß-Filme sind genauso spannend wie Farbfilme. (*Black-and-white movies are just as exciting as movies in Technicolor.*) This one works in the reverse order, too.

Je qualifizierter man ist, desto mehr verdient man. (*The more qualified one is, the more one earns.*) This statement has tricky word order and doesn't make sense in reverse.

Das Wetter in Deutschland ist so schön wie das Wetter in Neuengland. (*The weather in Germany is as nice as the weather in New England.*) This one also works in reverse.

Identifying Unique Adjective and Adverb Groups

The structure and usage of some adjectives and adverbs is unique. These types include adjectives used as nouns, participles used as adjectives or adverbs, and adverbs that modify adjectives. Most are fairly easy to remember because they have parallel meanings and structures in English.

You need to know these three groups because they're high-frequency words and expressions that you come across in everyday language, and they help you express yourself more clearly. This section takes a closer look at the following three unique groups and explains how to use them in sentences:

- **Adjectives used as nouns:** Naturally, these adjectives stand in for the noun. In other words, they omit the noun — for example, **das Richtige** (*the right thing/decision/choice*).

- **Participles that function as adjectives or adverbs:** An example is **am motiviertesten** (*the most motivated*). The present participle of **motivieren** (*to motivate*) is **motivierend** (*motivating*), and the past participle is **motiviert** (*motivated*).

- **Adverbs that modify adjectives:** The combination of adverb + adjective here serves to make the adjective more descriptive; for example, in the expression **wirklich interessant,** you use the word **wirklich** (*really, absolutely*) to modify **interessant** (*interesting*).

Adjectives that act as nouns

Sometimes adjectives replace a noun to represent an abstract idea, a person, an object, and so on. The noun that the adjective replaces may be singular or plural, and it may be the subject or the object of a sentence; in short, the adjective functions just as the noun does. The same structure exists in English and German for adjectives that take over as nouns; for example, *the poor, the brave, the lonely one, the new ones*. The only difference is that in German, nouns are capitalized and the spelling reflects gender, number, and case. In addition, German doesn't have an equivalent for *one/ones*, so the German adjective stands alone to represent the noun.

To understand how such adjectives work, imagine you're discussing with your friend which cat you want to take home from the animal shelter. You talk about **die Große, die Braune,** and **die Ruhige** (*the little one, the brown one, the quiet one*). You're replacing the word **Katze** (*cat*) by describing a characteristic of each cat and using that adjective to represent that cat. You use the feminine article **die** because **Katze** is a feminine noun. If you're talking about taking home a dog, **der Hund,** instead, you refer to each one as **der Große, der Braune,** and **der Ruhige.** When you make your decision, you may say something like **Ich nehme den Braunen.** (*I'll take the brown one [dog].*) The adjective has the accusative masculine singular case ending **-en** to reflect the noun it's replacing.

Look at these example sentences:

> **Ich wünsche euch das Beste.** (*I wish you the best.*) **Das Beste** is a noun.

> **Kennst du die Kleine da drüben?** (*Do you know the small [woman] over there?*) The article **die** combines with **Kleine** to stand in for the noun *woman* (**die Frau**).

Note: **Die Kleine** doesn't necessarily have to refer to a small woman. However, if it's used to refer to a woman, it's colloquial, a bit like saying *that babe*.

Participles that function as adjectives or adverbs

In German, as in English, present and past participles can function as adjectives or adverbs. If the adjectives precede a noun, they agree in gender, number, and case with the noun they modify. In English, a *present participle* is the infinitive (for instance, *fly, tumble,* or *seethe*) with the ending *-ing*. When you use it as an adjective, you combine it with the noun you want to modify; for example, *the flying squirrels, the tumbling acrobats,* or *the seething volcano*.

To create the present participle in German, start with a verb, such as **laufen** (*to run*). Then drop the infinitive ending **-en** and add **-end** to the infinitive form (**lauf- + -end = laufend**). The present participle of **laufen** is **laufend** (the closest thing to the English word *running*). Look at this example:

> **Er erzählte Witze am laufenden Band.** (*He told an endless stream of jokes.* Literally: *He told jokes on a running band/belt.*)

A *past participle* of a regular verb in English is the infinitive of a verb with *-ed* or *-d* added. For an irregular verb, it's the form such as *eaten, hidden,* or *seen* that you use to form the present perfect tense and other compound verb tenses. (An example of the present perfect tense is *Scruffy has already eaten,* where you combine the past participle *eaten* with the auxiliary verb *have.*) You can also use the past participle as a descriptive word; for example, *the drenched cat, sunken treasure,* or *forbidden fruit.*

In German, verbs form past participles differently, depending on the verb type (see Book IV, Chapter 4); for instance, the past participle of **pflegen** is **gepflegt** (*groomed, taken care of*). The phrases **gepflegtes Essen** (*first-rate food*) and **gepflegte Weine** (*quality wines*) are typical descriptions that restaurants use to impress their clientele. Literally speaking, these expressions mean *groomed food/wines* in the sense that the restaurant has a carefully selected menu or wine list.

Some German verbs, namely the verbs ending in **-ieren,** are cognates — in other words, they have the same meanings in English — making them easily recognizable. The past participle form of these verbs is formed with **-iert** at the end; the ending is the same, regardless of whether you're using the past participle as an adjective or adverb.

Many of these common adjectives have comparative and superlative forms: Some common adjectives with this structure are **dekoriert** (*decorated*), **diszipliniert** (*disciplined*), **fasziniert** (*fascinated*), **frustriert** (*dissastisfied, frustrated*), **interessiert** (*interested*), **motiviert** (*motivated*), **organisiert** (*organized*), and **talentiert** (*talented*). They can all form comparative and superlative adjectives (and possibly adverbs):

> **Der Gefreite Schwarz war der disziplinierteste Soldat in seiner Kompanie.** (*Private Schwarz was the most disciplined soldier in his company.*) **Diszipliniertest-** is a superlative adjective.

> **In der Schule war ich motivierter als meine Schwester.** (*I was more motivated than my sister when I was in school.*) **Motivierter** is a comparative adjective.

> **Wir schauten die Olympische Spiele fasziniert zu.** (*We watched the Olympic Games with fascination.*) **Fasziniert** is an adverb describing how we watched.

Some frequently used adjectives derived from past participles don't have comparative forms. Among the more common are **ausprobiert** (*tested*), **diskutiert** (*discussed*), **fotografiert** (*photographed*), and **probiert** (*tried/ tested*). See the earlier section "Comparing with Regular Adjectives and Adverbs: Fast, Faster, Fastest" for more on comparatives.

Adverbs that modify adjectives

Adverbs often modify verbs, but they can also modify adjectives. For instance, to express that something or someone is *quite good, especially interesting,* or *really motivated,* you use adverbs to modify the adjective. The adverbs frequently used with adjectives in German are **besonders** (*especially*), **etwas** (*somewhat*), **relativ** (*relatively*), **sehr** (*very*), **viel** (*much, a lot*), **wirklich** (*absolutely, really*), and **ziemlich** (*quite*). The good news here is that they don't have any changes in the endings.

To use an adverb to modify an adjective, just place the adverb in front of the adjective it's modifying, and voilà! To see how this works, imagine you're talking about the hotels you stayed at on your last trip to Europe. One hotel was especially luxurious. To express this in German, you place the adverb **wirklich** (*really*) in front of **luxuriös** (*luxurious*), and if the adjective precedes the noun that it modifies, add the appropriate adjective ending; for example, **Wir haben zwei Nächte in einem wirklich luxuriösen Hotel übernachtet.** (*We spent two nights in a really luxurious hotel.*) Here are two more examples:

> **Der Sommer war etwas wärmer als in vergangenen Jahren.** (*The summer was somewhat warmer than in previous years.*) The adverb **etwas** modifies the adjective **wärmer,** which is in the comparative form. The adjective **wärmer** needs no ending because it doesn't precede the noun that it modifies, **der Sommer.**

> **Letztes Jahr hatten wir einen ziemlich langen Winter.** (*Last year we had quite a long winter.*) The adverb **ziemlich** modifies the adjective **lang: einen ziemlich langen.** *Winter* is the direct object of the sentence, so the other modifiers — **einen** and **langen** — have masculine, singular, accusative endings to reflect **(der) Winter.**

Book III

Assembling the Grammatical Foundations for Communication

Chapter 6

Modifying Verbs with Helpers: The Modal Auxiliaries

I hope you're in a good mood as you start this chapter about modal auxiliary verbs. I'm talking about attitude with a capital *A* in the next few pages. In grammar mumbo jumbo, *modals* are auxiliary (helping) verbs that indicate an attitude about the main verb, even though they don't directly alter the main verb's action.

This motley band of modal verbs helps set the mood of the sentence. They can, at times, be quite influential in their mood-altering abilities — and all without illegal substances. *Mood* is grammarspeak for how something is expressed in a sentence: The mood of a verb indicates a wide range of, yes, moods such as probability, impossibility, certainty, doubt, or even just plain old facts, without all the **Schnickschnack** (*bells and whistles*).

If you're asking yourself whether you can get by without using modals, the answer is plain and simple: No way, José — not unless you're willing to put up with being misunderstood in daily situations in which the modals should make your intended thought clear to the listener. In this chapter, you find out what the seven modal verbs are, together with their equivalents in English, and you discover the importance of modal verbs in everyday situations. You get the present-tense conjugation of these verbs and the particulars on important characteristics of these verbs.

Grasping the Basics of Modal Verbs

Modal verbs modify the main verb in the sentence. Here's how they work: You take a plain old verb or phrase like *eat, sleep, walk, plant a garden, play tennis, learn how to play chess,* or *do nothing.* Then you think about your attitude toward these activities, and you decide you want to say <u>*I like to*</u> *eat, I* <u>*must*</u> *sleep more, I* <u>*would like to*</u> *walk every day, I* <u>*should*</u> *plant a garden, I* <u>*can*</u> *play tennis well, I* <u>*want to*</u> *learn how to play chess,* or *I* <u>*may*</u> *do nothing.* The underlined modal verbs offer you a wide range of ways to express your attitude toward actions such as *eat, sleep, play,* and *learn.*

You find modals working their magic in sentences in the *indicative mood.* This type of mood is for stating facts. Modal verbs also crop up in sentences expressed in the *subjunctive mood.* That's what you use when you want to sound polite when requesting or suggesting something or when you want to make hypothetical statements. (Chapter 7 of Book IV is where you find out about the subjunctive.) This section gives you a quick overview of what modal verbs are and how they work. The rest of this chapter focuses on the seven specific modal verbs.

Identifying modals: Assistants with attitude

Modals are your ticket to conveying your attitude or how you feel about an action. They usually accompany another verb and appear in the second position of a sentence. The main verb they assist generally appears at the end of the clause.

Table 6-1 shows the German modal verbs in infinitive form and the English translation, followed by a statement using the modal verb. Look at the various ways of modifying the statement **Ich lerne Deutsch** (*I learn German*) with the modal verbs. Notice that the modal verb is in second position in the sentence, and the main verb gets booted to the end.

Table 6-1	German Modal Verbs		
German Modal Verb	**Translation**	**Example**	**English Equivalent**
dürfen	*may, to be allowed to*	Ich **darf** Deutsch lernen.	*I may/am allowed to learn German.*
können	*can, to be able to*	Ich **kann** Deutsch lernen.	*I can/am able to learn German.*

German Modal Verb	Translation	Example	English Equivalent
mögen	*to like to*	Ich **mag** Deutsch lernen.	*I like to learn German.*
möchten	*would like to*	Ich **möchte** Deutsch lernen.	*I would like to learn German.*
müssen	*must, to have to*	Ich **muss** Deutsch lernen.	*I must/have to learn German.*
sollen	*should, to be supposed to*	Ich **soll** Deutsch lernen.	*I am supposed to/should learn German.*
wollen	*to want to*	Ich **will** Deutsch lernen.	*I want to learn German.*

These verbs all have regular verb endings in their plural forms (**wir, ihr, sie,** and **Sie**). Most of them also have irregular verb changes, some of which you can see in the examples in Table 6-1. As you go through **Die Glorreichen Sieben** (*The Magnificent Seven* — modal verbs, that is) in this chapter, you see the irregular verb endings of these verbs in the present tense.

In English, you typically have two verbs in a sentence that has a modal verb; the second one is the *main verb.* In German, however, the modal verb may be the only verb. The one true rogue is the verb **mögen,** which frequently stands alone, and to a lesser extent, its cousin **möchten.** (Check out the sections "I Like That: **Mögen,** the Likeable Verb" and "What Would You Like? **Möchten,** the Preference Verb" for more information on these two.)

Book III

Assembling the Grammatical Foundations for Communication

Understanding word order and modals

In terms of word order for modals, German uses pretty much the same order as for other verbs that require an auxiliary verb to complete the meaning of the main verb. The present perfect and the future tenses also use a secondary, auxiliary verb to complete the main verb's meaning. With these verb types (and tenses), you conjugate the auxiliary verb, put it in second position in the sentence, and generally put the main verb at the end of the clause or phrase. (See Chapter 4 of Book IV for present perfect verbs and Chapter 6 of Book IV for future tense verbs and their word order.)

Look at the examples in Table 6-1. The conjugated, active verb is in second position in the sentence. It directly follows the subject or other elements, such as a reference to time or a prepositional phrase. When you need more than one verb, the others go to the very end of the sentence.

Questions follow a slightly different word order (inverted word order) if they're the type of question that can be answered with *yes, no,* or *maybe.* See Chapter 4 of Book III for info on forming questions.

May I? Dürfen, the Permission Verb

Some people feel rules and customs crimp their personal style, but such guidelines give people an idea of what they can expect from each other. The rules of the road allow you to do something (or not) — you may proceed with caution at a yield sign, but you're not allowed to cross the double yellow line. And being polite by asking permission — *May I use your bathroom? May I have another cookie?* — is certainly not limited to young boys and girls. Adults in all parts of the world know that asking for and granting permission is part of the code of polite interaction.

Forming dürfen

You use the modal verb **dürfen** to ask for and grant permission. Look at the conjugation of **dürfen.** It's irregular in the singular forms: **ich, du,** and **er/sie/es.** In the table, the irregular forms are bold, and the regular forms show the endings in bold.

dürfen *(may, to be allowed to, to be permitted to)*	
ich **darf**	wir dürf**en**
du **darfst**	ihr dürf**t**
er/sie/es **darf**	sie dürf**en**
Sie dürf**en**	
Sie **dürfen** dort nicht parken. (*You're not allowed to park there.*)	

Using dürfen

German uses **dürfen** in a wide variety of everyday situations. Table 6-2 lists four common idiomatic expressions with **dürfen,** followed by an example sentence in German and the English equivalent. You frequently hear these expressions in polite exchanges between people who don't know each other well.

Table 6-2	Uses of Dürfen in Polite Conversation	
Situation	*Example*	*English Equivalent*
to ask whether a customer needs assistance	Was **darf** es sein?	*May I help you?*
to signal someone to do a favor such as opening the door	**Darf** ich Sie bitten?	*May I trouble you?*
to say that you'd like to introduce two people to each other	**Darf** ich Ihnen Frau Feuerstein vorstellen?	*May I introduce you to Mrs. Feuerstein?*
to explain that something is not allowed	Das Obst **dürfen** Sie nicht anfassen.	*You may not/must not touch the fruit.*

Generally speaking, German and English use **dürfen** (*may, to be allowed to, to be permitted to*) in very similar ways: to ask for permission, to grant permission, and to state that something is (or is not) permitted or allowed.

German sometimes uses the impersonal form **man** (*it, one, you*) with **dürfen,** as in the following example sentence: **Man darf hier nicht parken.** For the equivalent in English, you use the passive construction (*parking/passing/ stopping isn't allowed here*), or you simply say *no parking/passing/stopping (allowed here)*.

English uses *may* to express possibility, whereas **dürfen** doesn't have this meaning. Instead, you'd use **vielleicht** (*maybe/perhaps*) to express possibility or chance. For instance, you can translate **Vielleicht komme ich spät nach Hause** as *I may come home late.* However, *Perhaps I'll come home late* is closer to the word-for-word translation, even though German doesn't use the future tense in the example sentence. (For information on the present tense, see Chapter 3 of Book III.)

Watch out for false friends (which we discuss in Chapter 1 of Book I). The modal verb **müssen** looks somewhat similar to the English *must,* which is the correct meaning in English; however, you express *must not* in German with **nicht dürfen: Sie dürfen hier nicht rauchen.** (*You must not/are not allowed to smoke here.*)

Look at the following example sentences with **dürfen:**

> **Sie darf das nicht tun.** (*She is not allowed to do that.*)

> **Darf ich Sie daran erinnern?** (*May I remind you of that?*)

Book III

Assembling the Grammatical Foundations for Communication

Wir dürfen das nicht vergessen. (*We must not forget that.*)

Das dürfen wir nicht vergessen. (*We must never forget that.*) The message is the same as with the previous sentence, but the word order is slightly different: **Das** (*that*) and **wir** (*we*) are switched. The modal auxiliary verb, **dürfen**, is in the second position in both sentences.

Er hätte so etwas nicht machen dürfen. (*He should never have been allowed to do that.*) This sentence contains three verbs, and **hätte** (*should have*) is the conjugated verb. The other two verbs, **machen** (*to make*) and **dürfen** (*to be allowed to*), are at the end.

Ich bin sehr dankbar, dich zu meinen Freunden zählen zu dürfen. (*I am very grateful to be able to count you among my friends.*) The verb **zählen** (*to count*) is followed by **zu dürfen** (*to be allowed to*).

These phrases can combine with an idea that follows:

Wenn ich fragen darf . . . (*If you don't mind my asking . . .*) With the word order here, the verb **dürfen** needs to be at the end of the phrase; **wenn** (*when*) sends the verb to the end. The phrase that completes the thought is most likely in the form of a question.

Ich darf wohl sagen, dass . . . (*I dare say that . . .*) The conjunction **dass** (*that*) needs to be followed by a phrase that has the verb at the end. (For information on conjunctions like **dass,** check out Chapter 1 of Book IV.)

Wir dürfen sicher sein, dass . . . (*We may be certain that . . .*)

Sie dürfen damit rechnen, dass . . . (*You may rest assured that . . .*)

You Can Do It! Können, the Ability Verb

Can you run a marathon barefoot? Do you know how to play chess (and win) against a computer? Are you able to make a five-course dinner for 12 guests without batting an eye? No matter what your hidden talents may be, if you have a healthy ego, then chances are you enjoy talking about yourself. Know-how, ability, and can-do attitude — all are expressed with the verb **können**.

As one of the seven players in the modal verb dugout, **können** (*can, to be able to, to know how to*) is a true champ. In general, German and English use **können** in similar ways. The verb goes up to bat whenever you need to express that

- You *can* or *can't* do something: **Kannst du Tennis/Tischtennis/ Volleyball/Schach/Poker spielen?** (*Can you play tennis/table tennis/ volleyball/chess/poker?*)

✔ You *know* or *don't know how to* do something: **Er kann Geige/Klavier/ Keyboards/Gitarre/Klarinette/Saxophon spielen.** (*He knows how to play the violin/piano/keyboards/guitar/clarinet/saxophone.*) In German, you don't use the definite article **der, die, das** [*the*] to talk about playing an instrument.

✔ You *are able to* do something: **Ich kann bis Mittag schlafen.** (*I'm able to/ can sleep until noon.*)

✔ You want to request or offer help in a polite but direct way: **Können Sie mir sagen, wo der Bahnhof/die Straßenbahnhaltestelle/das Hotel Blaue Gans/das Kunstmuseum ist?** (*Can you tell me where the train station/the streetcar stop/the Hotel Blaue Gans/the art museum is?*)

Note: Notice the comma after the first clause. In German, you need this comma to separate the subordinate clause (**. . . wo der Bahnhof ist?**) from the main clause (**Können Sie mir sagen, . . .**). Subordinate clauses often begin with words like **wo** (*where*), **was** (*what*), **wie viel** (*how much*), **wer** (*who*), and **warum** (*why*). The conjugated verb in the subordinate clause, **ist** (*is*), gets the boot and lands at the end of the sentence. (For information on subordinate clauses, see Chapter 1 of Book IV.)

Forming können

Look at the conjugation of **können.** It's irregular in the singular forms: **ich, du,** and **er/sie/es.** The irregular forms are bold, and the regular forms show the endings in bold.

können (*can, to be able to, to know how to*)	
ich **kann**	wir könn**en**
du **kannst**	ihr könn**t**
er/sie/es **kann**	sie könn**en**
Sie könn**en**	
Ich **kann** Ihnen mit ihrem Gepäck helfen. (*I can help you with your luggage.*)	

Using können

One striking difference between English and German is that German sometimes describes what can or can't be done using **können** but no main verb. Typically, you hear the following expressions in spoken, casual conversation. Table 6-3 lists the situation, an example sentence in German, and its equivalent in English.

Book III

Assembling the Grammatical Foundations for Communication

Table 6-3	Uses of Können without a Main Verb	
Situation	**Example**	**English Equivalent**
to say someone can speak a language	Meine Frau **kann** sehr gut Französisch.	*My wife can speak French very well.*
to say that you give up trying	Ich **kann nicht** weiter. Es ist zu schwer.	*I can't go on. It's too difficult.*
to explain that you can't help doing (excusing yourself for taking a third piece of chocolate cake)	Ich **kann nichts** dafür. Es schmeckt so gut!	*I can't help it. It tastes so good!*
to interject that you can do something	Das **kann** ich wohl!	*Of course I can do that!*

A number of common **können** expressions are reflexive (they use a reflexive pronoun [*me, you, us,* and so on] with the verb) in German but not in English. German uses the reflexive much more frequently than English. (For information on reflexive verbs, check out Chapter 3 of Book IV.) Table 6-4 lists these common expressions, an example sentence in German, and the English translation.

Table 6-4	Uses of Können with a Reflexive Verb	
Situation	**Example**	**English Equivalent**
to say you can('t) decide	Ich **kann mich** nicht entscheiden.	*I can't decide.*
to express that you can get away with something	Wie **kannst** du **dir** so etwas erlauben?	*How can you get away with something like that?*
to be able (or unable) to afford something	Wir **können uns** kein teueres Auto leisten.	*We can't afford an expensive car.*
to give assurance that someone/something can be trusted	Sie **können sich** auf mich verlassen.	*You can depend on me.*

Notice the word order in the following expressions. When there are two verbs, the main verb (the one that's in infinitive form) gets kicked to the end of the sentence. (Harsh treatment for some decent, upstanding verbs, but it's true!)

Sie kann Klarinette spielen. (*She can play the clarinet.*) The word order needs to have the conjugated verb **kann** in second position and the main verb **spielen** (in the infinitive form) at the end of the sentence.

Können Sie mir helfen? (*Can you help me?*) **Können** is the conjugated verb, and in a yes/no question, it's first; the verb **helfen** needs to be at the end.

Könnt ihr gut Tennis spielen? (*Can you play tennis well?*) **Könnt** is the conjugated verb. This is a yes/no question, so it's in first position. The verb **spielen** needs to be at the end.

Ich kann Englisch, Deutsch, und Spanisch. (*I can speak English, German, and Spanish.*) **Können** needs no other verb here. However, you can add **sprechen** (*to speak*) at the end of the sentence, especially if you want to go on and say something different about another language: **Ich kann Französisch verstehen, aber nicht sprechen.** (*I can understand French but not speak it.*)

Ich kann Fußball spielen. (*I can play soccer.*) In this word order, the conjugated modal verb **kann** is in second position, and the main verb **spielen** (in infinitive form) is at the end of the sentence.

1 Like That: Mögen, the Likeable Verb

Book III

Assembling the Grammatical Foundations for Communication

Want to talk about likes and dislikes? **Mögen** is the verb for you. Consider these sentences: **Magst du kaltes Wetter?** (*Do you like cold weather?*) **Nein, ich mag den Winter überhaupt nicht.** (*No, I don't like the winter at all.*) Want to express your feelings toward someone? Try **ich mag dich** (*I like you*).

The main definition of **mögen** is that of liking or disliking someone or something. When talking about such preferences, you usually don't need an additional verb:

Magst du diese Sängerin? (*Do you like this female singer?*)

Er mag kein Starkbier. (*He doesn't like strong beer.*)

The modal verb **mögen** comes as a double dipper. Why? Because **mögen** (*to like, to care for*) is so likeable that it has a cousin, **möchten** (*would like, would like to do*), which is similar in meaning to **mögen**. (Check out the later section for more on **möchten**.)

Forming mögen

This verb table shows you the conjugation of **mögen**. It follows the typical pattern of modal verbs: the singular verb forms are the irregular ones — **ich mag, du magst, er/sie/es mag.** The irregular forms are shown in bold, and the regular forms show the endings in bold.

mögen (to like, to care for)	
ich **mag**	wir mög**en**
du **magst**	ihr mög**t**
er/sie/es **mag**	sie mög**en**
Sie mög**en**	
Ich **mag** klassische Musik. (*I like classical music.*)	

When you want to express dislike for someone or something, you put **nicht** at the end of the sentence when no other verb is along for the ride:

Ihr mögt diese Farbe nicht. (*You don't like this color.*)

Mögen sie Schokoladeneis nicht? (*Don't they like chocolate ice cream?*)

Using mögen

To add some oomph to **mögen,** you can use a number of expressions with **gern** (**gern** is similar to *a lot* when you add it to other words). We've arranged the list in order of most positive to most negative:

- ✔ **mögen . . . besonders gern** (*to especially like*): **Ich mag Bratkartoffeln besonders gern.** (*I especially like roasted potatoes.*) They're similar to home fries.

- ✔ **mögen . . . (sehr) gern** (*to like [very much]*): **Ich mag Kartoffelklöße (sehr) gern.** (*I like potato dumplings very much.*) In southern Germany and Austria, **Klöße** are referred to as **Knödel,** both of which are *dumplings.*

- ✔ **mögen . . . nicht gern** (*not to like very much*): **Ich mag Pommes frites nicht gern.** (*I don't like French fries very much.*)

- ✔ **mögen . . . überhaupt nicht gern** (*not to like at all*): **Ich mag Salzkartoffeln überhaupt nicht gern.** (*I don't like boiled potatoes at all.*)

A few idiomatic expressions use **mögen:**

- ✔ **Das mag sein.** (*That could be true.*)

- ✔ **Ich mag ihn leiden.** (*I care for him.*) You can also leave off **leiden** without changing the meaning much, but **leiden** stresses the emotion of caring.

- ✔ **Darin mögen Sie Recht haben.** (*You have a point there.*)

What Would You Like? Möchten, the Preference Verb

Life is full of choices, and you're likely to have some opinions on what you like best. When the **Kellner/Kellnerin** (*waiter/waitress*) in a German restaurant asks you, **"Was möchten Sie?"** (*What would you like?*), make sure you order something to drink first — **"Ich möchte eine Apfelsaftschorle."** (*I'd like an apple juice/mineral water drink.*) That way, you have time to peruse the eight-page menu and order the meal later.

To say you'd like [to do] something in German, you use the modal verb **möchten.**

Forming möchten

Although **möchten** (*would like [to do]*) is often lumped together with **mögen** (*to like, to care for*) (see the preceding section for more info), it's definitely important enough to get top billing in the modal verb lineup. Technically speaking, **möchten** is the *subjunctive* form of **mögen;** it expresses a wish rather than reality. (Check out Book IV, Chapter 7 for more on the subjunctive.) Look at the conjugation of **möchten.** The verb endings are in bold.

Book III

Assembling the Grammatical Foundations for Communication

möchten (*would like [to]*)	
ich möcht**e**	wir möcht**en**
du möcht**est**	ihr möcht**et**
er/sie/es möcht**e**	sie möcht**en**
Sie möcht**en**	
Ich **möchte** am Wochenende Rad fahren. (*I'd like to go bicycling on the weekend.*)	

Using möchten

The important similarity that **möchten** and **mögen** share, aside from their meanings, is that neither modal verb needs a main verb to express something clearly. For instance, when ordering in a restaurant, the context can typically indicate what you'd like to have. Using **möchten** as the modal verb, you can omit the following main verbs:

- **essen** (*to eat*)
- **trinken** (*to drink*)
- **haben** (*to have*)
- **fahren** (*to drive*)
- **gehen** (*to go, to walk*)

Look at the two example sentences, one with and one without a main verb. Assuming you know they're spoken in a restaurant, the meaning of the first sentence, which has no main verb, is clear:

Ich möchte ein Glas Rotwein, bitte. (*I'd like a glass of red wine, please.*)

Ich möchte ein Glas Rotwein trinken, bitte. (*I'd like to drink a glass of red wine, please.*) Or you can use **haben** (*to have*) instead of **trinken,** and you'd still get a glass of red wine.

German often expresses a preference by using **möchten** in combination with **lieber** (*rather*). The following example dialogue shows **haben** in parentheses to indicate that it's not necessary in the context of the situation:

Möchten Sie einen Fensterplatz (haben)? (*Would you like a window seat?*)

Nein, ich möchte lieber einen Gangplatz (haben). (*No, I'd rather have an aisle seat.*)

The following examples show more ways to use **möchten:**

Ich möchte eine Tasse Kaffee. (*I'd like a cup of coffee.*)

Ich möchte eine Pizza, bitte. (*I'd like a pizza, please.*)

Wir möchten Deutsch lernen. (*We'd like to learn German.*)

Ich möchte zu Hause bleiben. (*I'd like to stay at home.*)

Sie möchte mit Andreas tanzen. (*She'd like to dance with Andreas.*)

Möchtest du ein Glas Wasser? (*Would you like a glass of water?*)

Do 1 Have To? Müssen, the Verb of Necessity

As a child, you may have heard something along the lines of "No, you don't have to finish your broccoli au gratin, but you have to try at least three bites." So now that you've grown up — or at least other people think you have — far more serious obligations haunt you, such as paying taxes, mowing the lawn, and having the first local strawberries of the season before anyone else.

Müssen bears a vague resemblance to *must*, making it easier to get down to the nitty-gritty of how this modal works, when you *need* it, when you *have to* use it, when it's a *must*, and when you *don't have to* deal with it. What about *must not?* Oddly enough, *must not* is **darf nicht** in German, with the modal verb **dürfen** (*to be allowed to*). (Check out the earlier section on **dürfen** if you're a bit foggy on the difference between the two verbs.)

Book III

Assembling the Grammatical Foundations for Communication

Forming müssen

Take a look at the conjugation of **müssen.** Like most of its fellow modal verbs, it's irregular in the singular forms: **ich, du,** and **er/sie/es.** The irregular forms are in bold, and the regular forms show the endings in bold.

müssen (*must, to have to, to need to*)	
ich **muss**	wir müss**en**
du **musst**	ihr müss**t**
er/sie/es **muss**	sie müss**en**
Sie müss**en**	
Er **muss** morgen früh aufstehen. (*He has to get up early tomorrow.*)	

Using müssen

Necessity and obligation are the core meanings of **müssen** in both English and German, although in the English-speaking world and among North Americans in particular, there's a tendency to downplay the use of *must* because it sounds so strong to the ear. *Do I have to?* works just fine at getting the obligation message across (especially when uttered by whining 10-year-olds after you've told them to turn off the TV and go to bed).

Don't get lulled into thinking that **muss nicht** is equivalent to *must not*. When you turn **müssen** into a negative expression, the similarities between German and English go down the drain. German has two expressions for indicating whether something is forbidden or simply not necessary:

- ✔ **nicht dürfen** (*not allowed, must not, not permitted*): A no-no; strong prohibition, such as **Du darfst das nicht trinken.** (You *mustn't* drink that.)

- ✔ **nicht müssen** (*not necessary, don't need to*): An absence of necessity or obligation, such as **Du musst das nicht trinken.** (You *don't need to* drink that.)

The following sentences show how to use the modal auxiliary verb **müssen**:

Ich muss jetzt gehen. (*I have to leave now.*)

Sie muss das sehr genau machen. (*She has to do that very precisely.*)

Wir müssen eine Entscheidung treffen. (*We have to come to a decision.*)

Er muss im Bett bleiben. (*He has to stay in bed.*)

Sie muss das Haus hüten. (*She has to stay at home.*)

Ich muss damit rechnen. (*I have to face that.*)

Wir müssen sparen. (*We have to save [money].*)

Following are some commonly used fixed expressions using **müssen**:

Sie müssen Farben bekennen. (*You have to show your true colors.*)

Wir müssen zusammenhalten. (*We have to stick together.*)

Sie müssen die Folgen tragen. (*She has to bear the consequences.*)

Er muss sich entscheiden. (*He has to reach a decision.*)

Muss das sein? (*Is that really necessary?*) This expression in the form of a question is typically used to indicate that you call into question or disapprove of someone else's actions.

These beginning phrases can combine with an idea that follows. The second phrase in the sentence uses the conjunction **dass** (*that*), which needs to be followed by a phrase that has the verb at the end. (For information on conjunctions like **dass,** check out Chapter 1 of Book IV.)

> **Ich muss zugeben, dass . . .** (*I have to admit that . . .*)
>
> **Wir müssen bedenken, dass . . .** (*We have to consider that . . .*)
>
> **Sie müssen wissen, dass . . .** (*You have to know that . . .*)

Should 1 or Shouldn't 1? Sollen, the Duty Verb

There are things in life that you have to do and things you're supposed to do. We prefer the latter because they're easier to put off. But wasting valuable vacation time to accomplish everything on your checklist is something you really shouldn't do. So the to-do list just gets longer and longer until the day it fortuitously gets lost in the trash.

When you want to describe an action you *should* or *shouldn't do* or that you're *supposed to* or *not supposed to do,* **sollen** is the verb to use.

Book III

Assembling the Grammatical Foundations for Communication

Forming sollen

Look at the conjugation of this modal verb in the table that follows. **Sollen** is irregular only in two places — the **ich** and **er/sie/es** forms. The irregular forms are in bold, and the regular forms show the endings in bold.

sollen (*should, to be supposed to*)	
ich **soll**	wir soll**en**
du soll**st**	ihr soll**t**
er/sie/es **soll**	sie soll**en**
Sie soll**en**	
Du **sollst** die Katze füttern. (*You should feed the cat.*)	

Using sollen

Nonnative speakers of German should be careful not to sound too forceful when it isn't necessary. **Sollen,** the modal duty verb, is the verb you use for giving advice or expressing a duty that's an expected, right-kind-of-thing-to-do action. The negative version, **nicht sollen,** expresses what you shouldn't do. The cousin **müssen** is the modal verb of necessity and strong directives — see the earlier section on **müssen.**

Check out the examples with **sollen** and **nicht sollen:**

> **Ich soll etwas trinken. Ich habe Durst.** (*I should drink something. I'm thirsty.*)

> **Wir sollen unsere Schuhe putzen. Sie sind schmutzig.** (*We should clean our shoes. They're dirty.*)

> **Du sollst nicht spät ins Bett gehen. Du siehst sehr müde aus.** (*You shouldn't go to bed late. You look very tired.*)

> **Ich soll den neuen Film sehen. Er ist super.** (*I should see the new movie. It's super.*)

> **Maria soll ein kleineres Auto kaufen. Das Benzin ist sehr teuer.** (*Maria should buy a smaller car. Gas is very expensive.*)

> **Du sollst nicht zum Konzert gehen. Die Gruppe ist wirklich schlecht.** (*You shouldn't go to the concert. The group is really bad.*)

> **Was soll das bedeuten?** (*What's that supposed to mean?*) (This is an idiomatic expression.)

I Want to Be Famous: Wollen, the Intention Verb

When you were little, did you want to travel around the world in a hot air balloon? Chances are, by now you've scaled back such grand intentions: You wish you could just remember the names of three famous movie stars. However, you do intend to travel more — to your son's soccer games. No matter how grandiose or mundane your wants and desires may be, you can express them all with **wollen,** the intention verb. Expressing your wants (as well as intentions, desires, and a secret wish or two) in German is simple when you know how to use **wollen.**

Forming wollen

Like some others in the band of modal verbs, **wollen** is irregular in the following forms: **ich, du,** and **er/sie/es** — the singular forms. The irregular forms are in bold, and the regular forms show the endings in bold. Look at the verb conjugation.

wollen (*to want to, to intend to, to wish*)	
ich **will**	wir woll**en**
du **willst**	ihr woll**t**
er/sie/es **will**	sie woll**en**
Sie woll**en**	
Ich **will** jetzt nach Hause fahren. (*I want to drive home now.*)	

Note: Although **(ich) will** can easily be mistaken as meaning (*I*) *will*, it's the verb **werden** that means *will.* You use **werden** as a helping verb to speak about the future. (Go to Book IV, Chapter 6 for more on using **werden** to form the future.)

Using wollen

When you're expressing something you *want to do* or *intend to do,* you can substitute **möchten** for **wollen** and come up with virtually the same results (see the earlier section "What Would You Like? **Möchten,** the Preference Verb"). Look at the following examples. The difference between them is minimal in both languages. The speaker could be talking to someone or doing some wishful thinking:

> **Ich will ein neues Auto kaufen.** (*I want to buy a new car.*)

> **Ich möchte ein neues Auto kaufen.** (*I would like to buy a new car.*)

When you want something from someone else, the two verbs are not interchangeable. **Wollen** is direct: You *want* something. **Möchten** does express a *want* in the form of *would like to,* but it carries the ring of politeness. Compare the two example sentences that follow. The speaker is a dinner guest in someone's living room.

> **Ich will fernsehen.** (*I want to watch TV.*) The guest is simply stating what he or she wants or intends to do. There's no hint, direct or indirect, of a request.

> **Ich möchte fernsehen.** (*I would like to watch TV.*) The guest sounds polite by using **möchte.** A request is likely to follow the stated intention with a question, such as **Haben Sie etwas dagegen?** (*Do you mind?*)

Book III

Assembling the Grammatical Foundations for Communication

The expressions using **wollen** in the following sentences show how its meaning can bend slightly in conjunction with another word or words:

- ✔ **wollen . . . gern + infinitive:** Stresses desire. (*Note:* Look at the earlier section in this chapter on **mögen** for more ways to use **gern.**) For example, **Er will gern Musik hören** (*He feels like listening to music*).

- ✔ **wollen . . . unbedingt:** Underscores that you absolutely want something, without fail, such as **Ich will unbedingt nach Australien reisen** (*I'm dying to travel to Australia*).

- ✔ **wie + subject + wollen:** Notes that a decision is up to somebody else, such as **Wie Sie wollen** (*It's up to you*). The German title of Shakespeare's *As You Like It* is **Wie Ihr Wollt.**

- ✔ **wollen . . . nicht + past participle + haben/sein:** Expresses that someone doesn't want to admit having done something, as in **Sie wollen den Unfall nicht gesehen haben** (*They claim not to have seen the accident*). In other words, they don't want to admit to having seen the accident. (See Chapter 4 of Book IV for info on past participles.)

- ✔ **wollen nichts damit zu tun haben:** Notes that the subject doesn't want to be involved with something, as in **Ich will nichts damit zu tun haben** (*I want no part of that* or *I don't want anything to do with it*).

Look at the examples of sentences with **wollen:**

Du willst einen Salat machen. (*You want to make a salad.*)

Ich will morgen um 17.00 Uhr Tennis spielen. (*I want to play tennis tomorrow at 5 p.m.*)

Wir wollen Orangensaft (trinken). (*We want to drink [some] orange juice.*)

Ihr wollt in die Stadt gehen. (*You want to go into the city.*)

Heidi und Thomas wollen heute Abend ins Restaurant gehen. (*Heidi and Thomas want to go to a/the restaurant this evening.*)

Sophie will ein Stück Apfelkuchen essen. (*Sophie wants to eat a piece of apple cake.*)

Chapter 7

Instructing and Commanding: The Imperative Mood

*W*hen you need help, you can ask for it in several ways. You could simply state something like *I need some help.* But if you're surfing and a shark is after you, you're more likely to be shouting at the top of your lungs, *Help! Shark!* In that panic-stricken moment, you're commanding the attention of the others on the beach to help you. And although most of them will run the other way, the lifeguard will hopefully rush out to rescue you before the shark has you for dinner.

In the unlikely event that you need to shout out a warning in German, you want to know how to use the *imperative form,* also called the *command form.* You can also use the imperative form in other situations, such as giving instructions, offering encouragement, making suggestions, and persuading people. Unexpected situations may happen when you're among German-speaking people, and understanding what's going on is useful. Someone may be commanding a group of people you're among to get out of the way, or a helpful pedestrian may be telling you that you need to get out of the street because a bus is approaching behind you.

This chapter gives the lowdown on the imperative in its varied forms. You find out how to use the command form, understand warning signs, read instructions, and direct people's attention to lend you a hand.

Getting into the Imperative Mood

When telling someone to do something, you use the imperative. Note that the *imperative* is not a verb tense; it's actually what's known as a *mood*. So what's that? *Mood* is the means by which the speaker perceives the action of the sentence — in other words, the verb. (A *verb tense,* on the other hand, is the way in which the speaker expresses the past, present, or future.)

When issuing commands, you need to use the correct verb form and punctuation so the person you're talking to understands. (However, that still doesn't mean he'll do what you say.) Keep reading to see how to use the imperative correctly.

Grasping the three imperative forms

English has one verb form for the imperative — *stop* here please, *get* me a pen please, *go* home, *watch* out! You may be talking to one person, several people, a bus driver, a friend, or your neighbor's dog. On the other hand, German has three forms, depending on whom you're addressing. They correspond to the three German pronouns that represent *you* — **Sie, ihr,** and **du.**

An imperative sentence begins with the verb, followed by the pronoun. However, only imperatives in the **Sie** form use the pronoun. Table 7-1 shows examples of the three imperative forms and explains how to form the verbs.

Table 7-1		The Three German Imperative Forms of *You*		
German Pronoun	*Translation*	**German Example Sentence**	*Translation*	**How to Form the Verb**
Sie	*you* (formal, singular or plural)	**Zeigen Sie mir, bitte!** **(zeigen)**	*Please show me.*	Same as present-tense **Sie** form
ihr	*you* (informal, plural = *y'all*)	**Öffnet bitte die Fenster!** **(öffnen)**	*Please open the windows.*	Same as present-tense **ihr** form
du	*you* (informal, singular)	**Fahr vorsichtig!** **(fahren)**	*Drive carefully.*	Stem of a verb (+e)

We explain when to use each form of the imperative later in this chapter. But first, we explain how to punctuate imperatives and form them from regular and irregular verbs.

Punctuating commands

When you write a command in German, you generally put an exclamation mark at the end of the phrase. It isn't intended to make the command sound like a do-or-die situation, and when you read the written words out loud, you don't need to sound like a drill sergeant (unless the situation merits that emphasis). The exclamation mark is simply a grammatical element of the imperative form, just as a question mark belongs at the end of a question. By contrast, in written English, you reserve the use of the exclamation mark for situations when you're trying to add a sense of real urgency, threat, or anger to the meaning of a sentence.

The liberal use of exclamation marks on German signage as a means of signaling warning can be a bit overwhelming at first. **Rasen nicht betreten!** (*Don't walk on the grass*) may seem threatening, but don't let it give you the impression that you'll go straight to jail if you dare to place even one toe on the grass. The exclamation mark is meant to draw your attention to the sign so you recognize it as a directive that you need to adhere to.

Grammatically speaking, the format of **Rasen nicht betreten!** is an imperative, but you more often see the infinitive form on signs, and it often takes the form of a prohibition with **nicht** preceding the infinitive. **Nicht hinauslehnen!** (*Don't lean out!*) is an example of a sign posted on a train window. The exclamation mark adds strength to the message.

Not all commands need an exclamation mark. There are several ways to grab someone's attention or get your message across, and whether you use an exclamation mark depends on how you want to emphasize the message. For example, when giving instructions in German, you may use a form of the imperative, yet you don't need to drive home the information with an exclamation mark.

When you're telling someone what to do, your tone of voice is every bit as important as the actual words you utter. You can turn your message into something that sounds more like a question than a command by raising your voice at the end of your statement, just as you would when you're asking a question.

Book III

Assembling the Grammatical Foundations for Communication

Commanding with regular verbs

Most German verbs are regular in the sense that they follow a standard pattern of conjugation, so that's good news. For the imperative, you need only three forms, as Table 7-1 indicates — **Sie, ihr,** and **du** — in the present tense. (For information on present-tense conjugation, go to Chapter 3 of Book III.)

Within this large group of regular verbs, German verbs are classified into other groups, two of which are the separable-prefix verbs (Chapter 8 of Book III) and reflexive verbs (Chapter 3 of Book IV). For all verbs, you start the imperative/command phrase with the verb. When you want to form the imperative of separable-prefix verbs and reflexive verbs, you need to know some details about word order and how the verbs work in a sentence.

The verbs in the following commands are separable-prefix verbs. When you use separable-prefix verbs in a command, the prefix needs to go to the end of the sentence. For reference, the infinitive form of the German verb follows the English translation of the sentence.

Stehen Sie jetzt auf! (*Get up now.*) **aufstehen** (*to get up*).

Kommt her! (*Come here.*) **herkommen** (*to come here*).

Passen Sie auf! (*Look out./Watch out.*) **aufpassen** (*to look out/to watch out*).

Ruf doch mal an. (*Give a call.*) **anrufen** (*to call*). Gentle reminders like this don't need an exclamation mark — unless you're agitated! It's a message used by the **Deutsche Telekom** (*German Telecommunications Company*) to promote business.

Bringen Sie eine Flasche Wein mit. (*Bring a bottle of wine along.*) **mitbringen** (*to bring along*). Using an exclamation mark here isn't likely to get you far with a request like this.

Zieh dich warm an! (*Dress warmly.*) **anziehen** (*to dress, to get dressed*). The separable-prefix verb **anziehen** is used reflexively here.

In the following list of commands, the verb is a reflexive verb. Word order for sentences with reflexive verbs is simple: You begin the sentence as usual, with the imperative form of the verb, followed by the corresponding reflexive pronoun, for example, **sich** (*you*). When using the formal imperative form, you do, however, place the formal pronoun **Sie** in second place directly after the verb. Look at these example sentences:

Putz dir die Zähne. (*Brush your teeth.*)

Schauen Sie sich im Spiegel an. (*Look at yourself in the mirror.*) In addition to being used reflexively here, the verb **anschauen** (*to look at*) is a separable-prefix verb.

Beeilt euch! (*Hurry up!*)

Wasch dir gründlich die Hände. (*Wash your hands thoroughly.*)

Commanding with irregular verbs

As is the situation with many verbs in both German and English, a few way-ward souls don't particularly care to adhere to the standard pattern of con-jugation. The good news is that for German imperative verbs, the irregular forms are mostly limited to the **du** form.

Normally, the **du** imperative form is straightforward: verb stem + **-e** (for example, **geh** + **-e** = **gehe** [*go*]). Here are the three **du** imperative exceptions:

- ✔ In informal German, the **-e** is often dropped: **pass auf** (*watch out*).
- ✔ In verbs with a stem ending in **-d** or **-t,** you often *don't* drop the **-e**: **arbeite** (*work*).
- ✔ If the verb has a stem-vowel change, the imperative has this vowel change and does *not* have **-e** at the end of the verb: **essen = iss** (*eat*). (See Chapter 3 of Book III for verbs with stem-vowel changes.)

The verb **sein** (*to be*) is irregular (of course!) in the imperative:

- ✔ Sie form: **seien Sie**
- ✔ ihr form: **seid**
- ✔ du form: **sei**

The following examples show command forms with verbs that have a stem ending in **-d** or **-t**, verbs with stem-vowel changes, and the verb **sein**:

Arbeite schneller! (*Work faster!*)

Wirf mir den Ball! (*Throw me the ball!*)

Seien Sie ruhig! (*Be quiet!*)

Seid still! (*Be quiet!*)

Nimm noch ein Stuck Kuchen. (*Have another piece of cake.*)

Sprich nicht so laut. (*Don't speak so loud.*)

Lies weiter. (*Continue reading.*)

Grasping Formal Commands

Many situations in daily life involve understanding both written and spoken commands. When someone is giving you directions on how to get to that cozy restaurant you've been hunting for, you may hear something like, **Gehen Sie geradeaus, und an der Kreuzung, gehen Sie nach links.** (*Go straight ahead, and at the intersection, go to the left.*) (For details on following directions on the street, go to Chapter 1 of Book II.) You may be on a plane or a ferry, and a crew member is giving instructions about what to do in case of an emergency. In German, you use the formal **Sie** command form when dealing with public officials, service personnel, and people you don't know well. You also see formal commands on street signs and signs in public buildings; being familiar with them enables you to navigate smoothly and confidently.

The next sections delve into the world of formal commands and give you the language essentials you need in order to deal with such situations in German-speaking regions.

Using the formal "you" form: Sie

When you want to use a formal command when speaking German, you need to be certain about the effect of your words. Expressing yourself in forceful-sounding language may be tricky. You generally have the alternative of softening your message by throwing a **bitte** into the mix. Other alternatives include the question-command hybrids. (For info on this type of language, go to the later section "Giving Directives Politely and Making Suggestions.")

Look at the examples of formal commands you may find useful in times of need:

> **Helfen Sie mir, bitte.** (*Please help me.*)
>
> **Zeigen Sie mir, bitte.** (*Show me, please.*)
>
> **Lassen Sie mich in Ruhe!** (*Leave me alone!*)

The formal **Sie** command form sounds more respectful than the **du** form, so if you really want someone to leave you alone in no uncertain terms, use one of these commands in the **du** form:

> **Lass mich in Ruhe!** (*Leave me alone!*)
>
> **Hau ab!** (*Get lost!*)
>
> **Hör auf damit!** (*Stop doing that!*)

The following commands are fixed expressions you may hear in conversation. They may have a strong effect on the listener just as they would in English, so be careful about using them until you're sure they're appropriate in a given situation:

Schießen Sie los! (*Fire away!*)

Reißen Sie sich zusammen! (*Pull yourself together!*)

Schieben Sie die Schuld nicht auf mich! (*Don't lay the blame on me!*)

Schämen Sie sich! (*[You should] be ashamed of yourself!*)

The following formal expressions all use the verb **sein:**

Seien wir ehrlich. (*Let's be honest.*)

Seien Sie mir nicht böse. (*Don't be angry with me.*)

Seien Sie offen zu mir! (*Be frank with me!*)

Seien Sie auf der Hut! (*Watch out!/Be on your guard!*)

Obeying orders

Book III

Assembling the Grammatical Foundations for Communication

You've just boarded Lufthansa 235 to Frankfurt and the crew is about to go through the safety precautions. You have several options: Dig into some music on your iPod, glance at the card with safety precaution pictograms in the seat pocket in front of you, wait for the English instructions, or focus on the crew's instructions in German. Obviously, the most useful means of boosting your German is the latter, so why not give it a try?

To better understand all those long-winded instructions, grab that card and follow along as you listen to the verbiage. Anticipate hearing verbs like **möchten** (*would like*) or **können** (*can/to be able to*), commonly referred to as *modal auxiliary verbs* mixed in with the instructions. (Chapter 6 of Book III has information on modal auxiliaries.) Check out these annotated examples:

Wir möchten Ihnen zeigen, wie Sie ihren Sitzgurt richtig öffnen und schließen können. (*We would like to show you how to fasten and unfasten your seat belts correctly.*) Although you may not understand all the words that follow **möchten** (*would like*), when you grasp that **möchten** is a polite means of inviting you to do something, then you know that the rest is more or less optional.

Sie können ihr persönliches elektronisches Gerät nach dem Erreichen der Flughöhe und nach Erlöschen der Anschnallzeichen über Ihren Sitzen gerne wieder benutzen. (*You can use your own electronic equipment after takeoff when the plane has reached cruising altitude and the fasten seat belt signs have been switched off.*) This sentence may sound incredibly long and convoluted, but when you hear **können** (*can/to be able to*), you understand that the rest of the information is not obligatory.

Also recognize that in the case of commands or instructions, the verb is likely to come first in the sentence or phrase. The following onboard safety instructions use this word order:

Stellen Sie bitte die Rückenlehne senkrecht und klappen Sie bitte die Tische zurück. (*Please make sure that your seat back is in the upright position and your tray table is closed.*)

Ziehen sie bitte eine der Masken zu sich heran. (*Pull one of the masks toward you.*)

Drücken Sie die Maske fest auf Mund und Nase. (*Press the mask firmly over your mouth and nose.*)

Ziehen Sie die Schwimmweste über den Kopf. (*Slip the life vest over your head.*)

Ziehen Sie die Gurte straff. (*Pull the straps tight.*)

Ziehen Sie an den roten Griffen, um die Weste aufzublasen. (*Inflate the vest by pulling down on [one of] the red tabs.*)

When instructions begin with **bitte** (*please*), you have a chance to focus your attention on some key information that immediately follows — namely, the verb telling you what to do or not to do. The following instructions begin with **bitte** and follow with the verb:

Bitte prägen Sie sich die Lage der Notausgänge ein. (*Please remember the location of the emergency exits.*)

Wir bitten Sie sich wieder zu Ihren Plätzen zu begeben und sich anzuschnallen. (*Please return to your seat and fasten your seat belt.*)

Bitte bleiben Sie noch so lange angeschnallt auf Ihren Plätzen sitzen bis wir unsere entgultige Parkposition erreicht haben. (*Please remain seated with your seat belt fastened until the aircraft has come to a complete stop.*)

Bitte vergessen Sie keine Gepäckstücke in den Ablagen über Ihnen oder in den Sitztaschen vor Ihnen. (*Please do not forget any baggage in the compartment over you or the seat pockets in front of you.*)

Understanding signs

When you're traveling in German-speaking regions, you're likely to see a great number of warning signs. Although you may think that the sheer number of these signs far surpasses the number you see in a comparable English-speaking country, the main difference may be in the content of the message, not in the quantity. For one, that exclamation mark does grab your attention.

No less striking are the words of warning that seem to pop up everywhere. When you're aware of the most frequently seen words, you're well on your way to understanding how to react when you see such signs. Here are some familiar words you may see on signs:

> **Achtung!** (*Attention/Caution*)
>
> **Kein** (*No, not*)
>
> **Nicht** (*No, not*)
>
> **Verboten!** (*Forbidden*)
>
> **Freihalten** (*Keep clear*)
>
> **Vorsicht** (*Careful*)

You may find signs like these in public places:

> **Kein Eingang!** (*No entry*)
>
> **Kein Zutritt!** (*No entry*)
>
> **Kein Ausgang!** (*No exit*)
>
> **Kein Zugang!** (*No access*)
>
> **Kein Trinkwasser** (*Water not potable*)
>
> **Nicht rauchen!** (*No smoking*)

You may see the following signs in museums or other public venues:

> **Berühren verboten!** (*Do not touch*)
>
> **Anfassen verboten!** (*Do not handle*)
>
> **Fotografieren verboten!** (*No photos*)

Book III

Assembling the Grammatical Foundations for Communication

Zutritt für Unbefugte verboten! (*Unauthorized persons not allowed/ No trespassing*)

Mobilfunk verboten (*No cellphones*)

Mobiltelefone benutzen verboten (*No cellphone use*)

Achtung! Tür schließt automatisch (*Attention! Door closes automatically*)

Tür bitte freihalten! (*Please keep door clear*)

Bitte Tür schließen (*Please close door*)

Bitte Tür geschlossen halten! (*Please keep door closed at all times*)

Für Garderobe keine Haftung (*Not responsible for items in cloakroom*)

Vorsicht Stufe! (*Caution: Step*)

Eltern haften für ihre Kinder! (*Parents responsible for children*)

When you see any of the following signs on the street, make sure you follow their instructions:

Zufahrt/Einfahrt freihalten (*Keep entrance clear*)

Ausfahrt freihalten (*Keep exit clear*)

Feuerwehrzufahrt freihalten (*Fire department entrance — keep clear*)

Parken verboten (*No parking*)

Durchfahrt verboten (*Not a thruway*)

Schritt fahren (*Drive slowly*)

Achtung! Schranke schließt nach jedem Fahrzeug (*Attention! Gate closes after each vehicle*)

Hunde müssen draußen bleiben (*Dogs have to stay outdoors*)

Plakate ankleben verboten! (*Do not put up posters here*)

These signs warn against trespassing:

Betreten auf eigene Gefahr! (*Enter at your own risk*)

Betreten der Baustelle verboten! (*No trespassing on construction site*)

Betreten des Grundstückes verboten! (*No trespassing on property*)

Betreten verboten! Lebensgefahr! (*No entry! Highly dangerous!*)

Das Betreten der Anlage ist streng verboten! (*Trespassing strictly forbidden*)

You may find warning signs like these in public places such as hospitals or factories:

Kein Zutritt Röntgen (*No entry: X-ray lab*)

Nur für Mitarbeiter! (*Employees only*)

Dieser Bereich wird durch Video überwacht! (*Area under surveillance cameras*)

Hochspannung! Lebensgefahr! (*High voltage! Danger to life!*)

Achtung! Nicht unter Spannung ausstecken (*Attention! Do not unplug [before switching off the machine]*)

Reading instructions

You find the command, or imperative, form in written instructions such as the type you find for assembling a bookshelf, setting up a tent, or following a recipe. These step-by-step instructions typically use a variation of the word order for the imperative form: the verb comes at the very end of each step in the sequence of instructions. The verb is generally written in the infinitive form — for example, **aufstellen** (*to assemble*) or **kochen** (*to cook*).

The following instructions from a recipe for making **Kartoffelsalat** (*potato salad*) are arranged with each step on a separate line so you can easily identify the verb at the end of each step. In English, the word order for the equivalent information puts the verb at the beginning. Look at the line-by-line instructions:

Kartoffeln ca. 20 Min. in Salzwasser gar kochen, (*Boil potatoes approximately 20 minutes in salt water until cooked,*)

etwas abkühlen lassen, (*let [them] cool,*)

dann pellen (*[and] then peel*)

und in Scheiben schneiden. (*and cut into slices.*)

Die heiße Gemüsebrühe darüber gießen (*Pour hot vegetable broth over [the potatoes]*)

und etwas durchziehen lassen. (*and let stand awhile.*)

Anschließend die übrigen Zutaten dazugeben (*Afterward, add the remaining ingredients*)

und unterheben. (*and mix gently.*)

Mit Salz und Pfeffer abschmecken. (*Add salt and pepper to taste.*)

Book III

Assembling the Grammatical Foundations for Communication

Giving Informal Directives

When you know someone well enough to speak informally together, use the casual **du** form. You generally use the **du** form with people you know well, people who have communicated to you that they want to be on informal **du** terms, and with animals and children under the age of around 16. (For more information on using the informal **du**, go to Chapter 3 of Book I.) In any situation where you don't really know whether to use the **Sie** or **du** form, stick to the **Sie** form. When you're sure you're on **du** (or its plural form, **ihr**) speaking terms, however, you can go ahead and use the informal means of addressing someone.

Imagine you're driving on the **Autobahn** (*highway*) with your long-lost German uncle, with whom you're on **du** speaking terms, and he's trying to impress you with his Mercedes XXLQRS7000 by taking it up to 180 — kilometers per hour, that is — or even faster. You're more likely to get a helpful reaction from him if you say **Fahr bitte nicht so schnell** (*Please don't drive so fast*) in a neutral tone of voice than if you raise your voice and blurt out the **Sie** version: **Fahren Sie nicht so schnell!** (*Don't drive so fast!*) After all, the last thing you want to do is get him rattled while he's behind the wheel.

The following sections give you some pointers about issuing commands when using the informal *you* in either the singular or plural form.

Using the singular "you" form: du

Here are some imperative **du** forms with verbs that have no spelling change:

> **Fahr vorsichtig.** (*Drive carefully.*)
>
> **Bleib bis neun Uhr im Bett.** (*Stay in bed until 9 a.m.*)
>
> **Trink mehr Wasser.** (*Drink more water.*)
>
> **Mach es so.** (*Do it like this.*)
>
> **Mach, was du willst.** (*Do what you like.*)

The following examples of **du** imperatives have spelling changes. For reference, you see the infinitive form of the verb following the command and its English equivalent.

> **Nimm eine Aspirin.** (*Take an aspirin.*) **nehmen** (*to take*)
>
> **Lies meine E-mails.** (*Read my e-mails.*) **lesen** (*to read*)

Vergiss es. (*Forget it.*) **vergessen** (*to forget*)

Hilf mir. (*Help me.*) **helfen** (*to help*)

Gib Gas! (*Step on it!*) **geben** (*to give*); **Gas geben** is a colloquial expression

Using the plural informal "you" form: ihr

When you want to make a command using the **ihr** form, you use the present tense **ihr** form of the verb. The following examples show how the **ihr** form of a command looks in a sentence:

Kommt schnell! (*Come quickly!*)

Helft mir! (*Help me!*)

Macht die Tür auf! (*Open the door!*)

Trinkt nicht so viel. (*Don't drink so much.*)

Beeilt euch! (*Hurry up!*)

Stellt die Flaschen im Kühlschrank. (*Put the bottles in the fridge.*)

Macht nicht so viel Lärm! (*Don't make so much noise!*)

Giving Directives Politely and Making Suggestions

In some cases, the imperative walks the fine line between asking and telling someone to do something. Both have inverted word order with the verb first, followed by the subject. Look at the following examples of questions and imperative sentences:

Können Sie das bitte machen? (*Could you do that, please?*) You're asking someone to do something, so you formulate your request more politely by using a helping verb such as **können** (*could*). In addition, you end the request in a rising voice and use a question mark.

Machen Sie das, bitte. (*Please do that.*) By contrast, when you want to tell someone to do something in more direct but polite language, you make a request with the imperative form. Your voice falls at the end, and you use a period.

Book III

Assembling the Grammatical Foundations for Communication

Können Sie mir bitte helfen? (*Could you help me, please?*) The question form, **können,** and **bitte** indicate a request that you're asking someone (politely) to do something. When you say it, your voice rises at the end.

Helfen Sie mir, bitte. (*Please help me./Give me a hand, please.*) The imperative form is a request in more direct language, but **bitte** makes it sound polite. This is probably something you'd say, not write.

Another use of the imperative is to make suggestions. When referring to **wir** (*we*) as the people who may follow the suggestion, the German looks like this: **Fahren wir Fahrrad.** (*Let's go bicycling.*) It's the **wir** verb form with inverted word order.

The following suggestions use **wir:**

Gehen wir! (*Let's go!*) **Gehen** indicates going on foot.

Fahren wir jetzt! (*Let's go now!*) **Fahren** refers to driving a car, riding a bicycle, or taking some sort of transportation.

Fahren wir mit dem Taxi zum Flughafen. (*Let's take a taxi to the airport.*)

Schauen wir uns das Fußballspiel an. (*Let's watch the soccer game.*)

Bleiben wir noch eine Stunde. (*Let's stay another hour.*)

Gehen wir zur Party. (*Let's go to the party.*)

The German verb **lassen** (*to let, to leave, to allow*) is another way to make a suggestion. When you translate the following examples of suggestions into English, the equivalent often involves *let's,* yet the German sentence structure looks different from the English. How so? The German word order comes into play. The second verb gets kicked to the end of the sentence. (For information on word order, go to Chapter 1 of Book III.) Look at the following examples:

Lassen wir das Thema fallen. (*Let's drop the subject.*)

Lassen wir uns bald wiedersehen. (*Let's meet again soon.*)

Lassen Sie von sich hören. (*Let us hear from you.*)

Lassen Sie mich an der Kreuzung aussteigen. (*Let me [get] out at the intersection.*)

Lassen Sie den Toast nicht anbrennen. (*Don't let the toast burn.*)

Lassen Sie mich nicht im Stich! (*Don't leave me in the lurch!/Don't leave me high and dry!*)

Leben und leben lassen. (*Live and let live.*)

Check out the following polite directives that use **Sie:**

> **Helfen Sie mir bitte mit dem Gepäck.** (*Please help me with the luggage.*)
>
> **Bitte wecken Sie mich morgen um sechs Uhr.** (*Please wake me tomorrow at 6 a.m.*)
>
> **Vergessen Sie bitte nicht, uns anzurufen.** (*Please don't forget to call us.*)
>
> **Schauen Sie sich das an**. (*Take a look at that.*)
>
> **Probieren Sie eine dieser Pralinen.** (*Try one of these chocolates.*)

Chapter 8

Sorting Out Separable- and Inseparable-Prefix Verbs

In This Chapter

▶ Juggling separable-prefix verbs

▶ Keeping it together with inseparable-prefix verbs

▶ Rounding up dual-prefix verbs

All you couch potatoes: Use it or lose it! *Get up* off the couch, *put* your shoes *on,* *breathe* some air *in,* and get ready to *work out!* Why the exercise hype in a chapter on separable- and inseparable-prefix verbs? Wouldn't it be more appropriate as a pep talk in a health magazine? Actually, the verbs we deal with in this chapter are the types you see in italics here. In English, they're called *two-part* or *phrasal verbs,* and their German counterparts are called *separable-* or *inseparable-prefix verbs. Separable prefixes* can separate from the verb itself, depending on the verb tense you use, while *inseparable prefixes* never separate from the verb. These verb types are equally common in German and English.

This chapter deals with three categories of verbs: separable-prefix verbs, inseparable-prefix verbs, and dual-prefix verbs, which we dub the *double-crossers* because the prefixes can be separable or inseparable.

Looking at the Prefix

Two-part verbs in English are generally exactly that — in two parts: *get* + *up* = *get up.* They're a dime a dozen: *turn away, put on, take off* . . . you get the picture. The German equivalent of a two-part verb has a prefix attached directly to an infinitive (the base verb form). The prefix, which corresponds to the second part of a two-part verb in English, may stand for a preposition like *up* or an adverb like *away*. (Refer to Book IV, Chapter 2 for info on prepositions.) For example, **aufstehen** (*to get up*) has the prefix **auf-**; literally, **auf-** + **stehen** is *up* + *stand*. Such German verbs are extremely common. The prefix alters the meaning of the original verb, sometimes only slightly, sometimes radically.

To remember whether verbs are separable- or inseparable-prefix verbs, practice pronouncing them aloud. The separable-prefix verbs stress the prefix in spoken German, but the inseparable-prefix verbs don't stress the prefix. For instance, **umsteigen** (*to change [trains, planes, and so on]*) is separable, so when you say it, stress the prefix **um-** like this: ***um*-steig-en. Unterbrechen** (*to interrupt*) is inseparable, so you don't stress the prefix, but you do stress the first syllable of the verb **brechen** like this: **un-ter-*brech*-en.**

You can remember verbs with prefixes using two approaches. First, find out the meanings of the prefixes, and second, know what the prefix and verb mean together. Prefixes can alter the verb's meaning logically, for example, when you add the prefixes **an** (*at, to, on*) or **aus** (*from, out*) to **machen** (*to make*), you get **anmachen** (*to turn on*) and **ausmachen** (*to turn off*). Idiomatically speaking, the meanings change and you get **anmachen** (*to make a pass at someone*, as well as *to mix/dress [a salad]*), and **ausmachen** (*to arrange, to plan*). With the prefix/verb lists in this chapter, you can try both methods at the same time. Although this may sound complicated, a great deal of these verbs (sans prefix) are garden-variety types you encounter often in German.

Parting Ways: Simplifying Separable-Prefix Verbs

With separable-prefix verbs, the verb and the prefix can — drum roll please — split up (surprise, surprise). For example, **aufstehen** (*to get up*) is a separable-prefix verb. Its prefix, **auf-**, means *up* in this context, and the verb **stehen** means *to stand* or *to stay*. Notice that the prefix **auf-** appears at the end of the sentence: **Ich stehe meistens um sechs Uhr auf.** (*I usually get up at 6 a.m.*)

Of the three groups of verbs that we discuss in this chapter, this group is the largest because it has the largest number of prefixes as well as the largest number of verbs that connect with these prefixes.

The following sections introduce you to separable prefixes and show you how to use separable-prefix verbs in the present tense. (For information on forming separable-prefix verbs in the simple past, go to Book IV, Chapter 5, and for the present perfect, go to Book IV, Chapter 4.)

Getting the hang of separable prefixes

You get your money's worth with the prefixes in this section. They're a great help when you're expanding your vocabulary. Why? Not only do they combine with verbs, but some also combine with nouns and adjectives. Most verb prefixes have more than one specific meaning, and as you become familiar with them, you start seeing a pattern in the way a prefix alters the meaning of the verbs it combines with. When you come across a new German verb with the same prefix, you can make an educated guess about its meaning. These itty bitty sound bites are very influential, so start your own collection right away.

Table 8-1 shows separable prefixes, their English meanings, and some verbs that use each prefix. Knowing the meaning of the verb without the prefix can help, but make sure you also know the separable-prefix verb and its English meaning. Although this prefix list is fairly extensive, the number of separable-prefix verbs is huge. This sample list contains high-frequency verbs.

Table 8-1	Separable Prefixes and Verb Combinations		
Prefix	*English Definition*	*Example Verb*	*English Equivalent*
ab-	*from*	**abblenden**	*to shade, to dim (lights)*
		abbrechen	*to break away, to stop*
		abnehmen	*to lose weight, to reduce, to diminish*
		abschaffen	*to do away with*
		abziehen	*to deduct, to print (photos)*
an-	*at, to, on*	**anbauen**	*to grow, to plant*
		anbringen	*to install, to fasten*
		anfangen	*to begin, to start*
		anhaben	*to have on, to wear*
		ankommen	*to arrive, to catch on*
		anrufen	*to phone*
		anschauen	*to look at, to examine*

(continued)

Book III

Assembling the Grammatical Foundations for Communication

Table 8-1 *(continued)*

Prefix	English Definition	Example Verb	English Equivalent
auf-	on, out, up	aufbauen	to put up, to build up
		aufdrehen	to turn on, to wind up
		auffallen	to be noticeable, to stand out
		aufgeben	to give up, to check (bags)
		aufschließen	to unlock, to open up
		aufstehen	to get up, to stand up
aus-	from, out	ausatmen	to exhale
		ausbilden	to train, to educate
		ausfallen	to cancel, to fall out (hair)
		ausgehen	to go out
		ausmachen	to put out (fire), to turn off (lights), to discern, to make plans, to amount to
		aussehen	to look (like), to appear
		auswechseln	to replace (parts)
bei-	with, along	beibringen	to teach, to inflict
		beilegen	to insert (in a document)
		beisetzen	to bury
		beitragen	to contribute (to)
		beitreten	to join, to enter into (a pact)
da-	there	dableiben	to stay behind
		dalassen	to leave there
dabei-	there	dabeibleiben	to stay with, to stick with (it)
daran-	on	daranmachen	to get down to (it)

Prefix	English Definition	Example Verb	English Equivalent
ein-	in, into, down	einatmen	to inhale
		einbrechen	to break in, to cave in
		einkaufen	to go shopping, to buy
		einladen	to invite
		einschlafen	to go to sleep
		einsteigen	to board (plane)
entgegen-	against, toward	entgegenarbeiten	to oppose, to work against
		entgegenkommen	to approach, to accommodate
fehl-	wrong	fehlschlagen	to go wrong
fest-	fixed	festhalten	to hold on, to keep hold of
		festlegen	to establish
		festsitzen	to be stuck, to be stranded
fort-	onward, away	fortbilden	to continue education
		fortführen	to carry on, to continue
		fortpflanzen	to reproduce, to propagate
		fortsetzen	to continue
		forttreiben	to drive away
gegenüber-	across from	gegenüberliegen	to face, to be opposite
		gegenüberstehen	to confront, to face
gleich-	equal	gleichstellen	to treat as equal
her-	from, here	herfahren	to pull up, to get here
		herstellen	to manufacture, to establish
heraus-	from, out of	herausfinden	to find out
		herausreden	to talk one's way out of
		herausfordern	to challenge

Book III

Assembling the Grammatical Foundations for Communication

(continued)

Table 8-1 *(continued)*

Prefix	English Definition	Example Verb	English Equivalent
hin-	*to, toward, there*	hinfahren	*to drive there, to go there*
hinzu-	*in addition*	hinzufügen	*to add (details), to enclose*
kennen-	*know*	kennenlernen	*to get to know, to meet*
los-	*start, away*	losbrechen	*to break off*
		losfahren	*to drive off*
		loslassen	*to let go of*
mit-	*along, with* (similar to English prefix *co-*)	mitarbeiten	*to collaborate*
		mitbringen	*to bring along*
		mitfahren	*to go with, to get a ride*
		mitmachen	*to go along with, to join in*
		mitteilen	*to inform (someone)*
nach-	*after, copy* (similar to English prefix *re-*)	nachahmen	*to imitate*
		nachfragen	*to ask, to inquire*
		nachfüllen	*to refill, to top off*
		nachgeben	*to give way, to give in*
		nachlassen	*to loosen, to decrease (price)*
statt-	no equivalent	stattfinden	*to take place (event)*
		stattgeben	*to grant*
vor-	*before* (similar to English prefixes *pre-* and *pro-*)	vorbereiten	*to prepare*
		vorführen	*to present, to perform*
		vorgehen	*to proceed, to go first*
		vorlegen	*to submit, to present*
		vorlesen	*to read aloud*
		vormachen	*to show someone how to do something, to fool someone*

Prefix	English Definition	Example Verb	English Equivalent
weg-	away, off	wegbleiben	to stay away
		wegfahren	to drive off, to leave
		wegfallen	to be discontinued
		wegnehmen	to take away
		wegwerfen	to throw away
zu-	shut, to, upon	zudecken	to cover up
		zulassen	to authorize, to license
		zumachen	to close
		zusichern	to assure someone
		zusteigen	to get on, to board
zurück-	back	zurückgehen	to go back
		zurückkommen	to return, to come back
		zurückschlagen	to strike back
		zurücksetzen	to put back, to reverse
		zurücktreten	to step back, to resign
		zurückzahlen	to pay back
zusammen-	together	zusammenarbeiten	to work together
		zusammenfassen	to summarize
		zusammenreißen	to pull oneself together
		zusammenstoßen	to crash, to clash
		zusammenwachsen	to grow together
zwischen-	between	zwischenlanden	to stop over (flight)

Book III

Assembling the Grammatical Foundations for Communication

Using separable-prefix verbs in the present tense

When you write an e-mail to your friend in Berlin or speak to your German boss, you'll probably end up using separable-prefix verbs in the present tense. When doing so, word order is a really big deal. Why? If you mix up word order, the reader or listener may not get your intended message. Also, keep in mind that the prefix alters the basic verb's meaning, so if you leave it out, you're likely to cause confusion. (For more on word order in present tense, see Book III, Chapter 3.)

With separable-prefix verbs in the present tense, keep the following points in mind:

- ✔ The prefix — such as **fest-** in **festhalten** (*to hold on*) — goes to the end of the sentence. In spoken German, you stress the prefix.

- ✔ The verb itself, which is the part you conjugate, is generally in second position in the sentence, as in **Ich halte mich fest.** (*I'm holding on tight.*) **Halte,** the conjugated part of the verb, is in second position.

Here are some guidelines for word order, depending on the type of sentence:

- ✔ **Statements, both positive and negative:** The verb is generally in second position, such as in **Wir haben viel vor.** (*We're planning to do a lot [of activities].*) The verb is **vorhaben** (*to plan*). The verb **haben** is in second position, and the prefix **vor-** is at the end of the sentence. The same sentence expressed negatively would look like this: **Wir haben nicht viel vor.** (*We're not planning to do much.*)

- ✔ **Yes/no questions and commands:** The verb and subject are inverted, meaning that the verb is first, followed by the subject, such as with **Kommst du am Sonntag vom Urlaub zurück?** (*Are you coming back from vacation on Sunday?*) The verb is **zurückkommen** (*to come back*). **Kommst,** the conjugated part of the verb **zurückkommen,** is in first position in a yes/no question, and the prefix **zurück** is at the end of the question.

- ✔ **Sentences or questions with a modal verb (such as dürfen or möchten) in addition to the separable-prefix verb:** *Modal verbs* are helping verbs that modify an attitude about the main verb. Conjugate the modal verb, put it in second position (usually), and place the separable-prefix verb in the infinitive form at the end of the phrase, such as in **Alle Gäste dürfen mitmachen.** (*All the guests may join in.*) The verb is **mitmachen** (*to join in*). The modal verb **dürfen** (*may, to be allowed to*) is in second position, and **mitmachen,** the infinitive form of the separable-prefix verb, goes to the end of the sentence. (See Book III, Chapter 6 for info on modal verbs.)

- ✔ **Sentences with multiple clauses:** For sentences that have more than one clause, the guidelines follow those for two-part sentences. See Book IV, Chapter 1 for details.

The following pairs of sentences show how the separable-prefix verbs work with and without a modal auxiliary verb. When you have a modal in the sentence, the separable-prefix verb goes to the end of the sentence or clause.

It's in the infinitive form, meaning the verb is in one piece, with the prefix attached. When the sentence has only one verb (the separable-prefix verb), the prefix goes to the end of the sentence or clause.

> **Die Regierung soll das Gesetz abschaffen.** (*The government should do away with [repeal] the law.*)

> **Die Regierung schafft das Gesetz ab.** (*The government is doing away with [repealing] the law.*)

> **Um wie viel Uhr möchten Sie aufstehen?** (*What time would you like to get up?*)

> **Um wie viel Uhr stehen Sie auf?** (*What time are you getting up?*)

> **Das Konzert kann nur bei schönem Wetter stattfinden.** (*The concert can only take place with good weather.*)

> **Das Konzert findet nur bei schönem Wetter statt.** (*The concert only takes place with good weather.*)

> **Muss der Präsident zurücktreten?** (*Does the president have to resign?*)

> **Tritt der Präsident zurück?** (*Is the president resigning?*)

> **Ich darf nicht einschlafen.** (*I must not fall asleep.*)

> **Ich schlafe nicht ein.** (*I'm not falling asleep.*)

> **Können Sie mir bitte die Details mitteilen?** (*Could you send me the details, please?*)

> **Teilen Sie mir bitte die Details mit.** (*Please send me the details.*)

Book III

Assembling the Grammatical Foundations for Communication

Together Forever: Investigating Inseparable-Prefix Verbs

Although the number of inseparable-prefix verbs isn't as large as that of separable-prefix verbs, you still need to be aware of these verbs so you can include them in your writing and speech. The good news is that many of these inseparable-prefix verbs are common German verbs. More good news: As you may rightly assume from their name, the prefix doesn't separate from the verb, no matter how the verb is used. In addition, some equivalent verbs in English have the same prefix. For these reasons, recognizing many of these inseparable-prefix verbs is fairly simple.

In the following sections, we introduce the inseparable prefixes and then show you how to use inseparable verbs in the present tense. (For information on forming inseparable-prefix verbs in the simple past, go to Book IV, Chapter 5, and for the present perfect, go to Book IV, Chapter 4.)

Understanding inseparable-prefix combinations

Inseparable-prefix verbs are easier to spot in a sentence than separable-prefix verbs because the verb appears together with its prefix. What you still need to keep in mind is that the prefix alters the original meaning of the verb.

Table 8-2 lists inseparable prefixes, their English meanings, and some verbs that use the prefix. A number of the prefixes have direct comparable uses in English, and many of the verbs are frequently used. **Erkennen Sie einige Verben?** (*Do you recognize some verbs?*) But as with separable prefixes, each prefix may have several meanings, and a few inseparable prefixes, such as **emp-** and **ge-,** have no English equivalent.

Table 8-2	Inseparable Prefixes and Verb Combinations		
Prefix	*English Definition*	*Example Verb*	*English Equivalent*
be-	similar to English prefix *be-*	**sich befinden** (reflexive)	*to be located*
		befreunden	*to befriend*
		begegnen	*to meet*
		bekommen	*to get*
		bemerken	*to notice*
emp-	no equivalent	**empfangen**	*to receive (signal, visitor), to welcome someone*
		empfehlen	*to recommend*
		empfinden	*to feel*

Prefix	English Definition	Example Verb	English Equivalent
ent-	similar to English prefixes *de-* and *dis-*	entbehren	*to do without*
		entdecken	*to discover*
		entfernen	*to remove*
		entkommen	*to escape*
		entlassen	*to discharge (someone)*
		entstehen	*to originate*
		entwerten	*to cancel (ticket)*
er-	sometimes no equivalent, sometimes similar to the English prefix *re-* or the meaning of *fatal*	erhängen	*to hang (execute)*
		erholen	*to recover*
		sich erinnern (reflexive)	*to remember*
		erkennen	*to recognize*
		erklären	*to explain, to declare*
		erschiessen	*to shoot dead*
		ertrinken	*to drown*
		erzählen	*to tell*
ge-	no equivalent	gebrauchen	*to use, to make use of*
		gefallen	*to like*
		gehören	*to belong to*
		gelangen	*to arrive at, to attain*
		genesen	*to recover*
		gestalten	*to form, to shape*
		gestehen	*to confess*

(continued)

Book III

Assembling the Grammatical Foundations for Communication

Table 8-2 *(continued)*

Prefix	English Definition	Example Verb	English Equivalent
miss-	similar to English prefix *mis-*	missachten	to disregard
		missbrauchen	to misuse, to abuse
		misstrauen	to mistrust
		missverstehen	to misunderstand
ver-	similar to English prefix *for-*	verbieten	to forbid
		vergeben	to forgive
		vergessen	to forget
ver-	*(go) awry*	verachten	to despise
		sich verfahren (reflexive)	to get lost
		verkommen	to go to ruin
		verschlafen	to oversleep
ver-	*away, lose*	verdrängen	to block out, to push aside
		verlassen	to leave, to abandon
		verlieren	to lose
ver-	no equivalent	verbinden	to link, to join, to bandage
		vergrößern	to enlarge
		verfhaften	to arrest
		versprechen	to promise
voll-	*complete*	vollenden	to complete, to come to an end
		vollführen	to execute, to perform
zer-	*completely (ruin)*	zerbrechen	to shatter
		zerstören	to destroy

Putting inseparable-prefix verbs into the present tense

After you grasp the meaning of an inseparable-prefix verb (or any other word, for that matter), you can try your hand at plugging it into a meaningful sentence. The following points define the use of *inseparable-prefix verbs:*

✔ You don't stress the prefix in spoken German.

✔ Unlike the separable-prefix verbs, these verbs remain as one word. Word order follows the usual German rule of thumb for verbs: In a simple sentence with only one verb, that verb is in second position.

Look at the example sentences with the inseparable-prefix verb in its usual second position:

Ich verspreche dir einen Rosengarten. (*I promise you a rose garden.*) The verb is **versprechen** (*to promise*).

Viele Fluggäste vergessen ihre Geräte während der Landung auszuschalten. (*Many air passengers forget to turn off their devices while landing.*)

Ich empfehle Ihnen diesen österreichischen Weißwein. (*I recommend this Austrian white wine.*)

Wie gefällt Ihnen dieses Restaurant? (*How do you like this restaurant?*) With this type of information question, the inseparable-prefix verb **gefallen** (*to like*) is in second position following the question word **wie** (*how*).

Sentences with modal auxiliary verbs, commands, and yes/no questions put the inseparable-prefix verb in a position other than the second position. Here are some example sentences:

Erklären Sie das bitte noch einmal. (*Please explain that again.*) **Erklären** (*to explain*) is an inseparable-prefix verb used as a command. With the command (imperative) form, the verb is at the beginning of the sentence.

Sie will ihren Mann verlassen. (*She wants to leave her husband.*) The conjugated verb is the modal auxiliary verb **wollen** (*to want to*), and it's in second position. The inseparable-prefix verb **verlassen** (*to leave*) is in the infinitive form at the end of the sentence.

Verfahren viele Touristen sich in der Stadt? (*Do many tourists get lost in the city?*) The verb **verfahren** means *to get lost*. In yes/no questions, the verb is at the beginning of the question.

Double-Crossers: Dealing with Dual-Prefix Verbs

The *dual-prefix verbs,* the ones we call the *double-crossers,* are characterized by having a prefix that can combine to make both separable-prefix verbs and inseparable-prefix verbs. This means that with some main verbs, the prefix is separable, and with other main verbs, the same prefix is inseparable. For example, you can use the prefix **unter-** (*down*) to form the verb **unterzeichnen** (*to sign [a document]*), which is an inseparable-prefix verb. You can also combine **unter-** with **bringen** (*to bring*) to form **unterbringen** (*to accommodate*), a separable-prefix verb. The list of these prefixes is short. Without the prefix, many of the verbs are high-frequency types that you may already be familiar with.

Grasping dual-prefix verb distinctions

Follow these guidelines to help you remember dual-prefix verbs:

- **Memorize whether the prefix is usually separable or inseparable.** Some dual prefixes are mainly separable, and others are mainly inseparable:

  - **Um-** is a prefix that is mainly separable. **Umziehen** (*to move*), with the prefix **um-** (*around*), is an example of a separable-prefix verb: **Wann ziehst du um?** (*When are you moving?*)

  - **Über-** is a prefix that is mainly inseparable. **Übernachten** (*to sleep*), with the prefix **über-** (*over, across*), is an inseparable-prefix verb: **Im Sommer übernachten wir oft im Zelt.** (*We often sleep in a tent in the summer.*)

- **Think about whether the meaning is literal or figurative.** Some dual-prefix verbs are both separable and inseparable. Generally speaking, the verb in its literal meaning has a separable prefix, such as with **Die Fähre setzt uns ans andere Ufer über.** (*The ferry is taking us across to the other bank [side].*) **Übersetzen** (*to ferry across*) is a separable-prefix verb. The prefix **über-** (*over, across*) is at the end of the sentence. The literal meaning involves physical movement from one place to another: *to cross over, travel across, go across.*

  The verb in its figurative meaning has an inseparable prefix, such as with **Sie übersetzt sehr schnell.** (*She translates very quickly.*) **Übersetzen** (*to translate*), with the prefix **über-** (*over, across*), is an inseparable-prefix verb. The figurative meaning involves changing over: *to translate from one language to another.*

Table 8-3 provides a list of dual prefixes and their English definitions, a sampling of dual-prefix verbs, indicating whether they're separable- or inseparable-prefix verbs, and the English verb equivalents. Five verb pairs have both separable (sep.) and inseparable (insep.) prefixes. Notice that the last two prefixes, **wider-** (*against*) and **wieder-** (*again*), have two separate meanings and spellings.

Table 8-3	Dual Prefixes and Verb Combinations		
Prefix	*English Definition*	*Example Verb*	*English Equivalent*
durch- (usually sep.)	*through*	**durchbringen** (sep.)	*to get through*
		durchfahren (sep.)	*to drive through*
		durchkommen (sep.)	*to come through*
hinter-	*behind*	**hinterlassen** (sep.)	*to let someone go behind*
		hinterlassen (insep.)	*to leave, to bequeath*
über- (usually insep.)	*over, across*	**überfahren** (sep.)	*to ferry across, to cross (over)*
		überfahren (insep.)	*to run over*
		überfallen (insep.)	*to attack, to hold up (a bank and so on)*
		übernachten (insep.)	*to sleep (in a hotel and such)*
		übersetzen (insep.)	*to translate*
		übersetzen (sep.)	*to ferry across*
um- (usually sep.)	*around*	**umbauen** (sep.)	*to renovate*
		umbauen (insep.)	*to enclose, to build around*
		umsteigen (sep.)	*to change (trains)*
		umziehen (sep.)	*to move (to a new home), to change (clothes)*
unter-	*down, under*	**unterbrechen** (insep.)	*to interrupt, to disconnect*
		untergehen (sep.)	*to sink, to go down*
		unterkommen (sep.)	*to find accommodation*
		unternehmen (insep.)	*to do, to undertake*

(continued)

Book III

Assembling the Grammatical Foundations for Communication

Table 8-3 *(continued)*

Prefix	English Definition	Example Verb	English Equivalent
wider- (usually insep.)	*against* (similar to English prefix *re-*)	**widerrufen** (insep.)	*to recall (product), to withdraw*
		widersprechen (insep.)	*to contradict*
		widerstehen (insep.)	*to resist, to withstand*
wieder-	*again*	**wiedergeben** (sep.)	*to give back, to play back, to restore*
		wiederholen (insep.)	*to repeat*
		wiederholen (sep.)	*to get back*
		wiedersehen (sep.)	*to see again, to meet again*

Looking at dual-prefix verbs in the present tense

Dual-prefix verbs follow the guidelines for formation, usage, and word order according to whether the prefix is separable or inseparable. As is the case with the separable-prefix verbs, the dual-prefix verbs that are separable follow the same guidelines for pronunciation: when speaking, the separable prefix is stressed. (For more information on usage, look at the guidelines in the earlier two sections for separable- and inseparable-prefix verbs.)

The following examples show how the dual-prefix verbs play out when you use them in a present-tense sentence:

> **Ich steige im nächsten Bahnhof um.** (*I'm changing [trains] at the next station.*) The dual-prefix verb **umsteigen** (*to change [train, plane]*) is separable.

> **Wiederholen Sie bitte ihre Telefonnummer.** (*Please repeat your phone number.*) The verb **wiederholen** (*to repeat*) has an inseparable prefix when it means *to repeat*. This meaning of the verb is very frequently used.

Hilfe! Das Schiff geht unter! (*Help! The ship is sinking!*) The dual-prefix verb **untergehen** (*to sink*) is separable.

Die Firma widerruft alle defekten Produkte. (*The company is recalling all of the defective products.*) **Widerrufen** (*to recall*) is the dual-prefix verb and it's inseparable.

Mein Freund baut sein altes Haus um. (*My friend is renovating his old house.*) The dual-prefix verb **umbauen** can be either separable or inseparable depending on the meaning. Here, **umbauen** (*to renovate*) is separable.

Book IV
Building Detail and Precision in Your Communication

Two-Way Prepositions That Work in Both the Accusative and Dative Cases	
Preposition	*English Equivalent(s)*
an	at, on, to
auf	on, onto, to
hinter	behind, to the back of
in	in, into, to
neben	beside, next to
über	above, over
unter	under, underneath
vor	in front of
zwischen	between

To improve your chances of being understood when communicating in German, you have to speak or write your words in a particular order. Head to www.dummies.com/extras/germanaio for a free article about the basic guidelines for German word order.

Contents at a Glance

Chapter 1

Tying Ideas Together with Conjunctions and Relative Pronouns

. . . .

In This Chapter

▶ Getting to know different sentence parts and the conjunctions that hold them together

▶ Connecting phrases and clauses with coordinating conjunctions

▶ Forming sentences with subordinating conjunctions

▶ Joining sentences with relative pronouns

. . . .

Conjunctions are the glue that connects parts of a sentence, such as clauses, phrases, or words, together to reach beyond basic sentence structure to form more sophisticated sentences. German uses two types of conjunctions: *coordinating conjunctions,* such as **oder** (*or*), and *subordinating conjunctions,* such as **weil** (*because*). Which type you use depends on the structure of the clauses, phrases, and words that you're joining together. In the first part of this chapter, you find out the difference between these two types of conjunctions, and then you discover how to use the most common German conjunctions to express your ideas clearly and intelligently.

Relative pronouns are another type of glue used to connect sentence parts. These words — *who, whose, whom, which,* and *that* — generally appear at the beginning of a relative clause, and they refer back to the noun or pronoun in the main clause. At the end of this chapter, you find out how to identify German relative pronouns and how to use them to link parts of a sentence together.

Conjunctions and Clauses: Reviewing the Terminology

Before you can master the art of using conjunctions , you need to get a handle on some basic grammatical vocab. You may already be familiar with many of the following terms, but here's a quick recap of the differences among phrases, clauses, and sentences — just in case you've forgotten:

✔ **Phrase:** A group of connected words that has neither a subject nor a verb, such as **nach Zürich** (*to Zürich*).

✔ **Clause:** A group of related words that has a subject and a verb, such as **Ich fliege** (*I'm flying*). Clauses come in several varieties:

- **Main clause (independent clause):** This clause can stand on its own; it has a sentence structure, as in **der Nachrichtensprecher war enttäuscht** (*the newscaster was disappointed*). This is just about the same as a sentence, except it doesn't have a proper beginning (a capitalized **D** in **der**) or a punctuation mark at the end (a period in this example).

- **Subordinate clause (dependent clause):** This clause has a sentence structure with a subject and a verb, but it can't stand on its own. It needs some help from its friends, the independent clause and the conjunction. If you see such a clause alone without a main clause — for example, **weil er seine Stimme verloren hat** (*because he lost his voice*) — you're left waiting to find out more information.

- **Relative clause (dependent clause):** This type of clause can't stand on its own even though it has a sentence structure with a subject and a verb. Relative clauses modify nouns or pronouns, as well as whole phrases. The modifying clause begins with a relative pronoun, such as *who, which,* or *that*. In English, the relative pronoun may be left out; that's not the case in German. For example, **Wo ist das Hotel, das er uns empfohlen hat?** (*Where's the hotel [that] he recommended us?*) The second **das** in the sentence is the relative pronoun **das** (*that*).

✔ **Sentence:** A group of words that has it all: a subject, a verb, a capital letter at the beginning, and an ending like a period, exclamation point, or question mark. In other words, a sentence is the whole shebang. For example, **Ich fliege nächste Woche nach Zürich.** (*I'm flying to Zürich next week.*)

Conjunctions are the connectors, the cement, the super glue that you use to combine sentence parts. Here are the two types of conjunctions:

- ✔ **Coordinating:** A coordinating conjunction joins main clauses, phrases, or words. For example:

    Der Nachrichtensprecher hat seine Stimme verloren, und er musste zu Hause bleiben. (*The newscaster lost his voice, and he had to stay home.*) The coordinating conjunction **und** (*and*) combines the two main clauses; a comma placed before **und** separates the two clauses.

    Martin ging nach Hause und machte sich ein Käsebrot zum Abendessen. (*Martin went home and made [himself] a cheese sandwich for supper.*) **Und** (*and*) is a coordinating conjunction; it combines two actions (verbs) that Martin did.

- ✔ **Subordinating:** This type of conjunction introduces a subordinate clause and relates it to another clause in the sentence. For example:

    Der Nachrichtensprecher war enttäuscht, weil er seine Stimme verloren hat. (*The newscaster was disappointed because he lost his voice.*) **Weil** (*because*) is the subordinating conjunction. The subordinate clause **weil er seine Stimme verloren hat** (*because he lost his voice*) has complete meaning when it's connected to **der Nachrichtensprecher war enttäuscht** (*the newscaster was disappointed*).

    Martin ging nach Hause, obwohl er sehr einsam war. (*Martin went home, although he was very lonely.*) The subordinating conjunction **obwohl** (*although*) introduces the subordinate clause that follows it and connects the two parts of the sentence — **Martin ging nach Hause** and **er sehr einsam war.**

In English, conjunctions such as *and, because, but, or,* and *when* are simple to use in a sentence; the word order comes naturally for fluent speakers. Using German conjunctions correctly, however, requires a conscious effort on your part to keep in mind which type of conjunction you're dealing with and how to get the word order straight. You also need to remember the comma. Keep reading to find out how to correctly use these two types of conjunctions.

Book IV

Building Detail and Precision in Your Communication

Connecting with Coordinating Conjunctions

The *coordinating conjunctions,* the ones that join main clauses, phrases, or words, are the easier of the two types to master. The number of German coordinating conjunctions is small, and they correspond well to their English counterparts in meaning and usage — except for a few easy-to-understand differences.

Table 1-1 shows the common coordinating conjunctions, along with their English equivalents and comments related to how you use them in a sentence.

Note: In German, you don't use a comma in front of **und** in a series (or list of words), although this practice is common in English. Example: **Wir haben Kartoffelbrei, Spinat und Kabeljau gegessen.** (*We ate mashed potatoes, spinach, and cod.*)

Table 1-1	Common Coordinating Conjunctions		
German	*English Equivalent*	*Does a Comma Separate Joined Sentence Parts?*	*Comment*
aber	*but*	yes	Used the same way in English.
denn	*for, because*	yes	**Denn** is also used as a flavoring particle, often to interest the listener; **weil,** a subordinating conjunction, also means *because,* but it has a different word order.
oder	*or*	no (unless the writer chooses a comma for clarity)	Used the same way in English.
sondern	*but (rather)*	yes	Used to express *on the contrary, rather,* or *instead;* it's preceded by a clause that makes a negative statement.
und	*and*	no (unless the writer chooses a comma for clarity)	Used the same way in English.

Using coordinating conjunctions

Incorporating coordinating conjunctions into your writing and speech isn't too difficult. You just combine two sentence parts by using the coordinating conjunction that fits what you intend to say about the relationship between them.

Keep in mind that in German, **oder** and **und** don't need a comma preceding them, although you can use a comma to improve clarity. On the other hand, **aber, sondern,** and **denn** do require a preceding comma to connect clauses, phrases, and words. Here are some examples:

> **Ich gehe zur Bank, denn ich brauche Geld.** (*I'm going to the bank because I need some money.*)

> **Esssen wir heute Abend bei dir oder bei mir?** (*Are we having dinner at your place or my place tonight?*)

> **Heute esse ich ein saftiges Steak im Restaurant oder ich mache Spaghetti zu Hause.** (*Today I'll have a juicy steak in a restaurant, or I'll make spaghetti at home.*)

Sondern and **aber** both mean *but;* however, their uses differ. You use **sondern** to express *but rather* in cases where the first clause has a negative expression and where the two ideas cancel each other. For example:

> **Ich wohne nicht in der Stadtmitte, sondern am Stadtrand.** (*I live not downtown but [rather] on the outskirts of the city.*)

The main clause in the beginning (**Ich wohne nicht in der Stadtmitte**) contains a negative, **nicht,** and the two ideas are mutually exclusive. **Sondern** links the prepositional phrase **am Stadtrand** to the rest of the sentence. You use **aber** in the same manner as in English — to connect two ideas that aren't mutually exclusive. The following sentences show you how to use the coordinating conjunctions **sondern** and **aber:**

> **Ich möchte gern ins Theater gehen, aber ich habe kein Geld.** (*I'd really like to go to the theater, but I don't have any money.*)

> **Ich fliege nicht am Samstag, sondern am Sonntag.** (*I'm flying not on Saturday but rather on Sunday.*)

> **Der Film hatte nicht nur gute Schauspieler, sondern auch hervorragende Musik.** (*The movie had not only good actors but also excellent music.*)

Book IV

Building Detail and Precision in Your Communication

Working on word order

When you form German sentences with coordinating conjunctions, the separate sentence parts maintain their word order. For both English and German, the standard word order looks like this: Take the subject + the verb + additional information, like an object or a prepositional phrase, and then add the conjunction to combine the other sentence part. (Keep in mind that in German, the active, conjugated verb always goes in the second position.) Now you have two parts combined into one sentence:

> **Luca geht ins Kaufhaus, aber sein Hund bleibt zu Hause.** (*Luca goes to the department store, but his dog stays home.*) **Aber** (*but*) is the coordinating conjunction.

Although the preceding word order is exactly the same in English and German, that's not always the case. Other German sentences using a coordinating conjunction have a different word order from the standard subject + verb + other information structure. (Go to Book III, Chapter 1 for more on word order.)

For example, in sentences where *time expressions* (descriptions of time, such as *this morning, in the eighteenth century, at five o'clock,* and so on) take the place of the subject, the verb is still in second position, but the subject goes behind the verb. Here's what this word order change looks like:

> **Wir fahren heute mit dem Zug nach Hamburg, denn morgen früh möchten wir zum Fischmarkt gehen.** (*We're taking the train to Hamburg today because tomorrow morning we'd like to go to the fish market.*) The time expression **morgen früh** immediately follows the coordinating conjunction **denn.**

This change in word order is important because it distinguishes coordinating conjunctions from their cousins, the subordinating conjunctions. (See the later section "Using subordinating conjunctions" for details on the differences between these two types of conjunctions.)

When you want to add more detail to a German sentence (as part of the "additional information" that comes after the subject and verb), remember the mantra *time, cause, manner, place.* This mantra reminds you how to position information that describes when, why, how, and where. The standard word order is

1. Time (tells when)
2. Cause (tells why)
3. Manner (tells how)
4. Place (tells where)

Take a look at the enhancement to the example sentence from earlier in this section:

Wir fahren heute wegen des Fischmarkts mit dem Zug nach Hamburg, denn schon um 5 Uhr in der Früh beginnt der Fischmarkt. (*We're taking the train to Hamburg today because of the fish market, for the market opens already at 5 a.m.*)

In the first clause, **heute** = time, **wegen des Fischmarkts** = cause, **mit dem Zug** = manner, and **nach Hamburg** = place. In the second clause, **schon um 5 Uhr in der Früh** describes time and is in first place in front of the verb.

The following sentences demonstrate German word order with the coordinating conjunctions **und, aber,** and **denn:**

Ich möchte schwimmen, aber das Wasser ist zu kalt. (*I'd like to go swimming, but the water is too cold.*)

Kai hat zwei Brüder und Stefanie hat drei Schwestern. (*Kai has two brothers, and Stefanie has three sisters.*)

Sven ist sehr intelligent, aber er ist nicht amüsant. (*Sven is very intelligent, but he is not amusing.*)

Heike und Georg wohnen in einem sehr kleinen Haus, aber sie sind glücklich darin. (*Heike and Georg live in a very small house, but they're happy in it.*)

Heute arbeite ich nicht, denn ich habe eine Erkältung. (*I'm not working today because I have a cold.*)

Getting Support from Subordinating Conjunctions

Subordinating conjunctions are a little trickier to use than their coordinating cousins, but that's partly because there are more of them to keep straight. As long as you follow the guidelines covered in this section, you'll be able to use subordinating conjunctions in German as well as (or maybe even better than) you do in English.

Book IV

Building Detail and Precision in Your Communication

Table 1-2 presents a list of commonly used German subordinating conjunctions with their English equivalents and comments on their usage.

Table 1-2	Common Subordinating Conjunctions	
German	**English Equivalent**	**Comment**
als	*as, when*	Describes an event in the past. Example: **Als ich elf Jahre alt war . . .** (*When I was eleven . . .*)
bevor	*before*	Used the same way in English
da	*since (inasmuch as)*	Not to be confused with the preposition **seit** (*since* + a point in time) or **da** (*there*)
damit	*so that*	Used to express *in order that . . .*; not to be confused with **damit**, a compound of **da + mit** to express with *that/it/them*
dass	*that*	Rarely begins a sentence; in English, you can leave out the conjunction *that*, but you can't in German. Example: **Ich wusste, dass er krank war . . .** (*I knew [that] he was sick . . .*)
falls	*in case*	Used to describe *in the situation/event that . . .*
ob	*if, whether*	Not interchangeable with **wenn**; **ob** can be used to begin an indirect yes/no question
obwohl	*although*	Used the same way in English
weil	*because*	Same meaning as **denn** (coordinating conjunction) but with a different word order in the subordinate clause
wenn	*if, when, whenever*	Not interchangeable with **ob**; **wenn** starts a clause that stipulates the condition of something possibly happening or not, such as *if A, then B*

Using subordinating conjunctions

Subordinating conjunctions have some similarities to coordinating conjunctions: Both types of conjunctions link ideas together, both introduce one of the ideas, and both generally use commas to separate the two ideas. The distinguishing characteristics of subordinating conjunctions are as follows:

- A subordinating conjunction begins a subordinate clause. **Ich hoffe, dass du kommst.** (*I hope that you come.*) **Dass** is the subordinating conjunction, and the subordinate clause is **dass du kommst.**

- A comma always separates the main clause from the subordinate clause. **Ich hoffe** (main clause) + , (comma) + **dass** . . . (subordinate clause).

- Subordinating conjunctions affect word order of verbs. They push the conjugated (main) verb to the end of the subordinate clause.

Als and **wenn** have similar meanings; they can both mean *when*. However, **als** describes a single event in the past, and **wenn** functions the way it does in English — to describe an action that's repeated in any verb tense. Here are two examples to help you keep these two conjunctions straight:

> **Als ich in der Stadt lebte, hatte ich kein Auto.** (*When I lived in the city, I didn't have a car.*) You don't live in the city anymore; that event is over.

> **Wenn ich nicht mehr arbeite, möchte ich noch fit bleiben.** (*When I'm no longer working, I'd like to stay in shape.*) This sentence is in present tense; it describes an imagined scenario in the future.

Ob and **wenn** are similar because they can both mean *if*. However, **ob** can begin an indirect yes/no question, and **wenn** starts a clause that stipulates the condition of something possibly happening or not. **Falls** and **wenn** are also similar. **Falls** can be used in such situations when you want to express *in case* or *in the case that*. Consider these examples:

> **Ich weiß nicht, ob das richtig ist.** (*I don't know if that's right.*) You're posing a question to yourself that would have a yes/no answer.

> **Wenn/Falls es morgen regnet, bleiben wir zu Hause.** (*If/In case it rains tomorrow, we'll stay home.*)

Look at the following examples of how you use **da, bevor,** and **damit** in German sentences. You find example sentences with **dass, obwohl,** and **weil** in the next section.

> **Da ich wenig Geld habe, hoffe ich einen reichen Partner zu finden.** (*Since I have little money, I hope to find a rich partner.*) You can also use **weil** in place of **da** in this sentence when you want to express *because*.

> **Bevor ich den richtigen Mann finde, werde ich meine Freiheit genießen.** (*Before I find the right man, I'll enjoy my freedom.*)

> **Ich brauche viel Geld, damit ich Luxusartikeln kaufen kann.** (*I need a lot of money so I can buy luxury goods.*)

Putting words in the proper order

Clarity is the name of the game when you're using subordinating conjunctions. To achieve that clarity, you need to make sure you put everything in its proper order:

✔ Throw the conjugated verb to the end of the subordinate clause, as in **Ich hoffe, dass sie das Basketballspiel gewinnen.** (*I hope [that] they win the basketball game.*) The verb **gewinnen** (*win*) is at the end of the subordinate clause, which begins with the word **dass. Dass** very rarely begins a sentence.

✔ When a subordinate clause begins a sentence, place the conjugated verb of the main clause directly following the subordinate clause. Why? Because the whole subordinate clause counts as one sentence element (one unit), the verb in the main clause is in its usual second position: **Wenn ich zu spät aufstehe, verpasse ich den Zug.** (*When I get up too late, I miss the train.*) The verb **verpasse** (*miss*, as in *to miss an opportunity*) directly follows the subordinate clause.

Look at the annotated examples of three sentences that use subordinating conjunctions:

> **Ich hoffe, dass sie das Basketballspiel gewinnen.** (*I hope [that] they win the basketball game.*) The main clause comes first, followed by the subordinate clause.

> 1. **Ich hoffe** (*I hope*) = main clause
>
> 2. **dass** (*that*) = subordinating conjunction introducing the subordinate clause
>
> 3. **sie** (*they*) = subject

4. **das Basketballspiel** (*the basketball game*) = direct object, in accusative case

5. **gewinnen** (*win*) = verb at the end of the subordinate clause

Obwohl ich oft zu spät aufstehe, erreiche ich den Zug. (*Although I often get up too late, I catch the train.*) The subordinate clause comes first, followed by the main clause.

1. **Obwohl** (*although*) = subordinating conjunction introducing the sentence

2. **ich oft zu spät** (*I often too late*) = subject and other information

3. **aufstehe** (*get up*) = verb at the end of the subordinate clause

4. **erreiche** (*catch*) = verb at the beginning of the independent clause (counts as second position in the sentence)

5. **ich den Zug** (*I the train*) = subject and direct object, in accusative case

Weil ich viel zu spät aufgestanden bin, habe ich den Zug verpasst. (*Because I [have gotten] got up much too late, I [have] missed the train.*) The subordinate clause comes first, with the main clause in second position; both clauses use the present perfect verb tense (see Book IV, Chapter 4 for more on the present perfect). In the subordinate clause, the two verb parts are at the end of the clause, with the past participle (**aufgestanden**) preceding the conjugated verb (**bin**). In the main clause (**habe ich den Zug verpasst**), the word order of the verbs follows that of present perfect in a sentence with only one clause: The conjugated verb is in second position (**habe**), and the past participle is at the end of the clause/sentence. Remember that the whole subordinate clause functions as a subject, or as one unit of information, with a comma separating the two clauses. The conjugated verb is, grammatically speaking, in second position.

1. **Weil** (*because*) = subordinating conjunction introducing the sentence

2. **ich zu spät** (*I too late*) = subject and other information

3. **aufgestanden** (*got up*) = past participle of **aufstehen** (*to get up*)

4. **bin** (*have;* Literally: *am*) = conjugated verb thrown to the end of the subordinate clause so it follows the past participle **aufgestanden** (*got up*)

5. **habe** (*have*) = conjugated verb at the beginning of the main clause

6. **ich den Zug** (*I the train*) = subject and direct object, in accusative case

7. **verpasst** (*missed*) = past participle of **verpassen** (*to miss*)

Book IV

Building Detail and Precision in Your Communication

The following sentences show how word order plays out with the subordinating conjunction **dass:**

> **Ich weiss, dass Sie gut Deutsch sprechen.** (*I know that you speak good German.*)

> **Ich möchte, dass du morgen mit mir kommst.** (*I'd like you to come with me tomorrow.* Literally: *I would like that you come with me tomorrow.*)

> **Es ist gut, dass er am Freitag Zeit hat.** (*It's good that he has time on Friday.*)

> **Wir möchten, dass sie den Vertrag unterschreiben.** (*We want them to sign the contract.* Literally: *We would like that they sign the contract.*)

> **Es ist nicht gut, dass Norbert heute Abend allein ist.** (*It's not good that Norbert's alone tonight.*)

Joining with Relative Pronouns

When you want to include more information in a sentence than just a subject, verb, and possibly an object, you may need the help of a relative clause, which uses a relative pronoun (like *who, whom, which,* or *that*) to link two sentence parts. (For more information on relative pronouns, refer to Book III, Chapter 2.) This section explains what the German relative pronouns look like, how they differ from their English counterparts, and how to use them in sentences.

Knowing how to make the connection with relative pronouns

The most important factors that determine which form of the German relative pronoun to use are gender and case. For your reference, Table 1-3 shows the breakdown of the relative pronouns by gender and case. Remember that these relative pronouns can mean *who, whom, whose, which,* or *that* in English.

Table 1-3	Relative Pronouns			
Gender/Number of Noun Being Replaced	**Nominative Case**	**Accusative Case**	**Dative Case**	**Genitive Case**
Masculine (m.)	der	den	dem	dessen
Feminine (f.)	die	die	der	deren
Neuter (n.)	das	das	dem	dessen
Plural (pl.)	die	die	denen	deren

As Table 1-3 shows, the German relative pronouns take a number of different forms, depending on their function in the relative clause. To form a relative clause, keep in mind the following points:

✔ Relative clauses need a relative pronoun; English doesn't always use a relative pronoun.

✔ Relative clauses are set off by commas; English doesn't always need commas.

✔ Selecting the correct form of the relative pronoun depends on gender, number, and case. In English, you only have case with *who, whom,* and *whose.*

✔ The information preceding the relative clause determines the gender and number of the relative pronoun. In English, you aren't concerned with either gender or number.

✔ The relative pronoun's case is determined by its function in the relative clause. The same thing goes for English with *who, whom,* and *whose.*

Forming sentences with relative clauses

When you know the details of how relative pronouns work, you're ready to form your own sentences with relative clauses. Look at the following two short sentences that both have to do with **der Mann** (*the man*):

Das ist der Mann. Ich habe gestern mit ihm gesprochen. (*That is the man. I spoke with him yesterday.*)

Book IV

Building Detail and Precision in Your Communication

To put these two bits of information together into a single sentence, you use the corresponding relative pronoun that links the two sentences. The resulting single sentence with a relative clause sounds more natural than the two short sentences:

> **Das ist der Mann, mit dem ich gestern gesprochen habe.** (*That is the man [that] I spoke to yesterday.*) The relative clause begins with **mit dem** (*with whom*). **Dem** refers to **der Mann,** so it's singular, and it's dative because it's connected to the dative preposition **mit** (*with*). The more formal-sounding English equivalent of the sentence looks like this: *That is the man with whom I spoke yesterday.*

The following example sentences each have a relative clause. After the English translation, you see an explanation for the relative pronoun used in the sentence. As you look at the sentences, notice that the relative clause directly follows the noun to which it refers.

> **Das ist die Frau, in deren Frühstückspension wir übernachten.** (*That's the woman whose bed and breakfast we're staying at.*) The relative pronoun **deren** is in the genitive case, and it's feminine singular.

> **Ich habe einen Freund, dessen Sohn in Kiev lebt.** (*I have a friend whose son lives in Kiev.*) The relative pronoun **dessen** is in the genitive case, and it's masculine singular.

> **Das Auto, das ich kaufen möchte, kostet mehr als $50,000.** (*The car [that] I want to buy costs more than $50,000.*) **Das** is a singular, neuter relative pronoun, and it's in the accusative case. The relative clause interrupts the main clause to modify **Das Auto.**

> **Das Holz, aus dem dieser Schreibtisch gemacht wurde, stammt aus Indonesien.** (*The wood that this desk was made of comes from Indonesia.*) **Dem** is a singular, neuter pronoun, and it's in the dative case. The relative clause interrupts the main clause to modify **Das Holz.**

> **Kennst du Männer, die Frauennamen haben?** (*Do you know [any] men who have women's names?*) The relative pronoun **die** is in the nominative case, and it's plural.

> **Wie finden Sie die Musik, die diese Gruppe spielt?** (*What do you think of the music [that] this band is playing?*) The relative pronoun is the second **die,** the one that follows the comma. **Die** is feminine singular, and it's in the accusative case.

> **Der grosse Hund, der gerade bellt, hat mich letzte Woche gebissen.** (*The big dog that is barking right now bit me last week.*) The relative pronoun **der** is masculine, singular, and it's in the nominative case.

> **Es gibt viele Länder, denen wir mehr Entwicklungshilfe geben sollten.** (*There are many countries to whom we should give more economic aid.*) The relative pronoun **denen** is in the dative case, and it's plural.

Chapter 2

Specifying Relationships with Prepositions

*W*hat's in a preposition? **Zwischen** (*between*) by any other name would sound as strange. A *preposition* is a small word that shows the relationship between its object (a noun) and another word or words in the sentence. It's part of a *prepositional phrase,* which starts with a preposition and includes a noun and maybe an article and other words.

In this chapter, you find out just how important these little guys are in expressing such things as

✔ Place/where something is located, as with **in** (*in*): **Es gibt eine Fliege in meiner Suppe.** (*There's a fly in my soup.*)

✔ Movement/the direction where something is going, as with **unter** (*under*): **Eine Maus läuft unter meinen Stuhl.** (*A mouse is running under my chair.*)

✔ Information showing relationships, as with **trotz** (*in spite of*): **Trotz dieser Überraschungen, schmeckt mir das Essen.** (*In spite of these surprises, the food tastes good.*)

Here, we break down German prepositions into four groups: accusative, dative, genitive, and accusative/dative. The prepositions in the latter group are what we call the *two-timers* because they can be either accusative or dative. You find an easy and logical explanation for these wise guys in the section pertaining to them. Plus, you get a rundown on the preposition combinations or fixed expressions like **zu Hause** (*at home*) and **nach Hause** (*to home [going home]*).

Prepping for Prepositions with a Few Basic Guidelines

Prepositions, such as *around, before*, and *with,* combine with other words to form prepositional phrases that provide information on where (*around the corner*), when (*before noon*), who (*with you*), and much more. Prepositions perform incredible tasks when they combine with other words — notably nouns and verbs — to create a diverse range of expressions. But all those possibilities come at a price. Prepositions are finicky little critters, much more so in German than in English. So how in the world do you get to feel even remotely comfortable with understanding, let alone using, German prepositions with the right case? For starters, look at these basic grammar guidelines.

Grasping the importance of case

In German, case is one key to perfecting the fine art of prepositioning. Both English and German have many prepositions, and both languages use prepositions in similar ways. However, English doesn't have much to do with cases and case endings. In fact, if you bring up the subject of case in English grammar, some people may tell you to go home, lie down for a while, and forget all about it. But case is hugely important to using German prepositions correctly in a prepositional phrase.

As with other German words like nouns, adjectives, and verbs, you have to understand prepositions in conjunction with the other trappings of language. After all, a lowly two-letter preposition like **in** (*in, into, to*) has so much power that it forces the rest of the prepositional phrase — the noun and other words following the preposition — to take the same case endings. The preposition doesn't change; it "tells" the words that follow it to use the same case that it uses. The result is that the case endings in the prepositional phrase help you to

- Recognize the links between the preposition and the words in the phrase.
- Understand the prepositional phrase in context of the whole sentence.

The three cases that prepositions identify with are accusative, dative, and genitive, though some prepositions may use accusative or dative case, depending on meaning. The following examples show all four groups of prepositions. (Book III, Chapter 2 deals with the basics of case.)

- Accusative: **Mein Hund Bello läuft gern durch den Wald.** (*My dog Bello likes to run through the woods.*)

  The prepositional phrase is **durch den Wald** (*through the woods*). Because **durch** is in the accusative case, **der Wald** changes to the accusative form **den Wald.**

✔ Dative: **Ich laufe gern mit ihm (Bello).** (*I like to run with him.*)

The phrase is **mit ihm** (*with him*). The preposition **mit** is in the dative case, so the personal pronoun **er** changes to the dative form **ihm.**

✔ Genitive: **Während des Winters bleiben Bello und ich oft zu Hause.** (*During the winter, Bello and I often stay at home.*)

The phrase is **während des Winters** (*during the winter*). Because **während** is a genitive preposition, **der Winter** in nominative case changes to **des Winters** in genitive case.

✔ Accusative/dative: **Meistens liege ich allein auf der Couch, aber manchmal springt Bello auf die Couch.** (*I usually lie on the couch alone, but sometimes he jumps onto the couch.*)

Auf der Couch (*on the couch*) is dative case; **auf die Couch** (*onto the couch*) is accusative case. The first denotes place, and the second describes movement.

Check out the section "Accusative, Dative, and Genitive Cases: How the Rest of the Phrase Shapes Up" for a complete discussion of case and a look at why case is important when using prepositions.

Understanding where meaning fits in

Meaning is another key to using German prepositions successfully. Know that the rules of mathematics don't apply here — the prepositions and their English counterparts aren't always equal. The preposition **in** looks like the English preposition *in*. Indeed, you can use it the same way in both languages: **Wie viele Fernseher haben Sie in Ihrem Haus?** (*How many TVs do you have in your house?*) However, **in** in German can also mean *into* or *to*. Another preposition, **bei,** sounds like *by* but has a variety of meanings, including *at, near,* and *with*: **Bei mir gibt es keine Flimmerkisten.** (*There aren't any boob tubes at my place.*)

Prepositions crop up in places you'd never suspect, and they take on new meanings in combinations with other words that can be surprising. Don't assume there's a parallel in meaning between German prepositions that resemble English prepositions, either in spelling, pronunciation, or both, because one preposition may have several different meanings. Often, these meanings don't parallel the way the preposition is used in English.

The trick to taming these preposition beasties is remembering them in commonly used phrases, fixed idioms, or standard prepositional phrases — not all alone and naked. So memorize one or two common phrases or words that combine with each preposition to get a feeling for the various meanings a preposition may have.

Book IV

Building Detail and Precision in Your Communication

When you come across an unfamiliar expression that includes a preposition, look at (or listen to) the context of the phrase. You can often make an accurate guess of the meaning by checking whether the literal meaning or the figurative meaning makes more sense. Your experience in your own language can help you make the leap of faith to understanding figurative meaning.

Accusative, Dative, and Genitive Cases: How the Rest of the Phrase Shapes Up

When you use prepositions in your German writing and speech, you want to use them correctly, right? If so (hopefully you said *yes!*), this section is key because it explains the role that cases play in using prepositions. So what exactly is case? *Case* is like a marker, a tag, or an ID for a word; it shows the word's role in relationship to other words in the sentence. The three groups of prepositions are organized by the case that they require to form phrases. These three cases are accusative, dative, and genitive. Having said that, by far the most frequently used group of prepositions is yet another group, namely those that use both accusative and dative cases (fondly called the *two-way prepositions*); we deal with these two-timers in the later section "Tackling Two-Way Prepositions: Accusative/Dative."

As you go through this section, keep in mind that prepositions pop up everywhere in German (and English, for that matter), so be patient and take your time to master the cases one by one. In addition, remember that the context of the phrase influences the meaning of the preposition. For example, **nach** can mean three different things in English — *after, past,* or *to* — yet **nach dem Weg fragen** (*to ask for directions*) doesn't even translate using one of those three prepositions.

No finger pointing: Accusative prepositions

Accusative prepositions express movement, opposition to something, and acts of excluding or receiving. The small band of accusative prepositions, which are strictly linked to the accusative case, includes **bis, durch, für, gegen, ohne,** and **um.** Look in Table 2-1 for a list of these prepositions, their English equivalents, and a few sample phrases.

Table 2-1		Accusative Prepositions	
Preposition	*English Equivalent(s)*	*Sample Phrases*	*English Equivalent*
bis	*till, until* (also: conjunction *until)*	**bis nächsten Sonntag**	*until next Sunday*
durch	*through, by*	**durch die Stadt**	*through the city*
		(jemanden) durch einen Freund kennenlernen	*meet (someone) through a friend*
für	*for*	**für Sie**	*for you*
		für meine Freunde	*for my friends*
gegen	*against, for*	**gegen die Regeln**	*against the rules*
		etwas gegen Kopfschmerzen nehmen	*take something for a headache*
ohne	*without*	**ohne mich**	*without me*
		ohne Herrn Adler	*without Herr Adler*
um	*around, for, at*	**um das Haus**	*around the house*
		Ich bewerbe mich um die Stelle.	*I'm applying for the job.*

To form phrases with accusative prepositions, start with the preposition and add the information that the preposition links to the rest of the sentence — the preposition's object (noun) and any modifiers. If necessary, change the endings of any articles, pronouns, adjectives, and nouns following the preposition to the accusative case. Here's what needs to change:

✔ Some definite articles change. The definite articles are easy because the only change is **der** → **den**. **Die** (feminine and plural) and **das** don't change. (See Book III, Chapters 1 and 2 for details on definite articles.)

Book IV

Building Detail and Precision in Your Communication

✔ Some accusative prepositions may be expressed as contractions with **das:**

- **durch + das = durchs**
- **für + das = fürs**
- **um + das = ums**

These contractions are very common in spoken, colloquial German but not so common in written German.

✔ Most of the pronouns change. The personal pronouns in accusative (direct object) case are **mich** (*me*), **dich** (*you*), **ihn/sie/es** (*him/her/it*), **uns** (*us*), **euch** (*you*), **sie** (*them*), and **Sie** (*you*). (See Book III, Chapter 2 for details on pronouns.)

✔ Adjectives may or may not undergo an ending change. (See Book III, Chapter 5 for the skinny on adjectives.)

✔ A few nouns undergo an ending change. (See Book III, Chapters 1 and 2 for more on nouns.)

Here are some examples of these changes in action:

Sammy das Stinktier sitzt ganz allein, ohne seine Freunde. (*Sammy the skunk is sitting all alone without his friends.*) The preposition **ohne** is followed by **seine Freunde;** both words have accusative plural endings.

Dann läuft er durch den Garten der Familie Finkenhuber. (*Then he runs through the Finkenhuber's garden.*) The preposition **durch** (*through* in this context) indicates movement. **Den Garten** is the masculine singular form of **der Garten** in the accusative case.

Sammy läuft um den Hund Bello und . . . psst! (*Sammy runs around Bello the dog and . . . psst!*) The preposition **um** (*around*) indicates movement. **Den Hund** is the masculine singular form of **der Hund** in the accusative case.

Dative prepositions

Dative prepositions include some heavy hitters. Most *dative prepositions* express relationships of time (when), motion (where to), and location (where). Some have surprising variations in meaning. Nine prepositions are on the dative hit list: **aus, außer, bei, gegenüber, mit, nach, seit, von,** and **zu.** These particular prepositions have an exclusivity clause with the dative case. Table 2-2 shows the nine dative prepositions, their English equivalents, and some sample phrases for each.

Table 2-2		Dative Prepositions	
Preposition	*English Equivalent(s)*	*Sample Phrases*	*English Equivalent*
aus	*from, out of*	**aus den USA**	*from the U.S.A.*
		aus der Arbeit	*from/out of work*
außer	*besides, except for*	**außer uns**	*besides/except for us*
		außer den Kindern	*except for the children*
bei	*at* (a home of, a place of business), *near, with*	**bei Katharina**	*at Katharina's (place)*
		bei der Straße	*near the street*
		Es ist anders bei mir.	*It's different with me.*
		bei schlechtem Wetter	*in bad weather*
mit	*with, by* (means of transportation)	**mit dem Hund**	*with the dog*
		mit dem Zug	*by train*
nach	*after, past, to*	**nach einer Stunde**	*after an hour*
		Es ist fünf nach vier.	*It's five past four.*
		nach Moskau (no article for cities and countries in German)	*to Moscow*
seit	*for, since*	**seit zwanzig Jahren**	*for 20 years*
		seit dem Krieg	*since the war*
von	*by, from, of*	**von einem deutschen Maler**	*by a German artist (created by someone)*
		ein Geschenk von dir	*a present from you*
		am Ende vom Film	*at the end of the movie*
zu	*to* (with people and certain places)	**zur Universität**	*to the university*
		Was gibt's zum Abendessen?	*What's for dinner?*

Book IV

Building Detail and Precision in Your Communication

To form phrases with dative prepositions, start with the preposition and add the information that the preposition connects to the rest of the sentence (the object of the preposition and any articles or adjectives that modify it). Change the endings of any articles, pronouns, adjectives, and nouns following the preposition — if necessary — to the dative case. Here's a list of what needs to change:

- The definite articles change like this (see Book III, Chapters 1 and 2 for more on definite articles):

    - **der** → **dem**

    - **die** → **der** (feminine)

    - **das** → **dem**

    - **die** → **den** (plural)

    Note: Not all prepositional phrases need an article (**dem, einen,** and so on) with the noun, although those that don't are generally fixed expressions such as clock times like **es ist Viertel nach acht** (*it's quarter past eight*) or other types like **zu Hause** (*at home*).

- The contractions that dative prepositions build are

    - **bei + dem = beim**

    - **von + dem = vom**

    - **zu + dem = zum**

    - **zu + der = zur**

    These contractions are very common in spoken, colloquial German, but they're not as common in written German.

- All the pronouns change. The personal pronouns in the dative case are **mir** (*me*), **dir** (*you*), **ihm/ihr/ihm** (*him/her/it*), **uns** (*us*), **euch** (*you*), **ihnen** (*them*), and **Ihnen** (*you*). (See Book III, Chapter 2 for details on pronouns.)

- Adjectives may or may not undergo an ending change. (See Book III, Chapter 5 for more on adjectives.)

- A few nouns undergo an ending change. (See Book III, Chapters 1 and 2 for the lowdown on nouns.)

Take a look at these examples:

Essen wir heute Abend bei dir? (*Shall we have dinner at your place tonight?*) **Bei** is a true chameleon as far as variations in meanings go. In this example, take **bei,** add the dative pronoun **dir,** and presto! You end up with **bei dir** = *at your place.*

Nein, ich möchte lieber zum Restaurant um die Ecke gehen. (*No, I'd rather go to the restaurant around the corner.*) This example uses the contraction of **zu + dem = zum.**

Luigis? Es ist seit einem Monat geschlossen. (*Luigi's? It's been closed for a month.*) **Einem Monat** is the masculine dative case of the indefinite article **ein** combined with the masculine noun **Monat.**

Wichtig ist nur, ich esse mit dir. (*It's only important that I eat with you.*) **Dir** is the dative form of the pronoun *you* that combines with the dative preposition **mit.**

Genitive prepositions

The list of genitive prepositions may be small, but these prepositions are used almost as frequently as the others in this chapter. The *genitive prepositions* describe duration of time, reasons for something, or opposition to something. Most expressions with genitive prepositions are equivalent to English expressions that include *of: instead of, because of*, and *inside* or *outside of*. The genitive prepositions include **anstatt/statt, außerhalb, innerhalb, trotz, während,** and **wegen.** A few other genitive prepositions exist, but they're used less frequently.

Table 2-3 shows the six most common genitive prepositions, along with their English equivalents and sample phrases.

Table 2-3	Genitive Prepositions		
Preposition	*English Equivalent(s)*	*Sample Phrases*	*English Equivalent*
(an)statt (no difference between **anstatt** and **statt**)	*instead of*	**(an)statt meines Autos**	*instead of my car*
außerhalb	*outside of*	**außerhalb des Hauses**	*outside of the house*
innerhalb	*inside of*	**innerhalb der Firma**	*within the company*
trotz	*in spite of, despite*	**trotz des Wetters**	*despite the weather*
		trotz des Lärms	*in spite of the noise*
während	*during*	**während des Tages**	*during the day*
wegen	*because of, on account of*	**wegen der Kosten**	*on account of the costs*
		wegen mir	*because of me*

Book IV

Building Detail and Precision in Your Communication

To form genitive prepositional phrases, begin with the preposition and then add the information that the preposition links to the rest of the sentence. Change the endings of any articles, pronouns, adjectives, and nouns following the preposition — if necessary — so they're also in the genitive case. (See Book III, Chapter 2 for more on cases.) Here are a few examples of what needs to change:

- ✔ Definite articles: Masculine and neuter articles change from **der/das** to **des.** Feminine and plural articles change from **die/die** to **des.**

- ✔ Indefinite articles: Masculine and neuter articles change from **ein/ein** to **eines.** Feminine and plural articles change from **eine/eine** to **einer.**

- ✔ Adjectives: Almost all adjectives, singular and plural, add the **-en** ending to the adjective.

Take a look at a couple of example sentences:

> **Wegen der Hitze gehen wir nicht spazieren.** (*We're not going for a walk because of the heat.*) **Die Hitze** in nominative case becomes **der Hitze** in genitive case.

> **Während des Winters bleiben wir meistens zu Hause.** (*We usually stay at home during the winter.*) **Der Winter** in nominative case becomes **des Winters** in genitive case.

Note: Especially in spoken German, but also in casual written German, some genitive prepositions — **anstatt/statt, trotz, wegen,** and **während** — are typically used with the dative case. This is generally true in central Germany and in the south and southwest German-speaking regions — **Bayern, Österreich, und die Schweiz** (*Bavaria, Austria, and Switzerland*). **Während** uses dative case less frequently in colloquial German than the other three. The meaning of these prepositions doesn't change when you use dative case.

Tackling Two-Way Prepositions: Accusative/Dative

The nine *two-way prepositions* in this section can use either accusative or dative case, depending on meaning. Here are the main differences:

- ✔ The preposition in the *accusative case* describes movement, shows a change of location, is used for dynamic, change-of-place verbs, and answers the question **wohin?** (*where to?*)

- ✔ The preposition in the *dative case* describes position, refers to a static location, and answers the question **wo?** (*where?*)

English sometimes has two different prepositions that do the work of one German two-way preposition. Take *in* and *into*, for example: *In* expresses where something is (dative), and *into* refers to the movement from one place *into* the other (accusative). The German preposition **in** can therefore use either accusative or dative case, depending on whether it expresses position (location) or movement (from one location to another). For example, **Ich sitze im Kino** (*I'm sitting in the cinema*) expresses location, so the preposition uses the dative case, and **Ich gehe ins Kino** (*I'm going to the cinema*) expresses movement, so the preposition uses the accusative case.

To determine whether you need to use a preposition in accusative or dative case, visualize what you want to say. These prepositions indicate concrete spatial relationships, not intangible concepts, which makes it simple to imagine the difference between a cat lying *on* the table — **eine Katze liegt auf dem Tisch** (location = dative case) — and a cat jumping *onto* the table — **eine Katz springt auf den Tisch** (movement = accusative case).

Table 2-4 shows the two-way prepositions, their English equivalents, and a sample phrase for each one with the English translation. ***Remember***: German doesn't have a present continuous, so the present tense (*the mouse runs*), present continuous (*the mouse is running*), or both may be logical translations.

Table 2-4		Two-Way Prepositions	
Preposition	*English Equivalent(s)*	*Accusative Example*	*Dative Example*
an	*at, on, to*	**Die Katze geht ans (an + das) Fenster.** (*The cat walks to the window.*)	**Die Katze sitzt am Fenster.** (*The cat is sitting at the window.*)
auf	*on, onto, to*	**Die Katze springt auf den Tisch.** (*The cat jumps onto the table.*)	**Die Katze steht auf dem Tisch.** (*The cat is standing on the table.*)
hinter	*behind, to the back of*	**Die Katze geht hinter die Couch.** (*The cat is going behind the couch.*)	**Die Katze sitzt hinter der Couch.** (*The cat is sitting behind the couch.*)
in	*in, into, to*	**Die Katze läuft in die Küche.** (*The cat is running into the kitchen.*)	**Die Katze ist in der Küche.** (*The cat is in the kitchen.*)

(continued)

Book IV

Building Detail and Precision in Your Communication

Table 2-4 *(continued)*

Preposition	English Equivalent(s)	Accusative Example	Dative Example
neben	*beside, next to*	**Der Hund legt sich neben die Katze hin.** (*The dog lays itself down next to the cat.*)	**Die Katze liegt neben dem Hund.** (*The cat is lying next to the dog.*)
über	*above, over*	**Eine Maus läuft über den Teppich.** (*A mouse is running over the carpet.*)	**Eine Lampe hängt über dem Tisch.** (*A lamp is hanging over the table.*)
unter	*under, underneath*	**Die Maus läuft unter den Teppich.** (*The mouse runs under the carpet.*)	**Der Teppich liegt unter dem Tisch.** (*The carpet is lying under the table.*)
vor	*in front of*	**Die Maus läuft vor die Katze.** (*The mouse is running in front of the cat.*)	**Der Hund sitzt vor dem Fernseher.** (*The dog is sitting in front of the TV.*)
zwischen	*between*	**Die Katze legt sich zwischen die Pfoten des Hundes.** (*The cat lies down between the dog's paws.*)	**Der Hund steht zwischen der Maus und der Katze.** (*The dog is standing between the mouse and the cat.*)

To form phrases with accusative/dative prepositions, follow the guidelines I describe in the previous two sections for accusative prepositions and dative prepositions. The following two-way prepositions combine with articles to make contractions, though they're mostly used in spoken, colloquial German:

- **an + das = ans**
- **an + dem = am**
- **auf + das = aufs**
- **in + das = ins**
- **in + dem = im**

Other contractions that aren't as frequently used with **das** and **dem** include **hinters, hinterm, übers, überm, unters, unterm, vors,** and **vorm.**

The following examples clarify how to form and use these prepositions correctly:

Die Kinder sind im Bett. (*The children are in bed.*) The preposition **in** (here it means *in*) uses dative case here to express location. Where are the children? In bed.

Die Kinder gehen ins Bett. (*The children are going to bed.*) The preposition **in** (here it means *into*) uses accusative case to express movement. Where are the children going? To bed.

Ich wohne über einer Buchhandlung. (*I live above a bookstore.*) The preposition **über** (*over*) describes where it is. *Where* describes location, so it takes the dative case.

Der Zeppelin fliegt über die Stadt. (*The zeppelin [blimp] is flying over the city.*) The preposition **über** (*over*) describes movement, so it's in the accusative case.

Understanding Quirky Combinations

German has several quirky yet important prepositional phrases that you encounter on a regular basis. These phrases are easiest to remember in verb/preposition combinations. *Verb/preposition combinations* are high-frequency expressions that combine verbs with prepositions. (Refer to Book IV, Chapter 3 for details on verb/preposition combinations.) To understand what sets these prepositional phrases apart from the others in this chapter, consider the following descriptions and sample sentences:

✔ **Zu Hause** and **nach Hause** are two prepositional phrases that are often confused. **Zu Hause** means *at home*. It indicates location. **Nach Hause** means *going home*. It implies movement — motion in the direction of home.

> **Wo ist Birgit? Sie ist zu Hause.** (*Where's Birgit? She's at home.*)

> **Wohin geht Lars? Er geht nach Hause.** (*Where is Lars going? He's going home.*)

✔ **Bis** (*till, until*) is an accusative preposition. What makes it different is the fact that it's used most often in combination with other prepositions, not as a standalone. Look at the following expressions:

> **von 8.30 Uhr bis 19.00 Uhr** (*from 8:30 a.m. till 7 p.m.*): The preposition combo here is **von** (*from*) together with **bis** (*till/to*). This expression represents a sign on a store posting opening hours; clock time expressions don't need an article.

> **bis zum bitteren Ende** (*until the bitter end*): This idiom has the preposition combination **bis zu** (*until*). **Zu** takes dative case: **zu + dem = zum.**

Book IV

Building Detail and Precision in Your Communication

> **bis ins kleinste Detail** (*in[to] the smallest detail*): This is an idiom, and the preposition combo consists of **bis in** (*in[to]*). **Ins = in + das,** the accusative case.

> **bis in (den Abend) hinein** (*on into the [evening]*): When you tack **hinein** (*into*) at the end of **bis in + den Abend,** or a similar time frame, you're emphasizing the length of time. The phrase is in accusative case.

✔ **Entlang** (*along, down*) is the preposition that works the case crowd. It actually has three case combinations: accusative, dative, and genitive. In addition, **entlang** often follows the information it modifies. (And it also functions as an adverb!) Look at these three examples of **entlang,** each of which uses a different case:

> **Gehen Sie den Weg entlang.** (*Walk along the path.*) **Den Weg** is accusative case. You use the accusative case here because you're describing the motion of walking along.

> **Die Grenze verläuft entlang dem Fluß.** (*The border follows the river.*) **Dem Fluß** is dative case because you're describing the place, the location where the border is.

> **Entlang des Ufers gibt es viele Schwäne.** (*There are a lot of swans along the shore.*) The use of the genitive case, **Des Ufers,** is a regional variation on the dative case usage. Using **entlang** in genitive case is typical in southern Germany and Austria.

✔ **Gegenüber** (*across from, opposite*) is another oddity among prepositions. A true multitasker, **gegenüber** works as a dative preposition and combines with verbs as a separable-prefix verb in **gegenüberstehen —** **Er steht mir gegenüber.** (*He's standing opposite me.*) As a preposition, it can be in front of or after its object; it makes no difference in meaning:

> **Wir wohnen gegenüber dem Park.** (*We live across from the park.*) The object, **dem Park,** follows **gegenüber.**

> **Der Präsident stand mir gegenüber.** (*The president was standing opposite me.*) The object, **mir,** precedes **gegenüber.** Technically speaking, prepositions that combine with verbs belong in a separate group called *prefix verbs.* (See Book III, Chapter 8 for the lowdown on separable- and inseparable-prefix verbs.)

Chapter 3

Using Reflexives and Other Verb Combinations

*W*hat, exactly, marks the difference between the dabbler in German who's struggling to order a cup of coffee at a local café and the customer in a three-star restaurant who has the wait staff surrounding the table, offering yet another sample from the chef's newest concoction? The customer's sway over the servers may have to do with his command of native German expressions.

You can notice how well a person has mastered German — or any language — by observing the timely use of *idiomatic expressions,* or fixed expressions whose meanings you can't necessarily figure out based on the meanings of the words that make them up. To correctly insert idiomatic expressions into spoken and written German with ease, you have to know the meaning of the whole expression (not just the words in it). This chapter takes a closer look at the expressions that involve verbs, including those that use reflexive verbs. By using these expressions in your writing and speech, you can take your German to the next level and come across sounding like a native speaker.

Identifying Types of Idiomatic Verb Expressions

Idiomatic German flows easily from the mouths of native speakers, who know when and how much to season their language with verb expressions. You can add some flair to your own German speech and writing by using one of the following major types of idiomatic verb expressions:

✔ **Reflexive verbs:** Verbs are *reflexive* when you use them with reflexive pronouns, which include words such as *myself, themselves,* and *himself* in English. Look at the following example: **Ich erinnere mich an unserem ersten Tanz.** (*I remember our first dance.* Literally: *I recall to myself at our first dance.*) German expresses a great deal of actions by linking reflexive pronouns to the verb, a practice that English uses much less often.

✔ **Verbs associated with certain prepositions:** In this chapter, you find out about idiomatic expressions that pair the verb with a particular preposition in either the dative or accusative case. For instance, the preposition **vor** usually means *in front of,* but in the example **Ich habe Angst vor Schlangen** (*I'm afraid of snakes*), the fixed expression combines the verb **haben** (*to have*) with **Angst** (*fear*) and the dative preposition **vor.**

✔ **Verbs with separable or inseparable prefixes:** A *separable-prefix verb* is a verb with a prefix that detaches from the verb when it's conjugated. These verb combinations can be confusing because more often than not, the prefixes are nothing more than prepositions in disguise. Some reflexive verbs have separable or inseparable prefixes. (For more on verbs with separable and inseparable prefixes, see Book III, Chapter 8.)

To make things even more confusing, you find combos of combos; some verb/preposition combos are actually separable or inseparable verb combos at the same time. In the following verb/preposition expression, the verb **ankommen** (*to arrive*) is a case in point because it has a separable verb prefix **an-.** When you add the preposition **auf** (*on*) to the expression, the meaning changes. Look at the example: **Es kommt darauf an.** (*It depends.*) The prefix **an-** is separated from **-kommen,** the word **darauf** (literally: *on it*) accompanies the verb, and the sum of its parts is no longer *arrive* but rather *depend on.* The preposition **auf** (*on*) in the word **darauf** is a combination of **da-** + **(r)** + **auf.** (See Book III, Chapter 4 for more on expressions using **da-.**)

In the rest of this chapter, you discover various ways of using verb combinations to talk about yourself, others, and things. These groups of idiomatic expressions combine a verb with another word (or words), such as a reflexive pronoun or a preposition, to form expressions.

In the Looking Glass: Reflecting on Reflexive Verbs

Look at yourself in the mirror and smile. What do you see (besides a stunningly beautiful or handsome person)? You are, grammatically speaking, *reflecting on yourself. Reflexive verbs* have a subject that carries out an action directed at itself. Typically, the verb combines with a reflexive pronoun to describe that action. The reflexive pronoun refers back to the subject of the sentence, which is carrying out the action indicated by the verb.

German and English both have reflexive verbs, but German uses them much more liberally. To make a long story short, your German can benefit from flexing (yourself) at the reflexive verb gym. This section introduces you to reflexive verbs and shows you how to use them correctly in your writing and speech.

Self-ish concerns: Meeting the reflexive pronouns

A reflexive verb has two elements: the verb and the reflexive pronoun. In English, a reflexive pronoun has the ending *-self* (*myself, yourself*) for singular forms and *-selves* for plural forms (*ourselves, yourselves*). Both English and German have two cases of reflexive pronouns: the accusative and the dative case. The two cases are identical in English. German has only two variations between the two cases, namely in the first- and second-person singular forms.

Table 3-1 lists the reflexive pronouns together with their translations. (Notice how frequently **sich** appears in the right two columns.) As a guide, you see the corresponding nominative pronouns in the left-hand column. Here's the key to the abbreviations: s. = singular, pl. = plural, inf. = informal, and form. = formal.

Book IV

Building Detail and Precision in Your Communication

Table 3-1	Reflexive Pronouns: Accusative and Dative Case	
Nominative (nom.) Pronouns for Reference	**Accusative (acc.)**	**Dative (dat.)**
ich (*I*)	**mich** (*myself*)	**mir** (*myself*)
du (*you*) (s., inf.)	**dich** (*yourself*)	**dir** (*yourself*)
er/sie/es (*he/she/it*)	**sich** (*himself/herself/itself*)	**sich** (*himself/herself/ itself*)
wir (*we*)	**uns** (*ourselves*)	**uns** (*ourselves*)
ihr (*you*) (pl., inf.)	**euch** (*yourselves*)	**euch** (*yourselves*)
sie (*they*)	**sich** (*themselves*)	**sich** (*themselves*)
Sie (*you*) (s. or pl., form.)	**sich** (*yourself* or *yourselves*)	**sich** (*yourself* or *yourselves*)

On the case! Choosing the right form of reflexive pronoun

Reflexive pronouns are in either the accusative case or the dative case. Which case you use depends on how the pronoun functions in the sentence. It may be the direct object (accusative case) or the indirect object (dative case). Case shows the relationship of words to each other in a sentence — for instance, who's doing what (where the reflexive pronoun is in the accusative case) or who's doing what to what/whom (where the reflexive pronoun is in the dative case).

Consider this example:

> **Ich putze mir die Zähne.** (*I brush my teeth.*)

It explains who's doing what to what, so German expresses this activity with a reflexive pronoun in dative case — **mir.** **Die Zähne** is the direct object, the receiver of the action, and it's in the accusative case. (See Book III, Chapter 2 for more on cases.)

Here are two more examples:

> **Ich fühle mich viel besser.** (*I feel/I'm feeling much better.*) **Mich** (*myself*) is the accusative form of the reflexive pronoun; it's the direct object that refers back to the subject performing the action of the verb **fühlen.** (The information answers the question *who's doing what?* Therefore, the reflexive pronoun is in the accusative case.)

> **Ich ziehe mir eine Jeans an.** (*I put on/I'm putting on a pair of jeans.*) **Mir** is the dative form of the reflexive pronoun; **eine Jeans** is the direct object (accusative case) in the sentence. (The information answers the question *who's doing what to what/whom?* Therefore, the reflexive pronoun is in the dative case.)

The verbs using the dative reflexive pronoun are those in sentences that have a separate direct object; the verbs using an accusative reflexive pronoun have no separate direct object in the sentence.

The reflexive pronoun can also be part of a *verb + preposition* expression, and certain prepositions can require either the accusative or the dative case, as with **Wir freuen uns auf den Feiertag nächste Woche.** (*We're happy about the holiday next week.*) The preposition **auf** (*about*) requires the accusative case, as do time expressions. (Find out more about verb/preposition idioms in the section "Combining Verbs with Prepositions.")

Putting the pronoun in the proper place

Word order plays an important role when you're constructing sentences with reflexive pronouns. Keep in mind the following important points related to word order and reflexive pronouns:

- In a statement, the reflexive pronoun immediately follows the conjugated verb. **Sich** comes right after **haben** in this example: **Die Touristen haben sich die schöne Umgebung angesehen.** (*The tourists looked at the beautiful surroundings.*)

- In a question, if the subject is a pronoun (**ihr** [*you*]), then you place the reflexive pronoun (**euch** [*you*]) directly after it. For example, **Habt ihr euch beide schon wieder erkältet?** (*Have you both caught a cold again?*)

- In the present tense, you push the prefix of a separable-prefix verb to the end of the sentence. In the following example, the verb **anziehen** (*to get dressed*) is a separable-prefix verb; the reflexive pronoun **mich** comes after the conjugated verb **ziehe** and before the prefix **an-: Ich ziehe mich an.** (*I get/I'm getting dressed.*) (Refer to Book III, Chapter 8 for more on separable-prefix verbs.)

Identifying which verbs need to be reflexive

A surprisingly large number of German verbs require a reflexive pronoun such as **mich** (*myself*), **dich** (*yourself*), or **uns** (*ourselves*) in situations when you don't use a reflexive pronoun in English, as in the sentence **Beeilen Sie sich!** (*Hurry up!*)

In German, you frequently find the reflexive in describing personal care routines. These reflexive verbs often describe what you do to yourself when you're in the bathroom. For example, shaving (**sich rasieren** [*to shave oneself*]) is a reflexive verb. In English, you can say that the *man shaved himself* or that *he shaved*, period. The first version is expressed reflexively using *himself*. The second statement, *he shaved,* is just as understandable, and it isn't reflexive in structure. But German has only one, reflexive way of expressing this action: **Er rasiert sich.** (*He shaves himself.*)

Book IV

Building Detail and Precision in Your Communication

To further add to the mix, some German verbs can go either way: with or without the reflexive pronoun. With such verbs, the reflexive format is different from the verb without the reflexive pronoun. The next three examples show you **waschen** (*to wash*) expressed first with a reflexive pronoun in the accusative case, then in the dative case, and finally without a reflexive pronoun; notice the difference in meaning:

Ich wasche mich am Abend. (*I wash myself in the evening.*) **Mich,** the reflexive pronoun in accusative case, refers back to the subject of the sentence, **ich.** And **ich** (*I*) is carrying out the action on **mich** (*myself*).

Waschbären waschen sich oft die Hände. (*Raccoons often wash their hands.*) Notice that German speakers express *their hands* with **die Hände** (*the hands*), so if you want to say *I wash my hands* in German, it looks like this: **Ich wasche mir die Hände. Mir** is the dative case reflexive pronoun *myself,* and **die Hände** is the accusative case (direct object) *the hands.*

Christian wäscht sein Auto jeden Samstag. (*Christian washes his car every Saturday.*) In both the English and the German sentences, the verb **wäscht** (*washes*) is followed by a direct object that refers to another living being or thing.

Table 3-2 lists some of the more common reflexive verbs that have to do with personal hygiene. In German, you express the verbs in this list with a reflexive pronoun. The helpful grammar details give you clues about case and whether you have a separable-prefix verb.

Table 3-2	Reflexive Verbs: Personal Hygiene	
German Expression	**English Equivalent**	**Helpful Grammar Details**
sich abschminken (acc.)	*to take off one's makeup*	Separable-prefix verb; accusative reflexive pronoun
sich abtrocknen (acc.)	*to dry oneself off*	Separable-prefix verb; accusative or dative reflexive pronoun
sich (die Hände) abtrocknen (dat.)	*to dry (one's hands)*	
sich anziehen (acc.)	*to get dressed*	Separable-prefix verb; accusative or dative reflexive pronoun
sich (das Hemd) anziehen (dat.)	*to put on (one's shirt)*	

German Expression	English Equivalent	Helpful Grammar Details
sich ausziehen (acc.) **sich (die Stiefel) ausziehen** (dat.)	*to get undressed* *to take off (one's boots)*	Separable-prefix verb; accusative or dative reflexive pronoun
sich duschen (acc.)	*to take a shower*	Accusative reflexive pronoun
sich kämmen (acc.) **sich (die Haare) kämmen** (dat.)	*to comb oneself* *to comb (one's hair)*	Accusative or dative reflexive pronoun
sich die Zähne putzen (dat.)	*to brush one's teeth*	Dative reflexive pronoun
sich rasieren (acc.) **sich (das Gesicht) rasieren** (dat.)	*to shave oneself* *to shave (one's face)*	Accusative or dative reflexive pronoun
sich schminken (acc.)	*to put on one's makeup*	Accusative reflexive pronoun
sich waschen (acc.) **sich das Gesicht waschen** (dat.) **sich die Haare waschen** (dat.) **sich die Hände waschen** (dat.)	*to wash oneself* *to wash (one's face)* *to wash (one's hair)* *to wash (one's hands)*	Accusative or dative reflexive pronoun

Many German reflexive verbs have to do with actions other than personal hygiene. They include verbs such as **sich entscheiden** (*to make up one's mind, to decide*) or **sich befinden** (*to be located, to find oneself [somewhere]*). These verbs are common in everyday German, so you can really boost your language ability by familiarizing yourself with such verbal expressions. For the most part, these reflexive verbs have the reflexive pronoun in the accusative case, meaning the reflexive pronoun refers back to the subject of the sentence.

Table 3-3 shows some of the commonly used reflexive verbs that revolve around activities in daily life. Note that all the verbs in this list use the accusative reflexive pronoun, and any prepositions used with these verbs take the accusative case.

Table 3-3	Reflexive Verbs: Daily Life
German Expression	*English Equivalent*
sich ärgern (acc.) **(über)**	*to be angry, upset (about)*
sich bedienen (acc.)	*to serve oneself*
sich beeilen (acc.)	*to hurry (up)*
sich befinden (acc.)	*to be located*
sich bewegen (acc.)	*to move*
sich eignen (acc.)	*to be suited (for)*
sich entscheiden (acc.)	*to decide*
sich erholen (acc.)	*to get better, to recover*
sich erinnern (acc.) **(an)**	*to remember, to recollect*
sich freuen auf (acc.)	*to look forward to something*
sich freuen über (acc.)	*to be happy about something*
sich gewöhnen an (acc.)	*to get used to something*
sich handeln um (acc.)	*to be about*
sich interessieren für (acc.)	*to be interested in*
sich konzentrieren auf (acc.)	*to focus on*
sich setzen (acc.)	*to sit down*
sich vergewissern (acc.)	*to make sure (of)*
sich verlassen auf (acc.)	*to rely on*
sich verlieben in (acc.)	*to fall in love with*
sich vorbereiten auf (acc.)	*to get ready for*
sich vorstellen (acc.)	*to introduce oneself*
sich wundern über (acc.)	*to be amazed at*

Combining Verbs with Prepositions

Prepositions are short, cute words that can have a great influence on other parts of the sentence. Some German prepositions and their English counterparts look similar at times: **in** (*in*), **an** (*on*), and **für** (*for*). However, they can also be sly little creatures that change their tune when they hook up with different verbs, changing the verb's meaning.

Certain prepositions that work together with certain verbs make for powerful, effective means of expression in German and English. You may refer to them as *idioms, idiomatic expressions,* or the bare bones term — *verb/preposition combos.* When you want to sound like your mother tongue is German, you need to acquire as many of these combos as you can fit into your repertoire.

Seeing how prepositions transform verbs

Verb/preposition combinations are more than the sum of their parts. Why? These prepositions are slick: When combined with a verb to form a fixed expression, they can alter the meaning of the verb they appear with. That's why memorizing the verb/preposition combos as a unit is important. You can't predict which preposition partners with which verb, and you can't determine the meaning of the whole phrase, even if you know the meaning of the verb alone (without the preposition).

Table 3-4 lists some of the most frequently used German prepositions that change their meaning in combination with a verb. Notice that the English equivalent of the preposition itself isn't always the same as the translation of the verbal expression. The third column gives an example of a verb/preposition combo, and the fourth column shows an example sentence with its English translation. As you look through the example sentences and their English equivalents, notice that the preposition generally changes its original meaning. Here's what the abbreviations in the table mean: acc. = accusative, dat. = dative.

Table 3-4	Prepositions Used in Idiomatic Verb Expressions		
Preposition	*Usual English Equivalent*	*Example Verbal Expression/English Translation*	*Example Sentence*
an (acc./dat.)	*on, at, to*	**denken an** (acc.) (*to think of/about*)	**Er denkt oft an seinen Eltern.** (acc.) (*He often thinks of his parents.*)
auf (acc./dat.)	*on top of, to*	**warten auf** (acc.) (*to wait for*)	**Sie warten auf den Zug.** (acc.) (*They're waiting for the train.*)
aus (dat.)	*out of, from*	**bestehen aus** (dat.) (*to consist of*)	**Die Uhr besteht aus vielen kleinen Teilen.** (*The clock consists of many small parts.*)
für (acc.)	*for*	**halten für** (acc.) (*to take someone for, to consider*)	**Ich halte ihn für einen engen Freund.** (*I consider him a close friend.*)
in (acc./dat.)	*in, inside of*	**sich verlieben in** (acc.) (*to fall in love with*)	**Sie hat sich in ihn verliebt.** (acc.) (*She fell in love with him.*)
mit (dat.)	*with*	**fahren mit** (dat.) (*to go with*)	**Ich fahre gern mit der U-Bahn.** (*I like to take the subway.*)
über (acc.)	*over, above*	**reden über** (acc.) (*to talk about*)	**Wir reden über dich.** (*We're talking about you.*)
um (acc.)	*around*	**bitten um** (acc.) (*to ask for*)	**Er bittet um Hilfe.** (*He's asking for help.*)
von (dat.)	*from, of*	**sprechen von** (dat.) (*to speak about/of*)	**Wir sprechen von dem/vom Präsidenten. (von + dem = vom)** (*We're talking about the president.*)
vor (dat.)	*in front of*	**Angst haben vor** (dat.) (*to be afraid of*)	**Hast du Angst vor Spinnen?** (*Are you afraid of spiders?*)

All German prepositions dictate the case of and control the relationship they have with other parts of the sentence, namely as objects of the preposition. Some of the prepositions that pair with verbs use the accusative case, while others use the dative case. Another group, the *two-way prepositions,* can work in the accusative or dative case. (This is true of some other prepositions as well, including those that don't partner with verbs to form idiomatic expressions.) The following sections group some common verbal expressions according to what case their preposition takes to help you remember them. (Check out Book IV, Chapter 2 for more information on prepositions.)

Knowing common combos in the accusative case

Verbs that combine with prepositions using the accusative case add real German sparkle to your written and spoken language. These common verb/preposition combos are fixed expressions, so you have to remember which preposition partners with which verb, which case the preposition takes (accusative for this list), and what the expression means.

Table 3-5 lists the commonly used verb/preposition combos with prepositions in the accusative case. Used alone, these prepositions may be able to use either accusative or dative, but in combination with these verbs, they work as accusatives. The expressions are listed alphabetically by verb.

Table 3-5 Idiomatic Verb Expressions with Accusative Prepositions

Verbal Expression	Example Sentence	English Equivalent
ankommen auf (*to depend on*) (***Note:*** **Ankommen** has a separable prefix **an-**.)	**Es kommt auf das Wetter an.**	*It depends on the weather.*
bitten um (*to ask for*)	**Wir bitten um Ihre Unterstützung.**	*We're asking for your support.*
denken an (*to think of/about*)	**Denkst du oft an deine Kindheit?**	*Do you often think about your childhood?*
gespannt sein auf (*to be excited about*)	**Ich bin gespannt auf die Reise.**	*I'm excited about the trip.*
glauben an (*to believe in*)	**Sie glauben nicht an Gott.**	*They don't believe in God.*

(continued)

Table 3-5 *(continued)*

Verbal Expression	*Example Sentence*	*English Equivalent*
halten für (*to take someone for, to consider*)	**Hältst du ihn für einen Dieb?**	*Do you take him for a thief?*
reden über (*to talk about*)	**Sie redet über diverse Themen.**	*She talks about different topics.*
schreiben an (*to write to*)	**Ich schreibe an die Zeitung.**	*I'm writing to the newspaper.*
schreiben über (*to write about*)	**Schreibst du über mich?**	*Are you writing about me?*
sorgen für (*to take care of*)	**Wir sorgen für unsere Oma.**	*We're taking care of our grandma.*
sich verlieben in (*to fall in love with*)	**Ich habe mich in ihn verliebt.**	*I fell in love with him.*
verzichten auf (*to do without*)	**Ich kann auf meinen Urlaub verzichten.**	*I can do without my vacation.*
warten auf (*to wait for*)	**Wartest du auf uns?**	*Are you waiting for us?*

Eyeing common combos in the dative case

When you know how to incorporate verbs that combine with prepositions in the dative case into your written and spoken German, you're well on your way to sounding like you're originally from a German-speaking country. The frequently used verb/preposition combos covered in this section are fixed expressions, so get ready to memorize which preposition combines with which verb, which case the preposition takes (dative for this list), and what the expression means.

Table 3-6 lists some commonly used verb expressions with prepositions in the dative case. Used alone, these prepositions may be accusative or dative, but in these expressions, they require the dative. The table lists the expressions alphabetically by verb.

Table 3-6   Idiomatic Verb Expressions with Dative Prepositions

Verbal Expression	Example Sentence	English Equivalent
abhängen von (*to depend on*) (***Note:* Abhängen** has a separable prefix **ab-**.)	**Es hängt von dem Wetter ab.**	*It depends on the weather.*
Angst haben vor (*to be afraid of*)	**Hast du Angst vor Grizzlybären?**	*Are you afraid of grizzly bears?*
arbeiten an (*to work on*)	**Ich arbeite sehr fleißig an dem Projekt.**	*I'm working very diligently on the project.*
bestehen aus (*to consist of*)	**Die Schweiz besteht aus vier Sprachregionen.**	*Switzerland consists of four language regions.*
erzählen von (*to talk about*)	**Er erzählt oft von seinen Reisen.**	*He often talks about his trips.*
fahren mit (*to go, to ride with*)	**Ich fahre mit dir.**	*I'll go (or ride) with you.*
gehören zu (*to belong to*)	**Sie gehören zu unserer Mannschaft.**	*They belong to our team.*
halten von (*to think of, to have an opinion about*)	**Sie hält nicht viel von der neuen Regierung.**	*She doesn't think much of the new government.*
rechnen mit (*to count on*)	**Sie rechnen mit einer langen Nacht.**	*They're counting on a long night.*
sprechen von (*to talk about*)	**Ich spreche nicht von dir.**	*I'm not talking about you.*
studieren an (*to study at*)	**Viele Studenten studieren an technischen Universitäten.**	*Many students study at technical universities (usually: engineering schools).*
verstehen von (*to understand about*)	**Verstehst du etwas von Motorrädern?**	*Do you know something about motorcycles?*

Book IV

Building Detail and Precision in Your Communication

Chapter 4

Conversing about the Past: The Present Perfect and Past Perfect

*P*resent perfect in German is commonly described as the *conversational past* because — naturally — you use it in conversation. You also typically see present perfect in informal writing such as personal letters and e-mails. German uses the present perfect to talk about all actions or states in the past, finished or unfinished. English, on the other hand, tends to use the present perfect for actions that began in the past but have a link to the present.

The present perfect in German has two elements:

✔ An auxiliary verb, also known as a *helping verb.* (English present perfect uses *have.*)

✔ A past participle. (English examples are *gone, been,* and *known.*)

German uses the two auxiliary verbs **haben** (*to have*) and **sein** (*to be*) to form the present perfect. First, you conjugate the auxiliary in the present tense, and then you add the past participle of the verb (**gelebt** [*lived*]; **gewesen** [*been*]; **geschwommen** [*swum*]).

This chapter shows you how to form and use the present perfect in German and explains how the present perfect differs between German and English. You also get a quick look at the German past perfect, a verb tense that isn't used nearly as frequently as the present perfect.

Forming the Present Perfect with Haben

The majority of verbs form the present perfect with the auxiliary verb **haben** (*to have*) plus the past participle of the action verb you want to use. The two main categories of verbs are classified by the way you form the past participle. They're called *weak* and *strong* verbs. (Don't worry — you don't have to go to the gym to find the strong verbs!) Check out the next sections for more information on weak and strong verbs.

To conjugate a verb in the present perfect with **haben,** you choose the simple present-tense form of **haben — ich habe, du hast, er/sie/es hat, wir haben, ihr habt, sie haben,** or **Sie haben —** and then add the past participle of the verb. Check out the following example of **wohnen** (*to live, to reside*) in the present perfect.

wohnen (*to live*)	
ich **habe gewohnt**	wir **haben gewohnt**
du **hast gewohnt**	ihr **habt gewohnt**
er/sie/es **hat gewohnt**	sie **haben gewohnt**
Sie **haben gewohnt**	
Ich **habe** ein Jahr in Paris **gewohnt.** (*I lived in Paris for a year.*)	

German word order follows specific rules. When you form a sentence with two verbs, the conjugated verb (**haben** [*to have*], **sein** [*to be*], **werden** [*will*], **möchten** [*would like*], and so on) takes second position in the sentence, and you push the past participle to the end of the sentence. (See Book III, Chapter 1 for more info on word order.)

Forming the present perfect with regular weak verbs

Regular weak verbs are the largest group of verbs. To form the past participle, take the unchanged present-tense stem and add the **ge-** prefix and the ending **-t** or **-et.** You need the **-et** ending in the following cases:

- ✔ For verbs whose stem ends in **-d** or **-t:** For example, **heiraten** (*to marry*) becomes **geheiratet** (*married*).

- ✔ For some verbs whose stem ends in **-m** or **-n:** For example, **regnen** (*to rain*) becomes **geregnet** (*rained*).

- ✔ For verbs recently taken over from English: For example, **flirten** (*to flirt*) changes to **geflirtet** (*flirted*).

Note: The verbs ending in **-ieren** — such as, **interpretieren** (*to interpret*), which changes to **interpretiert** (*interpreted*) — don't add the prefix **ge-**. (Get the lowdown on these verbs that have no **ge-** prefix in the later section "Forming the present perfect with verbs ending in **-ieren**.")

So with the verb **arbeiten** (*to work*), you conjugate **haben** in the appropriate person and then add the past participle. To create the past participle, you chop off the ending **-en,** take the stem **arbeit,** and add **ge-** and **-et** like this: **ge- + arbeit + -et = gearbeitet.**

arbeiten (*to work*)	
ich **habe gearbeitet**	wir **haben gearbeitet**
du **hast gearbeitet**	ihr **habt gearbeitet**
er/sie/es **hat gearbeitet**	sie **haben gearbeitet**
Sie **haben gearbeitet**	
Sie **hat** im Herbst bei der Filmgesellschaft **gearbeitet.** (*She worked at the film company in the fall.*)	

Table 4-1 shows some regular weak verbs with the German and English infinitives, followed by the German and English past participles.

Table 4-1	Past Participles of Regular Weak Verbs		
Infinitive	*Past Participle*	*Infinitive*	*Past Participle*
arbeiten (*to work*)	**gearbeitet** (*worked*)	**lieben** (*to love*)	**geliebt** (*loved*)
brauchen (*to need*)	**gebraucht** (*needed*)	**lernen** (*to learn*)	**gelernt** (*learned*)
chatten (*to chat*)	**gechattet** (*chatted*)	**machen** (*to make*)	**gemacht** (*made*)
drucken (*to print*)	**gedruckt** (*printed*)	**passen** (*to fit*)	**gepasst** (*fit*)
feiern (*to celebrate*)	**gefeiert** (*celebrated*)	**regnen** (*to rain*)	**geregnet** (*rained*)
fragen (*to ask*)	**gefragt** (*asked*)	**sagen** (*to say*)	**gesagt** (*said*)
führen (*to lead*)	**geführt** (*led*)	**schenken** (*to give [a present]*)	**geschenkt** (*given*)
glauben (*to believe*)	**geglaubt** (*believed*)	**schmecken** (*to taste*)	**geschmeckt** (*tasted*)

(continued)

Book IV

Building Detail and Precision in Your Communication

Table 4-1 (continued)

Infinitive	Past Participle	Infinitive	Past Participle
hören (to hear)	**gehört** (heard)	**schneien** (to snow)	**geschneit** (snowed)
hoffen (to hope)	**gehofft** (hoped)	**spielen** (to play)	**gespielt** (played)
jobben (to do odd jobs)	**gejobbt** (did odd jobs)	**suchen** (to look for, to search)	**gesucht** (looked for, searched)
kaufen (to buy)	**gekauft** (bought)	**surfen** (to surf)	**gesurft** (surfed)
kochen (to cook)	**gekocht** (cooked)	**tanzen** (to dance)	**getanzt** (danced)
kosten (to cost)	**gekostet** (cost)	**töten** (to kill)	**getötet** (killed)
kriegen (to get)	**gekriegt** (gotten/got)	**wohnen** (to live)	**gewohnt** (lived)
lächeln (to smile)	**gelächelt** (smiled)	**zahlen** (to pay)	**gezahlt** (paid)
leben (to live)	**gelebt** (lived)		

Forming the present perfect with irregular weak verbs

A few weak verbs are irregular, because although they have the prefix **ge-** and the ending **-t,** they don't follow the same pattern as the regular weak verbs. The present-tense stem changes when you put it in the past participle. The good news is there aren't many of these rebels. The bad news: The only way to really identify them is to memorize their past participles because they don't follow any recognizable pattern.

To form these irregular weak verbs in the present perfect, conjugate **haben** in the present tense and then add the past participle. Check out the following example with the verb **denken** (to think).

denken (to think)	
ich **habe gedacht**	wir **haben gedacht**
du **hast gedacht**	ihr **habt gedacht**
er/sie/es **hat gedacht**	sie **haben gedacht**
Sie **haben gedacht**	
Luka **hat** oft an seine Frau **gedacht.** (Luka often thought about his wife.)	

Table 4-2 shows irregular weak verbs with the German and English infinitives, followed by the German and English past participles.

Table 4-2	Past Participles of Irregular Weak Verbs
Infinitive	*Past Participle*
brennen (*to burn*)	**gebrannt** (*burned*)
bringen (*to bring*)	**gebracht** (*brought*)
denken (*to think*)	**gedacht** (*thought*)
kennen (*to know a person*)	**gekannt** (*known a person*)
nennen (*to name, to call*)	**genannt** (*named, called*)
wissen (*to know information*)	**gewusst** (*known information*)

Forming the present perfect with strong verbs

Identifying a *strong verb* is fairly easy. Its past participle ends in **-en.** (The one exception is the verb **tun** [*to do*], whose past participle is **getan** [*done*].) In most strong verbs, the past participle begins with **ge-.** Many of these past participles can seem pesky at first. Why? They often have vowels and consonants that differ from those in the infinitive. Here's some good news, though: A lot of the verbs whose past participles go through these spelling contortions are high-frequency verbs. To form the present perfect with strong verbs, you conjugate **haben** in the appropriate person and then add the past participle. Take a look at the following table to see an example.

trinken (*to drink*)	
ich **habe getrunken**	wir **haben getrunken**
du **hast getrunken**	ihr **habt getrunken**
er/sie/es **hat getrunken**	sie **haben getrunken**
Sie **haben getrunken**	
Wir **haben** gestern viel Mineralwasser **getrunken**. (*We drank a lot of mineral water yesterday.*)	

Table 4-3 lists some other strong verbs with their infinitives, past participles, and English translations.

Table 4-3		Past Participles of Strong Verbs	
Infinitive	**Past Participle**	**Infinitive**	**Past Participle**
backen (*to bake*)	**gebacken** (*baked*)	**schreiben** (*to write*)	**geschrieben** (*written*)
beginnen (*to begin*)	**begonnen** (*begun*)	**singen** (*to sing*)	**gesungen** (*sung*)
essen (*to eat*)	**gegessen** (*eaten*)	**sitzen** (*to sit*)	**gesessen** (*sat*)
finden (*to find*)	**gefunden** (*found*)	**sprechen** (*to speak, to talk*)	**gesprochen** (*spoken, talked*)
geben (*to give*)	**gegeben** (*given*)	**stehen** (*to stand*)	**gestanden** (*stood*)
halten (*to hold*)	**gehalten** (*held*)	**tragen** (*to wear*)	**getragen** (*worn*)
heißen (*to be called*)	**geheißen** (*been called*)	**treffen** (*to meet*)	**getroffen** (*met*)
helfen (*to help*)	**geholfen** (*helped*)	**trinken** (*to drink*)	**getrunken** (*drunk*)
lassen (*to leave, to let*)	**gelassen** (*left, let*)	**tun** (*to do*)	**getan** (*done*)
lesen (*to read*)	**gelesen** (*read*)	**verlassen** (*to leave*)	**verlassen** (*leave*)
liegen (*to lie, to be located*)	**gelegen** (*lain, been located*)	**verlieren** (*to lose*)	**verloren** (*lost*)
nehmen (*to take*)	**genommen** (*taken*)	**verstehen** (*to understand*)	**verstanden** (*understood*)
rufen (*to call*)	**gerufen** (*called*)	**waschen** (*to wash*)	**gewaschen** (*washed*)
schlafen (*to sleep*)	**geschlafen** (*slept*)	**ziehen** (*to pull*)	**gezogen** (*pulled*)

You can easily remember the meanings of many strong verbs because they're reasonably similar to the English verbs. Another plus is that you can even find similar patterns to the English past participle forms. Take a look at these examples: **beginnen, begonnen** (*begin, begun*); **singen, gesungen** (*sing, sung*); and **trinken, getrunken** (*drink, drunk*).

Forming the present perfect with verbs ending in -ieren

The **-ieren** verbs are easy to spot because when you take away the **-ieren**, they generally look like verbs you may be familiar with in English. These verbs are different from other German verbs for several reasons. First, they end in **-ieren,** unlike mainstream verbs, which end in **-en.** In addition, they form the past participle without the prefix **ge-** but with **-t** at the end.

You can usually recognize the meanings of these verbs, and the English equivalent of the infinitive often ends in *-ify* (**identifizieren** = *to identify;* **verifizieren** = *to verify*), *-ize* (**idealisieren** = *to idealize;* **sozialisieren** = *to socialize*), or *-ate* (**aktivieren** = *to activate;* **vibrieren** = *to vibrate*). When forming the present perfect with **-ieren** verbs, all you need to know is this:

- You form the past participle without **ge-.**
- You form the past participle with **-t.**

Look at how easily you can use these verbs:

- **fotografieren** (*to photograph*): Der Journalist **hat** die Demonstration **fotografiert.** (*The journalist photographed the demonstration.*)
- **dekorieren** (*to decorate*): Vor dem Neujahrsfest **haben** wir das Wohnzimmer **dekoriert.** (*Before the New Year's Eve party, we decorated the living room.*)
- **probieren** (*to try, to sample*): **Hast** du die Torte schon **probiert?** Sie ist lecker! (*Have you tried the torte [cake] yet? It's delicious!*)

Forming the Present Perfect with Sein

Some verbs form the present perfect with the auxiliary verb **sein** (*to be*) plus the past participle of the verb you want to use. All the verbs that use **sein** have two similarities:

- They don't have a direct object, which means they're *intransitive.* For example, the verb **laufen** (*to run*) is intransitive: **Wir sind schnell gelaufen.** (*We ran fast.*) An example of a transitive verb (with a direct object) is **trinken** (*to drink*), and it looks like this: **Ich habe eine Tasse Tee getrunken.** (*I drank a cup of tea.*)
- They show a change in some condition, as with **werden** (*to become*), or some motion to or from a place, as with **kommen** (*to come*).

Generally, you form the past participle with **ge-** + the stem from the infinitive + the ending **–en.** For example, **kommen** (*to come*) becomes **gekommen** (*come*). However, some verbs in this group have past participles with spelling changes from the original infinitive form. For instance, **gehen** (*to go, to walk*) changes to **gegangen** (*gone, walked*).

Of course, this verb group includes a few rogues, as well. For instance, the verbs **bleiben** (*to stay*) and **sein** (*to be*) don't meet the second criterion, but they still need **sein** to form the present perfect. Adding to the group of wayward verbs are the ones that use **sein** but have a **-t** ending in the past participle.

These include **joggen** (*to jog*), which changes to **gejoggt** (*jogged*), **reisen** (*to travel*), which changes to **gereist** (*traveled*), and **rennen** (*to run, to race*), which changes to **gerannt** (*run, raced*).

To form the present perfect with **sein,** you first conjugate the present tense of the verb **sein** and then add the right past participle, as you can see in the following conjugation of **fahren** (*to drive*).

fahren (*to drive*)	
ich **bin gefahren**	wir **sind gefahren**
du **bist gefahren**	ihr **seid gefahren**
er/sie/es **ist gefahren**	sie **sind gefahren**
Sie **sind gefahren**	
Bist du die ganze Nacht **gefahren?** (*Did you drive all night?*)	

Even in conversation, it's a lot more common to use the simple past of **sein** than the present perfect; for example, **Wie war der Flug von Zürich nach San Francisco?** (*How was the flight from Zürich to San Francisco?*) (For more information on how to form and use the simple past, check out Book IV, Chapter 5.)

Look at Table 4-4 for a list of verbs that use **sein** in the present perfect. Some past participles have no stem change; others go through contortions to form the past participle, so you need to memorize them.

Table 4-4   Verbs Conjugated with Sein in the Present Perfect

Infinitive	*Sein + Past Participle*	*Infinitive*	*Sein + Past Participle*
bleiben (*to stay, to remain*)	**ist geblieben** (*stayed, remained*)	**reiten** (*to ride [horseback]*)	**ist geritten** (*ridden*)
fahren (*to drive*)	**ist gefahren** (*driven*)	**schwimmen** (*to swim*)	**ist geschwommen** (*swum*)
fallen (*to fall*)	**ist gefallen** (*fallen*)	**sein** (*to be*)	**ist gewesen** (*been*)
fliegen (*to fly*)	**ist geflogen** (*flown*)	**steigen** (*to climb*)	**ist gestiegen** (*climbed*)
fließen (*to flow, to run*)	**ist geflossen** (*flowed, run*)	**sterben** (*to die*)	**ist gestorben** (*died*)

Infinitive	Sein + Past Participle	Infinitive	Sein + Past Participle
gehen (*to go, to walk*)	**ist gegangen** (*gone, walked*)	**wachsen** (*to grow*)	**ist gewachsen** (*grown*)
kommen (*to come*)	**ist gekommen** (*come*)	**werden** (*to become*)	**ist geworden** (*become*)
laufen (*to run, to walk*)	**ist gelaufen** (*run, walked*)		

Eyeing the Present Perfect: German versus English

In the present perfect, German and English have some similarities and some differences. In both languages, you use the present perfect to talk about past activities, and you use them both in conversation. Also, the construction looks similar, at least when you use the auxiliary verb **haben;** for example, **Ich habe einen Kojoten gesehen.** (*I have seen a coyote.*)

The differences in the present perfect come about when you want to add a time element, such as **gestern** (*yesterday*): **Gestern habe ich einen Kojoten gesehen.** (*Yesterday I saw a coyote.*) You use the present perfect in German, but in English, you use *saw* (the simple past). On the other hand, when you want to describe a past action that's still going on, you say something like **Seit einigen Jahren sehe ich Kojoten.** (*I've been seeing coyotes for a few years.*) Here, German uses the simple present, yet English uses the present perfect continuous. In this section, you get familiar with these differences in verb tense usage.

One for all: Representing three English tenses

Both English and German use the present perfect in conversation. The distinction is that in German, you use it a lot more frequently in conversation and informal written language. Look at this example, which uses present perfect in German but simple past in English because *last night* is finished:

> **Was hast du gestern Abend im Fernsehen gesehen?** (*What did you see on TV last night?*)

German has only the one verb tense, the present perfect, to represent three tenses in English. For example, here are three acceptable translations of **Sie haben in Wien gelebt:**

- **Present perfect:** *They have lived in Vienna.* (This one expresses that they may still live there.)
- **Simple past:** *They lived in Vienna.* (This version says they no longer live there.)
- **Past continuous:** *They were living in Vienna.* (This tense talks about a relationship between two completed past actions. Usually one is longer than the other; the other past action may be described in a previous or subsequent sentence or in the same sentence.)

Look at the sentence *They were living in Vienna.* Because you don't even have past continuous in German (or any other continuous forms, for that matter), you use the present perfect as the pinch hitter, like so: **Während des kalten Krieges haben sie in Wien gelebt.** (*During the Cold War, they were living in Vienna.*)

As soon as you understand how to form the present perfect, you'll find yourself using it frequently to describe a great deal of situations in the past. In fact, unless you intend to pursue a career in German journalism, you won't have much use for the simple past or other past-tense verb forms.

Opting for the German present

Look at the following two German sentences with their literal and real English translations. You may be surprised (and relieved) that in German, you can get by with the simple present in some situations where you have to use the present perfect in English. To make things even simpler, you express both *since* and *for* with **seit** in German.

> **Seit wie lange warten Sie auf die U-Bahn?** (*How long have you been waiting for the subway?* Literally: *Since how long wait you for the subway?*)

> **Wir stehen hier seit zehn Minuten.** (*We've been standing here for ten minutes.* Literally: *We stand here for ten minutes.*)

Using Modal Auxiliary Verbs in Present Perfect

When you're dealing with modal verbs — such as **sollen** (*should, to be supposed to*) or **wollen** (*to want*) — in the present perfect, you need to be aware of word order. Some sentences with a modal verb in the present perfect may have three verb components; others may have only two parts. This section gives you the lowdown on forming modal verbs and using them in the present perfect tense.

Forming modal verbs in present perfect

When modal verbs stand alone without modifying an infinitive verb in present perfect, they look and act like other strong verbs in present perfect. **Mögen** (*to like*) is the modal verb that most often appears alone without another verb.

To form the present perfect of a modal verb, you first conjugate the auxiliary verb **haben** (*to have*) in the present tense — for example, **ich habe** (*I have*). Then you add the past participle form of the modal verb — for example, the past participle form of **mögen** is **gemocht** (*liked*). Consider this example sentence: **Ich habe ihn gemocht.** (*I liked him.*)

Table 4-5 lists the infinitives and past participles of the modal verbs.

Table 4-5	Past Participles of Modal Verbs
Infinitive	*Past Participle*
dürfen (*may, to be allowed to*)	**gedurft** (*was allowed to*)
können (*can, to be able to*)	**gekonnt** (*could, was able to*)
mögen (*to like to*)	**gemocht** (*liked*)
müssen (*must, to have to*)	**gemusst** (*had to*)
sollen (*should, to be supposed to*)	**gesollt** (*was supposed to*)
wollen (*to want to*)	**gewollt** (*wanted to*)

Understanding word order with modal verbs

For situations in which modal verbs don't modify an infinitive verb in the present perfect, the conjugated auxiliary verb goes in second position in the sentence, and the past participle goes at the end of the sentence. The following sentences show you what this word order looks like. Notice that each of the sentences has two verb parts (the auxiliary verb and the past participle of the modal verb).

> **Am Anfang habe ich diese Kollegin nicht gemocht.** (*In the beginning, I didn't like that colleague.*)

> **In früheren Zeiten haben die Bauer viele Kinder gewollt.** (*In former times, farmers wanted [to have] a lot of children.*)

Book IV

Building Detail and Precision in Your Communication

> **Wir haben vor Mitternacht nach Hause gemusst.** (*We had to be home before midnight.*)

> **Er hat Pasta nie gemocht.** (*He never liked pasta.*)

When the modal verb combines with another verb (in addition to the auxiliary **haben**) in present perfect tense, they form a double infinitive. In such sentences, the main verb and the modal verb appear together at the end of the clause or sentence in their infinitive forms, with the main verb preceding the modal verb. As is the case with other verbs in the present perfect, you conjugate the auxiliary verb **haben** in the present tense and place it in second position in the sentence. The following examples illustrate the correct word order for modals that are double infinitives. Notice that each sentence has three verb parts, and remember only the first (**haben**) is conjugated.

> **Wir haben den Film sehen wollen, aber er war schon ausverkauft.** (*We wanted to see the movie, but it was already sold out.*)

> **Die Kinder haben am Silvesterabend bis Mitternacht aufbleiben dürfen.** (*The children were allowed to stay up until midnight on New Year's Eve.*)

> **Er hat im Ausland studieren müssen.** (*He had to study abroad.*)

> **Sie haben noch eine Nacht im Hotel verbringen können.** (*They were able to stay one more night in the hotel.*)

One more thing when you're dealing with modal verbs in the present perfect tense: When you have a dependent clause that has a subordinating conjunction, such as **dass** (*that*) or **obwohl** (*although*), or a relative pronoun, such as **wer** (*who*) or **das** (*that*), you have to put all the verb parts at the end of the clause. (For more info on subordinating conjunctions and relative pronouns, see Book IV, Chapter 1.) In other words, the conjugated auxiliary verb goes in second-to-last position, and the past participle — or the infinitives, if the clause includes a double infinitive — goes in last place. The following sentences show you how this word order looks when using double infinitives with the modal verb:

> **Ich wusste, dass er die Prüfung hat bestehen können.** (*I knew that he could have passed the test.*)

> **Ich verstehe immer noch nicht, warum sie so etwas hat machen müssen.** (*I still don't understand why she had to do that.*)

> **Es war unklar, wer von uns hat gehen sollen.** (*It was unclear which one of us should have gone.*)

Using Separable- and Inseparable-Prefix Verbs in Present Perfect

You have to do a bit of juggling with some German verbs that have prefixes when you form the present perfect. The two types of prefix verbs are

- **Separable-prefix verbs:** These are the verbs that have a prefix, such as **auf-,** that separates from the base, or stand-alone verb, in some verb tenses. In the infinitive form, the prefix is added to the front of the verb; for example, **geben** (*to give*) becomes **aufgeben** (*to give up, to check [luggage]*). These verbs may have either strong or weak endings in the past participle, which you use to form the present perfect, but they all have the **ge-** prefix, as in **aufgegeben.**

- **Inseparable-prefix verbs:** These verbs have a prefix, such as **be-,** that doesn't separate from the base, or stand-alone verb, such as **kommen** (*to come*): **bekommen** (*to get*). They may have either strong or weak endings in the past participle, which is used to form the present perfect, but they lack the **ge-** prefix: **bekommen.**

In this section, you identify these two types of prefix verbs and find out how to form them in the present perfect. (For more on verbs with prefixes, go to Book III, Chapter 8.)

Separable-prefix verbs

With separable-prefix verbs, you form the past participle by leaving the prefix at the front of the verb, squishing **ge-** in the middle, and following up with the rest of the participle. Most of the commonly used verbs in this group resemble strong verbs (past participle ending in **-en**); others resemble weak verbs (past participle ending in **-t** or **-et**). And just to keep you on your toes, although most of these verbs use the auxiliary **haben,** a few verbs use the auxiliary verb **sein.** (See Book III, Chapter 8 for more on separable-prefix verbs.)

You form the present perfect of separable-prefix verbs by conjugating **haben** or **sein** in the present tense and adding the past participle. So if the infinitive is **anrufen** (*to call [on the phone]*), you get the past participle **angerufen** (*called*), which has the three elements **an + ge + rufen.** Take a look at the conjugation of **fernsehen** (*to watch TV*).

Book IV

Building Detail and Precision in Your Communication

fernsehen (*to watch TV*)	
ich **habe ferngesehen**	wir **haben ferngesehen**
du **hast ferngesehen**	ihr **habt ferngesehen**
er/sie/es **hat ferngesehen**	sie **haben ferngesehen**
Sie **haben ferngesehen**	
Habt ihr am Wochenende **ferngesehen?** (*Did you watch TV on the weekend?*)	

You pronounce the separable-prefix verbs with the stress on the first syllable, which is the prefix.

Table 4-6 shows you what the past participles for some common separable-prefix verbs look like. I've included **ist** before the past participles that need the verb **sein**.

Table 4-6	Past Participles of Separable-Prefix Verbs		
Infinitive	*Past Participle*	*Infinitive*	*Past Participle*
anfangen (*to begin, to start*)	**angefangen** (*begun, started*)	**mitbringen** (*to bring along*)	**mitgebracht** (*brought along*)
ankommen (*to arrive*)	**ist angekommen** (*arrived*)	**mitmachen** (*to join in*)	**mitgemacht** (*joined in*)
anrufen (*to call*)	**angerufen** (*called*)	**stattfinden** (*to take place*)	**stattgefunden** (*taken place*)
aufgeben (*to give up, to check [luggage]*)	**aufgegeben** (*given up, checked [luggage]*)	**vorhaben** (*to plan*)	**vorgehabt** (*planned*)
aussehen (*to look [like]*)	**ausgesehen** (*looked [like]*)	**zurückgehen** (*to decline, to go back*)	**ist zurückgegangen** (*declined, gone back*)
einkaufen (*to go shopping*)	**eingekauft** (*gone shopping*)	**zusammenfassen** (*to summarize*)	**zusammengefasst** (*summarized*)
einladen (*to invite*)	**eingeladen** (*invited*)	**zusammenkommen** (*to meet*)	**ist zusammengekommen** (*met*)
fernsehen (*to watch TV*)	**ferngesehen** (*watched TV*)		

Inseparable-prefix verbs

With inseparable-prefix verbs, the past participle can have a strong verb ending (**-en**) or a weak verb ending (**-t** or **-et**), but the rest is relatively easy. To help you distinguish how these verbs differ from separable-prefix verbs, just look at these three characteristics for the past participle of inseparable-prefix verbs:

- The prefix always sticks to the rest of the verb, including the past participle.
- You don't add the prefix **ge-** to the past participle.
- You don't stress the prefix. Look at the infinitive **erkennen** (*to recognize*) and its past participle **erkannt** (*recognized*).

You put together the present perfect of inseparable-prefix verbs by conjugating **haben** in the present tense and adding the past participle. Check out the conjugation of **bekommen** (*to get, to receive*).

bekommen *(to get, to receive)*	
ich **habe bekommen**	wir **haben bekommen**
du **hast bekommen**	ihr **habt bekommen**
er/sie/es **hat bekommen**	sie **haben bekommen**
Sie **haben bekommen**	
Warum **hast** du die Zeitung heute nicht **bekommen?** (*Why didn't you get the newspaper today?*)	

Table 4-7 lists some other inseparable-prefix verbs with their past participles. Notice how similar the two forms of the verbs are; a few are exactly the same.

Table 4-7	Past Participles of Inseparable-Prefix Verbs		
Infinitive	*Past Participle*	*Infinitive*	*Past Participle*
beantworten (*to answer*)	**beantwortet** (*answered*)	**gebrauchen** (*to use, to make use of*)	**gebraucht** (*used, made use of*)
bekommen (*to get, to receive*)	**bekommen** (*gotten, received*)	**gefallen** (*to like*)	**gefallen** (*liked*)
besuchen (*to visit*)	**besucht** (*visited*)	**gehören** (*to belong to*)	**gehört** (*belonged to*)

(continued)

Book IV

Building Detail and Precision in Your Communication

Table 4-7 *(continued)*

Infinitive	Past Participle	Infinitive	Past Participle
bezahlen (*to pay*)	**bezahlt** (*paid*)	**gewinnen** (*to win*)	**gewonnen** (*won*)
erkennen (*to recognize*)	**erkannt** (*recognized*)	**missverstehen** (*to misunderstand*)	**missverstanden** (*misunderstood*)
erklären (*to explain*)	**erklärt** (*explained*)	**vergessen** (*to forget*)	**vergessen** (*forgotten*)
erzählen (*to tell*)	**erzählt** (*told*)	**verlieren** (*to lose*)	**verloren** (*lost*)

Describing with Past Perfect

The difference between the past perfect and the present perfect is that the past perfect describes an action that began and ended in the past. The present perfect may describe an action that has ended in the past, but in English, it's also somehow connected to the present. The past perfect tense works the same way in both German and English. Generally, you use it to express a past event that happened before another event that took place in the past. That second event may be stated or simply implied from the context of the sentence. In both English and German, the past perfect can appear in a sentence without a second, accompanying past action.

To form the past perfect in English, you use the auxiliary verb *had* (the simple past form of *have*) and combine it with the past participle of the verb; for example, *I had lived* or *they had seen*. German is the same, except that you use one of two auxiliary verbs. To conjugate a verb in the past perfect in German, you choose the simple past tense form of the auxiliary verb **haben** (*to have*) or **sein** (*to be*). You then add the past participle of the verb. (To see how to conjugate **haben** and **sein** in simple past, go to Book IV, Chapter 5.)

In the following example sentence, the verb in the past perfect describes an event that happened before another event that's in the present perfect tense:

> **Hubert hatte bereits zwei Konzertkarten gekauft, bevor seine Freundin erkrankt ist.** (*Hubert had already bought two concert tickets before his girlfriend became ill.*)

First Hubert bought two concert tickets, so this action is in the past perfect — **hatte . . . gekauft** (*had bought*). In the second part of the sentence, the verb **ist erkrankt** (*became ill*) is in present perfect in German, indicating that the event happened after the tickets were bought. Notice that the English equivalent, *became ill*, is in simple past. English uses the simple past to describe past, finished actions, whereas German uses the present perfect or, in some cases, the present tense. (For details on using simple present to describe past events, go to Book III, Chapter 3.)

The distinction in the time frame between the two past events may be implied, as in the following examples:

> **Wir hatten eine bessere Leistung von den Schauspielern erwartet.** (*We had expected a better performance by the actors.*)

> **Sie hatten bereits sehr viel über die moderne Kunst erfahren.** (*They had already learned a lot about modern art.*)

> **Das hatte ich nicht gewusst.** (*I hadn't known that/didn't know that.*)

Or the time frame can be stated outright in the sentence. Look at the following example sentences with past perfect. They contain another verb in a clause that's linked to the main part of the sentence by a subordinating conjunction. (Check out Book IV, Chapter 1 for more info on subordinating clauses and subordinating conjunctions.)

> **Sie waren bereits abgereist als wir ankamen.** (*They had already left by the time we arrived.*)

> **Trixi war so müde gewesen, dass sie auf der Couch eingeschlafen ist.** (*Trixi was so tired that she fell asleep on the couch.*)

> **Ich hatte nicht geahnt, dass das Studium so lange dauern würde.** (*I had not suspected that the course of studies would take so long.*)

Book IV

Building Detail and Precision in Your Communication

Chapter 5

Narrating the (Simple) Past: Fact and Fiction

In This Chapter

▶ Forming the simple past

▶ Comparing simple past with present perfect and past perfect

Master storytellers and journalists both have an incredible knack for drawing their audience into a narrative. Storytellers lend a façade of reality to the wildest tales as they twist and turn, fold and unfold in front of rapt listeners (or readers), and journalists rivet readers' attention with their well-written news reports of violence, natural disasters, and human prowess. What these two narrators have in common is a command of the *simple past tense,* also referred to as the *imperfect* or the *narrative past.*

To describe any events or stories, you need verbs — and lots of them. In German, the verb tense of choice when narrating fact or fiction is the simple past tense — for example, **er ging** (*he went*), **wir mussten** (*we had to*), or **ich sprach** (*I spoke*). This chapter compares the simple past tense to the other past tenses and helps improve your German by focusing on forming and using the simple past tense.

To remember the difference in usage between the simple past and the present perfect in German, think of the simple past as the narrative past; you run across it more frequently in written German. Think of the present perfect as the conversational past, the one you hear in offices, cafés, and on the streets. (Check out Book IV, Chapter 4 for more on the present perfect.)

Conjugating the Simple Past

To write or talk formally about something that happened, you need to know how to conjugate verbs in the simple past tense. However, before you dive into conjugations, you need to understand how the simple past relates to English.

Although you may know that the simple past in German translates as the simple past in English, you may not be aware of other ways to render it. In some respects, the simple past is a gold mine for expressing various verb tenses in English. Table 5-1 shows the four different English equivalents for the same German phrase, along with the context for these differences in English translation.

Table 5-1	English Equivalents for the German Simple Past		
German Phrase in the Simple Past	**English Equivalent**	**English Verb Tense**	**Context/ Intended Idea**
Fritz **spielte** sehr gut Gitarre.	Fritz *played* the guitar very well.	Simple past.	Commenting about Fritz — he played very well last night.
Fritz **spielte** sehr gut Gitarre.	Fritz *was playing* the guitar very well.	Past continuous; this verb tense doesn't exist in German.	Fritz was playing very well, when all of a sudden lightning struck the amplifiers.
Fritz **spielte** sehr gut Gitarre.	Fritz *used to play* the guitar very well.	*Used to* + verb to describe habitual actions that no longer apply. The *used to* + *verb* isn't described verbally in German; instead, you use **damals** (*then*).	Telling about Fritz's former talents; he's 78 years old now, and he's lost his edge.
Fritz **spielte** sehr gut Gitarre.	Fritz *did play* the guitar very well.	Simple past, emphatic form; the emphatic form is described with **doch** (*indeed/ really*) in German.	Fritz did indeed play well; he was working up a storm on Saturday night.

The simple past verb form isn't too difficult to master. You just need to know that there are several types of endings according to which of the following categories the verb falls into:

- Regular verbs (also called *weak verbs*)
- Irregular verbs (also known as *strong verbs*)
- Other irregular verbs like **sein, haben,** and the modal verbs (also called *auxiliary* or *helping verbs*)

Note: A fourth category of verbs, the *separable-prefix verbs,* includes verbs that have a prefix like **ab-** or a preposition like **mit-** in front of the verb; these verbs may be regular or irregular. The prefix is separated when you conjugate the verb, and it's generally placed at the end of the phrase. Two examples are **abfahren** (*to leave*) and **mitkommen** (*to come along*). Book III, Chapter 8 deals with separable- and inseparable-prefix verbs.

The applications of the simple past are quite different when you compare German and English. The single most important aspect of the simple past in English is that it describes an action that was completed in the past, often with a reference to the past, like *last month, in 2012,* or *when I was 13.* English uses the simple past in a great number of situations: to describe past events of both formal and informal (casual) nature, as well as for spoken and written language. German, on the other hand, tends to use the simple past in written language, especially newspapers, books, written texts, narrated stories, and even fairy tales. In German, the simple past is also a means of describing past events not connected to the present.

This section shows you how to conjugate different German verbs, including regular (weak) and irregular (strong), **haben** and **sein,** and modals. After you read this section, you can write about the past with eloquence and style.

Forming regular (weak) verbs in simple past

Regular verbs are verbs that don't have a stem change between the present tense and the simple past tense. For example, the present tense stem of **wohnen** is **wohn-,** and the simple past stem is also **wohn-.** The endings are what make the difference between the two tenses.

Here's how to form the simple past of regular verbs:

1. Drop the **-en** from the infinitive.

2. Add **-te,** which you can think of as the *-te tense marker.*

3. Add the additional endings (with the exception of the **ich** and **er/sie/es** forms, which have no ending other than **-te**). The endings are as follows: nothing, **-st,** nothing, **-n, -t, -n,** and **-n.**

To see an example, compare the present and the simple past of the verb **wohnen** (*to live*). The present form is in parentheses after the simple past.

Book IV

Building Detail and Precision in Your Communication

wohnen (*to live*) — Simple Past (Present)	
ich wohn**te** (wohn**e**)	wir wohn**ten** (wohn**en**)
du wohn**test** (wohn**st**)	ihr wohn**tet** (wohn**t**)
er/sie/es wohn**te** (wohn**t**)	sie wir wohn**ten** (wohn**en**)
Sie wohn**ten** (wohn**en**)	
Ich **wohnte** in Dortmund. (*I lived in Dortmund.*)	

A second group of regular verbs are those with a stem ending in **-d** or **-t**. A small number of verbs with the stem ending in **-fn** or **-gn** also fall into this category. With these verbs, for the purpose of making them easier to pronounce, you put an additional **e** in front of the **-te** tense marker. Taking **arbeiten** (*to work*) as an example, you form the simple past like this: **ich arbeit + e + te = ich arbeitete.** Compare the present and the simple past.

arbeiten (*to work*) — Simple Past (Present)	
ich arbeit**ete** (arbeit**e**)	wir arbeit**eten** (arbeit**en**)
du arbeit**etest** (arbeit**est**)	ihr arbeit**etet** (arbeit**et**)
er/sie/es arbeit**ete** (arbeit**et**)	sie arbeit**eten** (arbeit**en**)
Sie arbeit**eten** (arbeit**en**)	
Du **arbeitetest** sehr schnell. (*You worked very fast.*)	

The following example sentences show you how to use simple past with regular (weak) verbs:

> **Wir bezahlten die Rechnung.** (*We paid the bill.*)

> **Wie lange dauerte die Reise?** (*How long did the trip take?*)

> **Gestern kaufte ich neue Winterstiefel.** (*Yesterday I bought new winter boots.*)

> **Es regnete zwei Tage ohne Unterbrechung.** (*It rained for two days without stopping.*)

Forming irregular (strong) verbs in simple past

The verbs described in this section are called *irregular* because unlike regular verbs, these verbs have a variety of vowel changes in the simple past form.

The change may simply be one vowel change, such as **i** to **a**; for example, with the irregular verb **beginnen** (*to begin*), the simple past stem is **begann** (*began*). Unfortunately, you have to memorize the simple past stem for each irregular verb in order to add the simple past endings to it. But the good news is you encounter many of these verbs often, so you may already know their meanings and be familiar with the present tense forms of a number of them.

To conjugate irregular verbs in the simple past, keep in mind these points:

- ✔ These verbs have no endings in **ich** and **er/sie/es** forms.
- ✔ The other endings, those for **du, wir, ihr, sie,** and **Sie,** are the same as the present tense endings. The endings are nothing, **-st**, nothing, **-en, -t, -en,** and **-en.**

beginnen (*to begin*)	
ich begann	wir begann**en**
du begann**st**	ihr begann**t**
er/sie/es begann	sie begann**en**
Sie begann**en**	
Er **begann** zu laufen. (*He began to run.*)	

Luckily for you, German has only a relatively small number of irregular (strong) verbs for you to worry about when conjugating the simple past tense.

These verbs are fairly easy because with many of them, you can draw on your knowledge of English irregular verbs to help you recognize the German *cognates* (words that are the same or very close in spelling and meaning in two languages). Table 5-2 lists verbs that are irregular in both English and German; they're cognates or at least verbs that begin with the same letter in English and German and mean nearly the same thing. A couple of verbs — **kommen** (*to come*) and **trinken** (*to drink*) — are different in spelling but quite similar in pronunciation. The table lists the **er/sie/es** form of the simple past because it doesn't have any endings.

Book IV

Building Detail and Precision in Your Communication

Many irregular verbs are very common verbs, so you can familiarize yourself with them by *reading actively,* which involves thinking beyond the gist of the text. How? By slowing down your reading or by rereading a passage, you may notice how the verb stem is spelled differently from the present tense form. Try writing down the verbs as you come across them and figuring out the corresponding present tense; then you can familiarize yourself with the various spelling changes in the simple past.

Table 5-2	Simple Past of Irregular Verbs Resembling English Verbs		
Infinitive	*Simple Past (er/ sie/es Form)*	*Infinitive*	*Simple Past (er/ sie/es Form)*
beginnen (*to begin*)	**begann** (*began*)	**lassen** (*to let, to allow*)	**ließ** (*let, allowed*)
essen (*to eat*)	**aß** (*ate*)	**liegen** (*to lie [down]*)	**lag** (*lay*)
fallen (*to fall*)	**fiel** (*fell*)	**reiten** (*to ride [a horse or camel]*)	**ritt** (*rode*)
finden (*to find*)	**fand** (*found*)	**schwimmen** (*to swim*)	**schwamm** (*swam*)
fliegen (*to fly*)	**flog** (*flew*)	**sehen** (*to see*)	**sah** (*saw*)
geben (*to give*)	**gab** (*gave*)	**singen** (*to sing*)	**sang** (*sang*)
gehen (*to go*)	**ging** (*went*)	**sitzen** (*to sit*)	**saß** (*sat*)
halten (*to hold, to stop*)	**hielt** (*held, stopped*)	**sprechen** (*to speak*)	**sprach** (*spoke*)
kommen (*to come*)	**kam** (*came*)	**trinken** (*to drink*)	**trank** (*drank*)

The following example sentences use some of the irregular verbs from Table 5-2 in simple past to narrate a surprise ending to the tale of Little Red Riding Hood:

> **Der Wolf lag tot in Großmutters Bett.** (*The wolf lay dead in grandmother's bed.*)

> **Rotkäppchen und ihre Großmutter saßen im Wohnzimmer.** (*Little Red Riding Hood and her grandmother sat in the living room.*)

> **Sie aßen Kuchen und tranken Champagner.** (*They were eating cake and drinking champagne.*)

Table 5-3 lists some irregular verbs that are irregular in both English and German but that aren't cognates. What these verbs also have in common is that they're high-frequency verbs (verbs you encounter often in German). Try memorizing both the infinitive and simple past forms together.

Table 5-3	Simple Past of Common Irregular Verbs (Non-Cognates)		
Infinitive	*Simple Past (er/sie/es Form)*	*Infinitive*	*Simple Past (er/sie/es Form)*
fahren (*to drive, to ride a bike/ bus/train*)	**fuhr** (*drove, rode*)	**tragen** (*to wear, to carry*)	**trug** (*wore, carried*)
fangen (*to catch*)	**fing** (*caught*)	**treffen** (*to meet*)	**traf** (*met*)
gewinnen (*to win*)	**gewann** (*won*)	**tun** (*to do*)	**tat** (*did*)
laufen (*to run*)	**lief** (*ran*)	**vergessen** (*to forget*)	**vergaß** (*forgot*)
lesen (*to read*)	**las** (*read*)	**verlieren** (*to lose*)	**verlor** (*lost*)
nehmen (*to take*)	**nahm** (*took*)	**verstehen** (*to understand*)	**verstand** (*understood*)
schneiden (*to cut*)	**schnitt** (*cut*)	**wachsen** (*to grow*)	**wuchs** (*grew*)
schreiben (*to write*)	**schrieb** (*wrote*)	**werden** (*to become*)	**wurde** (*became*)

Forming haben and sein in simple past

When conjugating the two verbs **haben** (*to have*) and **sein** (*to be*) in simple past, you need to pay extra attention for two reasons:

✔ **Haben** and **sein** can function as auxiliary or helping verbs. Most verbs use the auxiliary verb **haben** to form the present perfect, but some irregular verbs use **sein**. (See Book IV, Chapter 4 for more on the present perfect.)

✔ Although German speakers usually use the present perfect tense in conversations about the past (see Book IV, Chapter 4), they use the simple past of **haben** and **sein** more frequently in conversation. (They also use the simple past of the modal verbs in conversation; check out the next section.)

You form the simple past of **haben** and **sein** with their respective stems **hatte** and **war.** Similar to the irregular (strong) verbs, the **ich** and **er/sie/es** forms have no verb endings. Look at the two conjugations, with the verb endings in bold.

haben (*to have*)	
ich hatt**e**	wir hatt**en**
du hatte**st**	ihr hatt**et**
er/sie/es hatt**e**	sie hatt**en**
Sie hatt**en**	
Ich **hatte** viel Zeit. (*I had a lot of time.*)	

sein (*to be*)	
ich war	wir war**en**
du war**st**	ihr war**t**
er/sie/es war	sie war**en**
Sie war**en**	
Sie **waren** zu Hause. (*They were at home.*)	

The following example sentences show **sein** and **haben** in the simple past tense:

> **Wie war der Film?** (*How was the film?*)
>
> **Er war nichts Besonderes.** (*It was nothing special.*)
>
> **Wo warst du heute Vormittag?** (*Where were you this morning?*)
>
> **Ich hatte einen Termin beim Zahnarzt.** (*I had an appointment at the dentist.*)
>
> **Letzte Woche hatten meine Frau und ich eine schwere Erkältung.** (*Last week, my wife and I had a bad cold.*)
>
> **Maximilian war zwei Wochen in Norwegen.** (*Maximilian was in Norway for two weeks.*)
>
> **Er hatte viel Glück mit dem Wetter. Es war sonnig und warm.** (*He was very lucky with the weather. It was sunny and warm.*) (The expression **Glück haben** (*to be lucky*) is, literally speaking, *to have luck.*)

Forming modals in simple past

The *modal verbs* are the small band of modifying or helping verbs. (See Book III, Chapter 6 for an in-depth look at modal verbs.) These verbs modify another verb, although sometimes they can stand alone. The list includes **dürfen** (*to be allowed to*), **können** (*can, to be able to*), **mögen** (*to like*), **müssen** (*to have to, must*), **sollen** (*to be supposed to, should*), and **wollen** (*to want to*).

Note: Although **möchten** is included in this elite group in the present tense, it falls by the wayside because of its meaning (*would like to*) and joins forces with **mögen** in the simple past tense. Both have the meaning *liked to* in the simple past.

German speakers prefer to use the modal verbs in the simple past form when conversing or telling stories. The modal verbs are reasonably easy to remember in the simple past form because they follow the same conjugation rules:

- The past stem changes have no umlaut.

- You add the **-te** stem marker onto the simple past stem. The additional endings are as follows: nothing, **-st**, nothing, **-n**, **-t**, **-n**, and **-n**.

Table 5-4 shows the modal verbs in the simple past tense.

Table 5-4			Modal Verbs in Simple Past Tense	
Infinitive	*Past Stem*	*Tense Marker*	*Simple Past (ich, er/sie/es Form)*	*English Equivalent of Simple Past*
dürfen	**durf-**	**-te**	**durfte**	*was allowed to*
können	**konn-**	**-te**	**konnte**	*was able to, could*
mögen	**moch-**	**-te**	**mochte**	*liked*
müssen	**muss-**	**-te**	**musste**	*had to*
sollen	**soll-**	**-te**	**sollte**	*was supposed to*
wollen	**woll-**	**-te**	**wollte**	*wanted to*

The following verb table shows the modal verb **können** conjugated, with the endings in bold, including the **-te** tense marker.

können (*to be able to, can*)	
ich konn**te**	wir konn**ten**
du konn**test**	ihr konn**tet**
er/sie/es konn**te**	sie konn**ten**
Sie konn**ten**	
Nach dem Skiurlaub **konnte** ich besser skifahren. (*I was able to ski better after the skiing vacation.*)	

The following example sentences show you how to use conjugated modal verbs in simple past. Notice that when you use a modal verb by itself, it goes in second position in the sentence.

> **Eine solche Überraschung wollten wir nicht.** (*We didn't want a surprise like that.*)
>
> **Er mochte sie gern.** (*He liked her a lot.*)
>
> **Ich musste schnell nach Hause.** (*I had to go home quickly.*)

When a sentence has two verbs — the modal verb and the verb it modifies — the modal goes in its usual second position, and the infinitive form of the action verb goes at the end of the sentence. The following examples show you what this order looks like:

> **Im Winter mochte ich nicht so früh aufstehen.** (*In the winter, I didn't like to get up so early.*)
>
> **Ich musste mich beeilen.** (*I had to hurry up.*)
>
> **Vor dem Spiel durften die Fussballfans Unterschriften sammeln.** (*Before the game, the soccer fans were allowed to collect signatures.*)
>
> **Sie konnte jeden Tag zehn Kilometer joggen.** (*She could jog ten kilometers every day.*)
>
> **Ich musste gestern länger bei der Arbeit bleiben.** (*I had to stay at work later yesterday.*)

Contrasting Tenses

In addition to the simple past (**Ich sah einen rosaroten Elefant** — *I saw a pink elephant*), two other verb tenses belong to the past tense club:

- ✔ The present perfect: **Ich habe einen rosaroten Elefant gesehen.** (*I have seen a pink elephant.*)

- ✔ The past perfect: **Ich hatte einen rosaroten Elefant gesehen.** (*I had seen a pink elephant.*)

This trio is the mainstay for describing events in the past in both English and German. However, you can often get away with using the present perfect or even the simple past in describing events that may actually call for the past perfect. In addition, the past perfect isn't used very frequently in either German or English, so it takes a back seat. In fact, that's a good way to remember when to use the past perfect — namely to describe events that happened way back before another past event. (Book IV, Chapter 4 deals with present perfect and past perfect in more detail.)

To help you keep the three past tenses straight, Table 5-5 compares their forms and applications (uses) and provides an example situation for each.

Table 5-5	German Usage of Past Tenses		
Past Tense	*How to Form*	*Use*	*Example Sentence/ Explanation*
Simple past (narrative past)	Use the simple past form of the verb.	Used in formal, written language; preferred in spoken language in northern Germany; used with **haben**, **sein**, and modal verbs	Der Orkan **dauerte** insgesamt zwei Wochen. (*The hurricane lasted two weeks altogether.*) **Dauerte** is the simple past, third-person singular of **dauern** (*to last*).
Present perfect (conversational past)	Combine the present tense of either **haben** or **sein** and a past participle of the verb.	Used in casual, informal, spoken language when talking about the past; preferred in southern German-speaking regions	Gestern **haben** wir einen guten Film **gesehen**. (*Yesterday we saw a good movie.*) **Haben** is the present tense, first-person plural of **haben**; **gesehen** is the past participle of **sehen** (*to see*).
Past perfect	Combine the simple past of either **haben** or **sein** and a past participle of the verb.	Used to describe a past event that happened before another past event, often with the two verbs in the same sentence	Nachdem sie das Telefon **aufgelegt hatte**, klingelte es nochmals. (*After she had hung up the phone, it rang again.*) **Hatte** is the simple past tense, third-person singular of **haben**, and **aufgelegt** is the past participle of **auflegen** (*to hang up*).

Book IV

Building Detail and Precision in Your Communication

Chapter 6

Looking to the Future (And Avoiding It)

In This Chapter

▶ Avoiding the future and sticking with the present

▶ Facing the future with **werden**

▶ Knowing when to use the future perfect

*W*hether you're the type to face the future head on, no holds barred, or you like to avoid the inevitable at all costs, this chapter has something for you. With all the complications of case endings and the three noun genders in German, at last the future pops up, simple and straightforward.

When you first read the chapter title, unless you've been dusting off (and reading) English grammar books lately, you're likely to say that the future is one verb tense — the one associated with *will* + a verb (as in, *I'll get the phone*). Actually, however, English has several ways to express the future. The good news is that in German you're on Easy Street because in a great deal of situations, you can avoid using the future tense altogether even when describing future events. In fact, German uses the future verb tenses far less frequently than English does.

Before you travel into the future, though, the first stop is the German present tense. In the beginning of this chapter, you find out how versatile the German present tense is for situations in which English uses various future tenses. Later in the chapter, you jump on the future bus and take a short and smooth ride through the future, looking at how to form it and when to use the future tense as well as the future perfect tense.

The Future Is Now: Using the Present Tense Instead

In general, you don't need to use the future in German when the context makes it clear that the action is describing something in future time. Imagine you're standing on the subway platform, and the train is coming into the station at Marienplatz in Munich. You have six bags and a broken arm, and someone behind you says **Ich helfe Ihnen** (Literally: *I help you*). In English, your helper would say *I'll help you.* This German do-gooder isn't grammar deficient; he or she is an angel speaking perfectly idiomatic German.

While English has a total of four ways to express the future, German has only two future tenses. In addition, the future tense usage in German is far less frequent than it is in English. Look at the following breakdown of how German and English express the future:

- First is the present tense used for schedules, like travel plans. This is the same in German: **Die Maschine startet um 7.40 Uhr.** (*The plane leaves at 7:40 a.m.*)

- Next in English is the *going to* future — *going to* + infinitive verb — as in *We're going to visit my cousins this weekend.* This future expression doesn't exist in German. You usually use the German present instead.

- English also uses the *present continuous* — *to be* + verb with *-ing* ending — as in *I'm taking the dog for a walk.* This verb tense is also nonexistent in German; instead, you can generally use the present for these situations.

- Last but not least is the *will* future verb form, which is equivalent to the German **werden** (*will*) + infinitive verb used to express the future. The usage is less frequent in German because the present tense can punt for the *will* future in many cases. (Check out the later section "Peering into the Future with **Werden**" for more details.)

This section more closely examines how German uses the present to express future actions.

Seeing when German present works perfectly

In English, you encounter all types of situations that require the future tense. But in German, you can state those same situations simply by using the present tense, especially when the context implies that you intend to express future time or when you use a time expression that indicates the future. (Book III, Chapter 3 deals solely with the present tense, in case you need a refresher.)

The following examples give you an overview of the range of situations where German uses the present to express the future. Keep in mind that in English, you generally use the future when you include an expression that refers to the future, such as *next week*.

> **Vielleicht ruft er morgen an.** (*Maybe he'll call tomorrow.*) **Morgen** (*tomorrow*) is an adverb of time that expresses the future.

> **Dieses Wochenende besuchen wir meine Kusinen.** (*We're going to visit my cousins this weekend.*) **Dieses Wochenende** (*this weekend*) refers to the coming weekend; also, German has no equivalent to the English verb form *going to* + verb.

> **Ich bleibe heute etwas länger im Büro.** (*I'm staying a bit longer in the office today.*) The reference to **heute** (*today*) in connection with **länger** (*longer*) indicates later on today; also, German has no *-ing* verb equivalent.

> **Ich glaube/Ich denke, ich bleibe zu Hause.** (*I think I'll stay home.*) German uses present tense here, but English expresses a spontaneous decision (*I think I'll . . .*) with the future.

> **Ich vergesse nicht/Ich werde nicht vergessen.** (*I won't forget.*) In English, you use the future for a promise. (If you say *I don't forget,* you're making a factual statement, not a promise.) In German, you have both options to make a promise.

Saying when: Using future time expressions with the present tense

When you talk about future events in English, you often include an expression of future time together with one of the future verb forms. Germans also use a wide range of future time expressions, such as **heute Abend** (*this evening*) or **morgen früh** (*tomorrow morning*). Here's good news for you: They frequently appear in combination with the present tense, as they cue the audience to a future time.

Take a look at some common future time expressions:

- ✔ **am Anfang der Woche** (*at the beginning of the week*)
- ✔ **am Dienstag** (*on Tuesday*)
- ✔ **diese Woche** (*this week*)
- ✔ **diesen Monat** (*this month*)
- ✔ **dieses Wochenende** (*this weekend*)
- ✔ **heute** (*today*)
- ✔ **heute Morgen** (*this morning*)

Book IV

Building Detail and Precision in Your Communication

- ✔ **im Frühling** (*in the spring*)

- ✔ **in vier Monaten** (*in four months*)

- ✔ **in vier Stunden** (*in four hours*)

- ✔ **morgen** (*tomorrow*)

- ✔ **morgen Nachmittag** (*tomorrow afternoon*)

- ✔ **nächsten Dienstag** (*next Tuesday*)

- ✔ **nächste Woche** (*next week*)

- ✔ **übermorgen** (*the day after tomorrow*)

You can express future events in German simply by using a future time expression together with a verb in the present tense. For example, **Ich fliege nächste Woche nach Frankfurt.** (*I'm flying to Frankfurt next week.*)

German word order is typically *time*, *manner*, and *place*. Here's the breakdown of the word order for a typical sentence:

1. Subject + active verb: **Ich fahre** (*I'm traveling*)

2. Time (when): **morgen Nachmittag** (*tomorrow afternoon*)

3. Manner (how): **mit dem Zug** (*by train*)

4. Place (where): **nach Hamburg** (*to Hamburg*)

Putting it all together, the sentence looks like this: **Ich fahre morgen Nachmittag mit dem Zug nach Hamburg.** (*I'm taking the train to Hamburg tomorrow afternoon.*)

When you're forming a sentence that has an expression of time such as **am Mittwoch** (*on Wednesday*) or **morgen** (*tomorrow*), as well as an expression of manner and/or place, you may want to be very clear about *when* something is happening. In this case, simply place the time expression at the very beginning of the sentence, followed by the verb and subject. Putting the time expression at the front of a sentence may also be easier if you have trouble remembering the correct word order for the trio of time, manner, and place. That way, you've taken care of the time, and you have to remember only that manner is before place.

The following example sentences show when various activities take place. All four sentences are in present in German, but they express the future four different ways in English. ***Note:*** You may have more than one future-tense alternative for translating the sentences into English, but all are in present tense in German.

> **Ich fliege am Dienstag nach Graz.** (*I'm flying to Graz on Tuesday.*)

> **Ich denke, ich arbeite dieses Wochenende zu Hause.** (*I think I'll work at home this weekend.*)

Übermorgen habe ich einen Termin mit einem neuen Kunden. (*The day after tomorrow I have an appointment with a new customer.*) **Der Kunde** means *the customer*. **Übermorgen** is at the beginning, so the verb comes in second position, followed by the subject.

Heute Abend telefoniere ich mit dem chinesischen Lieferanten. (*This evening I'm going to call the Chinese supplier.*) **Der Lieferant** means *the supplier*. The time element **heute Abend** is first, so the verb follows in second position, followed by the subject.

Peering into the Future with Werden

Sometimes you need to use the future tense in German. German speakers use the future to describe future events, either with or without a reference to time like **nächstes Jahr** (*next year*), although speakers of German prefer the present tense when they're using a time expression in the same sentence.

When you make no specific mention of when something will happen, you generally use **werden** to express the future. This section shows you how to conjugate the future tense and how to use it correctly in different circumstances.

Forming the future: Werden + infinitive verb

To form the future tense, you conjugate the auxiliary (helping) verb **werden** and add the infinitive form of the verb that you want to express in the future tense: **Ich werde bald nach Hause gehen.** (*I'm going home soon.*) In this context, **werden** means *going to* or *will*. Notice that the infinitive form of the action verb, **gehen,** is at the end of the sentence. This table shows how to conjugate the other forms of **werden gehen.**

werden gehen (*will go, going to go*)	
ich **werde** gehen	wir **werden** gehen
du **wirst** gehen	ihr **werdet** gehen
er/sie/es **wird** gehen	sie **werden** gehen
Sie **werden** gehen	
Ich **werde** bald nach Hause gehen. (*I'm going [to go] home soon.*)	

Book IV

Building Detail and Precision in Your Communication

Werden is a sneaky verb. It has several meanings. With the future, it means *will* or *going to*. However, when **werden** is the main verb, it means *to become* or *to get,* as in **Wir werden immer älter.** (*We're always becoming/getting older.*)

When some people see **will** in German, they equate it with **werden**. Watch out! *Will* indicates the future only in English; the German **will** means *to want*:

> **Ich will nach Hause gehen.** (*I want to go home.*) **Will** comes from **wollen:** *to want to.* It's a modal verb, which means it modifies the main verb. (For more on modal verbs, see Book III, Chapter 6.)

> **Ich werde nach Hause gehen.** (*I will go/am going home.*)

The following sentences give you a sense of how to use the future with **werden** in German:

> **Am Freitag Abend wird Gerhard Grossmann zu viel Bier trinken.** (*Gerhard Grossmann will drink too much beer on Friday evening.*)

> **Sie werden jetzt ganz still sein!** (*Be absolutely quiet now!*) (***Note:*** See Table 6-1 in the next section for details on why this particular example is in future tense.)

> **Mit einer Zigarre im Mund wirst du sicher keine Freunde machen.** (*You certainly won't make any friends with a cigar in your mouth.*)

> **Ihr werdet schon noch zwei Stunden Poker mit mir spielen.** (*For sure you'll play another two hours of poker with me.*)

> **Heute Abend werde ich alles gewinnen.** (*I'll win everything tonight.*)

As with any verb tense, you need to know how to get the right word order when you're formulating sentences in future tense. This can be a little tricky when you're talking about more than just future tense. The following sentences show you how to organize sentences that have future tense and a subordinating clause or a modal auxiliary verb:

> **Wenn sie in die Rente gehen, werden sie in Spanien überwintern.** (*When they retire, they'll spend their winters in Spain.*)

> **Heute Nachmittag wird der Präsident bekannt geben, ob er in der Politik bleibt.** (*This afternoon, the president will announce whether he'll stay in politics.*)

> **Ich werde ein Schloss kaufen, falls ich in der Lotterie gewinne.** (*I'll buy a castle if I win the lottery.*)

> **Wenn die Aussichten der Wirtschaft so düster bleiben, werden noch mehr junge Leute auswandern wollen.** (*If the prospects for the economy remain so dismal, even more young people will want to emigrate.*) ***Note:*** When you begin a sentence with a subordinating clause — the kind that has the verb at the end of the clause — the next clause begins with the conjugated verb. (For more information on subordinating clauses and conjunctions, go to Book IV, Chapter 1.)

Using the future: Assuming, hoping, and emphasizing intentions

German speakers use the future tense with **werden** in several different situations to express future action. Table 6-1 lists the uses for future tense, an example sentence in German, and the English equivalent. Notice that the infinitive verb is at the end of the sentence.

Table 6-1	Future Using Werden	
Use of Future Tense	*German Example Sentence*	*English Equivalent*
Emphasizing intention that an event will take place in the future	Ich **werde** ein erholsames Wochenende zu Hause **verbringen.**	*I'm going to have a restful weekend at home.*
Supposing, assuming, or hoping something will happen, expressed verbally	Ich hoffe, sie **wird** nicht **vergessen.**	*I hope she won't forget.*
Supposing, assuming, or hoping something will happen, expressed with an adverb	Sie **wird** wohl nicht **vergessen.**	*She probably won't forget.*
Giving strong advice or a stern warning	Du **wirst** jetzt ruhig (**sein**)! (You can express this without **sein.**)	*Be quiet!/You will be quiet!*
Indicating an event will happen after another event stated in the present tense	Joachim studiert sehr fleißig, und er **wird** später ein erfolgreicher Arzt.	*Joachim is studying very hard, and later he'll be a successful doctor.*

Just as German speakers use the **werden** future to emphasize that something will happen in the future, they also use it to say that something will *not* happen. The two alternatives are **werden** + **nicht** (*will not/won't*) + verb and **werden** + **kein** (*will not/won't*) + object, depending on what you're negating.

Here are the main differences in the use of **kein** and **nicht** (for more details on **kein** and **nicht,** turn to Book III, Chapter 4):

✔ **Kein** negates a noun, as in **keine Zeit** (*no time*). It has case and gender endings. For example:

> **Meine Freunde werden kein Geburtstagsfest für mich organisieren.**
> (*My friends aren't going to organize a birthday party for me.*) **Kein**

> negates **Geburtstagsfest**; it replaces **ein. Kein** is in the accusative case.
>
> ✔ **Nicht** generally negates a verb: **nicht gehen** (*to not go*). But it can also negate an adjective, like **nicht lustig** (*not funny*), or an adverb, like **nicht pünktlich** (*not on time*). **Nicht** has no case or gender endings. For example:
>
> > **Ich werde nicht hier bleiben.** (*I won't stay here.*) **Nicht** negates the information **hier bleiben.**

The following sentences provide more examples of how to use **kein** and **nicht** to talk about what's not going to happen:

> **Ich werde nicht reich sein, wenn ich 70 Jahre alt bin.** (*I won't be rich when I'm 70 years old.*)
>
> **Er wird kein Haus bauen.** (*He won't build a house.*)
>
> **Sie werden nicht in die Politik gehen.** (*They won't go into politics.*)
>
> **Sie wird nicht mit ihrer Familie nicht nach Tehachapi umziehen.** (*She won't move to Tehachapi with her family.*)
>
> **Ich werde nicht reisen, wenn ich nicht genug Geld habe.** (*I won't travel when I don't have enough money.*)
>
> **Ihr werdet keine Probleme haben.** (*You won't have any problems.*)

Using the future to express probability

When you aren't absolutely sure something will or won't happen in the future, you use expressions to describe probability. You may be confident that your favorite team will win a game, but you're not 100 percent certain, so you include words that express probability together with the future tense. Here are some common expressions:

✔ **bestimmt** (*certainly*)

✔ **eventuell** (*possibly, maybe*)

✔ **schon** (*probably*)

✔ **sicher** (*probably, definitely, certainly*)

✔ **vielleicht** (*perhaps, maybe*)

✔ **wahrscheinlich** (*probably*)

✔ **wohl** (*probably, no doubt, to be sure*)

Note: The elusive word **schon** can also mean *already* or *yet.*

Check out some examples:

> **Die Haffenreffers werden wohl eine neue Garage bauen.** (*The Haffenreffers are probably going to build a new garage.*)

> **Leander Haffenreffer wird sicher ein neues Auto kaufen.** (*Leander Haffenreffer will probably buy a new car.*)

> **Der Nachbar der Haffenreffers wird wahrscheinlich ein riesengroßes Schwimmbecken bauen.** (*The Haffenreffers' neighbor is probably going to build a gigantic swimming pool.*)

> **Wir werden eventuell bis Mitternacht spielen.** (*We might play until midnight.*)

> **Ich werde heute Abend bestimmt zu Hause sein.** (*I'll certainly be home this evening.*)

Talking about What Will Have Happened: The Future Perfect

English and German both use the future perfect tense to describe something that in the future will end up being a past event. The verb *will have seen* is the future perfect tense, and when you use it, you're predicting information that hasn't happened yet and talking about the future as a past event. This section shows you how to form the present perfect and how to use it.

Forming the future perfect

To form the future perfect, you need the following three parts:

- Conjugated present tense form of the verb **werden** (*will*)
- Past participle form of the verb that you're using
- Infinitive form of the auxiliary verb **haben** (*to have*) or **sein** (*to be*), depending on which auxiliary verb you need for the main verb you're using

The following conjugation tables show how the future perfect looks when you put all three elements together. The first future perfect conjugation is for the verb **lernen** (*to learn*); it uses the auxiliary verb **haben**. Only the auxiliary is conjugated and appears in second position.

Book IV

Building Detail and Precision in Your Communication

werde gelernt haben (*will have learned*)	
ich **werde gelernt haben**	wir **werden gelernt haben**
du **wirst gelernt haben**	ihr **werdet gelernt haben**
er/sie/es **wird gelernt haben**	sie **werden gelernt haben**
Sie **werden gelernt haben**	
Sie **werden** zwei Fremdsprachen **gelernt haben.** (*You will have learned two foreign languages.*)	

This table shows the future perfect conjugation of the verb **reisen** (*to travel*); it uses the auxiliary verb **sein.**

werde gereist sein (*will have traveled*)	
ich **werde gereist sein**	wir **werden gereist sein**
du **wirst gereist sein**	ihr **werdet gereist sein**
er/sie/es **wird gereist sein**	sie **werden gereist sein**
Sie **werden gereist sein**	
In zehn Jahren **werde** ich viel **gereist sein.** (*In ten years, I will have traveled a lot.*)	

For a refresher on which verbs use **sein** and which ones use **haben** with the German perfect tenses, turn to Book IV, Chapter 4.

Using the future perfect

Although the future perfect isn't by any means the most popular verb tense on the block, some situations definitely call for it in German. Here's a scenario: Imagine you're taking an extended trip to Europe next year. You're describing what you're planning to see and do, and you want to finish up by taking stock of all the places you intend to visit. You may say something like this: *By the time I get home, I will have seen many of the highlights of Europe, including the capitals of six major EU countries.*

When you're talking about something in the future, you're usually dealing with an element of probability or uncertainty. To express this uncertainty, you can use any of the words listed in the previous section "Using the future to express probability." In addition to these expressions, the German future perfect often uses one of the following two terms, both of which emphasize that something will have *already* happened by a certain point in the future:

✔ **bereits** (*already*)

✔ **schon** (*already*)

The following example sentences are in future perfect tense. They include some of the German words that describe probability as well as the expressions for *already*. The present tense conjugated form of **werden** is in second position in the main phrase.

Ich hoffe, Sie werden die Arbeit bis Freitag schon erledigt haben.
(*I hope they will have already finished the work by Friday.*)

Er wird die Nachrichten vielleicht gehört haben. (*Perhaps he will have heard the news.*)

In zwanzig Jahren werden die Bäume wahrscheinlich höher als das Haus gewachsen sein. (*In twenty years, the trees will probably have grown taller than the house.*)

Ich werde das ganze Haus eventuell aufgeräumt haben, bis du nach Hause kommst. (*I may possibly have straightened up the whole house by the time you get home.*)

Sie werden bestimmt gemerkt haben, dass der Zug ab und zu Verspätung hat. (*You will have certainly noticed that the train is late once in a while.*)

Chapter 7

Describing Your Mood: Summing Up the Subjunctive

Most English and German speakers who aren't used to analyzing their language — this group probably includes zillions of otherwise perfectly normal people — would be seriously challenged if they had to explain the ins and outs of the subjunctive. Although the word *subjunctive* may conjure up thoughts of doctors discussing an unpleasant eye infection, it's actually an innocuous description for the way verbs tell events that are contrary to fact. Consider the subjunctive as an umbrella term for describing all sorts of unreal situations, including hypothetical, unlikely, uncertain, potential, probable, or doubtful events.

In German, the subjunctive gets extra mileage because you also use it to describe polite requests. This chapter deals with how to construct the various forms of the subjunctive and how to use them in German. You also find out the differences between the subjunctive and conditional in German and English. To get you off and running, the next section explains the terminology surrounding the subjunctive.

Terms and Conditions: Unraveling Subjunctive Terminology

Discussing the subjunctive is pretty tough if you're not familiar with the lingo. The following sections help you keep the terms straight so you can better understand the subjunctive and its different uses.

Getting in the mood

If someone were to ask you what your mood is today, you probably wouldn't answer, "Oh, I'm in a real indicative mood today, but yesterday I was kind of subjunctive." But if sentences could speak about themselves, that's exactly what they'd say. See, a *mood* in language terms (as opposed to emotional terms) is the manner in which the speaker perceives an action. Take a look:

- ✔ **Indicative mood:** The indicative mood states a fact or deals with a real situation, usually in the form of a statement or a question, such as *I live in Waterford* or *Where are you from originally?*

- ✔ **Imperative mood:** This mood is the command form (which I discuss in Book III, Chapter 7), such as *Get out of here!*

- ✔ **Subjunctive mood:** The subjunctive mood expresses nonfactual, hypothetical, or similar "unreal" actions and thoughts as statements or questions. In German, you'd use the subjunctive form in these example sentences:

    I'd like 200 grams of that cheese, please.

    Would you marry someone 25 years younger than you?

Comparing subjunctive types and the conditional

In English grammar terms, the *conditional* can refer to a clause or a sentence that describes circumstances in varying stages of "reality." A typical example of a conditional sentence in English is the if-type question: *What would you do if you won a million dollars in the lottery?* The verb in the main clause *what would you do* is in the conditional.

In German, you use verbs in the subjunctive form in if-type conditional sentences that express a condition contrary to fact. But that's not the only use of the subjunctive — you find two subjunctive groups in German. Here's how they compare:

- ✔ **Subjunctive I:** People use Subjunctive I in indirect discourse (indirect speech), most often in the printed media to report what someone says. For this reason, when you do come across this subjunctive form, just try to recognize what the verbs mean; you'll probably never need to use Subjunctive I yourself.

- ✔ **Subjunctive II:** In terms of importance to you, Subjunctive I takes a back seat to Subjunctive II. You use Subjunctive II for expressing imagined things, describing information contrary to fact, or making wishes and requests.

Note: Both Subjunctive I and Subjunctive II forms can refer to events in the present, past, and future.

The common denominator of subjunctives in both English and German is that they express a specific mood, namely — you'll never believe it! — the subjunctive mood. Beyond that, in everyday German, the Subjunctive II form is very much alive and kicking, but in English, it's relegated to a dusty corner in terms of how often you use it.

Both groups, the German Subjunctive I and Subjunctive II, have definite differences in form and function from each other and from verbs in the indicative mood. In contrast, very few English verbs even have a special subjunctive form, so you may be using it without even realizing it. One example of the subjunctive in English is *if I were you.* In a sentence without *if,* you'd say *I was*, but with *if* (the element that adds unreality to the action), you use the subjunctive: *If I were you.*

In the following sections, you find out what you need to know about the present and past Subjunctive II forms so you can recognize them, form them, and use them in everyday spoken and written German. After that, you get a quick rundown of the present and past forms of the not-so-common Subjunctive I.

The Present Subjunctive II: Knowing How and When to Use It

When you pack your suitcase to travel to a German-speaking region, remember to include the Subjunctive II form. That way, you can order in a café — **Ich möchte eine Tasse Kaffee bitte** (*I'd like a cup of coffee*) — or agree with the tour guide's suggestion to visit the king's private quarters — **Ich hätte schon Interesse daran** (*I'd be really interested in that*). With a few more subjunctive expressions in your bag, you can express actions that are contrary to fact and more.

Even though the subjunctive is used a lot more frequently in German than in English, the average German speaker would probably get tangled up trying to explain the Subjunctive II, let alone list all its uses. It's so embedded in the language that its use isn't obvious to the native speaker. So relax, take a deep breath, and read on.

In this section, you discover two ways to form the present Subjunctive II to make hypothetical statements, request something, and express wishes. The most frequent form of present Subjunctive II is the construction of **würde** + infinitive. Look at this example: **Ich würde gerne nach Hamburg fahren.** (*I'd like to go to Hamburg.*) Most verbs use this two-part construction.

Book IV

Building Detail and Precision in Your Communication

The other means of forming the present Subjunctive II is common for only a small but important group of verbs. You form this subjunctive by putting the main verb itself into the subjunctive form. All verbs have subjunctive forms, but in formal written German, you find only a few; you encounter an even smaller number in everyday written and spoken German. The verbs that do commonly use the present Subjunctive II in the main verb are the modal verbs (see Book III, Chapter 6), the auxiliaries **haben** (*to have*) and **sein** (*to be*) (see Book III, Chapter 3), and a few others.

Creating the present Subjunctive II with würde

The present Subjunctive II form using **würde** + infinitive has many uses, including to make hypothetical statements, to request something, and to express wishes. For instance, you need to sound polite when making a request, especially when you're asking someone to do (or not do) something, so you use the present Subjunctive II form, like this: **Würden Sie mir bitte helfen?** (*Would you help me, please?*)

The common form of present subjunctive, using the **würde** construction, is easy to remember. It uses the simple past form of the infinitive **werden** (which translates to *will* in this context) plus an umlaut: **Wurde** changes to **würde,** the subjunctive of **werden,** and becomes equivalent to *would* in English. (In other words, it uses the present subjunctive form of **werden** like a modal verb — see Book III, Chapter 6 for more on modal verbs.) Add the infinitive form of the main verb you want to express in a subjunctive mood, and presto!

Look at the conjugation of **werden** in the following verb table. It builds the **würde** subjunctive construction in the present. You use the subjunctive form of **werden** plus the main verb in the infinitive. In the verb table, **arbeiten** (*to work*) is the main verb.

würde arbeiten (*would work*) — Present Subjunctive II	
ich **würde** arbeiten	wir **würden** arbeiten
du **würdest** arbeiten	ihr **würdet** arbeiten
er/sie/es **würde** arbeiten	sie **würden** arbeiten
Sie **würden** arbeiten	
Ich **würde** gerne in Wien **arbeiten**. (*I'd [really] like to work in Vienna.*)	

Here are some examples of present subjunctive with **würde:**

> **Würden Sie mir bitte mit meinem Koffer helfen?** (*Would you help me with my suitcase, please?*) The speaker is making a polite request.

Ich würde gerne nach Salzburg reisen. (*I'd love to travel to Salzburg.*)
The speaker is wishfully thinking of traveling to Salzburg.

An deiner Stelle würde ich lieber den Kilimanjaro anschauen. (*If I were you, I'd rather see Kilimanjaro.*) The speaker is making a hypothetical statement with the condition *if I were you*.

Note: The modal verbs **dürfen, können, mögen, müssen, sollen,** and **wollen,** as well as the auxiliaries **haben** and **sein,** don't generally use the subjunctive construction using **würde.** See the next section for details.

In the following example sentences, people are imagining they've made a windfall profit in the stock market. The sentences all answer the question **Was würden sie tun?** (*What would they do?*)

Die Großeltern würden nach Florida umziehen. (*The grandparents would move to Florida.*)

Helga würde ein kleines Segelboot kaufen. (*Helga would buy a small sailboat.*)

Du würdest das Geld auf die Bank bringen. (*You'd take the money to the bank.*)

Ihr würdet ein neues Auto kaufen. (*You'd buy a new car.*)

Johannes weiß nicht, was er machen würde. (*Johannes doesn't know what he'd do.*)

Marianne und Michael würden den ganzen Tag singen. (*Marianne and Michael would sing all day long.*)

Ich würde nicht alles ausgeben. (*I wouldn't spend all of it.*)

Der Nachbar würde eine gigantische Party organisieren. (*The neighbor would organize a gigantic party.*)

Forming the Subjunctive II of haben, sein, and modal verbs

Book IV

Building Detail and Precision in Your Communication

German speakers often use **haben** (*to have*) and **sein** (*to be*) in the present subjunctive form to express wishes, hypothetical situations, and things contrary to fact, such as **ich hätte mehr Zeit** (*I would have more time*) or **es wäre einfacher** (*it would be easier*). The modal auxiliary verbs use the present subjunctive for expressing wishes and other situations by combining with another verb in the infinitive form — for example, **Sie sollten vorsichtig fahren.** (*You/they should drive carefully.*) All these verbs — plus a few strong verbs — take the same subjunctive endings.

Haben and sein

To form the subjunctive with **haben** (*to have*), start with **hatte** (the simple past tense), remove the **-e**, and add an umlaut plus the appropriate subjunctive ending: **-e, -est, -e, -en, -et, -en,** and **-en**.

hätte (*would have*) — Present Subjunctive II	
ich hätt**e**	wir hätt**en**
du hätt**est**	ihr hätt**et**
er/sie/es hätt**e**	sie hätt**en**
Sie hätt**en**	
Ich **hätte** lieber ein umweltfreundliches Auto. (*I'd rather have an environmentally friendly car.*)	

As for **sein** (*to be*), to form the present subjunctive, start with **war** (the simple past tense) and add an umlaut and the appropriate subjunctive ending: **-e, -est, -e, -en, -et, -en,** and **-en**.

wäre (*would be*) — Present Subjunctive II	
ich wär**e**	wir wär**en**
du wär**est**	ihr wär**et**
er/sie/es wär**e**	sie wär**en**
Sie wär**en**	
Wir **wären** sicher reich. (*We'd certainly be rich.*)	

Modal verbs and other special verbs

German uses the present Subjunctive II with modal verbs (**dürfen, können, mögen, müssen, sollen,** and **wollen**) quite frequently. Lucky for you, forming the present subjunctive with these verbs isn't that difficult. Just take the simple past form of the verb, add an umlaut if there's one in the infinitive, and add the appropriate subjunctive endings: **-e, -est, -e, -en, -et, -en,** and **-en**. Only two modals — **sollen** and **wollen** — have no umlaut in the infinitive. (For information on simple past tense of modals, see Book IV, Chapter 5.) Take a look at the present Subjunctive II conjugation of **konnen**.

könnte (*could, would be able to*) — Present Subjunctive II	
ich könn**te**	wir könn**en**
du könn**test**	ihr könn**tet**
er/sie/es könn**te**	sie könn**en**
Sie könn**en**	
Sie **könnte** uns helfen. (*She could/would be able to help us.*)	

As you see in the three preceding verb tables, the meaning in the subjunctive is different from the present-tense indicative form. You see *would* in the English translation of the subjunctive verb. *Have* changes to *would have*, and *be* changes to *would be*. In the case of **können,** both of its meanings undergo a transformation: *Able to* changes to *would be able to*, and *can* changes to *could*.

Although all verbs have subjunctive forms of the main verb, only a few are common in informal written and spoken German. These verbs use the subjunctive form of the main verb instead of the **würde** + infinitive construction. The verbs you're most likely to come across include **gehen** (*to go*), **heißen** (*to be called*), **tun** (*to do*), **werden** (*to become*), and **wissen** (*to know [a fact]*). These verbs form the subjunctive as follows:

✔ For strong verbs, as with modal verbs, the present subjunctive is based on the simple past form of the verb + umlaut (when applicable) + subjunctive endings **-e, -est, -e, en, -et, -en,** and **–en**. For example, **gehen** (*to go*) becomes **ginge** (*would go*).

✔ For weak verbs, the present subjunctive is the same as the simple past (you use the same simple past endings). For example, **kaufen** (*to buy*) becomes **kaufte** (*would buy*). The context of the verb in the sentence generally shows whether you're using simple past or present subjunctive.

See Book IV, Chapters 4 and 5 and Appendix A for more on strong and weak verbs.

Book IV

Building Detail and Precision in Your Communication

Using the present Subjunctive II

This section breaks down the ways you can use the present Subjunctive II. In everyday German, you can use this multi-tasker to express a variety of contrary-to-fact situations. In addition, you can express wishes, make polite requests, describe a condition, and express your opinion. For example, imagine you're planning what to do during your three-day stay in **Wien** (*Vienna*).

You say, **Wir könnten die Spanische Reitschule sehen.** (*We could see the Spanish Riding School.*) In this example, you're making a polite request for what you *could* do while in Vienna; **könnten** is the subjunctive form (in the present) of the verb **können** (*can*).

Describing a hypothetical situation or a wish

When you want to express a hypothetical situation or a wish that can or can't be fulfilled, you often imagine a scenario. German uses the subjunctive in such situations:

> **Wenn ich nur etwas mehr Zeit hätte!** (*If only I had a little more time!*) You don't have more time, so you're wishing you did. **Hätte** (*had*) is the subjunctive form of **haben** (*to have*).

> **Ich wollte, ich hätte mehr Geschwister.** (*I wish I had more siblings.*) This sentence contains two subjunctives, **wollte** and **hätte**. If you want to get technical, **ich wollte** actually means *I would wish*.

Describing a condition

You use the subjunctive to talk about a condition that's contrary to fact — for example, when you're considering what you would (or wouldn't) do if something that isn't true now were true. (See the earlier section "Terms and Conditions: Unraveling Subjunctive Terminology" for more on conditional sentences with *if*.) Look at these examples:

> **Wenn du kein Affe wärest, würde ich dich heiraten.** (*If you weren't a monkey, I'd marry you.*) The verbs **wärest** (*were*) and **würde** (*would*) + infinitive **heiraten** (*to marry*) are both subjunctive forms. In English, the verb in the main clause (*I'd marry you*) is a conditional; technically speaking, the if-clause uses the subjunctive mood, expressed by *weren't*.

> **Hätte ich die Zeit, so würde ich den Roman lesen.** (*If I had time, I'd read that novel.*) Both verbs **hätte** (*had*) and **würde** (*would*) + infinitive **lesen** (*to read*) are in the subjunctive; in English, the verb in the main clause (*I'd read novels*) is a conditional; the if-clause uses the subjunctive mood, expressed by *had*.

Politely making a request

You use the subjunctive to make a polite request — for example, when you're hungry and you'd like to have something to eat:

> **Könnte ich noch ein Stück Fleisch nehmen?** (*Could I take another piece of meat?*) **Könnte** (*could*) is the subjunctive form of **können** (*can, to be able to*), and using it makes your request sound polite. **Kann ich. . . ?** (*Can I. . . ?*), where the verb is in the indicative mood, is direct; it lacks the politeness of the subjunctive **Könnte ich. . . ?**

Ich möchte die Speisekarte, bitte. (*I'd like the menu, please.*) The subjunctive **Ich möchte** (*I'd like*) is the polite way of ordering food, selecting an item in a store, and so on.

Expressing your feelings and/or opinion

When you state your feelings or express your opinion on something, you often use the subjunctive in German:

Das wäre prima! (*That would be fantastic!*) Your enthusiastic reply to someone's suggestion about going to hear your favorite band includes the subjunctive **wäre** (*would be*).

Wir sollten diese Wurst probieren. (*We should try this sausage.*) You think something would be a good idea, so you use the subjunctive. Here, the subjunctive is **sollten** (*should*) + infinitive **probieren** (*try*).

Forming and Using the Past Subjunctive II

When you want to express events that might have taken place in the past, you use the past Subjunctive II. Perhaps you wish you'd accomplished something, but you never got around to it. You may regret having done something — or the other way around. You use the past Subjunctive II for such situations.

Imagine you want to describe something that you would (or wouldn't) have done in a certain situation in the past; you say, **Ich hätte das nicht gemacht.** (*I wouldn't have done that.*) You form the past Subjunctive II with the present subjunctive form of either **haben** or **sein** + the past participle of the main verb that you want to express in the subjunctive. In the preceding example, the past subjunctive is **hätte** (*would have*) + **gemacht** (*done*).

This section runs through the details of forming and using the past Subjunctive II.

Forming the past Subjunctive II

The past subjunctive deals with past actions and events that might have happened in the past. At first glance, the past subjunctive seems to be a clone of the past perfect (see Book IV, Chapter 4). Indeed, it's the same, with the

Book IV

Building Detail and Precision in Your Communication

exception of an umlaut in **hätte** and **wäre.** You can simply remember that the past subjunctive is formed like this:

✔ Present subjunctive of **haben** = **hätte** + past participle **(geholfen)** = **hätte (geholfen)**

✔ Present subjunctive of **sein** = **wäre** + past participle **(gegangen)** = **wäre (gegangen)**

The endings for the present subjunctive are always the same (in this case, you add them to **hätt-** and **wär-**): **-e, -est, -e, -en, -et, -en, -en.**

Using the past Subjunctive II

Do you reflect on situations? Time slips by, and events, relationships, and memories drop off into oblivion. Before that happens, though, you may catch yourself saying, "I wouldn't have jumped into marriage so quickly," or "I might have dyed my hair green." The past subjunctive lets you do this type of reminiscing in German, describing scenarios that may or may not have happened. And even if you aren't the type to dwell on the past, you'll be able to understand what other people are talking about when they say **ich hätte sie angerufen.** (*I would have called her.*)

You can use three past-tense verb forms in the indicative, but you need only one form of the past subjunctive. Look at these examples:

✔ **Er hätte uns geholfen.** (*He would have helped us.*) This past Subjunctive II form stands in for three indicative sentences in the past:

> **Er hat uns geholfen.** (*He helped/has helped us.*)
>
> **Er half uns.** (*He helped us.*)
>
> **Er hatte uns geholfen.** (*He had helped us.*)

✔ **Sie wäre gegangen.** (*She would have gone.*) This past Subjunctive II form stands in for three indicative sentences in the past:

> **Sie ist gegangen.** (*She went/has gone.*)
>
> **Sie ging.** (*She went.*)
>
> **Sie war gegangen.** (*She had gone.*)

To get the hang of putting your ideas into the past Subjunctive II, try changing past actions from fact into a hypothetical situation; in other words, start with a sentence that describes something that did or didn't happen (that's the indicative mood). Write it down in German — for example, **Ich habe eine Katze gehabt.** (*I had a cat.*) Now imagine you didn't have a cat, but you *would've had* one if your parents hadn't had allergies. Change the verb as a fact (*had*) into past subjunctive (*would have had*) by changing **habe** to **hätte.** Now you have **Ich hätte eine Katze gehabt.** (*I would have had a cat.*)

With the following sentence pairs, you see sentences written first in the indicative mood, then in the past Subjunctive II. The first sentence describes some event that has happened. The second sentence, in the past subjunctive mood, indicates that these events could have happened in the past (but didn't).

Sascha hat einen Job gefunden. (*Sascha found a job.*)

Sascha hätte einen Job gefunden. (*Sascha would have found a job.*)

Liselotte und Heinz haben ein Haus in Ludwigshafen gekauft. (*Liselotte and Heinz bought a house in Ludwigshafen.*)

Liselotte und Heinz hätten ein Haus in Ludwigshafen gekauft. (*Liselotte and Heinz would have bought a house in Ludwigshafen.*)

Ich ging mit euch ins Theater. (*I went to the theater with you.*)

Ich wäre mit euch ins Theater gegangen. (*I would have gone to the theater with you.*)

Max und Moritz hatten uns im Sommer besucht. (*Max and Moritz visited us in the summer.*)

Max und Moritz hätten uns im Sommer besucht. (*Max and Moritz would have visited us in the summer.*)

Du hast die Reise besser geplant. (*You planned the trip better.*)

Du hättest die Reise besser geplant. (*You would have planned the trip better.*)

Jonas wanderte den ganzen Tag in den Bergen. (*Jonas hiked the whole day in the mountains.*)

Jonas wäre den ganzen Tag in den Bergen gewandert. (*Jonas would have hiked the whole day in the mountains.*)

Two-timing the past subjunctive: Using double infinitives

If only more wishful thinking using the subjunctive were coming your way . . . oh, it is! This time, the infinitive verb comes in a double pack, and one of the verbs is a modal verb — **dürfen, können, mögen, müssen, sollen,** or **wollen.** The purpose of adding the modal verb to another verb is to express what you *might have been allowed to do* (**hätte machen dürfen**), *could have done* (**hätte machen können**), and so on.

The construction consists of the present Subjunctive II, **hätte.** (**Wäre** doesn't combine with the modal verbs.) The two infinitive verbs are together at the

Book IV

Building Detail and Precision in Your Communication

end of the phrase, with the modal in the second position. Look at these two example sentences:

Ich hätte eine längere Reise machen können. (*I could have made/could have been able to make a longer trip.*) The word order follows the standard procedure, with the active verb **hätte** in second position in the sentence. The verb **machen** precedes the modal verb **können** at the end of the phrase.

Er hätte früher nach Hause fahren sollen. (*He should have driven home earlier.*) The word order follows the standard procedure with the active verb **hätte** in second position in the sentence. The main verb **fahren** and the modal **sollen** go to the very end of the sentence.

Subjunctive 1: Using It in Indirect Discourse

Another way to describe *indirect discourse* is *indirect speech*. It's the kind of information you read in print when someone writes something that someone else said, but it's not in quotation marks. Journalists use this form of writing to avoid quoting sources directly. Indirect speech frees the writer from taking responsibility for the statement's accuracy. As far as your needs go, you can leave its usage to the media pundits. Just get the hang of what it looks like by understanding how you form the Subjunctive I and knowing where you run across it and what it means, and you're all set.

Note: In English and German, you encounter this subjunctive form almost exclusively in the third-person singular — **er** (*he*), **sie** (*she*), **es** (*it*) — or the plural **sie** (*they*). In English, the present Subjunctive I is the infinitive form of the verb. In its rare appearances in English, it may be in a (somewhat obsolete) statement such as *so be it*, or it may invoke a higher power: *May the spirit of the holiday season be with you.*

Recognizing the present Subjunctive 1

As you read a German newspaper or magazine, you encounter the present Subjunctive I when the writer wants to report someone else's original statement. The information — an indirect quotation — may be an opinion, a fact, a plan, and so on, as in **Sie meinte, sie habe nicht genug Zeit.** (*She thought [that] she didn't have enough time.*) In German, you always use a comma to separate the indirect statement from the person who's telling the information.

You form the present Subjunctive I by taking the infinitive stem of the verb and adding the subjunctive verb endings: **-e, -est, -e, -en, -et, -en,** and **-en.** All verbs follow this pattern with one exception: **sein** (*to be*). Look at the verb table showing **gehen** (*to go, to walk*), paying special attention to the commonly used third-person forms. The infinitive stem is **geh-**. The endings are indicated in bold.

gehe (*go/walk*) — Present Subjunctive I	
ich geh**e**	wir geh**en**
du geh**est**	ihr geh**et**
er/sie/es geh**e**	sie geh**en**
Sie geh**en**	
Er sagte, er **gehe** nicht. (*He said he wasn't going.*)	

Look at the only irregular exception for present Subjunctive I, the verb **sein**:

sei (*am/is/are/was/were*) — Present Subjunctive I	
ich **sei**	wir **seien**
du **seist**	ihr **seiet**
er/sie/es **sei**	sie **seien**
Sie **seien**	
Sie sagte, es **sei** zu früh. (*She said it was too early.*)	

Note: In indirect speech in English, journalists often use the past tense to describe events that may still be occurring (to reflect that the original statement referred to events as they were at the time of speech). Thus, we use the past tense in the English translations.

Here are a few examples of present Subjunctive I:

> **Er sagte, er habe eine neue Freundin.** (*He said he had a new girlfriend.*) **Habe** is the present Subjunctive I form of **haben**. Although you say *He said he had . . .* , the information (usually) has present meaning.

> **Der Bundeskanzler sagte, er werde das Problem lösen.** (*The German Chancellor said he would solve the problem.*) **Werde** is the present Subjunctive I form of **werden**. This statement expresses a future event using **werde + lösen**.

Recognizing the past Subjunctive 1

The past Subjunctive I is the subjunctive you find in the press to describe what someone else has said about an event in the past. German uses the past subjunctive to describe three past tenses: simple past, present perfect, and

Book IV

Building Detail and Precision in Your Communication

past perfect. (Check out Book IV, Chapter 5 for details on simple past and Book IV, Chapter 4 for more on the two perfect tenses.)

You form the past Subjunctive I by using the appropriate conjugated form of the present subjunctive of **haben** (*to have*) or **sein** (*to be*) and adding the past participle (for more on past participles, see Book IV, Chapter 4). All verbs follow this pattern. Look at the past Subjunctive I conjugation of the verb **wohnen** (*to live, to reside*), which uses the auxiliary verb **haben.**

habe gewohnt (*had lived*) — Past Subjunctive I	
ich **habe gewohnt**	wir **haben gewohnt**
du **habest gewohnt**	ihr **habet gewohnt**
er/sie/es **habe gewohnt**	sie **haben gewohnt**
Sie **haben gewohnt**	
Sie sagte, sie **habe** in einer kleinen Wohnung **gewohnt.** (*She said she had lived in a small apartment.*)	

Look at the past Subjunctive I conjugation of **gehen,** which uses the auxiliary verb **sein.**

sei gegangen (*had gone*) — Past Subjunctive I	
ich **sei gegangen**	wir **seien gegangen**
du **seist gegangen**	ihr **seiet gegangen**
er/sie/es **sei gegangen**	sie **seien gegangen**
Sie **seien gegangen**	
Er sagte, er **sei** in die Stadt **gegangen.** (*He said he had gone into the city.*)	

Look at these examples of past Subjunctive I. The most common use for indirect discourse is to report what someone said.

> **Er sagte, er habe letzte Woche Golf gespielt.** (*He said he had played golf last week.*) To form the past Subjunctive I, you combine **habe,** the present Subjunctive I form of **haben,** with the past participle of **spielen: habe gespielt.**

> **Die Bundeskanzlerin sagte, sie sei nicht mit dem Verteidigungsminister geflogen.** (*The German Chancellor said she hadn't flown with the Defense Secretary.*) To form the past Subjunctive I, you combine **sei,** the present Subjunctive I form of **sein,** with the past participle of **fliegen: sei geflogen.**

Book V
The Appendixes

Contents at a Glance

Appendix A

Verb Tables and Case Charts

● ●

*1*n the first part of this appendix, we explain how to conjugate verbs and then provide tables showing sample conjugations. We list the conjugations for various verbs in order of the subject pronouns from first- to third-person singular, then from first- to third-person plural, and finally the formal second-person address: **ich, du, er/sie/es, wir, ihr, sie,** and **Sie.** For the imperative (used for suggestions and commands), the persons are **du, ihr, Sie.** As a bonus, you also find a table that contains the principal parts of high-frequency strong and irregular weak verbs.

The second part of this appendix deals with articles, pronouns, and adjectives. You find case charts showing the case, gender, and number endings for these parts of speech. A chart for prepositions also shows their usage by case to help you fit all these parts of speech in your sentences.

Verb Conjugation Basics

The following sections show you how to conjugate verbs so you can use them in your writing and speech. Later in this appendix, you find tables showing the conjugations of various example verbs.

Present and simple past tenses

You conjugate verbs in the present and simple past by combining the appropriate stem and ending for that verb. Table A-1 lists the endings. The patterns are as follows:

- ✔ **Present tense and simple past tense of weak regular verbs:** Start with the stem (the infinitive minus the **-en** ending); add the appropriate ending from Table A-1.

- ✔ **Simple past tense of weak irregular verbs and strong verbs:** Begin with the simple past stem; add the appropriate ending from Table A-1.

Table A-1 Verb Endings for Present Tense and Simple Past Tense

Subject Pronoun	Present: Most Verbs	Present: Stem Ending in d, t, fn, gn	Simple Past: Weak Verbs (Regular and Irregular)	Simple Past: Weak Verbs, Stem Ending in d, t, fn, gn	Simple Past: Strong Verbs
ich	-e	-e	-te	-ete	-
du	-st	-est	-test	-etest	-st
er/sie/es	-t	-et	-te	-ete	-
wir	-en	-en	-ten	-eten	-en
ihr	-t	-et	-tet	-etet	-t
sie	-en	-en	-ten	-eten	-en
Sie	-en	-en	-ten	-eten	-en

Present perfect tense

To form the present perfect, you conjugate the present tense of the auxiliary **haben** (*to have*) or **sein** (*to be*) and then add the past participle. Examples: **Ich habe gesehen** (*I [have] seen*) and **Ich bin gegangen** (*I have gone/went*).

To form the past participle of most weak verbs, take the prefix **ge-,** add the infinitive stem (formed by dropping the **-en** from the infinitive), and add the ending **-t.** Example: **ge-** + **wohn-** + **-t** = **gewohnt** (*lived*). Verbs with a stem that ends in **d, t, fn,** or **gn** add **-e** before the final **-t** ending. Example: **ge-** + **arbeit-** + **-et** = **gearbeitet** (*worked*).

Some other groups of verbs don't use the **ge-** prefix for the past participle. Examples include verbs with the infinitive ending **-ieren,** such as **informieren** (*to inform*) → **informiert** (*informed*) and **telefonieren** (*to telephone*) → **telefoniert** (*telephoned*). Some inseparable-prefix verbs that don't use the **ge-** prefix include **bekommen** (*to get*) → **bekommen** (*gotten*), **gehören** (*to belong to*) → **gehört** (*belonged to*), and **vergessen** (*to forget*) → **vergessen** (*forgotten*).

The past participle of most strong verbs begins with the prefix **ge-** and ends in **-en.** Many past participles have stem vowel changes, and some have both vowel and consonant changes. For example, **sehen** (*to see*) → **gesehen** (*seen*) has no stem change; **finden** (*to find*) → **gefunden** (*found*) has a vowel change; and **sitzen** (*to sit*) → **gesessen** (*sat*) has both vowel and consonant changes. Later in this chapter, Table A-2 shows the past participles for strong verbs and other kinds of verbs.

The past participles of irregular verbs such as auxiliaries may have different endings. We show these endings separately in the corresponding verb tables in this appendix.

Future tense

To form the future tense, conjugate the present tense of the auxiliary verb **werden — werde, wirst, wird, werden, werdet, werden, werden —** and add the infinitive form of the main verb. Example: **Ich werde fahren.** (*I will go/drive.*)

Subjunctive mood

In most cases of the present subjunctive, conjugate the subjunctive of the auxiliary verb **werden — würde, würdest, würde, würden, würdet, würden, würden —** and add the infinitive form of the main verb. Example: **Ich würde leben.** (*I would live.*)

Conjugations of Weak Verbs

Regular verbs (no stem change in the simple past)

wohnen (to live, to reside)

> **Present-Tense Stem:** wohn-
>
> **Simple Past (1st/3rd-person singular):** wohnte
>
> **Past Participle:** gewohnt; **Auxiliary Verb:** haben
>
> **Present Subjunctive:** würde wohnen
>
> **Present:** wohne, wohn**st**, wohn**t**, wohn**en**, wohn**t**, wohn**en**, wohn**en**
>
> **Simple Past:** wohn**te**, wohn**test**, wohn**te**, wohn**ten**, wohn**tet**, wohn**ten**, wohn**ten**
>
> **Imperative:** wohn, wohn**t**, wohn**en** Sie

Some other verbs like this are **brauchen** (*to need*), **feiern** (*to celebrate*), **glauben** (*to believe*), **hören** (*to hear*), **kaufen** (*to buy*), **lachen** (*to laugh*), **lernen** (*to learn*), **machen** (*to make, to do*), **sagen** (*to say*), and **spielen** (*to play*).

Regular verbs (with stem ending in -d, -t, -fn, or -gn)

arbeiten (to work)

Present-Tense Stem: arbeit-

Simple Past (1st/3rd-person singular): arbeit**ete**

Past Participle: gearbeitet; **Auxiliary Verb:** haben

Present Subjunctive: würde arbeiten

Present: arbeit**e**, arbeit**est**, arbeit**et**, arbeit**en**, arbeit**et**, arbeit**en**, arbeit**en**

Simple Past: arbeit**ete**, arbeit**etest**, arbeit**ete**, arbeit**eten**, arbeit**etet**, arbeit**eten**, arbeit**eten**

Imperative: arbeit**e**, arbeit**et**, arbeit**en** Sie

Some other verbs like this are **kosten** (*to cost*), **öffnen** (*to open*), **reden** (*to talk*), **regnen** (*to rain*), and **warten** (*to wait*).

Irregular weak verbs (stem change in the simple past)

denken (to think)

Present-Tense Stem: denk-

Simple Past (1st/3rd-person singular): dachte

Past Participle: gedacht; **Auxiliary Verb:** haben

Present Subjunctive: würde denken

Present: denk**e**, denk**st**, denk**t**, denk**en**, denk**t**, denk**en**, denk**en**

Simple Past: dach**te**, dach**test**, dach**te**, dach**ten**, dach**tet**, dach**ten**, dach**ten**

Imperative: denk, denk**t**, denk**en** Sie

Other verbs like this are in Table A-2.

Conjugations of Strong Verbs

Verbs with auxiliary haben

trinken (to drink)

Present-Tense Stem: trink-

Simple Past (1st/3rd-person singular): trank

Past Participle: getrunken; **Auxiliary Verb:** haben

Present Subjunctive: würde trinken

Present: trinke, trinkst, trinkt, trinken, trinkt, trinken, trinken

Simple Past: trank, trankst, trank, tranken, trankt, tranken, tranken

Imperative: trink, trinkt, trinken Sie

Other verbs like this are in Table A-2.

Verbs with auxiliary sein

kommen (to come)

Present-Tense Stem: komm-

Simple Past (1st/3rd-person singular): kam

Past Participle: gekommen; **Auxiliary Verb:** sein

Present Subjunctive: würde kommen

Present: komme, kommst, kommt, kommen, kommt, kommen, kommen

Simple Past: kam, kamst, kam, kamen, kamt, kamen, kamen

Imperative: komm, kommt, kommen Sie

Other verbs like this are in Table A-2.

Verbs with present-tense vowel change in second- and third-person singular

lesen (to read)

Present-Tense Stem: les-; **Present-Tense Vowel Change:** liest

Simple Past (1st/3rd-person singular): las

Past Participle: gelesen; **Auxiliary Verb:** haben

Present Subjunctive: würde lesen

Present: lese, **liest, liest,** lesen, lest, les**en,** lesen

Simple Past: las, las**est,** las, las**en,** las**t,** las**en,** las**en**

Imperative: lies, lest, lesen Sie

Other verbs like this are in Table A-2.

Conjugations of Separable-Prefix Verbs

mitbringen (to bring along)

Present-Tense Stem: bring- mit

Simple Past (1st/3rd-person singular): brachte mit

Past Participle: mitgebracht; **Auxiliary Verb:** haben

Present Subjunctive: würde mitbringen

Present: mitbringe, mitbring**st,** mitbring**t,** mitbring**en,** mitbring**t,** mitbring**en,** mitbring**en**

Simple Past: brach**te** mit, brach**test** mit, brach**te** mit, brach**ten** mit, brach**tet** mit, brach**ten** mit, brach**ten** mit

Imperative: bring mit, bringt mit, bringen Sie mit

Some other similar verbs are **anhaben** (*to wear*), **anrufen** (*to telephone*), **fernsehen** (*to watch TV*), and **vorhaben** (*to plan*).

Conjugations of Inseparable-Prefix Verbs

These verbs include those that have no **ge-** prefix in the past participle.

Verbs with a past participle ending in -t

bezahlen (to pay)

Present-Tense Stem: bezahl-

Simple Past (1st/3rd-person singular): bezahlte

Past Participle: bezahlt; **Auxiliary Verb:** haben

Present Subjunctive: würde bezahlen

Present: bezahle, bezahlst, bezahlt, bezahlen, bezahlt, bezahlen, bezahlen

Simple Past: bezahlte, bezahltest, bezahlte, bezahlten, bezahltet, bezahlten, bezahlten

Imperative: bezahl, bezahlt, bezahlen Sie

Some other verbs like this are **beantworten** (*to answer*), **besuchen** (*to visit*), **erklären** (*to explain*), **gehören** (*to belong to*), and **versuchen** (*to try*).

Verbs with a past participle ending in -en

gefallen (to like)

Present-Tense Stem: gefall-

Present-Tense Vowel Change (2nd/3rd-person singular): gefäll-

Simple Past (1st/3rd-person singular): gefiel

Past Participle: gefallen; **Auxiliary Verb:** haben

Present Subjunctive: würde gefallen

Present: gefalle, gefällst, gefällt, gefallen, gefallt, gefallen, gefallen

Simple Past: gefiel, gefielst, gefiel, gefielen, gefielt, gefielen, gefielen

Imperative: gefall, gefallt, gefallen Sie

Other verbs like this are in Table A-2.

Conjugations of Auxiliary Verbs Haben, Sein, and Werden

haben (to have)

Present (and auxiliary for verbs using haben in present perfect): habe, hast, hat, haben, habt, haben, haben

Simple Past (1st/3rd-person singular): hatte

Past Participle: gehabt; **Auxiliary Verb:** haben

Present Subjunctive (same as simple past with umlaut): hätte, hättest, hätte, hätten, hättet, hätten, hätten

Simple Past: hatte, hattest, hatte, hatten, hattet, hatten, hatten

Imperative: hab, habt, haben Sie

sein (to be)

Present (and auxiliary for verbs using sein in present perfect): bin, bist, ist, sind, seid, sind, sind

Simple Past (1st/3rd-person singular): war

Past Participle: gewesen; **Auxiliary Verb:** sein

Present Subjunctive (same as simple past with umlaut): wäre, wärest, wäre, wären, wäret, wären, wären

Simple Past: war, war**st**, war, war**en**, war**t**, war**en**, war**en**

Imperative: sei, seid, seien Sie

werden (to become, shall, will)

Present: werde, wirst, wird, werden, werdet, werden

Simple Past (1st/3rd-person singular): wurde

Past Participle: geworden; **Auxiliary Verb:** sein

Present Subjunctive (same as simple past with umlaut): würde, würdest, würde, würden, würdet, würden, würden

Simple Past: wurde, wurd**est**, wurde, wurd**en**, wurd**et**, wurd**en**, wurden

Imperative: werde, werdet, werden Sie

Note: The present of **werden** is the auxiliary verb for forming the future tense, and the present subjunctive is the auxiliary verb for many verbs in the present subjunctive.

Conjugations of Modal Auxiliary Verbs

dürfen (to be allowed, may)

Present: darf, darf**st**, darf, dürfen, dürf**t**, dürfen, dürfen

Simple Past (1st/3rd-person singular): durfte

Past Participle: gedurft; **Auxiliary Verb:** haben

Present Subjunctive (same as simple past with umlaut): dürfte

Simple Past: durfte, durftest, durfte, durften, durftet, durften, durften

können (to be able to, can, to know how to do something)

Present: kann, kann**st**, kann, könn**en**, könn**t**, könn**en**, könn**en**

Simple Past (1st/3rd-person singular): konnte

Past Participle: gekonnt; **Auxiliary Verb:** haben

Present Subjunctive (same as simple past with umlaut): könnte

Simple Past: konnte, konntest, konnte, konnten, konntet, konnten, konnten

mögen (to like [to], to want to)

Present: mag, magst, mag, mögen, mögt, mögen, mögen

Simple Past (1st/3rd-person singular): mochte

Past Participle: gemocht; **Auxiliary Verb:** haben

Present Subjunctive (same as simple past with umlaut): möchte (*would like to*)

Simple Past: mochte, mochtest, mochte, mochten, mochtet, mochten, mochte

müssen (to have to, must)

Present: muss, musst, muss, müssen, müsst, müssen, müssen

Simple Past (1st/3rd-person singular): musste

Past Participle: gemusst; **Auxiliary Verb:** haben

Present Subjunctive (same as simple past with umlaut): müsste

Simple Past: musste, musstest, musste, mussten, musstet, mussten, mussten

sollen (to be supposed to, should)

Present: soll, sollst, soll, sollen, sollt, sollen, sollen

Simple Past (1st/3rd-person singular): sollte

Past Participle: gesollt; **Auxiliary Verb:** haben

Present Subjunctive (same as simple past): sollte

Simple Past: sollte, solltest, sollte, sollten, solltet, sollten, sollten

wollen (to want to)

Present: will, willst, will, wollen, wollt, wollen, wollen

Simple Past (1st/3rd-person singular): wollte

Past Participle: gewollt; **Auxiliary Verb:** haben

Present Subjunctive (same as simple past): wollte

Simple Past: wollte, wolltest, wollte, wollten, wolltet, wollten, wollten

Principal Parts of Strong and Irregular Weak Verbs

Table A-2 contains the principal parts of verbs — the infinitive form, the simple past form, and the past participle. The second column shows the third-person singular present form for verbs that have a stem change. Included in this table are high-frequency strong verbs, irregular weak verbs, modal auxiliaries, common separable-prefix verbs whose base verb is not listed in this table, **haben** (*to have*), and **sein** (*to be*). The past participles that use the auxiliary **sein** are indicated by **ist** + past participle in the past participle column; the others use **haben.**

Table A-2	Principal Parts of Strong and Irregular Weak Verbs			
Infinitive	*Stem Change (3rd-Person Singular Present)*	*Simple Past*	*Past Participle*	*English Meaning*
anfangen	**fängt an**	**fing an**	**angefangen**	*to start, to begin*
anrufen		**rief an**	**angerufen**	*to telephone*
sich anziehen	**zieht an**	**zog an**	**angezogen**	*to get dressed*
sich aus-ziehen	**zieht aus**	**zog aus**	**ausgezogen**	*to get undressed*
beginnen		**begann**	**begonnen**	*to begin*
bekommen		**bekam**	**bekommen**	*to get*
bitten		**bat**	**gebeten**	*to request*
bleiben		**blieb**	**ist geblieben**	*to stay*
brechen	**bricht**	**brach**	**gebrochen**	*to break*
bringen		**brachte**	**gebracht**	*to bring*
denken		**dachte**	**gedacht**	*to think*
dürfen	**darf**	**durfte**	**gedurft**	*to be permitted to, may*
einladen	**lädt ein**	**lud ein**	**eingeladen**	*to invite*

Infinitive	Stem Change (3rd-Person Singular Present)	Simple Past	Past Participle	English Meaning
empfehlen	empfiehlt	empfahl	empfohlen	to recommend
entscheiden		entschied	entschieden	to decide
essen	isst	aß	gegessen	to eat
fahren	fährt	fuhr	ist gefahren	to go, to drive, to travel
fallen	fällt	fiel	ist gefallen	to fall
finden		fand	gefunden	to find
fliegen		flog	ist geflogen	to fly
geben	gibt	gab	gegeben	to give
gefallen	gefällt	gefiel	gefallen	to like
gehen		ging	ist gegangen	to go
genießen		genoss	genossen	to enjoy
gewinnen		gewann	gewonnen	to win
haben	hat	hatte	gehabt	to have
halten	hält	hielt	gehalten	to hold, to stop
heißen		hieß	geheißen	to be called, to be named
helfen	hilft	half	geholfen	to help
kennen		kannte	gekannt	to know (person)
klingen		klang	geklungen	to sound
kommen		kam	ist gekommen	to come
können	kann	konnte	gekonnt	to be able to, can
lassen	lässt	ließ	gelassen	to let
laufen	läuft	lief	ist gelaufen	to run
lesen	liest	las	gelesen	to read

(continued)

Table A-2 *(continued)*

Infinitive	Stem Change (3rd-Person Singular Present)	Simple Past	Past Participle	English Meaning
liegen		lag	gelegen	to lie (situated)
mögen	mag	mochte	gemocht	to like
müssen	muss	musste	gemusst	to have to, must
nehmen	nimmt	nahm	genommen	to take
nennen		nannte	genannt	to name
reiten		ritt	ist geritten	to ride (an animal)
rufen		rief	gerufen	to call
scheinen		schien	geschienen	to shine, to seem
schlafen	schläft	schlief	geschlafen	to sleep
schließen		schloss	geschlossen	to close
schneiden		schnitt	geschnitten	to cut
schreiben		schrieb	geschrieben	to write
schwimmen		schwamm	ist geschwommen	to swim
sehen	sieht	sah	gesehen	to see
sein	ist	war	ist gewesen	to be
singen		sang	gesungen	to sing
sitzen		saß	gesessen	to sit
sollen	soll	sollte	gesollt	to be supposed to, should
sprechen	spricht	sprach	gesprochen	to speak
stehen		stand	gestanden	to stand
sterben	stirbt	starb	ist gestorben	to die
tragen	trägt	trug	getragen	to wear, to carry
treffen	trifft	traf	getroffen	to meet

Infinitive	Stem Change (3rd-Person Singular Present)	Simple Past	Past Participle	English Meaning
treiben		trieb	getrieben	to engage in
trinken		trank	getrunken	to drink
tun		tat	getan	to do
vergessen	vergisst	vergaß	vergessen	to forget
verlieren		verlor	verloren	to lose
verstehen		verstand	verstanden	to understand
wachsen	wächst	wuchs	ist gewachsen	to grow
waschen	wäscht	wusch	gewaschen	to wash
werden	wird	wurde	ist geworden	to become, will
werfen	wirft	warf	geworfen	to throw
wissen	weiß	wusste	gewusst	to know (fact)
wollen	will	wollte	gewollt	to want (to)
ziehen		zog	gezogen	to pull

Case Charts

The following case charts are useful as a quick reference guide to articles, pronouns, and adjectives with case, gender, or number endings. You also find prepositions listed by case.

Articles

In this section, you find the definite articles **der, die,** and **das** (*the*) and the indefinite articles **ein** and **eine** (*a, an*). We also list the **ein-** words with the indefinite articles; they have the same case endings. (Go to Chapter 2 of Book III for details on articles.)

Definite articles (the)

Table A-3 shows all the ways to say *the* in German.

Table A-3		Definite Articles		
Case	*Masculine*	*Feminine*	*Neuter*	*Plural*
Nominative	der	die	das	die
Accusative	den	die	das	die
Dative	dem	der	dem	den
Genitive	des	der	des	der

Indefinite articles (a, an) and ein- words

Table A-4 shows the indefinite article **ein** (*a, an*) and the **ein-** words, which have the same case endings as **ein.** These words include **kein** (*no, not, not any*) and the possessive adjectives: **mein** (*my*), **dein** (*your*), **sein** (*his/its*), **ihr** (*her*), **unser** (*our*), **euer** (*your*), **ihr** (*their*), and **Ihr** (*your*). Each box in the table includes **ein** and the possessive adjectives **mein** and **unser.** All other possessive adjectives use these same endings. We indicate the case endings for all **ein-** words separately, as well as in each word, in bold.

Note: The word **ein** has no plural, so we put **kein** in the plural slot.

Table A-4		Ein, Kein, and Ein- Words		
Case	*Masculine*	*Feminine*	*Neuter*	*Plural*
Nominative	ein, mein, unser	eine, meine, unsere	ein, mein, unser	keine, meine, unsere
	-	-e	-	-e
Accusative	einen, meinen, unseren	eine, meine, unsere	ein, mein, unser	keine, meine, unsere
	-en	-e	-	-e
Dative	einem, meinem, unserem	einer, meiner, unserer	einem, meinem, unserem	keinen, meinen, unseren
	-em	-er	-em	-en
Genitive	eines, meines, unseres	einer, meiner, unserer	eines, meines, unseres	keiner, meiner, unserer
	-es	-er	-es	-er

Pronouns

In this section, you find the pronoun group: personal pronouns (in the nominative case: *I, you, he/she/it, we, you, they*), relative pronouns (*who, whom, whose, that*), demonstrative pronouns (*this, that, these, those*), reflexive pronouns (*myself, yourself, himself, herself, itself, ourselves, yourselves, themselves*), and the interrogative pronoun *who*. (Turn to Book III, Chapter 2 for more info on pronouns.)

Personal pronouns

Table A-5 shows the personal pronouns in three cases: nominative, accusative, and dative. In this section, we list the conjugations in order of the pronouns, from first- to third-person singular, then first- to third-person plural, and finally the formal second-person address (**Sie**). In order, the nominative case is **ich, du, er/sie/es, wir, ihr, sie, Sie.** Here's what the abbreviations in the table mean: s. = singular; pl. = plural; inf. = informal; form. = formal.

Table A-5	Personal Pronouns	
Nominative Case	*Accusative Case*	*Dative Case*
ich (*I*)	**mich** (*me*)	**mir** (*me*)
du (*you*) (s., inf.)	**dich** (*you*)	**dir** (*you*)
er (*he*)	**ihn** (*him*)	**ihm** (*him*)
sie (*she*)	**sie** (*her*)	**ihr** (*her*)
es (*it*)	**es** (*it*)	**ihm** (*it*)
wir (*we*)	**uns** (*us*)	**uns** (*us*)
ihr (*you*) (pl., inf.)	**euch** (*you*)	**euch** (*you*)
sie (*they*)	**sie** (*them*)	**ihnen** (*them*)
Sie (*you*) (s. or pl., form.)	**Sie** (*you*)	**Ihnen** (*you*)

Relative and demonstrative pronouns

The relative and demonstrative pronouns are the same in German (see Table A-6). In English, the relative pronouns are *who, whom, whose,* and *that,* and the demonstrative pronouns are *this, that, these,* and *those.*

Table A-6	Relative and Demonstrative Pronouns			
Case	*Masculine*	*Feminine*	*Neuter*	*Plural*
Nominative	der	die	das	die
Accusative	den	die	das	die
Dative	dem	der	dem	denen
Genitive (relative pronouns only)	dessen	deren	dessen	deren

Note: Another demonstrative pronoun, **dieser,** also has the same meanings in English: *this, that, these, those.* You can see it in Table A-7 with the **der-** words.

Der- words

The **der-** words all have the same case endings. They include **dieser** (*this, that, these, those*), **jeder** (*each, every*), **mancher** (*some*), **solcher** (*such*), and **welcher** (*which*). Table A-7 shows the endings in bold.

Table A-7	Der- Words			
Case	*Masculine*	*Feminine*	*Neuter*	*Plural*
Nominative	dies**er**	dies**e**	dies**es**	dies**e**
Accusative	dies**en**	dies**e**	dies**es**	dies**e**
Dative	dies**em**	dies**er**	dies**em**	dies**en**
Genitive	dies**es**	dies**er**	dies**es**	dies**er**

Reflexive pronouns

The reflexive pronouns include *myself, yourself, himself, herself, itself, ourselves, yourselves,* and *themselves.* Table A-8 also includes personal pronouns (nominative case) for reference. Here's what the abbreviations in the table mean: s. = singular; pl. = plural; inf. = informal; form. = formal.

Table A-8	Reflexive Pronouns	
Nominative of Personal Pronouns	*Accusative (Reflexive)*	*Dative (Reflexive)*
ich (*I*)	**mich** (*myself*)	**mir** (*myself*)
du (*you*) (s., inf.)	**dich** (*yourself*)	**dir** (*yourself*)
er (*he*)	**sich** (*himself*)	**sich** (*himself*)

Nominative of Personal Pronouns	Accusative (Reflexive)	Dative (Reflexive)
sie (*she*)	**sich** (*herself*)	**sich** (*herself*)
es (*it*)	**sich** (*itself*)	**sich** (*itself*)
wir (*we*)	**uns** (*ourselves*)	**uns** (*ourselves*)
ihr (*you*) (pl., inf.)	**euch** (*yourselves*)	**euch** (*yourselves*)
sie (*they*)	**sich** (*themselves*)	**sich** (*themselves*)
Sie (*you*) (s. or pl., form.)	**sich** (*yourself/yourselves*)	**sich** (*yourself/ yourselves*)

Interrogative pronoun who

Table A-9 shows the interrogative (question) pronoun *who*.

Table A-9	Interrogative Pronoun Who	
Case	*Pronoun*	*English Equivalent*
Nominative	**wer**	*who*
Accusative	**wen**	*whom/for*
Dative	**wem**	*(to) whom*
Genitive	**wessen**	*whose*

Adjectives

In this section, you find the adjective tables showing case endings for adjectives not preceded by an article and for preceded adjectives (after **der-** words and after **ein-** words). You also find a comparison table for irregular adjectives and adverbs. (Go to Chapter 5 of Book III for details on adjectives.)

Adjectives without der- or ein- words (not preceded)

Table A-10 shows endings for adjectives that aren't preceded by an article (**der/die/das** or **ein/eine**) or other modifiers (**der-** words, such as **dieser** and **solcher,** and **ein-** words, such as **mein** and **kein**). The endings for these adjectives indicate the noun's gender and case in the sentence. The endings are shown separately in bold.

Table A-10	Adjective Endings Not Preceded			
Case	*Masculine*	*Feminine*	*Neuter*	*Plural*
Nominative	gut**er** Käse	schmack- haf**te** Wurst	lecker**es** Brot	köstlich**e** Kuchen
	(*good cheese*)	(*tasty sausage*)	(*delicious bread*)	(*delicious cakes*)
	-er	**-e**	**-es**	**-e**
Accusative	gut**en** Käse	schmack- haf**te** Wurst	lecker**es** Brot	köstlich**e** Kuchen
	-en	**-e**	**-es**	**-e**
Dative	gut**em** Käse	schmack- haf**ter** Wurst	lecker**em** Brot	köstlich**en** Kuchen
	-em	**-er**	**-em**	**-en**
Genitive	gut**en** Käses	schmack- haf**ter** Wurst	lecker**en** Brotes	köstlich**er** Kuchen
	-en	**-er**	**-en**	**-er**

Preceded adjectives

Table A-11 shows endings for adjectives that are preceded by an article (**der/ die/das** or **ein/eine**) or other modifier (**der-** words or **ein-** words). The adjective endings are shown in bold.

Table A-11	Preceded Adjective Endings			
Case	*Masculine*	*Feminine*	*Neuter*	*Plural*
Nominative	**der** lustig**e** Mann	**die** glücklich**e** Frau	**das** brav**e** Kind	**die** lustig**en** Männer
	ein lustig**er** Mann	**eine** glücklich**e** Frau	**ein** brav**es** Kind	**keine** lusti- g**en** Männer
Accusative	**den** lustig**en** Mann	**die** glücklich**e** Frau	**das** brav**e** Kind	**die** lustig**en** Männer
	einen lustig**en** Mann	**eine** glücklich**e** Frau	**ein** brav**es** Kind	**keine** lustig**en** Männer

Case	Masculine	Feminine	Neuter	Plural
Dative	**dem** lustig**en** Mann	**der** glücklich**en** Frau	**dem** brav**en** Kind	**den** lustig**en** Männer**n**
	einem lustig**en** Mann	**einer** glücklich**en** Frau	**einem** brav**en** Kind	**keinen** lustig**en** Männer**n**
Genitive	**des** lustig**en** Mann**es**	**der** glückli-chen Frau	**des** brav**en** Kind**es**	**der** lustig**en** Männer
	eines lusti-g**en** Mann**es**	**einer** glück-lichen Frau	**eines** brav**en** Kind**es**	**keiner** lusti-g**en** Männer

Note: The plural endings for preceded adjectives are the same in masculine, feminine, and neuter.

Irregular comparison (adjectives and adverbs)

Table A-12 shows how you form the base, comparative, and superlative forms of irregular adjectives and adverbs.

Table A-12	Irregular Comparison Forms	
Base	**Comparative**	**Superlative**
bald (*soon*)	**eher** (*sooner*)	**am ehesten** (*soonest*)
gern (*like/enjoy [doing something]*)	**lieber** (*prefer*)	**am liebsten** (*like most of all*)
gut (*good*)	**besser** (*better*)	**am besten** (*best*)
hoch (*high*)	**höher** (*higher*)	**am höchsten** (*highest*)
nah (*near*)	**näher** (*nearer*)	**am nächsten** (*nearest*)
viel (*much*)	**mehr** (*more*)	**am meisten** (*most*)

Prepositions

German prepositions have a case: accusative, dative, or genitive. Some prep-ositions have two cases (accusative and dative). This section gives you the basics. (Go to Book IV, Chapter 2 for details on prepositions.)

Accusative, dative, and genitive prepositions

Table A-13 shows accusative, dative, and genitive prepositions and their English equivalents.

Table A-13	Accusative, Dative, and Genitive Prepositions
Preposition	*English Equivalent(s)*
Accusative	
bis	*till, until* (also: conjunction *until*)
durch	*through, by*
entlang	*along, down*
für	*for*
gegen	*against, for*
ohne	*without*
um	*around, for, at*
Dative	
aus	*from, out of*
außer	*besides, except for*
bei	*at* (a home of, a place of business), *near, with*
mit	*with, by* (means of transportation)
nach	*after, past, to* (no article for cities and countries)
seit	*for, since*
von	*by, from, of*
zu	*to* (with people and certain places)
Genitive	
(an)statt	*from, out of*
außerhalb	*besides, except for*
innerhalb	*at* (a home of, a place of business), *near, with*
trotz	*with, by* (means of transportation)
während	*after, past, to* (no article for cities and countries)

Note: **Entlang** (*along, down*) can be an accusative, dative, or genitive preposition.

Note: There's no difference between **anstatt** and **statt** (*instead of*), a genitive preposition.

Two-way prepositions: Accusative/dative

Table A-14 shows accusative/dative prepositions and their English equivalents. These prepositions can take the accusative case or the dative case, depending on how they're used in a sentence. Generally speaking, you use the accusative case to indicate motion, or a change of location, and the dative to indicate a static location.

Table A-14	Accusative/Dative Prepositions
Preposition	*English Equivalent(s)*
an	*at, on, to*
auf	*on, onto, to*
hinter	*behind, to the back of*
in	*in, into, to*
neben	*beside, next to*
über	*above, over*
unter	*under, underneath*
vor	*in front of*
zwischen	*between*

Appendix B

German-English Mini-Dictionary

Key: m = masculine, f = feminine, n = neuter, sing = singular, pl = plural, inf = informal, form = formal, dat = dative, acc = accusative

A

ab (âp): starting at, away, off

abfahren (*âp*-fahr-en): to depart (train)

ablaufen (*âp*-louf-en): to expire

Absender (*ap*-zên-der) m: sender

abwaschen (*âp*-vâsh-en): to do the dishes

alle (*âl*-e): all

allein (â-*layn*): alone

allergisch gegen (â-*lêr*-gish *gey*-gen): allergic to

als (âls): than, when

also (*âl*-zoh): so

alt (âlt): old

an (ân): at, by, to

Ananas (*ân*-ân-âs) f: pineapple

anfangen (*ân*-fâng-en): to begin

Angebot (*ân*-ge-boht) n: offer

Angestellte (*ân*-gê-shtêl-te) m: employee

ankommen (*ân*-kom-en): to arrive

anmelden (*ân*-mêl-den): to sign in

Ansichtskarte (*ahn*-ziHts-kâr-te) f: picture postcard

antworten (*ânt*-fort-en): to answer

Anzug (*ân*-tsook) m: suit (pants/jacket)

Apartment (â-*pârt*-ment) n: apartment (one room)

Apfel (*âp*-fel) m: apple

Apotheke (ah-poh-*tey*-ke) f: pharmacy

arbeiten (*âr*-bayt-en): to work

Arbeitskollege (*âr*-bayts-ko-*ley*-ge) m: coworker

Arbeitsplatz (*âr*-bayts-plâts) m: workplace

Arbeitszimmer (*âr*-bayts-tsi-mer) n: workroom, study

atmen (*aht*-men): to breathe

attraktiv (â-trâk-*teef*): attractive

Aubergine (oh-bêr-j*een*-e) f: eggplant

auf Wiederhören (ouf *vee*-der-herr-en): goodbye (on the phone)

aufmachen (*ouf*-mâH-en): to open

aufregend (*ouf*-rey-gent): exciting

Aufschnitt (*ouf*-shnit) m: cold cuts

aufstehen (*ouf*-shtey-en): to get up

aus (ous): from, out of

Ausflug (*ous*-floohk) m: excursion

aussteigen (*ous*-shtayg-en): to get off

Auster (*ous*-têr) f: oyster

Ausweis (*ous*-vays) m: ID card

Autounfall (*ou*-toh-oon-fâl) m: car accident

Autovermietung (*ou*-toh-fêr-*meet*-oong) f: car rental agency

Avocado (â-voh-*kah*-doh) f: avocado

B

Bäckerei (*bêk*-e-*ray*) f: bakery

Backofen (*bâk*-oh-fen) m: oven

Badeanzug (*bah*-de-ân-tsook) m: bathing suit

Badetuch (*bah*-de-toohH) n: bath towel

Badewanne (*bah*-de-wân-e) f: bathtub

bald (bâlt): soon

Balkon (bâl-*kohn*) m: balcony

Ballett (bâ-*lêt*) n: ballet

Banane (bâ-*nah*-ne) f: banana

Bargeld (*bâr*-gêlt) n: cash

Basketball (basketball [as in English]) m: basketball

Baustelle (*bou*-shtêl-e) f: construction site

beantragen (bê-*ân*-trah-gen): to apply for

Becher (*bêH*-er) m: mug

beige (beige [as in English]): beige

Beilage (*bay*-lah-ge) f: side dish

Bekannte (bê-*kân*-te) m: acquaintance

bekommen (be-*kom*-en): to get

Beleg (be-*leyk*) m: receipt, slip

Besprechung (be-*shprêH*-oong) f: informal meeting

Besteck (be-*shtêk*) n: cutlery

bestellen (be-*shtêl*-en): to order

bestimmt (be-*shtimt*): certainly

besuchen (be-*zooH*-en): to visit

Bett (bêt) n: bed

Bettuch (*bêt*-toohH) n: sheet

Bild (bilt) n: picture

billig (*bil*-iH): cheap, inexpensive

Birne (*birn*-e) f: pear

bis (bis): by, until

blau (blou): blue

Blaubeere (*blou*-beyr-e) f: blueberry

Blazer (*bley*-zer) m: blazer

Bleistift (*blay*-shtift) m: pencil

Blumenkohl (*bloom*-en-kohl) m: cauliflower

Bluse (*blooh*-ze) f: blouse

Boden (*boh*-den) m: floor

Bohne (*bohn*-e) f: bean

Börse (*bêr*-ze) f: stock market

botanisch (boh-*tân*-ish): botanical

Bratwurst (*braht*-voorst) f: fried sausage

brauchen (*brouH*-en): to need

braun (broun): brown

Brokkoli (*broh*-ko-lee) m: broccoli

Bruder (*brooh*-der) m: brother

Burg (boork) f: castle

Büro (bue-*roh*) n: office

C

Champignon (*shâm*-peen-yon) m: button mushroom

Chef (chêf) m: boss

Computer (computer [as in English]) m: computer

Cornflakes (cornflakes [as in English]) pl: cornflakes

Couch (couch [as in English]) f: couch

Couchtisch (*kouch*-tish) m: coffee table

Cousin (kooh-*zen*) m: cousin (male)

Cousine (kooh-*zeen*-e) f: cousin (female)

D

da (dâ): there, because

Dachboden (*dâH*-boh-den) m: attic

damit (dâ-*mit*): so that

dann (dân): then

darum (dâ-room): for that reason, therefore

das (dâs) n: the

dass (dâs): that

dauern (*dou*-ern): to last

Decke (*dêk*-e) f: blanket

dein (dayn): your (inf, sing)

denken (*dênk*-en): to think

Denkmal (*dênk*-mâl) n: memorial, monument

denn (dên): for, because

der (dêr) m: the

deshalb (*dês*-hâlp): therefore

dich (diH): you (inf, sing, acc)

die (dee) f: the

Dieb (deep) m: thief

dieser (*deez*-er): this, that, these, those

dir (deer): you (inf, sing, dat)

doch (doH): but, nevertheless

Doktor (*dok*-tohr) m: doctor

dolmetschen (*dol*-mêch-en): to interpret

Dolmetscher (*dol*-mêch-er) m: interpreter

draußen (*drous*-en): outside

dringend (*dring*-end): urgent, immediately

drinnen (*drin*-en): inside

Drogerie (droh-ge-*ree*) f: drugstore

drüben (*drue*-ben): over there

Drucker (*drook*-er) m: printer

du (dooh): you (inf, sing)

dunkel (*doon*-kêl): dark

durch (doorH): through, by

Durchfall (*doorH*-fâl) m: diarrhea

Durst (doorst) m: thirst

durstig (*doorst*-iH): thirsty

Dusche (*dooh*-she) f: shower

E

Eckbank (*êk*-bânk) f: corner bench

Ei (ay) n: egg

Eigentumswohnung (*ay*-gên-tooms-*vohn*-oong) f: condominium

Eilbrief (*ayl*-breef) m: express letter

ein (ayn): a, an

Einbahnstraße (*ayn*-bahn-*shtrah*-se) f: one-way street

einchecken (*ayn*-chêk-en): to check in

Einfahrt (*ayn*-fahrt) f: entrance ramp

Einfamilienhaus (*ayn*-fâ-*mi*-lee-en-hous) n: single-family house

eingelegt (*ayn*-ge-leygt): pickled

einkaufen (*ayn*-kouf-en): to go shopping

Einschreiben (*ayn*-shrayb-en) m: registered mail

einsteigen (*ayn*-shtayg-en): to get on, to get in

Eintrittskarte (*ayn*-trits-kar-te) f: entrance ticket

elegant (êl-ê-*gânt*): elegant

Eltern (*êl*-tern) pl: parents

E-Mail-Adresse (*e*-mail-ah-*drês*-e) f: e-mail address

Empfang (êm-*pfâng*) m: reception

Empfänger (êm-*pfêng*-er) m: addressee

endlich (*ênt*-liH): finally

Ente (*ên*-te) f: duck

enttäuschend (ênt-*toy*-shênt): disappointing

er (êr): he

Erbse (*erp*-se) f: pea

Erdbeere (*eyrt*-beyr-e) f: strawberry

ernst (êrnst): serious

erreichen (êr-*ayH*-en): to reach

es (ês): it

Essen (*ês*-en) n: meal

Esstisch (*ês*-tish) m: dining table

Esszimmer (*ês*-tsi-mer) n: dining room

etwa (*êt*-vâ): approximately

euch (oyH): you (inf, pl, acc/dat)

euer (*oy*-er): your (inf, pl)

eventuell (ê-vên-too-*êl*): possibly

F

Fahrplan (*fahr*-plân) m: train schedule

Fahrrad fahren (*fahr*-rât *fahr*-en): to ride a bike

fallen (*fâl*-en): to fall

falls (fâls): if, whether, in case

Farbe (*fâr*-be) f: color

Fasan (fâ-*zân*) m: pheasant

fast (fâst): almost

feiern (*fay*-ern): to celebrate

fernsehen (*fêrn*-zey-en): to watch TV

Fernseher (*fêrn*-zey-er) m: television

Fest (fêst) n: celebration, festival

Feuer! (*foy*-er!) n: fire!

finden (*fin*-den): to find

Flasche (*flâsh*-e) f: bottle

flexibel (flêx-*ee*-bel): flexible

Flunder (*floon*-der) f: flounder

Forelle (fohr-*êl*-e) f: trout

Fotokopierer (foh-toh-ko-*peer*-er) m: copy machine

Frau (frou) f: woman, wife

freundlich (*froynt*-liH): friendly

frisch (frish): fresh

frittiert (fri-*teert*): deep-fat fried

früh (frue): early

funktionieren (foonk-tsee-oh-*neer*-en): to function

Fußball (*foohs*-bâl) m: soccer

Fußgängerzone (*foohs*-gên-ger-*tsohn*-e) f: pedestrian zone

G

Galerie (gâl-êr-*ee*) f: gallery

Gang (gâng) m: hall

Gans (gâns) f: goose

Garage (gâ-*rah*-ge) f: garage

Gardine (gâr-*deen*-e) f: curtain

Garten (*gâr*-ten) m: garden

Gebäck (ge-*bêk*) n: cookies, pastries

gebacken (ge-*bâk*-en): baked

gebraten (ge-*brât*-en): roasted

Gebrauch (ge-*brouH*) m: use, purpose

Geburtsdatum (gê-*boorts*-dah-toohm) n: birth date

Geburtsort (gê-*boorts*-ort) m: place of birth

gedampft (ge-*dâmpft*): steamed

Geflügel (ge-*flueg*-el) n: poultry

gefüllt (ge-*fuelt*): stuffed

gekocht (ge-*koHt*): boiled, cooked

gelb (gêlp): yellow

gemischt (ge-*misht*): mixed

gemütlich (ge-*muet*-liH): cozy, comfortable

gerade (gê-*rah*-de): just, currently

geräuchert (ge-*royH*-êrt): smoked

Gericht (ge-*riHt*) n: dish (food)

gern (gêrn): gladly

Geschäftsfrau (gê-*shêfts*-frou) f: businesswoman

Geschäftsmann (gê-*shêfts*-mân) m: businessman

Geschenk (ge-*shênk*) n: gift

Geschirrspülmaschine (ge-*shir*-sphuel-mâ-*sheen*-e) f: dishwasher

Geschwister (ge-*shvis*-ter) pl: siblings

Gesellschaft (gê-*zêl*-shâft) f: society

Gesundheit (gê-*zoont*-hayt) f: health

gewiss (ge-*vis*): indeed, of course

gleich (glayH): alike, immediately

glücklich (*gluek*-liH): happy

gold (golt): gold

Golf (golf [as in English]) m: golf

grau (grou): gray

Großeltern (*grohs*-êl-tern) pl: grandparents

Großmutter (*grohs*-moot-er) f: grandmother

Großvater (*grohs*-fât-er) m: grandfather

grün (gruen): green

Grünkohl (*gruen*-kohl) m: kale

Gurke (*goork*-e) f: cucumber

Gürtel (*guer*-tel) m: belt

Guten Appetit (*gooh*-ten âp-e-*teet*): enjoy
your meal

H

Haarbürste (*hahr*-buers-te) f: hairbrush

Hackfleisch (*hâk*-flaysh) n: ground meat

Haferflocken (*hahf*-er-flok-en) pl: oatmeal

Hähnchen (*hain*-Hen) n: chicken

halten (*hâlt*-en): to hold, to stop

Handgepäck (*hând*-ge-pêk) n: carry-on
luggage

Handschuh (*hânt*-shooh) m: glove

Handtasche (*hânt*-tâsh-e) f: handbag

Haustier (*hous*-teer) n: family pet

Heilbutt (*hayl*-boot) m: halibut

heiß (hays): hot

heiter (*hayt*-er): cheerful

hell (hêl): light (color)

Hemd (hêmt) n: shirt

Herd (hêrt) m: stove

Hering (*hêr*-ing) m: herring

heutzutage (*hoyt*-tsooh-tah-ge):
nowadays

Himbeere (*him*-beyr-e) f: raspberry

hinterlassen (hin-ter-*lâs*-en): to leave
(behind)

hoch (hohH): high

hoffen (*hof*-en): to hope

hoffentlich (*hof*-ênt-liH): hopefully

höflich (*herf*-liH): polite

Honig (*hohn*-iH) m: honey

Hose (*hoh*-ze) f: pants

Hosenanzug (*hoh*-zen-ân-tsook)
m: (pant)suit

hübsch (huepsh): pretty

Hund (hoont) m: dog

Hunger (*hoong*-er) m: hunger

hungrig (*hoong*-riH): hungry

Hut (hooht) m: hat

I

ich (iH): I

ihm (eem): him, it

ihn (een): him

ihnen (*een*-en): them

Ihnen (*een*-en): you (form, sing/pl, dat)

ihr (eer): you (inf, pl), her, their

Ihr (eer): your (form, sing/pl, dat)

immer (*im*-er): always

in (in): in

in der Nähe (in dêr *nai*-he): nearby

in Ordnung (in *ord*-noong): okay

intelligent (in-têl-i-*gênt*): intelligent

irgendwo (*ir*-gênd-voh): somewhere,
anywhere

J

Jacke (*yâ*-ke) f: jacket

Jackett (jâ-*kêt*) n: jacket

Jeans (jeans [as in English]) f: jeans

jedenfalls (*yey*-den-fâls): anyway

jemals (*yey*-mâls): ever

jetzt (yêtst): now

jung (yoong): young

Junge (*yoong*-e) m: boy

K

Kabeljau (*kah*-bel-you) m: cod

Kalbfleisch (*kâlp*-flaysh) n: veal

Kamm (*kâm*) m: comb

Kaninchen (*kân-een*-Hen) n: rabbit

Karotte (*kâ-rot*-e) f: carrot

Kartoffel (*kâr-tof*-el) f: potato

Katze (*kâts*-e) f: cat

kaum (*koum*): hardly

Keller (*kêl*-er) m: cellar

Kellner (*kêl*-ner) m: waiter

Kind (*kint*) n: child

Kirsche (*kirsh*-e) f: cherry

Kiwi (*kee*-vee) f: kiwi

klar (*klahr*): of course

Kleid (*klayt*) n: dress

Kleiderschrank (*klay*-der-shrânk) m: (clothes) closet

Knoblauch (*knoh*-blouH) m: garlic

kochen (*koH*-en): to cook

Kohl (*kohl*) m: cabbage

Kohlrabi (kohl-*râ*-bee) m: kohlrabi

Kollege (ko-*ley*-ge) m: colleague

Kommode (ko-*moh*-de) f: dresser

Konditorei (kon-dee-to-*ray*) f: pastry shop

Kopfkissen (*kopf*-kis-en) n: pillow

Kopfsalat (*kopf*-zâ-laht) m: lettuce

Kostüm (kos-*tuem*) n: suit (dress/jacket)

Krabbe (*krâb*-e) f: shrimp

Kräuter (*kroyt*-er) pl: herbs

Krawatte (krâ-*vât*-e) f: tie

Krebs (*kreyps*) m: crab

Küche (*kueH*-e) f: kitchen

Kugelschreiber (*kooh*-gel-shray-ber) m, **Kuli** (*kooh*-lee) (colloquial) m: pen

kühl (*kuel*): cool

Kühlschrank (*kuel*-shrânk) m: refrigerator

Kultur (kool-*toohr*) f: culture

Kürbis (*kuer*-bis) m: pumpkin

Kurs (*koors*) m: course, class

L

Lachs (*lâx*) m: salmon

Lammfleisch (*lâm*-flaysh) n: lamb (meat)

Lampe (*lâm*-pe) f: lamp

langsam (*lâng*-zahm): slow(ly)

lassen (*lâs*-en): to let, to allow

Lauch (*louH*) m: leek

laufen (*louf*-en): to run

laut (*lout*): loud

Leitungswasser (*lay*-toongs-*vâs*-er) n: tap water

lernen (*lêrn*-en): to learn

liegen (*leeg*-en): to lie (down)

lila (*lee*-lâ): purple

M

Mädchen (*maid*-Hen) n: girl

man (*mân*): you (impersonal)

Mann (*mân*) m: man, husband

Mantel (*mân*-tel) m: coat

Margarine (mâr-gâr-*een*-e) f: margarine

mariniert (mâr-i-*neert*): marinated

Marmelade (mâr-me-*lah*-de) f: marmelade, jam

Meerrettich (*meyr*-rêt-iH) m: horseradish

Meeting (meeting [as in English]) n: meeting

mehr (*meyr*): more

Mehrwertsteuer (*meyr*-vêrt-shtoy-er) f: sales tax

Meldeschein (*mêl*-de-shayn) m: registration form

Melone (mê-*lohn*-e) f: melon

Metzgerei (mêts-ge-*ray*) f: butcher shop

mich (*miH*): me

Mietwohnung (*meet*-vohn-oong) f: rented apartment

Mikrowellenherd (meek-roh-*vêl*-en-hêrt) m: microwave oven

Mineralwasser (min-êr-*ahl*-vâs-er) n: mineral water

mir (mir): me

Mitarbeiter (*mit*-âr-bayt-er) m: associate

Monument (mon-oo-*mênt*) n: monument

Mülleimer (*muel*-aym-er) m: garbage can

Muschel (*moosh*-el) f: mussel

Müsli (*mues*-lee) n: muesli

Mutter (*moot*-er) f: mother

Mütze (*muetz*-e) f: cap

N

nach (nâH): after, to

Nachbar (*nâH*-bâr) m: neighbor

nachher (*nâH*-hêr): afterward

Nachspeise (*nâH*-shpayz-e) f: dessert

nah (nah): near

nämlich (*naim*-liH): namely

nass (nâs): wet

Natur (na-*toohr*) f: nature

nett (nêt): nice

neu (noy): new

neuerdings (*noy*-er-dings): recently

nicht nur (niHt noohr) . . . **sondern auch** (*zon*-dern ouH): not only . . . but also

niemals (*nee*-mâls): never

nirgendwo (*nir*-gênd-voh): nowhere

noch (noH): still, yet

Notruf (*noht*-roohf) m: emergency call

Nudeln (*nooh*-deln) pl: noodles

nur (noohr): only

O

ob (op): if, whether

oben (*oh*-ben): up

obwohl (op-*vohl*): although

oder (*oh*-der): or

oft (oft): often

ohne (*oh*-ne): without

Olive (oh-*leev*-e) f: olive

Onkel (*onk*-êl) m: uncle

orange (o-*rân*-je): orange (color)

Orange (o-*rân*-je) f: orange (fruit)

Ort (ort) m: place

P

Palast (pâ-*lâst*) m: palace

Papier (pâ-*peer*) n: paper

Paprika (*pâp*-ree-kah) m: bell pepper

Parkhaus (*pârk*-hous) n: parking garage

Passkontrolle (*pâs*-kon-trol-e) f: passport control

Pause (*pou*-ze) f: intermission, break

Person (pêr-*zohn*) f: person

persönlich (pêr-*zern*-lich): personal

Pfirsich (*pfir*-ziH) m: peach

Pflaume (*pflau*-me) f: plum

Pilz (pilts) m: mushroom

Platz (plâts) m: seat, place

Platzkarte (*plâts*-kâr-te) f: reserved seat

Politik (pol-i-*teek*) f: politics

Polizeirevier (po-li-*tsay*-re-veer) n: police station

Porto (*por*-toh) n: postage

Postleitzahl (*post*-layt-tsahl) f: area code

Preis (prays) m: price

Preiselbeere (*pray*-zêl-beyr-e) f: cranberry

Pulli (*poo*-lee) m: pullover

Pullover (poo-*loh*-ver) m: pullover

Pullunder (poo-*lun*-der) m: tank top

putzen (*poots*-en): to clean

R

Rasierapparat (râ-*zeer*-âp-â-*rât*) m: razor

Regal (rey-*gah*l) n: shelf

Regenmantel (*rey*-gen-*mân*-tel) m: raincoat

Rehfleisch (*rey*-flaysh) n: venison

Reihenhaus (*ray*-en-hous) n: town house

Reis (rays) m: rice

Reisebüro (*ray*-ze-bue-*roh*) n: travel agency

Rettungsdienst (*rêt*-oongs-deenst) m: emergency service

Rezept (rê-*tsêpt*) n: prescription, recipe

Rindfleisch (*rint*-flaysh) n: beef

Rock (rok) m: skirt

Roggenbrot (*rog*-en-broht) n: rye bread

roh (roh): raw

rosa (*roh*-zâ): pink

rot (roht): red

Rotkohl (*roht*-kohl) m: red cabbage

Rotwein (*roht*-vayn) m: red wine

rufen (*roohf*-en): to call, to summon

ruhig (*rooh*-iH): quiet

S

Sahne (*zahn*-e) f: cream

Salat (zâ-*laht*) m: salad

Sandale (zân-*dahl*-e) f: sandal

sauer (*zou*-er): sour

Sauerkraut (*zou*-er-krout) n: sauerkraut

Sauna (*zou*-nâ) f: sauna

Schal (shâl) m: scarf

Schellfisch (*shêl*-fish) m: haddock

schenken (*shênk*-en): to give (a present)

Schinken (*shin*-ken) m: ham

schlafen (*shlâf*-en): to sleep

Schlafzimmer (*shlahf*-tsi-mer) n: bedroom

schlank (shlânk): thin, slim

schlecht (shlêHt): bad

schließen (*shlees*-en): to close

Schloss (shlos) n: palace, castle

Schmuck (shmook) m: jewelry

schneiden (*shnay*-den): to cut

Schrank (shrânk) m: cabinet, cupboard, closet

Schrankwand (*shrânk*-vânt) f: wall unit

schreiben (*shray*-ben): to write

Schreibtisch (*shrayp*-tish) m: desk

Schublade (*shoob*-lâ-de) f: drawer

Schuh (shooh) m: shoe

schwach (shvâH): weak

schwarz (shvârts): black

Schwarzbrot (*shvârts*-broht) n: brown bread

Schweinefleisch (*shvayn*-e-flaysh) n: pork

Schwester (*shvês*-ter) f: sister

Seezunge (*zey*-tsoong-e) f: sole (fish)

sehenswert (*zey*-enz-vêrt): worth seeing

Seife (*zay*-fe) f: soap

sein (zayn): his, its

seit (zayt): since

Seite (*zay*-te) f: page

Sekretär (zê-krê-*têr*) m: secretary

Sellerie (zêl-êr-*ee*) m: celeriac

Serviette (sêr-vee-*êt*-e) f: napkin

Sessel (*zês*-el) m: armchair

setzen (*zêts*-en): to sit, to set

sharf (shârf): spicy

Shorts (shorts [as in English]) f: shorts

sich entschuldigen (ziH ênt-*shool*-di-gen): to excuse oneself

sich fühlen (ziH *fuel*-en): to feel

sicher (*ziH*-er): sure, certainly

sie (zee): she, her, they, them

Sie (zee): you (form, sing/pl)

silber (*zil*-ber): silver

Sinfonie (sin-foh-*nee*) f: symphony

so (*zoh*): such, thus, so, as

so (*zoh*) . . . **wie** (*vee*): as . . . as

Socke (*zok*-e) f: sock

Sofa (*zoh*-fâ) n: sofa

sofort (zo-*fort*): immediately

Sohn (*zohn*) m: son

sollen (*zol*-en): should

sondern (*zon*-dern): but rather

Sonnenbrille (*zon*-en-bril-e) f: sunglasses

sonnig (*zon*-iH): sunny

sonst (*zonst*): otherwise

Spargel (*shpâr*-gêl) m: asparagus

spät (*shpait*): late

Speck (*shpêk*) m: bacon

Spiegel (*shpee*-gel) m: mirror

Spiegelei (*shpee*-gel-ay) n: fried egg

Spinat (shpi-*naht*) m: spinach

Sport (*shport*) m: sports

sportlich (*shport*-liH): athletic

Spülbecken (*shpuel*-bêk-en) n: sink

Staatsangehörigkeit (*shtahts*-ân-ge-*her*-iH-kayt) f: nationality

Stadion (*shtah*-dee-on) n: stadium

stark (*shtârk*): strong

statt (*shtât*): instead of

Statue (*shtah*-too-e) f: statue

stellen (*shtêl*-en): to put, to place

Stereoanlage (*shtêr*-ee-oh-*ân*-lâ-ge) f: stereo

Stiefel (*shteef*-el) m: boot

Stimmt so (*shtimt zoh*): keep the change

Straßenbahnhaltestelle (*shtrah*-sen-bahn-*hâl*-te-shtêl-e) f: tram stop

Strickjacke (*shtrik*-yâ-ke) f: cardigan

Strumpf (*shtroohmpf*) m: stocking

Strumpfhose (*shtroohmpf*-hoh-ze) f: panty hose

Studentenwohnheim (shtoo-*dênt*-en-*vohn*-haym) n: dormitory

studieren (shtoo-*deer*-en): to study

Studio (*shtooh*-dee-oh) n: studio

Stuhl (*shtoohl*) m: chair

Sturm (*shtoorm*) m: storm

Suppe (*zoop*-e) f: soup

Suppenlöffel (*zoop*-en-*ler*-fel) m: soup spoon

Suppenteller (*zoop*-en-*têl*-er) m: soup bowl

Sweatshirt (sweatshirt [as in English]) n: sweatshirt

sympathisch (zerm-*pah*-tish): likeable, friendly

T

Tablette (tah-*blêt*-e) f: pill

Tante (*tân*-te) f: aunt

Tennis (tennis [as in English]) n: tennis

Teppich (*têp*-iH) m: carpet

Teppichboden (*têp*-iH-*boh*-den) m: wall-to-wall carpet

Termin (têr-*meen*) m: appointment

Terrasse (tê-*râs*-e) f: terrace

teuer (*toy*-er): expensive

Theke (*tey*-ke) f: counter

Thunfisch (*toohn*-fish) m: tuna

Tiefkühlfach (*teef*-kuel-fâH) n: freezer

Tierpark (*teer*-pârk) m: zoo

Tisch (*tish*) m: table

Tischdecke (*tish*-dêk-e) f: tablecloth

Tochter (*toH*-ter) f: daughter

tolerant (toh-lêr-*ânt*): tolerant

Tomate (toh-*mah*-te) f: tomato

treffen (*trêf*-en): to meet

Treppe (*trêp*-e) f: stairs

trocken (*trok*-en): dry

trotz (*trots*): in spite of

trotzdem (*trots*-deym): nevertheless

Truthahn (*trooht*-hahn) m: turkey

T-Shirt (T-shirt [as in English]) n: T-shirt

Tuch (toohH) n: towel
tun (toohn): to do
Tür (tuer) f: door
türkis (tuer-*kees*): turquoise

U

über (*ue*-ber): over
überbacken (ue-ber-*bâk*-en): scalloped
übermorgen (*ue*-ber-mor-gen): day after tomorrow
übersetzen (ue-ber-*zêts*-en): to translate
Übersetzer (ue-ber-*zêts*-er) m: translator
um (oom): around, at
um (oom) . . . **zu** (tsooh) . . . : in order to
Umgebung (oom-*gey*-boong) f: surroundings
Umschlag (*oom*-shlahk) m: envelope
Umwelt (*oom*-vêlt) f: environment
unbedingt (*oon*-be-dingt): absolutely
uns (oons): us
unser (*oons*-er): our
unten (*oon*-ten): down
unterhaltsam (oon-têr-*hâlt*-zâm): entertaining
Unterkunft (*oon*-ter-koonft) f: accommodation
Unterlagen (oon-ter-*lah*-gen) pl: documents
Unterteller (oon-ter-*têl*-er) m: saucer
Unterwäsche (*oon*-têr-*vaish*-e) f: underwear

V

Vater (*fât*-er) m: father
verbinden (fêr-*bin*-den): to connect
vergessen (fêr-*gês*-en): to forget
verletzt (fêr-*lêtst*): hurt
vernünftig (fêr-*nuenf*-tiH): sensible

verzollen (fêr-*tsol*-en): to declare (goods)
violett (vee-o-*lêt*): violet
Visitenkarte (vi-*zeet*-en-*kâr*-te) f: business card
Vogel (*foh*-gêl) m: bird
Volkstracht (*folks*-trâHt) f: folk costume
Volleyball (volleyball [as in English]) m: volleyball
von (fon): from
vor (fohr): before, in front of
vorgestern (*fohr*-gês-tern): day before yesterday
vorher (*fohr*-hêr): beforehand
Vorspeise (*fohr*-shpayz-e) f: appetizer

W

Wagen (*vah*-gen) m: car
während (*vair*-end): during
wahrscheinlich (vahr-*shayn*-liH): probably
Wand (vânt) f: wall
Wanderung (*vân*-der-oong) f: hike
Waren (*vahr*-en) pl: goods
warten (*vâr*-ten): to wait
warum (vâ-*roohm*): why
was für (vâs fuer): what kind of
Waschbecken (*vâsh*-bêk-en) n: sink (bathroom)
Wäsche (*vaish*-e) f: laundry
waschen (*vâsh*-en): to wash
Wasserhahn (*vâs*-er-hahn) m: faucet
wechseln (*vêk*-seln): to exchange
Wechselstube (*vêk*-sel-stooh-be) f: currency exchange office
Wecker (*vêk*-er) m: alarm clock
wegen (*vey*-gen): because of
weh tun (*vey* toohn): to hurt
weil (vayl): because
weiß (vays): white

Weißwein (*vays*-vayn) m: white wine

weit (vayt): far, loose (clothing)

welcher (*vêlH*-er): which

Welle (*vêl*-e) f: wave

wenig (*vey*-niH): little, few

wenn (vên): if, when

wer (vêr): who

werfen (*vêrf*-en): to throw

Weste (*vês*-te) f: vest

Wetter (*vêt*-er) n: weather

wie viel (vee feel): how much

wie viele (vee *fee*-le): how many

Wiese (*veez*-e) f: meadow

Wild (vilt) n: game (meat)

wir (veer): we

Wirtschaft (*virt*-shâft) f: economy

Wissenschaft (*vis*-en-shâft) f: science

witzig (*vits*-iH): funny

woanders (voh-*ân*-ders): somewhere else

woher (voh-*hêr*): from where

wohnen (*vohn*-en): to live

Wohnung (*vohn*-oong) f: apartment

Wohnzimmer (*vohn*-tsi-mer) n: living room

wolkig (*volk*-iH): cloudy

wunderschön (*voon*-der-shern): lovely, gorgeous

Wurst (voorst) f: sausage

Z

zahlen (*tsahl*-en): to pay

Zahnarzt (*tsahn*-ârtst) m: dentist

Zahnbürste (*tsahn*-buers-te) f: toothbrush

Zahnpaste (*tsahn*-pâs-te) f: toothpaste

Zimmer (*tsi*-mer) n: room

Zitrone (tsi-*trohn*-e) f: lemon

zu (tsooh): to, at, too

zu viel (tsooh feel): too much

zu viele (tsooh *fee*-le): too many

Zucchini (tsoo-*kee*-ni) f: zucchini

zum Wohl (tsoom vohl): cheers

zumachen (*tsooh*-mâH-en): to close

zurückrufen (tsoo-*ruek*-roohf-en): to call back

Zuschlag (*tsooh*-shlahk) m: surcharge

zuverlässig (*tsooh*-fêr-lês-iH): reliable

Zwiebel (*tsvee*-bel) f: onion

zwischen (*tsvish*-en): between

Appendix C

English-German Mini-Dictionary

Key: m = masculine, f = feminine, n = neuter, sing = singular, pl = plural, inf = informal, form = formal, dat = dative, acc = accusative

A

a, an: **ein** (ayn)

absolutely: **unbedingt** (*oon*-be-dingt)

accommodation: **Unterkunft** (*oon*-ter-koonft) f

acquaintance: **Bekannte** (bê-*kân*-te) m

addressee: **Empfänger** (êm-*pfêng*-er) m

after, to: **nach** (nâH)

afterward: **nachher** (*nâH*-hêr)

alarm clock: **Wecker** (*vêk*-er) m

alike, immediately: **gleich** (glayH)

all: **alle** (*âl*-e)

allergic to: **allergisch gegen** (â-*lêr*-gish *gey*-gen)

almost: **fast** (fâst)

alone: **allein** (â-*layn*)

although: **obwohl** (op-*vohl*)

always: **immer** (*im*-er)

answer: **antworten** (*ânt*-fort-en)

anyway: **jedenfalls** (*yey*-den-fâls)

apartment: **Wohnung** (*vohn*-oong) f

apartment (one room): **Apartment** (â-*pârt*-ment) n

appetizer: **Vorspeise** (*fohr*-shpayz-e) f

apple: **Apfel** (*âp*-fel) m

apply for: **beantragen** (bê-*ân*-trah-gen)

appointment: **Termin** (têr-*meen*) m

approximately: **etwa** (*êt*-vâ)

area code: **Postleitzahl** (*post*-layt-tsahl) f

armchair: **Sessel** (*zês*-el) m

around, at: **um** (oom)

arrive: **ankommen** (*ân*-kom-en)

as . . . as: **so** (zoh) **. . . wie** (vee)

asparagus: **Spargel** (*shpâr*-gêl) m

associate: **Mitarbeiter** (*mit*-âr-bayt-er) m

at, by, to: **an** (ân)

athletic: **sportlich** (*shport*-liH)

attic: **Dachboden** (*dâH*-boh-den) m

attractive: **attraktiv** (â-trâk-*teef*)

aunt: **Tante** (*tân*-te) f

avocado: **Avocado** (â-voh-*kah*-doh) f

B

bacon: **Speck** (shpêk) m

bad: **schlecht** (shlêHt)

baked: **gebacken** (ge-*bâk*-en)

bakery: **Bäckerei** (bêk-e-*ray*) f

balcony: **Balkon** (bâl-*kohn*) m

ballet: **Ballett** (bâ-*lêt*) n

banana: **Banane** (bâ-*nah*-ne) f

basketball: **Basketball** (basketball [as in English]) m

bath towel: **Badetuch** (*bah*-de-toohH) n

bathing suit: **Badeanzug** (*bah*-de-ân-tsook) m

bathroom sink: **Waschbecken** (*vâsh*-bêk-en) n

bathtub: **Badewanne** (*bah*-de-wân-e) f

bean: **Bohne** (*bohn*-e) f

because: **weil** (vayl)

because of, due to: **wegen** (*vey*-gen)

bed: **Bett** (bêt) n

bedroom: **Schlafzimmer** (*shlahf*-tsi-mer) n

beef: **Rindfleisch** (*rint*-flaysh) n

before, in front of: **vor** (fohr)

beforehand: **vorher** (*fohr*-hêr)

begin: **anfangen** (*ân*-fâng-en)

beige: **beige** (beige [as in English])

bell pepper: **Paprika** (*pâp*-ree-kah) m

belt: **Gürtel** (*guer*-tel) m

between: **zwischen** (*tsvish*-en)

bird: **Vogel** (*foh*-gêl) m

birth date: **Geburtsdatum** (gê-*boorts*-dah-toohm) n

black: **schwarz** (shvârts)

blanket: **Decke** (*dêk*-e) f

blazer: **Blazer** (*bley*-zer) m

blouse: **Bluse** (*blooh*-ze) f

blue: **blau** (blou)

blueberry: **Blaubeere** (*blou*-beyr-e) f

boiled, cooked: **gekocht** (ge-*koHt*)

boot: **Stiefel** (*shteef*-el) m

boss: **Chef** (chêf) m

botanical: **botanisch** (boh-*tân*-ish)

bottle: **Flasche** (*flâsh*-e) f

boy: **Junge** (*yoong*-e) m

breathe: **atmen** (*aht*-men)

broccoli: **Brokkoli** (*broh*-ko-lee) m

brother: **Bruder** (*brooh*-der) m

brown: **braun** (broun)

brown bread: **Schwarzbrot** (*shvârts*-broht) n

business card: **Visitenkarte** (vi-*zeet*-en-*kâr*-te) f

businessman: **Geschäftsmann** (gê-s*hêfts*-mân) m

businesswoman: **Geschäftsfrau** (gê-s*hêfts*-frou) f

but rather: **sondern** (*zon*-dern)

but, nevertheless: **doch** (doH)

butcher shop: **Metzgerei** (mêts-ge-*ray*) f

button mushroom: **Champignon** (s*hâm*-peen-y*on*) m

by, until: **bis** (bis)

C

cabbage: **Kohl** (kohl) m

cabinet, cupboard, closet: **Schrank** (shrânk) m

call back: **zurückrufen** (tsoo-*ruek*-roohf-en)

call, summon: **rufen** (*roohf*-en)

cap: **Mütze** (*muetz*-e) f

car: **Wagen** (*vah*-gen) m

car accident: **Autounfall** (*ou*-toh-*oon*-fâl) m

car rental agency: **Autovermietung** (*ou*-toh-fêr-*meet*-oong) f

cardigan: **Strickjacke** (s*htrik*-yâ-ke) f

carpet: **Teppich** (*têp*-iH) m

carrot: **Karotte** (kâ-*rot*-e) f

carry-on luggage: **Handgepäck** (*hând*-ge-pêk) n

cash: **Bargeld** (*bâr*-gêlt) n

castle: **Burg** (boork) f

cat: **Katze** (*kâts*-e) f

cauliflower: **Blumenkohl** (*bloom*-en-kohl) m

celebrate: **feiern** (*fay*-ern)

celebration, festival: **Fest** (fêst) n

celeriac: **Sellerie** (zêl-êr-*ee*) m

cellar: **Keller** (*kêl*-er) m

certainly: **bestimmt** (be-s*htimt*)

chair: **Stuhl** (shtoohl) m

cheap, inexpensive: **billig** (bil-iH)

check in: **einchecken** (ayn-chêk-en)

cheerful: **heiter** (hayt-er)

cheers: **zum Wohl** (tsoom vohl)

cherry: **Kirsche** (kirsh-e) f

chicken: **Hähnchen** (hain-Hen) n

child: **Kind** (kint) n

clean: **putzen** (poots-en)

close: **schließen** (shlees-en)

close: **zumachen** (tsooh-mâH-en)

closet (clothes): **Kleiderschrank** (klay-der-shrânk) m

cloudy: **wolkig** (volk-iH)

coat: **Mantel** (mân-tel) m

cod: **Kabeljau** (kah-bel-you) m

coffee table: **Couchtisch** (kouch-tish) m

cold cuts: **Aufschnitt** (ouf-shnit) m

colleague: **Kollege** (ko-ley-ge) m

color: **Farbe** (fâr-be) f

comb: **Kamm** (kâm) m

computer: **Computer** (computer [as in English]) m

condominium: **Eigentumswohnung** (ay-gên-tooms-vohn-oong) f

connect: **verbinden** (fêr-bin-den)

construction site: **Baustelle** (bou-shtêl-e) f

cook: **kochen** (koH-en)

cookies, pastries: **Gebäck** (ge-bêk) n

cool: **kühl** (kuel)

copy machine: **Fotokopierer** (foh-toh-ko-peer-er) m

corner bench: **Eckbank** (êk-bânk) f

cornflakes: **Cornflakes** (cornflakes [as in English]) pl

couch: **Couch** (couch [as in English]) f

counter: **Theke** (tey-ke) f

course, class: **Kurs** (koors) m

cousin (female): **Cousine** (kooh-zeen-e) f

cousin (male): **Cousin** (kooh-zen) m

coworker: **Arbeitskollege** (âr-bayts-ko-ley-ge) m

cozy, comfortable: **gemütlich** (ge-muet-liH)

crab: **Krebs** (kreyps) m

cranberry: **Preiselbeere** (pray-zêl-beyr-e) f

cream: **Sahne** (zahn-e) f

cucumber: **Gurke** (goork-e) f

culture: **Kultur** (kool-toohr) f

currency exchange office: **Wechselstube** (vêk-sel-stooh-be) f

curtain: **Gardine** (gâr-deen-e) f

cut: **schneiden** (shnay-den)

cutlery: **Besteck** (be-shtêk) n

D

dark: **dunkel** (doon-kêl)

daughter: **Tochter** (toH-ter) f

day after tomorrow: **übermorgen** (ue-ber-mor-gen)

day before yesterday: **vorgestern** (fohr-gês-tern)

declare (goods): **verzollen** (fêr-tsol-en)

deep-fat fried: **frittiert** (fri-teert)

dentist: **Zahnarzt** (tsahn-ârtst) m

depart (train): **abfahren** (âp-fahr-en)

desk: **Schreibtisch** (shrayp-tish) m

dessert: **Nachspeise** (nâH-shpayz-e) f

diarrhea: **Durchfall** (doorH-fâl) m

dining room: **Esszimmer** (ês-tsi-mer) n

dining table: **Esstisch** (ês-tish) m

disappointing: **enttäuschend** (ênt-toy-shênt)

dish (food): **Gericht** (ge-riHt) n

dishwasher: **Geschirrspülmaschine** (ge-shir-sphuel-mâ-sheen-e) f

do: **tun** (toohn)

do the dishes: **abwaschen** (âp-vâsh-en)

doctor: **Doktor** (dok-tohr) m

documents: **Unterlagen** (*oon*-ter-lah-gen) pl

dog: **Hund** (hoont) m

door: **Tür** (tuer) f

dormitory: **Studentenwohnheim** (shtoo-dênt-en-*vohn*-haym) n

down: **unten** (*oon*-ten)

drawer: **Schublade** (*shoob*-lâ-de) f

dress: **Kleid** (klayt) n

dresser: **Kommode** (ko-*moh*-de) f

drugstore: **Drogerie** (droh-ge-*ree*) f

dry: **trocken** (*trok*-en)

duck: **Ente** (*ên*-te) f

during: **während** (*vair*-end)

E

early: **früh** (frue)

economy: **Wirtschaft** (*virt*-shâft) f

egg: **Ei** (ay) n

eggplant: **Aubergine** (oh-bêr-*jeen*-e) f

elegant: **elegant** (êl-ê-*gânt*)

e-mail address: **E-Mail-Adresse** (e-mail-ah-*drês*-e) f

emergency call: **Notruf** (*noht*-roohf) m

emergency service: **Rettungsdienst** (*rêt*-oongs-deenst) m

employee: **Angestellte** (*ân*-gê-shtêl-te) m

enjoy your meal: **Guten Appetit** (*gooh*-ten âp-e-*teet*)

entertaining: **unterhaltsam** (oon-têr-*hâlt*-zâm)

entrance ramp: **Einfahrt** (*ayn*-fahrt) f

entrance ticket: **Eintrittskarte** (*ayn*-trits-kar-te) f

envelope: **Umschlag** (*oom*-shlahk) m

environment: **Umwelt** (*oom*-vêlt) f

ever: **jemals** (*yey*-mâls)

exchange: **wechseln** (*vêk*-seln)

exciting: **aufregend** (*ouf*-rey-gent)

excursion: **Ausflug** (*ous*-floohk) m

excuse oneself: **sich entschuldigen** (ziH ênt-*shool*-di-gen)

expensive: **teuer** (*toy*-er)

expire: **ablaufen** (*âp*-louf-en)

express letter: **Eilbrief** (*ayl*-breef) m

F

fall: **fallen** (*fâl*-en)

family pet: **Haustier** (*hous*-teer) n

far, loose (clothing): **weit** (vayt)

father: **Vater** (*fât*-er) m

faucet: **Wasserhahn** (*vâs*-er-hahn) m

feel: **sich fühlen** (ziH *fuel*-en)

finally: **endlich** (*ênt*-liH)

find: **finden** (*fin*-den)

fire!: **Feuer!** (*foy*-er!) n

flexible: **flexibel** (flêx-*ee*-bel)

floor: **Boden** (*boh*-den) m

flounder: **Flunder** (*floon*-der) f

folk costume: **Volkstracht** (*folks*-trâHt) f

for, because: **denn** (dên)

for that reason, therefore: **darum** (*dâ*-room)

forget: **vergessen** (fêr-*gês*-en)

freezer: **Tiefkühlfach** (*teef*-kuel-fâH) n

fresh: **frisch** (frish)

fried egg: **Spiegelei** (*shpee*-gel-ay) n

fried sausage: **Bratwurst** (*braht*-voorst) f

friendly: **freundlich** (*froynt*-liH)

from: **von** (fon)

from, out of: **aus** (ous)

from where: **woher** (voh-*hêr*)

function: **funktionieren** (foonk-tsee-oh-*neer*-en)

funny: **witzig** (*vits*-iH)

G

gallery: **Galerie** (gâl-êr-*ee*) f

game (meat): **Wild** (vilt) n

garage: **Garage** (gâ-*rah*-ge) f

garbage can: **Mülleimer** (*muel*-aym-er) m

garden: **Garten** (*gâr*-ten) m

garlic: **Knoblauch** (*knoh*-blouH) m

get: **bekommen** (be-*kom*-en)

get off: **aussteigen** (*ous*-shtayg-en)

get on, get in: **einsteigen** (*ayn*-shtayg-en)

get up: **aufstehen** (*ouf*-shtey-en)

gift: **Geschenk** (ge-*shênk*) n

girl: **Mädchen** (*maid*-Hen) n

give (a present): **schenken** (*shênk*-en)

gladly: **gern** (gêrn)

glove: **Handschuh** (*hânt*-shooh) m

go shopping: **einkaufen** (*ayn*-kouf-en)

gold: **gold** (golt)

golf: **Golf** (golf [as in English]) m

goodbye (on the phone): **auf Wiederhören** (ouf *vee*-der-*herr*-en)

goods: **Waren** (*vahr*-en) pl

goose: **Gans** (gâns) f

grandfather: **Großvater** (*grohs*-fât-er) m

grandmother: **Großmutter** (*grohs*-moot-er) f

grandparents: **Großeltern** (*grohs*-êl-tern) pl

gray: **grau** (grou)

green: **grün** (gruen)

ground meat: **Hackfleisch** (*hâk*-flaysh) n

H

haddock: **Schellfisch** (*shêl*-fish) m

hairbrush: **Haarbürste** (*hahr*-buers-te) f

halibut: **Heilbutt** (*hayl*-boot) m

hall: **Gang** (gâng) m

ham: **Schinken** (*shin*-ken) m

handbag: **Handtasche** (*hânt*-tâsh-e) f

happy: **glücklich** (*gluek*-liH)

hardly: **kaum** (koum)

hat: **Hut** (hooht) m

he: **er** (êr)

health: **Gesundheit** (gê-*zoont*-hayt) f

herbs: **Kräuter** (*kroyt*-er) pl

herring: **Hering** (*hêr*-ing) m

high: **hoch** (hohH)

hike: **Wanderung** (*vân*-der-oong) f

him: **ihn** (een)

him, it: **ihm** (eem)

his, its: **sein** (zayn)

hold, stop: **halten** (*hâlt*-en)

honey: **Honig** (*hohn*-iH) m

hope: **hoffen** (*hof*-en)

hopefully: **hoffentlich** (*hof*-ênt-liH)

horseradish: **Meerrettich** (*meyr*-rêt-iH) m

hot: **heiß** (hays)

how many: **wie viele** (vee *fee*-le)

how much: **wie viel** (vee feel)

hunger: **Hunger** (*hoong*-er) m

hungry: **hungrig** (*hoong*-riH)

hurt: **verletzt** (fêr-*lêtst*)

hurt: **weh tun** (vey toohn)

husband: **Mann** (mân) m

I

I: **ich** (iH)

ID card: **Ausweis** (*ous*-vays) m

if, when: **wenn** (vên)

if, whether: **ob** (op)

if, whether, in case: **falls** (fâls)

immediately: **sofort** (zo-*fort*)

in: **in** (in)

in order to: **um** (oom) . . . **zu** (tsooh) . . .

in spite of: **trotz** (trots)

indeed, of course: **gewiss** (ge-*vis*)

informal meeting: **Besprechung** (be-*shprêH*-oong) f

inside: **drinnen** (*drin*-en)

instead of: **statt** (shtât)

intelligent: **intelligent** (in-têl-i-*gênt*)

intermission, break: **Pause** (*pou*-ze) f

interpret: **dolmetschen** (*dol*-mêch-en)

interpreter: **Dolmetscher** (*dol*-mêch-er) m

it: **es** (ês)

J

jacket: **Jacke** (*yâ*-ke) f, **Jackett** (jâ-*kêt*) n

jeans: **Jeans** (jeans [as in English]) f

jewelry: **Schmuck** (shmook) m

just, currently: **gerade** (gê-*rah*-de)

K

kale: **Grünkohl** (*gruen*-kohl) m

keep the change: **Stimmt so** (shtimt zoh)

kitchen: **Küche** (*kueH*-e) f

kiwi: **Kiwi** (*kee*-vee) f

kohlrabi: **Kohlrabi** (kohl-*râ*-bee) m

L

lamb (meat): **Lammfleisch** (*lâm*-flaysh) n

lamp: **Lampe** (*lâm*-pe) f

last: **dauern** (*dou*-ern)

late: **spät** (shpait)

laundry: **Wäsche** (*vaish*-e) f

learn: **lernen** (*lêrn*-en)

leave (behind): **hinterlassen** (hin-ter-*lâs*-en)

leek: **Lauch** (louH) m

lemon: **Zitrone** (tsi-*trohn*-e) f

let, allow: **lassen** (*lâs*-en)

lettuce: **Kopfsalat** (*kopf*-zâ-laht) m

lie (down): **liegen** (*leeg*-en)

light (color): **hell** (hêl)

likeable, friendly: **sympathisch** (zerm-*pah*-tish)

little, few: **wenig** (*vey*-niH)

live: **wohnen** (*vohn*-en)

living room: **Wohnzimmer** (*vohn*-tsi-mer) n

loud: **laut** (lout)

lovely, gorgeous: **wunderschön** (*voon*-der-shern)

M

man: **Mann** (mân) m

margarine: **Margarine** (mâr-gâr-*een*-e) f

marinated: **mariniert** (mâr-i-*neert*)

marmelade, jam: **Marmelade** (mâr-me-*lah*-de) f

me: **mich** (miH), **mir** (mir)

meadow: **Wiese** (*veez*-e) f

meal: **Essen** (*ês*-en) n

meet: **treffen** (*trêf*-en)

meeting: **Meeting** (meeting [as in English]) n

melon: **Melone** (mê-*lohn*-e) f

memorial, monument: **Denkmal** (*dênk*-mâl) n

microwave oven: **Mikrowellenherd** (meek-roh-*vêl*-en-hêrt) m

mineral water: **Mineralwasser** (min-êr-*ahl*-vâs-er) n

mirror: **Spiegel** (*shpee*-gel) m

mixed: **gemischt** (ge-*misht*)

monument: **Monument** (mon-oo-*mênt*) n

more: **mehr** (meyr)

mother: **Mutter** (*moot*-er) f

muesli: **Müsli** (*mues*-lee) n

mug: **Becher** (*bêH*-er) m

mushroom: **Pilz** (pilts) m

mussel: **Muschel** (*moosh*-el) f

N

namely: **nämlich** (*naim*-liH)

napkin: **Serviett**e (sêr-vee-*êt*-e) f

nationality: **Staatsangehörigkeit** (*shtahts*-ân-ge-*her*-iH-kayt) f

nature: **Natur** (na-*toohr*) f

near: **nah** (nah)

nearby: **in der Nähe** (in dêr *nai*-he)

need: **brauchen** (*brouH*-en)

neighbor: **Nachbar** (*nâH*-bâr) m

never: **niemals** (*nee*-mâls)

nevertheless: **trotzdem** (*trots*-deym)

new: **neu** (noy)

nice: **nett** (nêt)

noodles: **Nudeln** (*nooh*-deln) pl

not only . . . but also: **nicht nur** (niHt noohr) . . . **sondern auch** (*zon*-dern ouH)

now: **jetzt** (yêtst)

nowadays: **heutzutage** (*hoyt*-tsooh-tah-ge)

nowhere: **nirgendwo** (*nir*-gênd-voh)

O

oatmeal: **Haferflocken** (*hahf*-er-flok-en) pl

of course: **klar** (klahr)

offer: **Angebot** (*ân*-ge-boht) n

office: **Büro** (bue-*roh*) n

often: **oft** (oft)

okay: **in Ordnung** (in *ord*-noong)

old: **alt** (âlt)

olive: **Olive** (oh-*leev*-e) f

one-way street: **Einbahnstraße** (*ayn*-bahn-*shtrah*-se) f

onion: **Zwiebel** (*tsvee*-bel) f

only: **nur** (noohr)

open: **aufmachen** (*ouf*-mâH-en)

or: **oder** (*oh*-der)

orange (color): **orange** (o-*rân*-je)

orange (fruit): **Orange** (o-*rân*-je) f

order: **bestellen** (be-*shtêl*-en)

otherwise: **sonst** (zonst)

our: **unser** (*oons*-er)

outside: **draußen** (*drous*-en)

oven: **Backofen** (*bâk*-oh-fen) m

over: **über** (*ue*-ber)

over there: **drüben** (*drue*-ben)

oyster: **Auster** (*ous*-têr) f

P

page: **Seite** (*zay*-te) f

palace: **Palast** (pâ-*lâst*) m

palace, castle: **Schloss** (shlos) n

pants: **Hose** (*hoh*-ze) f

panty hose: **Strumpfhose** (*shtroohmpf*-hoh-ze) f

paper: **Papier** (pâ-*peer*) n

parents: **Eltern** (*êl*-tern) pl

parking garage: **Parkhaus** (*pârk*-hous) n

passport control: **Passkontrolle** (*pâs*-kon-trol-e) f

pastry shop: **Konditorei** (kon-dee-to-*ray*) f

pay: **zahlen** (*tsahl*-en)

pea: **Erbse** (*erp*-se) f

peach: **Pfirsich** (*pfir*-ziH) m

pear: **Birne** (*birn*-e) f

pedestrian zone: **Fußgängerzone** (*foohs*-gên-ger-*tsohn*-e) f

pen: **Kugelschreiber** (*kooh*-gel-*shray*-ber) m, **Kuli** (*kooh*-lee) (colloquial) m

pencil: **Bleistift** (*blay*-shtift) m

person: **Person** (pêr-*zohn*) f

personal: **persönlich** (pêr-*zern*-lich)

pharmacy: **Apotheke** (ah-poh-*tey*-ke) f

pheasant: **Fasan** (fâ-*zân*) m

pickled: **eingelegt** (*ayn*-ge-leygt)

picture: **Bild** (bilt) n

picture postcard: **Ansichtskarte** (*ahn*-ziHts-kâr-te) f

pill: **Tablette** (tah-*blêt*-e) f

pillow: **Kopfkissen** (*kopf*-kis-en) n

pineapple: **Ananas** (*ân*-ân-âs) f

pink: **rosa** (*roh*-zâ)

place: **Ort** (ort) m

place of birth: **Geburtsort** (gê-*boorts*-ort) m

plum: **Pflaume** (*pflau*-me) f

police station: **Polizeirevier** (po-li-*tsay*-re-veer) n

polite: **höflich** (*herf*-liH)

politics: **Politik** (pol-i-*teek*) f

pork: **Schweinefleisch** (*shvayn*-e-flaysh) n

possibly: **eventuell** (ê-vên-too-*êl*)

postage: **Porto** (*por*-toh) n

potato: **Kartoffel** (kâr-*tof*-el) f

poultry: **Geflügel** (ge-*flueg*-el) n

prescription, recipe: **Rezept** (rê-*tsêpt*) n

pretty: **hübsch** (huepsh)

price: **Preis** (prays) m

printer: **Drucker** (*drook*-er) m

probably: **wahrscheinlich** (vahr-*shayn*-liH)

pullover: **Pulli** (*poo*-lee) m, **Pullover** (poo-*loh*-ver) m

pumpkin: **Kürbis** (*kuer*-bis) m

purple: **lila** (*lee*-lâ)

put, place: **stellen** (*shtêl*-en)

Q

quiet: **ruhig** (*rooh*-iH)

R

rabbit: **Kaninchen** (kân-*een*-Hen) n

raincoat: **Regenmantel** (*rey*-gen-*mân*-tel) m

raspberry: **Himbeere** (*him*-beyr-e) f

raw: **roh** (roh)

razor: **Rasierapparat** (râ-*zeer*-âp-â-*rât*) m

reach: **erreichen** (êr-*ayH*-en)

receipt, slip: **Beleg** (be-*leyk*) m

recently: **neuerdings** (*noy*-er-dings)

reception: **Empfang** (êm-*pfâng*) m

recipe, prescription: **Rezept** (rê-*tsêpt*) n

red: **rot** (roht)

red cabbage: **Rotkohl** (*roht*-kohl) m

red wine: **Rotwein** (*roht*-vayn) m

refrigerator: **Kühlschrank** (*kuel*-shrânk) m

registered mail: **Einschreiben** (*ayn*-shrayb-en) m

registration form: **Meldeschein** (*mêl*-de-shayn) m

reliable: **zuverlässig** (*tsooh*-fêr-lês-iH)

rented apartment: **Mietwohnung** (*meet*-vohn-oong) f

reserved seat: **Platzkarte** (*plâts*-kâr-te) f

rice: **Reis** (rays) m

ride a bike: **Fahrrad fahren** (*fahr*-rât *fahr*-en)

roasted: **gebraten** (ge-*brât*-en)

room: **Zimmer** (*tsi*-mer) n

run: **laufen** (*louf*-en)

rye bread: **Roggenbrot** (*rog*-en-broht) n

S

salad: **Salat** (zâ-*laht*) m

sales tax: **Mehrwertsteuer** (*meyr*-vêrt-shtoy-er) f

salmon: **Lachs** (lâx) m

sandal: **Sandale** (zân-*dahl*-e) f

saucer: **Unterteller** (*oon*-ter-*têl*-er) m

sauerkraut: **Sauerkraut** (*zou*-er-krout) n

sauna: **Sauna** (*zou*-nâ) f

sausage: **Wurst** (voorst) f

scalloped: **überbacken** (ue-ber-*bâk*-en)

scarf: **Schal** (shâl) m

science: **Wissenschaft** (*vis*-en-shâft) f

seat, place: **Platz** (plâts) m

secretary: **Sekretär** (zê-krê-*têr*) m

sender: **Absender** (*ap*-zên-der) m

sensible: **vernünftig** (fêr-*nuenf*-tiH)

serious: **ernst** (êrnst)

she, her, they, them: **sie** (zee)

sheet: **Bettuch** (*bêt*-toohH) n

shelf: **Regal** (rey-*gahl*) n

shirt: **Hemd** (hêmt) n

shoe: **Schuh** (shooh) m

shorts: **Shorts** (shorts [as in English]) f

should: **sollen** (*zol*-en)

shower: **Dusche** (*dooh*-she) f

shrimp: **Krabbe** (*krâb*-e) f

siblings: **Geschwister** (ge-*shvis*-ter) pl

side dish: **Beilage** (*bay*-lah-ge) f

sign in: **anmelden** (*ân*-mêl-den)

silver: **silber** (*zil*-ber)

since: **seit** (zayt)

single-family house: **Einfamilienhaus** (*ayn*-fâ-*mi*-lee-en-hous) n

sink: **Spülbecken** (*shpuel*-bêk-en) n

sister: **Schwester** (*shvês*-ter) f

sit, set: **setzen** (*zêts*-en)

skirt: **Rock** (rok) m

sleep: **schlafen** (*shlâf*-en)

slow, slowly: **langsam** (*lâng*-zahm)

smoked: **geräuchert** (ge-*royH*-êrt)

so: **also** (*âl*-zoh)

so that: **damit** (dâ-*mit*)

soap: **Seife** (*zay*-fe) f

soccer: **Fußball** (*foohs*-bâl) m

society: **Gesellschaft** (gê-*zêl*-shâft) f

sock: **Socke** (*zok*-e) f

sofa: **Sofa** (*zoh*-fâ) n

sole (fish): **Seezunge** (*zey*-tsoong-e) f

somewhere, anywhere: **irgendwo** (*ir*-gênd-voh)

somewhere else: **woanders** (voh-*ân*-ders)

son: **Sohn** (zohn) m

soon: **bald** (bâlt)

soup: **Suppe** (*zoop*-e) f

soup bowl: **Suppenteller** (*zoop*-en-*têl*-er) m

soup spoon: **Suppenlöffel** (*zoop*-en-*ler*-fel) m

sour: **sauer** (*zou*-er)

spicy: **sharf** (shârf)

spinach: **Spinat** (shpi-*naht*) m

sports: **Sport** (shport) m

stadium: **Stadion** (*shtah*-dee-on) n

stairs: **Treppe** (*trêp*-e) f

starting at, away, off: **ab** (âp)

statue: **Statue** (*shtah*-too-e) f

steamed: **gedampft** (ge-*dâmpft*)

stereo: **Stereoanlage** (*shtêr*-ee-oh-*ân*-lâ-ge) f

still, yet: **noch** (noH)

stock market: **Börse** (*bêr*-ze) f

stocking: **Strumpf** (shtroohmpf) m

storm: **Sturm** (shtoorm) m

stove: **Herd** (hêrt) m

strawberry: **Erdbeere** (*eyrt*-beyr-e) f

strong: **stark** (shtârk)

studio: **Studio** (*shtooh*-dee-oh) n

study: **studieren** (shtoo-*deer*-en)

stuffed: **gefüllt** (ge-*fuelt*)

such, thus, so, as: **so** (zoh)

suit (dress/jacket): **Kostüm** (kos-*tuem*) n

suit (pants/jacket): **Hosenanzug** (*hoh*-zen-*ân*-tsook) m

suit (pants/jacket): **Anzug** (*ân*-tsook) m

sunglasses: **Sonnenbrille** (*zon*-en-*bril*-e) f

sunny: **sonnig** (*zon*-iH)

surcharge: **Zuschlag** (*tsooh*-shlahk) m

sure, certainly: **sicher** (*ziH*-er)

surroundings: **Umgebung** (oom-*gey*-boong) f

sweatshirt: **Sweatshirt** (sweatshirt [as in English]) n

symphony: **Sinfonie** (sin-foh-*nee*) f

T

table: **Tisch** (*tish*) m

tablecloth: **Tischdecke** (*tish*-dêk-e) f

tank top: **Pullunder** (poo-*lun*-der) m

tap water: **Leitungswasser** (*lay*-toongs-*vâs*-er) n

television: **Fernseher** (*fêrn*-zey-er) m

tennis: **Tennis** (tennis [as in English]) n

terrace: **Terrasse** (tê-*râs*-e) f

than, when: **als** (âls)

that: **dass** (dâs)

the: **das** (dâs) n

the: **der** (dêr) m

the: **die** (dee) f

them: **ihnen** (*een*-en)

then: **dann** (dân)

there, because: **da** (dâ)

therefore: **deshalb** (*dês*-hâlp)

thief: **Dieb** (deep) m

thin, slim: **schlank** (shlânk)

think: **denken** (*dênk*-en)

thirst: **Durst** (doorst) m

thirsty: **durstig** (*doorst*-iH)

this, that, these, those: **dieser** (*deez*-er)

through, by: **durch** (doorH)

throw: **werfen** (*vêrf*-en)

tie: **Krawatte** (krâ-*vât*-e) f

to, at, too: **zu** (tsooh)

tolerant: **tolerant** (toh-lêr-*ânt*)

tomato: **Tomate** (toh-*mah*-te) f

too many: **zu viele** (tsooh *fee*-le)

too much: **zu viel** (tsooh feel)

toothbrush: **Zahnbürste** (*tsahn*-buers-te) f

toothpaste: **Zahnpaste** (*tsahn*-pâs-te) f

towel: **Tuch** (toohH) n

town house: **Reihenhaus** (*ray*-en-hous) n

train schedule: **Fahrplan** (*fahr*-plân) m

tram stop: **Straßenbahnhaltestelle** (*shtrah*-sen-bahn-*hâl*-te-shtêl-e) f

translate: **übersetzen** (ue-ber-*zêts*-en)

translator: **Übersetzer** (ue-ber-*zêts*-er) m

travel agency: **Reisebüro** (*ray*-ze-bue-*roh*) n

trout: **Forelle** (fohr-*êl*-e) f

T-shirt: **T-Shirt** (T-shirt [as in English]) n

tuna: **Thunfisch** (*toohn*-fish) m

turkey: **Truthahn** (*trooht*-hahn) m

turquoise: **türkis** (tuer-*kees*)

U

uncle: **Onkel** (*onk*-êl) m

underwear: **Unterwäsche** (*oon*-têr-*vaish*-e) f

up: **oben** (*oh*-ben)

urgent: **dringend** (*dring*-end)

us: **uns** (oons)

use, purpose: **Gebrauch** (ge-*brouH*) m

V

veal: **Kalbfleisch** (*kâlp*-flaysh) n

venison: **Rehfleisch** (*rey*-flaysh) n

vest: **Weste** (*vês*-te) f

violet: **violett** (vee-o-*lêt*)

visit: **besuchen** (be-*zooH*-en)

volleyball: **Volleyball** (volleyball [as in English]) m

W

wait: **warten** (*vâr*-ten)

waiter: **Kellner** (*kêl*-ner) m

wall: **Wand** (vânt) f

wall-to-wall carpet: **Teppichboden** (*têp*-iH-*boh*-den) m

wall unit: **Schrankwand** (*shrânk*-vânt) f

wash: **waschen** (*vâsh*-en)

watch TV: **fernsehen** (*fêrn*-zey-en)

wave: **Welle** (*vêl*-e) f

we: **wir** (veer)

weak: **schwach** (shvâH)

weather: **Wetter** (*vêt*-er) n

wet: **nass** (nâs)

what kind of: **was für** (vâs fuer)

which: **welcher** (*vêlH*-er)

white: **weiß** (vays)

white wine: **Weißwein** (*vays*-vayn) m

who: **wer** (vêr)

why: **warum** (vâ-*roohm*)

wife: **Frau** (frou) f

without: **ohne** (*oh*-ne)

woman: **Frau** (frou) f

work: **arbeiten** (*âr*-bayt-en)

workplace: **Arbeitsplatz** (*âr*-bayts-plâts) m

workroom, study: **Arbeitszimmer** (*âr*-bayts-tsi-mer) n

worth seeing: **sehenswert** (*zey*-enz-vêrt)

write: **schreiben** (*shray*-ben)

Y

yellow: **gelb** (gêlp)

you (form, sing/pl, dat): **Ihnen** (*een*-en)

you (form, sing/pl): **Sie** (zee)

you (impersonal): **man** (mân)

you (inf, pl), her, their: **ihr** (eer)

you (inf, pl, acc/dat): **euch** (oyH)

you (inf, sing): **du** (dooh)

you (inf, sing, acc): **dich** (diH)

you (inf, sing, dat): **dir** (deer)

young: **jung** (yoong)

your (form, sing/pl): **Ihr** (eer)

your (inf, pl): **euer** (*oy*-er)

your (inf, sing): **dein** (dayn)

Z

zoo: **Tierpark** (*teer*-pârk) m

zucchini: **Zucchini** (tsoo-*kee*-ni) f

Appendix D

Fun & Games

● ●

This appendix gives you the opportunity to challenge yourself and check just how much you remember from a given chapter. We hope the activities entertain you as you assess your skills. We provide you with translations and correct answers at the end of the appendix.

Book 1, Chapter 1: Warming Up to German Basics

The following story about Maria contains some of the words and expressions you find in Book I, Chapter 1. The sentences of the story are divided into two parts. The beginning of each sentence is numbered 1 through 14. The endings for these sentences are listed randomly with the letters A through N. As you read along, match the parts to make a logical story.

1. Maria ist 29 Jahre . . .

2. Sie lebt seit einem . . .

3. Maria findet München sehr interessant, aber das Wetter ist nicht . . .

4. Sie arbeitet in einem erstklass-igen Hotel . . .

5. Die Arbeit im Hotel gefällt Maria sehr gut, . . .

6. Heute ist . . .

7. Maria spricht am Handy . . .

8. Er ist ein sehr sympatischer . . .

9. Heute Nachmittag gehen Maria und Klaus . . .

10. Dort trinken sie Bier und essen . . .

11. Dann gehen sie wieder . . .

12. Es war ein sehr schöner . . .

13. Sie geht früh ins Bett, und schläft . . .

14. Morgen ist Montag, und die Arbeit . . .

A. . . . Mann, der auch im Hotel arbeitet.

B. . . . zusammen in den Biergarten.

C. . . . in der Stadtmitte.

D. . . . alt und kommt aus Amerika.

E. . . . Tag, aber Maria ist sehr müde.

F. . . . beginnt um 6 Uhr!

G. . . . Jahr in München.

H. . . . Bratwurst mit Sauerkraut.

I. . . . so schön wie in Amerika.

J. . . . wie ein Murmeltier.

K. . . . nach Hause.

L. . . . mit ihrem deutschen Freund Klaus.

M. . . . aber abends ist sie oft fix und fertig.

N. . . . Sonntag und die Sonne scheint.

Book 1, Chapter 2: Handling Numbers, Times, Dates, and Measurements

Alois Hailer needs to update his electronic calendar. Last week, the technology failed him, so to be on the safe side, he's writing out this week's appointments. Write each day, time, and appointment out as words. The activities are numbered in the calendar, and the first activity on Monday has already been done.

10 MO (1) 📱 Herr Hegele 8.00 (2) Meeting 10.30-11.30	14 FR (6) 🍽️ 20.00
11 DI (3) 🏒 9.45	15 SA (7) 🏮 12.00 HAUS DER KUNST (8) 🎭 19.30 FAUST
12 MI (4) 🚂 14.21 Dortmund	16 SO (9) 🍸 18.00 MIT ANDREA!
13 DO (5) ✈️ 7.40 Innsbrück	Nächste Woche Urlaub!

Illustration by Elizabeth Kurtzman

1. Montag, acht Uhr, Herr Hegele anrufen

2. _____

3. _____

4. _____

5. _____

6. _____

7. _____

8. _____

9. _____

Book 1, Chapter 3: Meeting and Greeting: Guten Tag!

It's Saturday and you're planning some outdoor activities for the next few days. Read the following four-day weather forecast and fill in the missing weather words.

Regen	schneit	Temperatur	Unwetter
donnert	regnen	unter	Null

1. Heute Nachmittag gibt es ein _____, und es blitzt und _____. (*This afternoon there'll be a _____, and there'll be lightning and _____.*)

2. Sonntag fällt die Temperatur _____ _____ (two words), und es _____ ein bisschen. (*On Sunday, the temperature will drop _____ _____, and it'll _____ a little bit.*)

3. Montag steigt die _____, und es fängt an zu _____. (*On Monday the _____ will rise, and it will start to _____.*)

4. In Berlin hört der _____ nicht vor Dienstag auf. (*In Berlin, the _____ won't stop before Tuesday.*)

Book 1, Chapter 4: Talking about Home, Family, Friends, and Daily Life

Name the rooms of the house that are illustrated in the following drawing.

Illustration by Elizabeth Kurtzman

A. _____

B. _____

C. _____

D. _____

E. _____

Book 1, Chapter 5: Talking Telecommunications, Business, and Current Events

The following picture shows the kinds of items you would find in a typical office. Write the German term for each item in the blank provided.

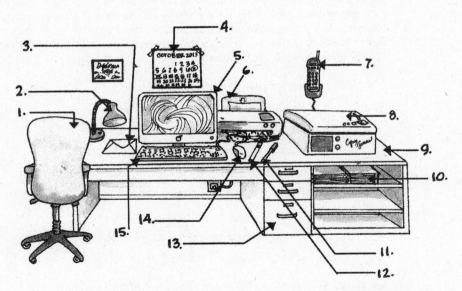

Illustration by Elizabeth Kurtzman

1. Office chair: _____
2. Lamp: _____
3. Envelope: _____
4. Calendar: _____
5. Computer: _____
6. Printer: _____
7. Telephone: _____
8. Copy machine: _____

9. Desk: _____
10. Paper: _____
11. Pen: _____
12. Pencil: _____
13. Files: _____
14. Mouse: _____
15. Keyboard: _____

Book 1, Chapter 6: Shopping Simplified

Imagine that you're shopping at a department store and you're trying to navigate the different floors of the store. Read the following phrases to decide which department belongs on which floor. Then write the correct German word for the department beside the floor number where it's located. Notice that sentence A gives a clue for sentence B; sentence C gives a clue for sentence D, and so on. (**Hint: Erdgeschoss/Parterre** is the North American first floor, **1. Etage** is the North American second floor, and so on. **Untergeschoss** is the German word for basement.)

A. Sie finden Schuhe im vierten Stock, und . . .

B. . . . die Kinderabteilung ist eine Etage tiefer.

C. Der Supermarkt ist im Untergeschoss, und . . .

D. . . . die Schmuckabteilung ist eine Etage höher.

E. Steve Jobs & Bill Gates sind im sechsten Stock, und . . .

F. . . . das Restaurant ist eine Etage höher.

G. Die Herrenabteilung ist im zweiten Stock, und . . .

H. . . . die Damenabteilung ist eine Etage tiefer.

I. TV/Telekommunikation sind im fünften Stock.

Kaufhaus Schlummer (*Department Store Schlummer*) **map**

Etage/Stock (floor)	Abteilung (department)
7	_____
6	_____
5	_____
4	_____

3 _____

2 _____

1 _____

Erdgeschoss _____

Untergeschoss _____

Book 1, Chapter 7: Dining Out and Buying Food: Guten Appetit!

You have just ordered a glass of water, a cup of coffee, soup, salad, steak, and mashed potatoes for lunch at a café. Identify everything on the table to make sure your server hasn't forgotten anything. Use the definite articles **der, die,** and **das** as needed.

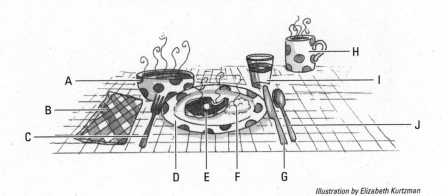

Illustration by Elizabeth Kurtzman

A. _____

B. _____

C. _____

D. _____

E. _____

F. _____

G. _____

H. _____

I. _____

J. _____

Book 11, Chapter 1: Locating Places

Match the descriptions to the pictures.

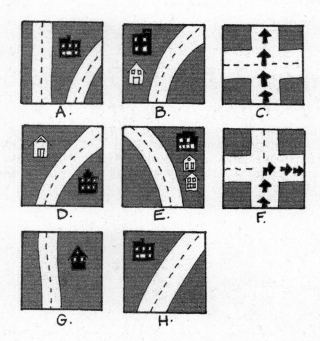

Illustration by Elizabeth Kurtzman

1. _____ Das Haus ist direkt gegenüber.

2. _____ Das Haus ist auf der rechten Seite.

3. _____ Es ist das dritte Haus auf der rechten Seite.

4. _____ Fahren Sie geradeaus.

5. _____ Das Haus ist auf der linken Seite.

6. _____ Es ist das zweite Haus auf der linken Seite.

7. _____ Das Haus ist zwischen den zwei Straßen.

8. _____ Biegen Sie rechts ab.

Book II, Chapter 2: Going Out on the Town

Many words in German have *cognates* (words similar in meaning and spelling) in English. In the following statements, some people are describing what they thought of an event. Decide which form of entertainment they're speaking of and then write that word at the beginning of the statement. Choose from the list of cognates shown here:

Museum   Ballett   Film

Oper   Party   Sinfonie

Illustrations by Elizabeth Kurtzman

1. _____ Die Ausstellung hat uns sehr gut gefallen.

2. _____ Die Zugabe war auch ausgezeichnet.

3. _____ Ich habe die Originalfassung gesehen.

4. _____ Die Tänzer haben mir gut gefallen.

5. _____ Die Sänger sind fantastisch gewesen.

6. _____ Wir haben viel gegessen und getrunken.

Book 11, Chapter 3: Planning a Pleasure Trip: Gute Reise!

Who doesn't like to count money — especially when it's their own? Count how much money is represented in the following pictures and write the correct amount in German words on the blank lines provided.

1.

_____

2.

_____

3.

_____

4.

_____

5.

_____

Illustrations by Elizabeth Kurtzman

Book 11, Chapter 4: Finding a Place to Stay: Gute Nacht!

Use the correct words to complete the questions:

Wo   Was für   Wie   Wann   Was

1. _____ kostet das Zimmer? (*How much is the room?*)
2. _____ lange bleiben Sie? (*How long are you going to stay?*)
3. _____ wird das Frühstück serviert? (*At what time is breakfast served?*)
4. _____ möchten Sie hin? (*Where would you like to go?*)
5. _____ ein Zimmer möchten Sie? (*What kind of room would you like?*)

You're checking into the **Hotel Schlumberger** and you need to fill out the following registration form — **Meldeschein** (*mēl*-de-shayn)/**Anmeldeformular** (*ān*-mēl-de-form-oo-lahr). In the blanks provided, write the English equivalents for the requested information shown in German.

Meldeschein

Hotel Schlumberger   Kirchheimstraße 34   83224 Grassau

1) Tag der Ankunft

_____

2) Familienname   3) Vorname   4) Beruf

_____   _____   _____

5) Geburtsdatum   6) Geburtsort   7) Staatsangehörigkeit

_____   _____   _____

8) Straße, Nummer (Nr.)   9) PLZ   10) Wohnort

_____   _____   _____

11) Ort/Datum   12) Unterschrift

_____   _____

Book II, Chapter 5: Getting Around

One part of driving safely is understanding and obeying road signs. To see how well you'd do on a German road, match each German road sign to its English translation.

A. Baustelle
B. Einbahnstraße
C. Umleitung
D. Vorsicht Glatte
E. Gesperrt
F. Autobahn
G. Ausfahrt
H. Autobahnkreuz oder Autobahndreieck
I. Einordnen
J. Fußgängerzone

Illustrations by Elizabeth Kurtzman

1. _____ Exit
2. _____ Slippery road
3. _____ One-way street
4. _____ Road closed, no entry
5. _____ Construction site
6. _____ Highway
7. _____ Pedestrians only
8. _____ Connecting highway
9. _____ Get in lane
10. _____ Detour

Book II, Chapter 6: Handling Emergencies: Hilfe!

Your friend Markus is a daredevil snowboarder, and as fate would have it, you're the first person to find him after he has crashed into a tree. He seems okay, but just to make sure, you ask him about each body part. To make sure you know the German words for the body parts, write them on the corresponding lines.

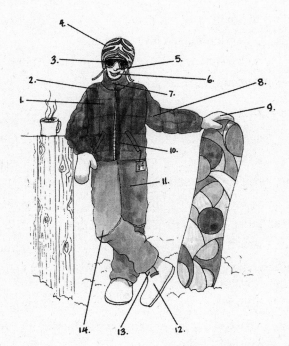

Illustration by Elizabeth Kurtzman

1. chest _____

2. shoulder _____

3. eye _____

4. head _____

5. nose _____

6. mouth _____

7. neck _____

8. arm _____

9. hand _____

10. stomach _____

11. leg _____

12. foot _____

13. ankle _____

14. knee _____

Book III, Chapter 1: Laying Out the Basics to Build Sentences

In the following exercise, each sentence has one word missing. Decide which word of the four choices is the correct one and write your answer in the space.

1. Viele Leute _____, dass München "die heimliche Hauptstadt Deutschlands" ist.

   a) behaupten   b) Sonne   c) der   d) vorwärts

2. Es gibt noch _____ Bezeichnungen für München.

   a) der   b) Personen   c) zwei   d) das

3. Die Einwohner sagen, München ist "die Weltstadt mit Herz," _____ "das Millionendorf."

   a) in   b) arbeiten   c) oder   d) interessant

4. In der Tat _____ die Stadt voller Überraschungen.

   a) von   b) ist   c) in   d) können

5. Jedes Jahr wird das grösste Volksfest der Welt in München _____.

   a) gehabt   b) Stein   c) geworden   d) gefeiert

6. Das Oktoberfest findet _____ 1810 in München statt.

   a) nun   b) seit   c) morgen   d) schön

7. Millionen Touristen kommen zum Oktoberfest, aber _____ Leute kommen zu spät. Warum?

   a) manche   b) haben   c) die   d) grün

8. Leider geht _____ Oktoberfest am ersten Sonntag im Oktober zu Ende.

   a) nur   b) in   c) das   d) von

Book III, Chapter 2: Sorting Out Word Gender and Case

In the following sentences, someone forgot to include the personal pronouns. Fill in the correct personal pronoun using the hints in parentheses (the *pronoun* in English/the case/the directives for *you*, if that's the word needed).

Here's the key for the hints in parentheses: nom. = nominative; acc. = accusative; dat. = dative; s. = singular; pl. = plural; form. = formal; inf. = informal.

1. Ich glaube, _____ arbeitet zu viel. (*you*/nom./pl., inf.)

2. Nein, _____ arbeiten nicht genug. (*we*/nom.)

3. Spielst _____ gern Karten? (*you*/nom./s., inf.)

4. Ja, _____ spiele gern Poker. (*I*/nom.)

5. Kennst du _____ ? (*him*/acc.)

6. Ich gehe ohne _____ in die Stadt. (*you*/acc./pl., inf.)

7. Wirklich? Ich dachte, du gehst mit _____. (*us*/dat.)

8. Wie gefällt _____ der neue Bürgermeister? (*you*/dat./s., form.)

Book III, Chapter 3: Dealing with the Here and Now: The Present Tense

Write the conjugated present tense form of each verb in parentheses in the blank space to complete each thought.

1. Ich _____ (kommen) aus Australien und . . .

2. . . . _____ (leben) seit einem Jahr in Heidelberg.

3. Die Stadt _____ (gefallen) mir sehr gut.

4. Heidelberg _____ (liegen) 80 Kilometer südlich von Frankfurt, im Bundesstadt Baden-Württemberg.

5. Hier _____ (geben) es ein berühmtes Schloss, eine wunderschöne Altstadt, und die älteste Universität Deutschlands.

6. Ich _____ (finden) das Leben in Deutschland sehr schön,

7. aber im Winter _____ (sein) das Wetter sehr kalt.

8. Es _____ (schneien) sehr oft!

9. Im Winter _____ (tragen) die Menschen warme Jacken und Stiefel.

10. Manchmal _____ (vermissen) ich das warme Wetter in Australien.

11. Aber wer _____ (wissen)?

12. Vielleicht _____ (bleiben) ich noch bis nächstes Jahr.

Book III, Chapter 4: Asking and Answering Questions

In the following exercise, add the correct ending to **kein** to fill in the blanks. To do so, you need to know the gender of the noun and, when a preposition is involved, the case the preposition takes. Here's the situation: Daniel is writing a good riddance letter to Susanne, who has run off with Jonas.

24/3/13

Liebe Susanne,

dieser Brief ist (1) _____ typischer Brief von mir. Ich

habe (2)_____ guten Worte für dich, und

(3) _____ Zeit, sehr lange zu schreiben. Du bist

(4) _____ Frau für mich, weil du (5) _____

Interesse mehr an mir hast. Warum bist du so? Ich habe mit

(6) _____ anderen Frau geflirtet.

Du hast (7)_____ Grund, mit Jonas zu flirten. Er schenkt

dir (8) _____ Blumen wie ich es immer tue, er hat (9)

_____ Auto, und noch schlimmer, er hat (10)_____

Arbeit. Ich sage dir, Jonas ist (11)_____ Mann für dich.

Veilleicht magst du mich nicht, weil ich (12)_____

Haare habe und auch (13) _____ Muskeln. Was kann ich

dazu sagen? Du bist auch (14) _____ Schönheit. Leb wohl.

Daniel

Book III, Chapter 5: Describing and Comparing with Adjectives and Adverbs

You're on vacation on the island of **Rügen, in der Ostsee** (*Rügen, in the Baltic Sea*), and you decide to write a letter to your friends Margit and Thomas, describing some activities you're doing there. Fill in the blanks, using the adjectives in parentheses. Be careful of the endings.

Hallo Margit und Thomas,

was macht ihr mit den (1) _____ (klein) Kindern zu Hause? Hier auf

der Insel Rügen gibt es leider keine (2) _____ (exotisch) Blumen,

aber gestern haben wir die (3) _____ (spektakular) (4) _____

(weiß) Felsen gesehen. Kennst du die Bilder von dem (5) _____

(bekannt) Maler Caspar David Friedrich? Diese (6) _____ (herrlich)

Landschaft hat er oft gemalt. Wir geniessen die (7) _____ (gesund)

Luft, und morgen machen wir einem (8) _____ (lang) Spaziergang

bei Binz. Heute Abend essen wir mit einem (9) _____ (interessant)

Ehepaar aus Ostdeutchland. Sie sagen, diese (10) _____

(wunderschön) Insel ist ihr Urlaubziel seit vielen Jahren. Am Donnerstag

fahren wir zu einer (11) _____ (klein) Insel mit einem (12) _____

(komisch) Namen - Hiddensee. Dort gibt es einen (13) _____ (lang)

Strand und einen (14) _____ (schön) Leuchturm.

Machts gut, Liesl und Hansi

Book III, Chapter 6: Modifying Verbs with Helpers: The Modal Auxiliaries

Karin and Alex are talking about their plans for the weekend. Write the correct form of the modal auxiliary verb in the sentence. The infinitive form of the modal auxiliary is in parentheses at the end of the sentence.

Karin: _____ du am Wochenende in die Berge fahren? (**wollen**)

Alex: Leider _____ ich nicht. (**können**) Am Samstag _____ ich zu Hause arbeiten. (**müssen**)

Karin: Das ist aber schade. Claudia und ich _____ eine lange Wanderung machen. (**möchten**) Du _____ doch mitkommen! (**sollen**)

Alex: Ich habe eine Idee. _____ ihr am Samstag Abend zu mir kommen? (**wollen**)

Karin: Das wäre doch toll. Was_____ wir mitbringen? (**sollen**)

Alex: Mmm . . . _____ du bitte eine Flasche Rotwein besorgen? (**können**)

Karin: Aber sicher!

Book III, Chapter 7: Instructing and Commanding: The Imperative Mood

Categorize the commands and instructions into the following five categories:

A. Signs in public places

B. Parent talking to a child

C. Tourist speaking to a hotel employee

D. Cooking instructions

E. Airplane safety instructions

1. _____ Bitte vergessen Sie keine Gepäckstücke.

2. _____ Die Kartoffeln pellen.

3. _____ Kein Zutritt!

4. _____ Sprechen Sie bitte etwas langsamer.

5. _____ Mit Salz und Pfeffer abschmecken.

6. _____ Iss nicht so schnell!

7. _____ Stellen Sie bitte die Rückenlehne senkrecht.

8. _____ Vorsicht Stufe!

9. _____ Wirf mir den Ball!

10. _____ Helfen Sie mir, bitte.

Book III, Chapter 8: Sorting Out Separable- and Inseparable-Prefix Verbs

You were about to read the synopsis of a German movie, but your puppy ripped it to shreds. Piece it back together by writing a number to the left of each letter to put the sentences in the correct order. After that, write an English summary of the story. **Hint:** It's a lowbrow love story with a tragic ending.

A. Der Film beginnt mit Leo der Lugner (*Leo the Liar*) als er aus einem Gefängnis (*prison*) **entkommt.**

B. Nach zwei Monaten zusammen, **verkommt** das Verhältnis (*relationship*) der beiden.

C. Am Anfang (*In the beginning*) **misstraut** er diese Frau in schwarz, . . .

D. Das Gefängnis **befindet sich** in der Nähe von der Lüneburger Heide im Norddeutschland.

E. Plötzlich (*Suddenly*) **bemerkt** er eine schöne Frau in einem schwarzen Kleid.

F. Bald kommt die Polizei und **verhaftet** Leo Lügner.

G. Eines Nachts (*One night*) **zerbricht** Leo eine Flasche (*bottle*) Bier über Silkes Kopf.

H. Dann **erschiesst** er die schöne Silke.

I. Leo Lügner **entdeckt** ein altes Fahrrad, in der Heide und fährt damit los.

J. . . . ich **werde** (*will*) dich nie (*never*) **verlassen**.

K. Die beiden (*The two of them*) sprechen über das Leben im Gefängnis, und **vergessen** ihre schreckliche Situation.

L. Schreckliche Silke sagt, "Ich **verspreche** dir. . .

M. . . . aber sie sagt, "Mein Name ist Schreckliche Silke (*Horrible Silke*), und ich bin aus dem Gefängnis **entkommen**."

N. Bald (*Soon*) **verfährt** er sich in der Heide.

Summary of the movie in English:

_____

_____

_____

_____

_____

_____

_____

_____

_____

_____

_____

Book IV, Chapter 1: Tying Ideas Together with Conjunctions and Relative Pronouns

Different people have different plans for how to spend their summer vacations. Match the following main clauses with their corresponding subordinate clauses. Look at how the conjunction or relative pronoun in the subordinate clause (A through E) logically connects with the first part of the sentence (1 through 5).

1. Wir fahren nicht nach Schweden, . . .

2. Meine Schwester sagt, . . .

3. Mein Bruder fliegt nach Australien . . .

4. Ich besuche meine Freunde, . . .

5. Die Familie Feldberg bleibt zuerst eine Woche in der Schweiz . . .

A. . . . die in Spanien leben.

B. . . . und dann eine Woche in Frankreich.

C. . . . sondern nach Italien.

D. . . . wenn er genug Geld hat.

E. . . . dass sie zu Hause bleibt.

Book IV, Chapter 2: Specifying Relationships with Prepositions

The following German proverbs are missing a preposition. They all have similar equivalents in English, although some details may be slightly different. Read each proverb and decide which of the following prepositions fits in the blanks. To help you out, some unfamiliar words appear in bold and have translations in parentheses.

zu   im   ins   vom (used twice)

in   mit   aus

1. Der Apfel fällt nicht weit _____ Stamm.

2. Aus den Augen, _____ dem **Sinn** (*mind*).

3. Wenn die Katze nicht _____ Hause ist, tanzen die Mäuse.

4. **Einem geschenkten Gaul** (*a gift horse*) schaut man nicht _____ **Maul** (*mouth [of an animal]*).

5. Besser ein Vogel in der Hand als zehn _____ der Luft.

6. **Ehen** (*marriages*) werden _____ **Himmel** (*heaven*) geschlossen.

7. Der Mensch lebt nicht _____ Brot allein.

8. Man soll das Kind nicht _____ dem Bade **ausschütten** (*throw out*).

Book IV, Chapter 3: Using Reflexives and Other Verb Combinations

The following love letter from Sarah has some missing verbal expressions that contain prepositions. Choose from the following list of verbal expressions to complete the love letter.

A. halten . . . für

B. auf . . . verzichten

C. denke . . . an

D. bitte um

E. rede . . . über

F. denkst . . .an

G. warte . . . auf

H. habe . . . in

Mein Liebling,

ich weiß, (1) du _____ oft _____ mich, und ich (2) _____ oft _____ dich. Jeden Tag (3) _____ ich _____ deinen Telefonanruf.

Ich kann nicht (4) _____ deine täglichen Anrufe_____ . In der Arbeit (5)_____ ich immer_____ dich. Meine Kollegen (6) _____ mich _____ eine Idiotin, aber das ist nicht wichtig. Wichtig ist nur eins: ich (7) _____ mich _____ dich verliebt. Ich (8) _____ _____ einen Anruf von dir heute Abend.

Deine Sarah

Book IV, Chapter 4: Conversing about the Past: The Present Perfect and Past Perfect

Some people are describing what they did last weekend, but the verbs are missing. Each sentence is in present perfect tense. Write the correct forms of the verbs in the blanks, using the verbs in parentheses.

1. Letztes Wochenende _____ ich meine Freunde in einem Restaurant _____. (treffen)

2. Markus _____ das Restaurant um 23.00 Uhr _____. (verlassen)

3. Janina _____ sehr spät nach Hause _____. (kommen)

4. Am nächsten Tag _____ Oliver und Helge _____. (joggen)

5. Die Nachbarn _____ uns zum Essen _____. (einladen)

6. Wir _____ in die Berge _____. (gefahren)

7. Thomas und Barbara _____ am Sonntag zu Hause _____. (bleiben)

8. Ich _____ ein Buch _____. (lesen)

Book IV, Chapter 5: Narrating the (Simple) Past: Fact and Fiction

Last month, Helmut and Hannelore drove to Spain for **der Urlaub** (*the vacation*). Hannelore wrote a diary while they were traveling. Read her diary, written in present tense; then fill in the missing verbs in the German simple past. Some sentences have strong and weak verbs, but the majority contain **sein** and **haben**.

den 11. August

Wir sind in Madrid — endlich! Das Wetter ist absolut wunderbar, und wir haben ein Zimmer in einem sehr schönen Hotel. Wir gehen zum Prado Museum. Am 12. August fahren wir nach Córdoba.

den 13. August

Ich habe viel Glück am 13.! Wir sind in einer billigen, aber netten Pension in Córdoba in der Nähe von der Mezquita (die Moschee im Zentrum). Sie ist sehr, sehr groß! In der Moschee ist es kühler als in der Sonne.

den 14. August

Wir fahren nach Sevilla, aber zuerst bin ich drei Stunden allein. Ich gehe einkaufen. Die Geschäfte sind sehr interessant. Ich suche nach Lederartikeln, aber der Preis für eine Lederjacke ist zu hoch für mich. Der Euro macht alles sehr teuer.

den 15. August

Das Wetter ist schrecklich. Es gibt viel Regen, es ist kühl, und Helmut hat Kopfweh. Wir sind den ganzen Tag in Cafés, essen spanische Spezialitäten, und trinken Rioja.

den 17. August

Der Regen ist zu viel! Helmut hat keine Lust, in Sevilla zu bleiben. Also wir fahren nach Málaga.

den 18. August

Es ist herrlich! In Málaga ist es sonnig und heiß! Ich gehe schwimmen, und Helmut hat eine deutsche Zeitung. Das Leben ist perfekt!

den 11. August

1. Wir _____ (sein) in Madrid — endlich!

2. Das Wetter _____ (sein) absolut wunderbar . . .

3. . . . und wir _____ (haben) ein Zimmer in einem sehr schönen Hotel.

4. Am 12. August _____ (fahren) wir nach Córdoba.

den 13. August

5. Wir _____ (sein) in einer billigen, aber netten Pension in Córdoba in der Nähe von der Mezquita (eine Moschee).

6. Sie _____ (sein) sehr, sehr groß!

den 14. August

7. Wir _____ (fahren) nach Sevilla.

den 15. August

8. Das Wetter _____ (sein) schrecklich.

9. Wir _____ (sein) den ganzen Tag in Cafés.

den 17. August

10. Der Regen _____ (sein) zu viel! Helmut _____ (haben) keine Lust, in Sevilla zu bleiben.

11. Also,wir _____ (fahren) nach Málaga.

den 18. August

12. Es _____ (sein) herrlich! In Málaga _____ (sein) es sonnig und heiß!

13. Das Leben _____ (sein) perfekt!

Book IV, Chapter 6: Looking to the Future (And Avoiding It)

You work at an international company. Your German boss, Herr Fleischmann, calls you on Monday morning and wants to know your plans for the next week. Using the following calendar and some future time expressions, describe what you're doing on the days you've made notes of your activities. Try using expressions other than dates (such as **am 20. Oktober**) whenever possible. Note that Question 9 covers more than one day.

Here's some useful vocabulary: **der Termin** (*the appointment*), **der Kunde** (*the customer*), **der Kollege** (*the colleague*), **die Messe** (*the trade fair*), **die Telekonferenz** (*the conference call*), and **der Bericht** (*the report*).

Note: German calendars begin the week with **Montag** (*Monday*).

Montag	Dienstag	Mittwoch	Donnerstag	Freitag	Samstag	Sonntag
1. nach Köln fliegen (Abend)	**2.** in Köln ankommen (früh!) **3.** 2 Termine mit Kunden (Nachmittag) **4.** Abend: mit dem Kollegen essen (Hotel-Restaurant)	**5.** nach Düsseldorf zur Messe (trade fair) fahren **6.** nach Hause fliegen	**7.** Telekonferenz mit Herrn Fleischmann & Kollegen	**8.** Fleischmann den vollen Bericht e-mailen (Nachmittag)	**9.** bei der Familie	**9.** bei der Familie

1. _____

2. _____

3. _____

4. _____

5. _____

6. _____

7. _____

8. _____

9. _____

Book IV, Chapter 7: Describing Your Mood: Summing Up the Subjunctive

Some employees are planning a party for Peter, a colleague who is relocating to India. It's supposed to be **eine Überraschung** (*a surprise*). Complete the sentences by filling in the forms of the subjunctive verbs, using the infinitive verbs in parentheses.

1. Walbie _____ (sollen) das Wohnzimmer dekorieren.

2. Hartmut und Richard _____ (sein) bereit, das Essen zu machen.

3. Wir _____ (dürfen) unsere Familien nicht einladen.

4. Es _____ (können) bis Mitternacht dauern . . .

5. . . . aber leider _____ (müssen) Peter früher nach Hause gehen.

6. Ich _____ (mögen) die Musik organisieren.

Answer Key

The following sections provide answers and translations for the activities in this appendix. The answers appear in boldface.

Book 1, Chapter 1: Warming Up to German Basics

Match the beginning and ending expressions to make a logical story.

1. **D. Maria ist 29 Jahre alt und kommt aus Amerika.** (*Maria is 29 years old and comes from the USA.*)

2. **G. Sie lebt seit einem Jahr in München.** (*She's been living in Munich for a year.*)

3. **I. Maria findet München sehr interessant, aber das Wetter ist nicht so schön wie in Amerika.** (*Maria thinks that Munich is very interesting, but the weather isn't as nice as it is in the USA.*)

4. **C. Sie arbeitet in einem erstklassigen Hotel in der Stadtmitte.** (*She works in a first-class hotel in the city center.*)

5. **M. Die Arbeit im Hotel gefällt Maria sehr gut, aber abends ist sie oft fix und fertig.** (*Maria likes the work at the hotel very much, but in the evenings she's often wiped out.*)

6. **N. Heute ist Sonntag und die Sonne scheint.** (*Today is Sunday and the sun's shining.*)

7. **L. Maria spricht am Handy mit ihrem deutschen Freund Klaus.** (*Maria's talking on her cellphone to her German friend Klaus.*)

8. **A. Er ist ein sehr sympatischer Mann, der auch im Hotel arbeitet.** (*He's a very likeable man who also works at the hotel.*)

9. **B. Heute Nachmittag gehen Maria und Klaus zusammen in den Biergarten.** (*This afternoon, Maria and Klaus are going to the beergarden together.*)

10. **H. Dort trinken sie Bier und essen Bratwurst mit Sauerkraut.** (*There they drink beer and eat fried sausage with sauerkraut.*)

11. **K. Dann gehen sie wieder nach Hause.** (*Then they return home.*)

12. **E. Es war ein sehr schöner Tag, aber Maria ist sehr müde.** (*It was a very pleasant day, but Maria's very tired.*)

13. **J. Sie geht früh ins Bett, und schläft wie ein Murmeltier.** (*She goes to bed early and sleeps like a log* [Literally: *sleeps like a woodchuck/marmot*].)

14. **F. Morgen ist Montag, und die Arbeit beginnt um 6 Uhr!** (*Tomorrow is Monday, and work starts at 6 a.m.!*)

Book 1, Chapter 2: Handling Numbers, Times, Dates, and Measurements

Write each day, time, and appointment out as words.

1. **Montag, acht Uhr, anrufen (call) Herr Hegele**
2. **Montag, zehn Uhr dreißig — elf Uhr dreißig, Meeting**
3. **Dienstag, neun Uhr fünfundvierzig, Golf**
4. **Mittwoch, ICE Zug (train) nach (to) Dortmund, vierzehn Uhr einundzwanzig**
5. **Donnerstag, fliegen (fly) nach (to) Innsbruck, sieben Uhr vierzig**
6. **Freitag, Abendessen (dinner), zwanzig Uhr**
7. **Samstag, Museum Haus der Kunst, zwölf Uhr**
8. **Samstag, Theater Faust, neunzehn Uhr dreißig**
9. **Sonntag, Cocktail mit (with) Andrea, achtzehn Uhr**

Book 1, Chapter 3: Meeting and Greeting: Guten Tag!

Fill in the missing weather words.

1. **Unwetter** (*storm*), **donnert** (*thunder*)
2. **unter Null** (*below zero*), **schneit** (*snow*)
3. **Temperatur** (*temperature*), **regnen** (*rain*) (verb)
4. **Regen** (*rain*) (noun)

Book 1, Chapter 4: Talking about Home, Family, Friends, and Daily Life

Name the rooms of the house.

A. **das Bad** (*bathroom*)
B. **das Schlafzimmer** (*bedroom*)
C. **das Esszimmer** (*dining room*)
D. **die Küche** (*kitchen*)
E. **das Wohnzimmer** (*living room*)

Book 1, Chapter 5: Talking Telecommunications, Business, and Current Events

Write the German term for each item in the blank provided.

1. der Bürostuhl
2. die Lampe
3. der Umschlag
4. der Kalender
5. der Computer
6. der Drucker
7. das Telefon
8. der Fotokopierer
9. der Schreibtisch
10. das Papier
11. der Kugelschreiber
12. der Bleistift
13. die Unterlagen
14. die Maus
15. die Tastatur

Book 1, Chapter 6: Shopping Simplified

Write the correct German word for the department beside the floor number where it's located.

7th floor: Restaurant (*Restaurant*)

6th floor: Computer (*Computers*)

5th floor: TV/Telekommunikation (*TV/Telecommunications*)

4th floor: Schuhe (*Shoes*)

3rd floor: Kinderabteilung (*Children's Department*)

2nd floor: Herrenabteilung (*Men's Department*)

1st floor: Damenabteilung (*Women's Department*)

Erdgeschoss: Schmuckabteilung (*Jewelry Department*)

Untergeschoss: Supermarkt (*Supermarket*)

Book 1, Chapter 7: Dining Out and Buying Food: Guten Appetit!

Identify everything on the table to make sure your server hasn't forgotten anything.

A. die Suppe

B. die Serviette

C. die Gabel

D. der Teller

E. das Steak

F. das Kartoffelpüree

G. das Messer

H. die Tasse Kaffee

I. das Glas Wasser

J. der Löffel

The waiter forgot **der Salat.**

Book 11, Chapter 1: Locating Places

Match the descriptions to the pictures.

1. **D** (*The house is directly opposite.*)

2. **G** (*The house is on the right side.*)

3. **E** (*It's the third house on the right side.*)

4. **C** (*Go [drive] straight.*)

5. **H** (*The house is on the left side.*)

6. **B** (*It's the second house on the left side.*)

7. **A** (*The house is between the two streets.*)

8. **F** (*Turn right.*)

Book 11, Chapter 2: Going Out on the Town

Decide which form of entertainment the people are speaking of and then write that word at the beginning of the statement.

1. Museum

2. Sinfonie

3. Film

4. Ballett

5. Oper

6. Party

Book II, Chapter 3: Planning a Pleasure Trip: Gute Reise!

Write the correct amount in German words for the euros shown in the pictures.

1. fünfhundertzehn Euro, dreißig Cent

2. zweihundertsechs Euro, sechzig Cent

3. sechshundert Euro, fünfzig Cent

4. zwölf Euro

5. zwei Euro, fünfzig Cent

Book II, Chapter 4: Finding a Place to Stay: Gute Nacht!

Use the correct words to complete the questions:

1. Was

2. Wie

3. Wann

4. Wo

5. Was für

In the blanks provided, write the English equivalents for the requested information shown in German.

1. Date of arrival

2. Last name

3. First name

4. Occupation

5. Birth date

6. Place of birth

7. Nationality

8. Street number

9. Zip code

10. City

11. Town/Date

12. Signature

Book II, Chapter 5: Getting Around

One part of driving safely is understanding and obeying road signs. To see how well you'd do on a German road, match each German road sign to its English translation.

1. G; 2. D; 3. B; 4. E; 5. A; 6. F; 7. J; 8. H; 9. I; 10. C

Book II, Chapter 6: Handling Emergencies: Hilfe!

Write the German words for the body parts on the corresponding lines.

1. die Brust
2. die Schulter
3. das Auge
4. der Kopf
5. die Nase
6. der Mund
7. der Nacken
8. der Arm
9. die Hand
10. der Bauch/der Magen
11. das Bein
12. der Fuß
13. der Fußgelenk/(Fuß-)knöchel
14. das Knie

Book III, Chapter 1: Laying Out the Basics to Build Sentences

Each sentence has one word missing. Decide which word of the four choices is the correct one and write your answer in the space.

1. a) behaupten
2. c) zwei
3. c) oder
4. b) ist
5. d) gefeiert
6. b) seit
7. a) manche
8. c) das

Book III, Chapter 2: Sorting Out Word Gender and Case

Fill in the correct personal pronoun using the hints in parentheses (the *pronoun* in English/the case/the directives for *you*, if that's the word needed).

1. **ihr** (*I think you work too much.*)
2. **wir** (*No, we don't work enough.*)
3. **du** (*Do you like to play cards?*)
4. **ich** (*Yes, I like to play poker.*)
5. **ihn** (*Do you know him?*)

6. **euch** (*I'm going downtown without you.*)

7. **uns** (*Really? I thought you were going with us.*)

8. **Ihnen** (*How do you like the new mayor?*)

Book III, Chapter 3: Dealing with the Here and Now: The Present Tense

Write the conjugated present tense form of each verb in parentheses in the blank space to complete each thought.

1. komme
2. lebe
3. gefällt
4. liegt
5. gibt
6. finde

7. ist
8. schneit
9. tragen
10. vermisse
11. weiß
12. bleibe

Book III, Chapter 4: Asking and Answering Questions

Add the correct ending to **kein** to fill in the blanks.

1. kein
2. keine
3. keine
4. keine
5. kein
6. keiner
7. keinen

8. keine
9. kein
10. keine
11. kein
12. keine
13. keine
14. keine

Book III, Chapter 5: Describing and Comparing with Adjectives and Adverbs

Fill in the blanks using the adjectives in parentheses.

Hallo Margit und Thomas,

was macht ihr mit den (1) **kleinen** Kindern zu Hause? Hier auf der Insel
Rugen gibt es leider keine (2) **exotischen** Blumen, aber gestern haben
wir die (3) **spektakularen** (4) **weißen** Felsen gesehen. Kennst du die Bilder
von dem (5) **bekannten** Maler Caspar David Friedrich? Diese (6) **herrliche**
Landschaft hat er oft gemalt. Wir geniessen die (7) **gesunde** Luft, und
morgen machen wir einem (8) **langen** Spaziergang bei Binz. Heute Abend
essen wir mit einem (9) **interessanten** Ehepaar aus Ostdeutchland. Sie
sagen, diese (10) **wunderschöne** Insel ist ihr Urlaubziel seit vielen Jahren.
Am Donnerstag fahren wir zu einer (11) **kleinen** Insel mit einem (12) **komischen**
Namen - Hiddensee. Dort gibt es einen (13) **langen** Strand und einen
(14) **schönen** Leuchturm.

Machts gut, Liesl und Hansi

Hi Margit and Thomas,

What are you doing with the little children at home? Here on the island of Rügen, there aren't any exotic flowers, but yesterday we saw the spectacular white cliffs. Do you know the paintings by the famous painter Caspar David Friedrich? He often painted this wonderful landscape. We're enjoying the healthy air, and tomorrow we're going on a long walk near Binz. This evening we're having dinner with an interesting couple from eastern Germany. They say this beautiful island is where they've been spending their vacations for many years. On Thursday we're going to a small island with a funny name — Hiddensee. There's a long beach there and a nice lighthouse.

See you soon, Liesl and Hansi

Book III, Chapter 6: Modifying Verbs with Helpers: The Modal Auxiliaries

Write the correct form of the modal auxiliary verb in the sentence.

Karin: **Willst** du am Wochenende in die Berge fahren? (*Do you want to go to the mountains on the weekend?*)

Alex: Leider **kann** ich nicht. (*Unfortunately, I can't*) Am Samstag **muss** ich zu Hause arbeiten. (*I have to work at home on Saturday.*)

Karin: Das ist aber schade. Claudia und ich **möchten** eine lange Wanderung machen. (*What a shame. Claudia and I would like to go on a long hike.*) Du **sollst** doch mitkommen! (*You should come along!*)

Alex: Ich habe eine Idee. **Wollt** ihr am Samstag Abend zu mir kommen? (*I have an idea. Do you want to come to my place on Saturday evening?*)

Karin: Das wäre doch toll. Was **sollen** wir mitbringen? (*That would be great. What should we bring?*)

Alex: Mmm . . . **kannst** du bitte eine Flasche Rotwein besorgen? (*Hmm . . . could you get a bottle of red wine?*)

Karin: Aber sicher! (*Of course!*)

Book III, Chapter 7: Instructing and Commanding: The Imperative Mood

Categorize the commands and instructions into the corresponding category.

1. **E. Airplane safety instructions** (*Please do not forget any baggage.*)

2. **D. Cooking instructions** (*Peel the potatoes.*)

3. **A. Signs in public places** (*No entry.*)

4. **C. Tourist speaking to a hotel employee** (*Please speak a bit slower.*)

5. **D. Cooking instructions** (*Add salt and pepper to taste.*)

6. **B. Parent talking to a child** (*Don't eat so fast!*)

7. **E. Airplane safety instructions** (*Please make sure that your seat back is straight up.*)

8. **A. Signs in public places** (*Caution: Step.*)

9. **B. Parent talking to a child** (*Throw me the ball!*)

10. **C. Tourist speaking to a hotel employee** (*Help me, please.*)

Book III, Chapter 8: Sorting Out Separable- and Inseparable-Prefix Verbs

Piece the movie summary back together by writing a number to the left of each letter to put the sentences in the correct order.

1. **A.** Der Film beginnt mit Leo der Lugner (*Leo the Liar*) als er aus einem Gefängnis (*prison*) **entkommt.**

2. **D.** Das Gefängnis **befindet sich** in der Nähe von der Lüneburger Heide im Norddeutschland.

3. **I.** Leo Lügner **endeckt** ein altes Fahrrad in der Heide, und fährt damit los.

4. **N.** Bald (*Soon*) **verfährt** er **sich** in der Heide.

5. **E.** Plötzlich (*Suddenly*) **bemerkt** er eine schöne Frau in einem schwarzen Kleid.

6. **C.** Am Anfang (*In the beginning*) **misstraut** er diese Frau in schwarz, . . .

7. **M.** . . . aber sie sagt, "Mein Name ist Schreckliche Silke (*Horrible Silke*), und ich bin aus dem Gefängnis **entkommen.**

8. **K.** Die beiden (*The two of them*) sprechen über das Leben im Gefängnis, und **vergessen** ihre schreckliche Situation.

9. **L.** Schreckliche Silke sagt, "Ich **verspreche** dir . . .

10. **J.** . . . ich **werde** (*will*) dich nie (*never*) **verlassen.**

11. **B.** Nach zwei Monaten zusammen, **verkommt** das Verhältnis (*relationship*) der beiden.

12. **G.** Eines Nachts (*One night*) **zerbricht** Leo eine Flasche Bier über Silkes Kopf.

13. **H.** Dann **erschiesst** er die schöne Silke.

14. **F.** Bald kommt die Polizei und **verhaftet** Leo.

Write a summary of the movie in English.

> *Leo Lügner escapes from a prison near the Lüneburger Heide, where he discovers a bicycle that he uses to escape. He soon gets lost in the heath, but all of a sudden, he notices a beautiful woman in a black dress; he's suspicious of her at first. However, when Leo discovers that this woman, named Schreckliche Silke, is also an escaped convict, they begin talking about life in prison and forget the terrible situation they're in. Silke promises Leo that she'll never leave him, but after two months together, their relationship falls apart. One night, Leo breaks a beer bottle over Silke's head and shoots her dead; soon, the police come and arrest Leo.*

Book IV, Chapter 1: Tying Ideas Together with Conjunctions and Relative Pronouns

Different people have different plans for how to spend their summer vacations. Match the following main clauses with their corresponding subordinate clauses. Look at how the conjunction or relative pronoun in the subordinate clause (A through E) logically connects with the first part of the sentence (1 through 5).

1. **C. Wir fahren nicht nach Schweden, sondern nach Italien.** (*We're not traveling to Sweden, but rather to Italy.*)

2. **E. Meine Schwester sagt, dass sie zu Hause bleibt.** (*My sister says that she's staying home.*)

3. **D. Mein Bruder fliegt nach Australien wenn er genug Geld hat.** (*My brother will fly to Australia if he has enough money.*)

4. **A. Ich besuche meine Freunde, die in Spanien leben.** (*I'm visiting my friends who live in Spain.*)

5. **B. Die Familie Feldberg bleibt zuerst eine Woche in der Schweiz und dann eine Woche in Frankreich.** (*The Feldbergs are staying [first] in Switzerland for a week and then in France for a week.*)

Book IV, Chapter 2: Specifying Relationships with Prepositions

Read each proverb and decide which preposition fits in the blank. The English equivalent follows the German proverb.

1. Der Apfel fällt nicht weit **vom** Stamm. (*The apple doesn't fall far from the tree.*)

2. Aus den Augen, **aus** dem Sinn. (*Out of sight, out of mind.*)

3. Wenn die Katze nicht **zu** Hause ist, tanzen die Mäuse. (*When the cat's away, the mice will play.*)

4. Einem geschenkten Gaul schaut man nicht **ins** Maul. (*Don't look a gift horse in the mouth.*)

5. Besser ein Vogel in der Hand als zehn **in** der Luft. (*A bird in the hand is worth two in the bush.*)

6. Ehen werden **im** Himmel geschlossen. (*Marriages are made in heaven.*)

7. Der Mensch lebt nicht **vom** Brot allein. (*Man does not live by bread alone.*)

8. Man soll das Kind nicht **mit** dem Bade ausschütten. (*Don't throw the baby out with the bathwater.*)

Book IV, Chapter 3: Using Reflexives and Other Verb Combinations

Put the verbal expressions into the correct sentence to complete the love letter.

Mein Liebling,

ich weiß, du (1) **denkst** oft an mich, und ich (2) **denke** oft an dich. Jeden Tag (3) **warte** ich **auf** deinen Telefonanruf. Ich kann nicht (4) **auf** deine täglichen Anrufe **verzichten.** In der Arbeit (5) **rede** ich immer **über** dich. Meine Kollegen (6) **halten** mich **für** eine Idiotin, aber das ist nicht wichtig. Wichtig ist nur eins: ich (7) **habe** mich in dich **verliebt.** Ich (8) **bitte um** einen Anruf von dir heute Abend.

Deine Sarah

My darling,

I know you often think about me, and I often think about you. Every day I wait for your telephone call. I can't do without your daily calls. At work I always talk about you. My colleagues take me for an idiot, but that's not important. Only one thing is important: I've fallen in love with you. I'm asking for a call from you this evening.

Your Sarah

Book IV, Chapter 4: Conversing about the Past: The Present Perfect and Past Perfect

Some people are describing what they did last weekend, but the verbs are missing. Each sentence is in present perfect tense. Write the correct forms of the verbs in the blanks, using the verbs in parentheses.

1. Letztes Wochenende **habe** ich meine Freunde in einem Restaurant **getroffen.** (*Last weekend I met my friends in a restaurant.*)

2. Markus **hat** das Restaurant um 23.00 Uhr **verlassen.** (*Markus left the restaurant at 11 p.m.*)

3. Janina **ist** sehr spät nach Hause **gekommen.** (*Janina came home very late.*)

4. Am nächsten Tag **sind** Oliver und Helge **gejoggt.** (*The next day Oliver and Helge jogged.*)

5. Die Nachbarn **haben** uns zum Essen **eingeladen.** (*The neighbors invited us for a meal.*)

6. Wir **sind** in die Berge **gefahren.** (*We drove to the mountains.*)

7. Thomas und Barbara **sind** am Sonntag zu Hause **geblieben.** (*Thomas and Barbara stayed home on Sunday.*)

8. Ich **habe** ein Buch **gelesen.** (*I read a book.*)

Book IV, Chapter 5: Narrating the (Simple) Past: Fact and Fiction

Last month, Helmut and Hannelore drove to Spain for **der Urlaub** (*the vacation*). Hannelore wrote a diary while they were traveling. Fill in the missing verbs in the German simple past.

1. **Wir waren in Madrid — endlich!** (*We were in Madrid — at last!*)

2. **Das Wetter war absolut wunderbar . . .** (*The weather was absolutely wonderful . . .*)

3. **. . . und wir hatten ein Zimmer in einem sehr schönen Hotel.** (*. . . and we had a room in a very pretty hotel.*)

4. **Am 12. August fuhren wir nach Córdoba.** (*On the 12th of August we drove to Córdoba.*)

5. **Wir waren in einer billigen, aber netten Pension in Córdoba in der Nähe von der Mezquita, eine Moschee.** (*We were in an inexpensive but nice pension in Córdoba, near the Mezquita, a mosque.*)

6. **Sie war sehr, sehr groß!** (*It was very, very big!*)

7. **Wir fuhren nach Sevilla.** (*We drove to Sevilla.*)

8. **Das Wetter war schrecklich.** (*The weather was awful [terrible].*)

9. **Wir waren den ganzen Tag in Cafés . . .** (*We were in cafés the whole day . . .*)

10. **Der Regen war zu viel! Helmut hatte keine Lust, in Sevilla zu bleiben.** (*The rain was too much! Helmut didn't feel like staying in Sevilla.*)

11. **Also wir fuhren nach Málaga.** (*So we drove to Málaga.*)

12. **Es war herrlich! In Málaga war es sonnig und heiß!** (*It was marvelous! It was sunny and hot in Málaga.*)

13. **Das Leben war perfekt!** (*Life was perfect!*)

Book IV, Chapter 6: Looking to the Future (And Avoiding It)

Describe what you're doing on the days you've made notes of your activities. Try using expressions other than dates whenever possible.

1. **Ich fliege heute Abend nach Köln.** (*I'm going to fly/I'm flying to Cologne this evening.*)

2. **Ich komme morgen früh/am Dienstag früh in Köln an.** (*I'll arrive in Cologne tomorrow morning/on Tuesday morning.*)

3. **Ich habe morgen Nachmittag/am Dienstagnachmittag zwei Termine mit Kunden.** (*I have two appointments with customers tomorrow afternoon/on Tuesday afternoon.*)

4. **Ich esse morgen Abend/am Dienstagabend mit dem Kollegen im Hotel-Restaurant.** (*I'm having dinner with the colleague in the hotel restaurant tomorrow evening/on Tuesday evening.*)

5. **Ich fahre übermorgen/am Mittwoch nach Düsseldorf zur Messe.** (*I'm going to the trade fair in Düsseldorf the day after tomorrow/on Wednesday.*)

6. **Ich fliege übermorgen/am Mittwoch nach Hause.** (*I'm flying home the day after tomorrow/on Wednesday.*)

7. **Ich habe am Donnerstag eine Telekonferenz mit Herrn Fleischmann und seinen Kollegen.** (*I have a conference call with Herr Fleischmann and his colleagues on Thursday.*)

8. **Ich e-maile Ihnen am Freitag Nachmittag den vollen Bericht.** (*I'll e-mail you the whole report on Friday afternoon.*)

9. **Ich bin dieses Wochenende/am Wochenende bei meiner Familie.** (*I'll be with my family this weekend/on the weekend.*)

Book IV, Chapter 7: Describing Your Mood: Summing Up the Subjunctive

Complete the sentences by filling in the forms of the subjunctive verbs, using the infinitive verbs in parentheses.

1. **Walbie sollte das Wohnzimmer dekorieren.** (*Walbie should decorate the living room.*)

2. **Hartmut und Richard wären bereit, das Essen zu machen.** (*Hartmut and Richard would be willing to make the food.*)

3. **Wir dürften unsere Familien nicht einladen.** (*We wouldn't be allowed to invite our families.*)

4. **Es könnte bis Mitternacht dauern . . .** (*It could last until midnight . . .*)

5. **. . . aber leider müsste Peter früher nach Hause gehen.** (*. . . but unfortunately Peter would have to go home earlier.*)

6. **Ich möchte die Musik organisieren.** (*I'd like to organize the music.*)

Appendix E

About the CD

· ·

*T*his appendix walks you through the CD that accompanies this book. The CD is audio-only, so it'll play in any standard CD player or in your computer's CD-ROM drive. *Note:* If you're using a digital version of this book, please go to `http://booksupport.wiley.com` for access to the additional content.

How to Use the CD

We recorded many of the Talkin' the Talk dialogues in this book to help you sharpen your listening skills. The written dialogues you encounter throughout the chapters will come to life when you listen to the CD. You're sure to discover more about pronunciation and oral communication by listening to these native German speakers.

You can use the CD to practice both your listening comprehension and your speech. If your goal is to work on pronunciation, start by listening to the tracks that accompany Chapter 1 of Book I and learn all those funny new sounds. Imitate the speakers on the CD and start to sound German.

Here are a couple of ways you can practice your listening comprehension:

- ✔ First, read a dialogue for comprehension. Then listen to the CD track without following the written script to see how much you understand without visual support. Repeat this exercise as many times as you like.

- ✔ Before you even read a dialogue, listen to it a couple of times and extract as many ideas as possible from it. Then check the written dialogue in your book to confirm how much you understood.

Here are some ways to practice your speaking ability:

- ✔ Read the dialogue in the book. Say one sentence at a time aloud before listening to that sentence to check whether it sounds the way you thought it would.

- ✔ Pick one of the speakers and pretend to be that person, allowing you to interact with the other person(s) in the conversation. Say your lines aloud as you play the audio track. You can even take turns being different characters.

Track Listing

The following is a list of the tracks that appear on this book's audio CD. You can also access the audio tracks at www.dummies.com/go/germanaio. **Viel Spaß!** (feel shpahs!) (*Have fun!*)

Track 1: The German alphabet (Book I, Chapter 1)

Track 2: Pronouncing German vowels (Book I, Chapter 1)

Track 3: Pronouncing vowels with umlauts (Book I, Chapter 1)

Track 4: Pronouncing diphthongs (Book I, Chapter 1)

Track 5: Pronouncing German consonants (Book I, Chapter 1)

Track 6: Pronouncing the German **r** and **l** (Book I, Chapter 1)

Track 7: Pronouncing consonant combinations (Book I, Chapter 1)

Track 8: Pronouncing German numbers (Book I, Chapter 2)

Track 9: Buying food, using the metric system (Book I, Chapter 2)

Track 10: Saying goodbye at the train station (Book I, Chapter 3)

Track 11: Formal greetings (Book I, Chapter 3)

Track 12: Informal greetings between friends (Book I, Chapter 3)

Track 13: Discussing jobs (Book I, Chapter 3)

Track 14: Chatting about family (Book I, Chapter 4)

Track 15: Making plans for the weekend (Book I, Chapter 4)

Track 16: Making a business call (Book I, Chapter 5)

Track 17: Buying a ladies' shirt (Book I, Chapter 6)

Track 18: Trying on a blouse (Book I, Chapter 6)

Track 19: Ordering a meal (Book I, Chapter 7)

Track 20: Paying the check and tipping (Book I, Chapter 7)

Track 21: Asking directions to a taxi stand (Book II, Chapter 1)

Track 22: Finding a friend's hotel (Book II, Chapter 1)

Track 23: Talking about the ballet (Book II, Chapter 2)

Track 24: Getting tourism information (Book II, Chapter 3)

Track 25: Exchanging money (Book II, Chapter 3)

Track 26: Checking in to a hotel (Book II, Chapter 4)

Track 27: Checking in at the airport (Book II, Chapter 5)

Track 28: Asking which bus to take (Book II, Chapter 5)

Track 29: Discussing symptoms with a doctor (Book II, Chapter 6)

You can access the following bonus tracks online at www.dummies.com/go/germanaio:

Bonus Track 1: Chatting about plans and the weather (Book I, Chapter 3)

Bonus Track 2: Being seated at a restaurant (Book I, Chapter 7)

Bonus Track 3: Making a date to go to the movies (Book II, Chapter 2)

Bonus Track 4: Booking a flight with a travel agent (Book II, Chapter 3)

Bonus Track 5: Reserving a hotel room (Book II, Chapter 4)

Customer Care

If you have trouble with the CD, please call Wiley Product Technical Support at 877-762-2974. Outside the United States, call 317-572-3993. You can also contact Wiley Product Technical Support at http://support.wiley.com. Wiley will provide technical support only for installation and other general quality control items.

To place additional orders or to request information about other Wiley products, please call 877-762-2974.

Index

• D •

• H •

• Q •

• R •

• U •

John Wiley & Sons, Inc.
End-User License Agreement

READ THIS. You should carefully read these terms and conditions before opening the software packet(s) included with this book "Book". This is a license agreement "Agreement" between you and John Wiley & Sons, Inc. "WILEY". By opening the accompanying software packet(s), you acknowledge that you have read and accept the following terms and conditions. If you do not agree and do not want to be bound by such terms and conditions, promptly return the Book and the unopened software packet(s) to the place you obtained them for a full refund.

1. **License Grant.** WILEY grants to you (either an individual or entity) a nonexclusive license to use one copy of the enclosed software program(s) (collectively, the "Software") solely for your own personal or business purposes on a single computer (whether a standard computer or a workstation component of a multi-user network). The Software is in use on a computer when it is loaded into temporary memory (RAM) or installed into permanent memory (hard disk, CD-ROM, or other storage device). WILEY reserves all rights not expressly granted herein.

2. **Ownership.** WILEY is the owner of all right, title, and interest, including copyright, in and to the compilation of the Software recorded on the physical packet included with this Book "Software Media". Copyright to the individual programs recorded on the Software Media is owned by the author or other authorized copyright owner of each program. Ownership of the Software and all proprietary rights relating thereto remain with WILEY and its licensers.

3. **Restrictions on Use and Transfer.**

    (a) You may only (i) make one copy of the Software for backup or archival purposes, or (ii) transfer the Software to a single hard disk, provided that you keep the original for backup or archival purposes. You may not (i) rent or lease the Software, (ii) copy or reproduce the Software through a LAN or other network system or through any computer subscriber system or bulletin-board system, or (iii) modify, adapt, or create derivative works based on the Software.

    (b) You may not reverse engineer, decompile, or disassemble the Software. You may transfer the Software and user documentation on a permanent basis, provided that the transferee agrees to accept the terms and conditions of this Agreement and you retain no copies. If the Software is an update or has been updated, any transfer must include the most recent update and all prior versions.

4. **Restrictions on Use of Individual Programs.** You must follow the individual requirements and restrictions detailed for each individual program in the "About the CD" appendix of this Book or on the Software Media. These limitations are also contained in the individual license agreements recorded on the Software Media. These limitations may include a requirement that after using the program for a specified period of time, the user must pay a registration fee or discontinue use. By opening the Software packet(s), you agree to abide by the licenses and restrictions for these individual programs that are detailed in the "About the CD" appendix and/or on the Software Media. None of the material on this Software Media or listed in this Book may ever be redistributed, in original or modified form, for commercial purposes.

5. **Limited Warranty.**

   (a) WILEY warrants that the Software and Software Media are free from defects in materials and workmanship under normal use for a period of sixty (60) days from the date of purchase of this Book. If WILEY receives notification within the warranty period of defects in materials or workmanship, WILEY will replace the defective Software Media.

   (b) WILEY AND THE AUTHOR(S) OF THE BOOK DISCLAIM ALL OTHER WARRANTIES, EXPRESS OR IMPLIED, INCLUDING WITHOUT LIMITATION IMPLIED WARRANTIES OF MERCHANTABILITY AND FITNESS FOR A PARTICULAR PURPOSE, WITH RESPECT TO THE SOFTWARE, THE PROGRAMS, THE SOURCE CODE CONTAINED THEREIN, AND/ OR THE TECHNIQUES DESCRIBED IN THIS BOOK. WILEY DOES NOT WARRANT THAT THE FUNCTIONS CONTAINED IN THE SOFTWARE WILL MEET YOUR REQUIREMENTS OR THAT THE OPERATION OF THE SOFTWARE WILL BE ERROR FREE.

   (c) This limited warranty gives you specific legal rights, and you may have other rights that vary from jurisdiction to jurisdiction.

6. **Remedies.**

   (a) WILEY's entire liability and your exclusive remedy for defects in materials and workmanship shall be limited to replacement of the Software Media, which may be returned to WILEY with a copy of your receipt at the following address: Software Media Fulfillment Department, Attn.: *German All-in-One For Dummies,* John Wiley & Sons, Inc., 10475 Crosspoint Blvd., Indianapolis, IN 46256, or call 1-800-762-2974. Please allow four to six weeks for delivery. This Limited Warranty is void if failure of the Software Media has resulted from accident, abuse, or misapplication. Any replacement Software Media will be warranted for the remainder of the original warranty period or thirty (30) days, whichever is longer.

   (b) In no event shall WILEY or the author be liable for any damages whatsoever (including without limitation damages for loss of business profits, business interruption, loss of business information, or any other pecuniary loss) arising from the use of or inability to use the Book or the Software, even if WILEY has been advised of the possibility of such damages.

   (c) Because some jurisdictions do not allow the exclusion or limitation of liability for consequential or incidental damages, the above limitation or exclusion may not apply to you.

7. **U.S. Government Restricted Rights.** Use, duplication, or disclosure of the Software for or on behalf of the United States of America, its agencies and/or instrumentalities "U.S. Government" is subject to restrictions as stated in paragraph (c)(1)(ii) of the Rights in Technical Data and Computer Software clause of DFARS 252.227-7013, or subparagraphs (c)(1) and (2) of the Commercial Computer Software - Restricted Rights clause at FAR 52.227-19, and in similar clauses in the NASA FAR supplement, as applicable.

8. **General.** This Agreement constitutes the entire understanding of the parties and revokes and supersedes all prior agreements, oral or written, between them and may not be modified or amended except in a writing signed by both parties hereto that specifically refers to this Agreement. This Agreement shall take precedence over any other documents that may be in conflict herewith. If any one or more provisions contained in this Agreement are held by any court or tribunal to be invalid, illegal, or otherwise unenforceable, each and every other provision shall remain in full force and effect.